BASARA™
Samurai Legends

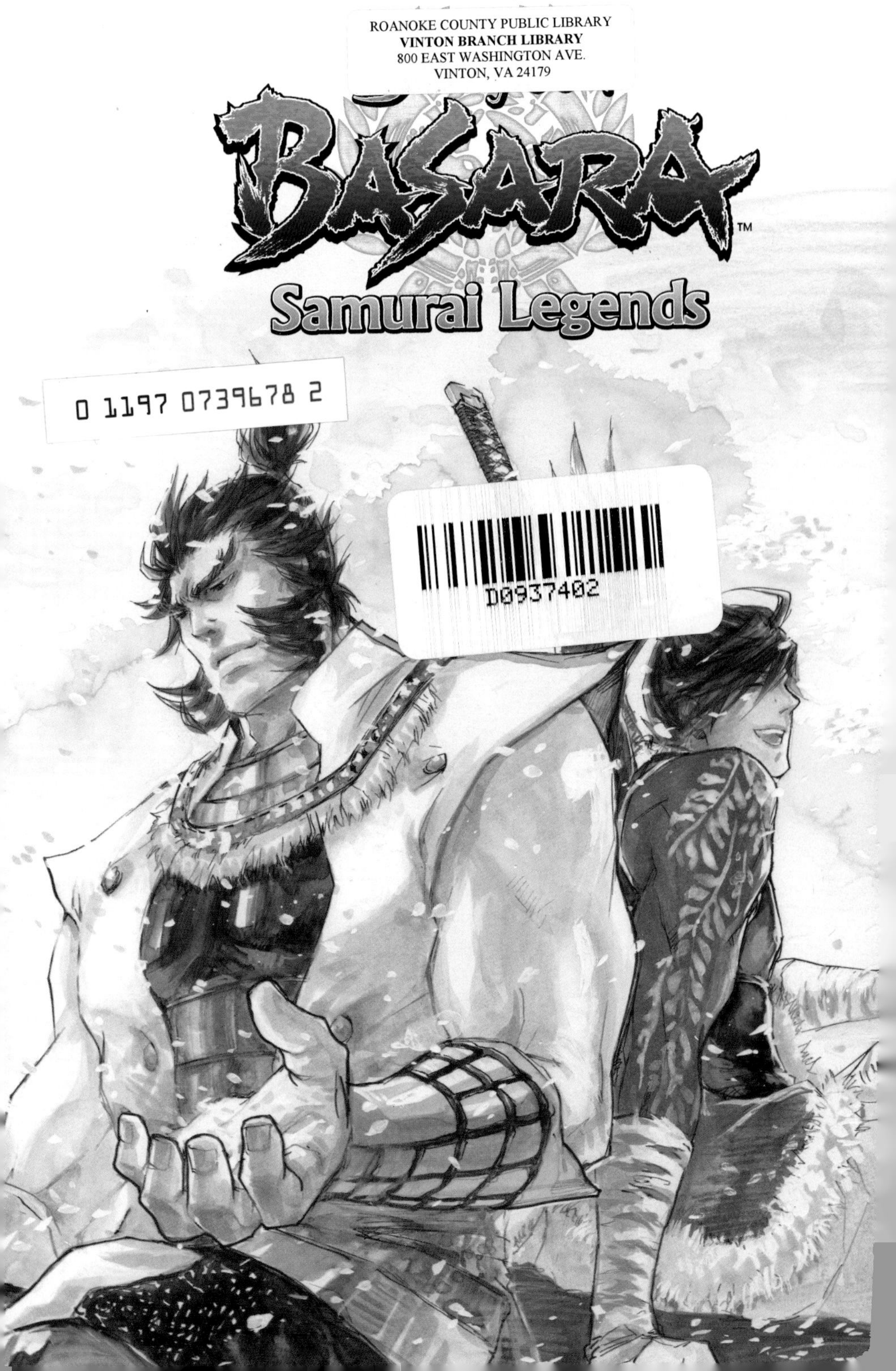

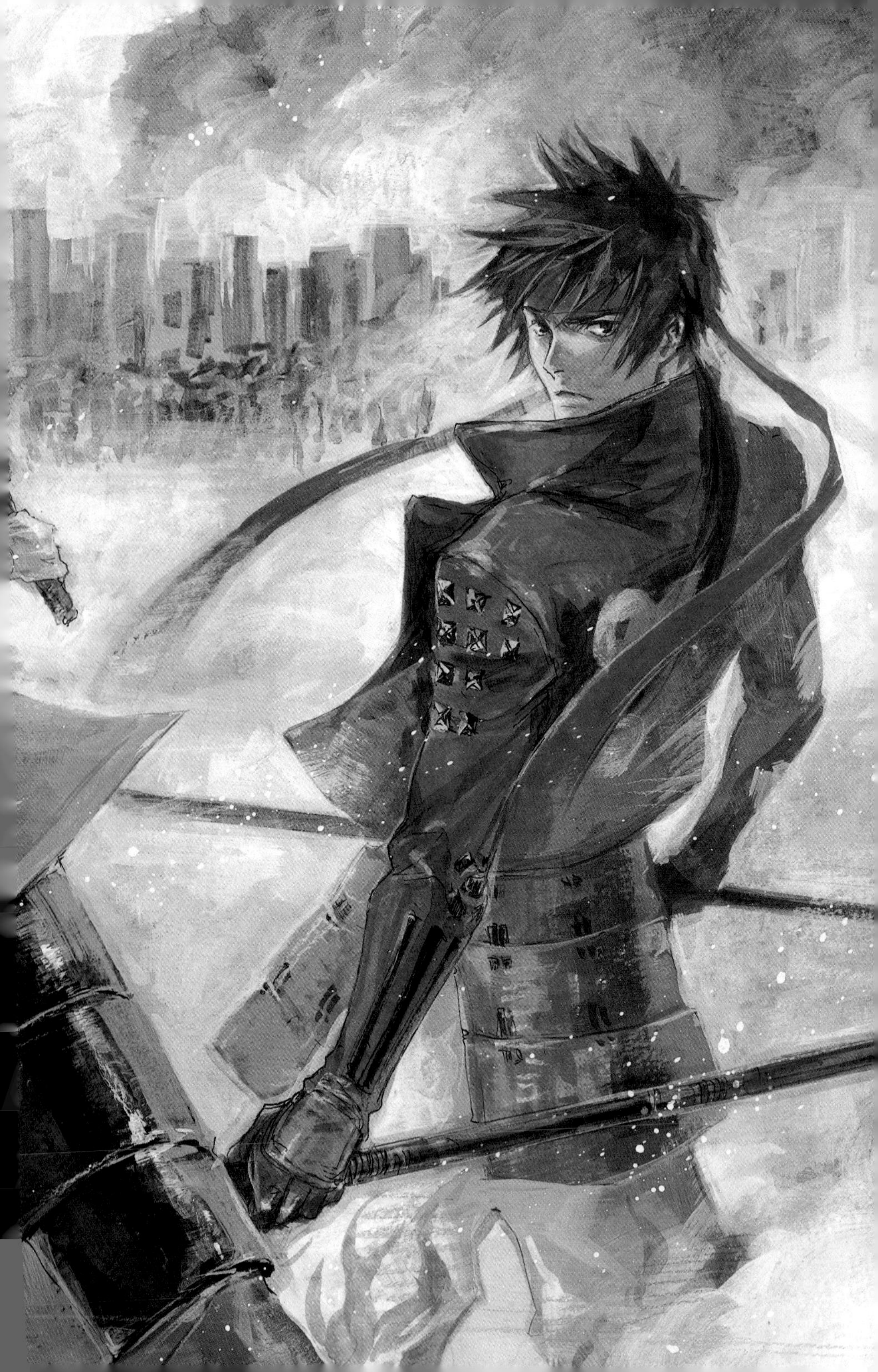

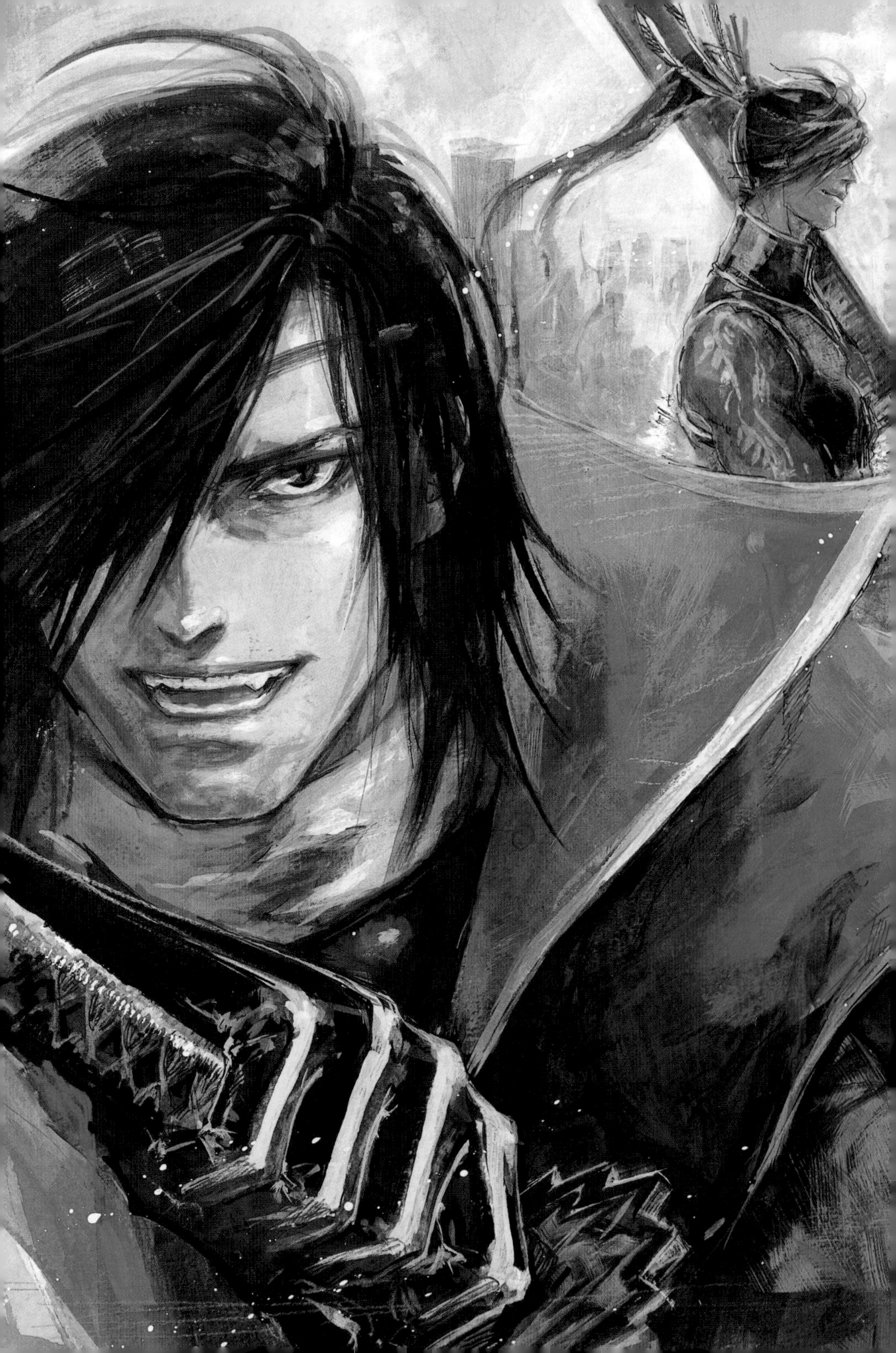

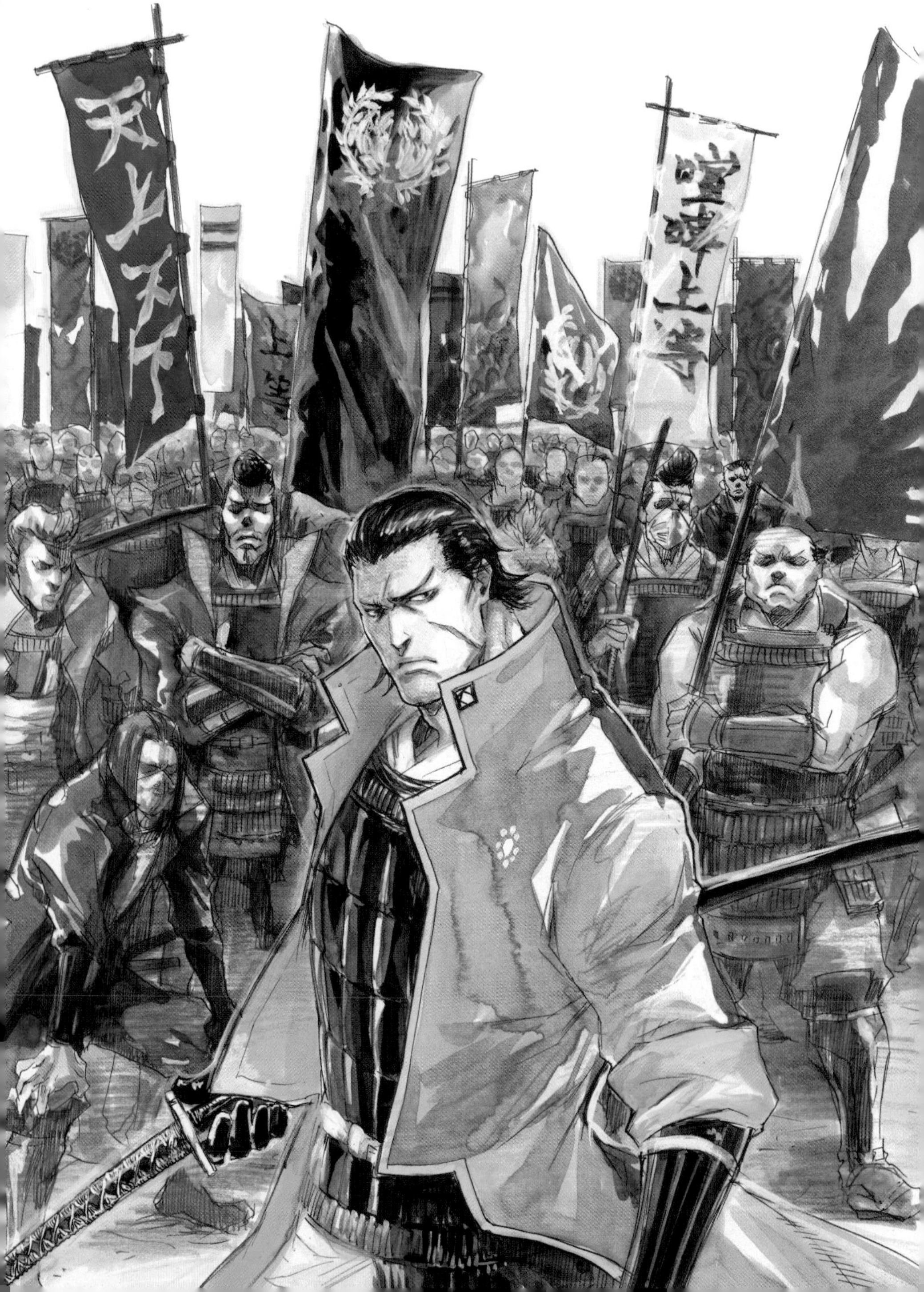
天上天下

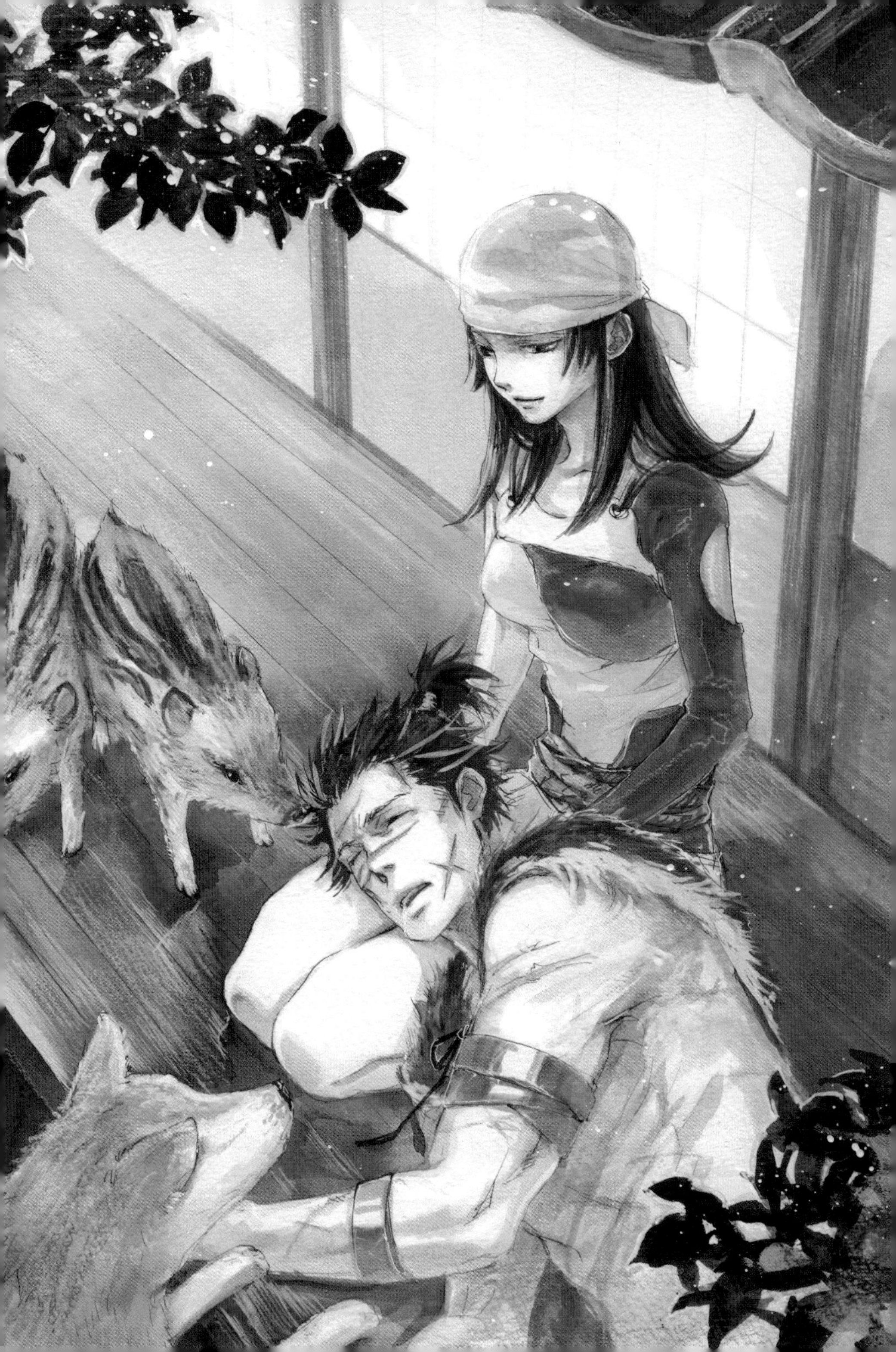

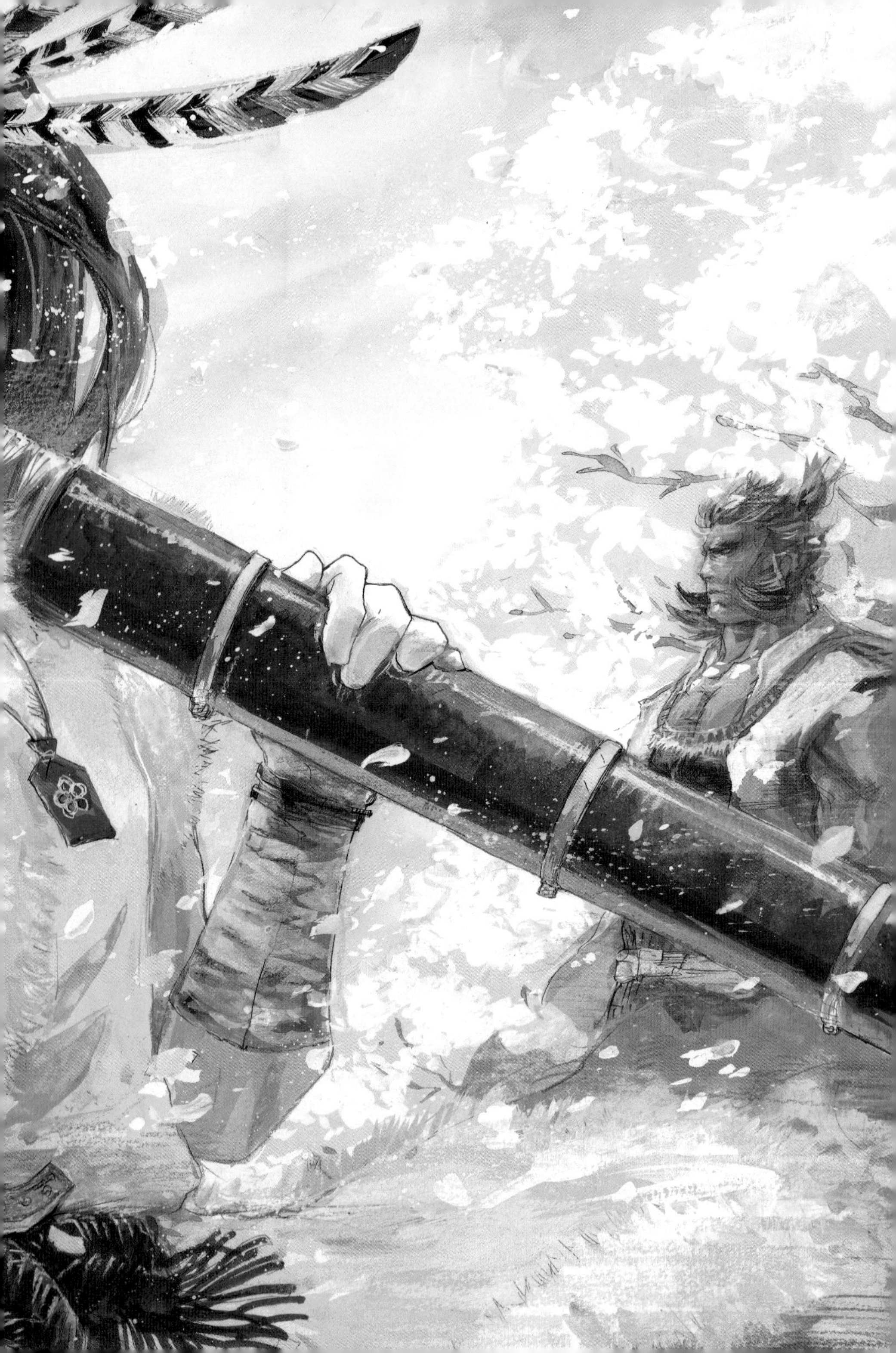

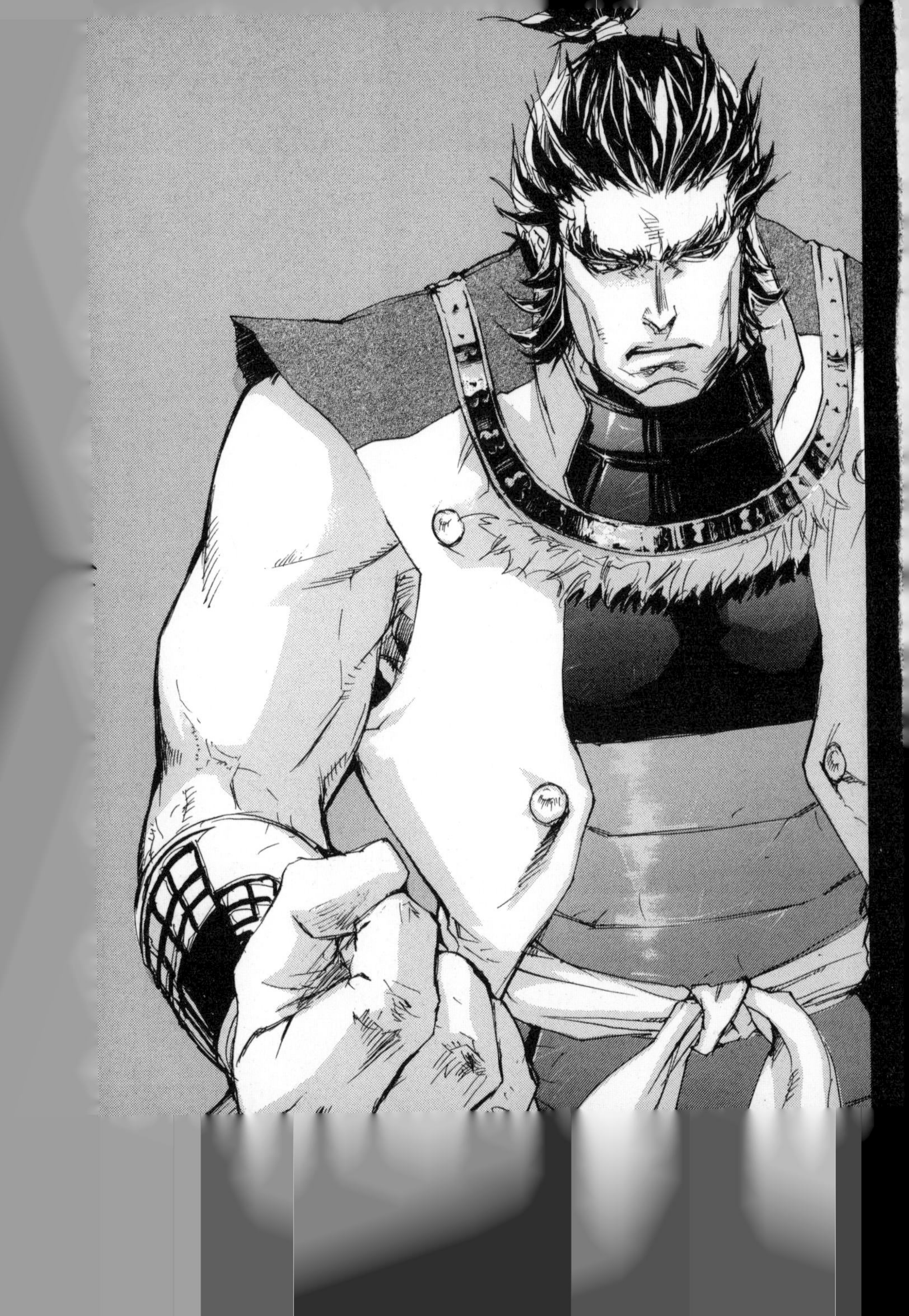

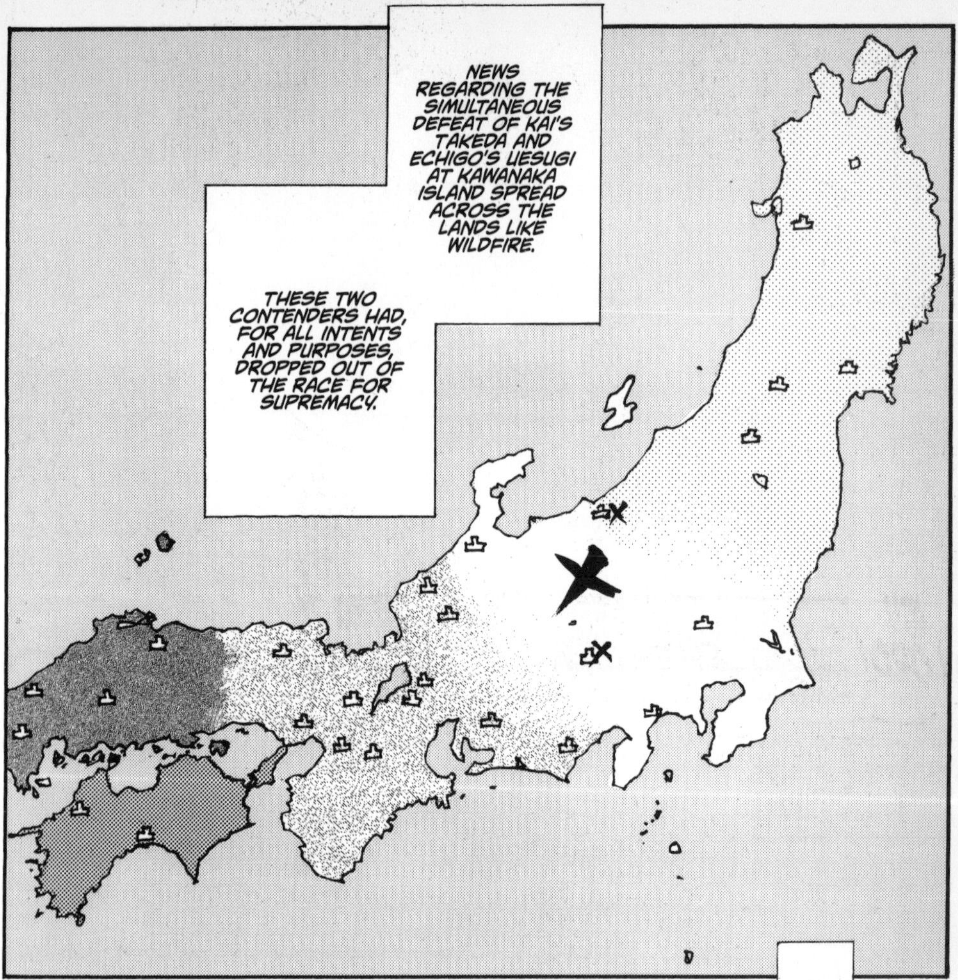
NEWS REGARDING THE SIMULTANEOUS DEFEAT OF KAI'S TAKEDA AND ECHIGO'S UESUGI AT KAWANAKA ISLAND SPREAD ACROSS THE LANDS LIKE WILDFIRE.
THESE TWO CONTENDERS HAD, FOR ALL INTENTS AND PURPOSES, DROPPED OUT OF THE RACE FOR SUPREMACY.

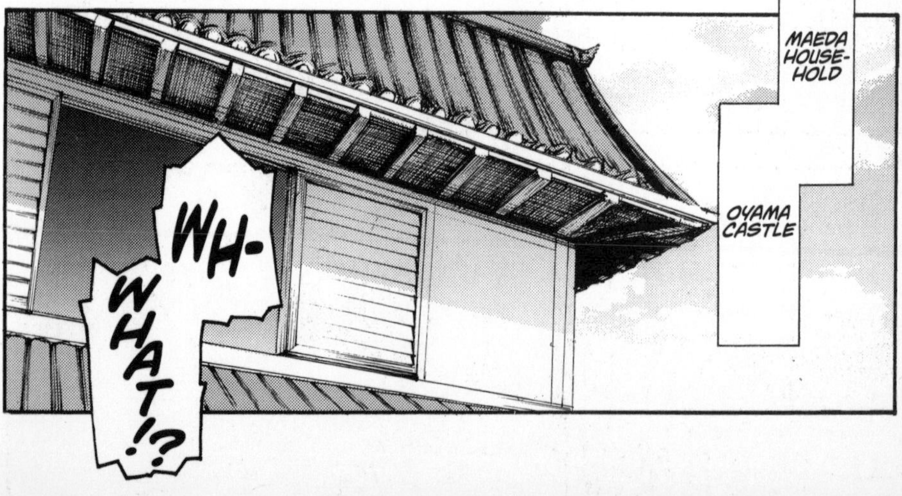
MAEDA HOUSEHOLD
OYAMA CASTLE
WH-WHAT!?

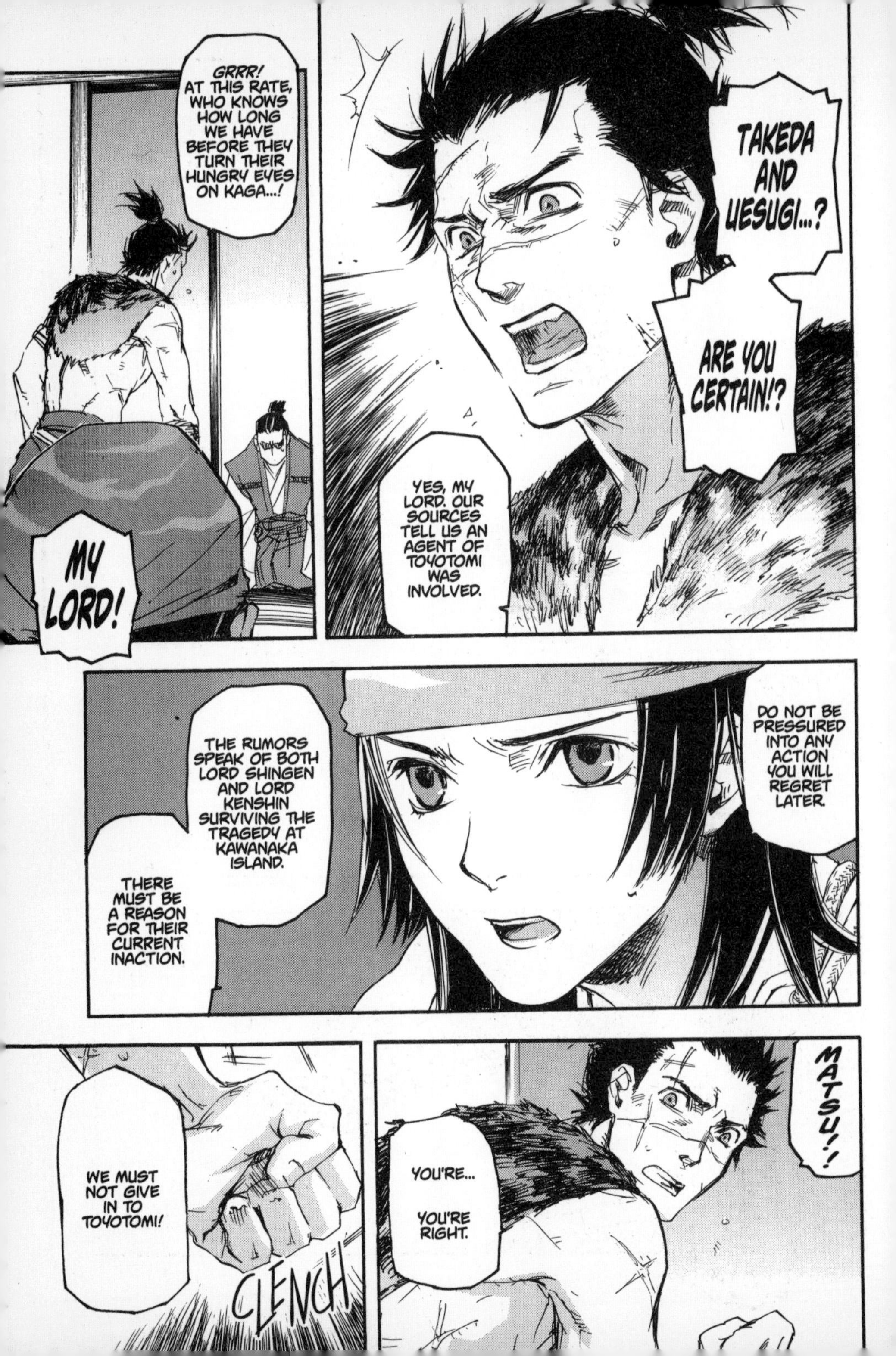
TAKEDA AND UESUGI...?
ARE YOU CERTAIN!?
YES, MY LORD. OUR SOURCES TELL US AN AGENT OF TOYOTOMI WAS INVOLVED.
GRRR! AT THIS RATE, WHO KNOWS HOW LONG WE HAVE BEFORE THEY TURN THEIR HUNGRY EYES ON KAGA...!
MY LORD!
DO NOT BE PRESSURED INTO ANY ACTION YOU WILL REGRET LATER.
THE RUMORS SPEAK OF BOTH LORD SHINGEN AND LORD KENSHIN SURVIVING THE TRAGEDY AT KAWANAKA ISLAND.
THERE MUST BE A REASON FOR THEIR CURRENT INACTION.
MATSU...!
YOU'RE...
YOU'RE RIGHT.
WE MUST NOT GIVE IN TO TOYOTOMI!
CLENCH

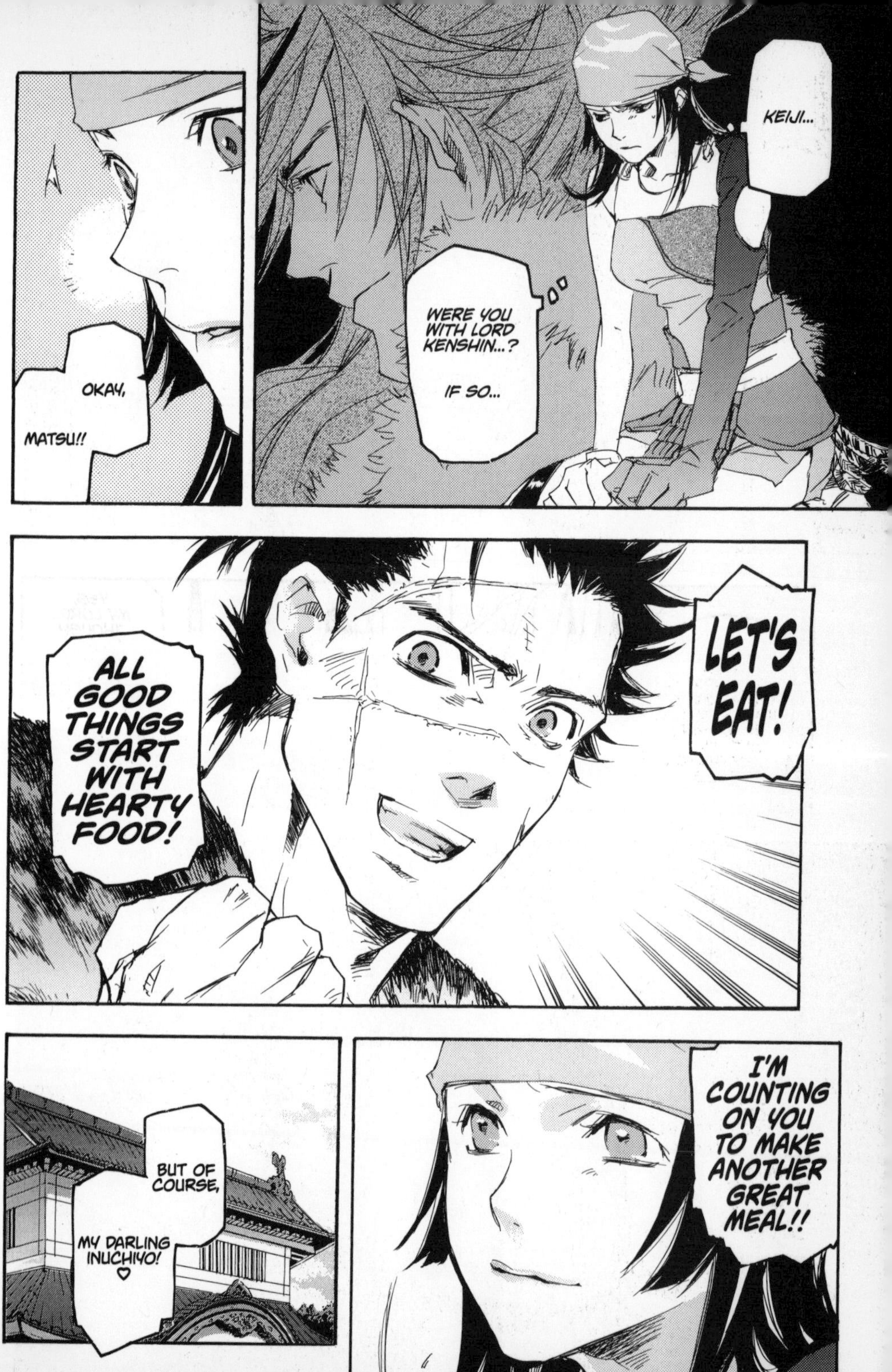
KEIJI...
WERE YOU WITH LORD KENSHIN...?
IF SO...
OKAY,
MATSU!!
LET'S EAT!
ALL GOOD THINGS START WITH HEARTY FOOD!
I'M COUNTING ON YOU TO MAKE ANOTHER GREAT MEAL!!
BUT OF COURSE,
MY DARLING INUCHIYO! ♡

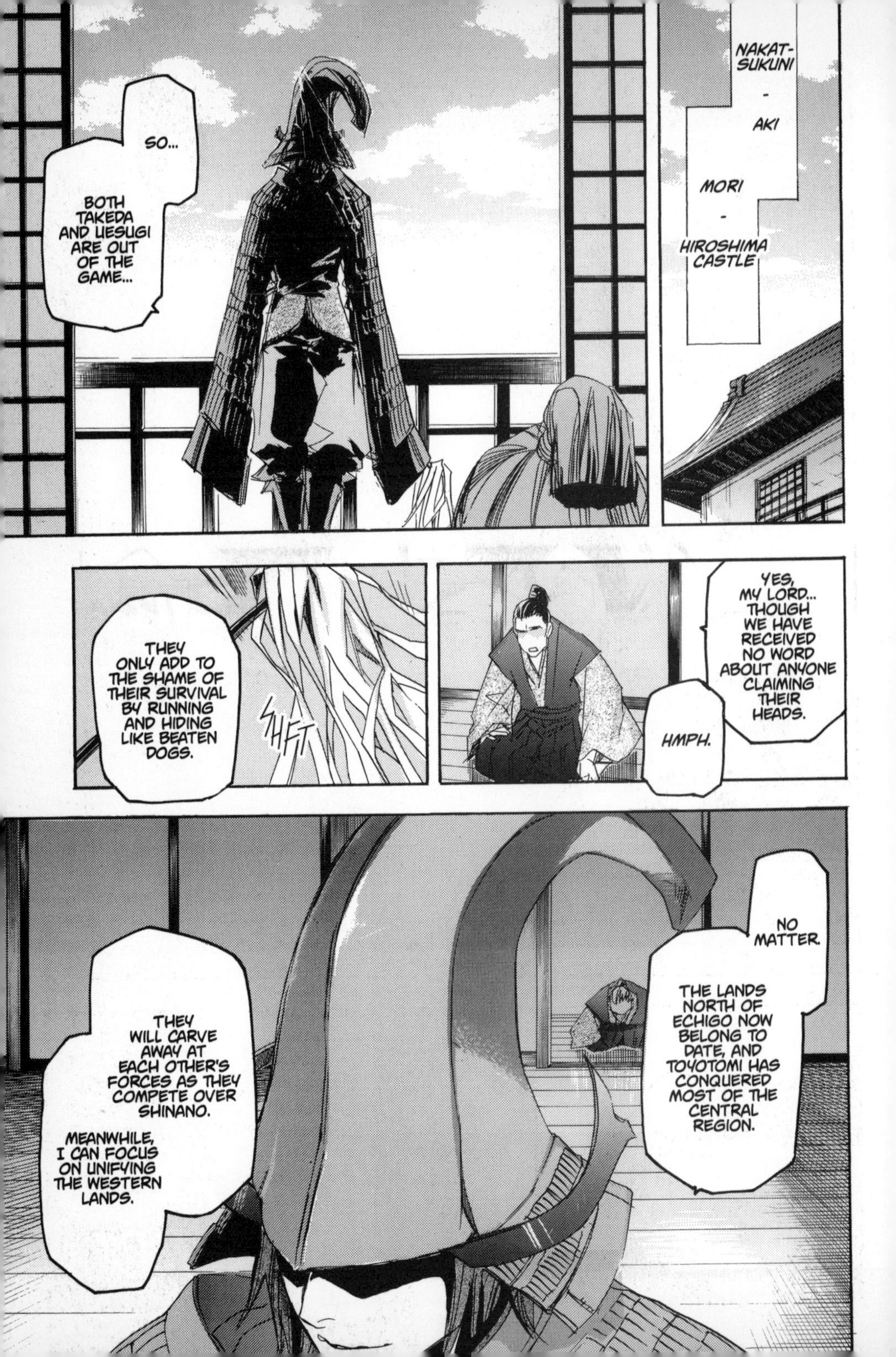
NAKATSUKUNI - AKI
MORI - HIROSHIMA CASTLE
SO...
BOTH TAKEDA AND UESUGI ARE OUT OF THE GAME...
YES, MY LORD... THOUGH WE HAVE RECEIVED NO WORD ABOUT ANYONE CLAIMING THEIR HEADS.
HMPH.
THEY ONLY ADD TO THE SHAME OF THEIR SURVIVAL BY RUNNING AND HIDING LIKE BEATEN DOGS.
SHFT
NO MATTER.
THE LANDS NORTH OF ECHIGO NOW BELONG TO DATE, AND TOYOTOMI HAS CONQUERED MOST OF THE CENTRAL REGION.
THEY WILL CARVE AWAY AT EACH OTHER'S FORCES AS THEY COMPETE OVER SHINANO.
MEANWHILE, I CAN FOCUS ON UNIFYING THE WESTERN LANDS.

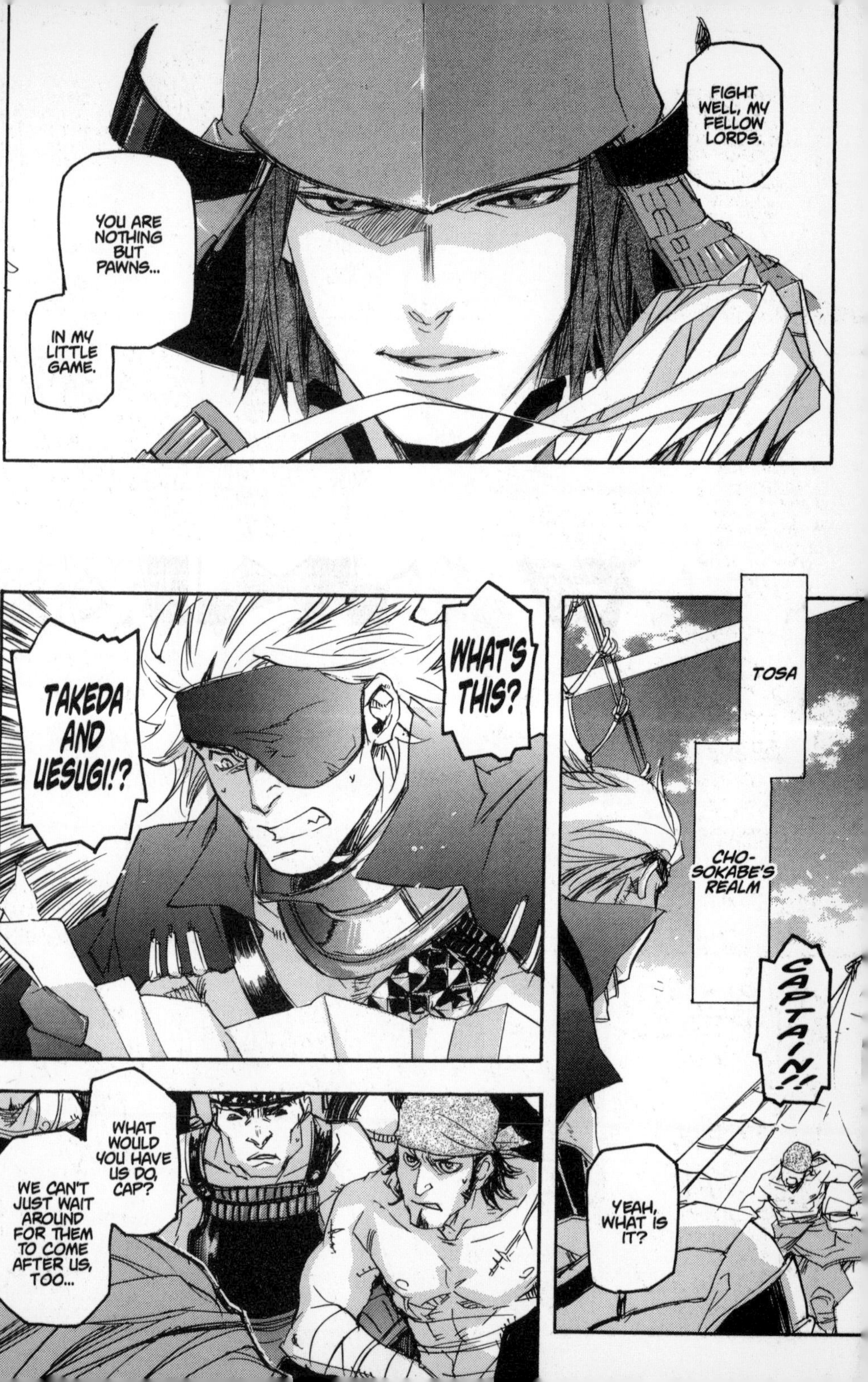
FIGHT WELL, MY FELLOW LORDS.
YOU ARE NOTHING BUT PAWNS...
IN MY LITTLE GAME.
TOSA
CHO-SOKABE'S REALM
CAPTAIN!!
YEAH, WHAT IS IT?
WHAT'S THIS?
TAKEDA AND UESUGI!?
WHAT WOULD YOU HAVE US DO, CAP?
WE CAN'T JUST WAIT AROUND FOR THEM TO COME AFTER US, TOO...

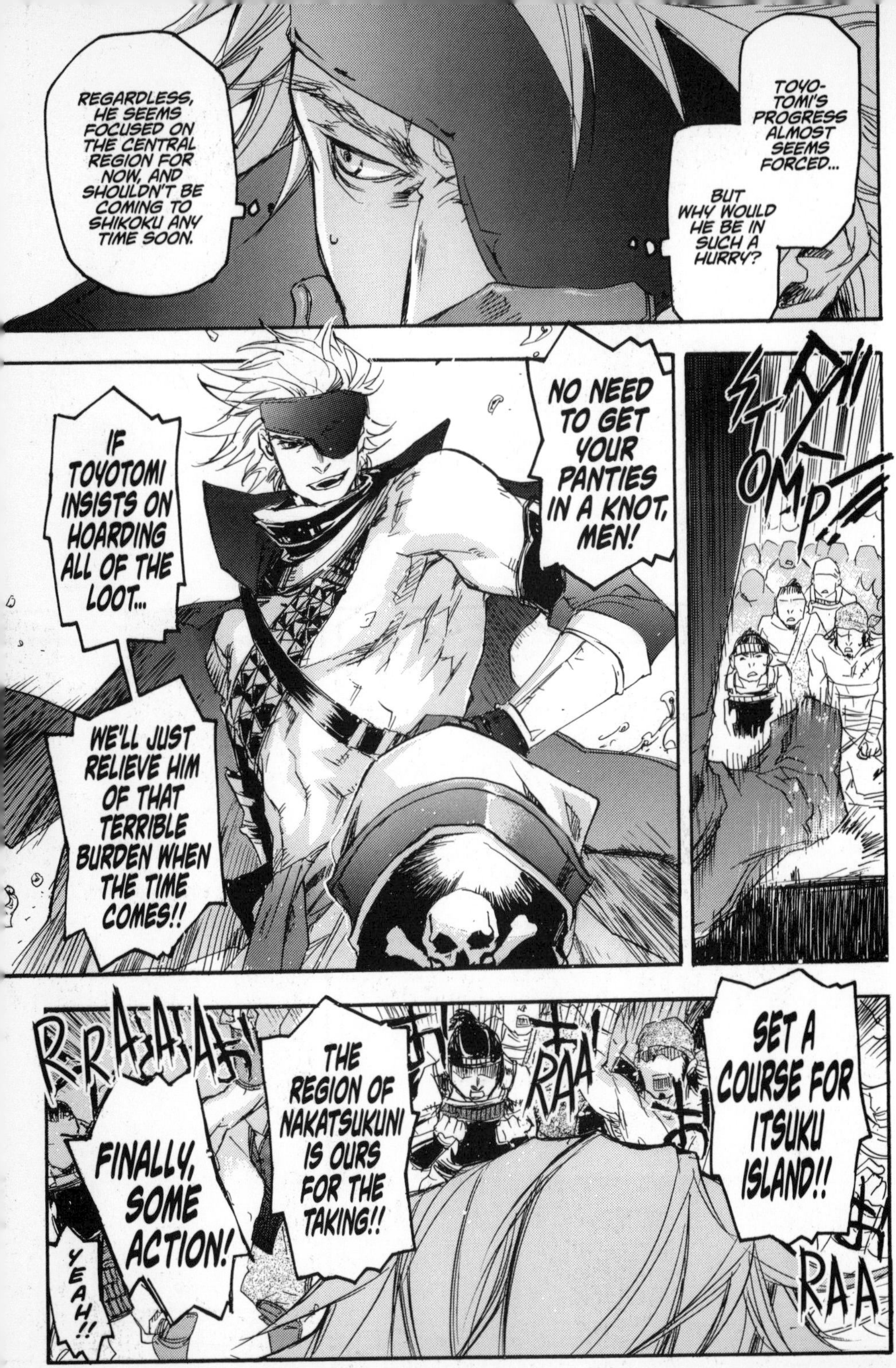
TOYOTOMI'S PROGRESS ALMOST SEEMS FORCED...
BUT WHY WOULD HE BE IN SUCH A HURRY?
REGARDLESS, HE SEEMS FOCUSED ON THE CENTRAL REGION FOR NOW, AND SHOULDN'T BE COMING TO SHIKOKU ANY TIME SOON.
STOMP
NO NEED TO GET YOUR PANTIES IN A KNOT, MEN!
IF TOYOTOMI INSISTS ON HOARDING ALL OF THE LOOT...
WE'LL JUST RELIEVE HIM OF THAT TERRIBLE BURDEN WHEN THE TIME COMES!!
SET A COURSE FOR ITSUKU ISLAND!!
RAA
RAA
THE REGION OF NAKATSUKUNI IS OURS FOR THE TAKING!!
RRAAAAH!
FINALLY, SOME ACTION!
YEAH!!

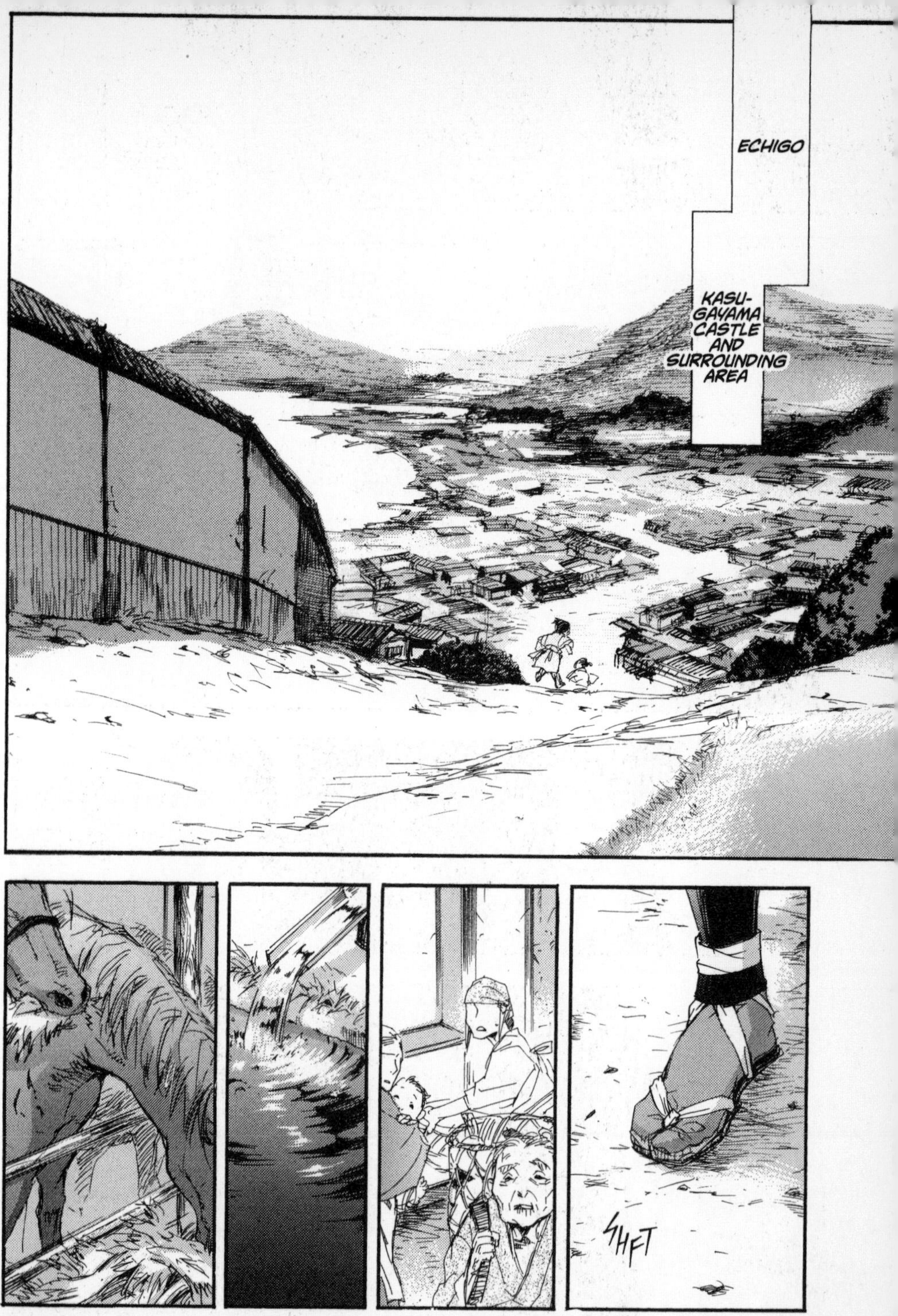
ECHIGO
KASU-GAYAMA CASTLE AND SURROUNDING AREA
SHFT

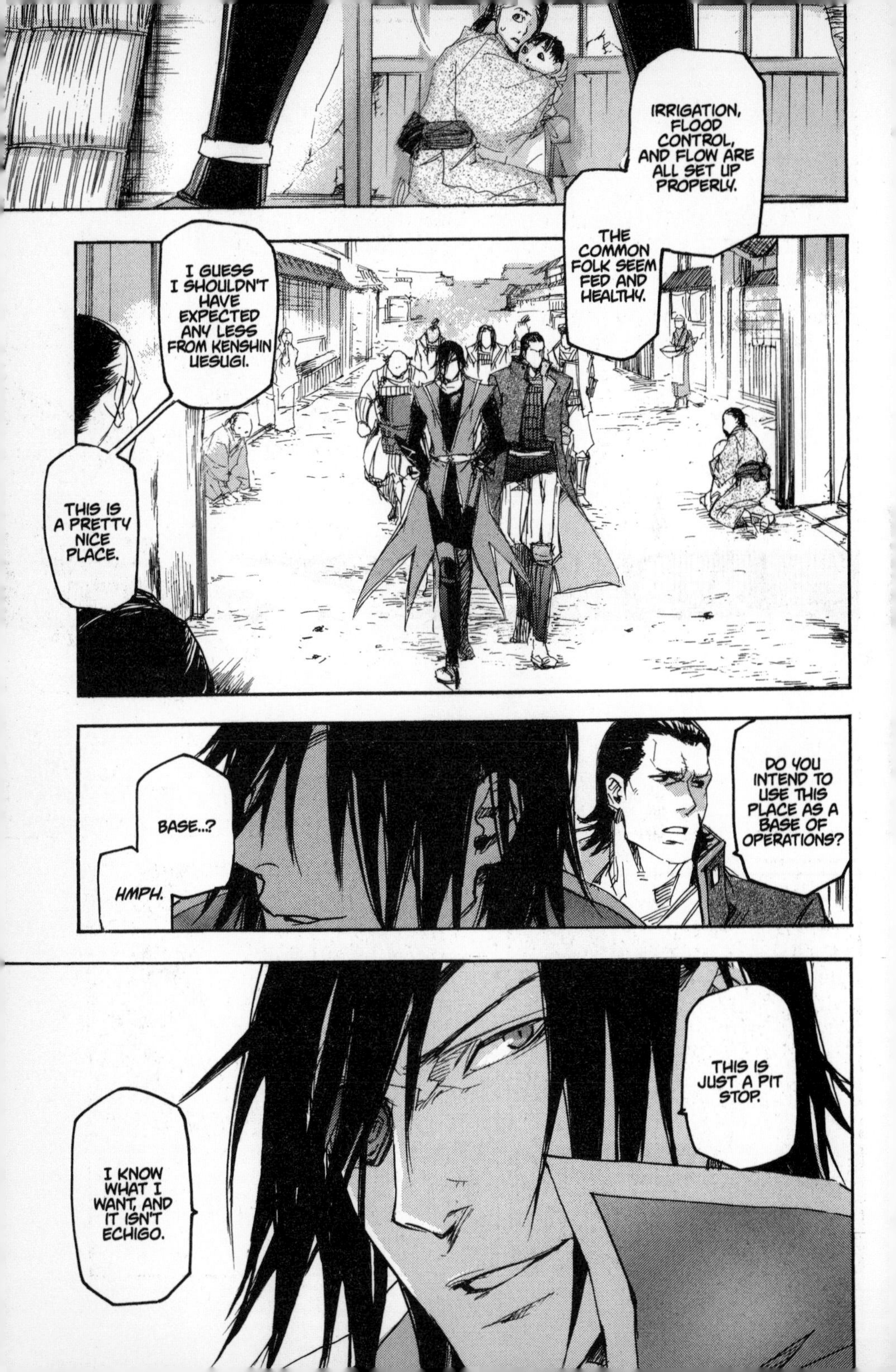
IRRIGATION, FLOOD CONTROL, AND FLOW ARE ALL SET UP PROPERLY.
THE COMMON FOLK SEEM FED AND HEALTHY.
I GUESS I SHOULDN'T HAVE EXPECTED ANY LESS FROM KENSHIN UESUGI.
THIS IS A PRETTY NICE PLACE.
DO YOU INTEND TO USE THIS PLACE AS A BASE OF OPERATIONS?
BASE...?
HMPH.
THIS IS JUST A PIT STOP.
I KNOW WHAT I WANT, AND IT ISN'T ECHIGO.

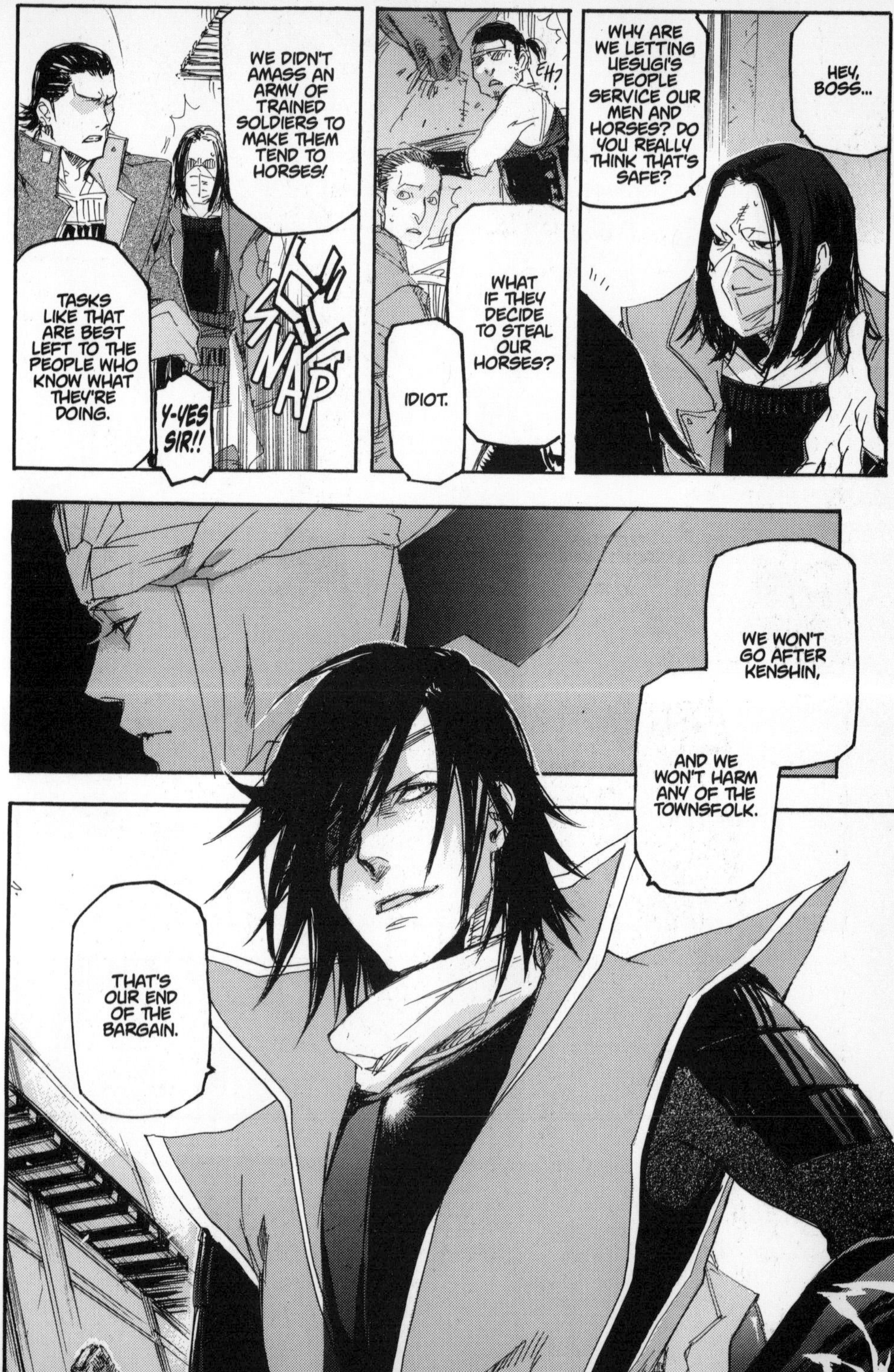
HEY, BOSS...
WHY ARE WE LETTING UESUGI'S PEOPLE SERVICE OUR MEN AND HORSES? DO YOU REALLY THINK THAT'S SAFE?
EH?
WHAT IF THEY DECIDE TO STEAL OUR HORSES?
IDIOT.
WE DIDN'T AMASS AN ARMY OF TRAINED SOLDIERS TO MAKE THEM TEND TO HORSES!
SNAP
TASKS LIKE THAT ARE BEST LEFT TO THE PEOPLE WHO KNOW WHAT THEY'RE DOING.
Y-YES SIR!!
WE WON'T GO AFTER KENSHIN,
AND WE WON'T HARM ANY OF THE TOWNSFOLK.
THAT'S OUR END OF THE BARGAIN.

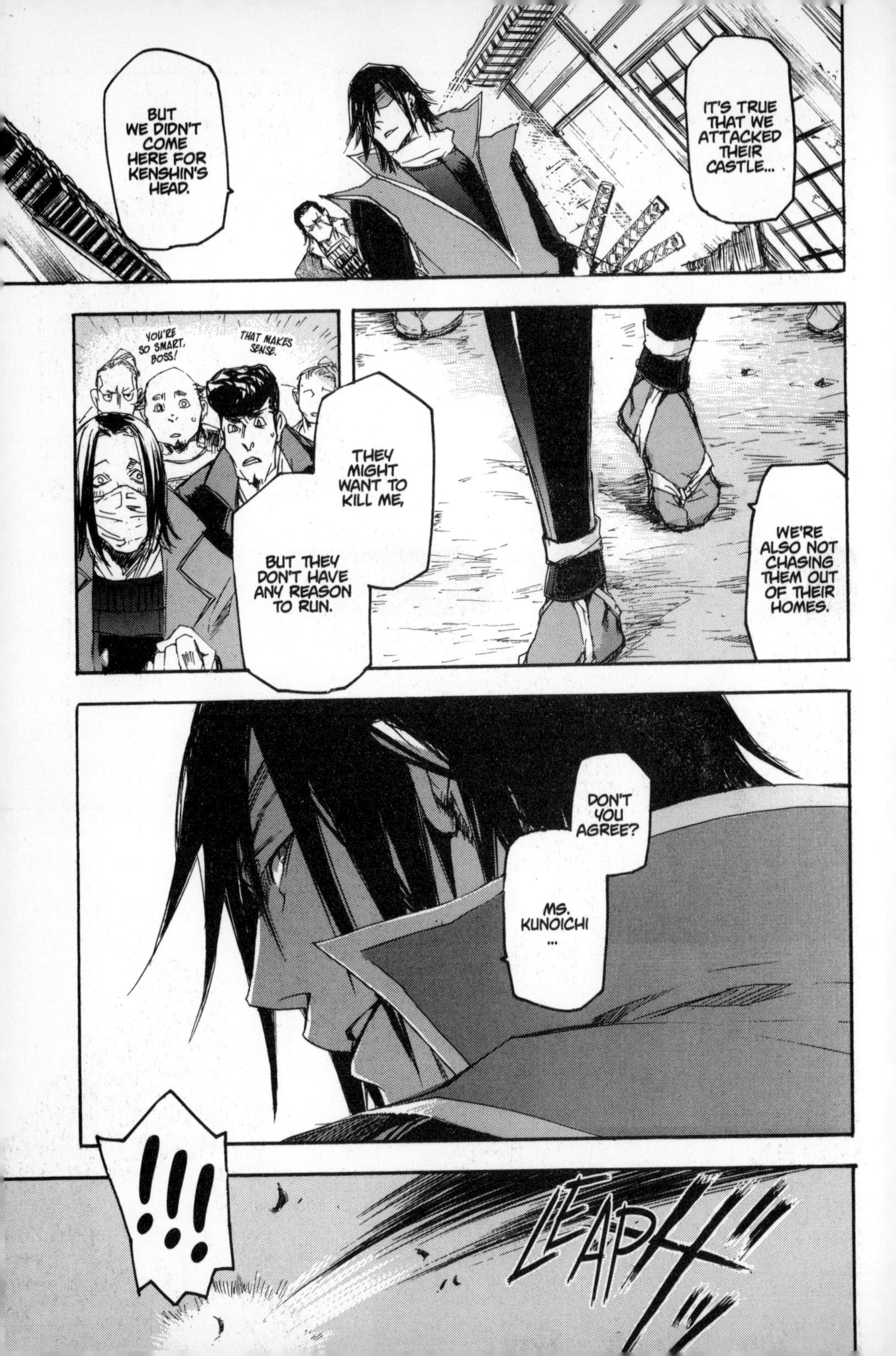
IT'S TRUE THAT WE ATTACKED THEIR CASTLE...
BUT WE DIDN'T COME HERE FOR KENSHIN'S HEAD.
WE'RE ALSO NOT CHASING THEM OUT OF THEIR HOMES.
THEY MIGHT WANT TO KILL ME,
BUT THEY DON'T HAVE ANY REASON TO RUN.
THAT MAKES SENSE.
YOU'RE SO SMART, BOSS!
DON'T YOU AGREE?
MS. KUNOICHI ...
LEAP!!
!!!

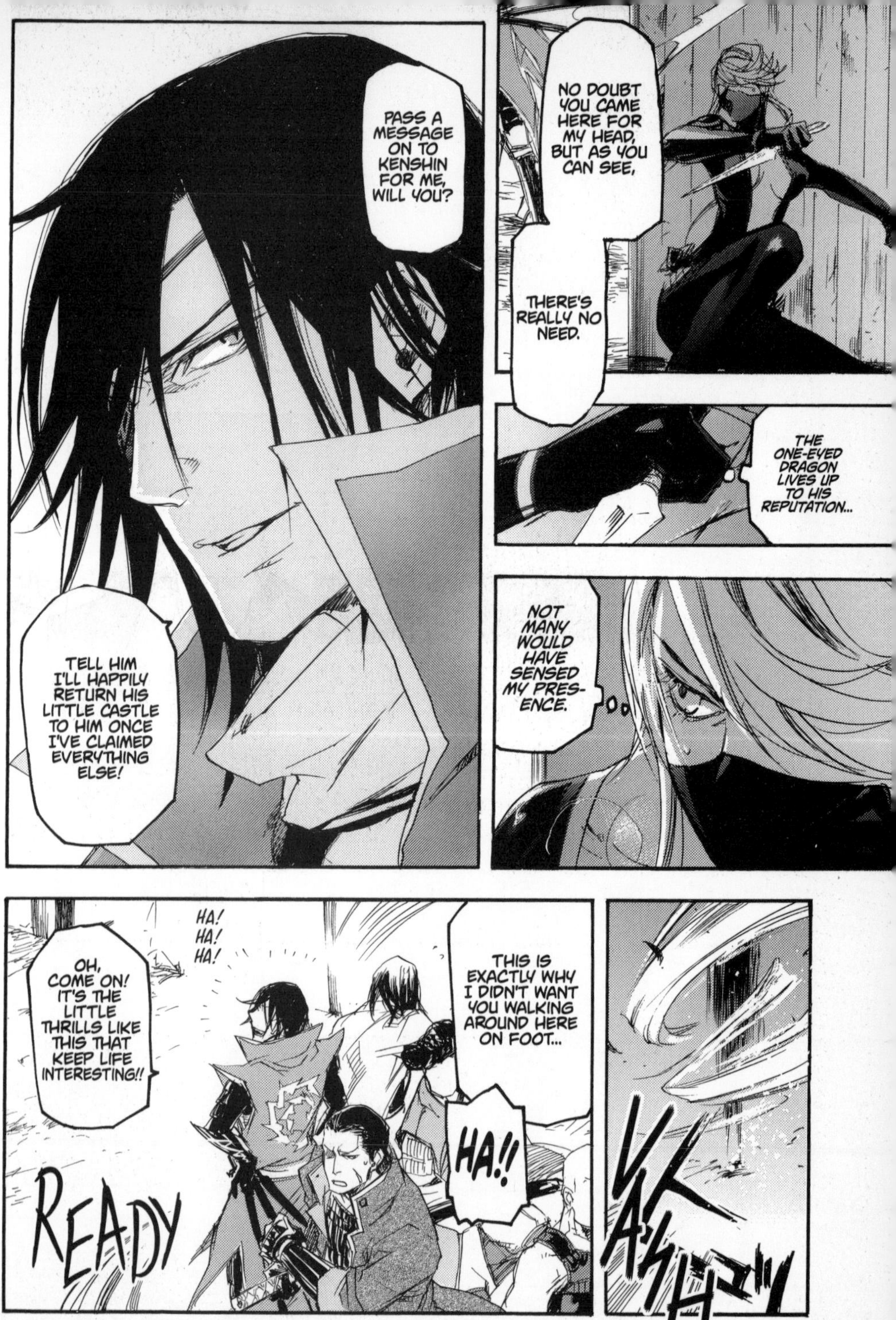
NO DOUBT YOU CAME HERE FOR MY HEAD, BUT AS YOU CAN SEE,
THERE'S REALLY NO NEED.
THE ONE-EYED DRAGON LIVES UP TO HIS REPUTATION...
NOT MANY WOULD HAVE SENSED MY PRES-ENCE.
PASS A MESSAGE ON TO KENSHIN FOR ME, WILL YOU?
TELL HIM I'LL HAPPILY RETURN HIS LITTLE CASTLE TO HIM ONCE I'VE CLAIMED EVERYTHING ELSE!
VASH
THIS IS EXACTLY WHY I DIDN'T WANT YOU WALKING AROUND HERE ON FOOT...
HA! HA! HA!
OH, COME ON! IT'S THE LITTLE THRILLS LIKE THIS THAT KEEP LIFE INTERESTING!!
HA!!
READY

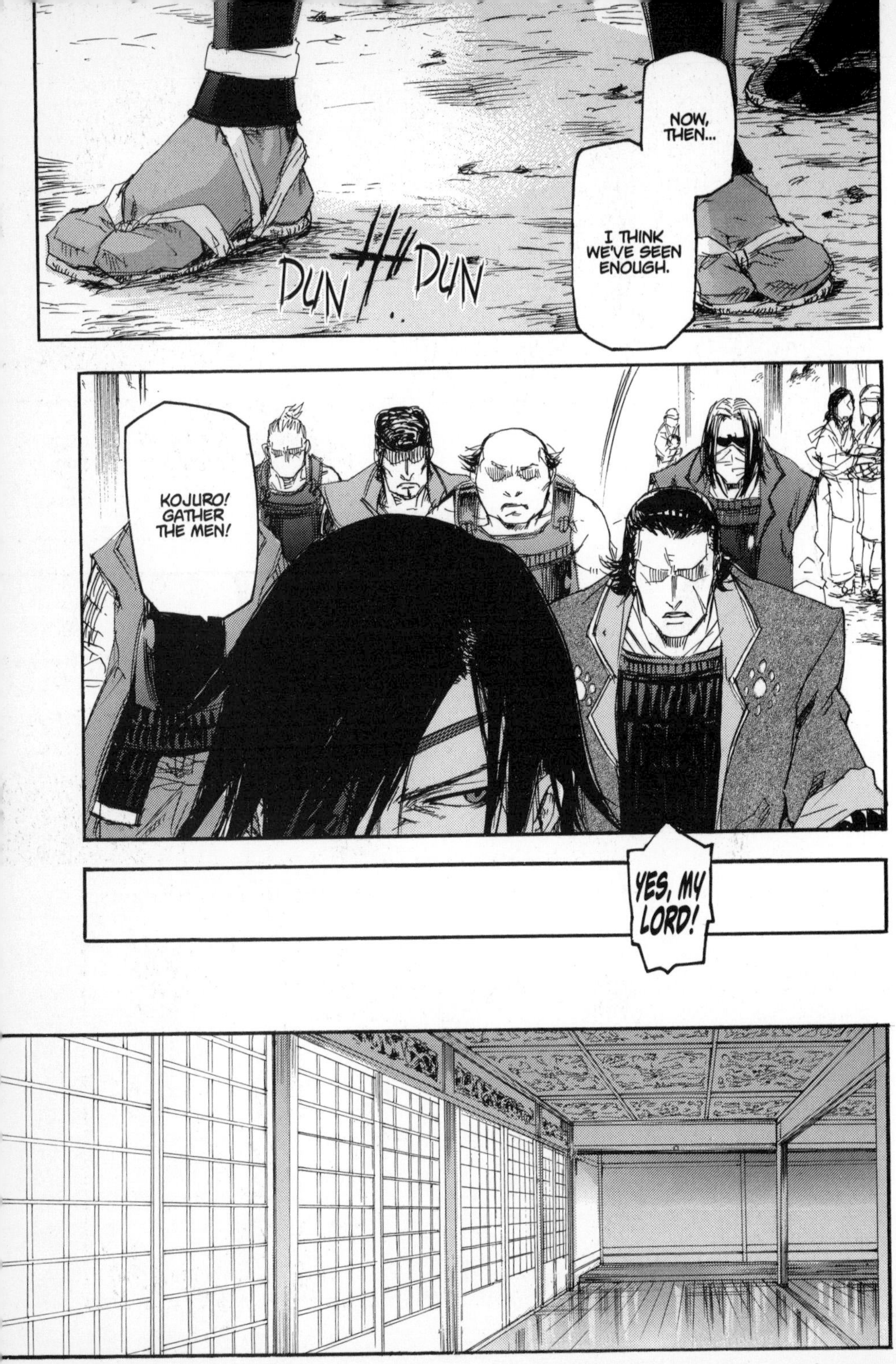
NOW, THEN...
I THINK WE'VE SEEN ENOUGH.
DUN DUN
KOJURO! GATHER THE MEN!
YES, MY LORD!

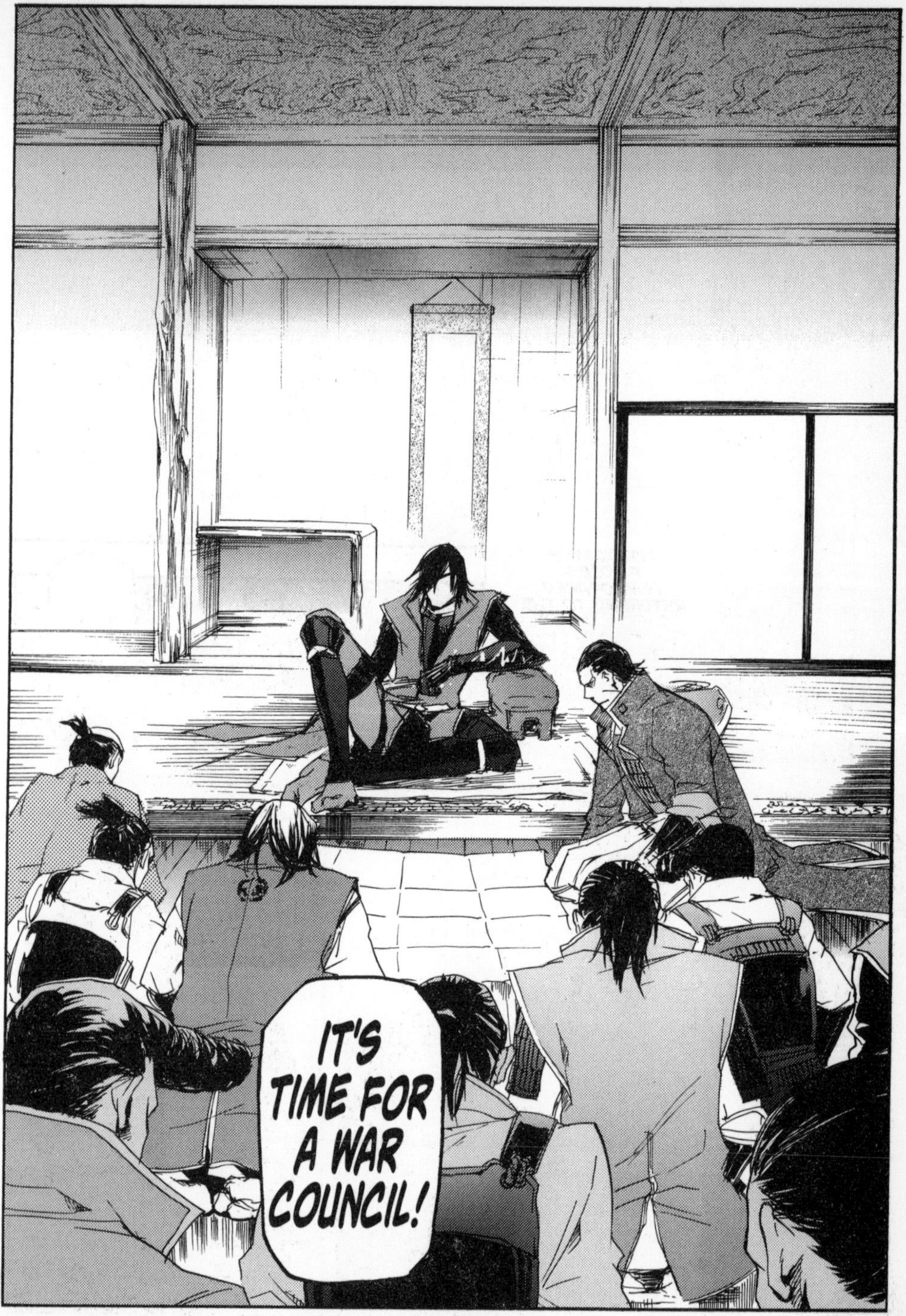
IT'S TIME FOR A WAR COUNCIL!

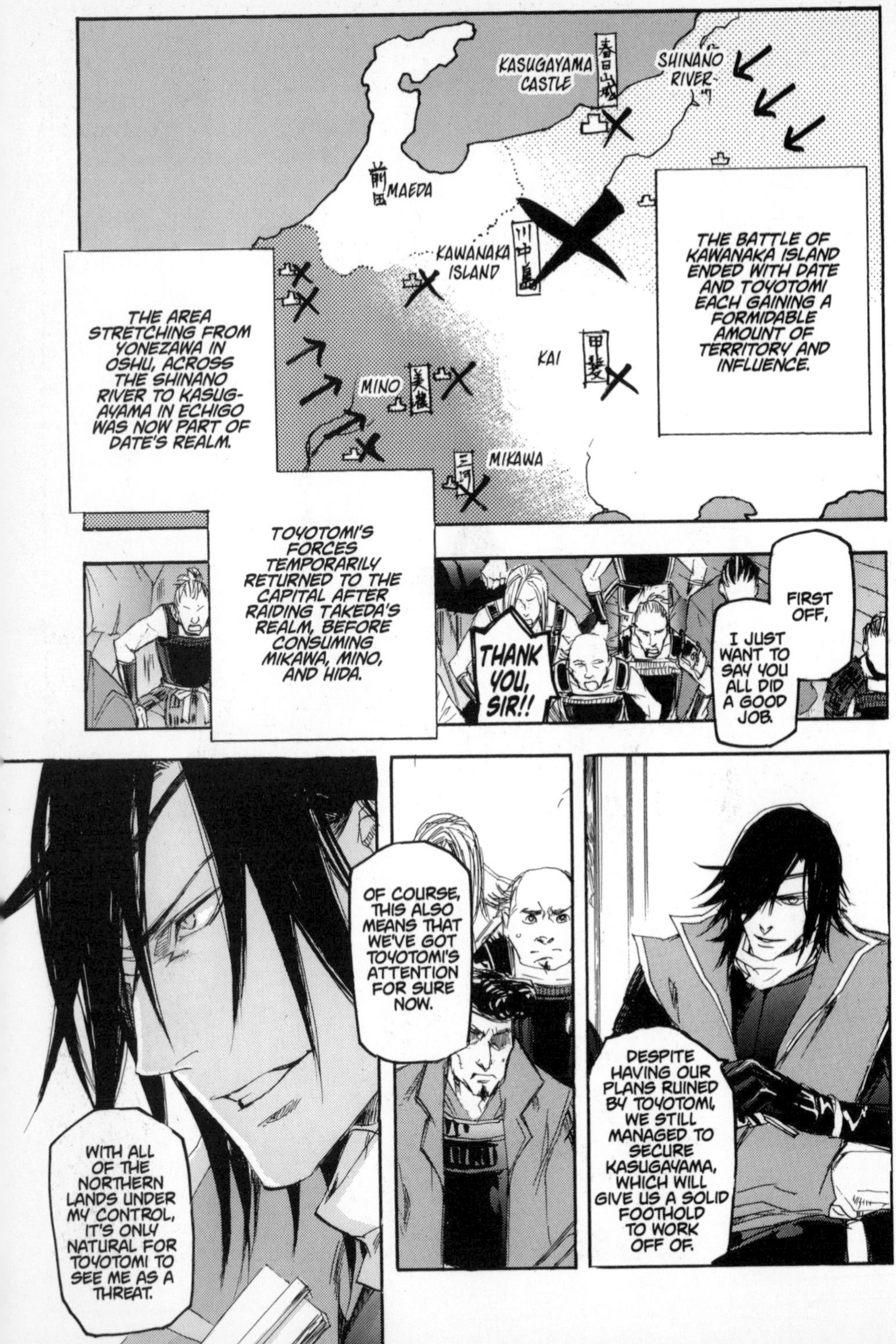
THE BATTLE OF KAWANAKA ISLAND ENDED WITH DATE AND TOYOTOMI EACH GAINING A FORMIDABLE AMOUNT OF TERRITORY AND INFLUENCE.
SHINANO RIVER
KASUGAYAMA CASTLE
春日山城
川中島
KAWANAKA ISLAND
MAEDA
前田
KAI
甲斐
美濃
MINO
三河
MIKAWA
THE AREA STRETCHING FROM YONEZAWA IN OSHU, ACROSS THE SHINANO RIVER TO KASUG-AYAMA IN ECHIGO WAS NOW PART OF DATE'S REALM.
TOYOTOMI'S FORCES TEMPORARILY RETURNED TO THE CAPITAL AFTER RAIDING TAKEDA'S REALM, BEFORE CONSUMING MIKAWA, MINO, AND HIDA.
FIRST OFF, I JUST WANT TO SAY YOU ALL DID A GOOD JOB.
THANK YOU, SIR!!
DESPITE HAVING OUR PLANS RUINED BY TOYOTOMI, WE STILL MANAGED TO SECURE KASUGAYAMA, WHICH WILL GIVE US A SOLID FOOTHOLD TO WORK OFF OF.
OF COURSE, THIS ALSO MEANS THAT WE'VE GOT TOYOTOMI'S ATTENTION FOR SURE NOW.
WITH ALL OF THE NORTHERN LANDS UNDER MY CONTROL, IT'S ONLY NATURAL FOR TOYOTOMI TO SEE ME AS A THREAT.

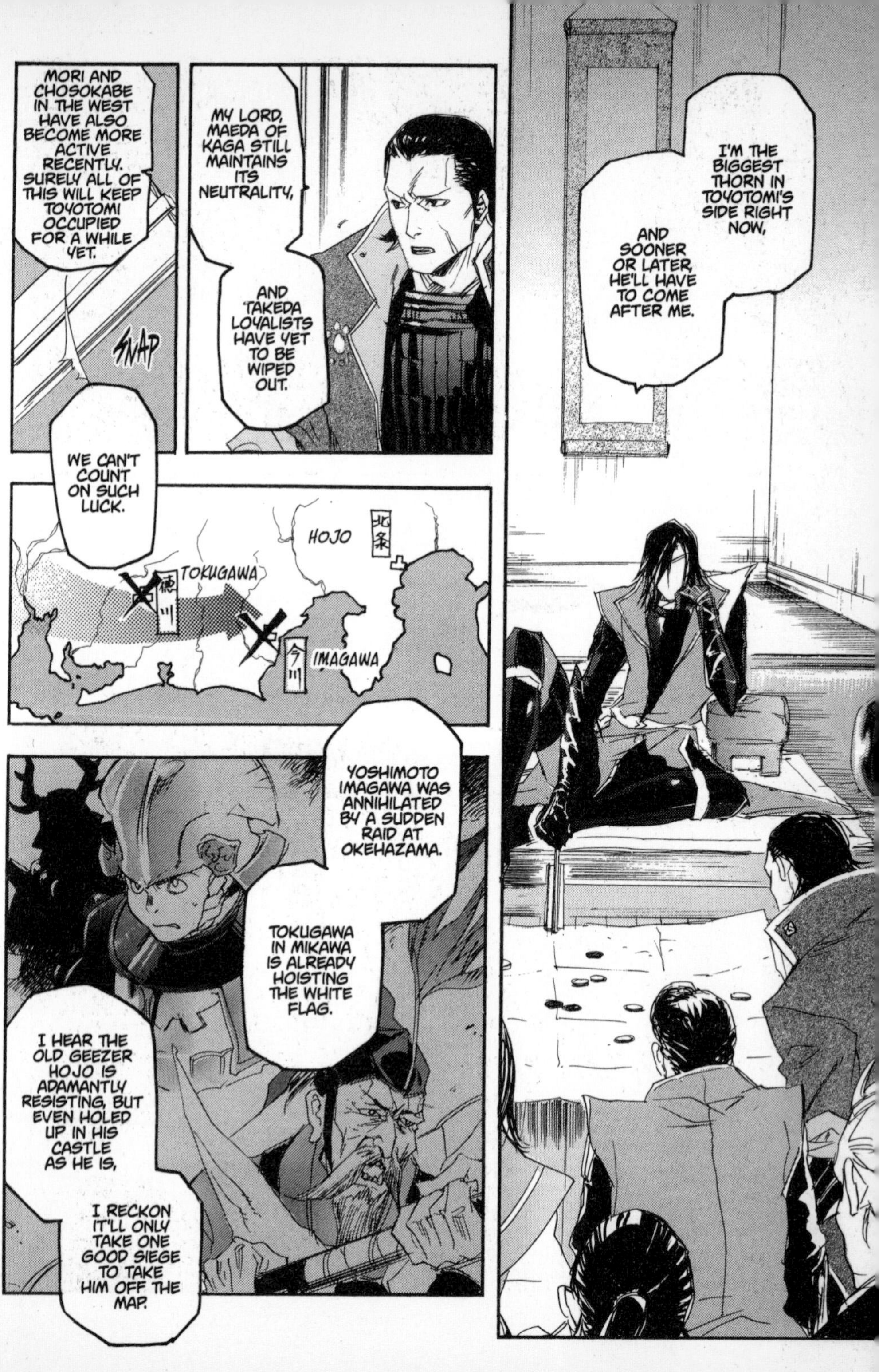
I'M THE BIGGEST THORN IN TOYOTOMI'S SIDE RIGHT NOW,
AND SOONER OR LATER, HE'LL HAVE TO COME AFTER ME.
MY LORD, MAEDA OF KAGA STILL MAINTAINS ITS NEUTRALITY,
AND TAKEDA LOYALISTS HAVE YET TO BE WIPED OUT.
MORI AND CHOSOKABE IN THE WEST HAVE ALSO BECOME MORE ACTIVE RECENTLY. SURELY ALL OF THIS WILL KEEP TOYOTOMI OCCUPIED FOR A WHILE YET.
SNAP
WE CAN'T COUNT ON SUCH LUCK.
北条
HOJO
徳川
TOKUGAWA
今川
IMAGAWA
YOSHIMOTO IMAGAWA WAS ANNIHILATED BY A SUDDEN RAID AT OKEHAZAMA.
TOKUGAWA IN MIKAWA IS ALREADY HOISTING THE WHITE FLAG.
I HEAR THE OLD GEEZER HOJO IS ADAMANTLY RESISTING, BUT EVEN HOLED UP IN HIS CASTLE AS HE IS,
I RECKON IT'LL ONLY TAKE ONE GOOD SIEGE TO TAKE HIM OFF THE MAP.

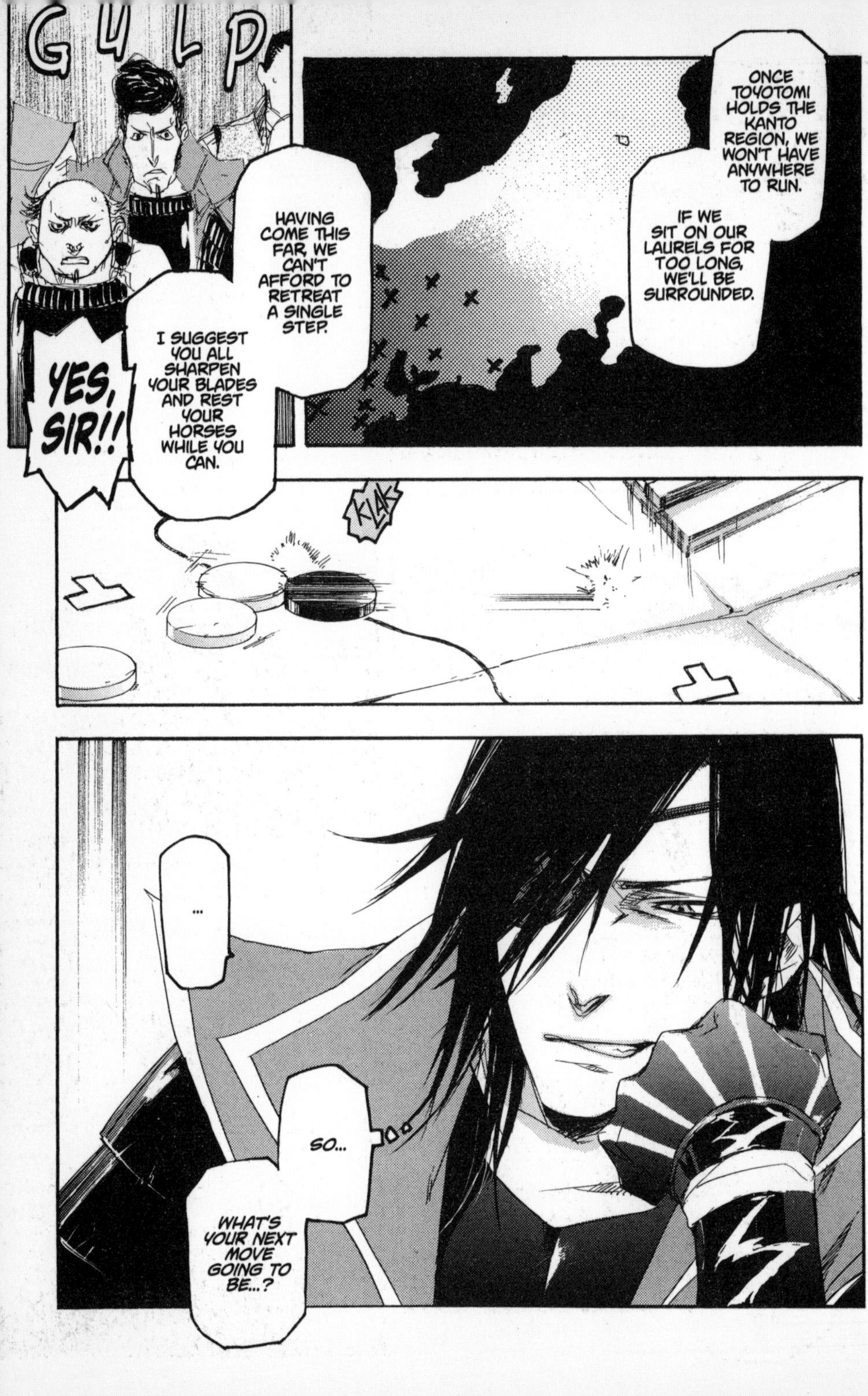

ONCE TOYOTOMI HOLDS THE KANTO REGION, WE WON'T HAVE ANYWHERE TO RUN.
IF WE SIT ON OUR LAURELS FOR TOO LONG, WE'LL BE SURROUNDED.
HAVING COME THIS FAR, WE CAN'T AFFORD TO RETREAT A SINGLE STEP.
I SUGGEST YOU ALL SHARPEN YOUR BLADES AND REST YOUR HORSES WHILE YOU CAN.
GULP
YES, SIR!!
KLAK
...
SO...
WHAT'S YOUR NEXT MOVE GOING TO BE...?

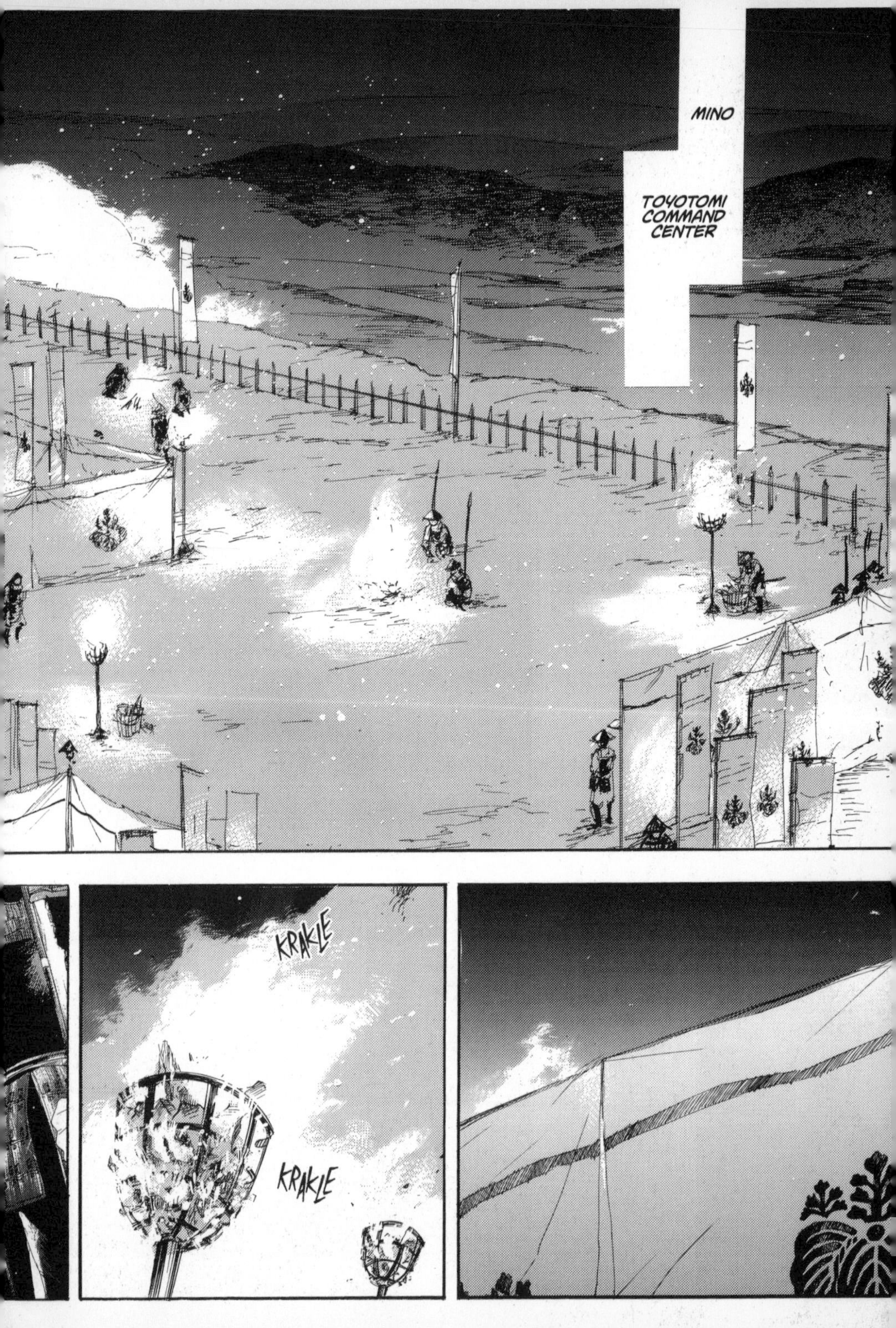
MINO
TOYOTOMI COMMAND CENTER
KRAKLE
KRAKLE

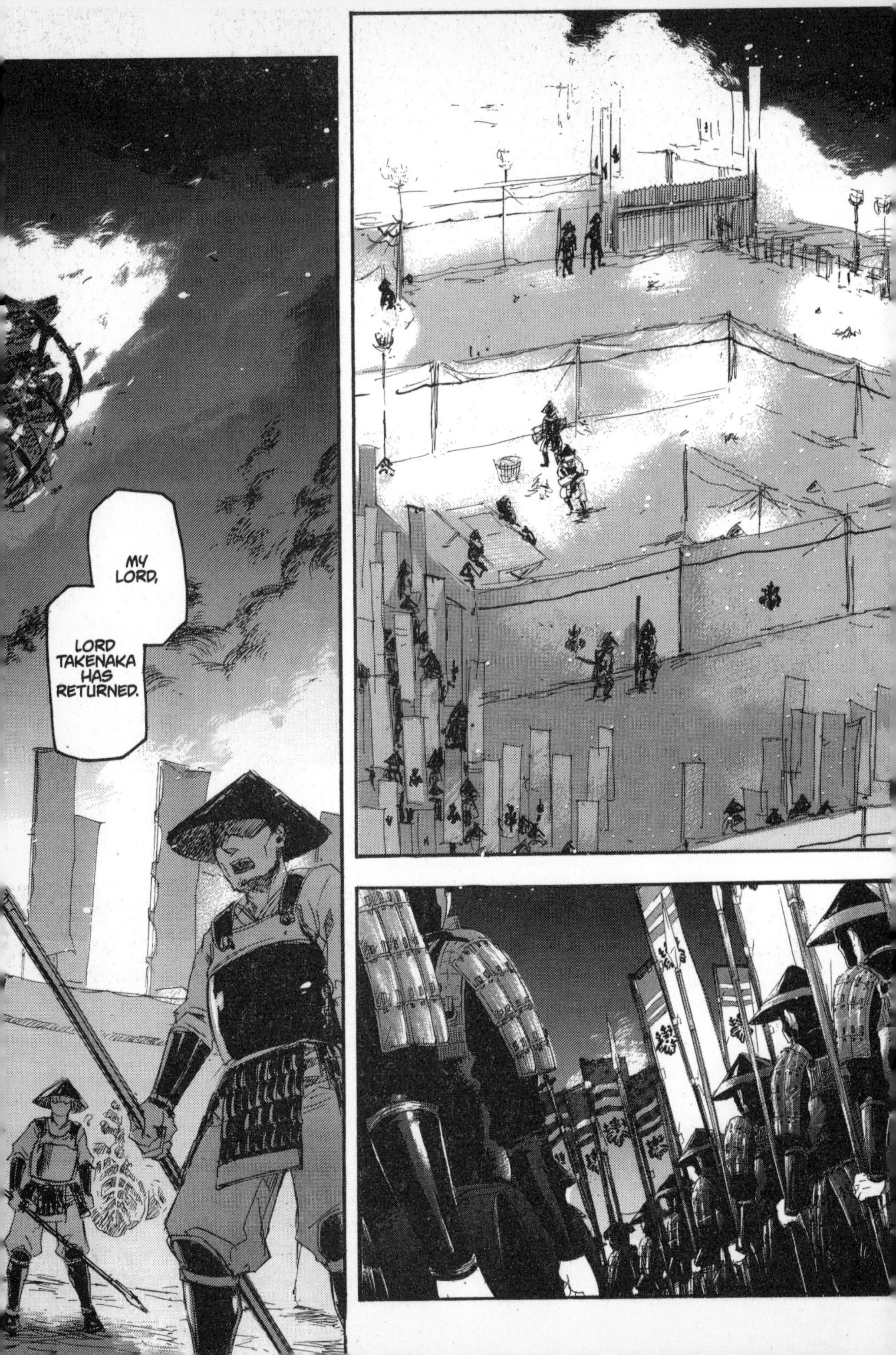
MY LORD,
LORD TAKENAKA HAS RETURNED.

WHERE IS HE, THEN?

MY LORD...

HE IS HAVING HIS WOUNDS TENDED.

WOUNDS?

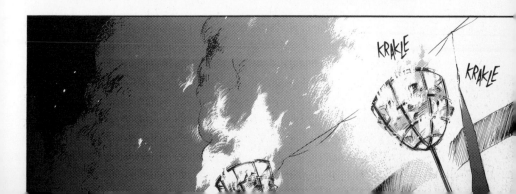

KRAKLE

KRAKLE

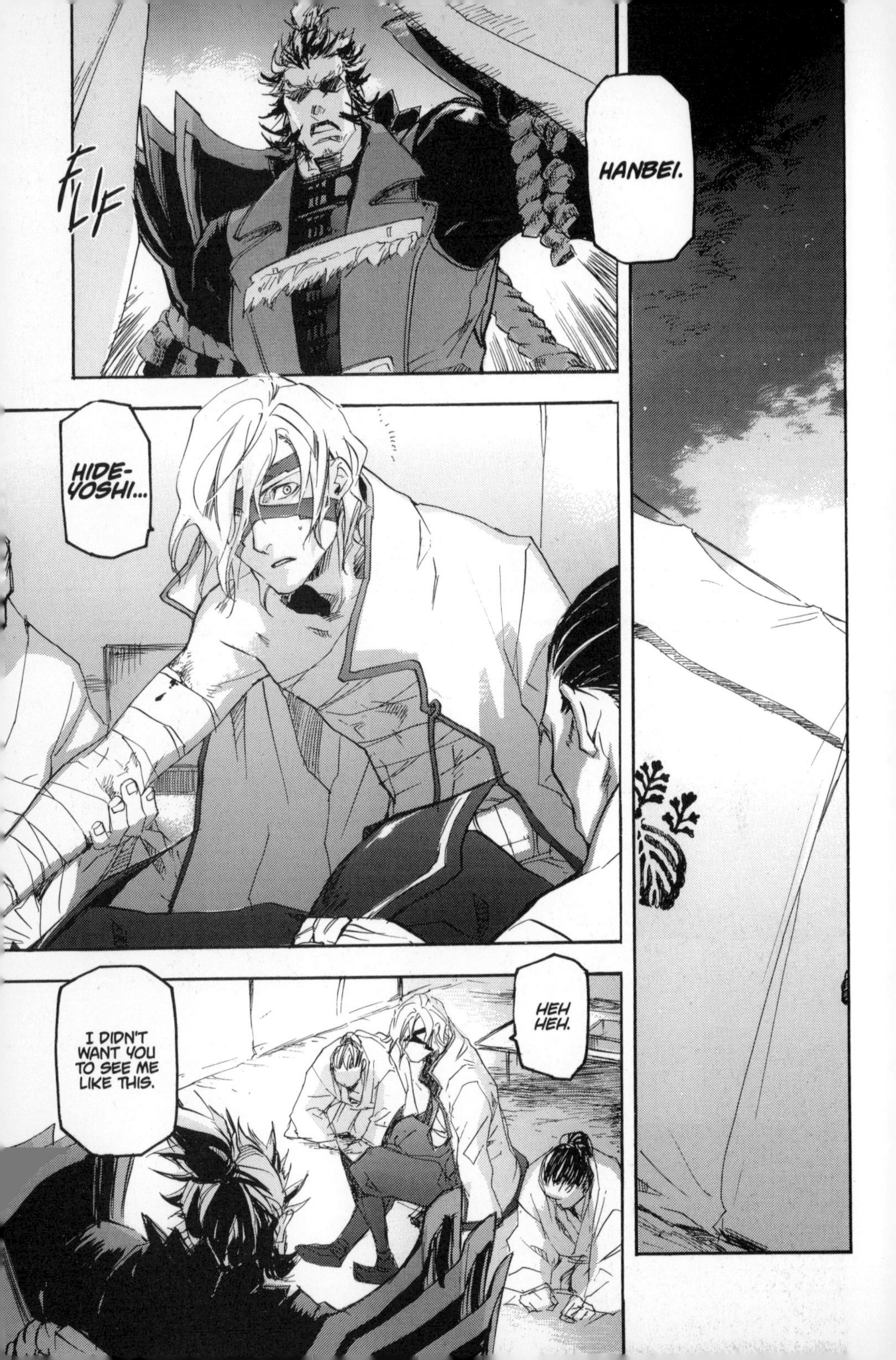
HANBEI.
FLIF
HIDE-YOSHI...
HEH HEH.
I DIDN'T WANT YOU TO SEE ME LIKE THIS.

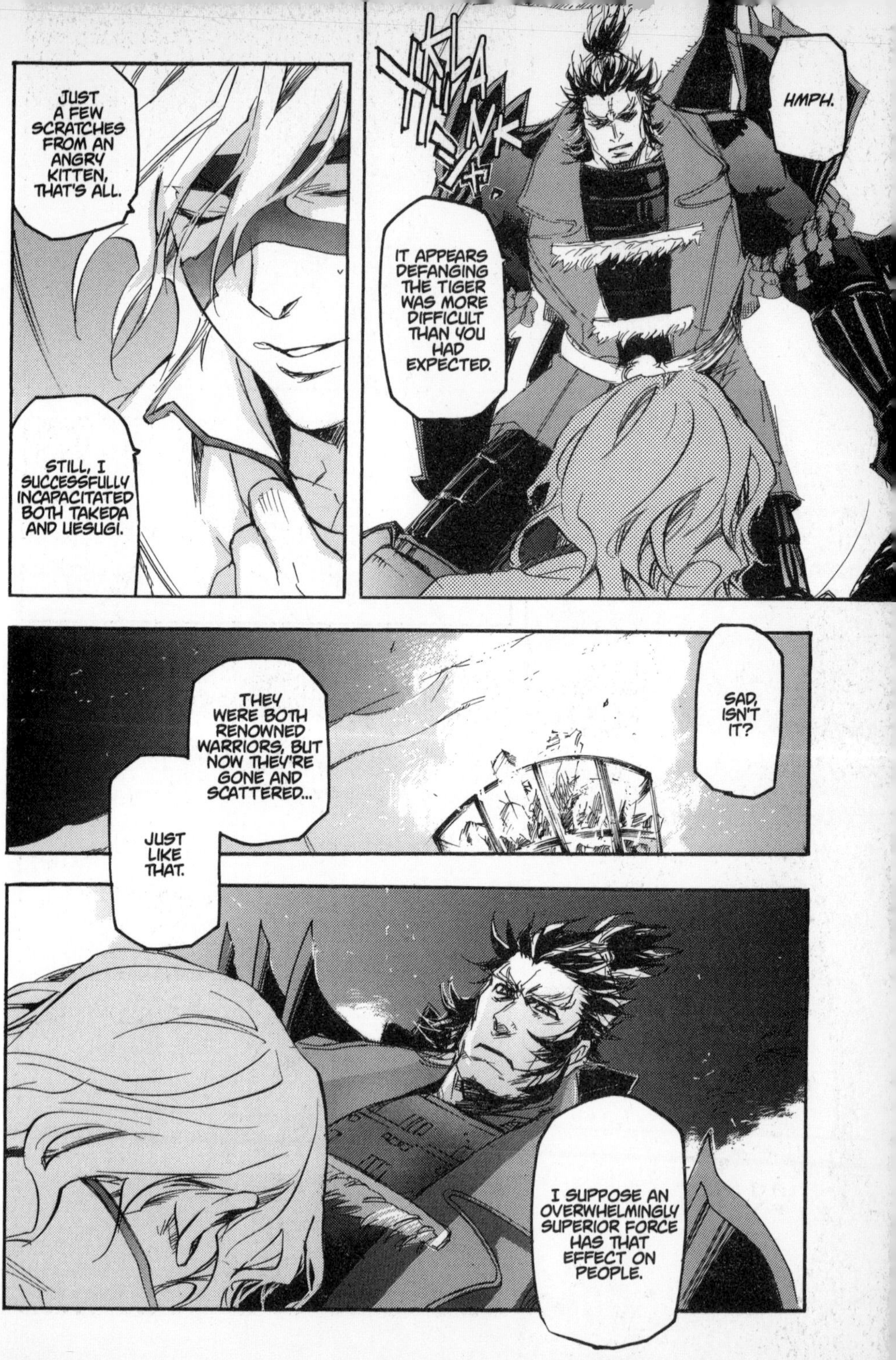
KLA-THUNK
HMPH.
IT APPEARS DEFANGING THE TIGER WAS MORE DIFFICULT THAN YOU HAD EXPECTED.
JUST A FEW SCRATCHES FROM AN ANGRY KITTEN, THAT'S ALL.
STILL, I SUCCESSFULLY INCAPACITATED BOTH TAKEDA AND UESUGI.
SAD, ISN'T IT?
THEY WERE BOTH RENOWNED WARRIORS, BUT NOW THEY'RE GONE AND SCATTERED...
JUST LIKE THAT.
I SUPPOSE AN OVERWHELMINGLY SUPERIOR FORCE HAS THAT EFFECT ON PEOPLE.

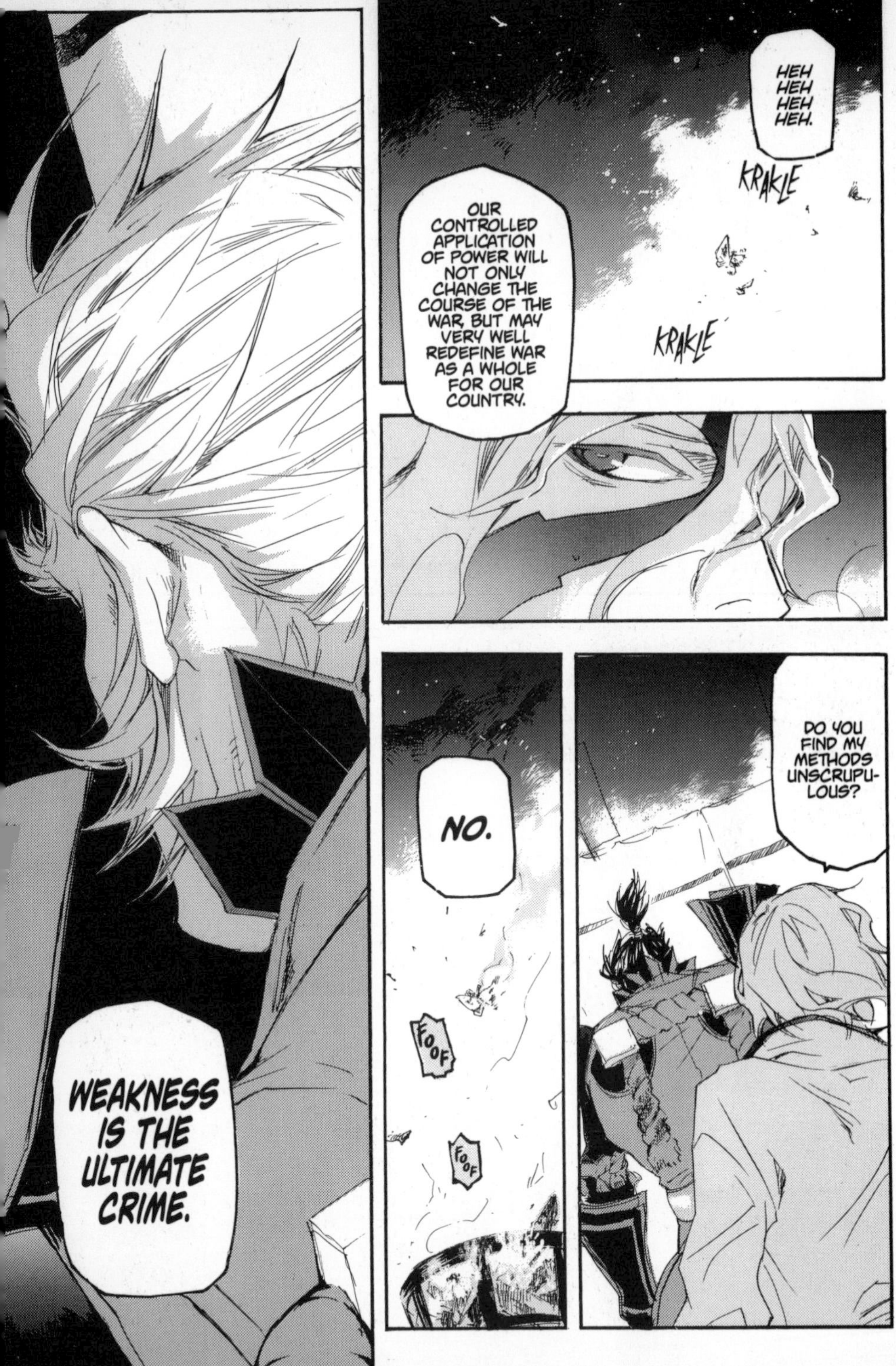

HEH HEH HEH HEH.
KRAKLE
OUR CONTROLLED APPLICATION OF POWER WILL NOT ONLY CHANGE THE COURSE OF THE WAR, BUT MAY VERY WELL REDEFINE WAR AS A WHOLE FOR OUR COUNTRY.
KRAKLE
DO YOU FIND MY METHODS UNSCRUPU-LOUS?
NO.
FOOF
FOOF
WEAKNESS IS THE ULTIMATE CRIME.

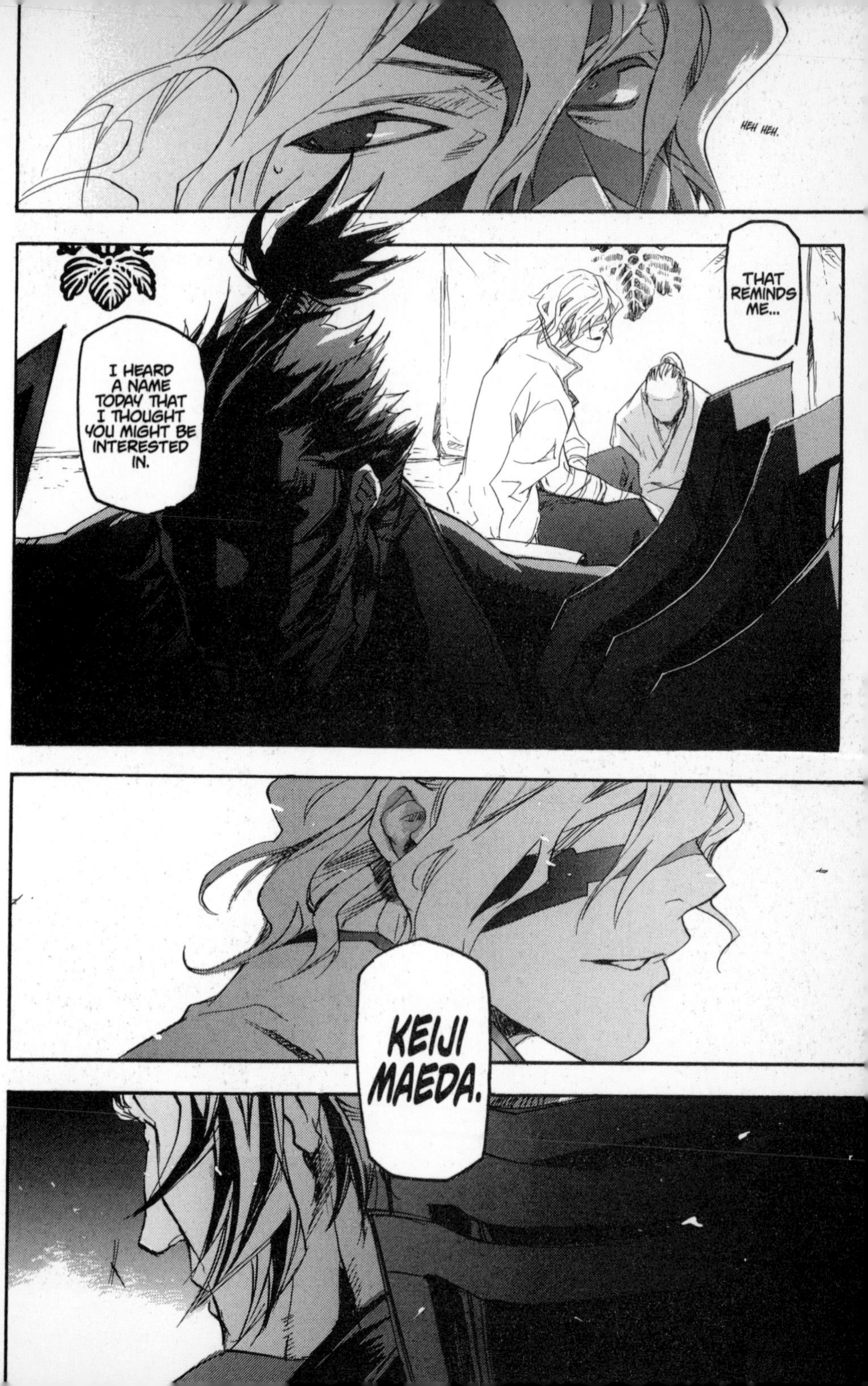
HEH HEH.
THAT REMINDS ME...
I HEARD A NAME TODAY THAT I THOUGHT YOU MIGHT BE INTERESTED IN.
KEIJI MAEDA.

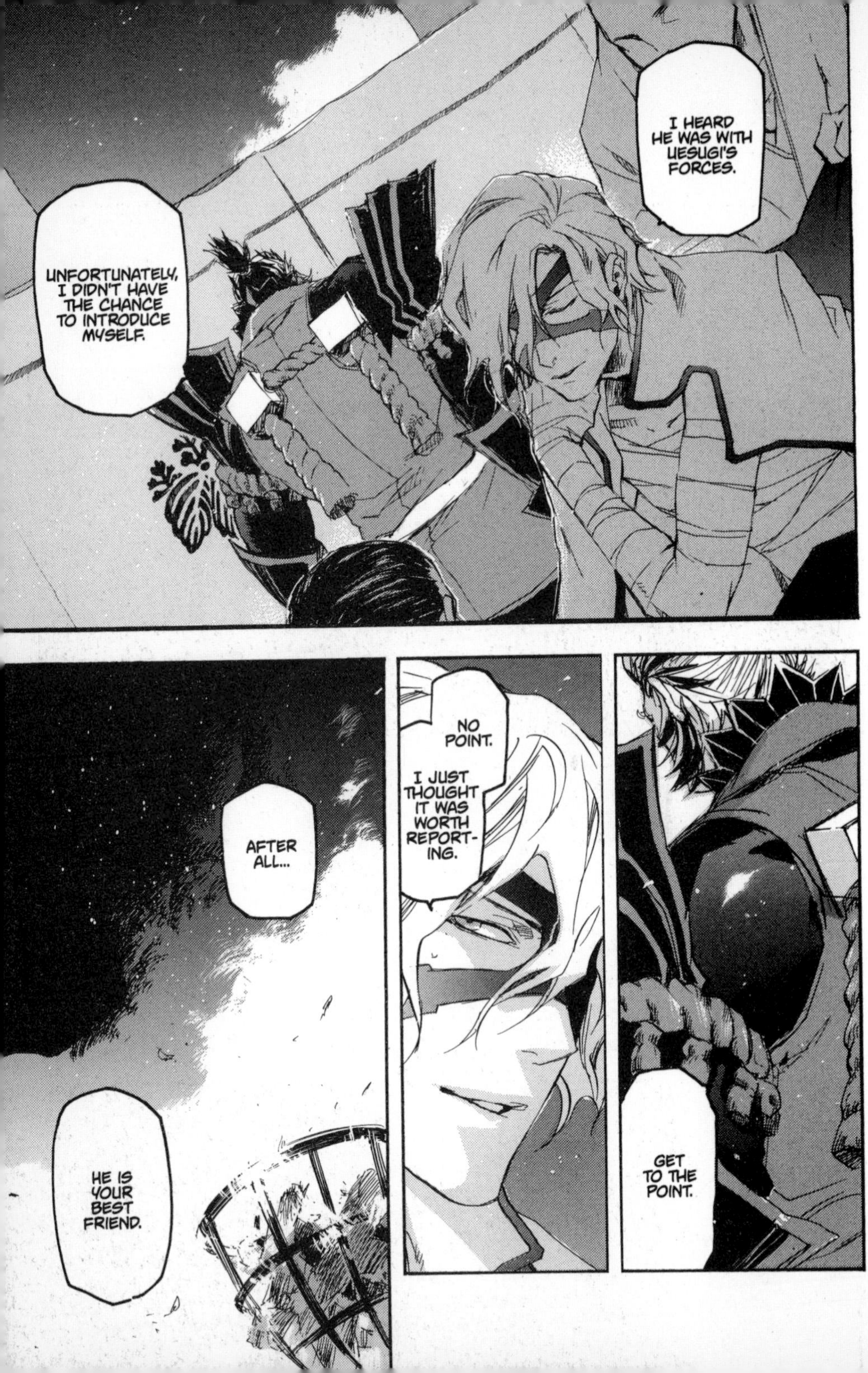
I HEARD HE WAS WITH UESUGI'S FORCES.
UNFORTUNATELY, I DIDN'T HAVE THE CHANCE TO INTRODUCE MYSELF.
GET TO THE POINT.
NO POINT.
I JUST THOUGHT IT WAS WORTH REPORTING.
AFTER ALL...
HE IS YOUR BEST FRIEND.

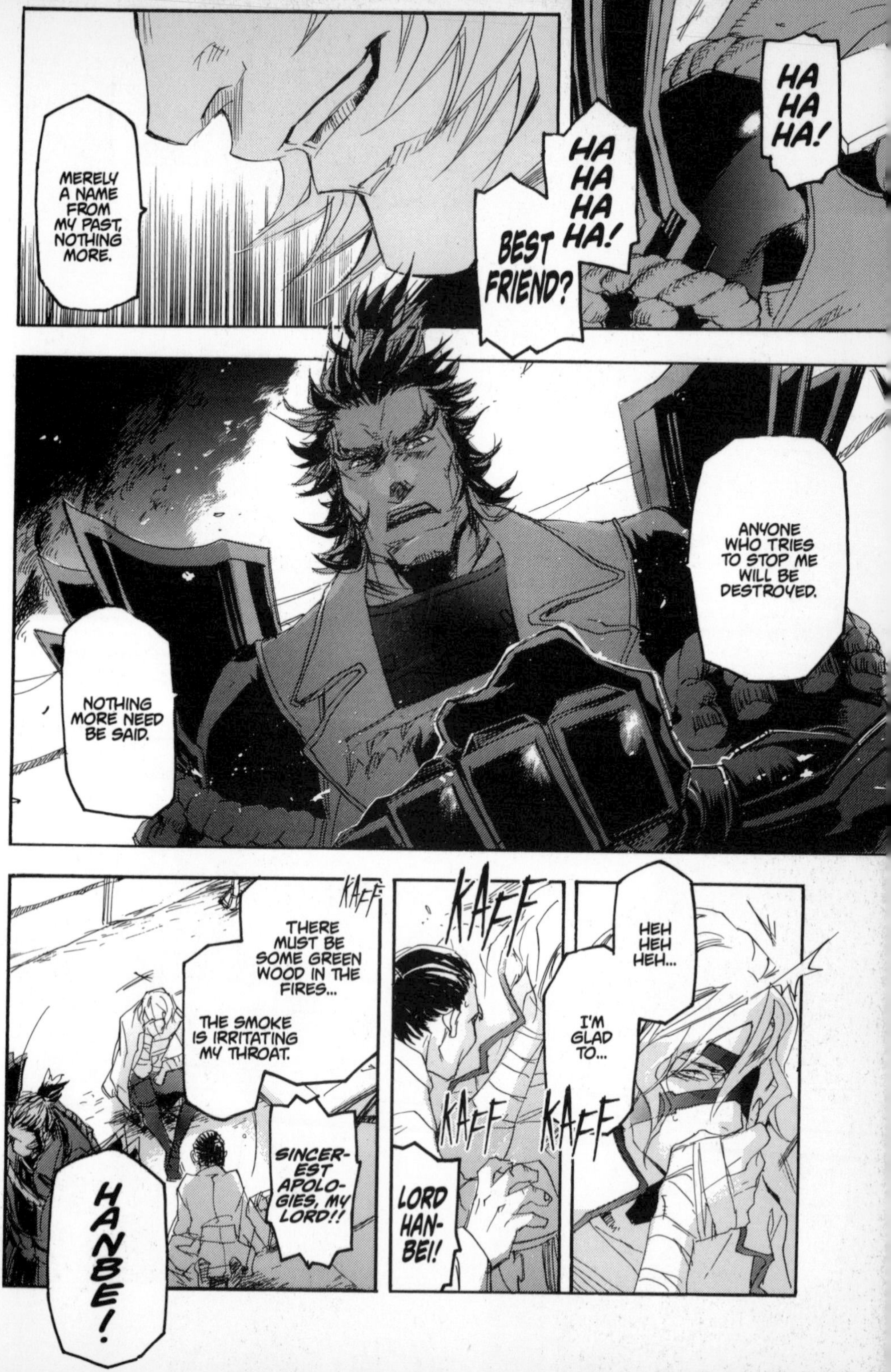
HA HA HA!
HA HA HA HA!
BEST FRIEND?
MERELY A NAME FROM MY PAST, NOTHING MORE.
ANYONE WHO TRIES TO STOP ME WILL BE DESTROYED.
NOTHING MORE NEED BE SAID.
HEH HEH HEH...
I'M GLAD TO...
KAFF
KAFF KAFF
LORD HAN-BEI!
KAFF
THERE MUST BE SOME GREEN WOOD IN THE FIRES...
THE SMOKE IS IRRITATING MY THROAT.
SINCER-EST APOLO-GIES, MY LORD!!
HANBE!

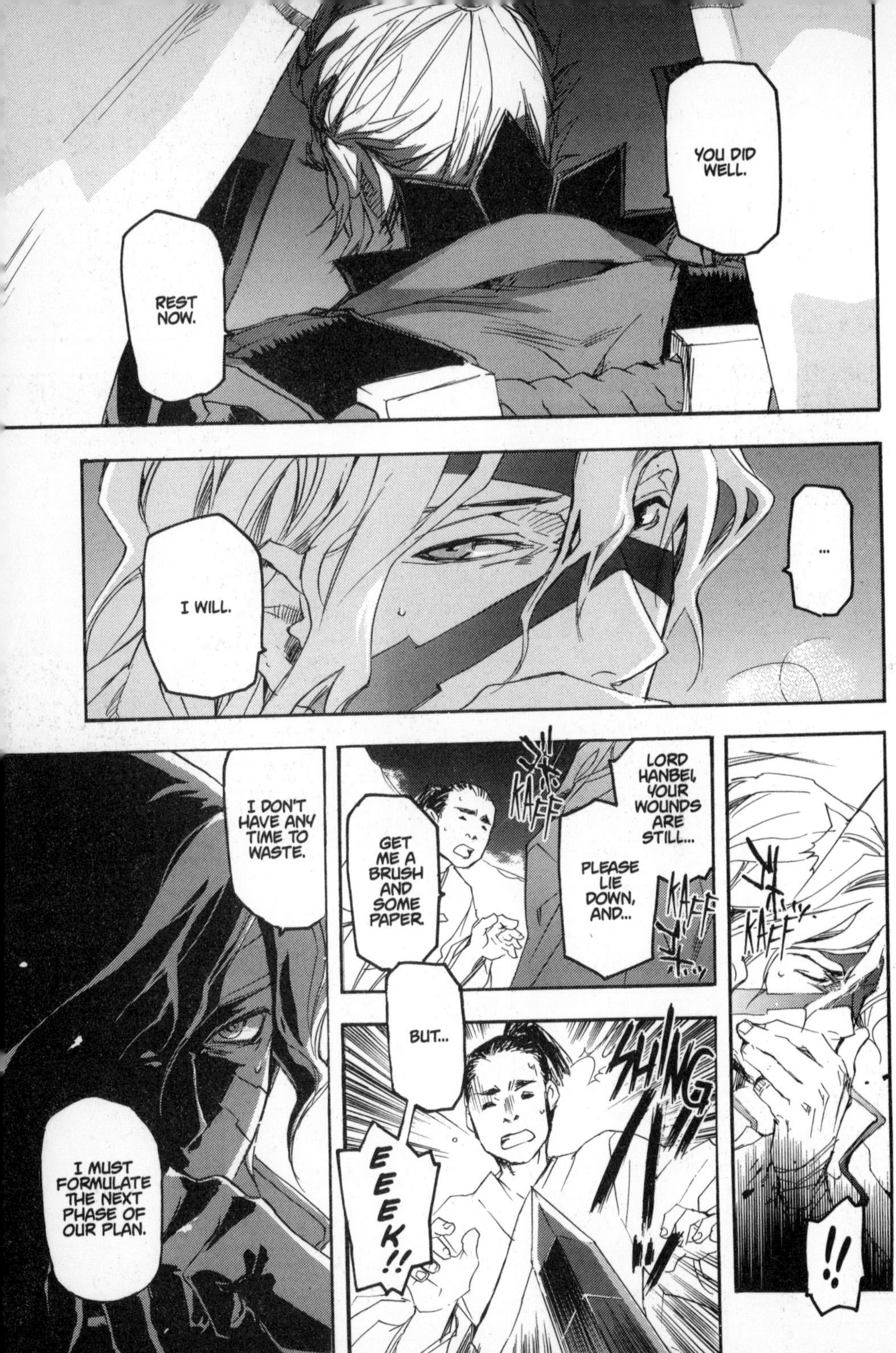

YOU DID WELL.
REST NOW.
...
I WILL.
KAFF
!!
LORD HANBEI, YOUR WOUNDS ARE STILL...
PLEASE LIE DOWN, AND...
KAFF
KAFF
GET ME A BRUSH AND SOME PAPER.
BUT...
SHING
EEEK!!
I DON'T HAVE ANY TIME TO WASTE.
I MUST FORMULATE THE NEXT PHASE OF OUR PLAN.

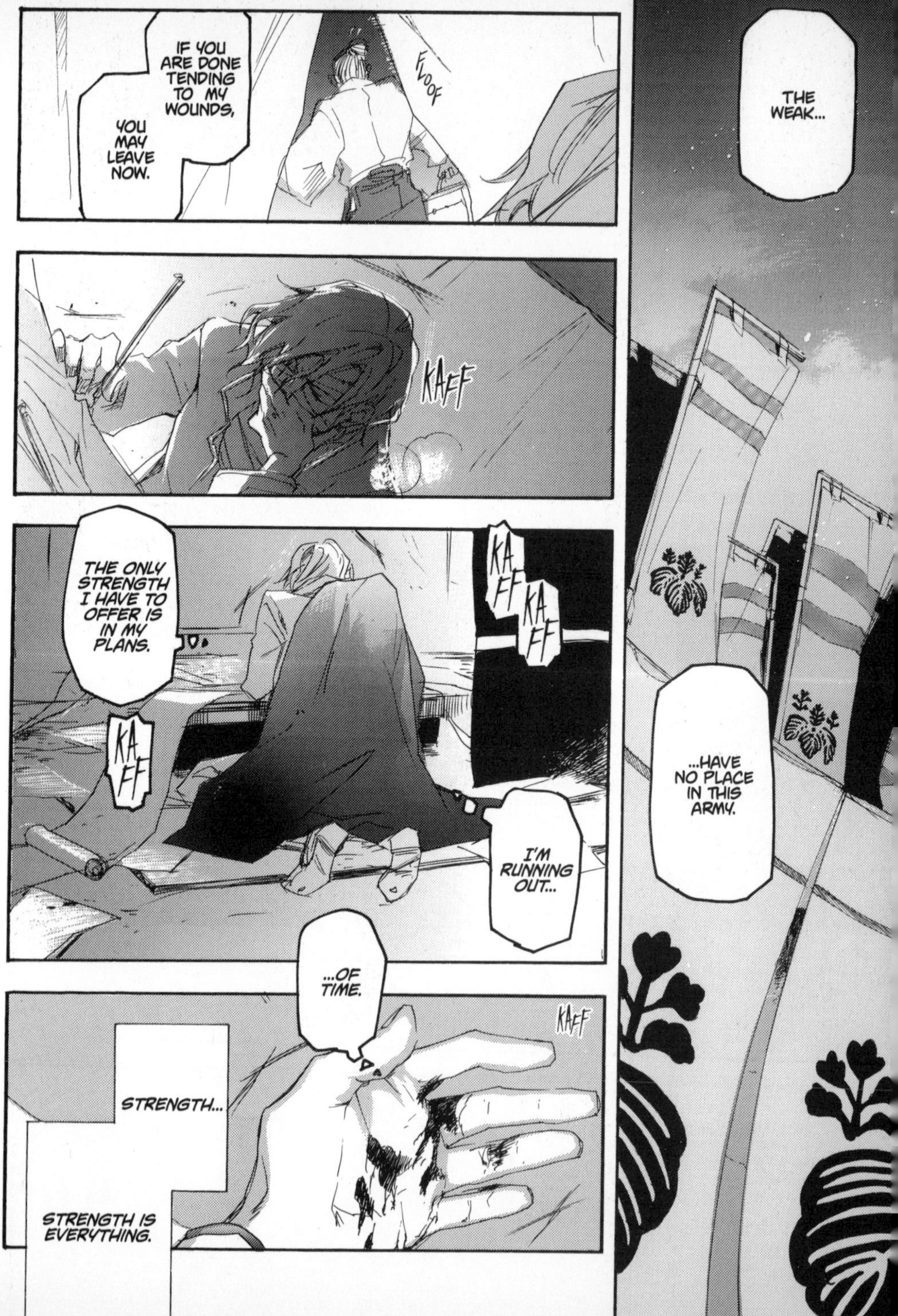
THE WEAK...
...HAVE NO PLACE IN THIS ARMY.
IF YOU ARE DONE TENDING TO MY WOUNDS,
YOU MAY LEAVE NOW.
FLOOF
KAFF
KAFF KAFF
THE ONLY STRENGTH I HAVE TO OFFER IS IN MY PLANS.
KAFF
I'M RUNNING OUT...
...OF TIME.
KAFF
STRENGTH...
STRENGTH IS EVERYTHING.

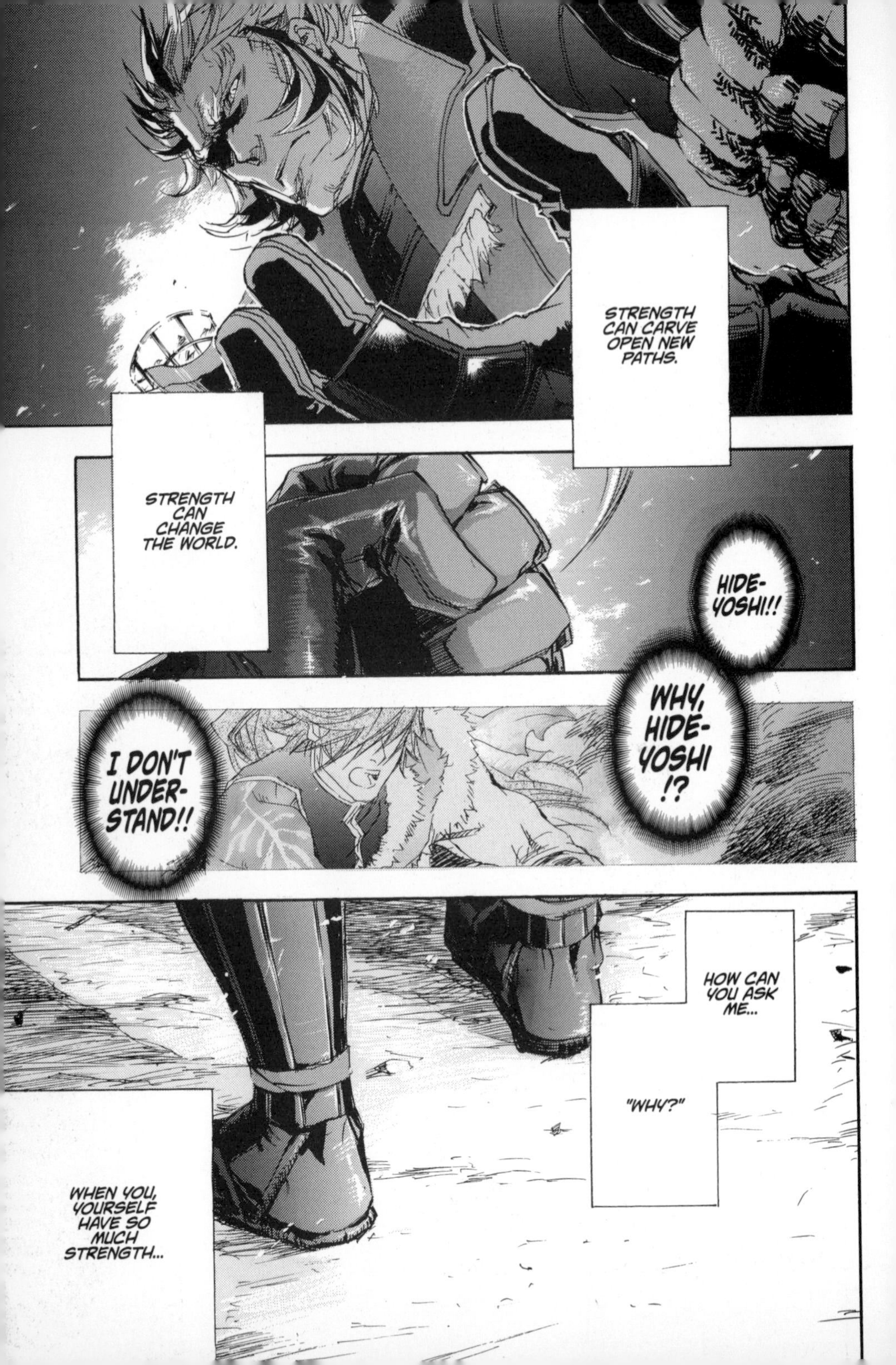
STRENGTH CAN CARVE OPEN NEW PATHS.
STRENGTH CAN CHANGE THE WORLD.
HIDE-YOSHI!!
WHY, HIDE-YOSHI!?
I DON'T UNDER-STAND!!
HOW CAN YOU ASK ME...
"WHY?"
WHEN YOU, YOURSELF HAVE SO MUCH STRENGTH...

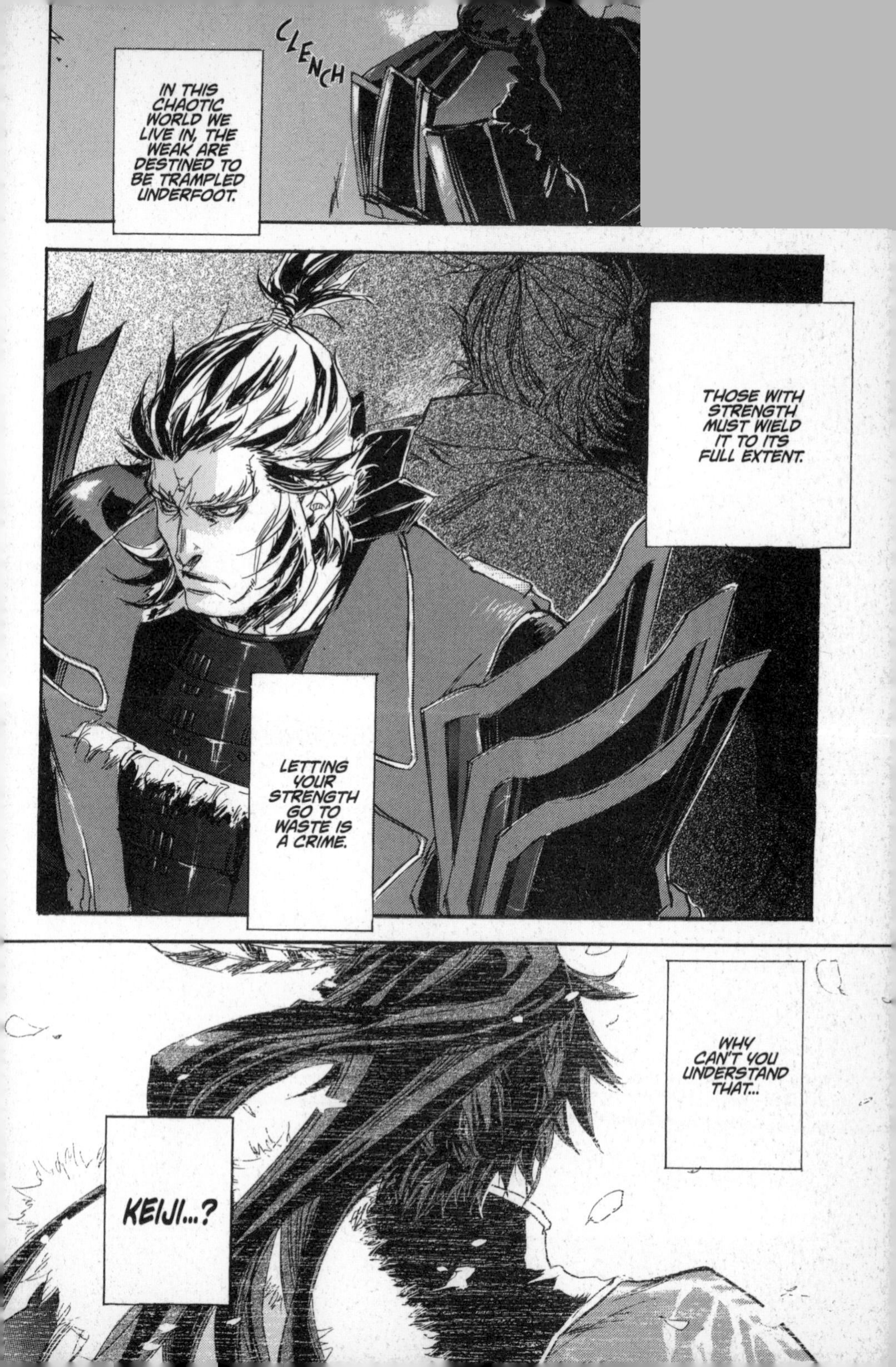
CLENCH
IN THIS CHAOTIC WORLD WE LIVE IN, THE WEAK ARE DESTINED TO BE TRAMPLED UNDERFOOT.
THOSE WITH STRENGTH MUST WIELD IT TO ITS FULL EXTENT.
LETTING YOUR STRENGTH GO TO WASTE IS A CRIME.
WHY CAN'T YOU UNDERSTAND THAT...
KEIJI...?

戦国BASARA2
SENGOKU BASARA2

ACT14:Quenchless

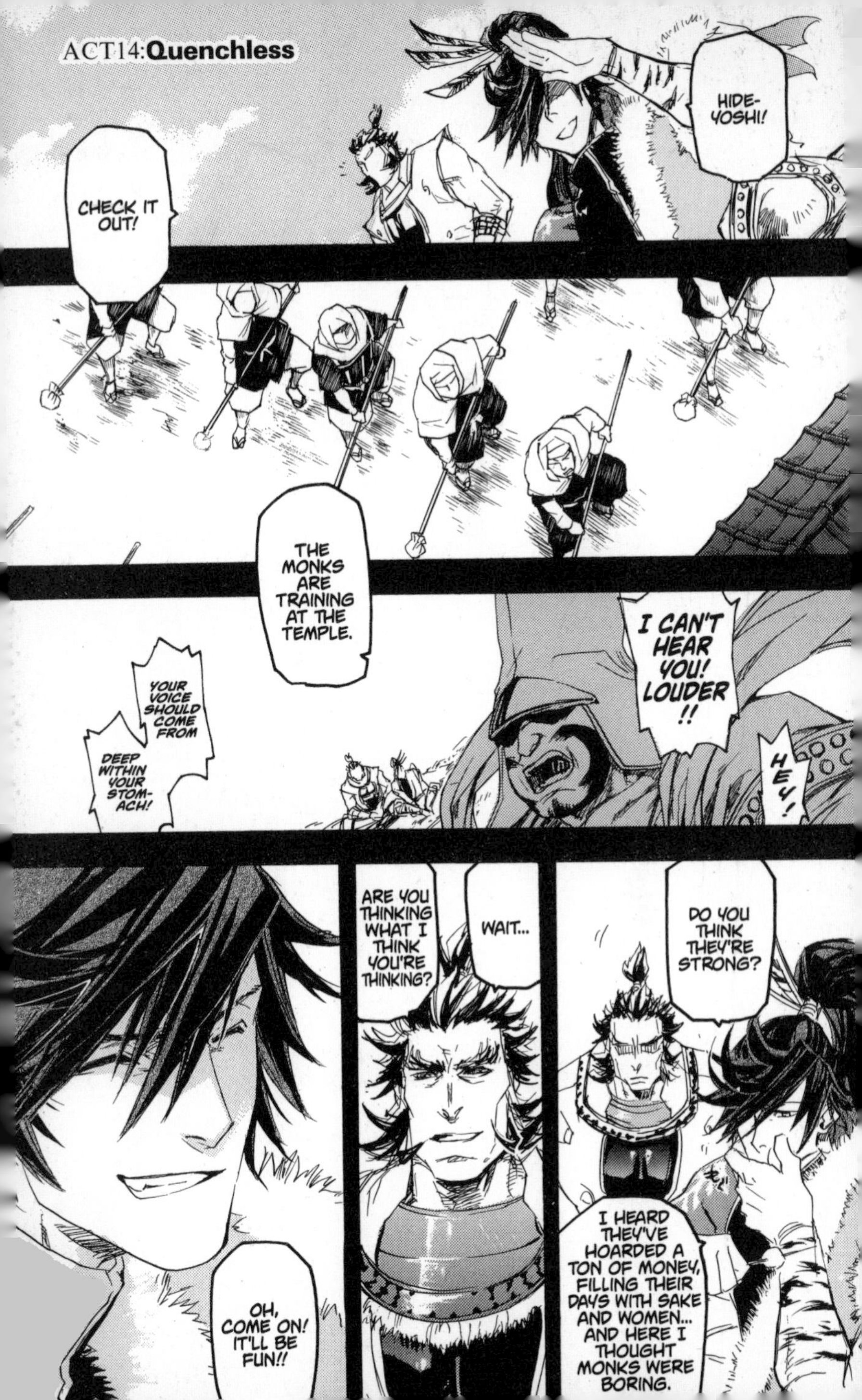
HIDE-YOSHI!
CHECK IT OUT!
THE MONKS ARE TRAINING AT THE TEMPLE.
HEY!
I CAN'T HEAR YOU! LOUDER!!
YOUR VOICE SHOULD COME FROM
DEEP WITHIN YOUR STOMACH!
DO YOU THINK THEY'RE STRONG?
I HEARD THEY'VE HOARDED A TON OF MONEY, FILLING THEIR DAYS WITH SAKE AND WOMEN... AND HERE I THOUGHT MONKS WERE BORING.
WAIT...
ARE YOU THINKING WHAT I THINK YOU'RE THINKING?
OH, COME ON! IT'LL BE FUN!!

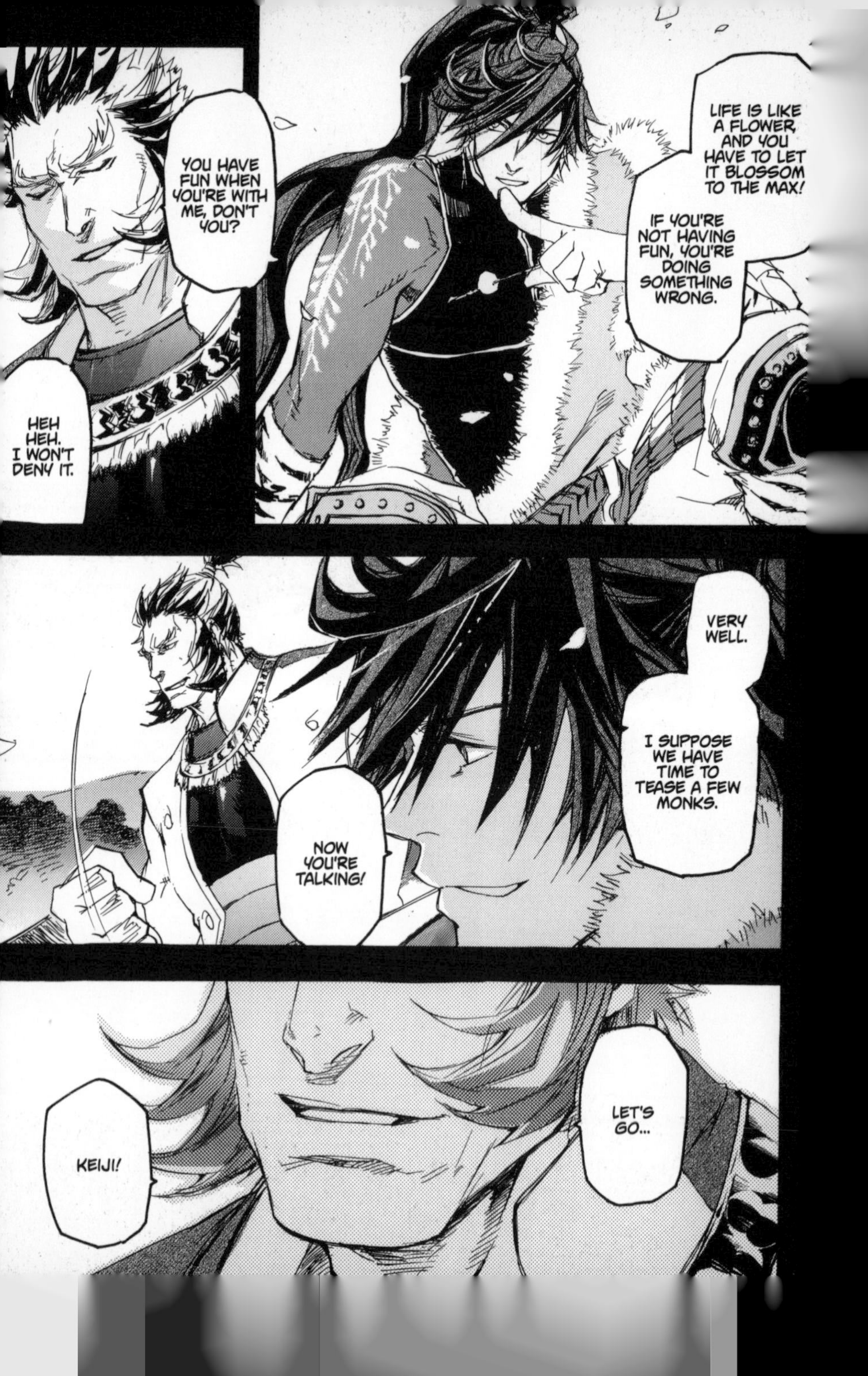
LIFE IS LIKE A FLOWER, AND YOU HAVE TO LET IT BLOSSOM TO THE MAX!
IF YOU'RE NOT HAVING FUN, YOU'RE DOING SOMETHING WRONG.
YOU HAVE FUN WHEN YOU'RE WITH ME, DON'T YOU?
HEH HEH. I WON'T DENY IT.
VERY WELL.
I SUPPOSE WE HAVE TIME TO TEASE A FEW MONKS.
NOW YOU'RE TALKING!
LET'S GO...
KEIJI!

ACT14:**Quenchless**

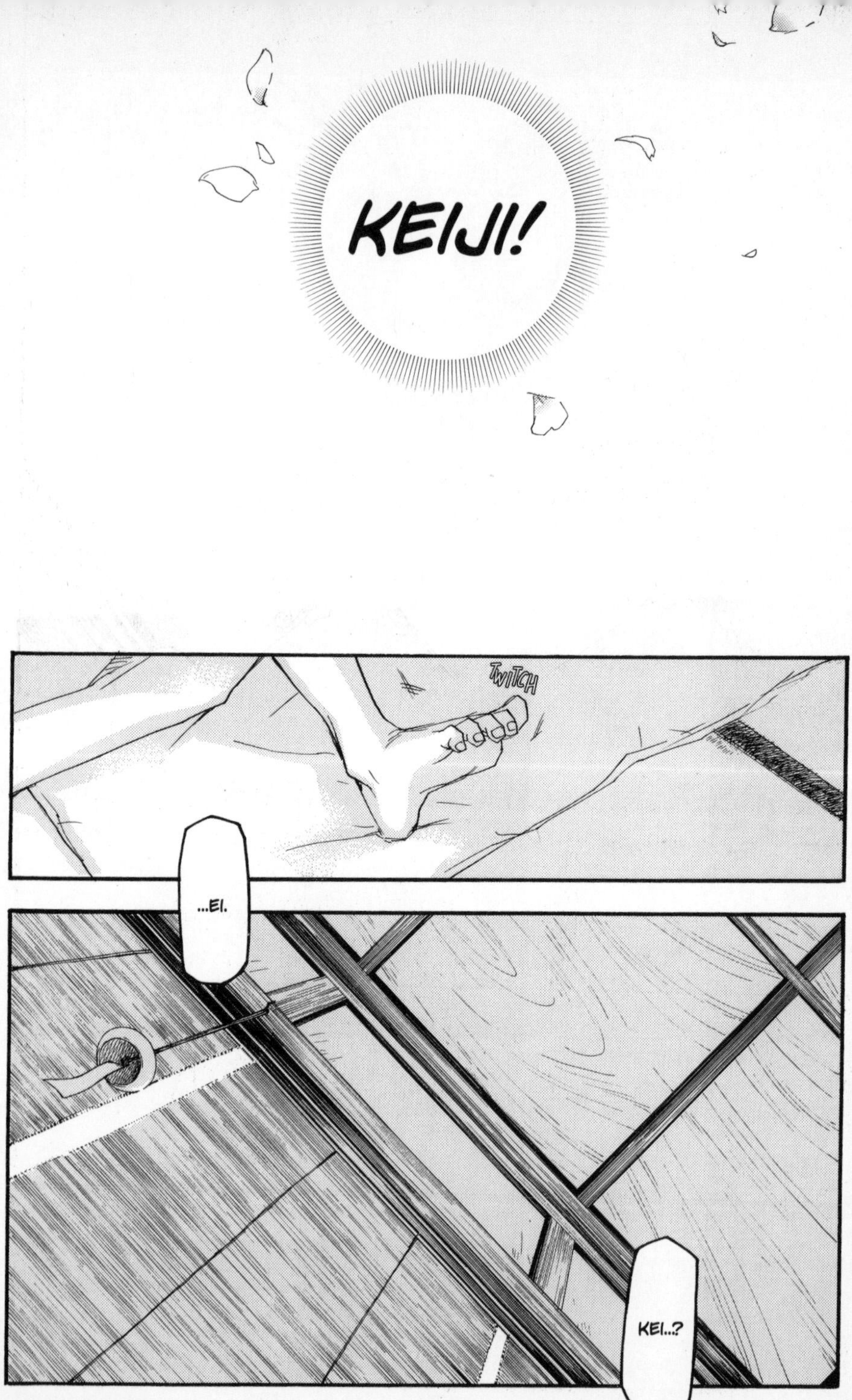
KEIJI!
TWITCH
...EI.
KEI...?

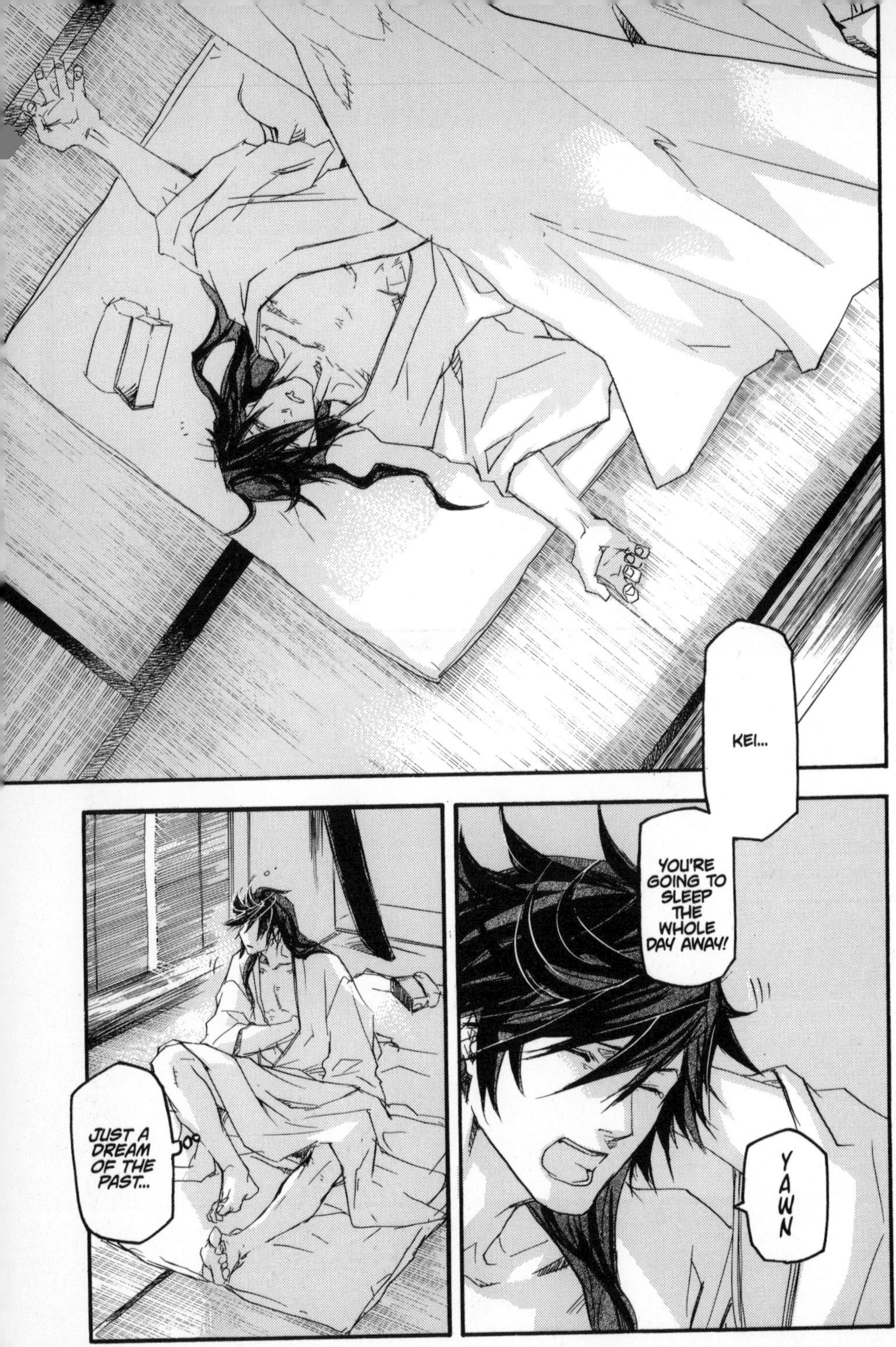
KEI...
YOU'RE GOING TO SLEEP THE WHOLE DAY AWAY!
YAWN
JUST A DREAM OF THE PAST...

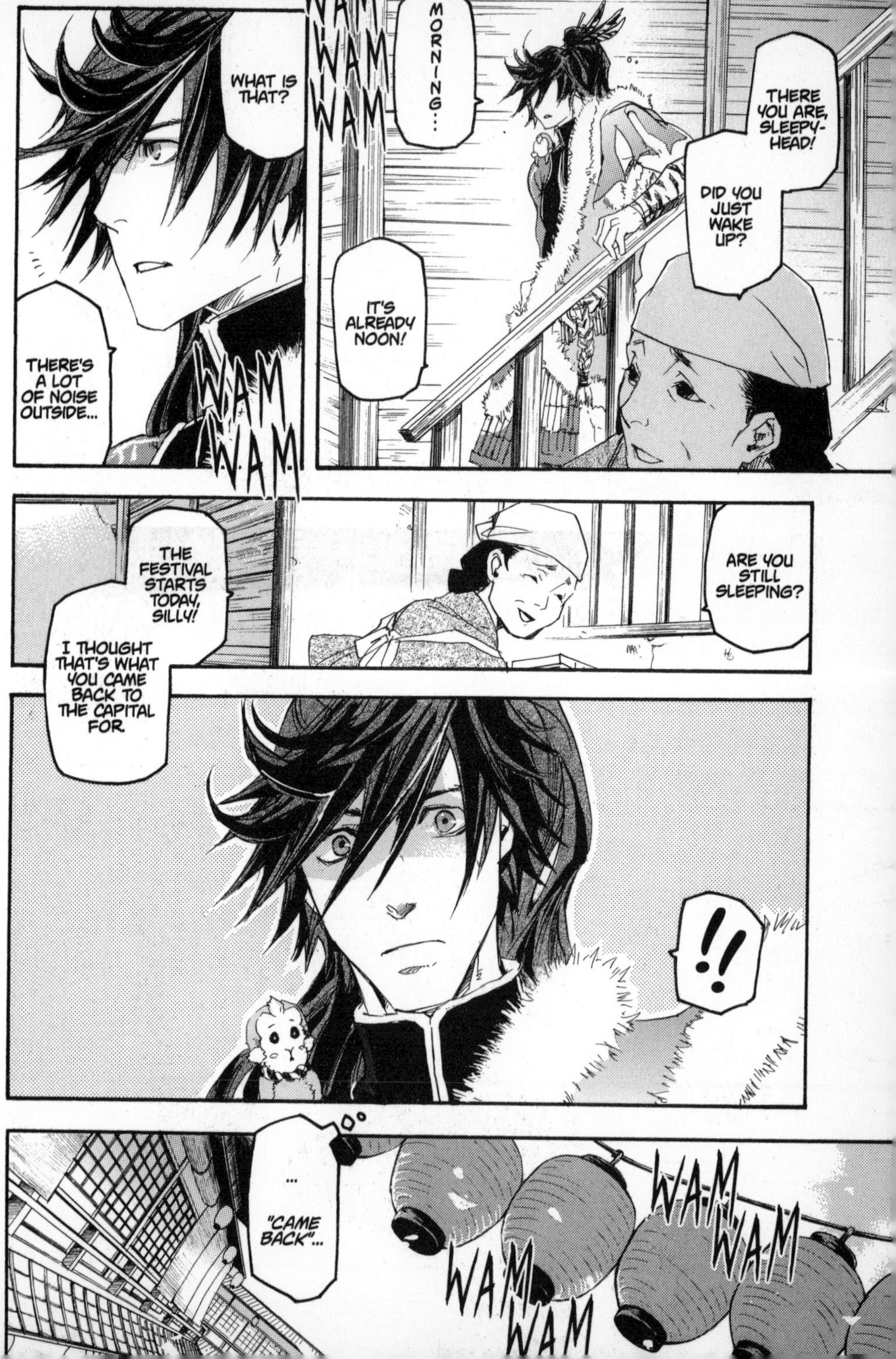
THERE YOU ARE, SLEEPY-HEAD!
DID YOU JUST WAKE UP?
MORNING...
WAM WAM WAM
IT'S ALREADY NOON!
WHAT IS THAT?
THERE'S A LOT OF NOISE OUTSIDE...
WAM WAM
ARE YOU STILL SLEEPING?
THE FESTIVAL STARTS TODAY, SILLY!
I THOUGHT THAT'S WHAT YOU CAME BACK TO THE CAPITAL FOR.
!!
... "CAME BACK"...
WAM WAM
WAM WAM

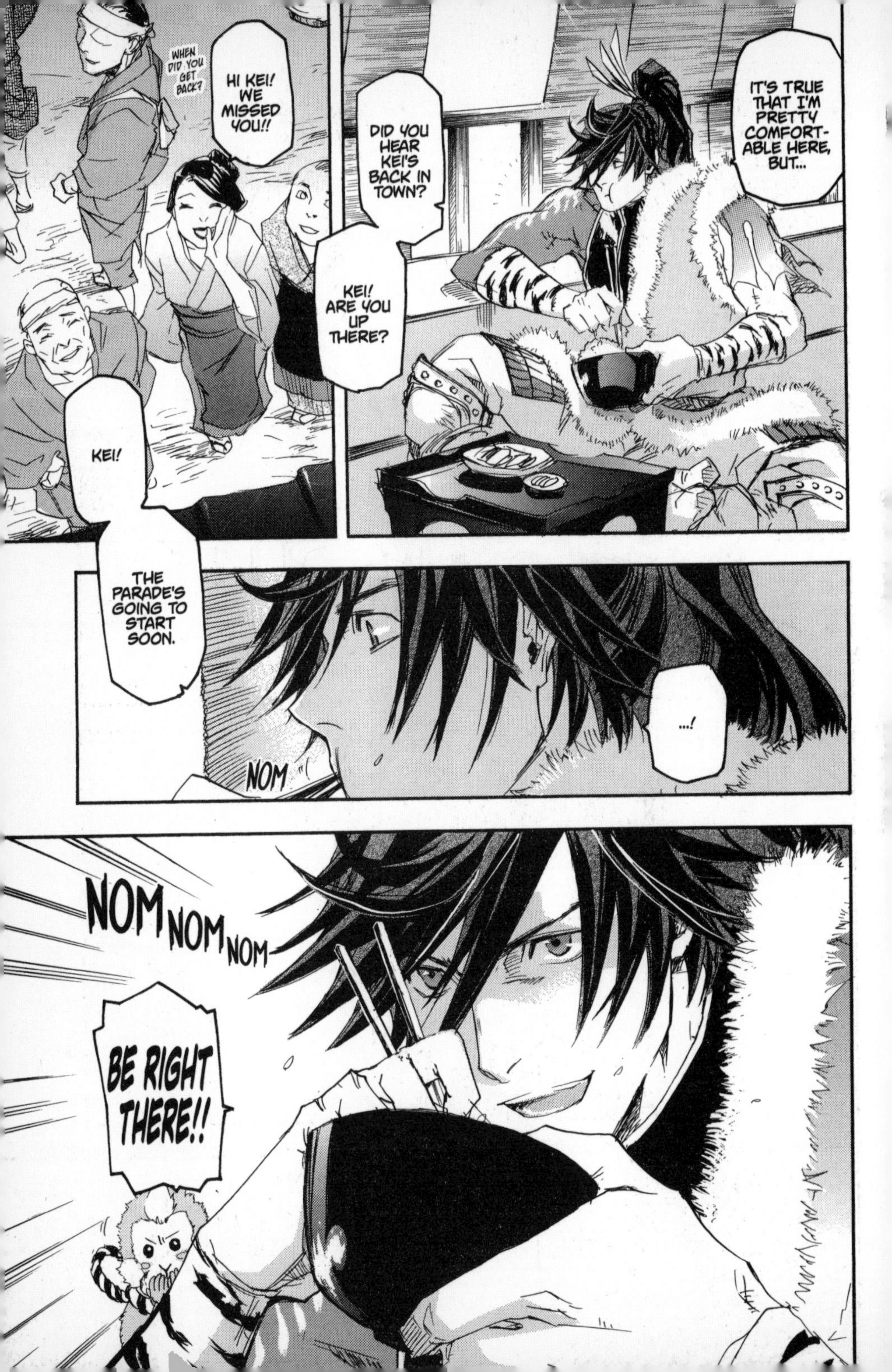
IT'S TRUE THAT I'M PRETTY COMFORTABLE HERE, BUT...
DID YOU HEAR KEI'S BACK IN TOWN?
KEI! ARE YOU UP THERE?
HI KEI! WE MISSED YOU!!
WHEN DID YOU GET BACK?
KEI!
THE PARADE'S GOING TO START SOON.
...!
NOM
NOM NOM NOM
BE RIGHT THERE!!

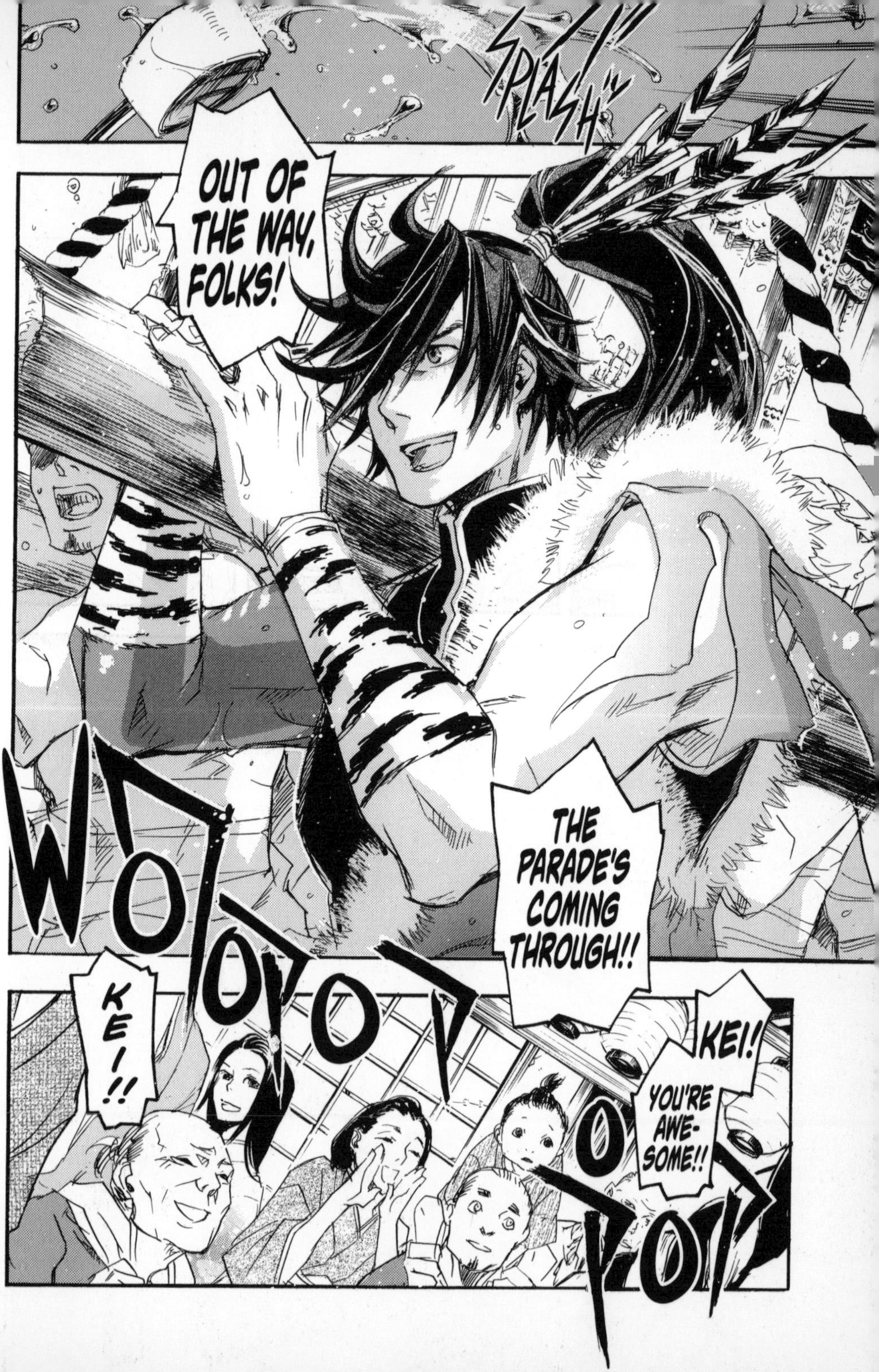
SPLASH
OUT OF THE WAY, FOLKS!
THE PARADE'S COMING THROUGH!!
KEI!
YOU'RE AWE-SOME!!
KEI!!

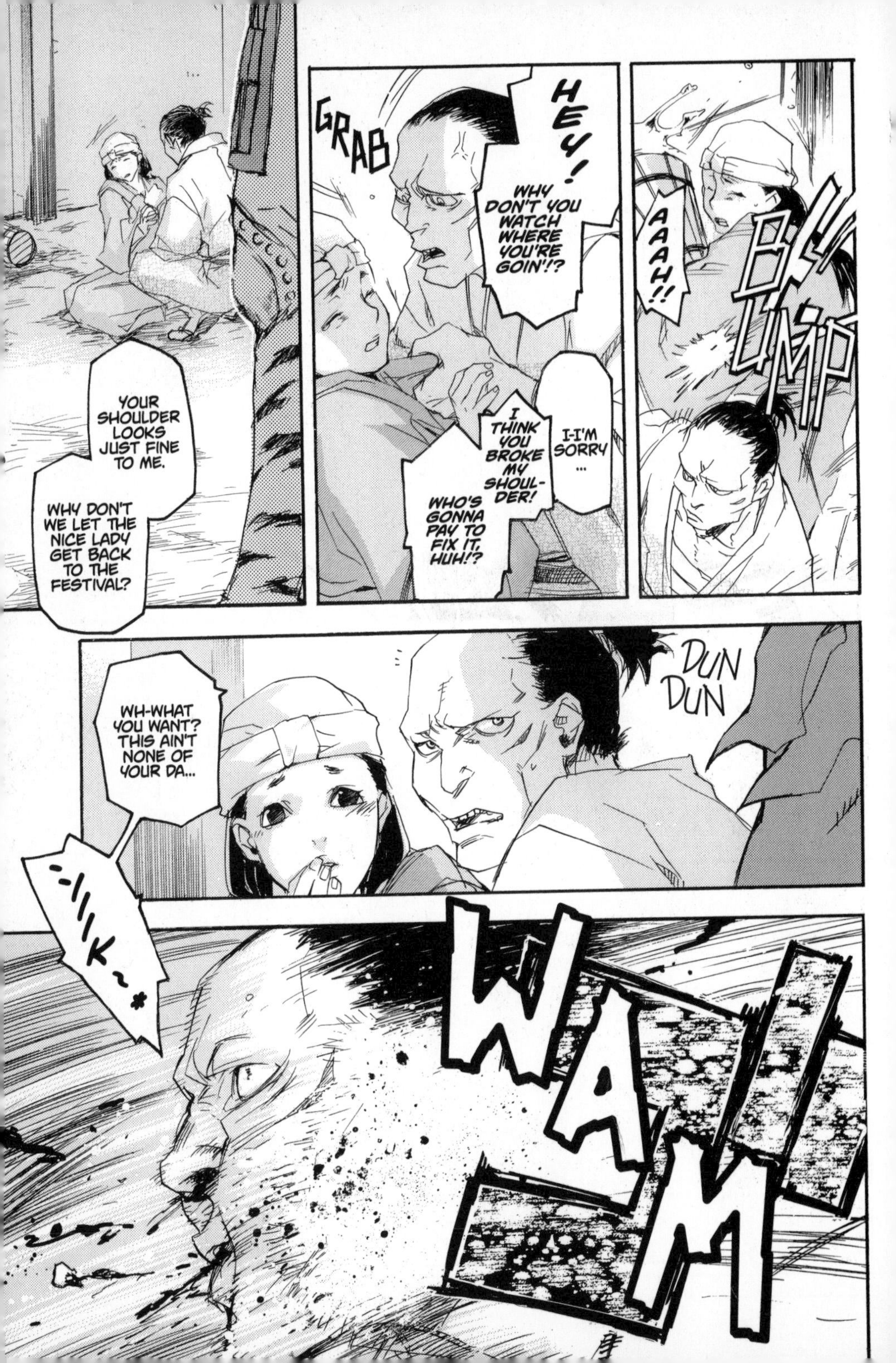
AAAH!!
BUMP
GRAB
HEY!
WHY DON'T YOU WATCH WHERE YOU'RE GOIN'!?
I-I'M SORRY...
I THINK YOU BROKE MY SHOULDER!
WHO'S GONNA PAY TO FIX IT, HUH!?
YOUR SHOULDER LOOKS JUST FINE TO ME.
WHY DON'T WE LET THE NICE LADY GET BACK TO THE FESTIVAL?
DUN DUN
WH-WHAT YOU WANT? THIS AIN'T NONE OF YOUR DA...
WAM!
--IIIK~*

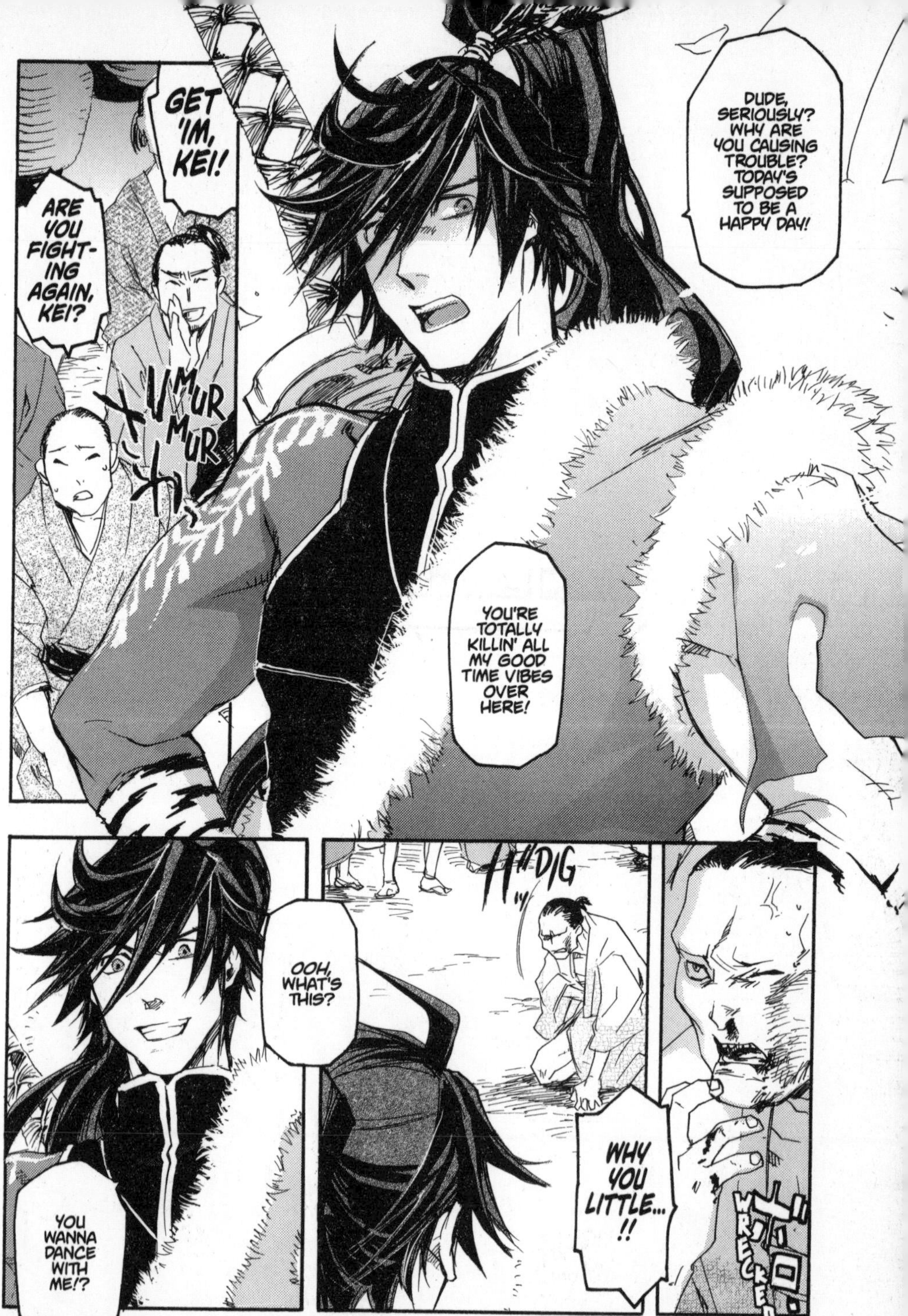
DUDE, SERIOUSLY? WHY ARE YOU CAUSING TROUBLE? TODAY'S SUPPOSED TO BE A HAPPY DAY!
YOU'RE TOTALLY KILLIN' ALL MY GOOD TIME VIBES OVER HERE!
GET 'IM, KEI!
ARE YOU FIGHT-ING AGAIN, KEI?
MUR MUR
WRECKED
WHY YOU LITTLE...!!
DIG
OOH, WHAT'S THIS?
YOU WANNA DANCE WITH ME!?

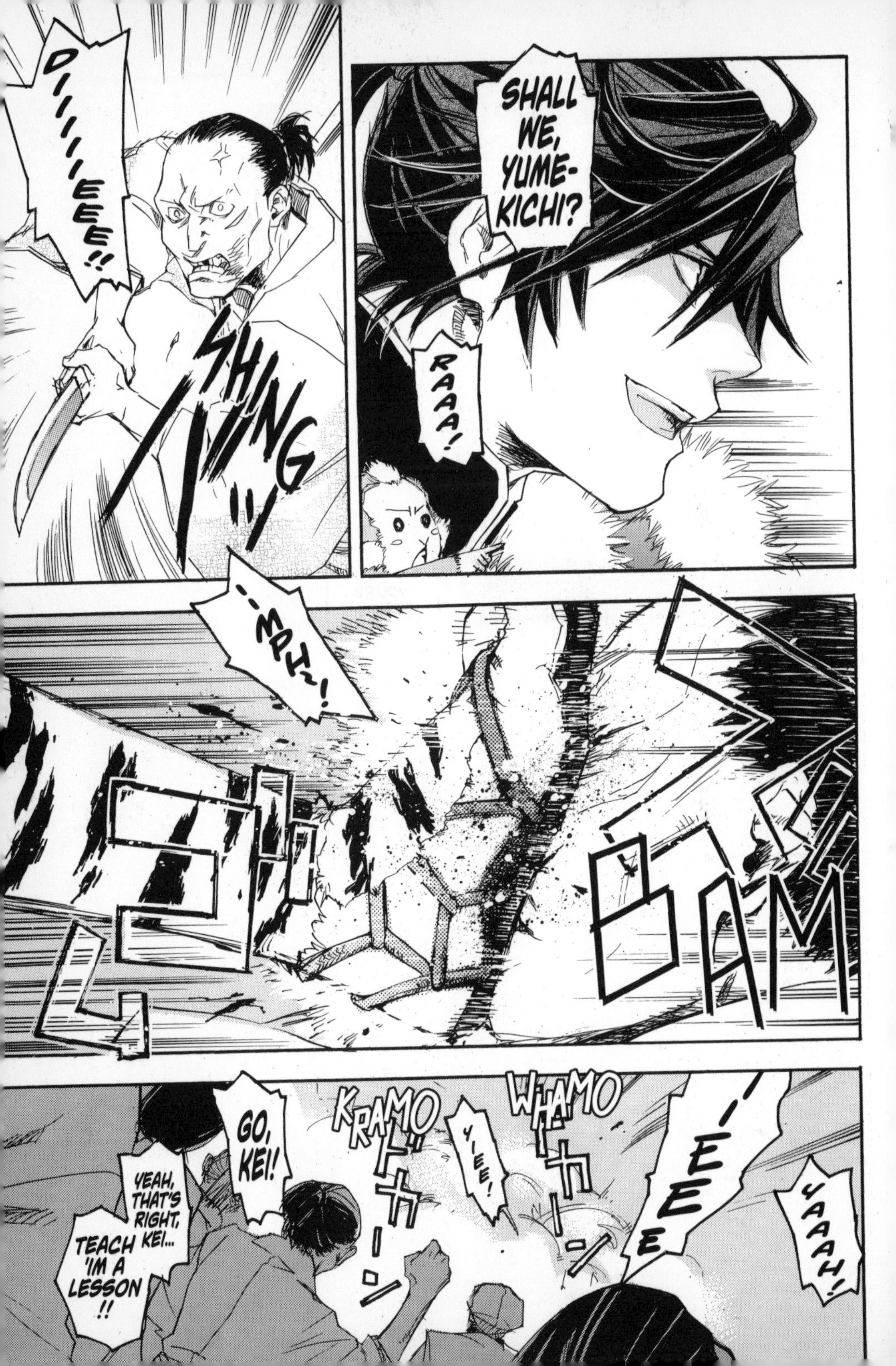
SHALL WE, YUME-KICHI?
RAAAA!
DIIIIIEEEE!!
SHING!!
...MPH?!
BAM
YAAAH!
...EEEE
WHAMO
YIEE!
KRAMO
GO, KEI!
YEAH, THAT'S RIGHT, KEI...
TEACH 'IM A LESSON!!

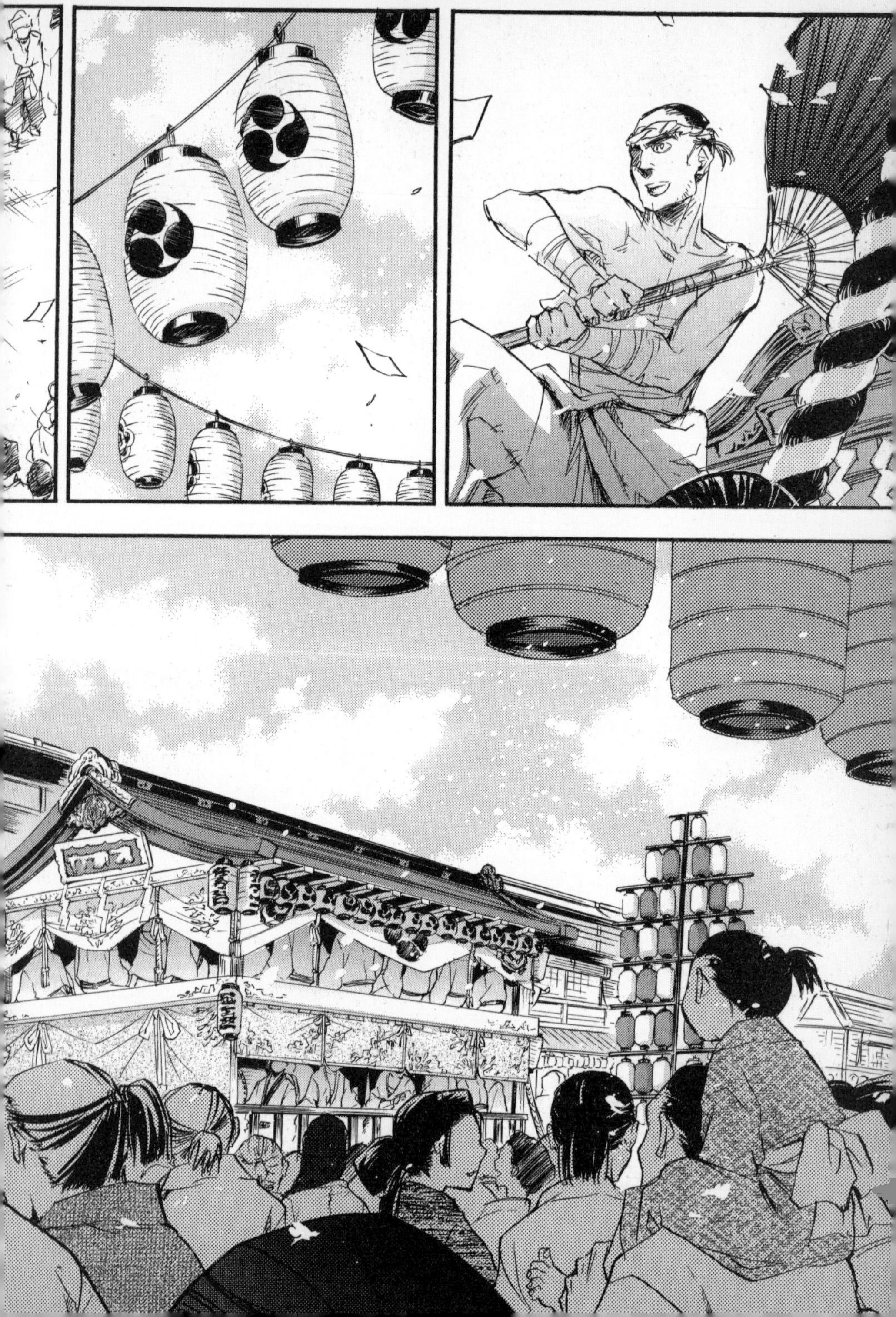

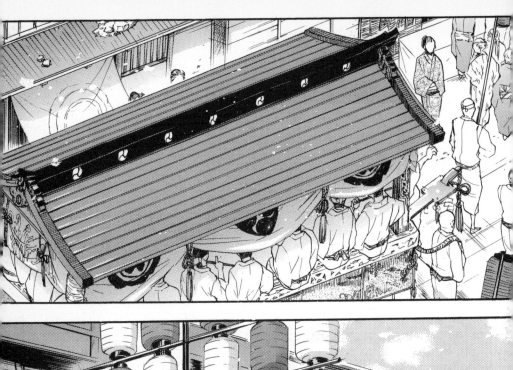

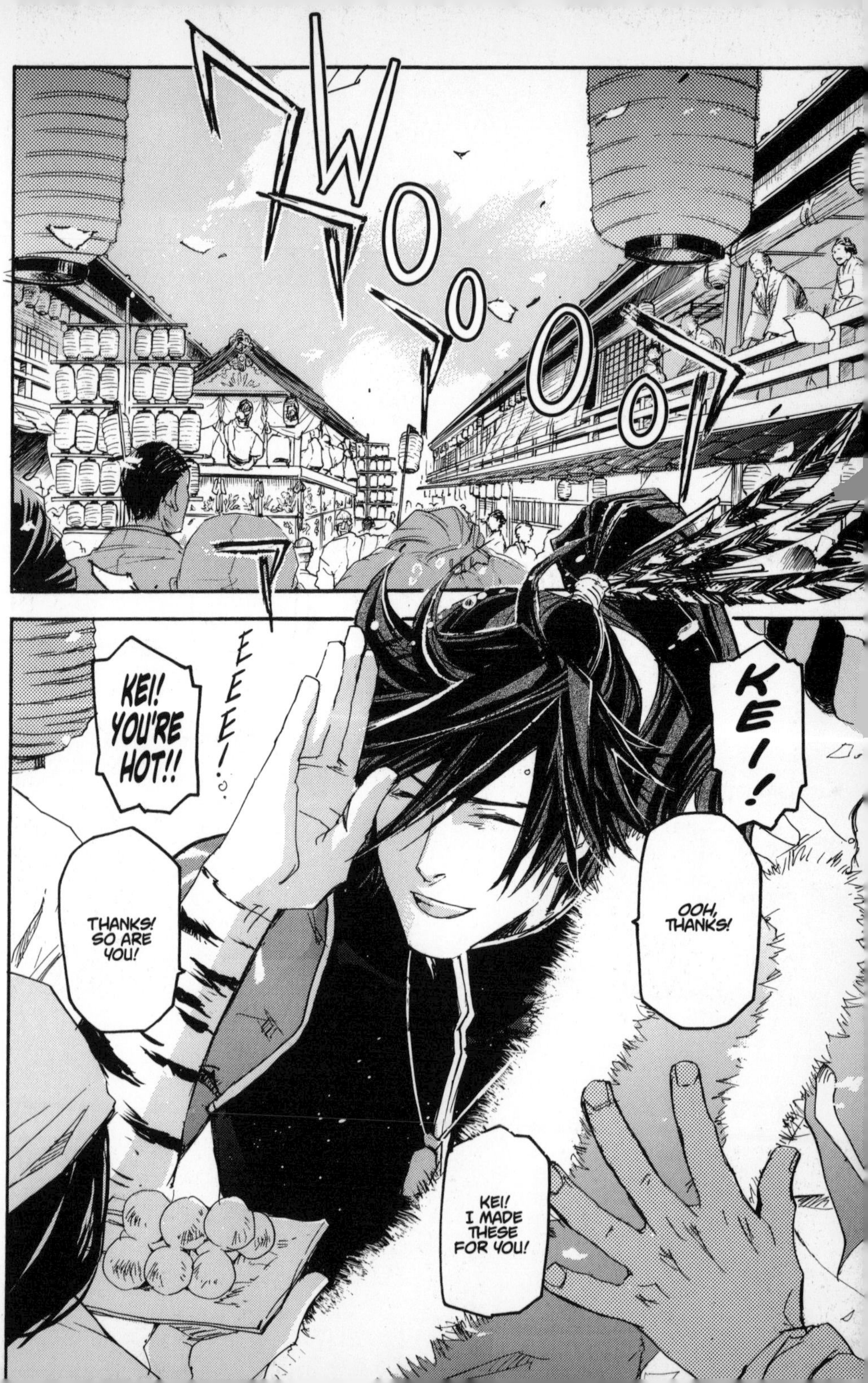
WOOOOOOO
EEEE!♡
KEI!!
OOH, THANKS!
KEI! YOU'RE HOT!!
THANKS! SO ARE YOU!
KEI! I MADE THESE FOR YOU!

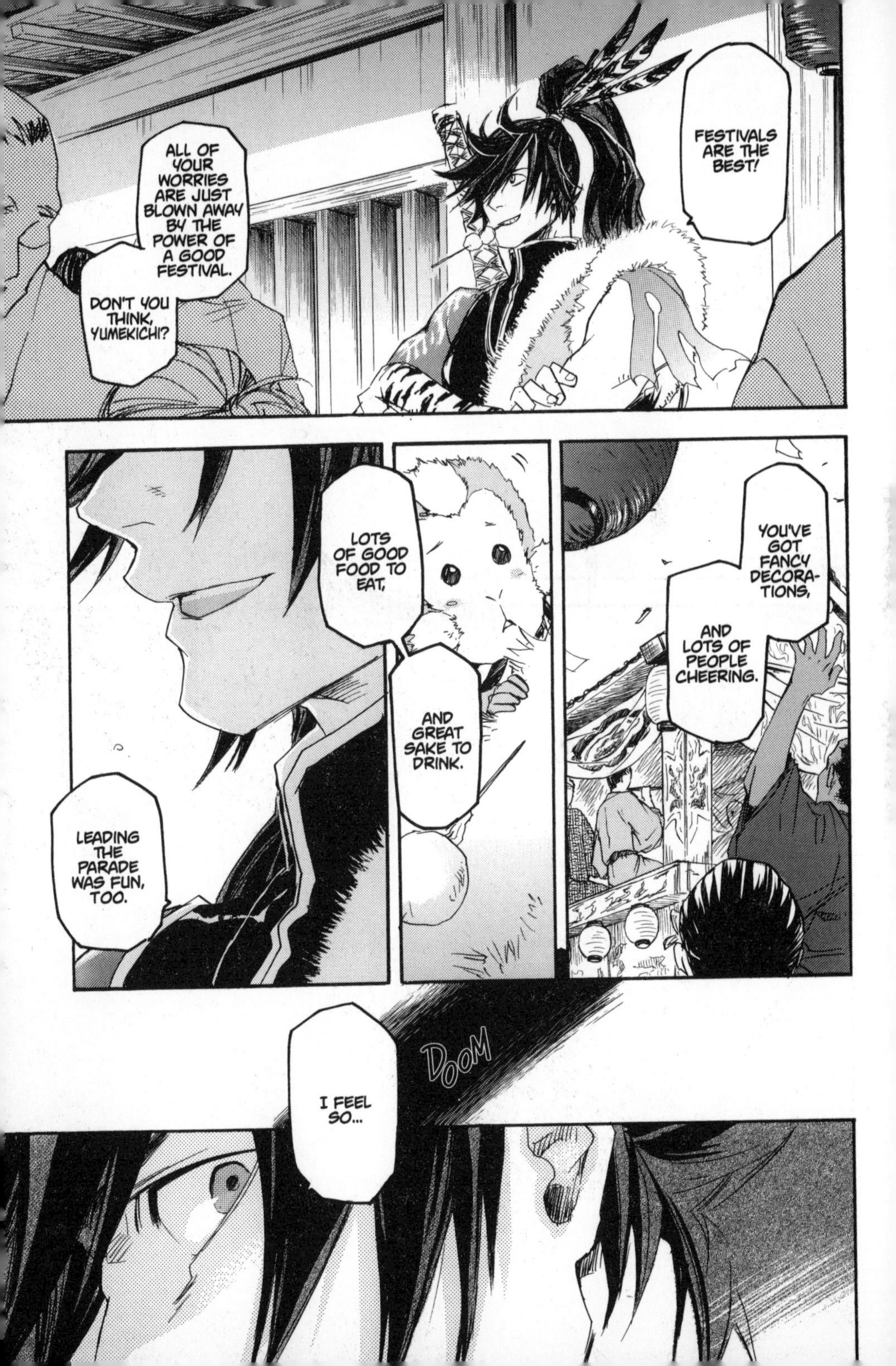
FESTIVALS ARE THE BEST!
ALL OF YOUR WORRIES ARE JUST BLOWN AWAY BY THE POWER OF A GOOD FESTIVAL.
DON'T YOU THINK, YUMEKICHI?
YOU'VE GOT FANCY DECORATIONS,
AND LOTS OF PEOPLE CHEERING.
LOTS OF GOOD FOOD TO EAT,
AND GREAT SAKE TO DRINK.
LEADING THE PARADE WAS FUN, TOO.
DOOM
I FEEL SO...

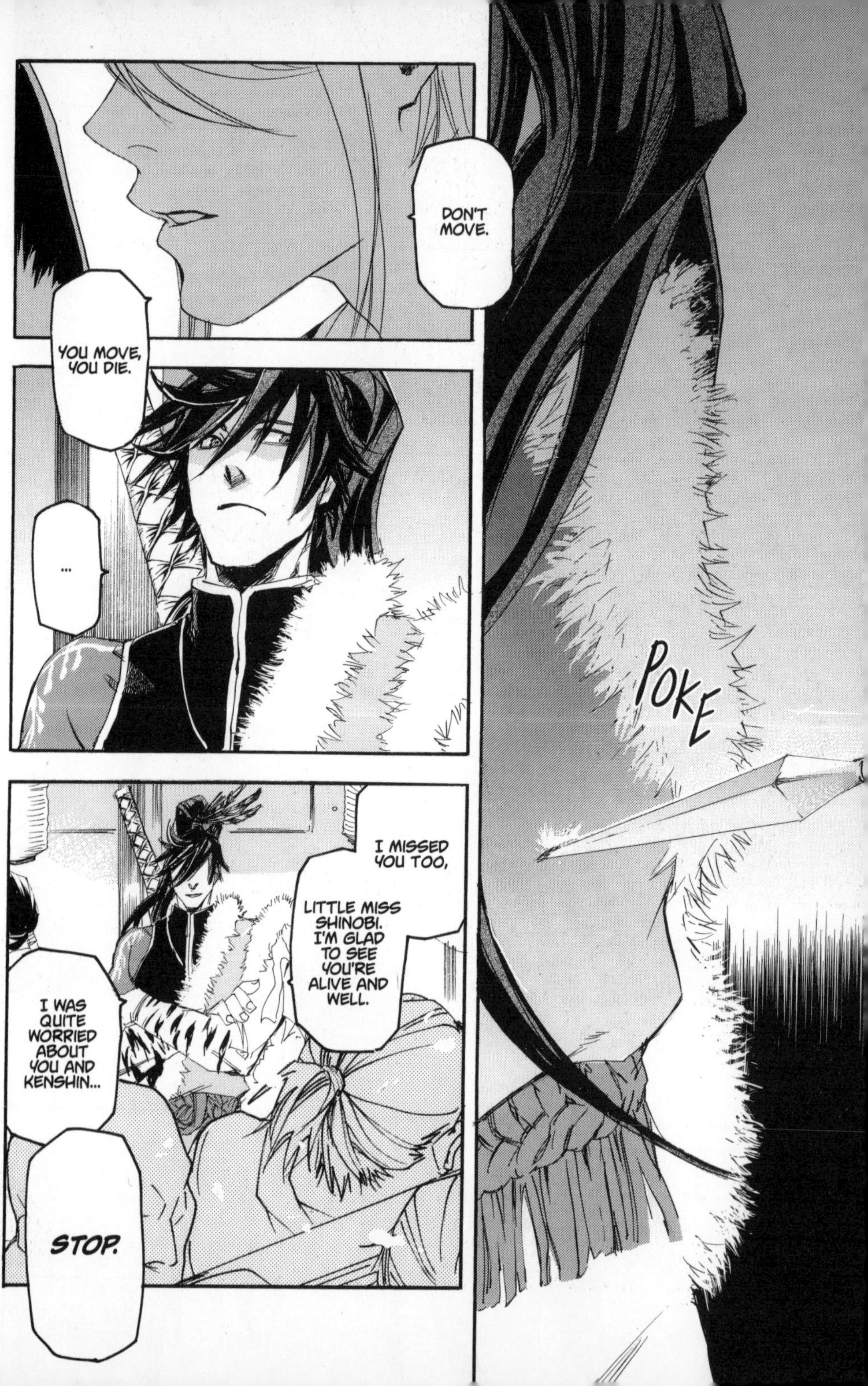
POKE
DON'T MOVE.
YOU MOVE, YOU DIE.
...
I MISSED YOU TOO,
LITTLE MISS SHINOBI. I'M GLAD TO SEE YOU'RE ALIVE AND WELL.
I WAS QUITE WORRIED ABOUT YOU AND KENSHIN...
STOP.

TELL ME...

WHAT ARE YOU DOING HERE?

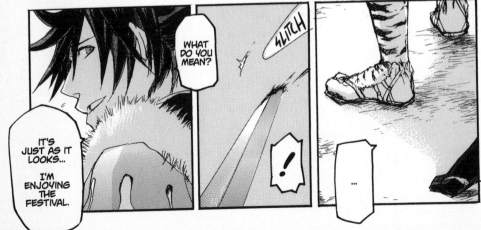

WHAT DO YOU MEAN?

SLITCH

IT'S JUST AS IT LOOKS... I'M ENJOYING THE FESTIVAL.

!

...

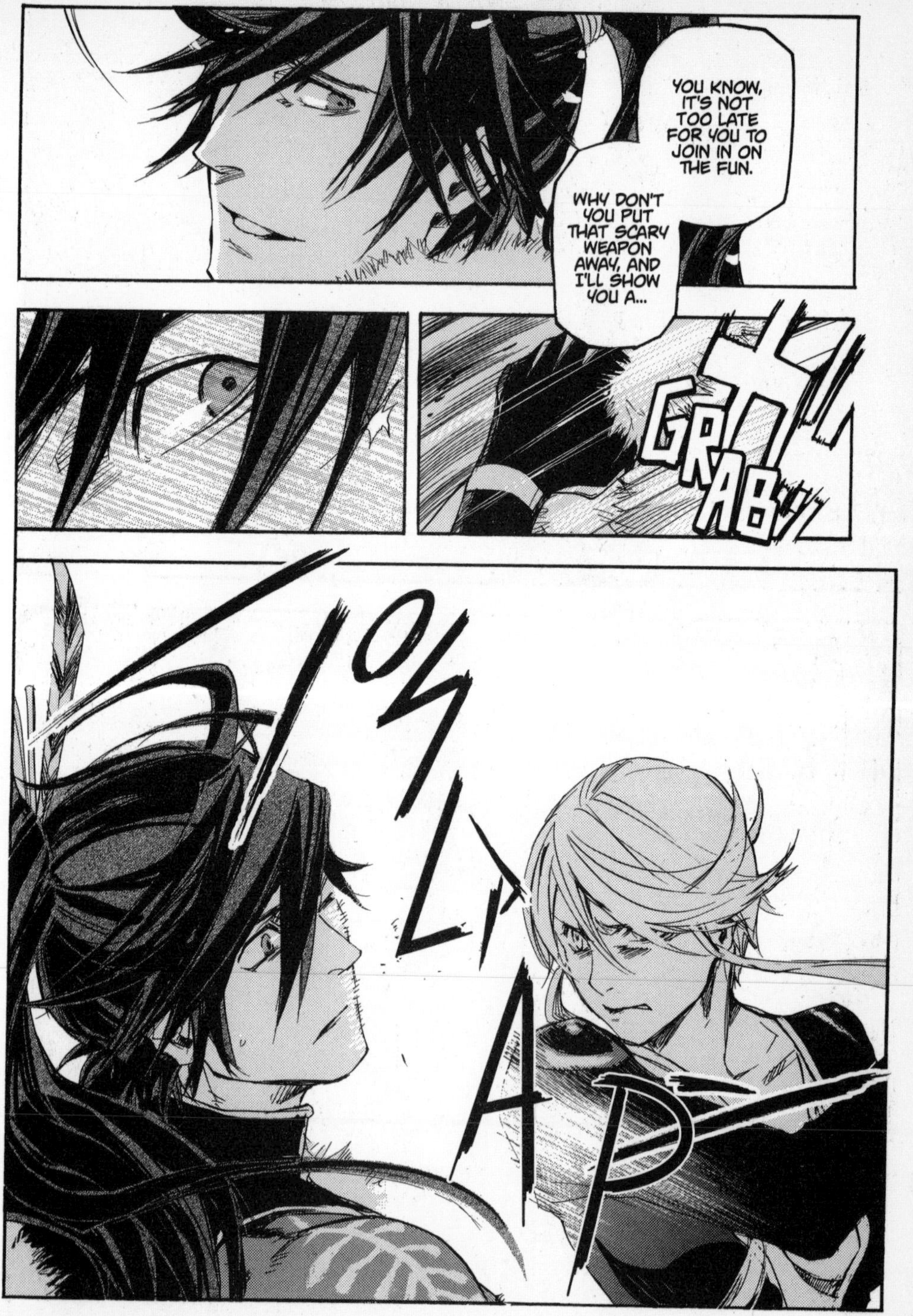

YOU KNOW, IT'S NOT TOO LATE FOR YOU TO JOIN IN ON THE FUN.
WHY DON'T YOU PUT THAT SCARY WEAPON AWAY, AND I'LL SHOW YOU A...
GRAB
SLAP

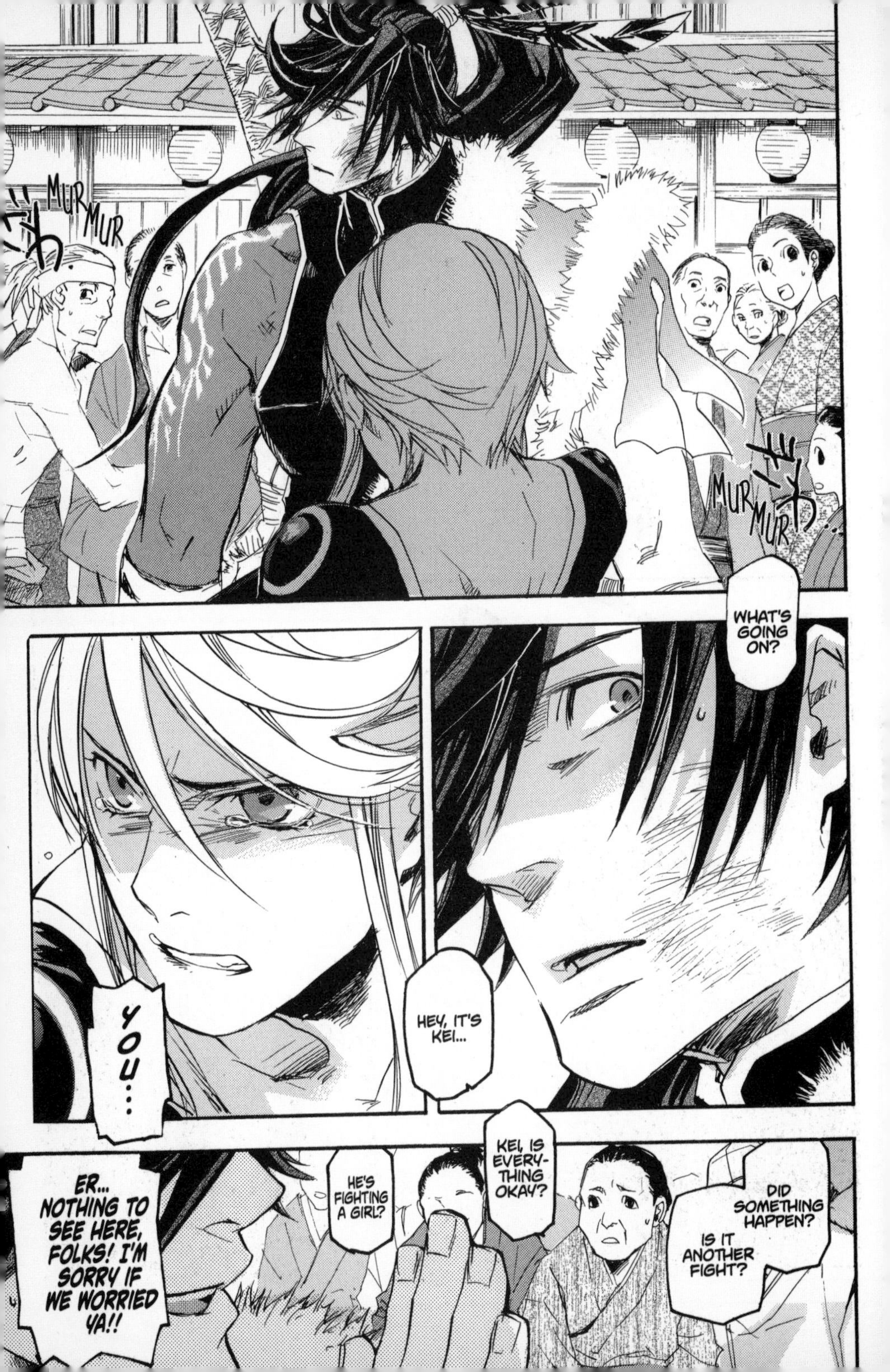

ざわ…
MUR MUR
ざわ
MUR MUR
WHAT'S GOING ON?
HEY, IT'S KEI...
YOU...
DID SOMETHING HAPPEN?
IS IT ANOTHER FIGHT?
KEI, IS EVERY-THING OKAY?
HE'S FIGHTING A GIRL?
ER... NOTHING TO SEE HERE, FOLKS! I'M SORRY IF WE WORRIED YA!!

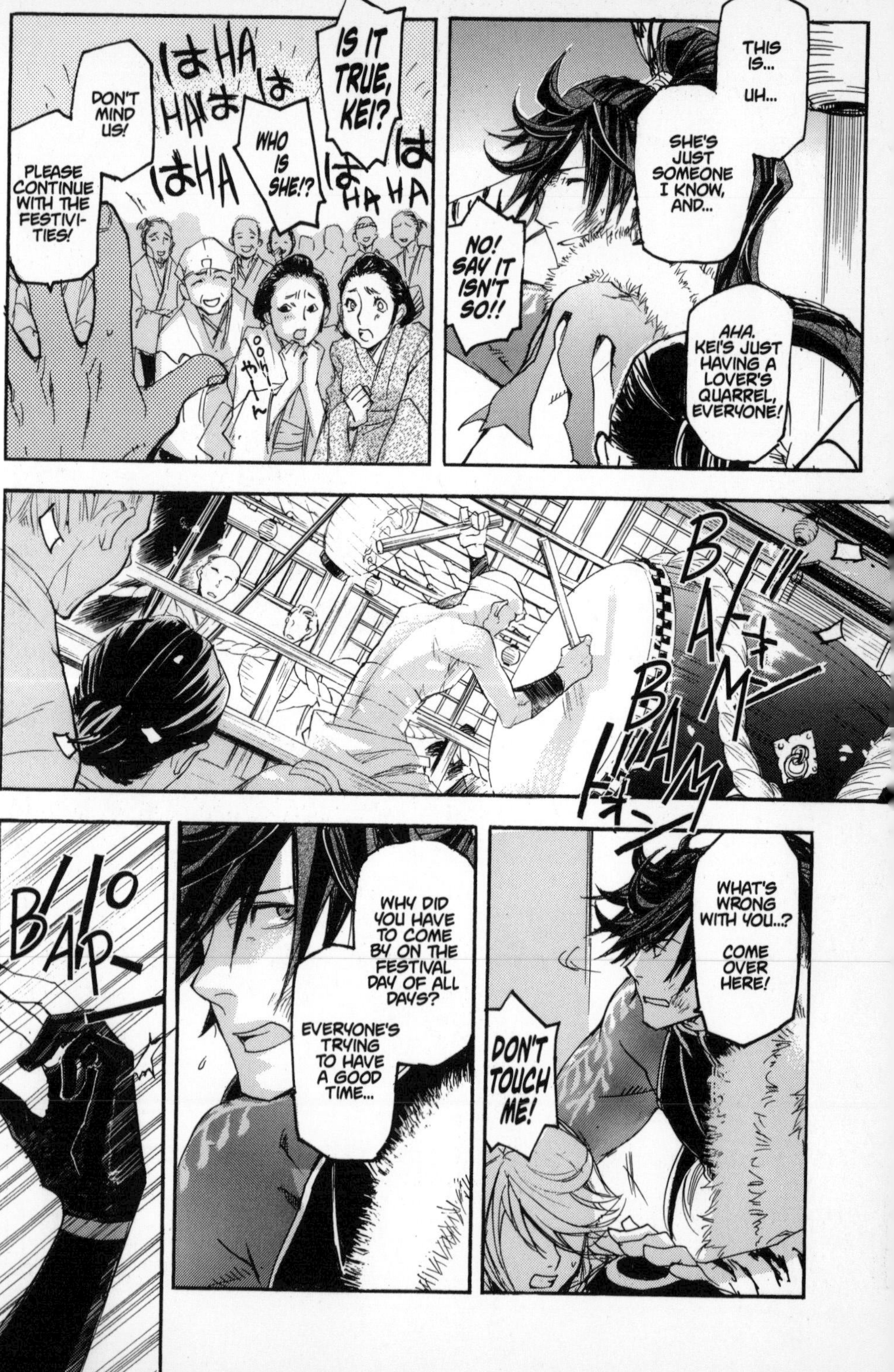
THIS IS... UH...
SHE'S JUST SOMEONE I KNOW, AND...
NO! SAY IT ISN'T SO!!
AHA. KEI'S JUST HAVING A LOVER'S QUARREL, EVERYONE!
IS IT TRUE, KEI?
WHO IS SHE!?
はHA はHA はHA はHA
DON'T MIND US!
PLEASE CONTINUE WITH THE FESTIVITIES!
BAM BAM
WHAT'S WRONG WITH YOU..?
COME OVER HERE!
DON'T TOUCH ME!
WHY DID YOU HAVE TO COME BY ON THE FESTIVAL DAY OF ALL DAYS?
EVERYONE'S TRYING TO HAVE A GOOD TIME...
BLAP

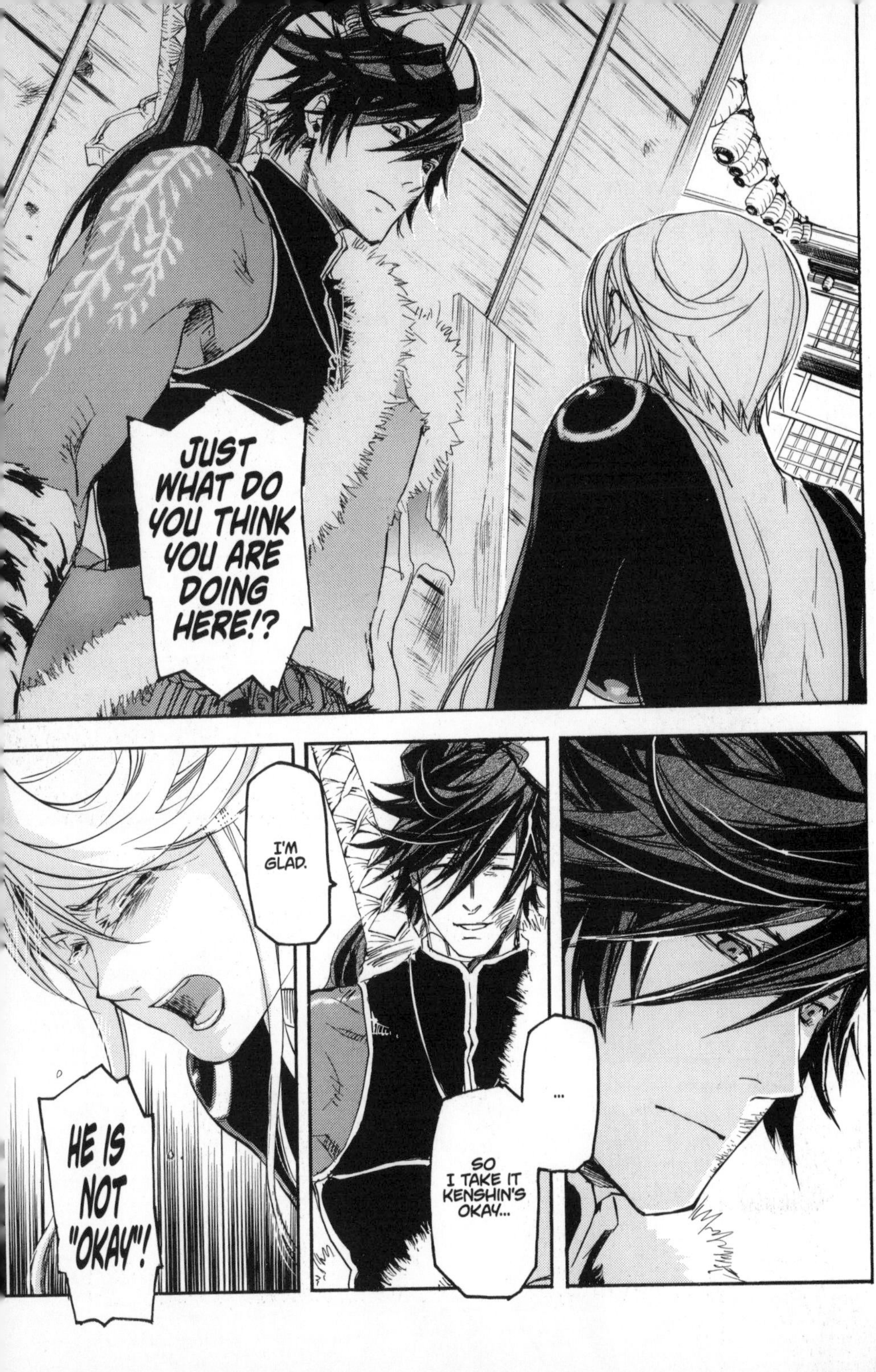
JUST WHAT DO YOU THINK YOU ARE DOING HERE!?
...
SO I TAKE IT KENSHIN'S OKAY...
I'M GLAD.
HE IS NOT "OKAY"!

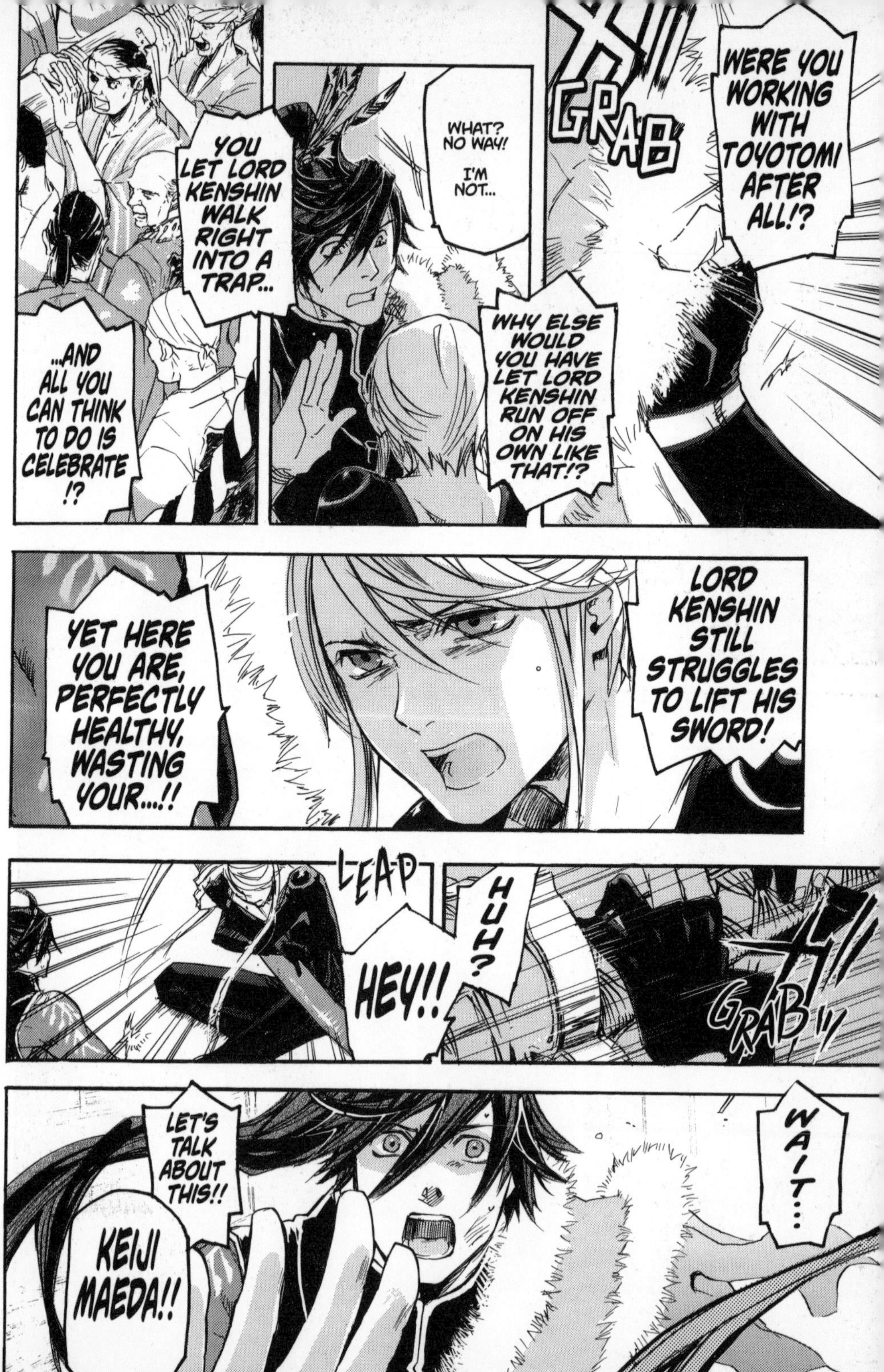
GRAB
WERE YOU WORKING WITH TOYOTOMI AFTER ALL!?
WHY ELSE WOULD YOU HAVE LET LORD KENSHIN RUN OFF ON HIS OWN LIKE THAT!?
WHAT? NO WAY! I'M NOT...
YOU LET LORD KENSHIN WALK RIGHT INTO A TRAP...
...AND ALL YOU CAN THINK TO DO IS CELEBRATE!?
LORD KENSHIN STILL STRUGGLES TO LIFT HIS SWORD!
YET HERE YOU ARE, PERFECTLY HEALTHY, WASTING YOUR...!!
GRAB
HUH?
LEAP
HEY!!
WAIT...
LET'S TALK ABOUT THIS!!
KEIJI MAEDA!!

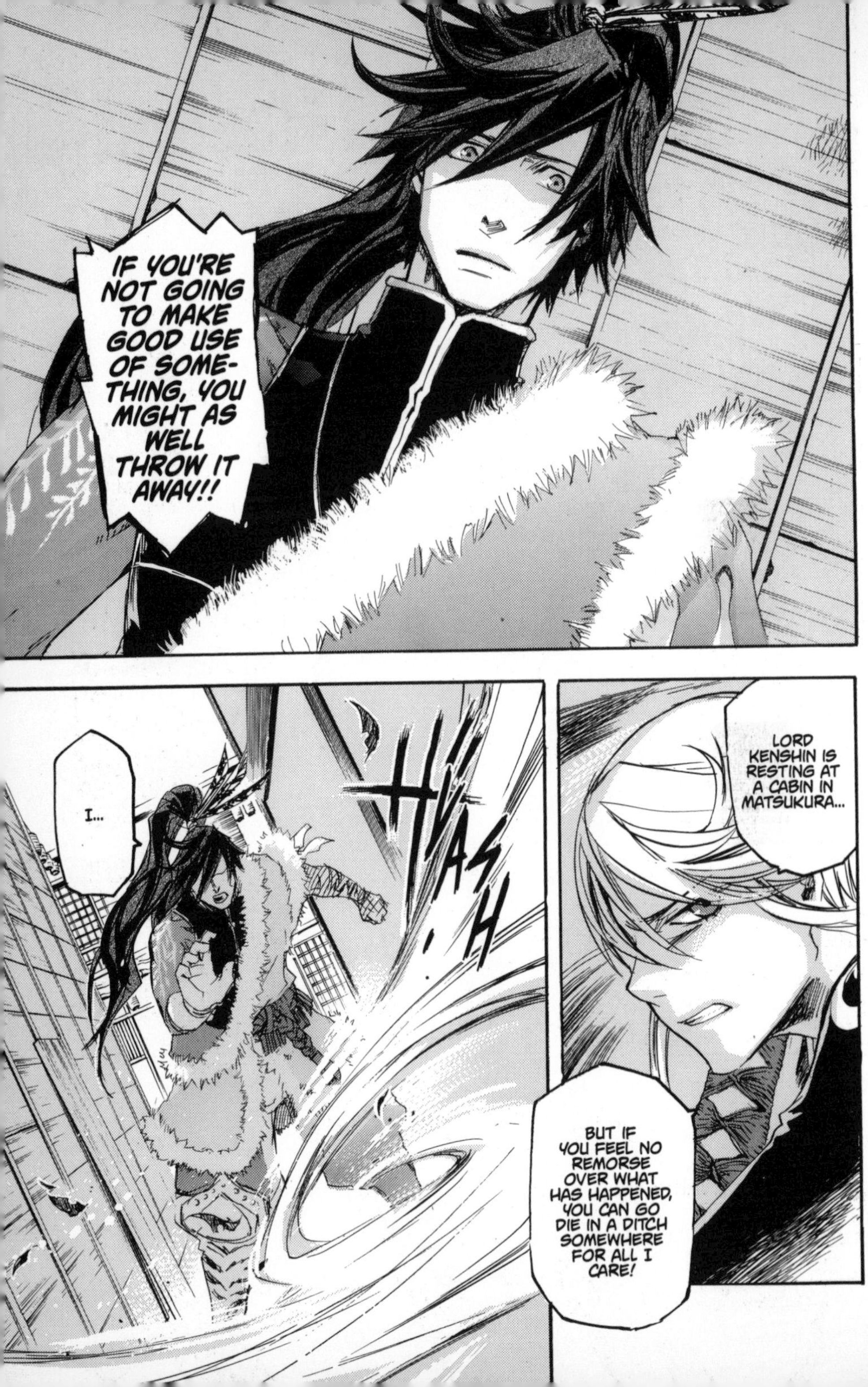
IF YOU'RE NOT GOING TO MAKE GOOD USE OF SOME-THING, YOU MIGHT AS WELL THROW IT AWAY!!
LORD KENSHIN IS RESTING AT A CABIN IN MATSUKURA...
BUT IF YOU FEEL NO REMORSE OVER WHAT HAS HAPPENED, YOU CAN GO DIE IN A DITCH SOMEWHERE FOR ALL I CARE!
I...
HWASH

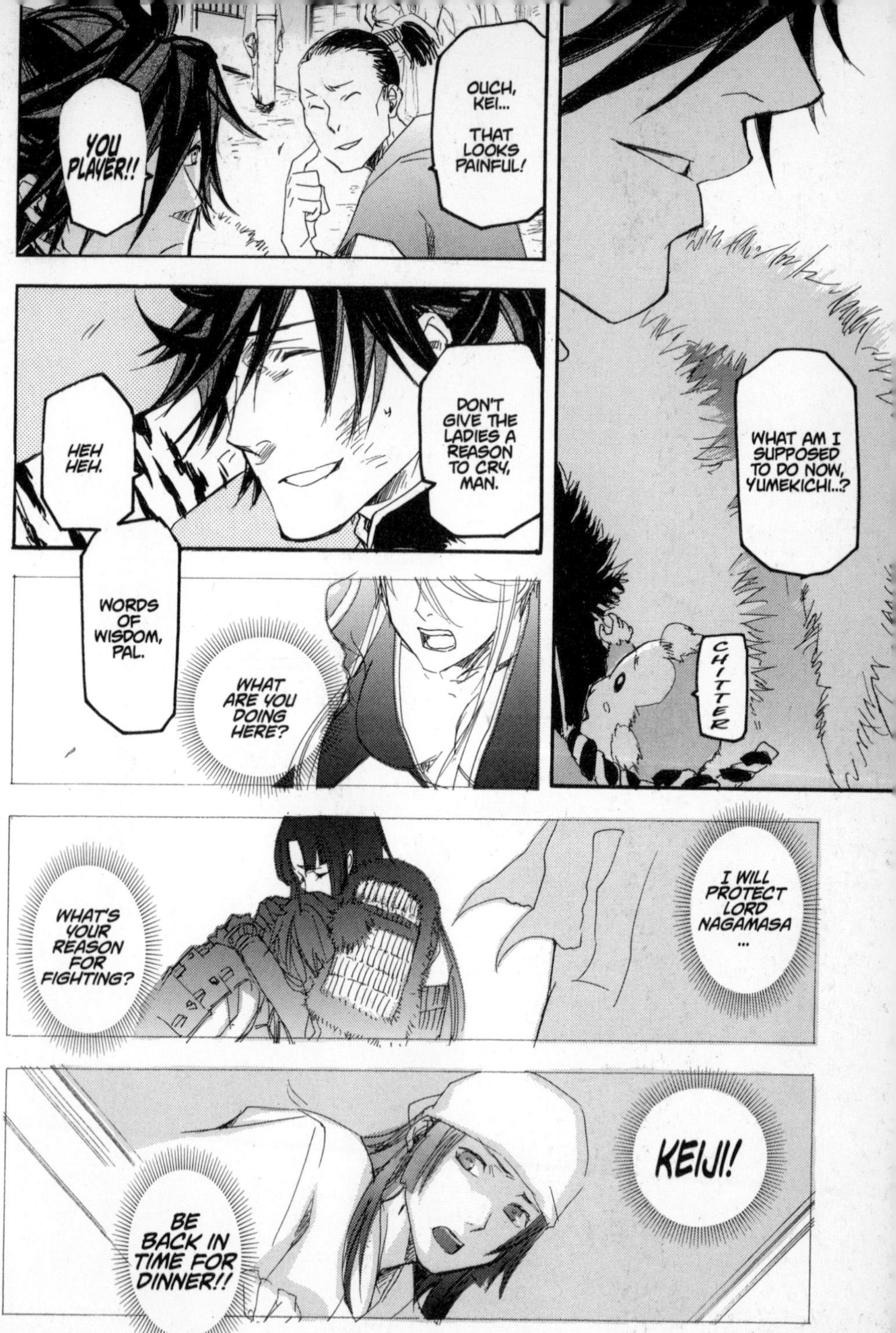
WHAT AM I SUPPOSED TO DO NOW, YUMEKICHI..?
CHITTER
OUCH, KEI... THAT LOOKS PAINFUL!
YOU PLAYER!!
DON'T GIVE THE LADIES A REASON TO CRY, MAN.
HEH HEH.
WORDS OF WISDOM, PAL.
WHAT ARE YOU DOING HERE?
I WILL PROTECT LORD NAGAMASA ...
WHAT'S YOUR REASON FOR FIGHTING?
KEIJI!
BE BACK IN TIME FOR DINNER!!

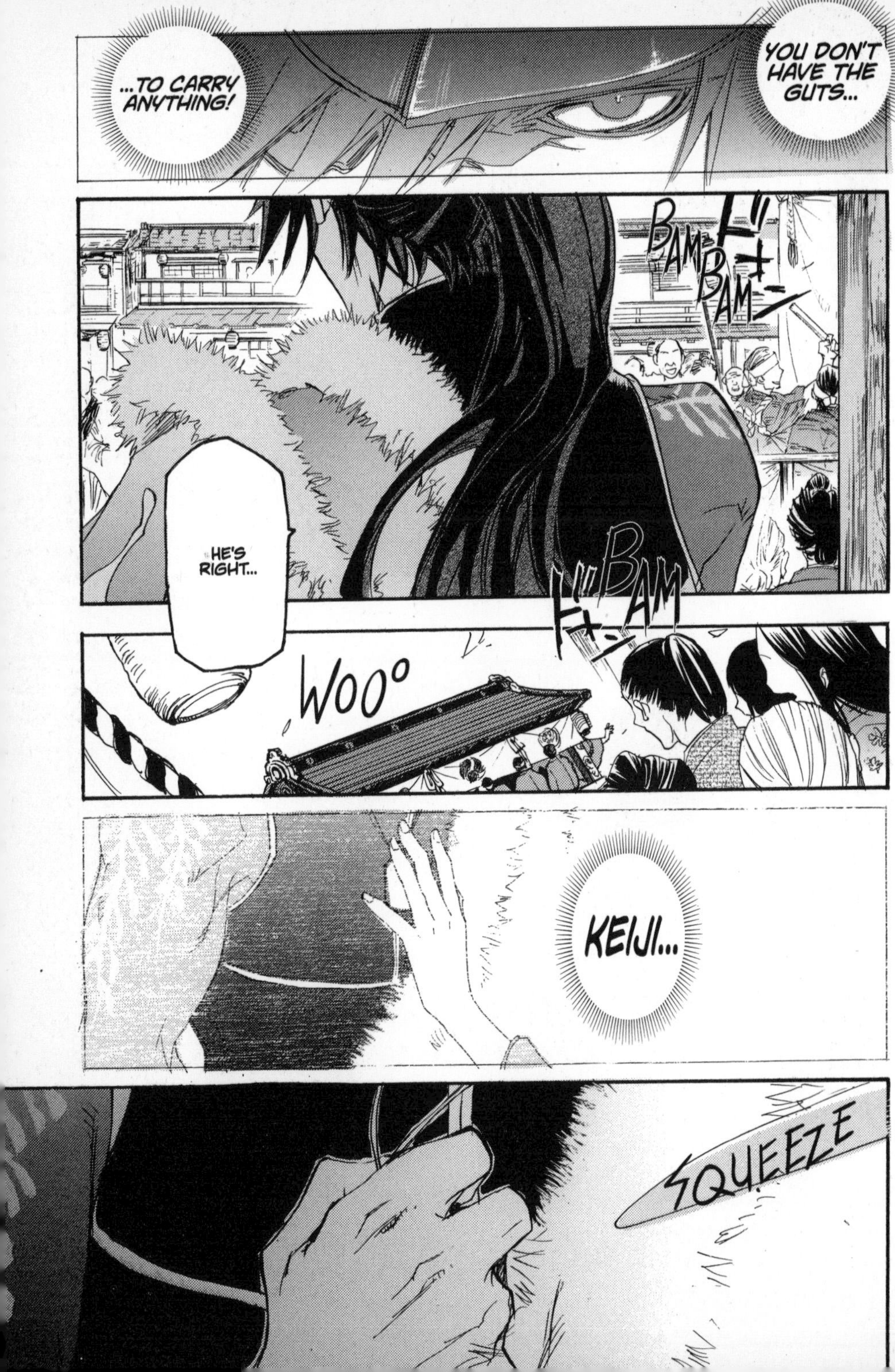
YOU DON'T HAVE THE GUTS...
...TO CARRY ANYTHING!
BAM BAM
HE'S RIGHT...
BAM
WOOO
KEIJI...
SQUEEZE

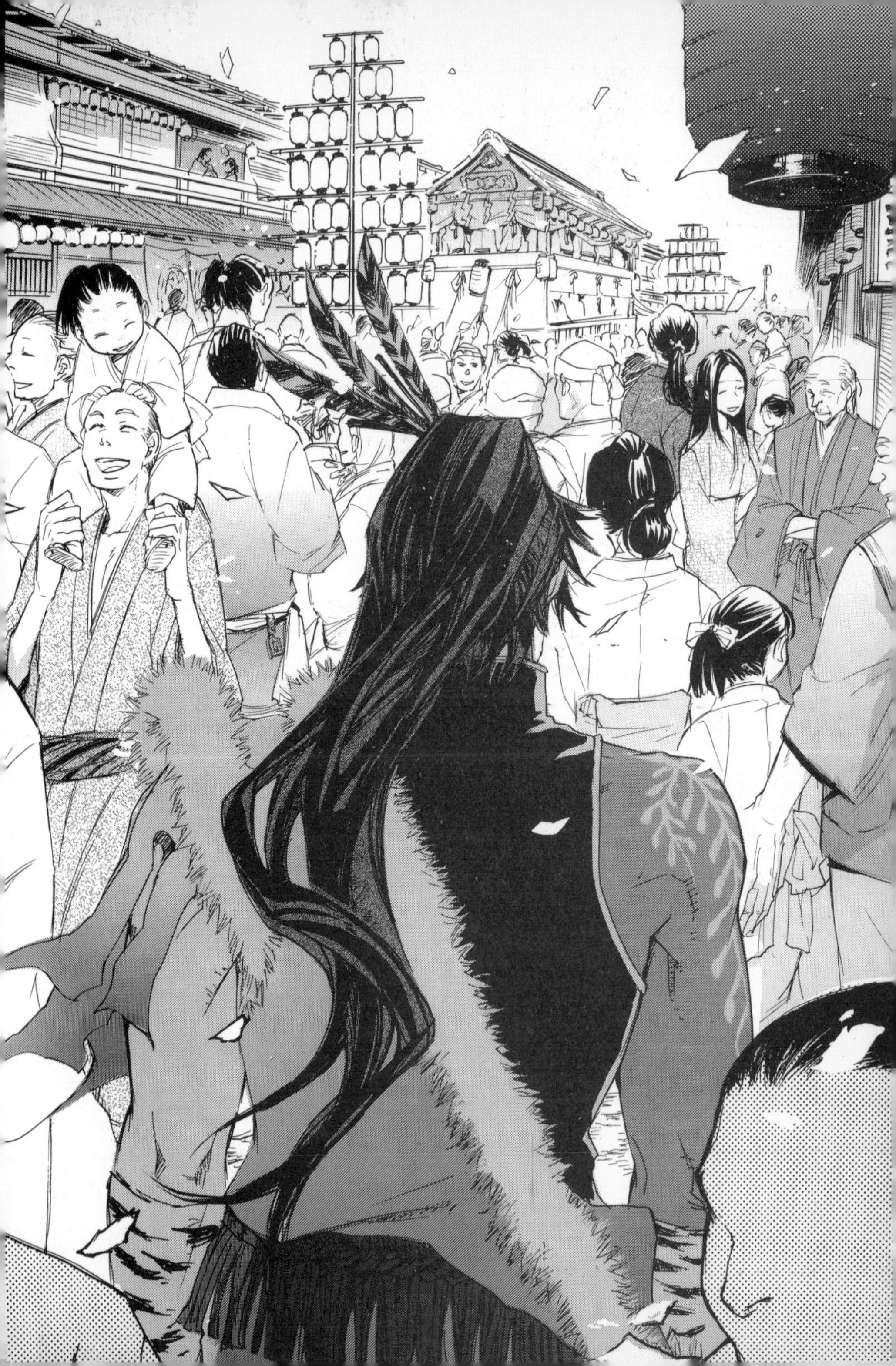

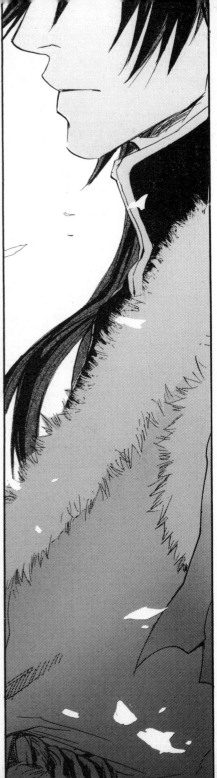

THERE YOU ARE!

WE'VE BEEN LOOKING ALL OVER FOR YOU!

KEI...!

SQUEAL

WHY DO YOU HAVE SUCH A SERIOUS LOOK ON YOUR FACE? IT DOESN'T SUIT YOU AT ALL!

COME ON, KEI...

...

KEI..?

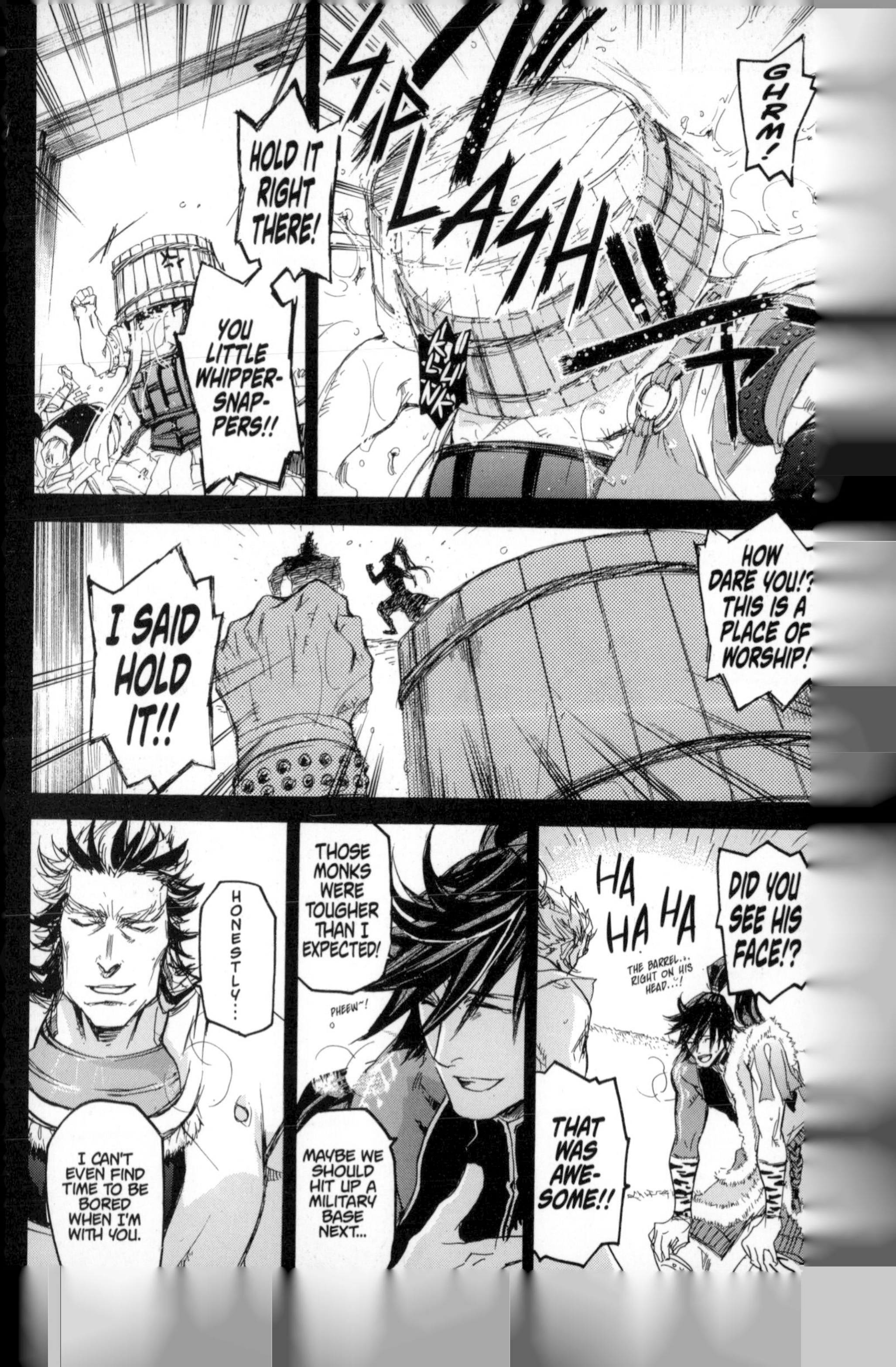

GHRM!
SPLASH!!
KLUNK
HOLD IT RIGHT THERE!
YOU LITTLE WHIPPER-SNAPPERS!!
HOW DARE YOU!? THIS IS A PLACE OF WORSHIP!
I SAID HOLD IT!!
DID YOU SEE HIS FACE!?
HA HA HA HA
THE BARREL... RIGHT ON HIS HEAD...!
THAT WAS AWE-SOME!!
THOSE MONKS WERE TOUGHER THAN I EXPECTED!
PHEEW~!
MAYBE WE SHOULD HIT UP A MILITARY BASE NEXT...
HONESTLY...
I CAN'T EVEN FIND TIME TO BE BORED WHEN I'M WITH YOU.

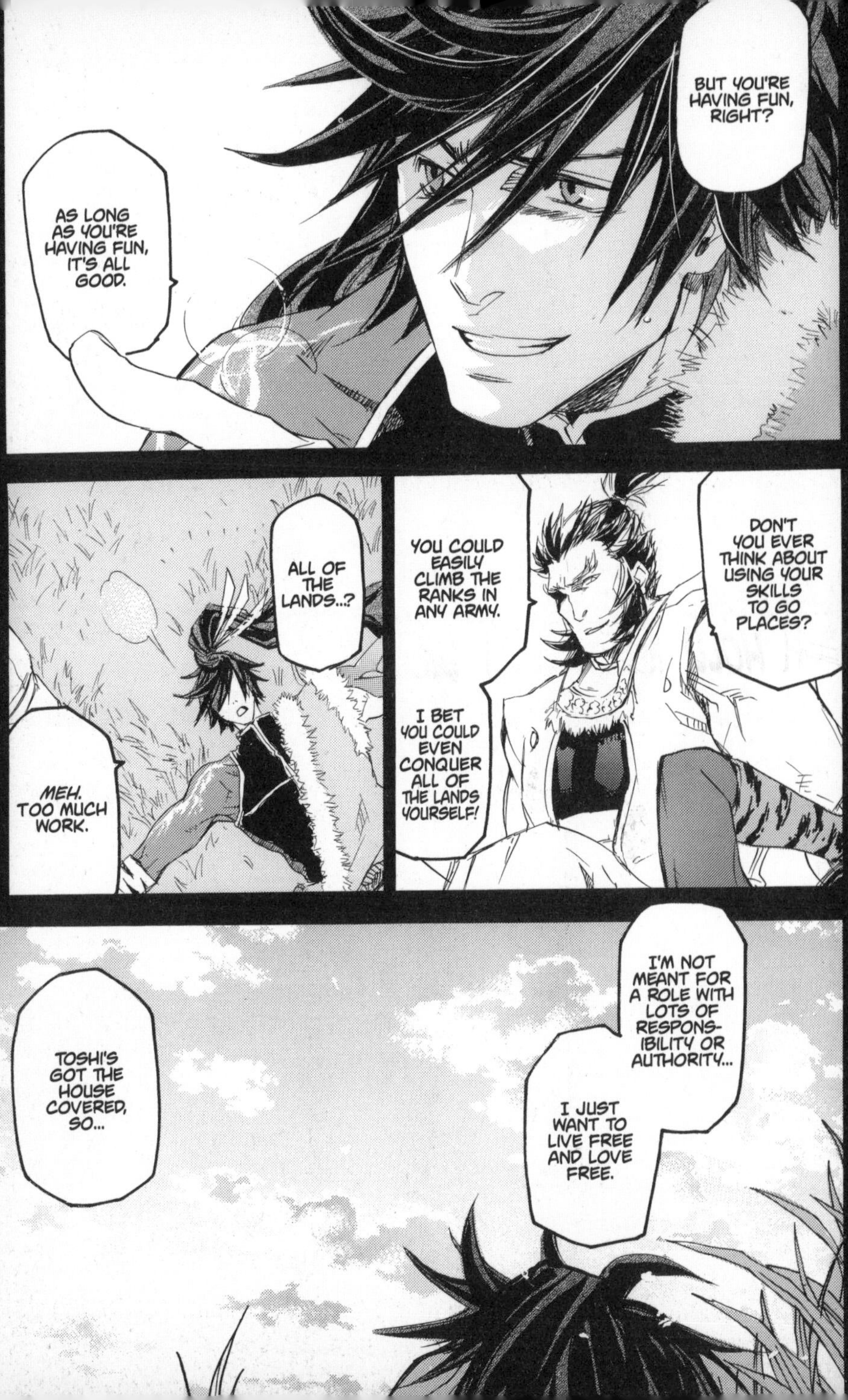
BUT YOU'RE HAVING FUN, RIGHT?
AS LONG AS YOU'RE HAVING FUN, IT'S ALL GOOD.
DON'T YOU EVER THINK ABOUT USING YOUR SKILLS TO GO PLACES?
YOU COULD EASILY CLIMB THE RANKS IN ANY ARMY.
I BET YOU COULD EVEN CONQUER ALL OF THE LANDS YOURSELF!
ALL OF THE LANDS...?
MEH. TOO MUCH WORK.
I'M NOT MEANT FOR A ROLE WITH LOTS OF RESPONS-IBILITY OR AUTHORITY...
I JUST WANT TO LIVE FREE AND LOVE FREE.
TOSHI'S GOT THE HOUSE COVERED, SO...

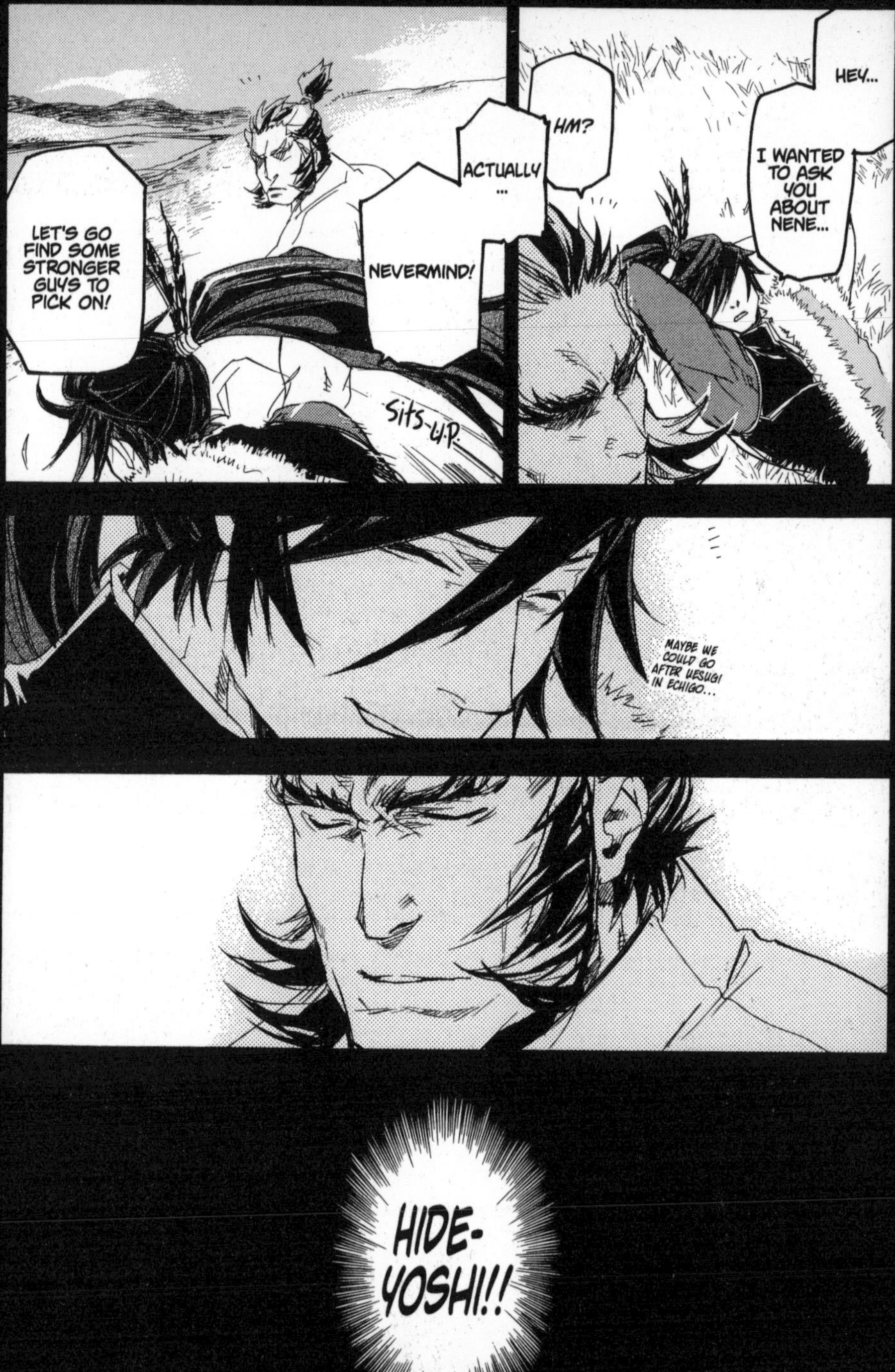
HEY...
I WANTED TO ASK YOU ABOUT NENE...
HM?
ACTUALLY ...
NEVERMIND!
LET'S GO FIND SOME STRONGER GUYS TO PICK ON!
Sits-up
MAYBE WE COULD GO AFTER UESUGI IN ECHIGO...
HIDE-YOSHI!!

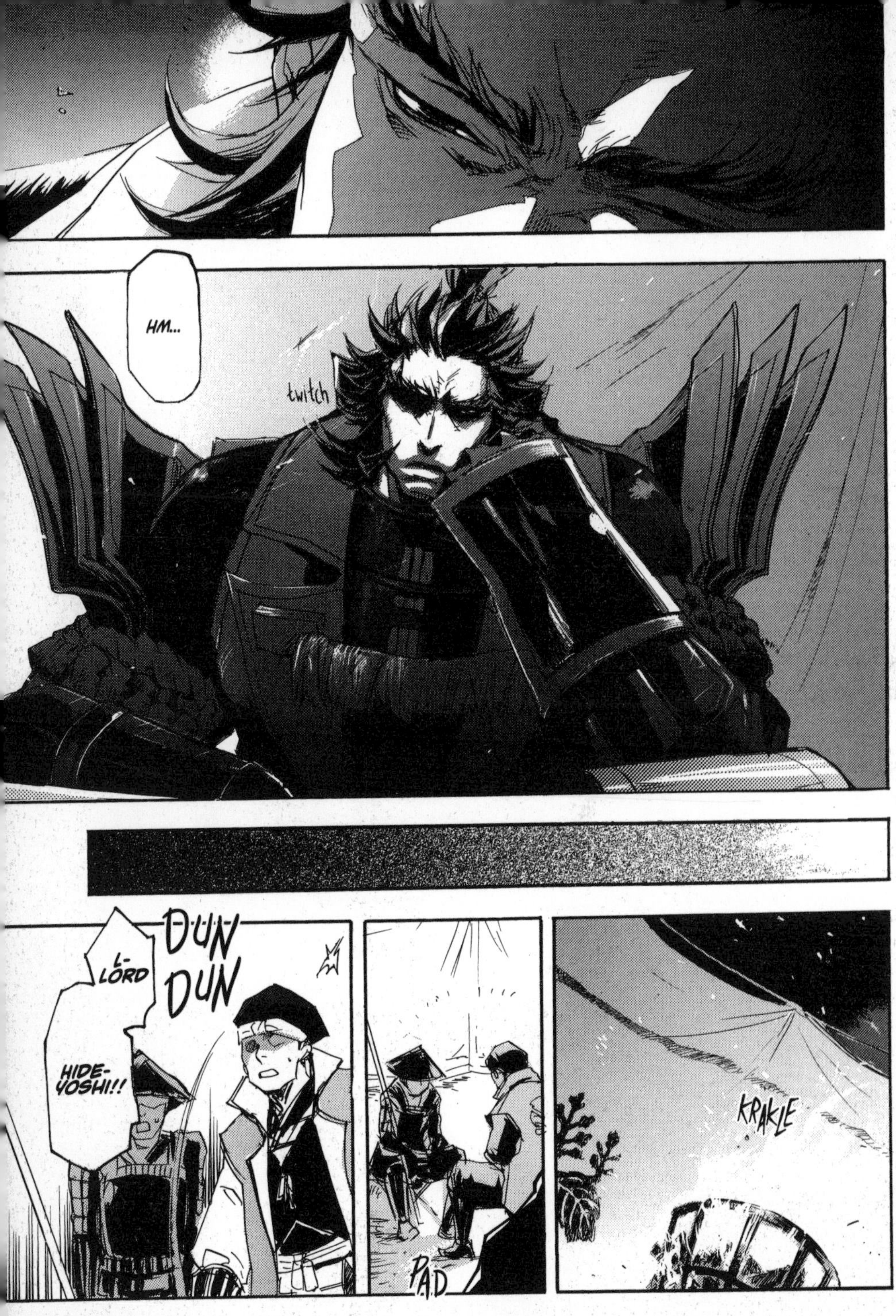
HM...
twitch
KRAKLE
PAD
L-LORD HIDE-YOSHI!!
DUN DUN

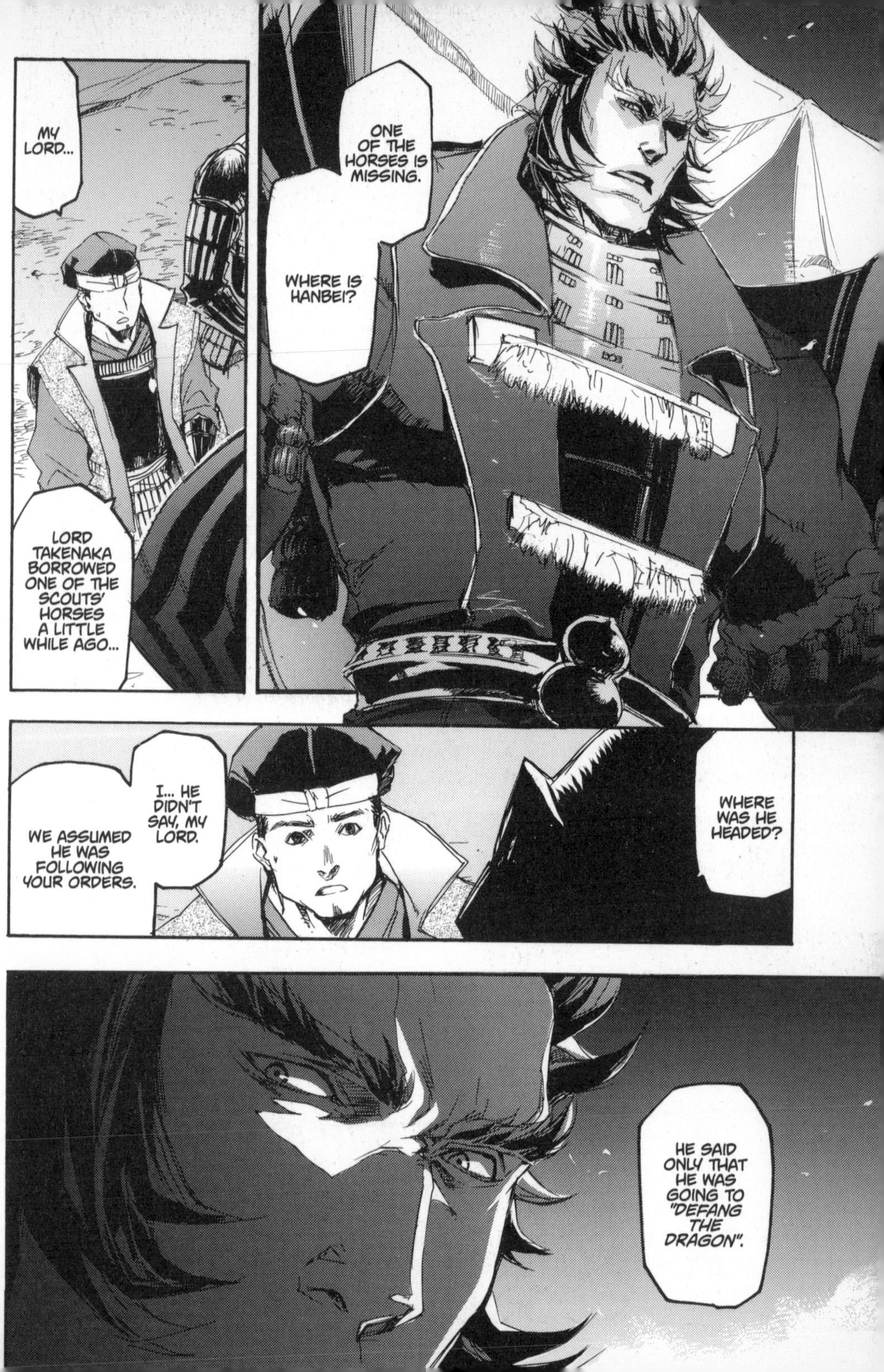
ONE OF THE HORSES IS MISSING.
WHERE IS HANBEI?
MY LORD...
LORD TAKENAKA BORROWED ONE OF THE SCOUTS' HORSES A LITTLE WHILE AGO...
WHERE WAS HE HEADED?
I... HE DIDN'T SAY, MY LORD.
WE ASSUMED HE WAS FOLLOWING YOUR ORDERS.
HE SAID ONLY THAT HE WAS GOING TO "DEFANG THE DRAGON".

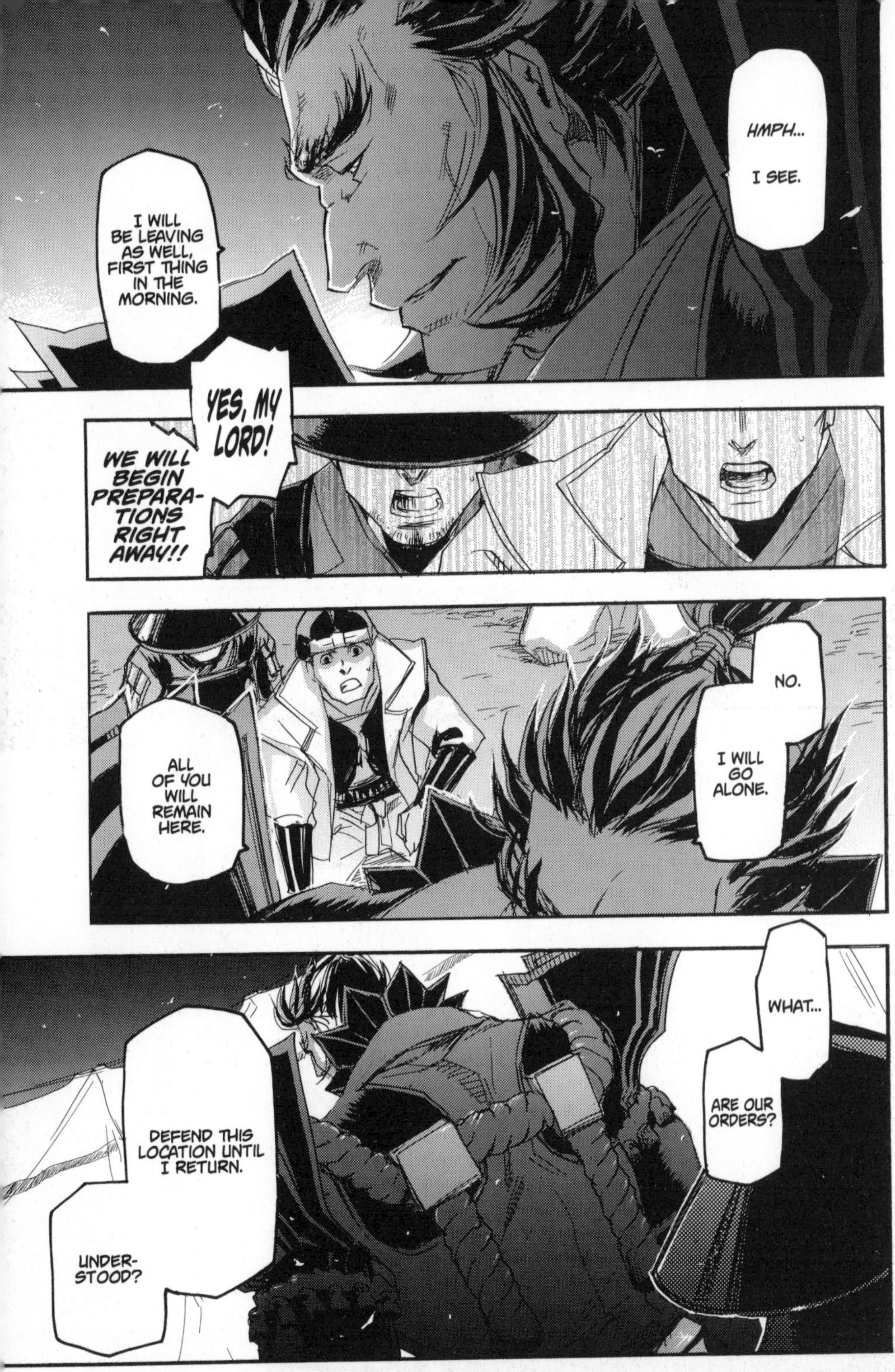
HMPH...
I SEE.
I WILL BE LEAVING AS WELL, FIRST THING IN THE MORNING.
YES, MY LORD!
WE WILL BEGIN PREPARATIONS RIGHT AWAY!!
NO.
I WILL GO ALONE.
ALL OF YOU WILL REMAIN HERE.
WHAT...
ARE OUR ORDERS?
DEFEND THIS LOCATION UNTIL I RETURN.
UNDERSTOOD?

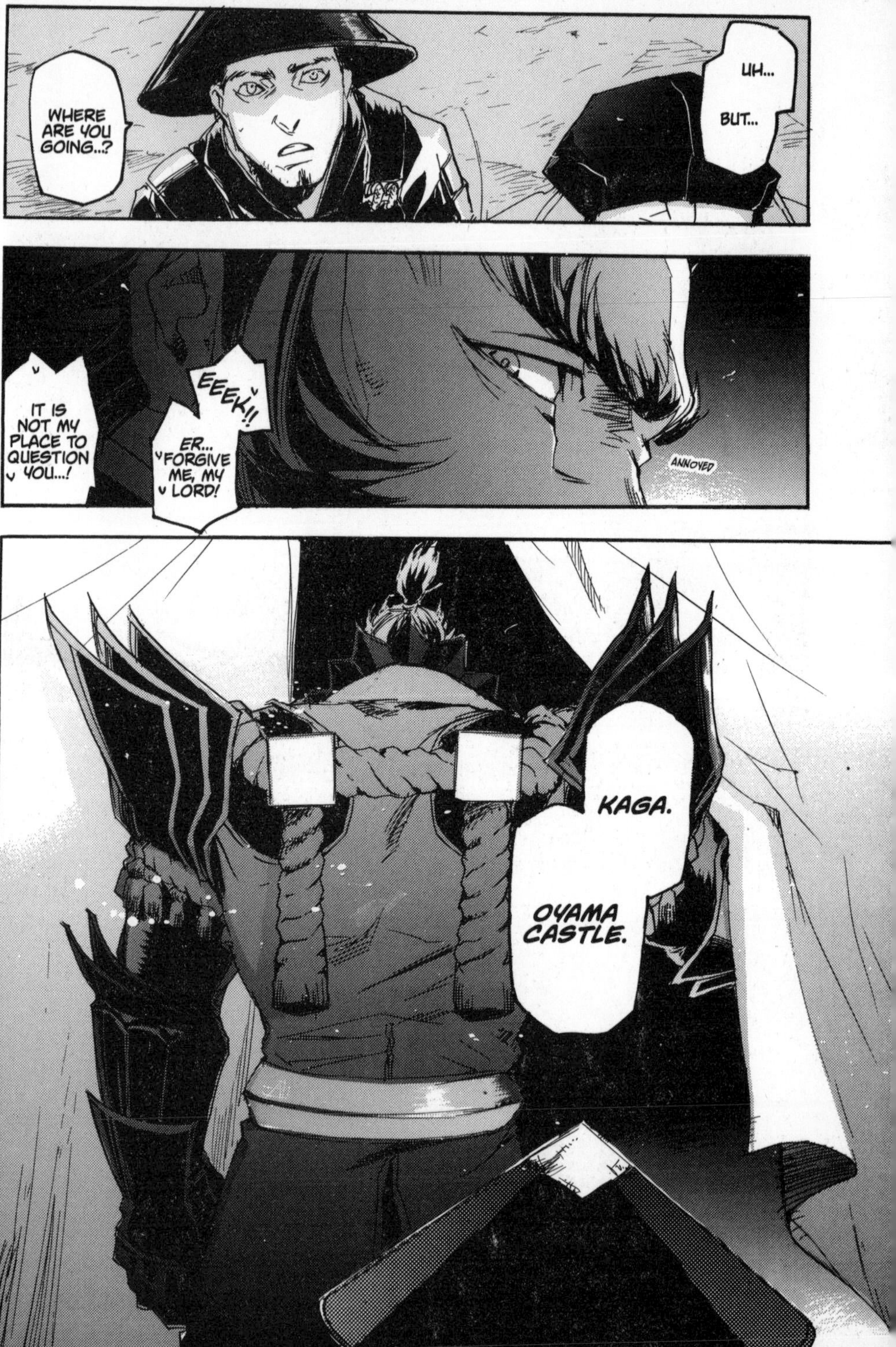
UH...
BUT...
WHERE ARE YOU GOING..?
ANNOYED
EEEK!!
ER... FORGIVE ME, MY LORD!
IT IS NOT MY PLACE TO QUESTION YOU...!
KAGA.
OYAMA CASTLE.

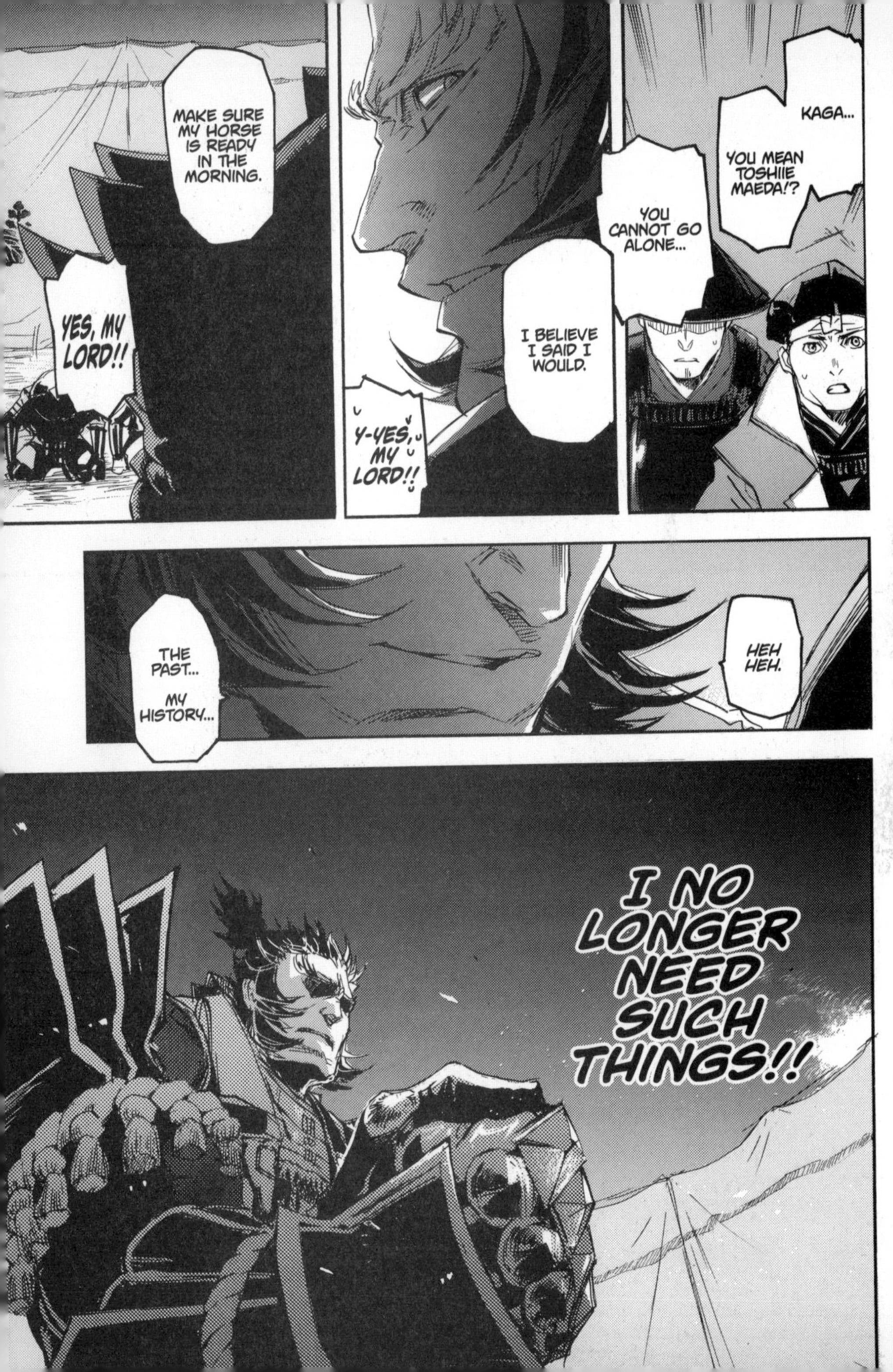
KAGA...
YOU MEAN TOSHIIE MAEDA!?
YOU CANNOT GO ALONE...
I BELIEVE I SAID I WOULD.
Y-YES, MY LORD!!
MAKE SURE MY HORSE IS READY IN THE MORNING.
YES, MY LORD!!
HEH HEH.
THE PAST...
MY HISTORY...
I NO LONGER NEED SUCH THINGS!!

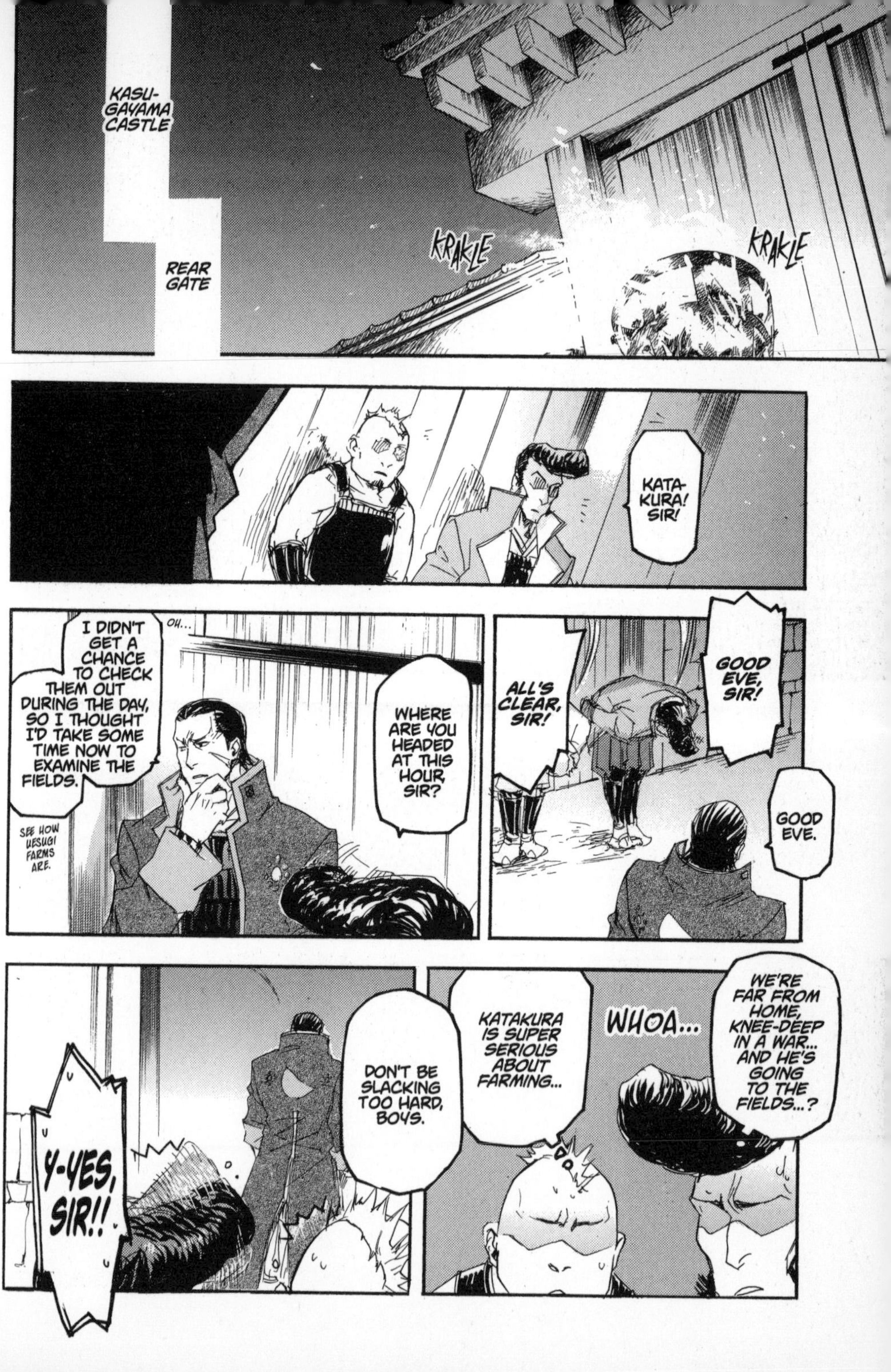
KASU-GAYAMA CASTLE
REAR GATE
KRAKLE
KRAKLE
KATA-KURA! SIR!
GOOD EVE, SIR!
ALL'S CLEAR, SIR!
GOOD EVE.
WHERE ARE YOU HEADED AT THIS HOUR, SIR?
OH...
I DIDN'T GET A CHANCE TO CHECK THEM OUT DURING THE DAY, SO I THOUGHT I'D TAKE SOME TIME NOW TO EXAMINE THE FIELDS.
SEE HOW UESUGI FARMS ARE.
WE'RE FAR FROM HOME, KNEE-DEEP IN A WAR... AND HE'S GOING TO THE FIELDS...?
WHOA...
KATAKURA IS SUPER SERIOUS ABOUT FARMING...
DON'T BE SLACKING TOO HARD, BOYS.
Y-YES, SIR!!

RUSTLE

GOOD SOIL...

GRIND

THIS LAND IS FERTILE.

GRAB

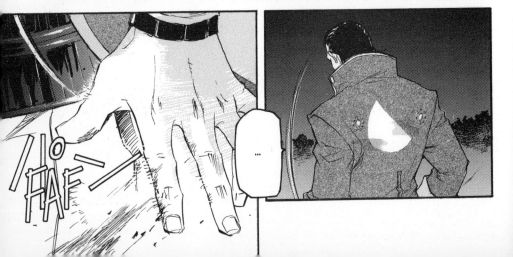

FAF

...

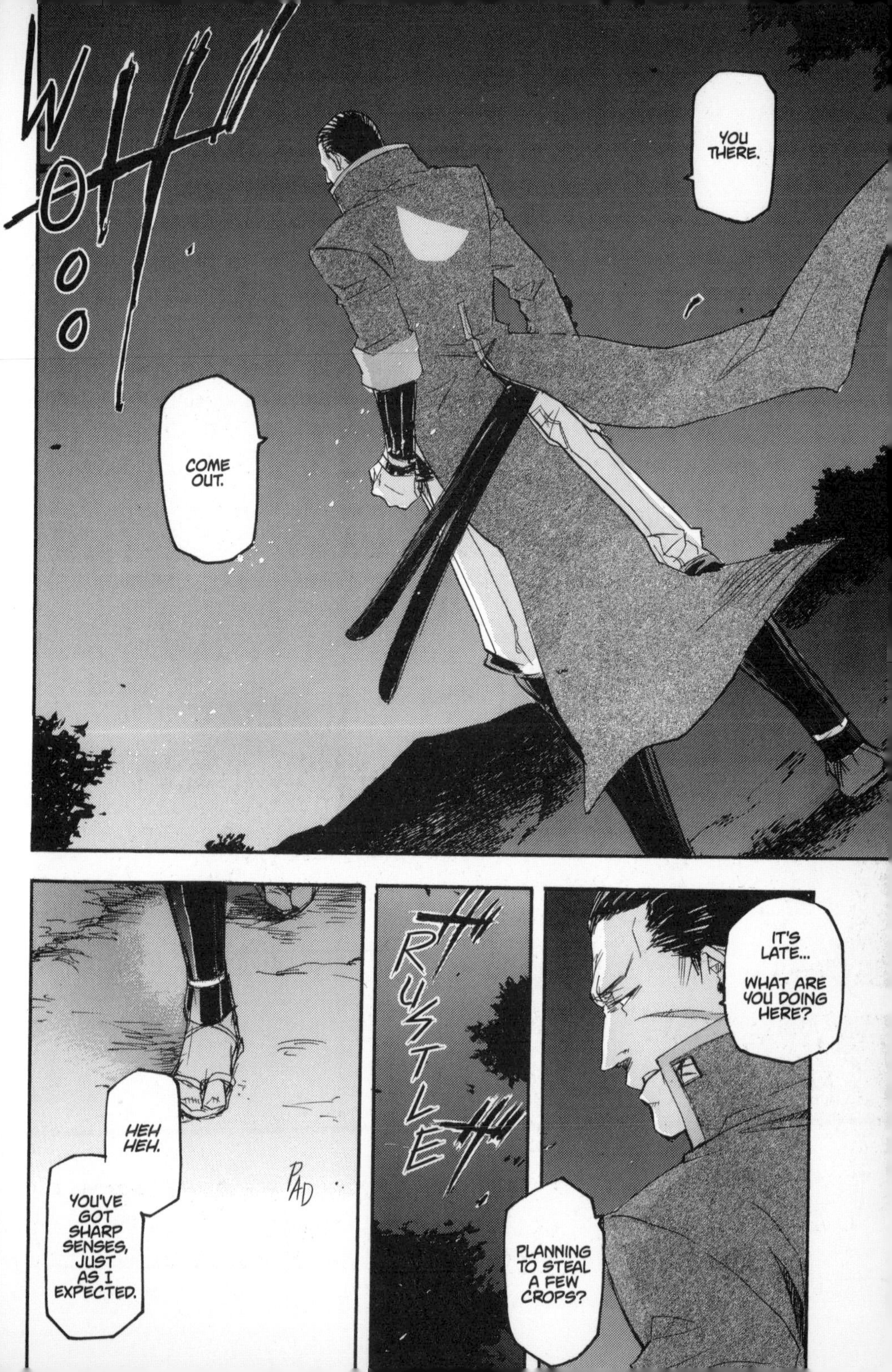

YOU THERE.
WHOOOO
COME OUT.
IT'S LATE... WHAT ARE YOU DOING HERE?
PLANNING TO STEAL A FEW CROPS?
RUSTLE
HEH HEH.
YOU'VE GOT SHARP SENSES, JUST AS I EXPECTED.
PAD

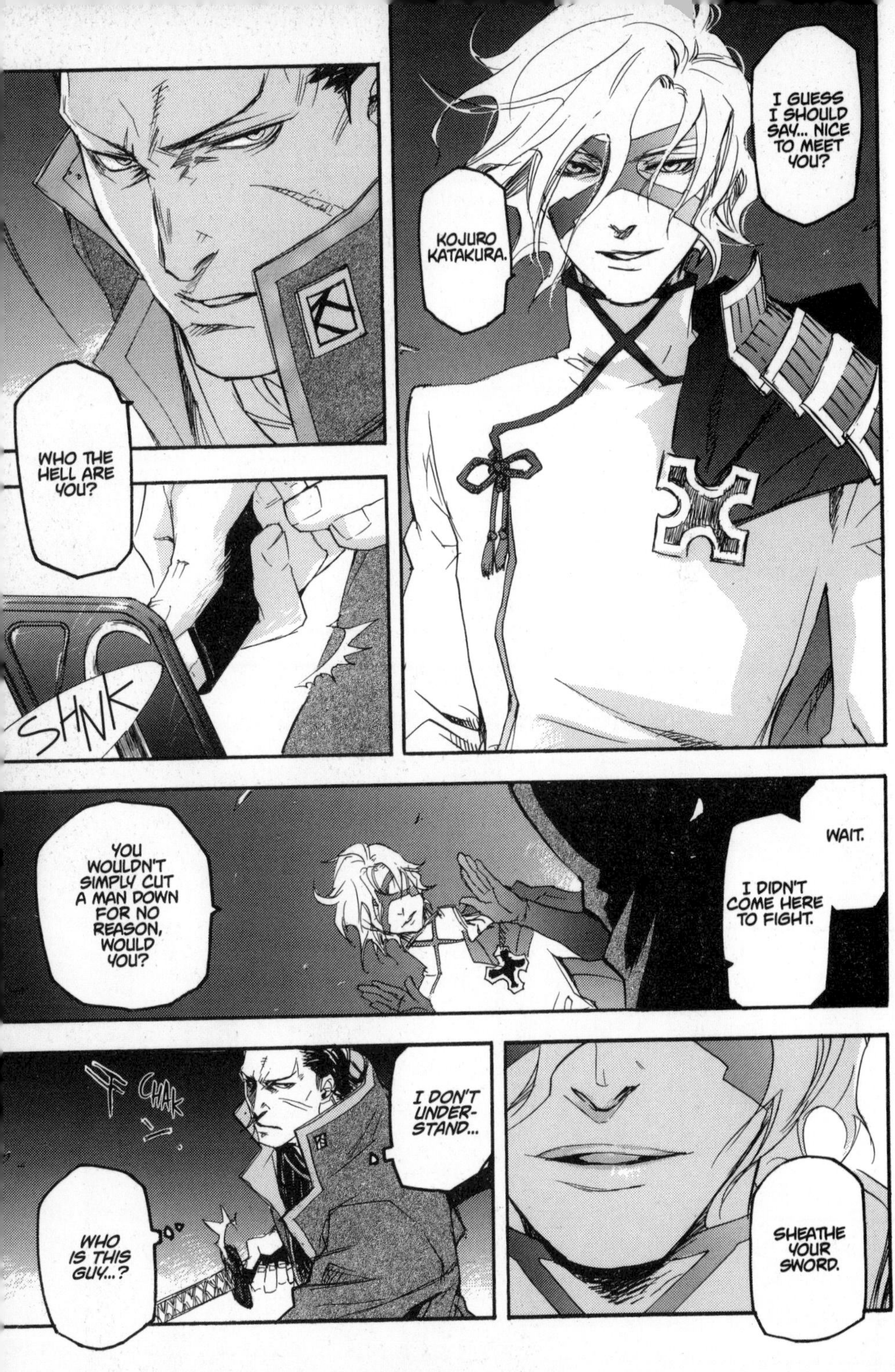
I GUESS I SHOULD SAY... NICE TO MEET YOU?
KOJURO KATAKURA.
WHO THE HELL ARE YOU?
SHNK
WAIT.
I DIDN'T COME HERE TO FIGHT.
YOU WOULDN'T SIMPLY CUT A MAN DOWN FOR NO REASON, WOULD YOU?
SHEATHE YOUR SWORD.
I DON'T UNDER-STAND...
CHAK
WHO IS THIS GUY...?

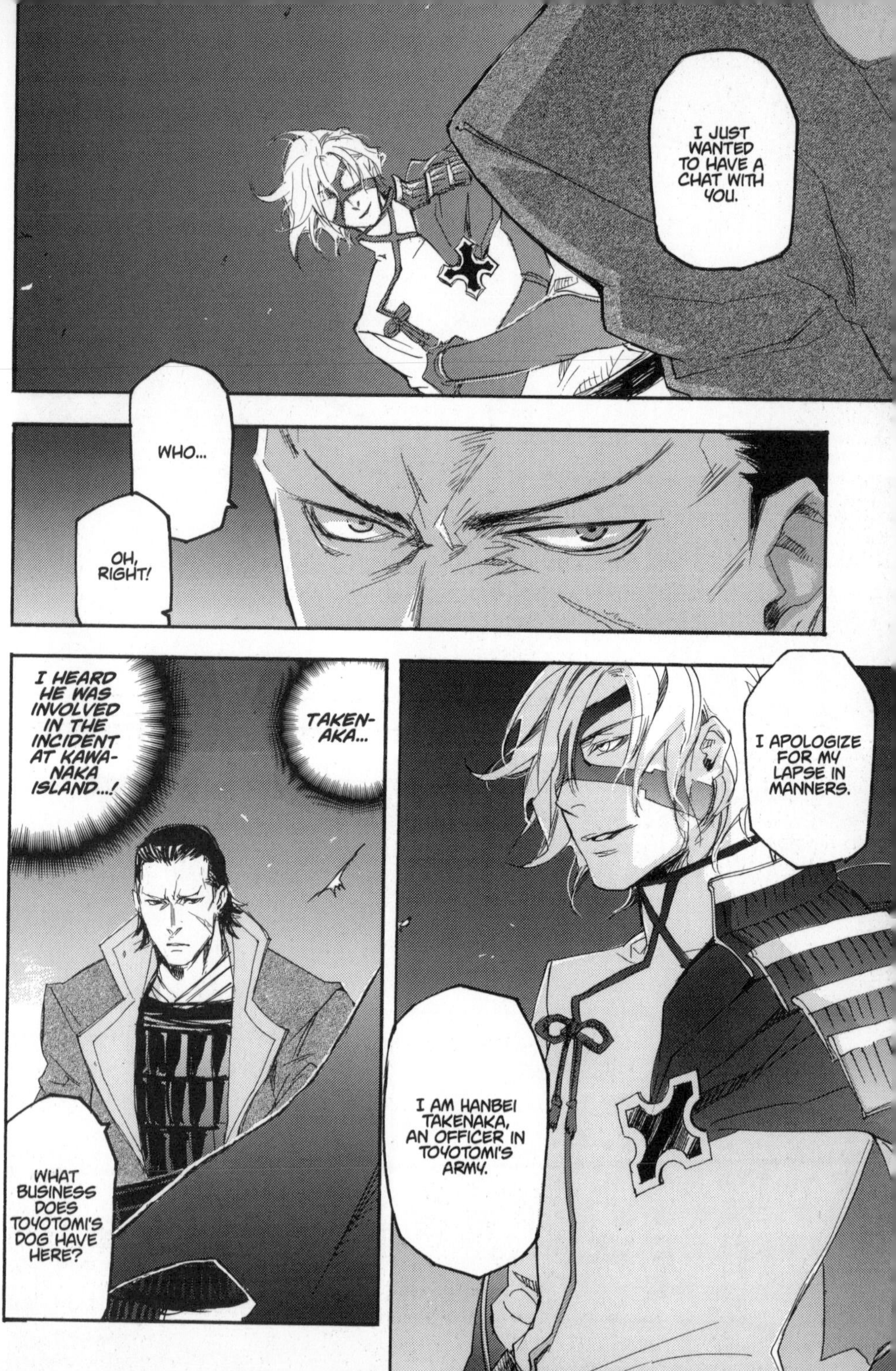
I JUST WANTED TO HAVE A CHAT WITH YOU.
WHO...
OH, RIGHT!
I APOLOGIZE FOR MY LAPSE IN MANNERS.
I AM HANBEI TAKENAKA, AN OFFICER IN TOYOTOMI'S ARMY.
TAKEN-AKA...
I HEARD HE WAS INVOLVED IN THE INCIDENT AT KAWA-NAKA ISLAND...!
WHAT BUSINESS DOES TOYOTOMI'S DOG HAVE HERE?

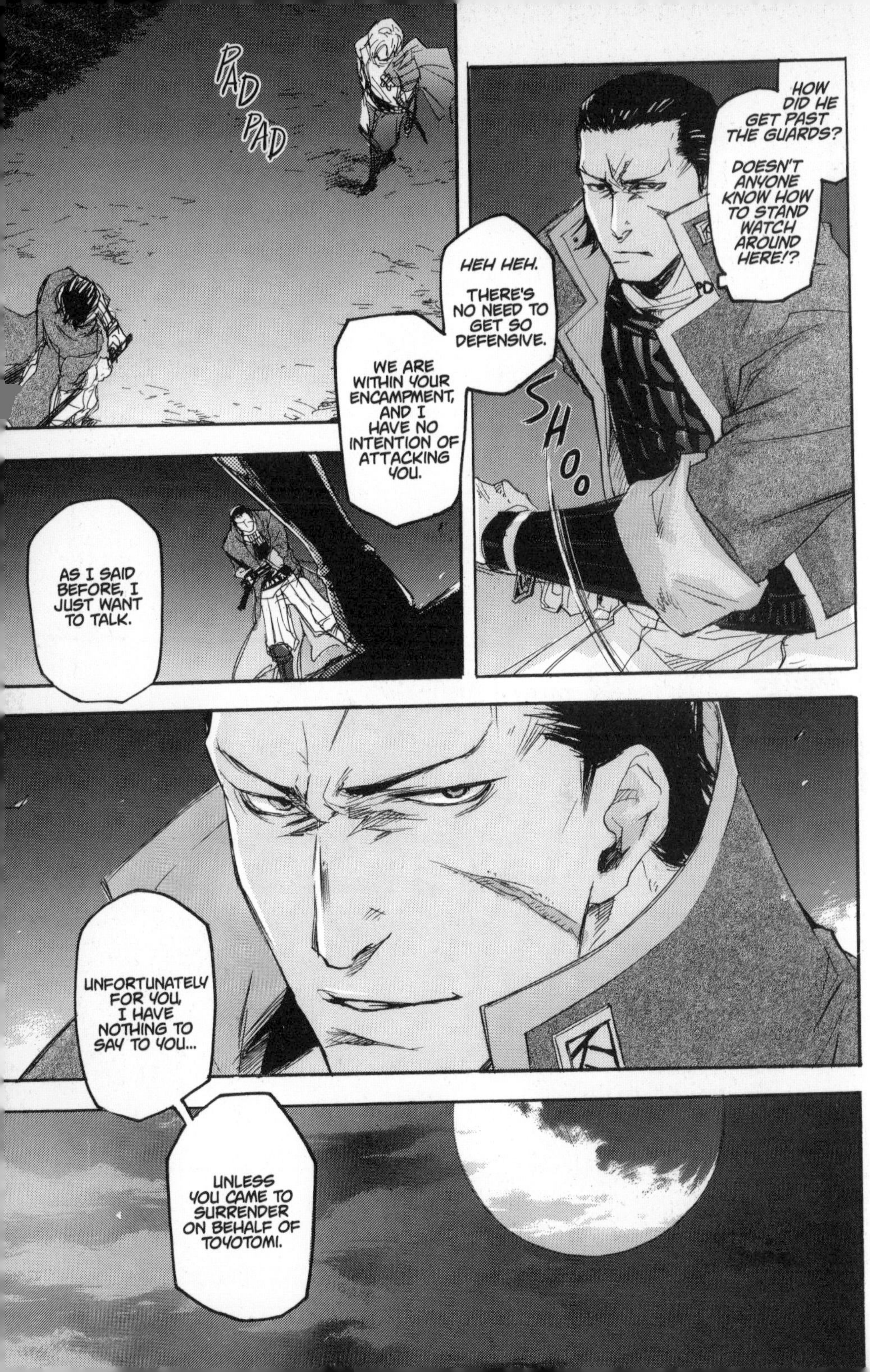
HOW DID HE GET PAST THE GUARDS?
DOESN'T ANYONE KNOW HOW TO STAND WATCH AROUND HERE!?
SHOOO
HEH HEH.
THERE'S NO NEED TO GET SO DEFENSIVE.
WE ARE WITHIN YOUR ENCAMPMENT, AND I HAVE NO INTENTION OF ATTACKING YOU.
PAD PAD
AS I SAID BEFORE, I JUST WANT TO TALK.
UNFORTUNATELY FOR YOU, I HAVE NOTHING TO SAY TO YOU...
UNLESS YOU CAME TO SURRENDER ON BEHALF OF TOYOTOMI.

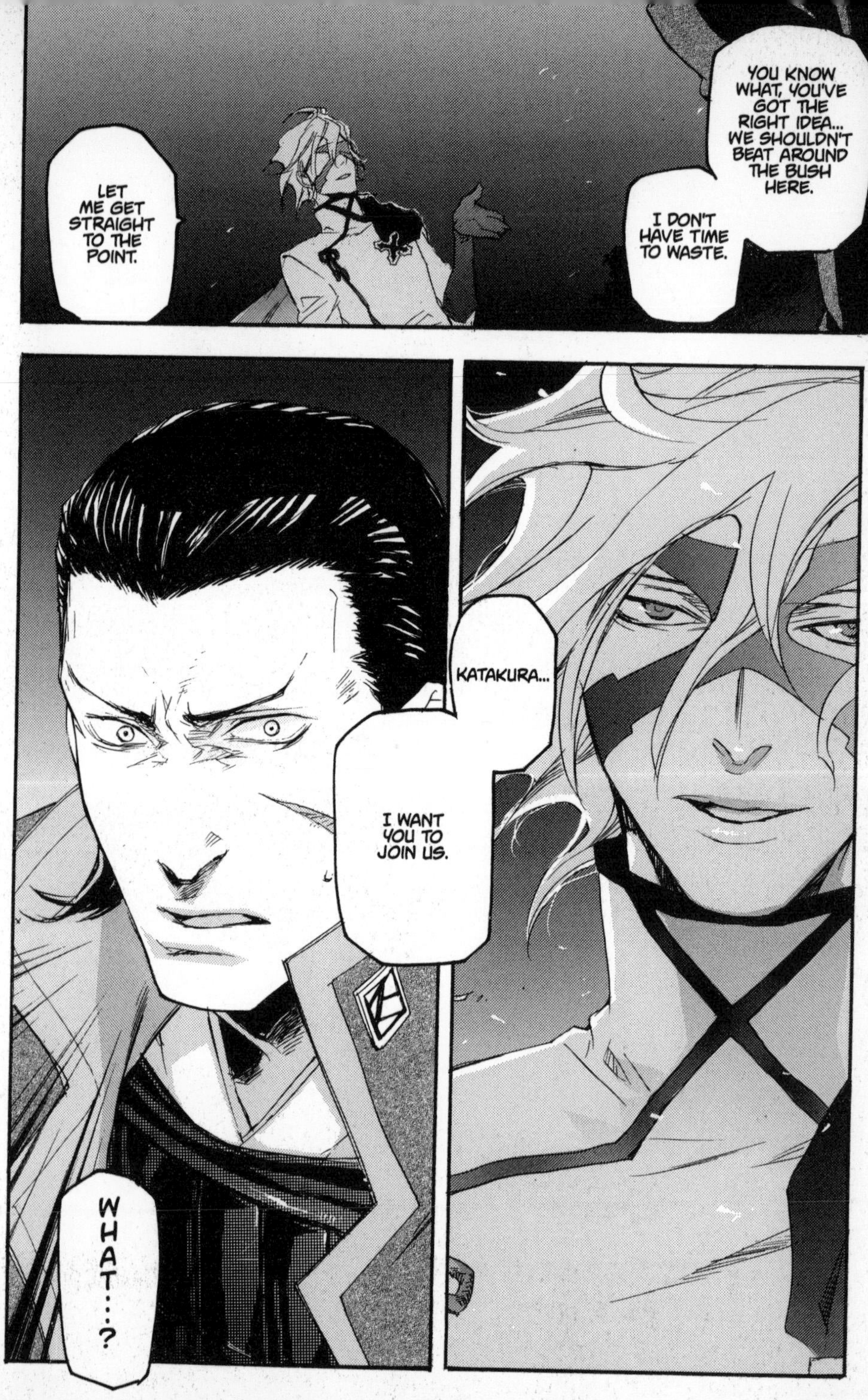
YOU KNOW WHAT, YOU'VE GOT THE RIGHT IDEA... WE SHOULDN'T BEAT AROUND THE BUSH HERE.
I DON'T HAVE TIME TO WASTE.
LET ME GET STRAIGHT TO THE POINT.
KATAKURA...
I WANT YOU TO JOIN US.
WHAT...?

ACT 4 **Ripples on the Water**

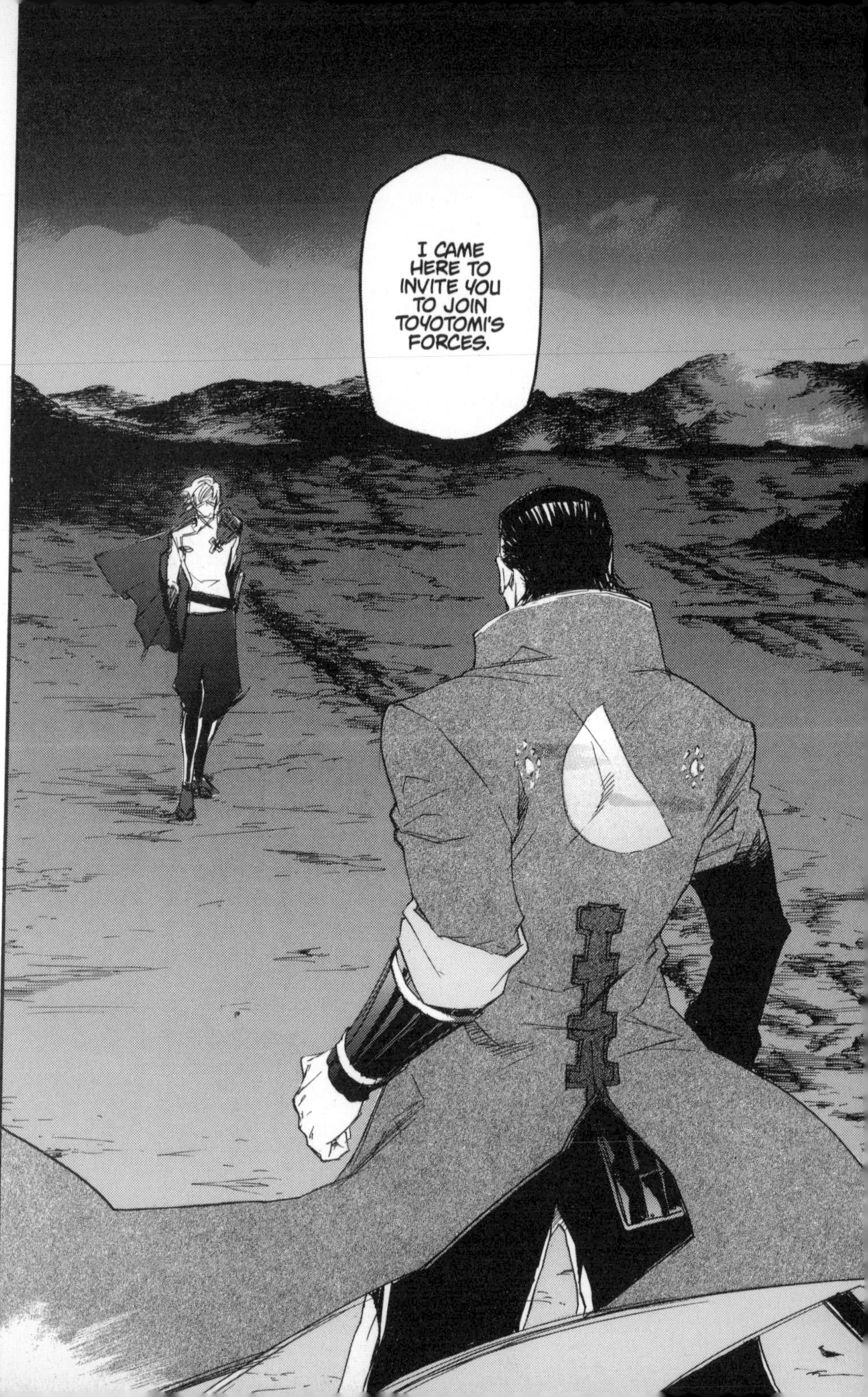
I CAME HERE TO INVITE YOU TO JOIN TOYOTOMI'S FORCES.

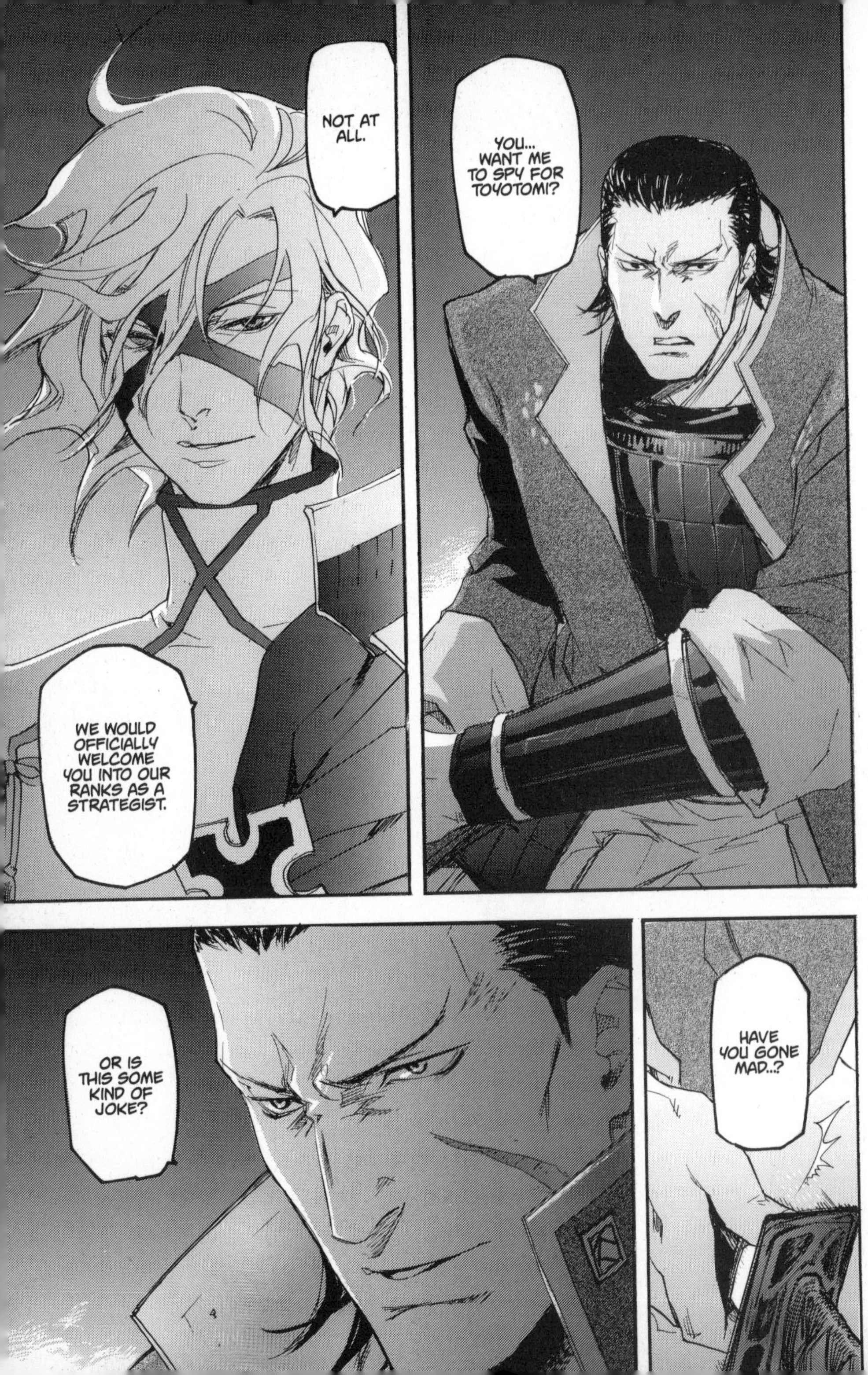
YOU... WANT ME TO SPY FOR TOYOTOMI?
NOT AT ALL.
WE WOULD OFFICIALLY WELCOME YOU INTO OUR RANKS AS A STRATEGIST.
HAVE YOU GONE MAD..?
OR IS THIS SOME KIND OF JOKE?

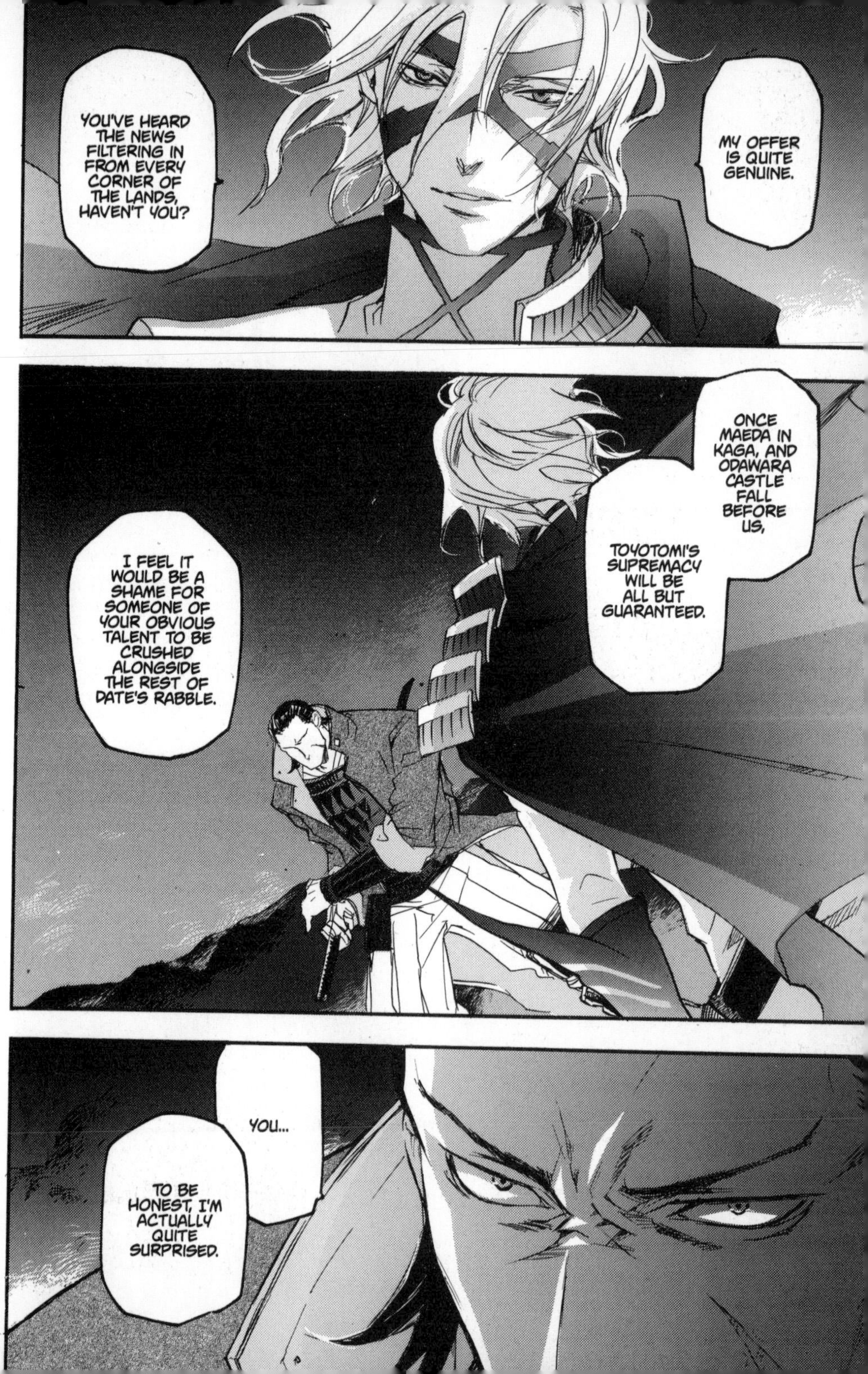
MY OFFER IS QUITE GENUINE.
YOU'VE HEARD THE NEWS FILTERING IN FROM EVERY CORNER OF THE LANDS, HAVEN'T YOU?
ONCE MAEDA IN KAGA, AND ODAWARA CASTLE FALL BEFORE US,
TOYOTOMI'S SUPREMACY WILL BE ALL BUT GUARANTEED.
I FEEL IT WOULD BE A SHAME FOR SOMEONE OF YOUR OBVIOUS TALENT TO BE CRUSHED ALONGSIDE THE REST OF DATE'S RABBLE.
YOU...
TO BE HONEST, I'M ACTUALLY QUITE SURPRISED.

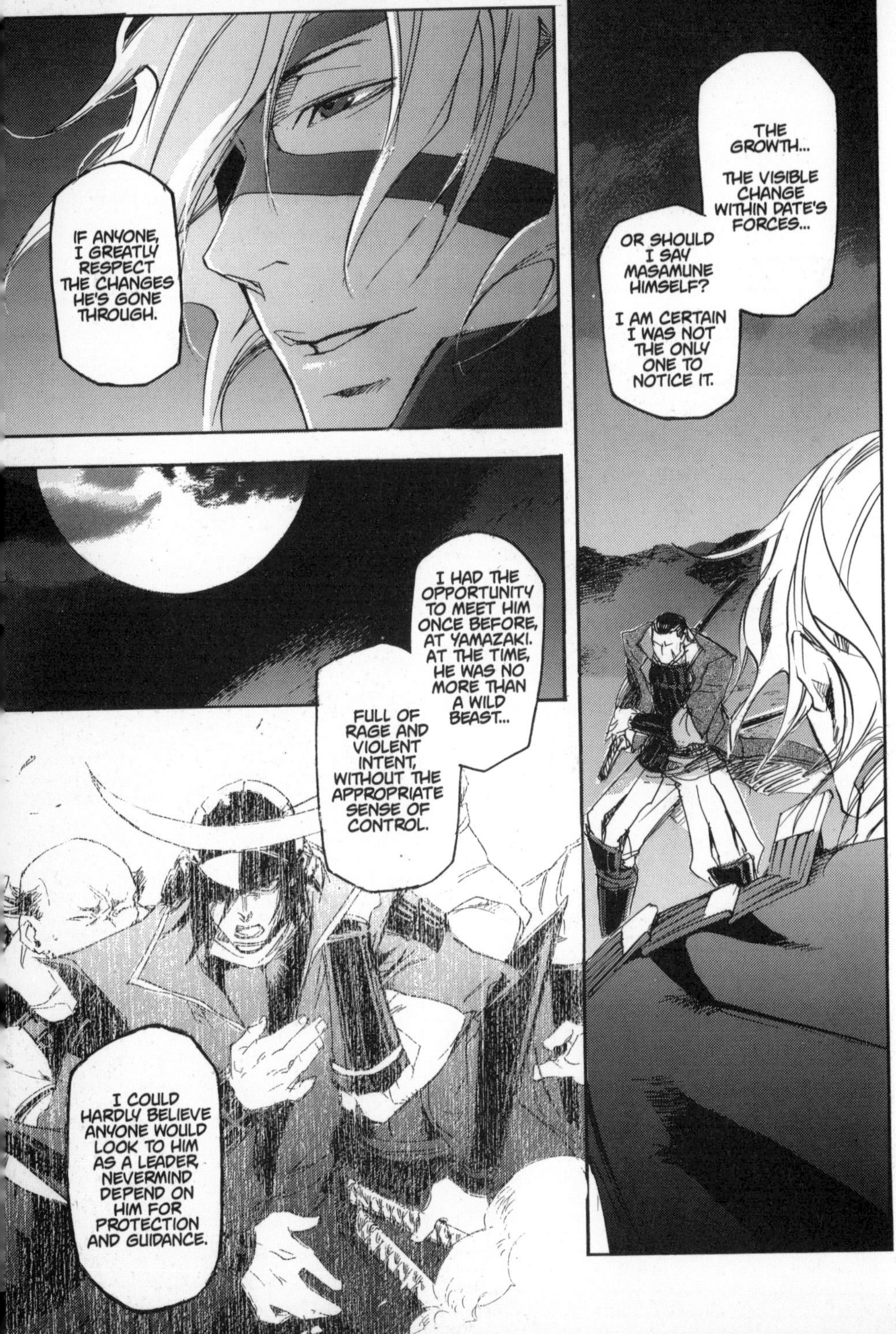
THE GROWTH... THE VISIBLE CHANGE WITHIN DATE'S FORCES...
OR SHOULD I SAY MASAMUNE HIMSELF? I AM CERTAIN I WAS NOT THE ONLY ONE TO NOTICE IT.
IF ANYONE, I GREATLY RESPECT THE CHANGES HE'S GONE THROUGH.
I HAD THE OPPORTUNITY TO MEET HIM ONCE BEFORE, AT YAMAZAKI. AT THE TIME, HE WAS NO MORE THAN A WILD BEAST...
FULL OF RAGE AND VIOLENT INTENT, WITHOUT THE APPROPRIATE SENSE OF CONTROL.
I COULD HARDLY BELIEVE ANYONE WOULD LOOK TO HIM AS A LEADER, NEVERMIND DEPEND ON HIM FOR PROTECTION AND GUIDANCE.

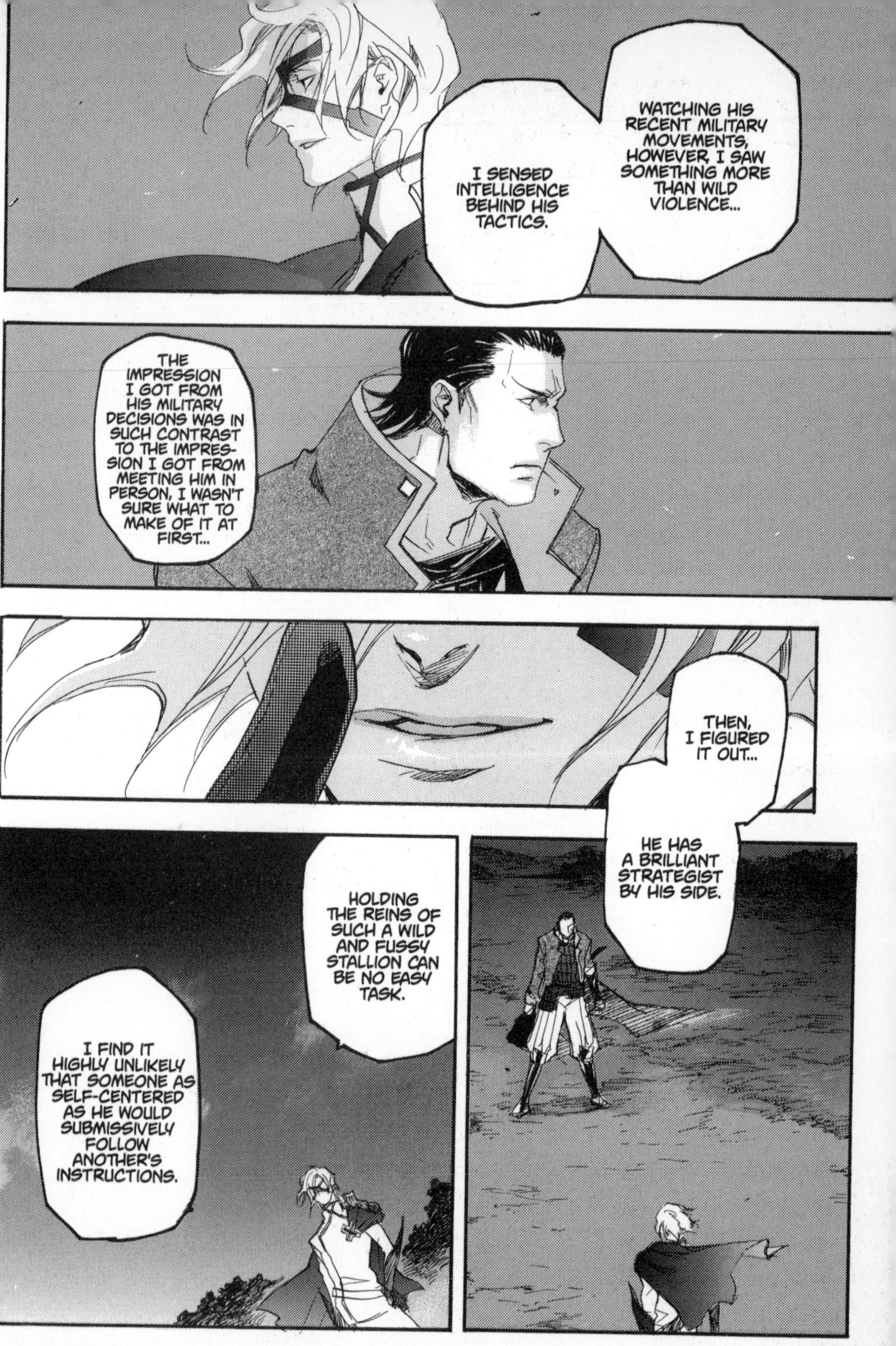
WATCHING HIS RECENT MILITARY MOVEMENTS, HOWEVER, I SAW SOMETHING MORE THAN WILD VIOLENCE...
I SENSED INTELLIGENCE BEHIND HIS TACTICS.
THE IMPRESSION I GOT FROM HIS MILITARY DECISIONS WAS IN SUCH CONTRAST TO THE IMPRESSION I GOT FROM MEETING HIM IN PERSON, I WASN'T SURE WHAT TO MAKE OF IT AT FIRST...
THEN, I FIGURED IT OUT...
HE HAS A BRILLIANT STRATEGIST BY HIS SIDE.
HOLDING THE REINS OF SUCH A WILD AND FUSSY STALLION CAN BE NO EASY TASK.
I FIND IT HIGHLY UNLIKELY THAT SOMEONE AS SELF-CENTERED AS HE WOULD SUBMISSIVELY FOLLOW ANOTHER'S INSTRUCTIONS.

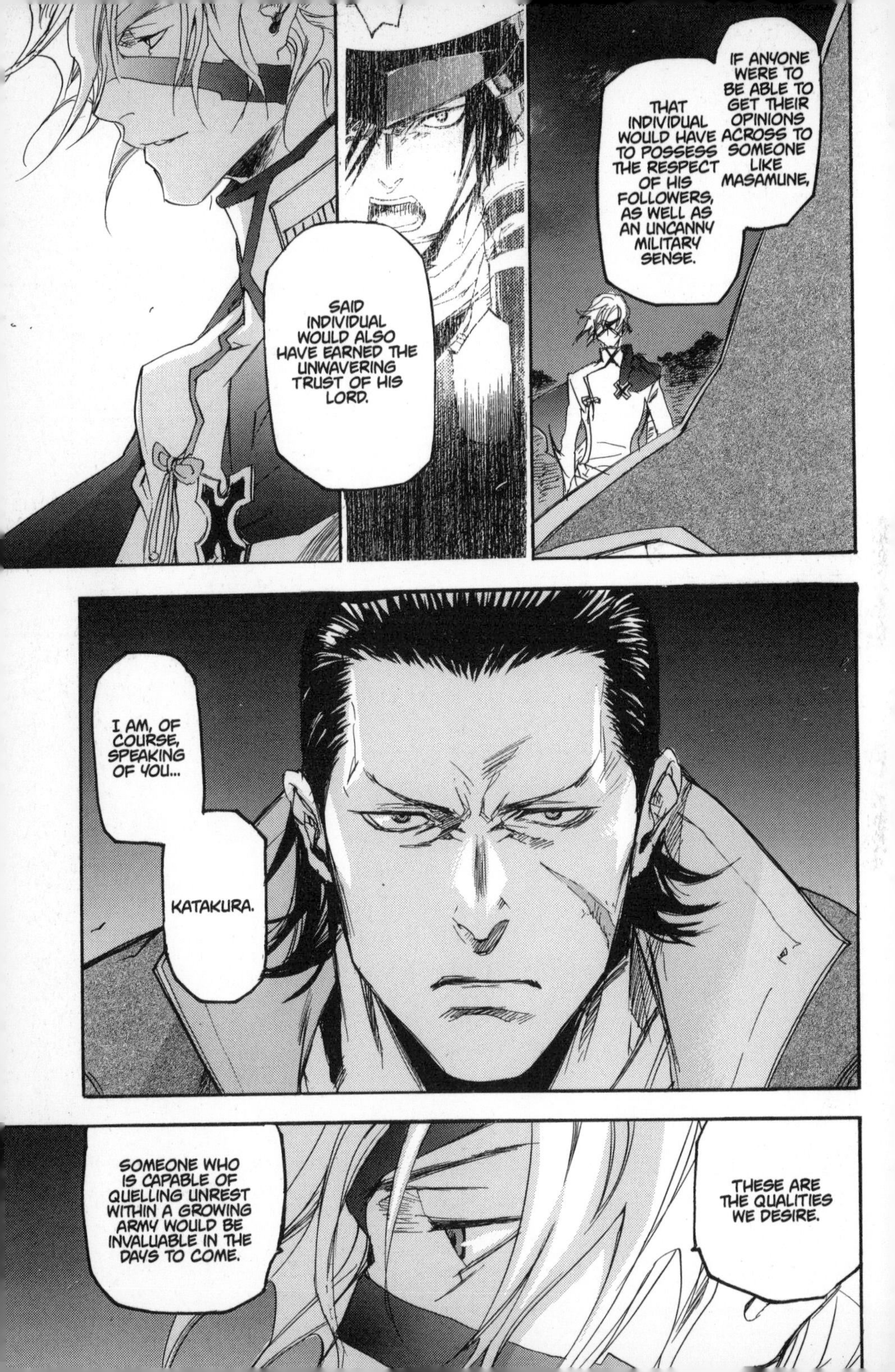
IF ANYONE WERE TO BE ABLE TO GET THEIR OPINIONS ACROSS TO SOMEONE LIKE MASAMUNE,
THAT INDIVIDUAL WOULD HAVE TO POSSESS THE RESPECT OF HIS FOLLOWERS, AS WELL AS AN UNCANNY MILITARY SENSE.
SAID INDIVIDUAL WOULD ALSO HAVE EARNED THE UNWAVERING TRUST OF HIS LORD.
I AM, OF COURSE, SPEAKING OF YOU...
KATAKURA.
THESE ARE THE QUALITIES WE DESIRE.
SOMEONE WHO IS CAPABLE OF QUELLING UNREST WITHIN A GROWING ARMY WOULD BE INVALUABLE IN THE DAYS TO COME.

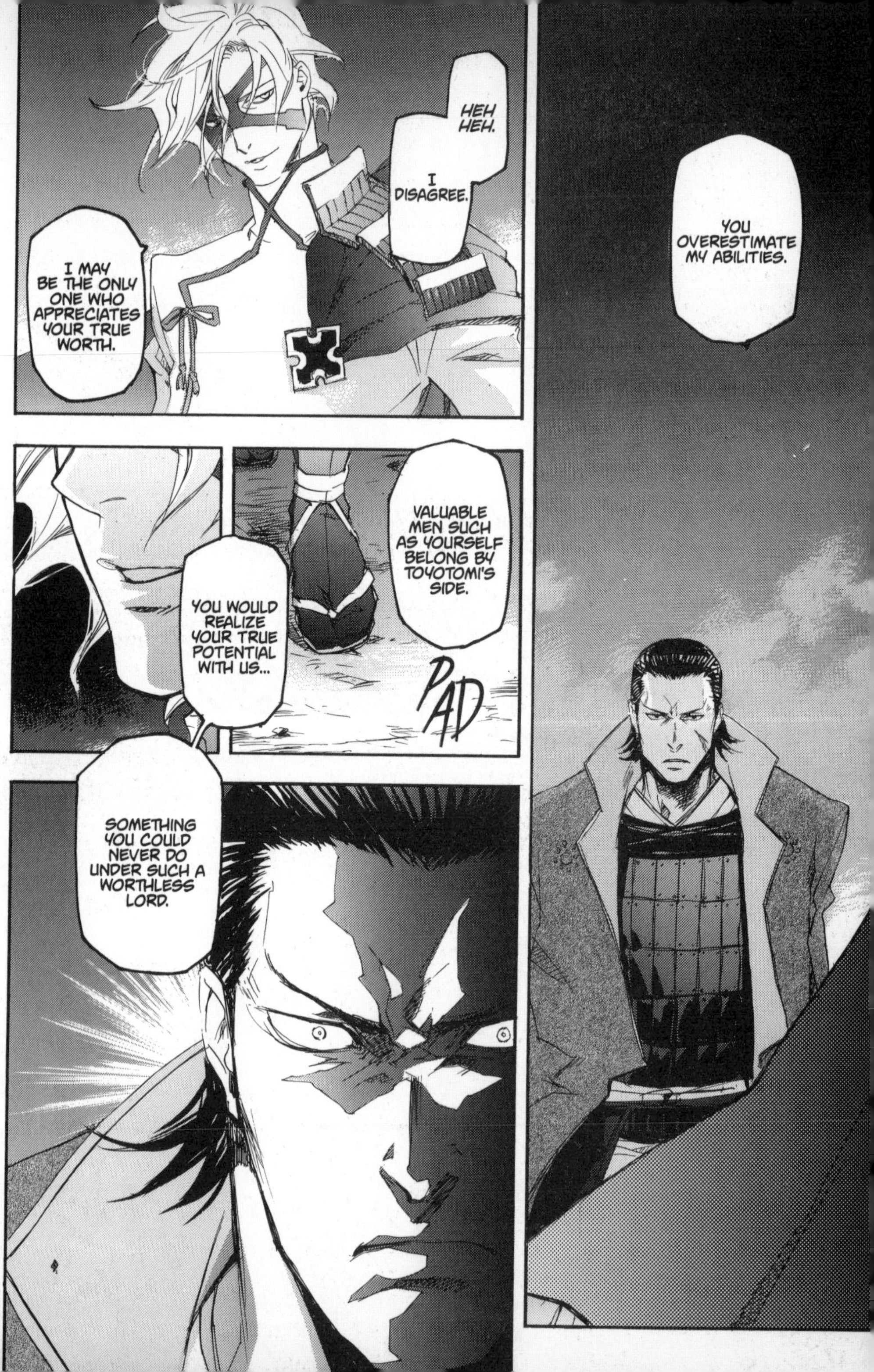
YOU OVERESTIMATE MY ABILITIES.
HEH HEH.
I DISAGREE.
I MAY BE THE ONLY ONE WHO APPRECIATES YOUR TRUE WORTH.
VALUABLE MEN SUCH AS YOURSELF BELONG BY TOYOTOMI'S SIDE.
PAD
YOU WOULD REALIZE YOUR TRUE POTENTIAL WITH US...
SOMETHING YOU COULD NEVER DO UNDER SUCH A WORTHLESS LORD.

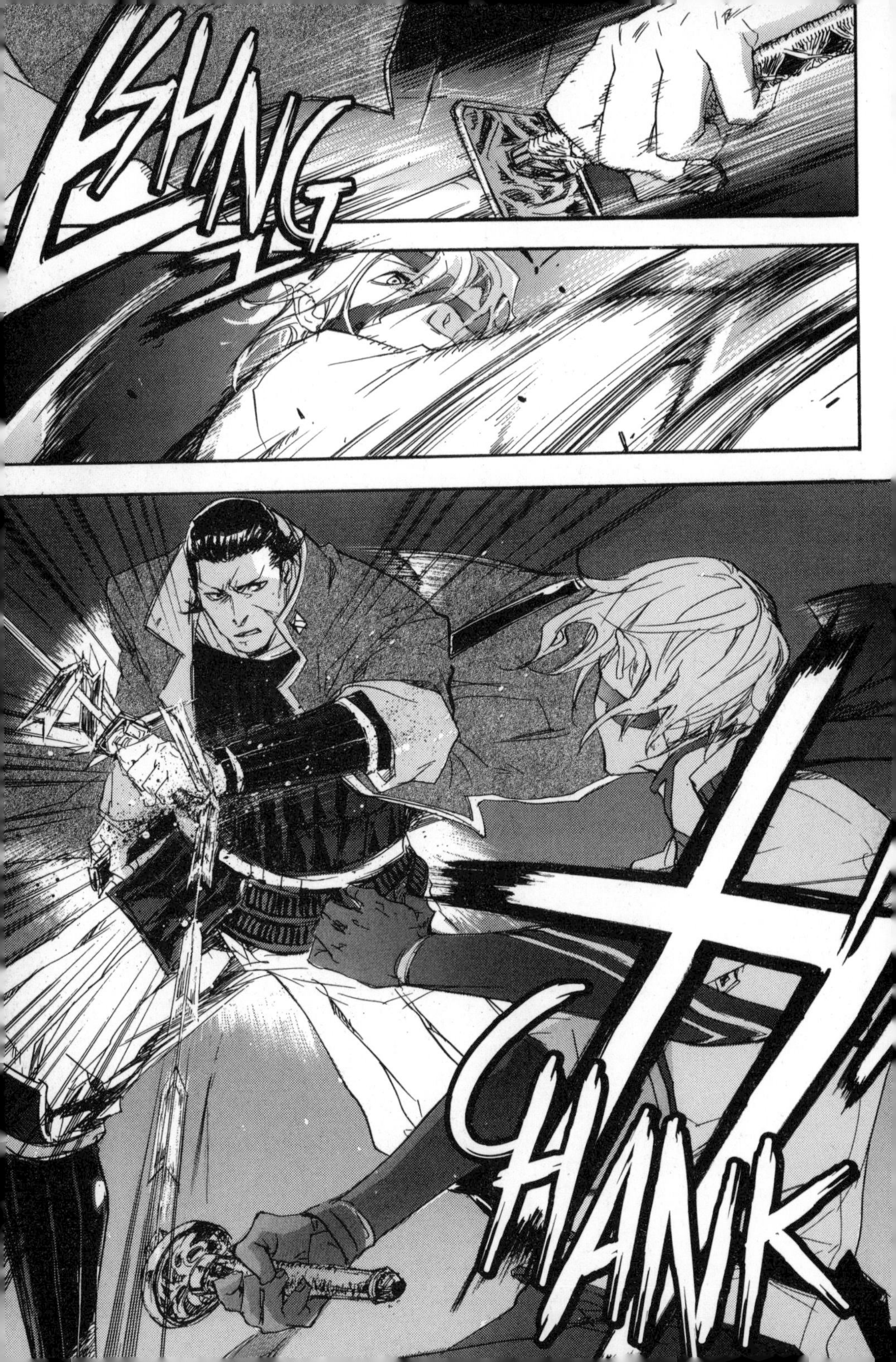
SHNG
CHANK

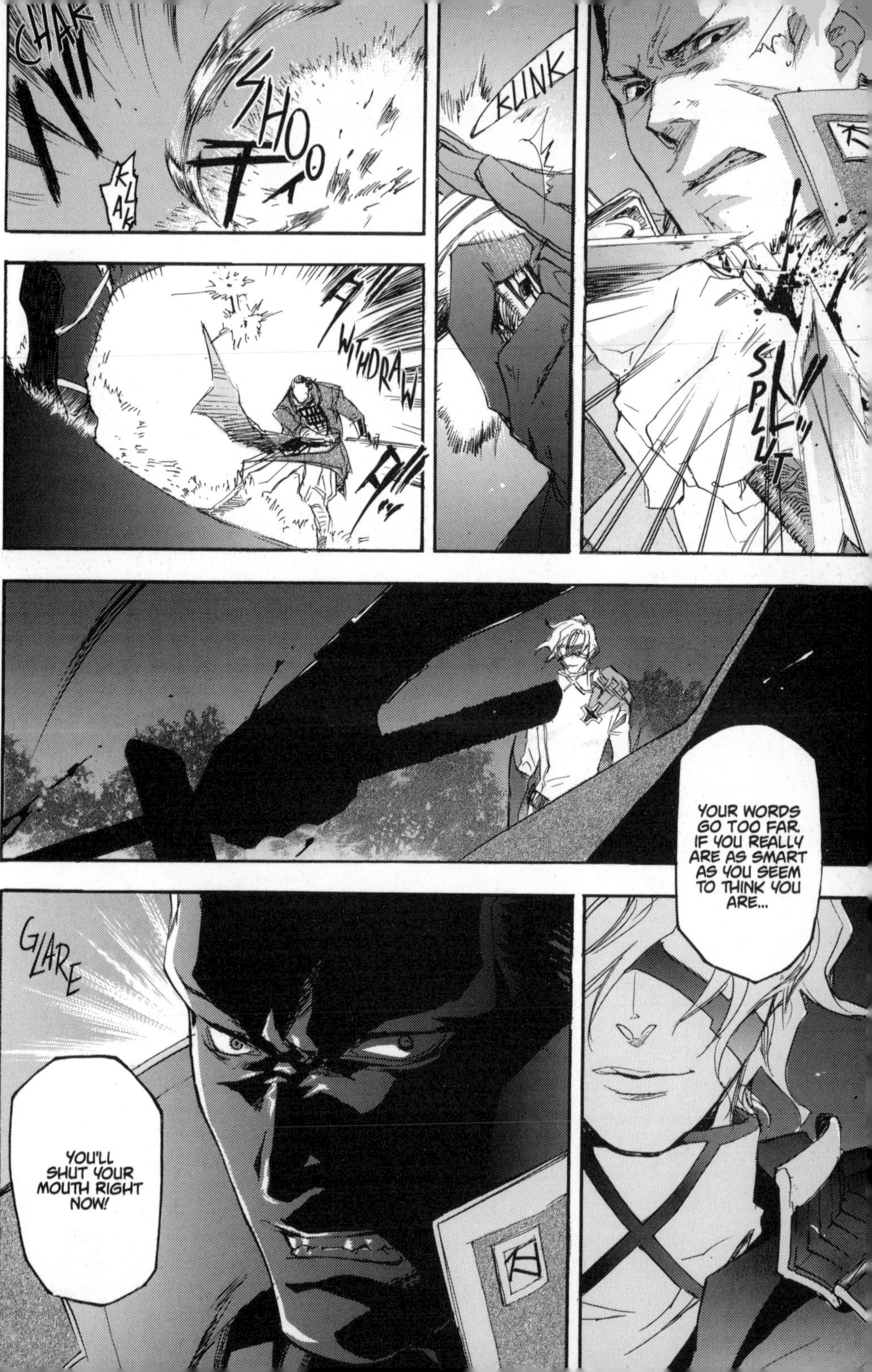
SPLUT
KLINK
CHAK
KLAK
SHOOT
WITHDRAW
YOUR WORDS GO TOO FAR. IF YOU REALLY ARE AS SMART AS YOU SEEM TO THINK YOU ARE...
GLARE
YOU'LL SHUT YOUR MOUTH RIGHT NOW!

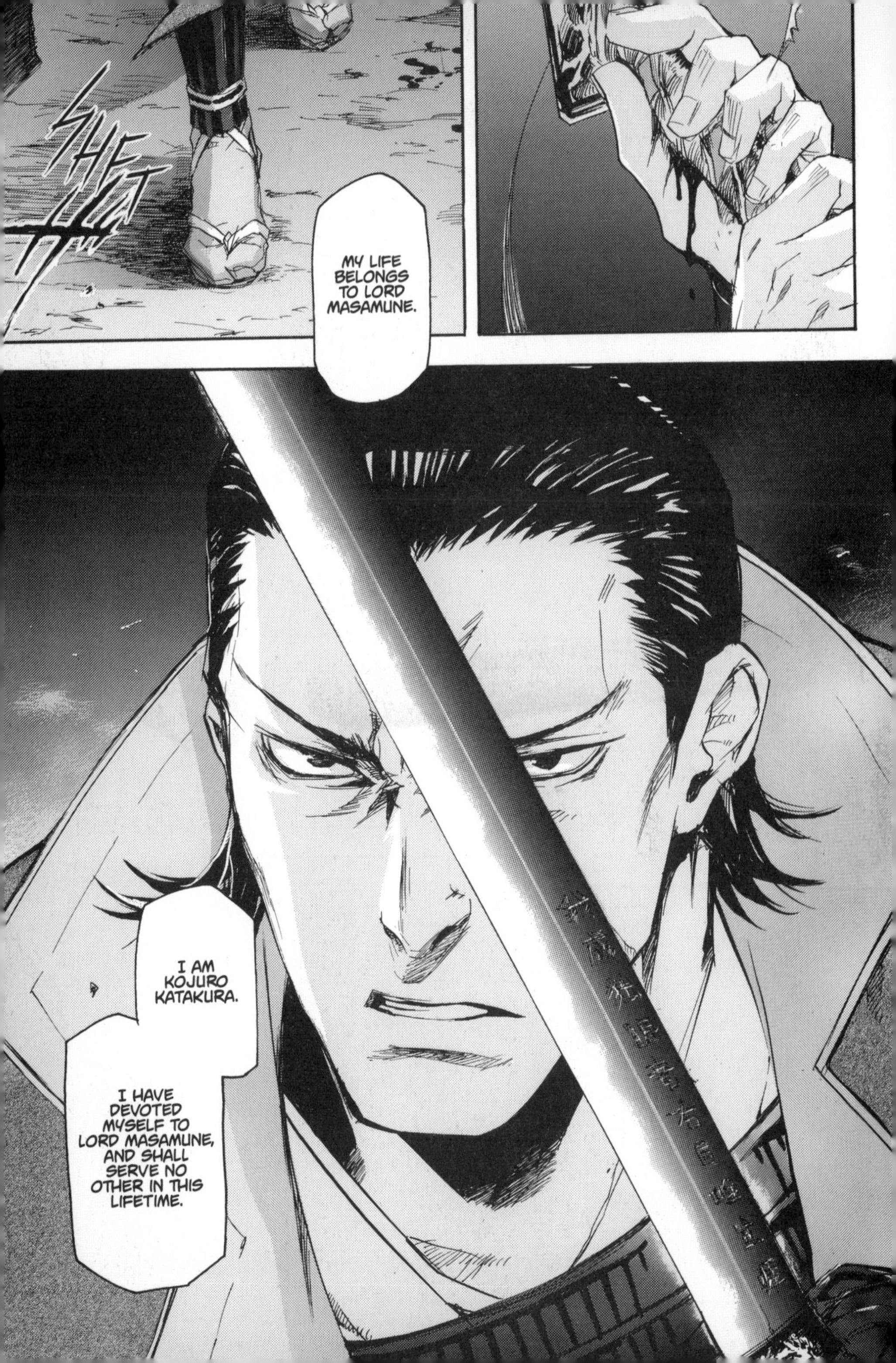
MY LIFE BELONGS TO LORD MASAMUNE.
I AM KOJURO KATAKURA.
I HAVE DEVOTED MYSELF TO LORD MASAMUNE, AND SHALL SERVE NO OTHER IN THIS LIFETIME.

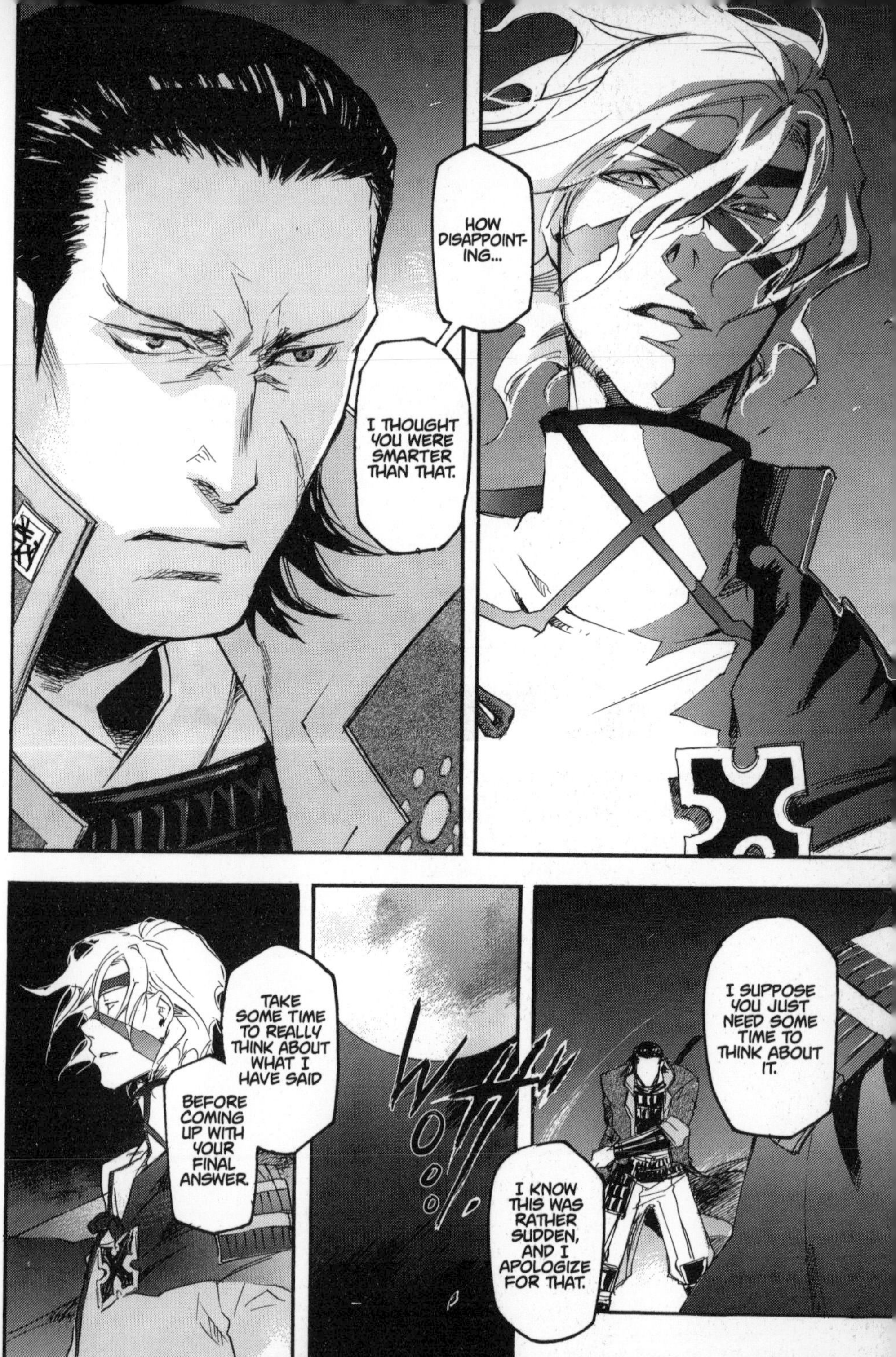
HOW DISAPPOINTING...
I THOUGHT YOU WERE SMARTER THAN THAT.
I SUPPOSE YOU JUST NEED SOME TIME TO THINK ABOUT IT.
I KNOW THIS WAS RATHER SUDDEN, AND I APOLOGIZE FOR THAT.
TAKE SOME TIME TO REALLY THINK ABOUT WHAT I HAVE SAID
BEFORE COMING UP WITH YOUR FINAL ANSWER.

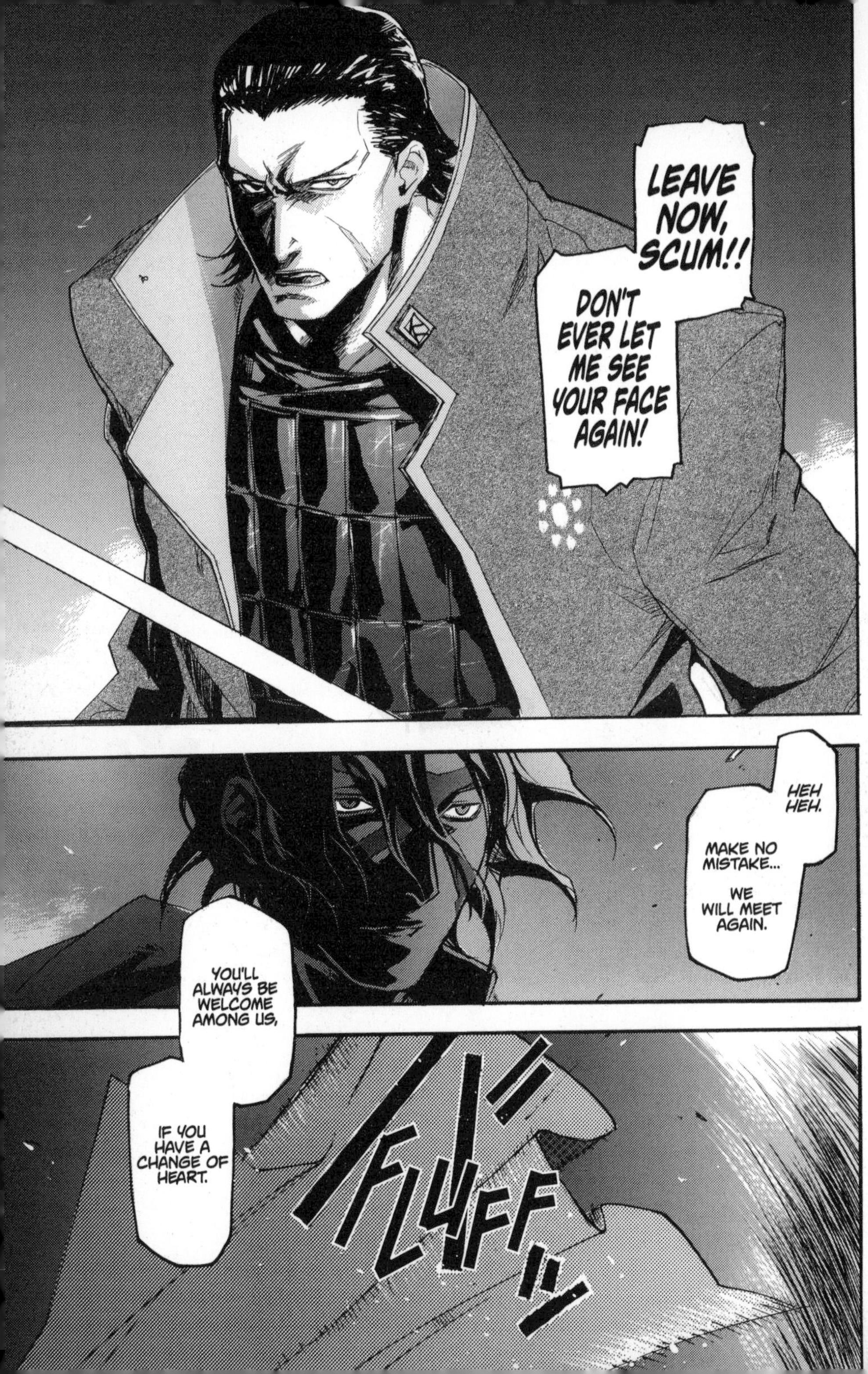
LEAVE NOW, SCUM!!
DON'T EVER LET ME SEE YOUR FACE AGAIN!
HEH HEH.
MAKE NO MISTAKE...
WE WILL MEET AGAIN.
YOU'LL ALWAYS BE WELCOME AMONG US,
IF YOU HAVE A CHANGE OF HEART.
FLUFF

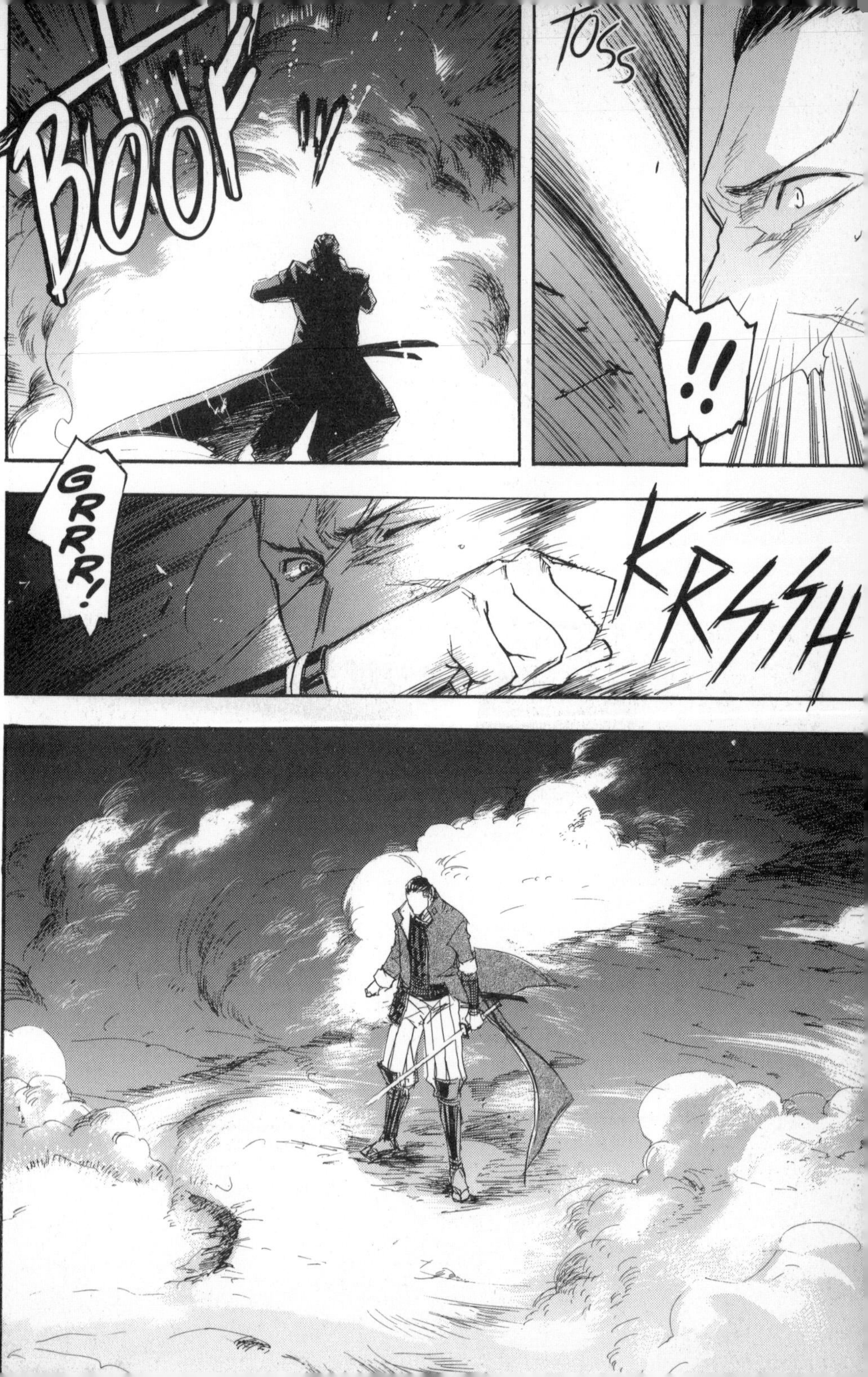
TOSS
!!
BOOF
KRSH
GRRR!

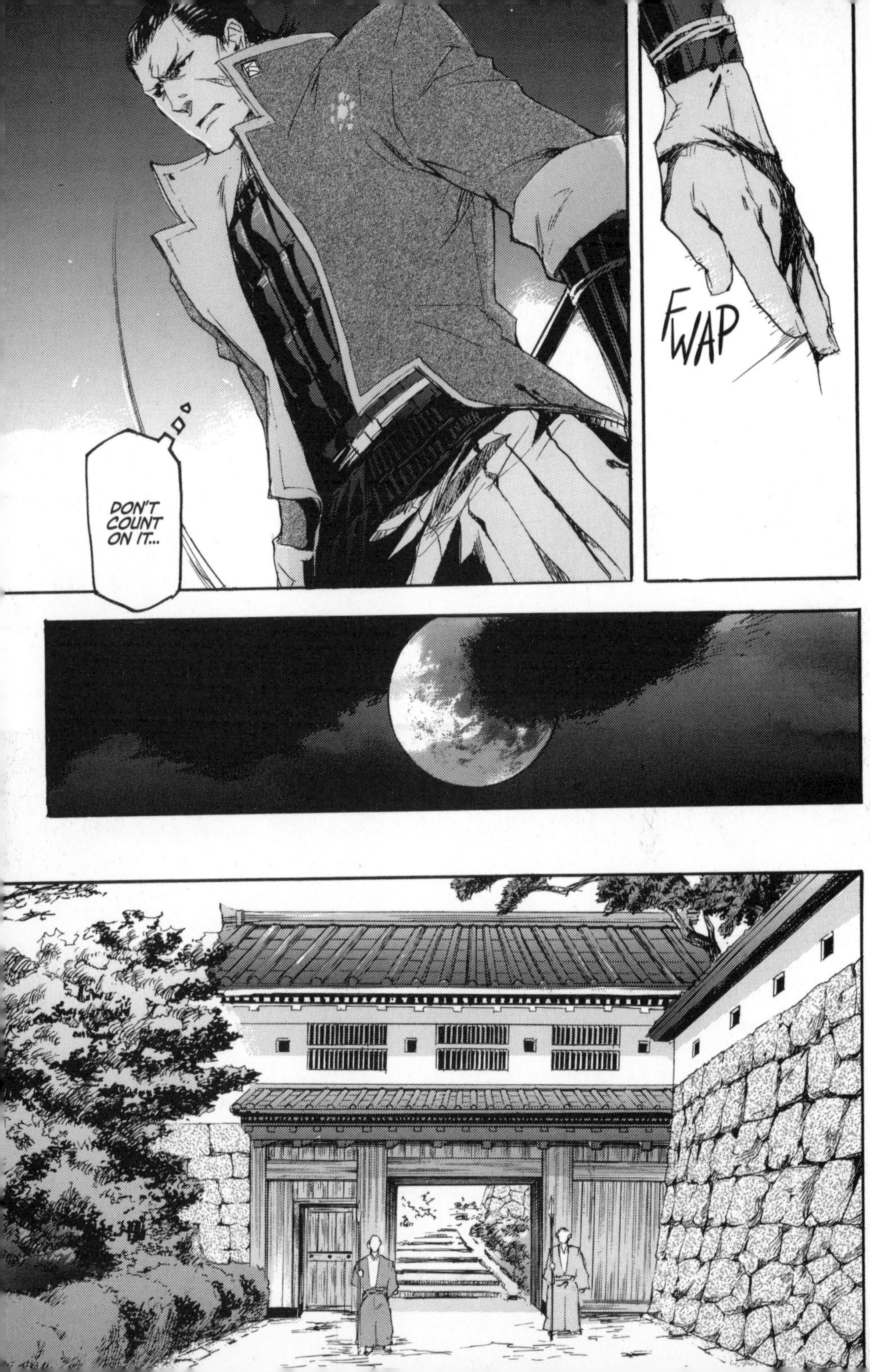
FWAP
DON'T COUNT ON IT...

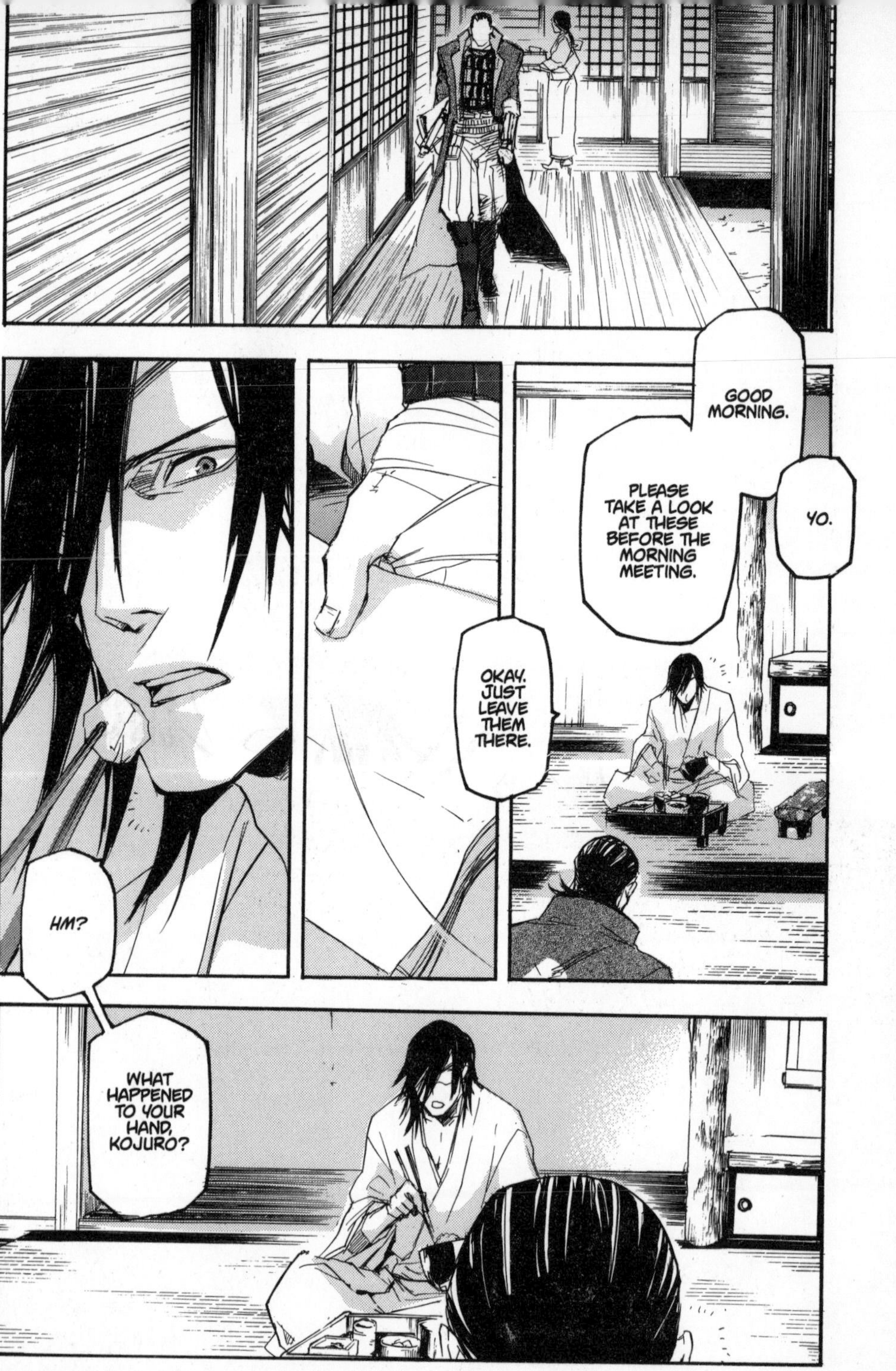
GOOD MORNING.
YO.
PLEASE TAKE A LOOK AT THESE BEFORE THE MORNING MEETING.
OKAY. JUST LEAVE THEM THERE.
HM?
WHAT HAPPENED TO YOUR HAND, KOJURO?

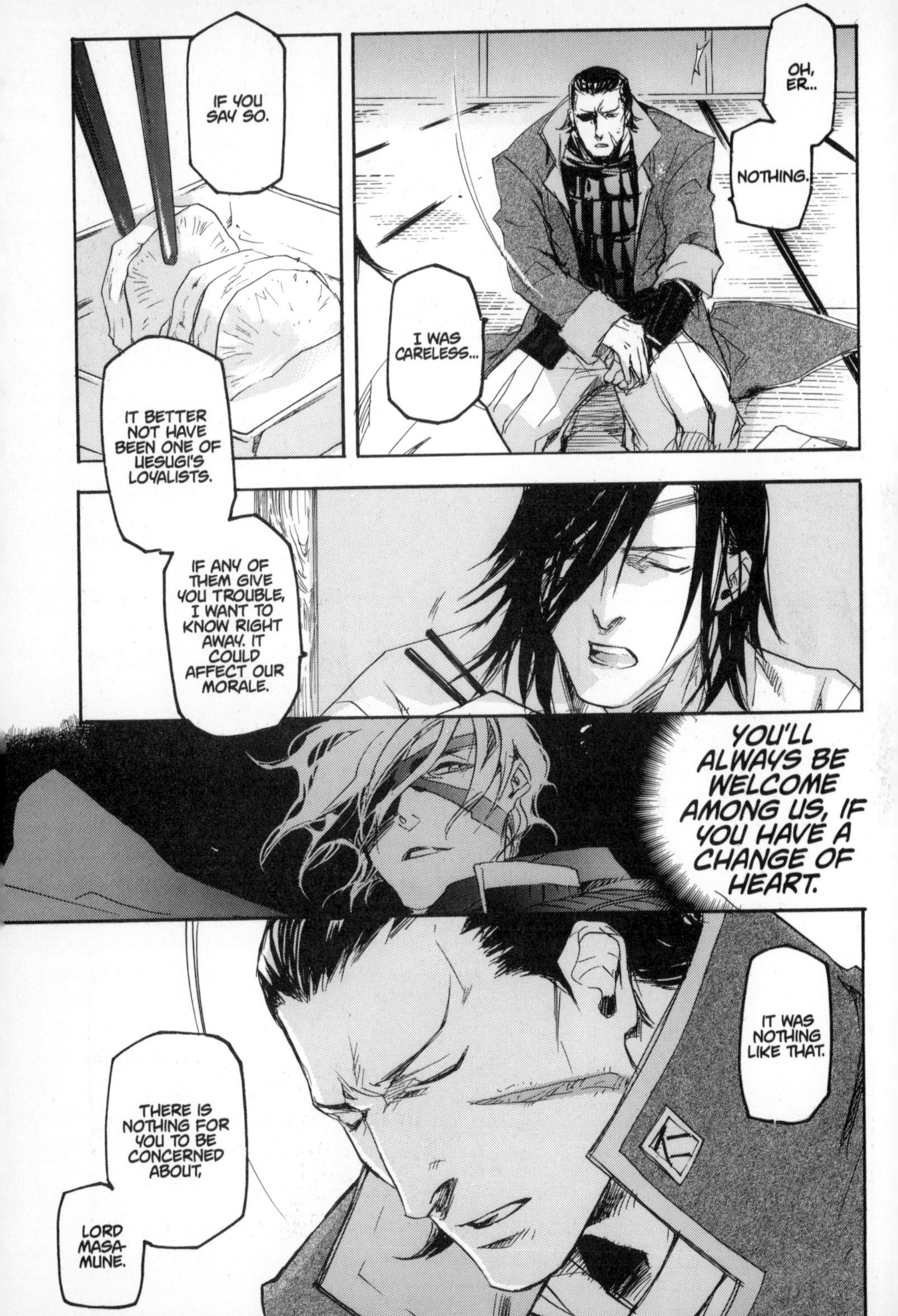
OH, ER...
NOTHING.
I WAS CARELESS...
IF YOU SAY SO.
IT BETTER NOT HAVE BEEN ONE OF UESUGI'S LOYALISTS.
IF ANY OF THEM GIVE YOU TROUBLE, I WANT TO KNOW RIGHT AWAY. IT COULD AFFECT OUR MORALE.
YOU'LL ALWAYS BE WELCOME AMONG US, IF YOU HAVE A CHANGE OF HEART.
IT WAS NOTHING LIKE THAT.
THERE IS NOTHING FOR YOU TO BE CONCERNED ABOUT,
LORD MASAMUNE.

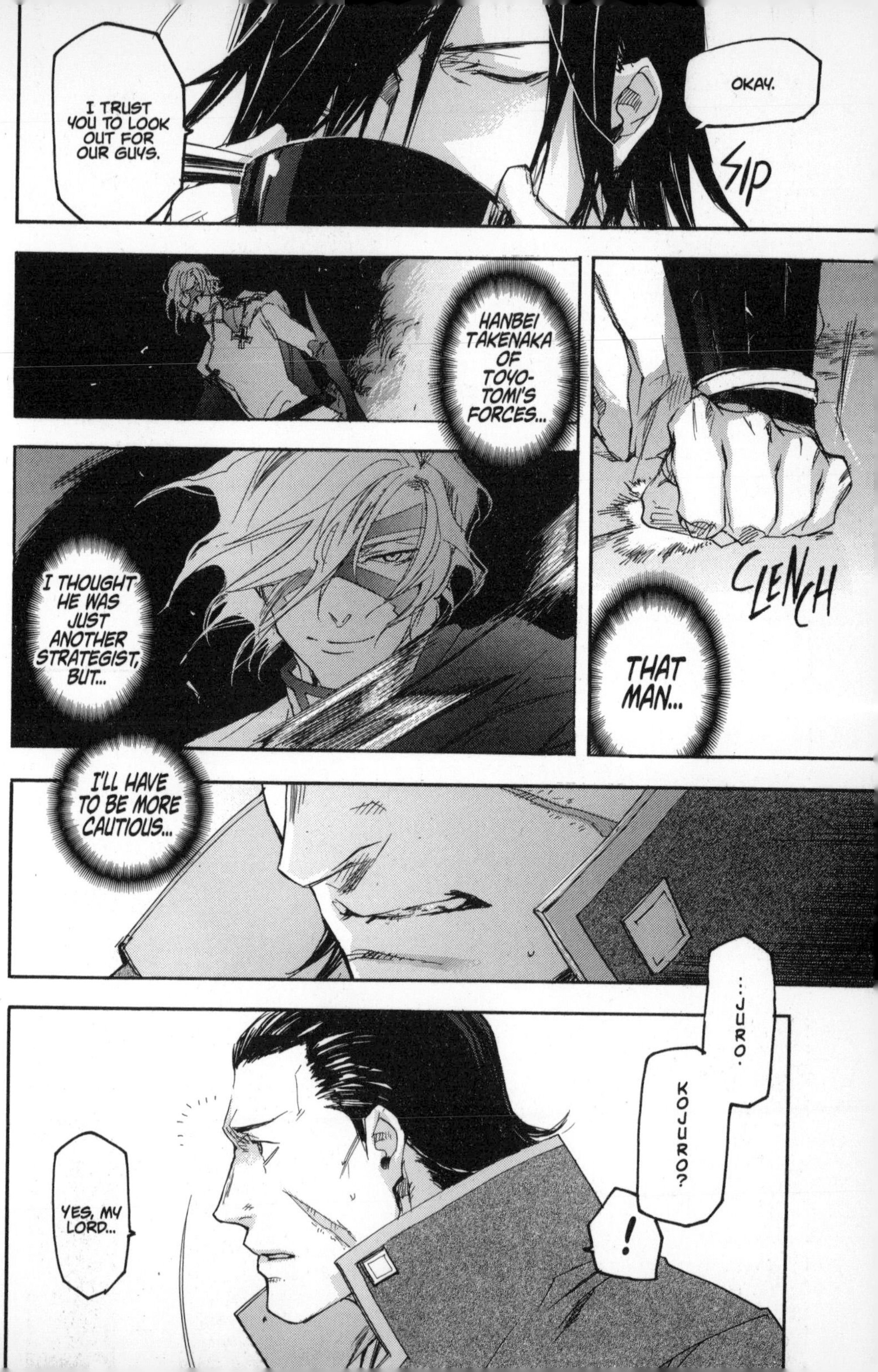
OKAY.
I TRUST YOU TO LOOK OUT FOR OUR GUYS.
SIP
CLENCH
THAT MAN...
HANBEI TAKENAKA OF TOYO-TOMI'S FORCES...
I THOUGHT HE WAS JUST ANOTHER STRATEGIST, BUT...
I'LL HAVE TO BE MORE CAUTIOUS...
...JURO. KOJURO?
!
YES, MY LORD...

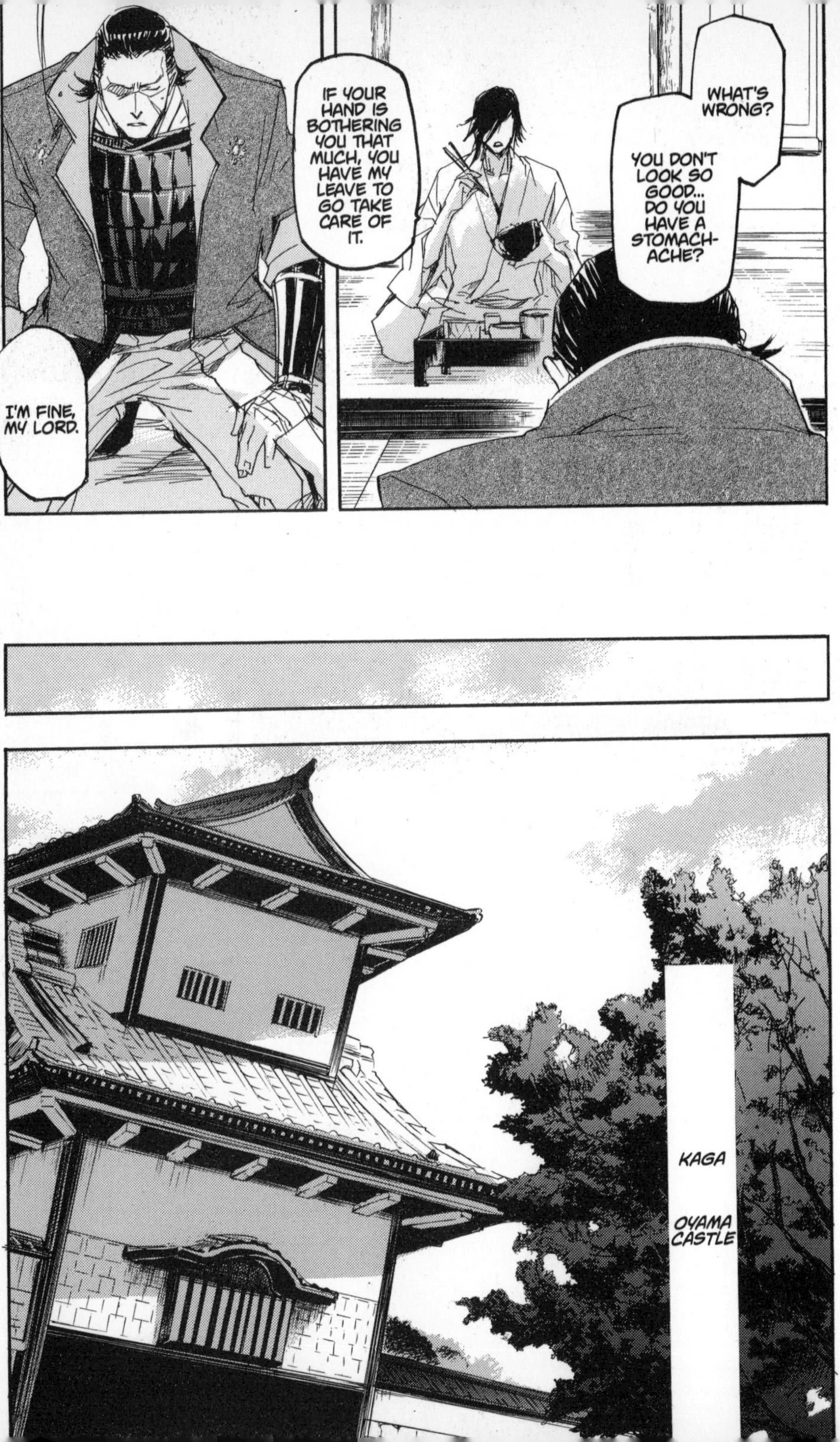
WHAT'S WRONG?
YOU DON'T LOOK SO GOOD... DO YOU HAVE A STOMACH-ACHE?
IF YOUR HAND IS BOTHERING YOU THAT MUCH, YOU HAVE MY LEAVE TO GO TAKE CARE OF IT.
I'M FINE, MY LORD.
KAGA
OYAMA CASTLE

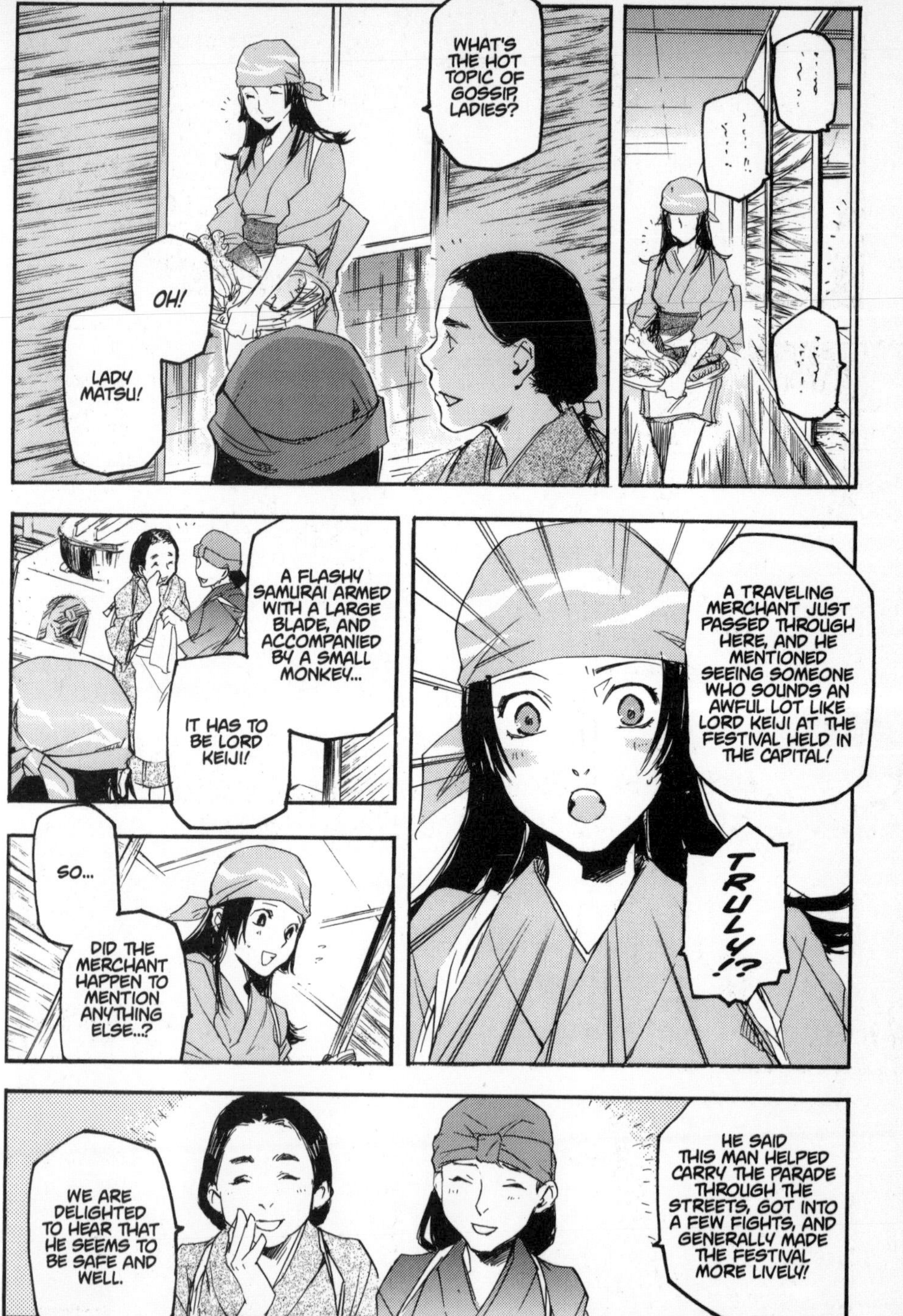
WHAT'S THE HOT TOPIC OF GOSSIP, LADIES?
OH!
LADY MATSU!
A TRAVELING MERCHANT JUST PASSED THROUGH HERE, AND HE MENTIONED SEEING SOMEONE WHO SOUNDS AN AWFUL LOT LIKE LORD KEIJI AT THE FESTIVAL HELD IN THE CAPITAL!
TRULY!?
A FLASHY SAMURAI ARMED WITH A LARGE BLADE, AND ACCOMPANIED BY A SMALL MONKEY...
IT HAS TO BE LORD KEIJI!
SO...
DID THE MERCHANT HAPPEN TO MENTION ANYTHING ELSE...?
HE SAID THIS MAN HELPED CARRY THE PARADE THROUGH THE STREETS, GOT INTO A FEW FIGHTS, AND GENERALLY MADE THE FESTIVAL MORE LIVELY!
WE ARE DELIGHTED TO HEAR THAT HE SEEMS TO BE SAFE AND WELL.

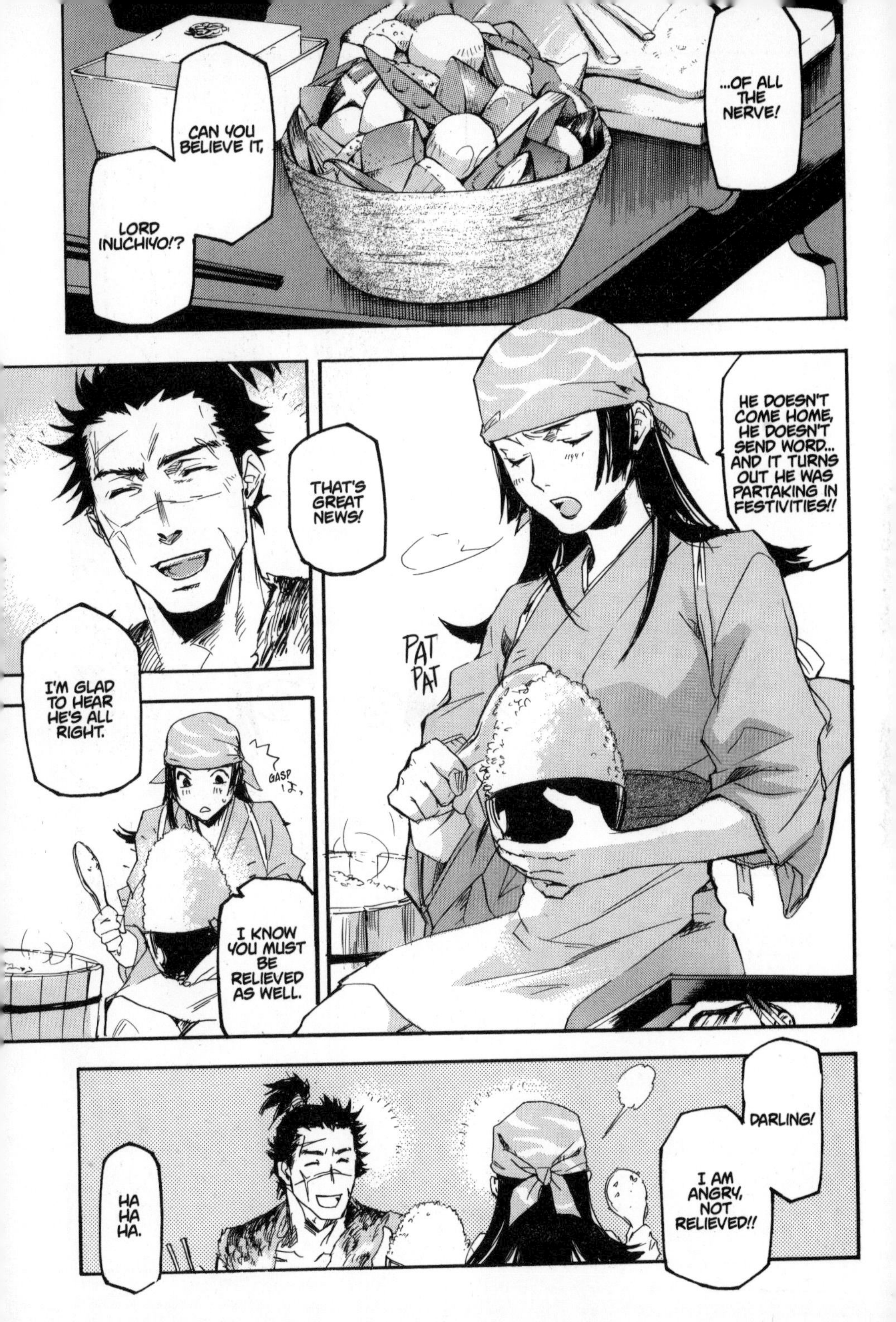

CAN YOU BELIEVE IT,
LORD INUCHIYO!?
...OF ALL THE NERVE!
HE DOESN'T COME HOME, HE DOESN'T SEND WORD... AND IT TURNS OUT HE WAS PARTAKING IN FESTIVITIES!!
PAT PAT
THAT'S GREAT NEWS!
I'M GLAD TO HEAR HE'S ALL RIGHT.
GASP
I KNOW YOU MUST BE RELIEVED AS WELL.
DARLING!
I AM ANGRY, NOT RELIEVED!!
HA HA HA.

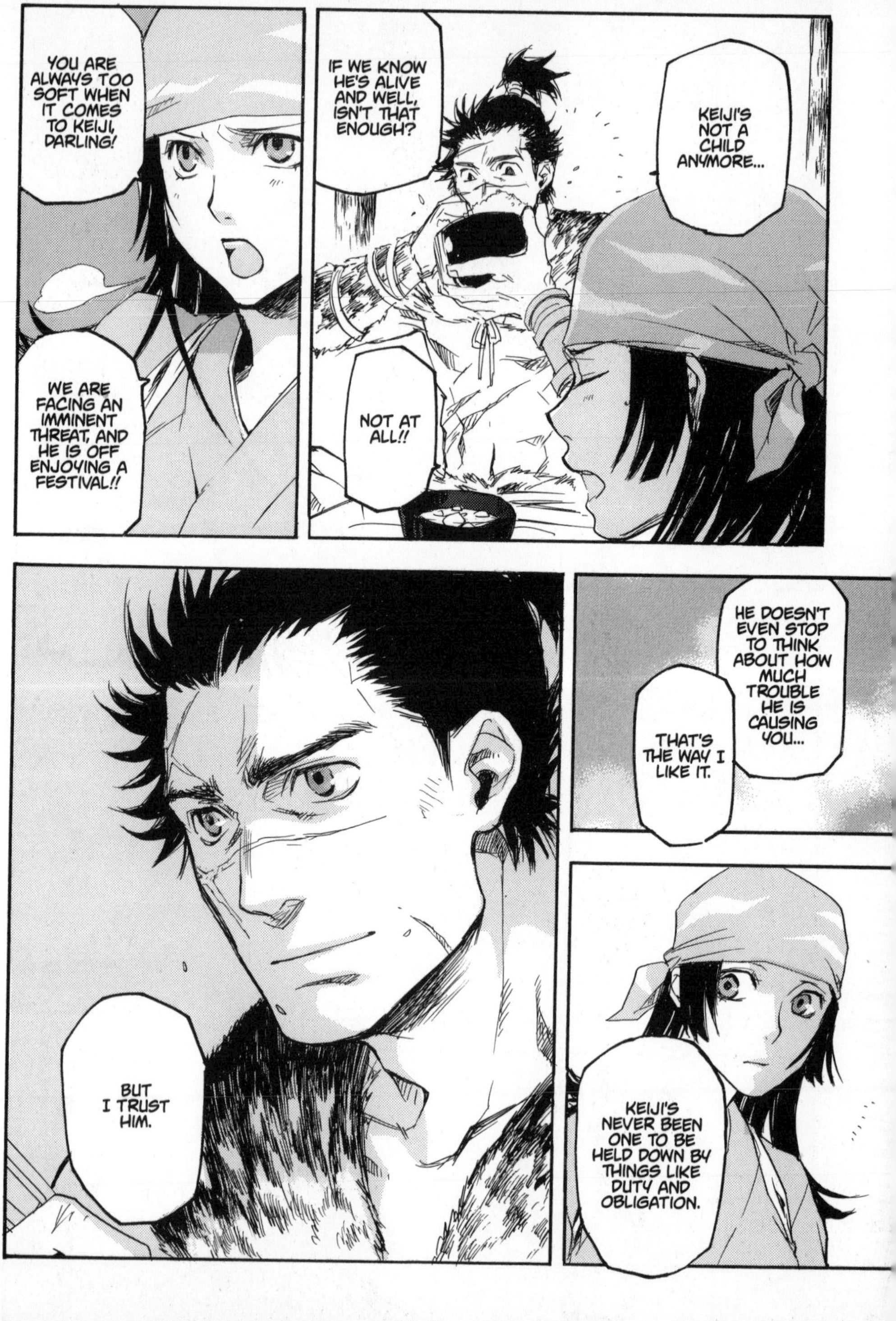
KEIJI'S NOT A CHILD ANYMORE...
IF WE KNOW HE'S ALIVE AND WELL, ISN'T THAT ENOUGH?
NOT AT ALL!!
YOU ARE ALWAYS TOO SOFT WHEN IT COMES TO KEIJI, DARLING!
WE ARE FACING AN IMMINENT THREAT, AND HE IS OFF ENJOYING A FESTIVAL!!
HE DOESN'T EVEN STOP TO THINK ABOUT HOW MUCH TROUBLE HE IS CAUSING YOU...
THAT'S THE WAY I LIKE IT.
KEIJI'S NEVER BEEN ONE TO BE HELD DOWN BY THINGS LIKE DUTY AND OBLIGATION.
BUT I TRUST HIM.

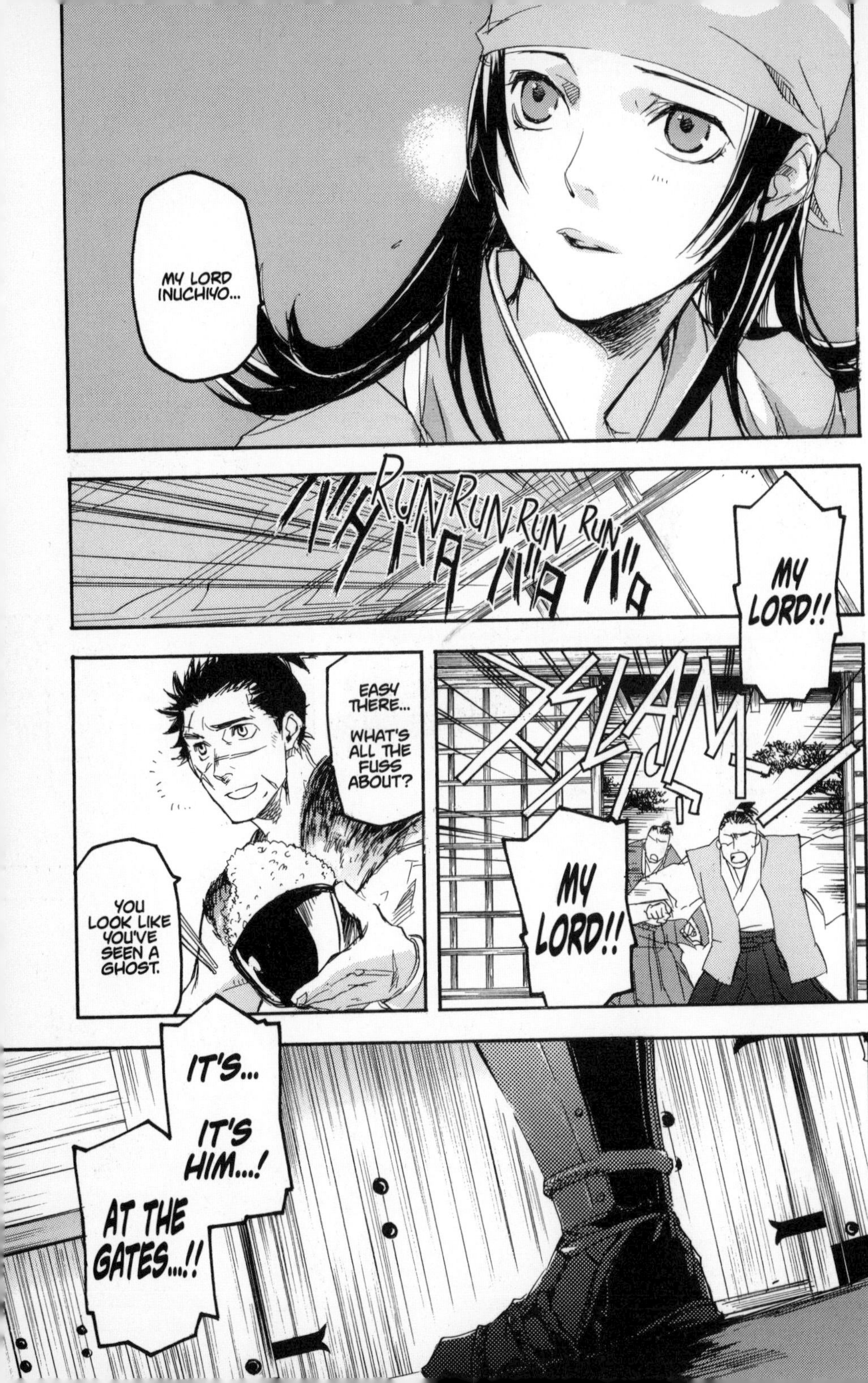
MY LORD INUCHIYO...
RUN RUN RUN RUN
MY LORD!!
SLAM
MY LORD!!
EASY THERE...
WHAT'S ALL THE FUSS ABOUT?
YOU LOOK LIKE YOU'VE SEEN A GHOST.
IT'S...
IT'S HIM...!
AT THE GATES...!!

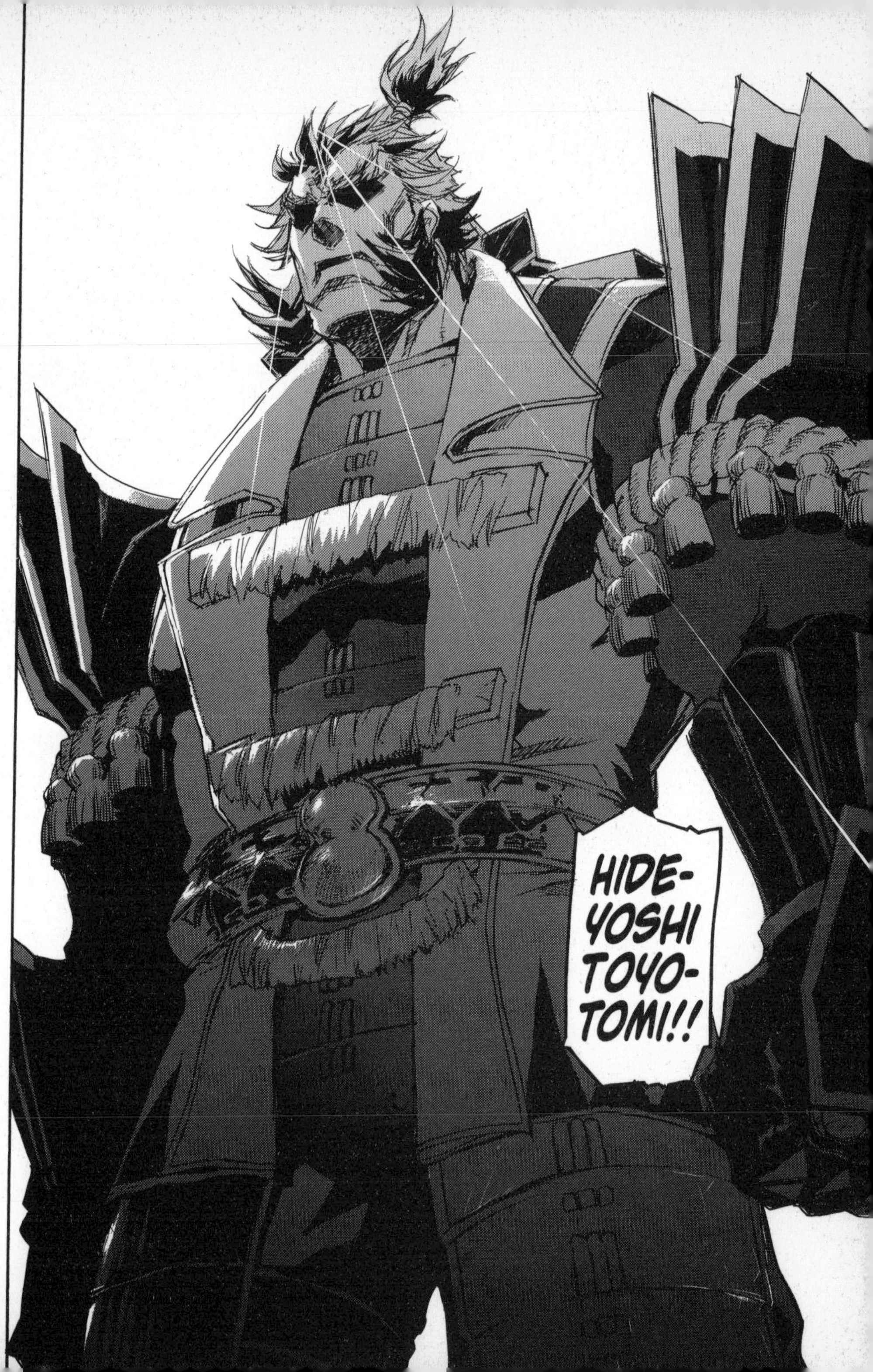
HIDE-YOSHI TOYO-TOMI!!

戦国BASARA2
SENGOKU BASARA2

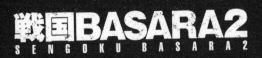

ACT 16: Symptom

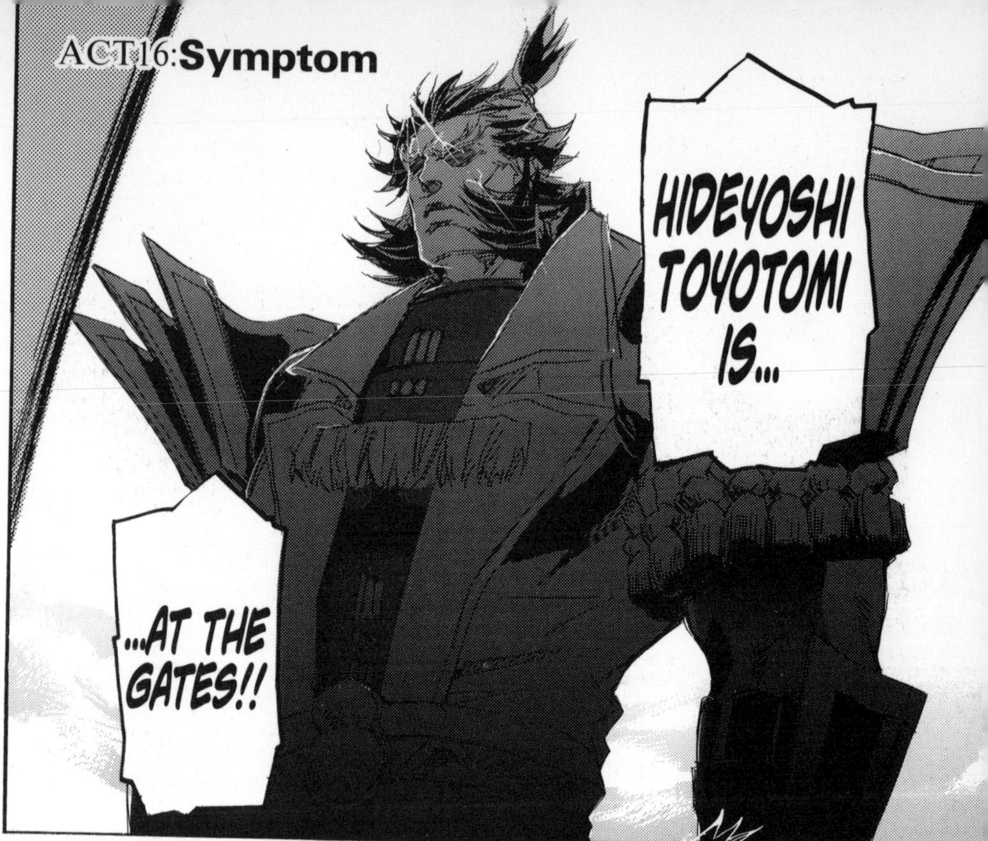
HIDEYOSHI TOYOTOMI IS...
...AT THE GATES!!

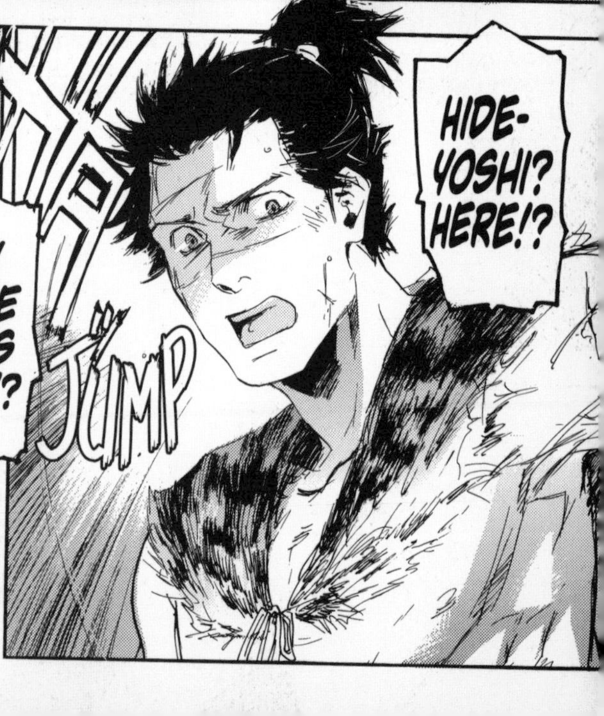
HIDE-YOSHI? HERE!?
JUMP
HOW LARGE IS HIS ARMY!?

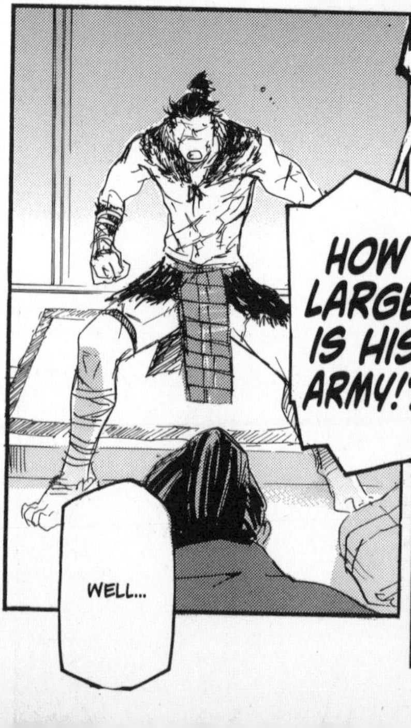
WELL...

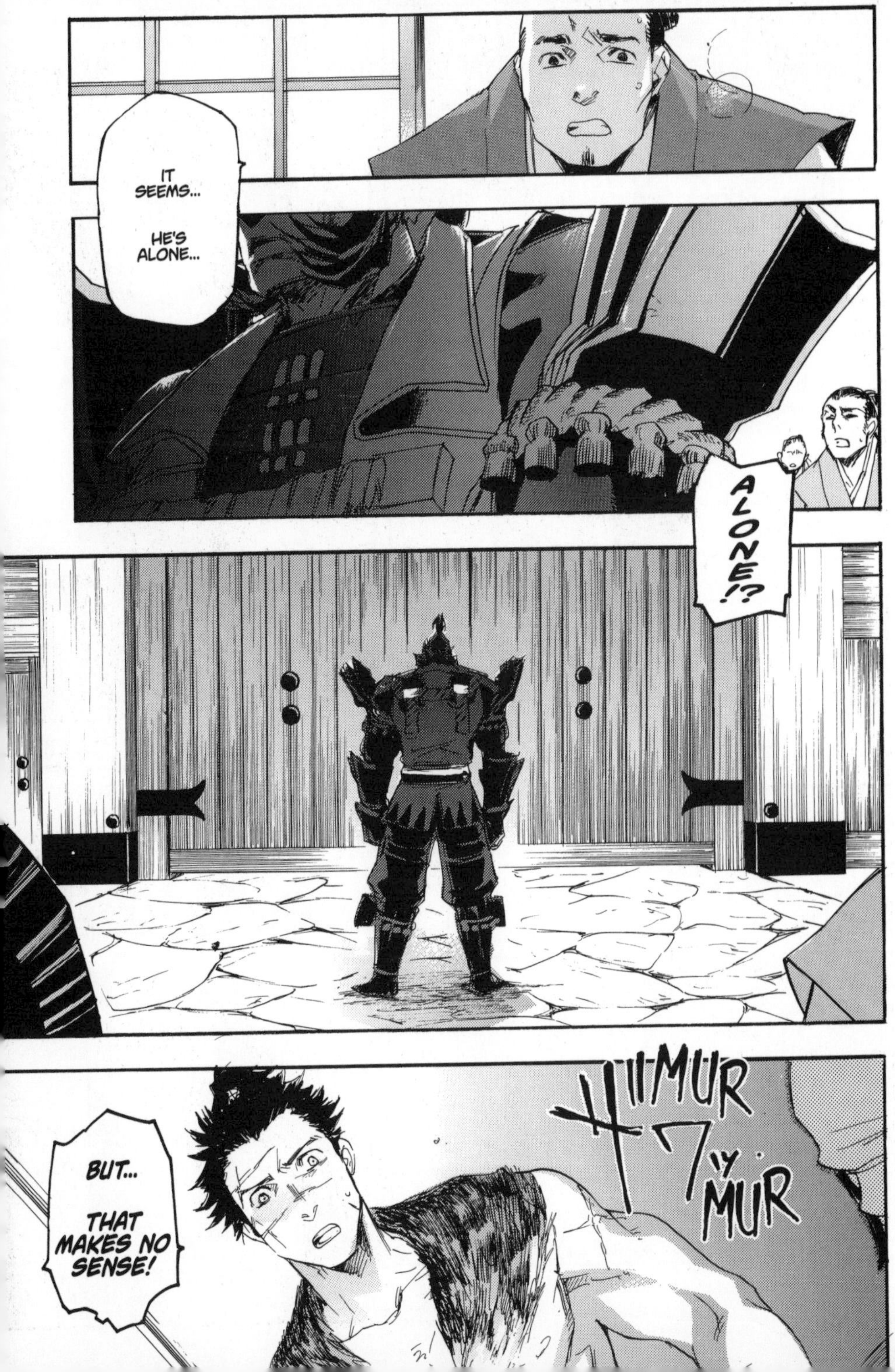

IT SEEMS...
HE'S ALONE...
ALONE!?
MUR MUR
BUT...
THAT MAKES NO SENSE!

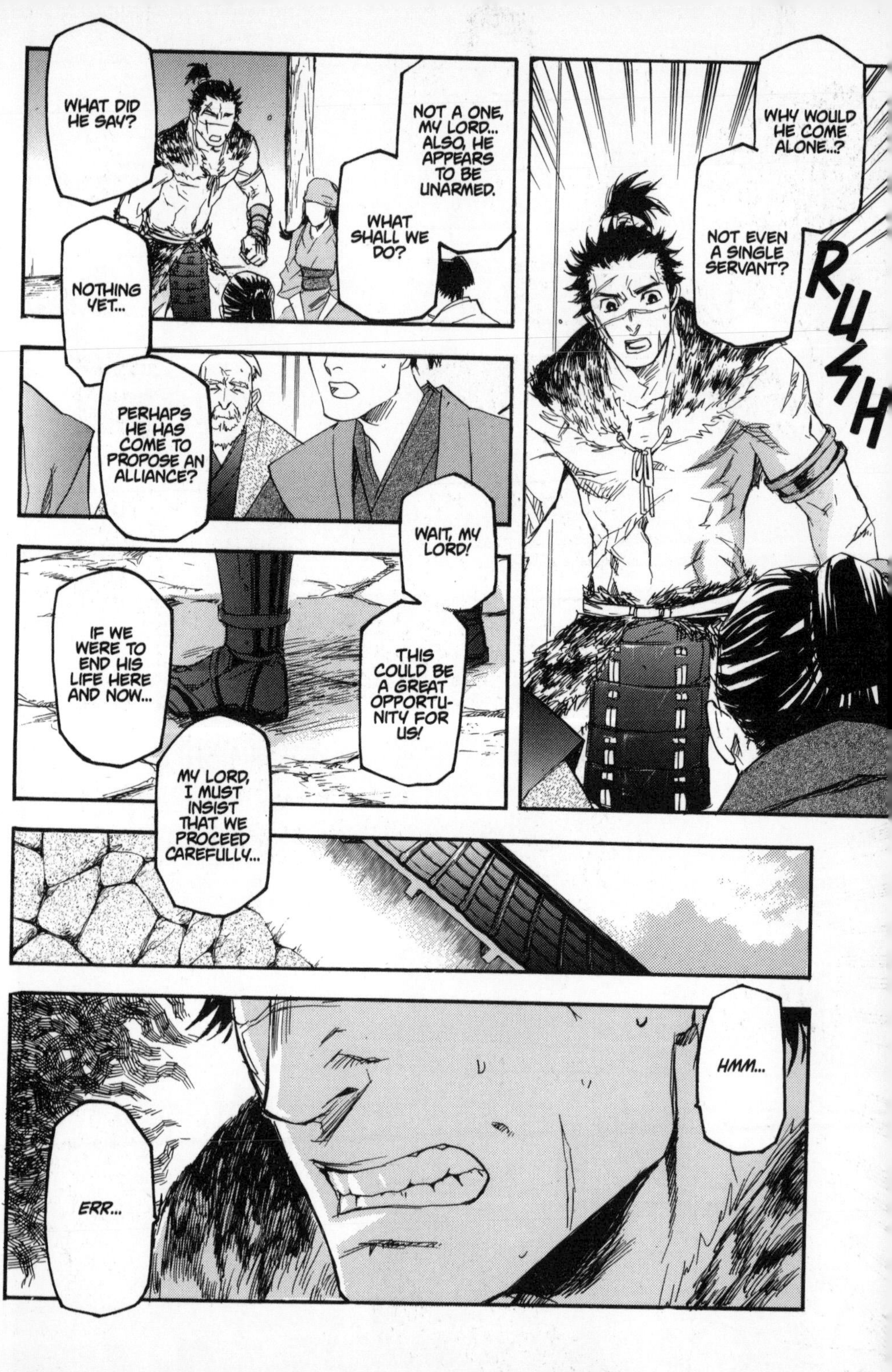

WHY WOULD HE COME ALONE..?
NOT EVEN A SINGLE SERVANT?
RUSH
NOT A ONE, MY LORD... ALSO, HE APPEARS TO BE UNARMED.
WHAT SHALL WE DO?
WHAT DID HE SAY?
NOTHING YET...
PERHAPS HE HAS COME TO PROPOSE AN ALLIANCE?
WAIT, MY LORD!
THIS COULD BE A GREAT OPPORTU-NITY FOR US!
IF WE WERE TO END HIS LIFE HERE AND NOW...
MY LORD, I MUST INSIST THAT WE PROCEED CAREFULLY...
HMM...
ERR...

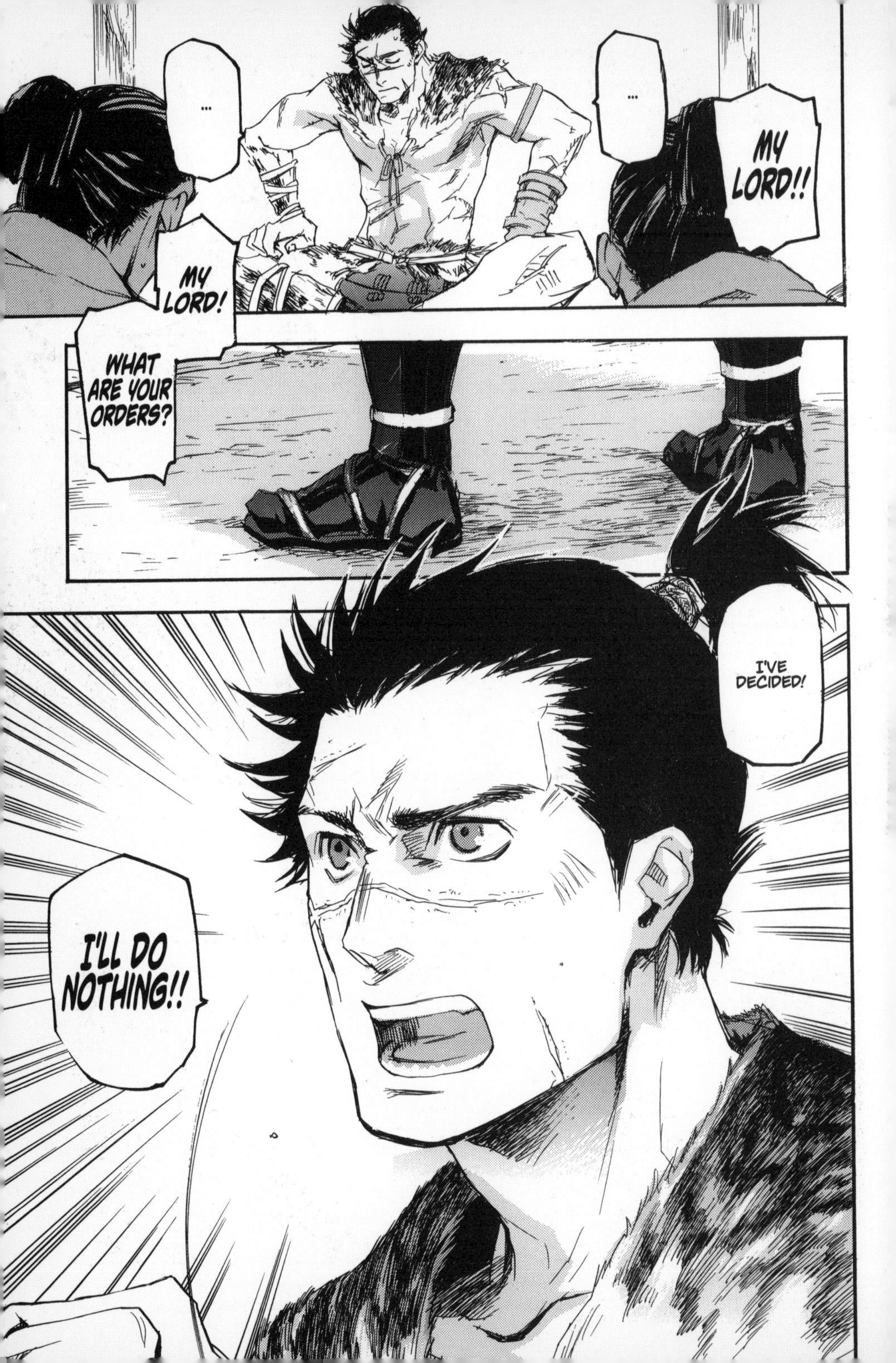
...
MY LORD!!
...
MY LORD!
WHAT ARE YOUR ORDERS?
I'VE DECIDED!
I'LL DO NOTHING!!

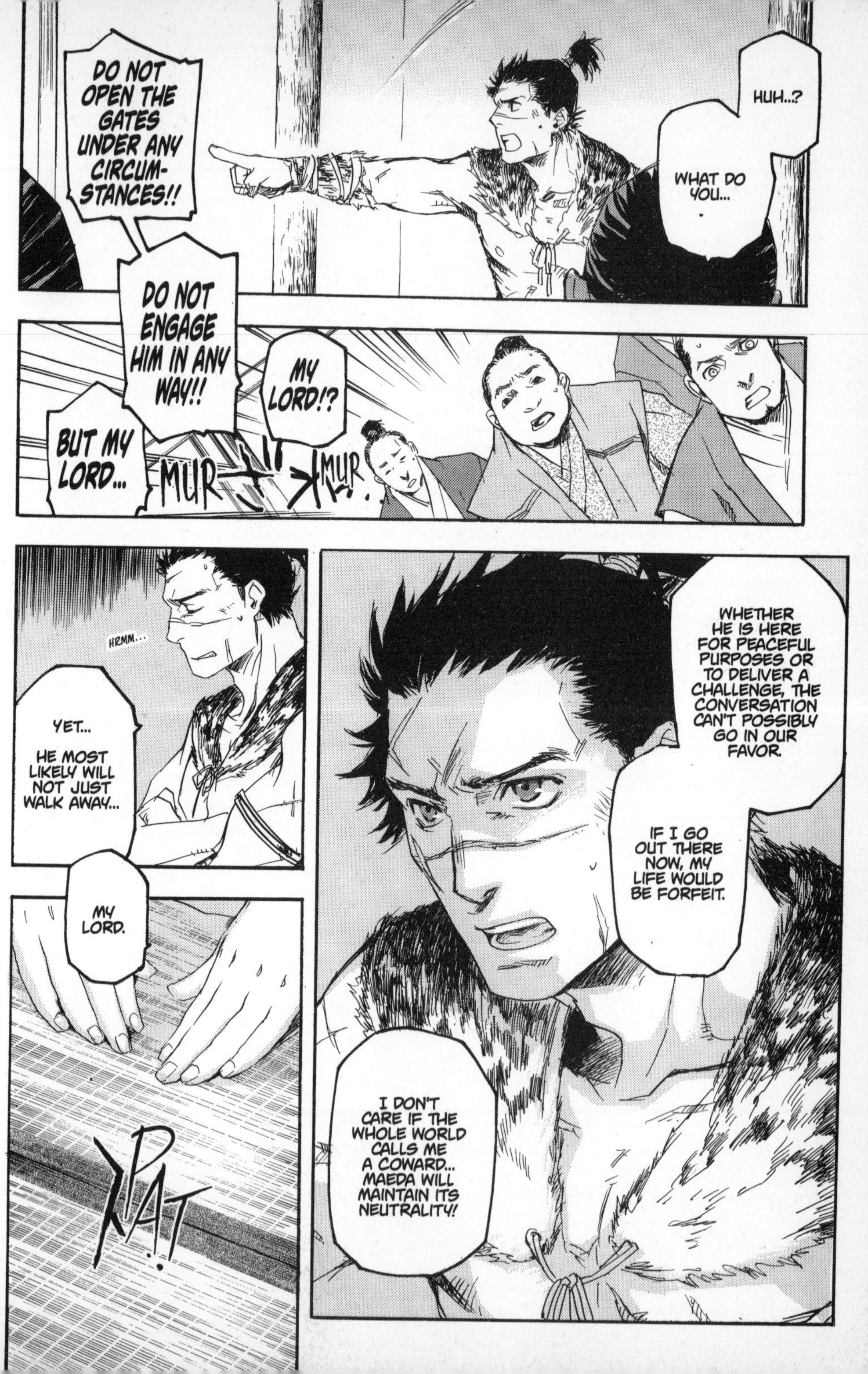
HUH..?
WHAT DO YOU...
DO NOT OPEN THE GATES UNDER ANY CIRCUM-STANCES!!
DO NOT ENGAGE HIM IN ANY WAY!!
MY LORD!?
BUT MY LORD...
MUR MUR
WHETHER HE IS HERE FOR PEACEFUL PURPOSES OR TO DELIVER A CHALLENGE, THE CONVERSATION CAN'T POSSIBLY GO IN OUR FAVOR.
IF I GO OUT THERE NOW, MY LIFE WOULD BE FORFEIT.
I DON'T CARE IF THE WHOLE WORLD CALLS ME A COWARD... MAEDA WILL MAINTAIN ITS NEUTRALITY!
HRMM...
YET...
HE MOST LIKELY WILL NOT JUST WALK AWAY...
MY LORD.
PAT

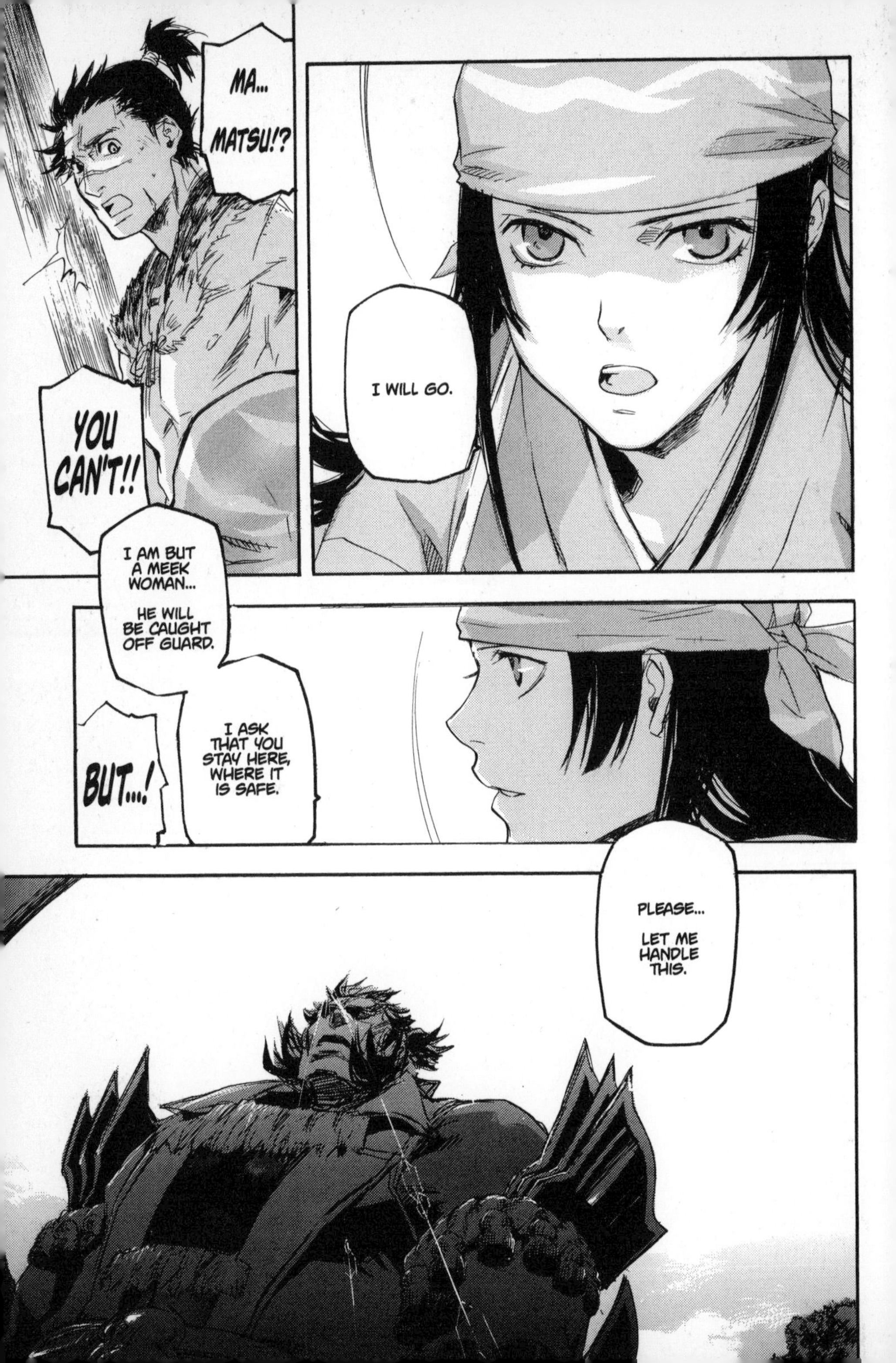
I WILL GO.
MA... MATSU!?
YOU CAN'T!!
I AM BUT A MEEK WOMAN... HE WILL BE CAUGHT OFF GUARD.
I ASK THAT YOU STAY HERE, WHERE IT IS SAFE.
BUT...!
PLEASE... LET ME HANDLE THIS.

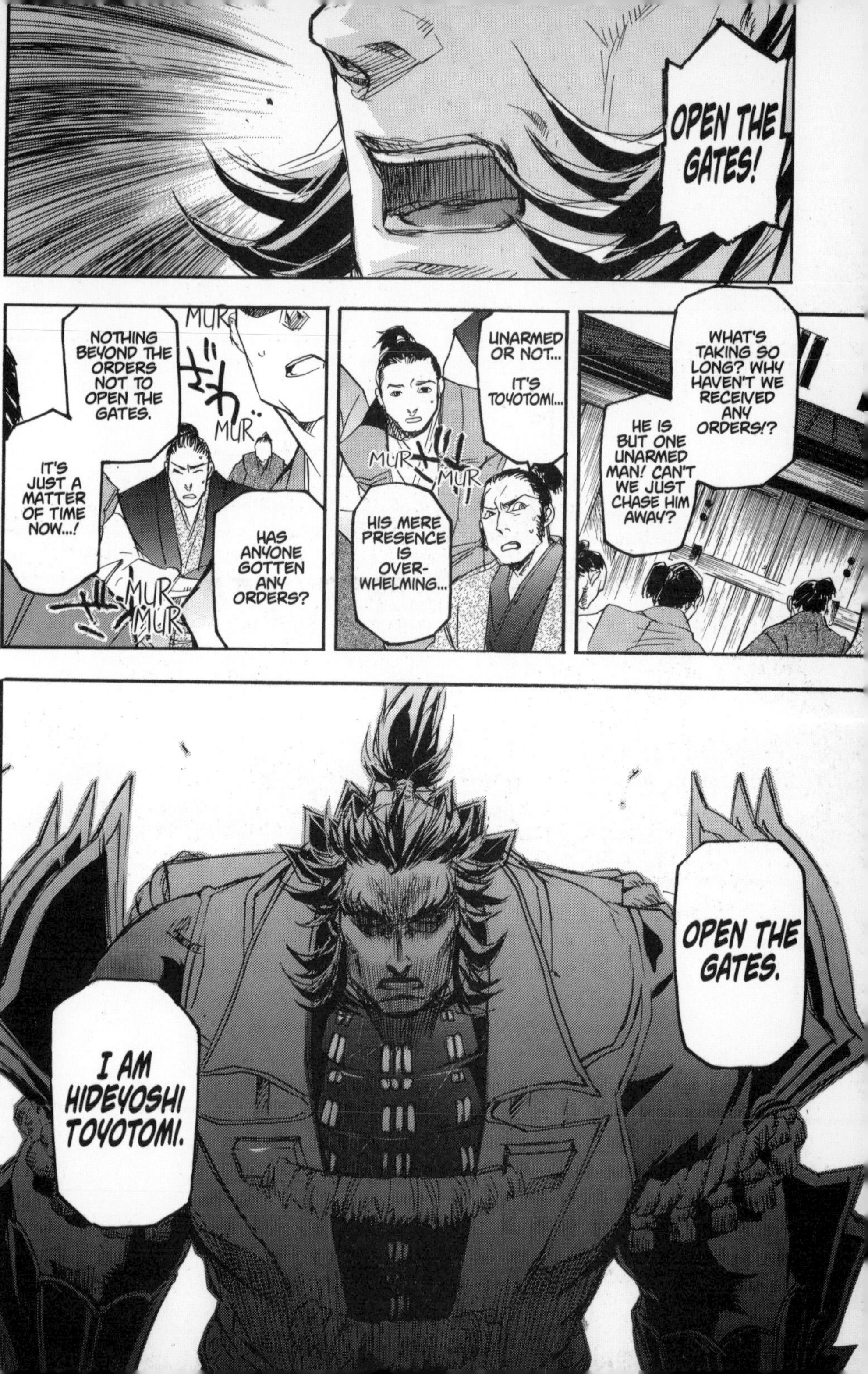
OPEN THE GATES!
WHAT'S TAKING SO LONG? WHY HAVEN'T WE RECEIVED ANY ORDERS!?
HE IS BUT ONE UNARMED MAN! CAN'T WE JUST CHASE HIM AWAY?
UNARMED OR NOT... IT'S TOYOTOMI...
MUR MUR
HIS MERE PRESENCE IS OVER-WHELMING...
MUR
ざわ
MUR
NOTHING BEYOND THE ORDERS NOT TO OPEN THE GATES.
IT'S JUST A MATTER OF TIME NOW...!
HAS ANYONE GOTTEN ANY ORDERS?
MUR MUR
OPEN THE GATES.
I AM HIDEYOSHI TOYOTOMI.

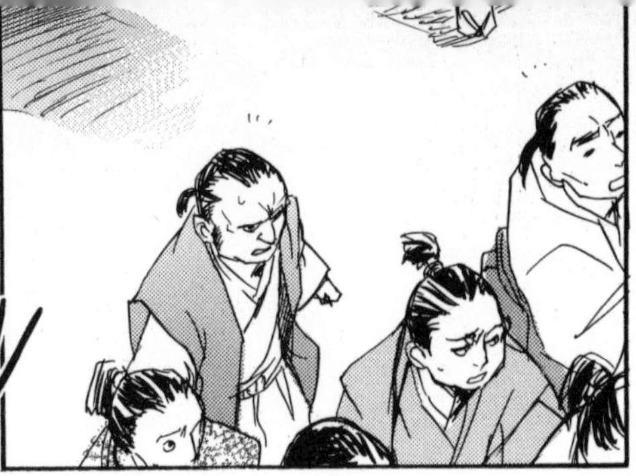

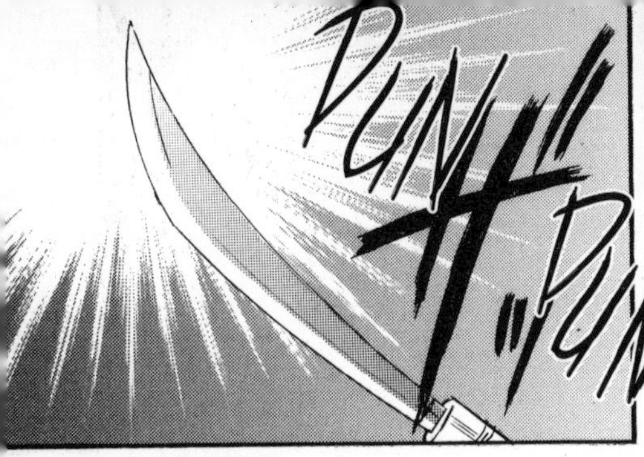
DUN
DUN

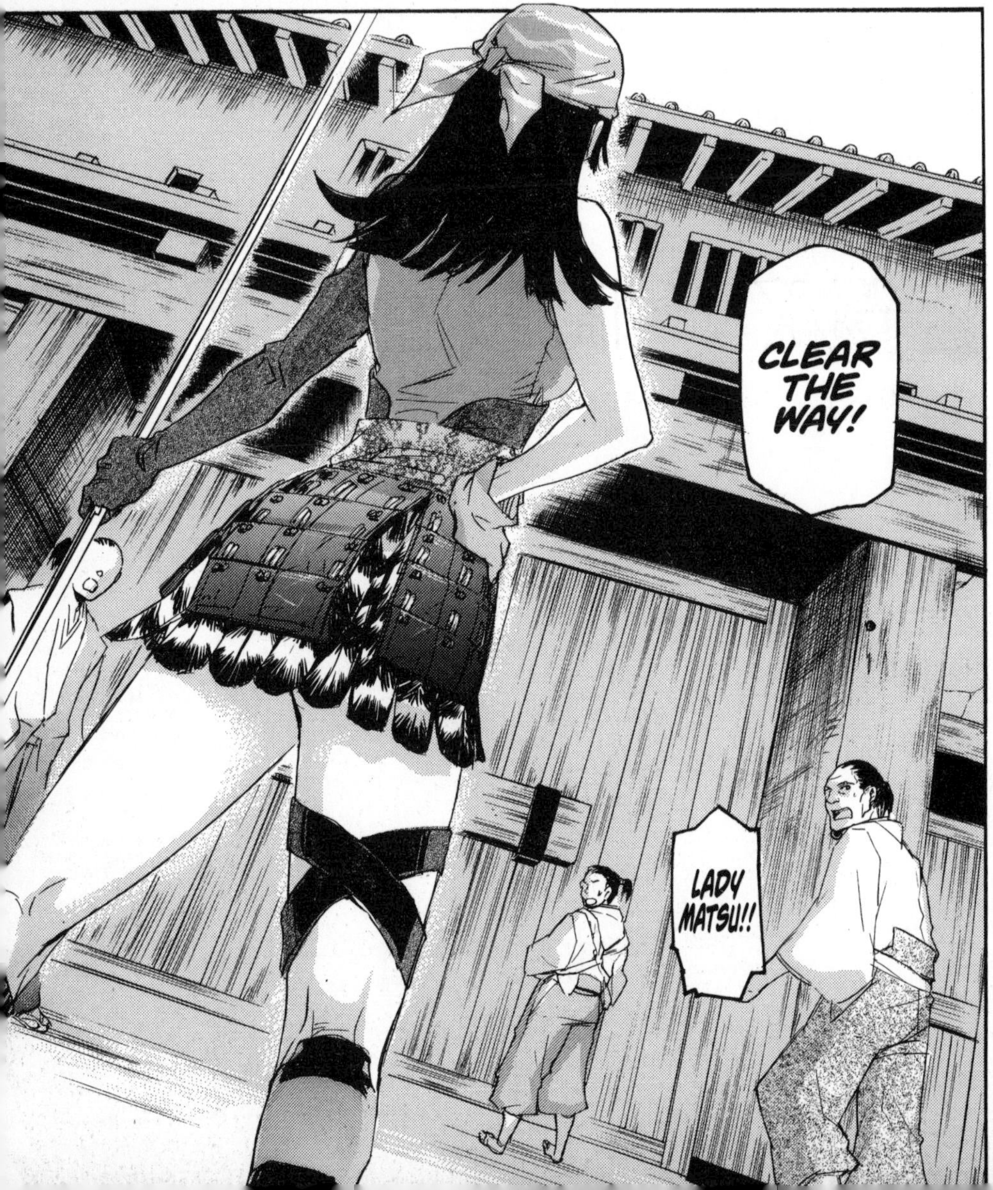
CLEAR THE WAY!
LADY MATSU!!

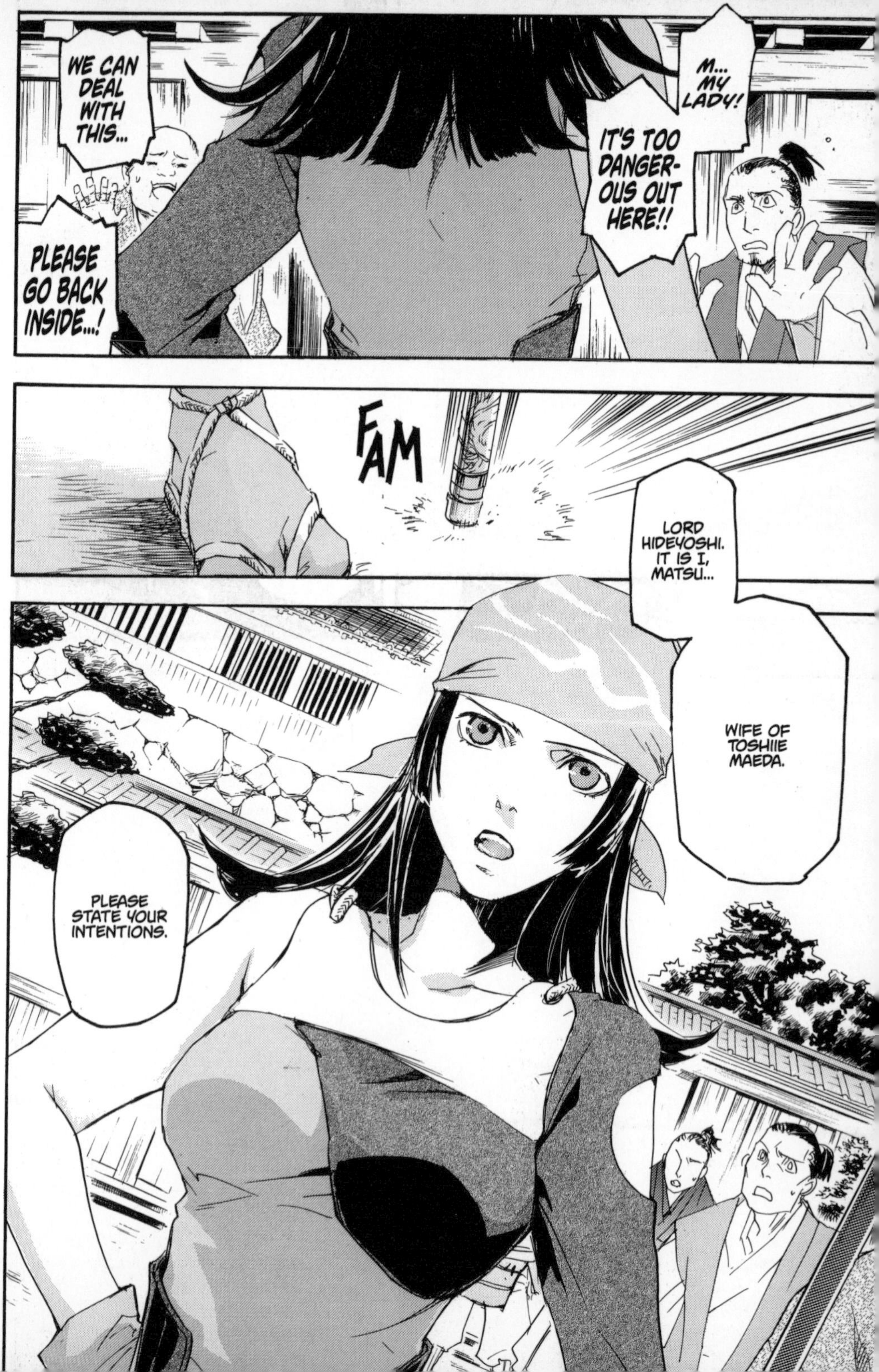
M... MY LADY!
IT'S TOO DANGER-OUS OUT HERE!!
WE CAN DEAL WITH THIS...
PLEASE GO BACK INSIDE...!
FAM
LORD HIDEYOSHI. IT IS I, MATSU...
WIFE OF TOSHIIE MAEDA.
PLEASE STATE YOUR INTENTIONS.

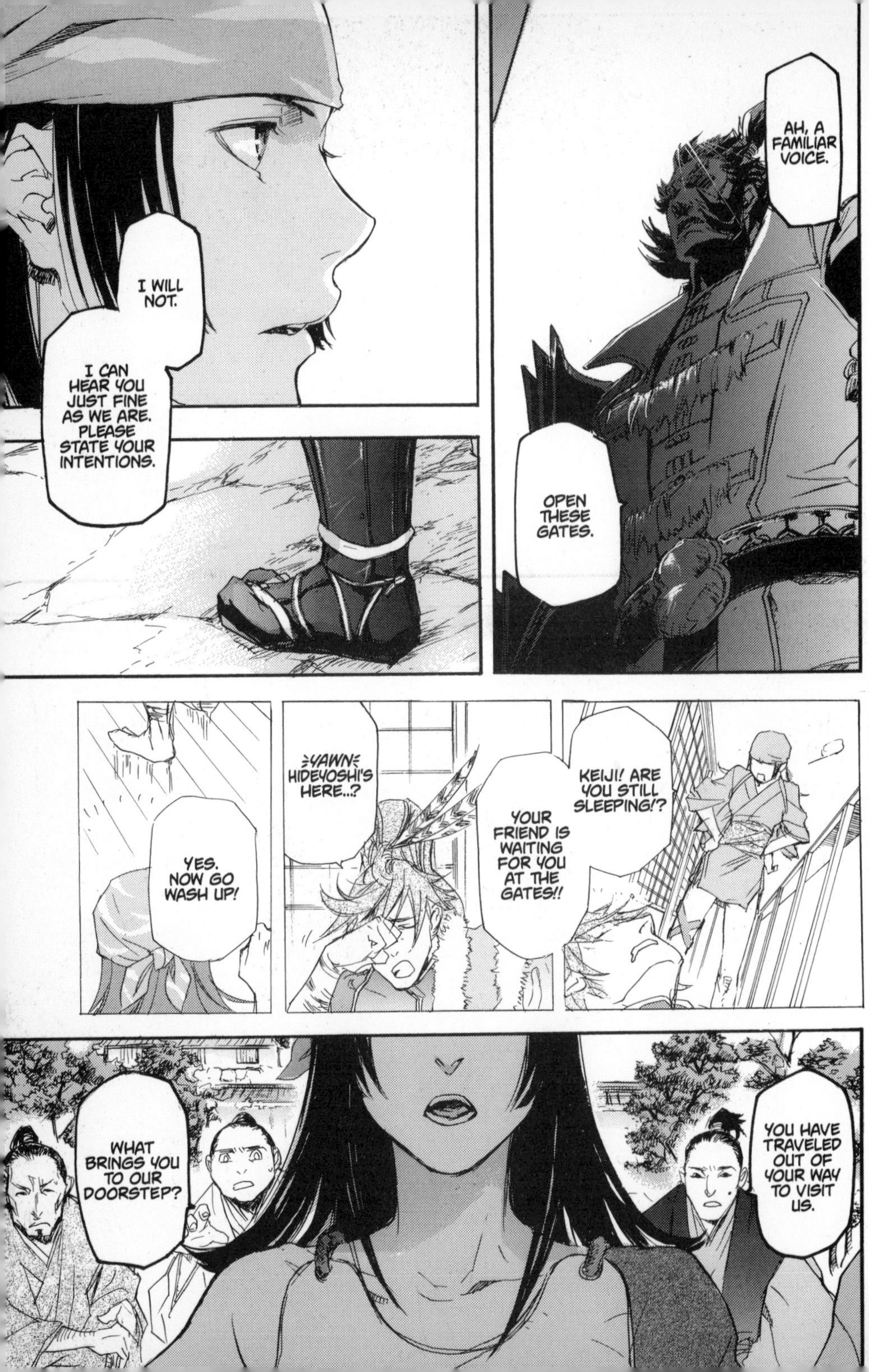
AH, A FAMILIAR VOICE.
OPEN THESE GATES.
I WILL NOT.
I CAN HEAR YOU JUST FINE AS WE ARE. PLEASE STATE YOUR INTENTIONS.
KEIJI! ARE YOU STILL SLEEPING!?
YOUR FRIEND IS WAITING FOR YOU AT THE GATES!!
≈YAWN≈ HIDEYOSHI'S HERE...?
YES. NOW GO WASH UP!
YOU HAVE TRAVELED OUT OF YOUR WAY TO VISIT US.
WHAT BRINGS YOU TO OUR DOORSTEP?

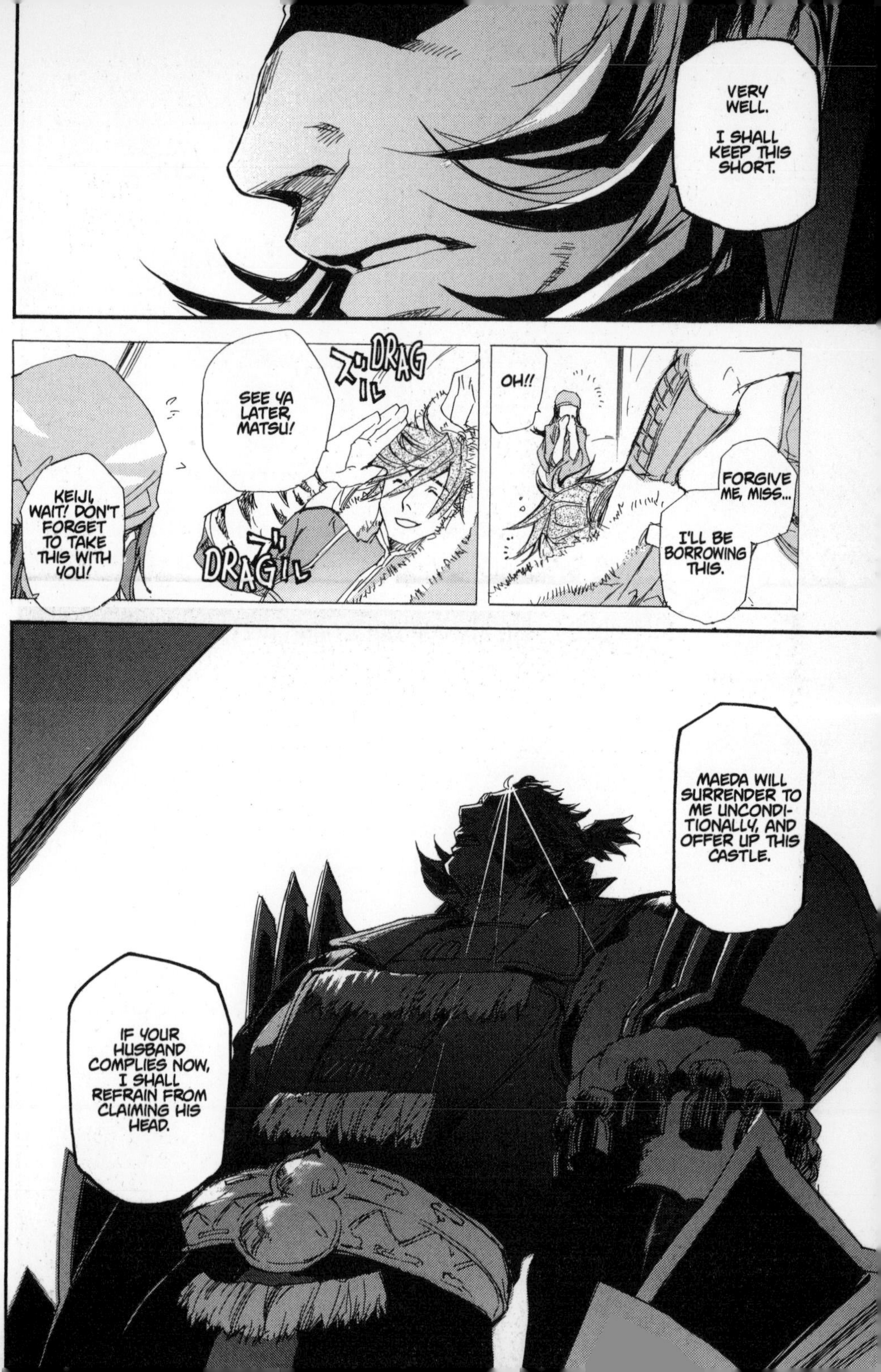
VERY WELL.
I SHALL KEEP THIS SHORT.
OH!!
FORGIVE ME, MISS...
I'LL BE BORROWING THIS.
DRAG
SEE YA LATER, MATSU!
KEIJI, WAIT! DON'T FORGET TO TAKE THIS WITH YOU!
DRAG
MAEDA WILL SURRENDER TO ME UNCONDITIONALLY, AND OFFER UP THIS CASTLE.
IF YOUR HUSBAND COMPLIES NOW, I SHALL REFRAIN FROM CLAIMING HIS HEAD.

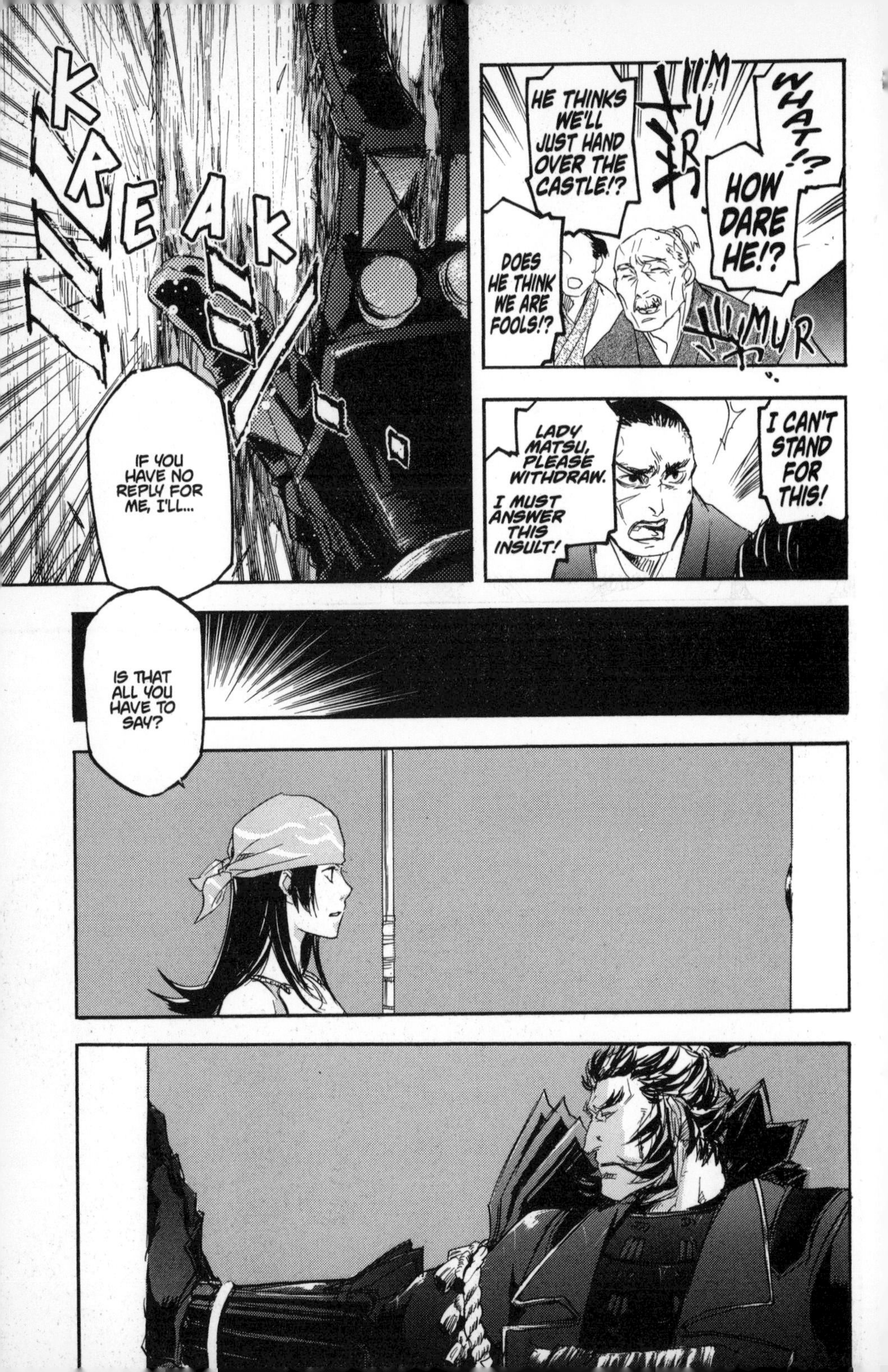
WHAT!? HOW DARE HE!?
MURMUR
HE THINKS WE'LL JUST HAND OVER THE CASTLE!?
DOES HE THINK WE ARE FOOLS!?
MUR
I CAN'T STAND FOR THIS!
LADY MATSU, PLEASE WITHDRAW.
I MUST ANSWER THIS INSULT!
KREAK
IF YOU HAVE NO REPLY FOR ME, I'LL...
IS THAT ALL YOU HAVE TO SAY?

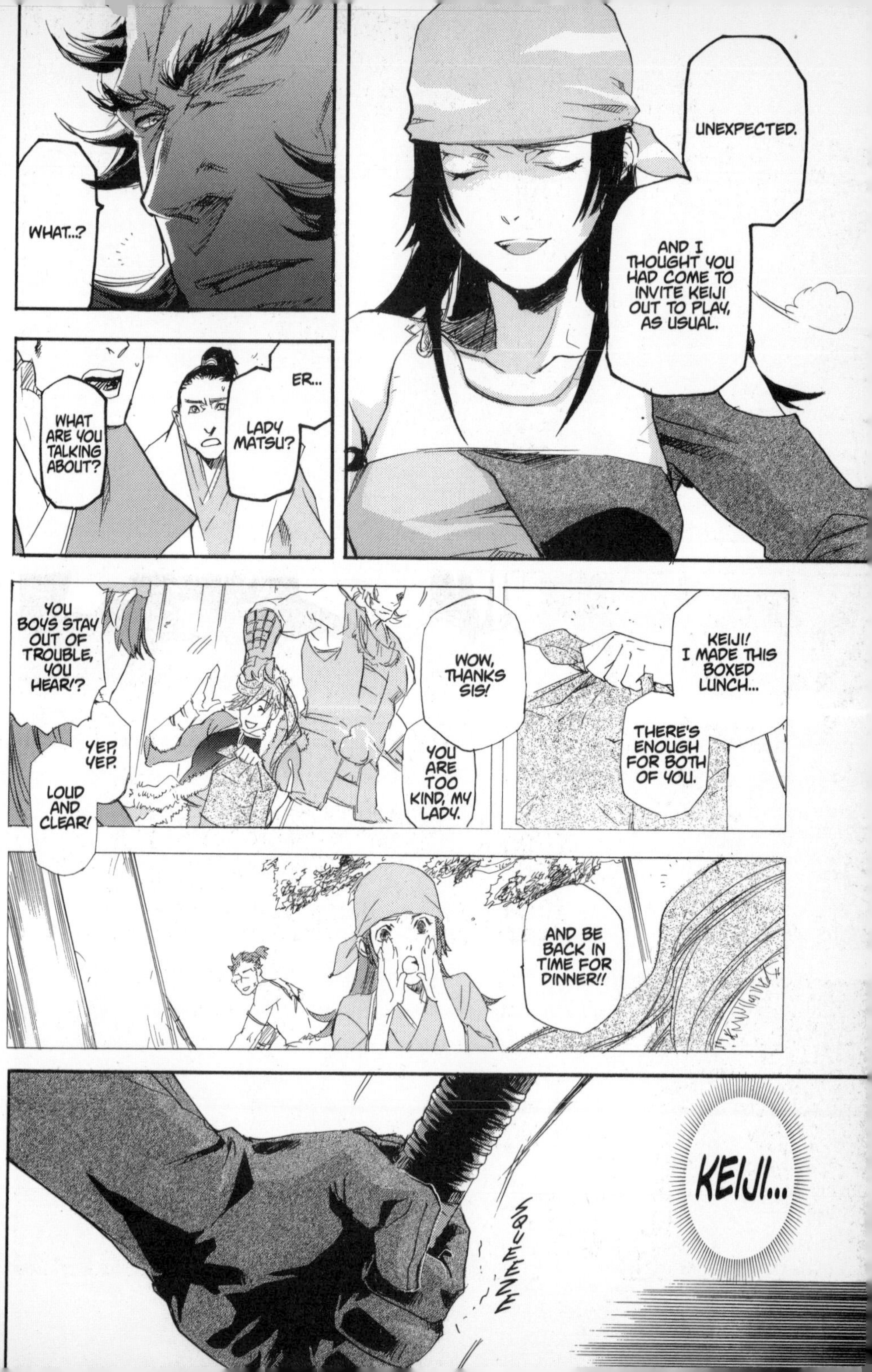
UNEXPECTED.
AND I THOUGHT YOU HAD COME TO INVITE KEIJI OUT TO PLAY, AS USUAL.
WHAT..?
ER...
LADY MATSU?
WHAT ARE YOU TALKING ABOUT?
KEIJI! I MADE THIS BOXED LUNCH...
THERE'S ENOUGH FOR BOTH OF YOU.
WOW, THANKS SIS!
YOU ARE TOO KIND, MY LADY.
YOU BOYS STAY OUT OF TROUBLE, YOU HEAR!?
YEP, YEP.
LOUD AND CLEAR!
AND BE BACK IN TIME FOR DINNER!!
KEIJI...
SQUEEZE

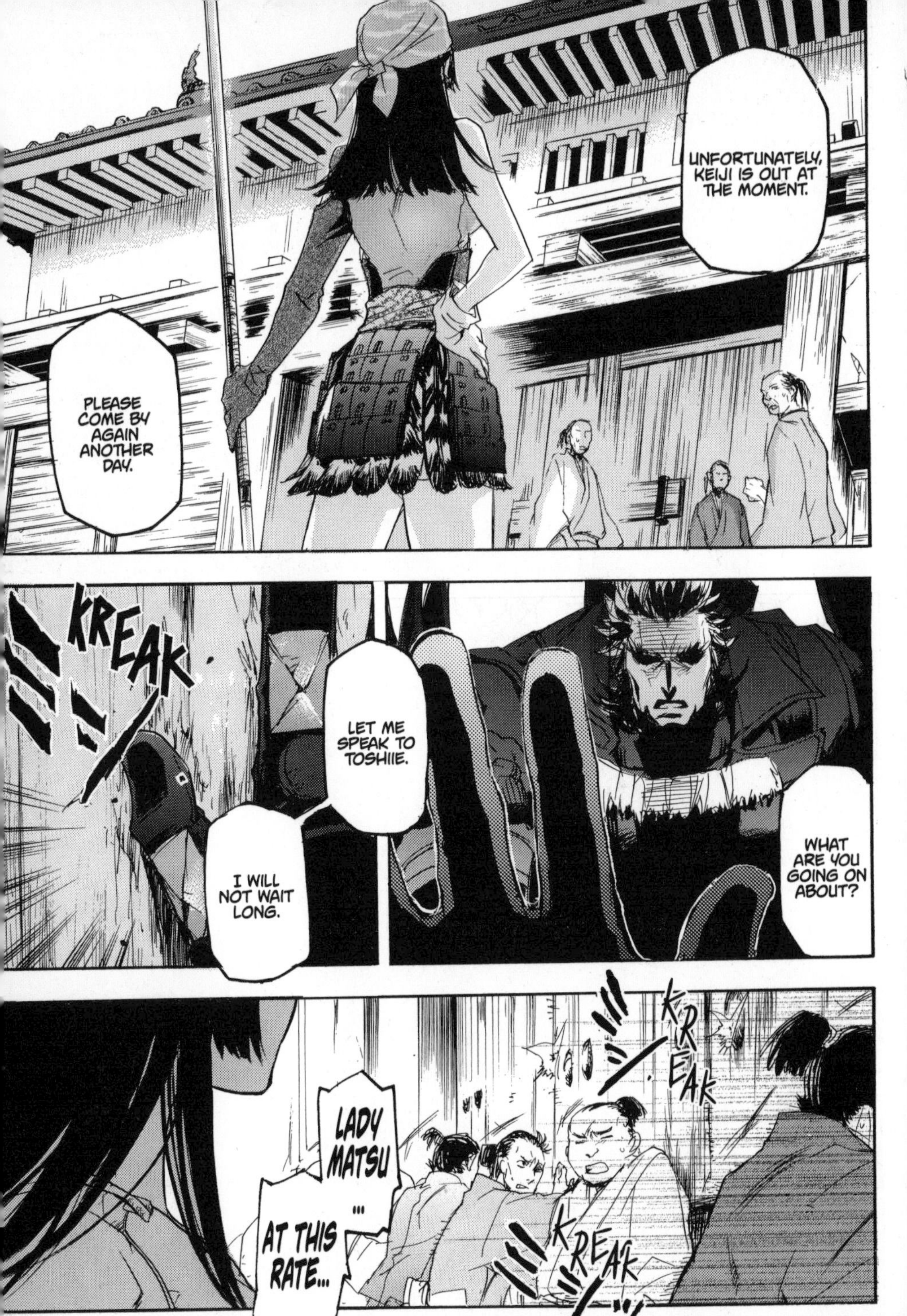
UNFORTUNATELY, KEIJI IS OUT AT THE MOMENT.
PLEASE COME BY AGAIN ANOTHER DAY.
WHAT ARE YOU GOING ON ABOUT?
KREAK
LET ME SPEAK TO TOSHIIE.
I WILL NOT WAIT LONG.
KREAK
KREAK
LADY MATSU ...
AT THIS RATE...

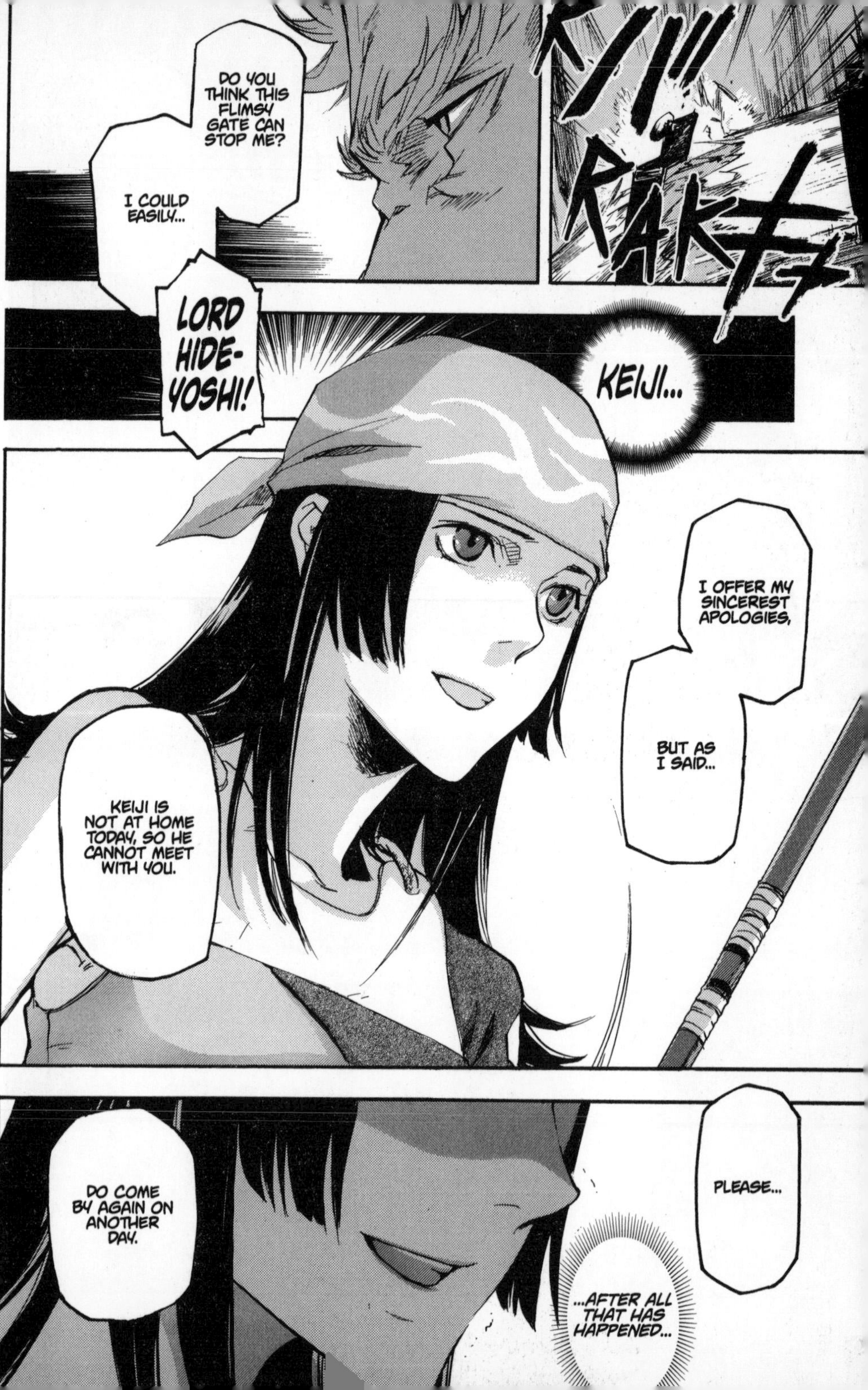
RAK
DO YOU THINK THIS FLIMSY GATE CAN STOP ME?
I COULD EASILY...
LORD HIDE-YOSHI!
KEIJI...
I OFFER MY SINCEREST APOLOGIES,
BUT AS I SAID...
KEIJI IS NOT AT HOME TODAY, SO HE CANNOT MEET WITH YOU.
PLEASE...
...AFTER ALL THAT HAS HAPPENED...
DO COME BY AGAIN ON ANOTHER DAY.

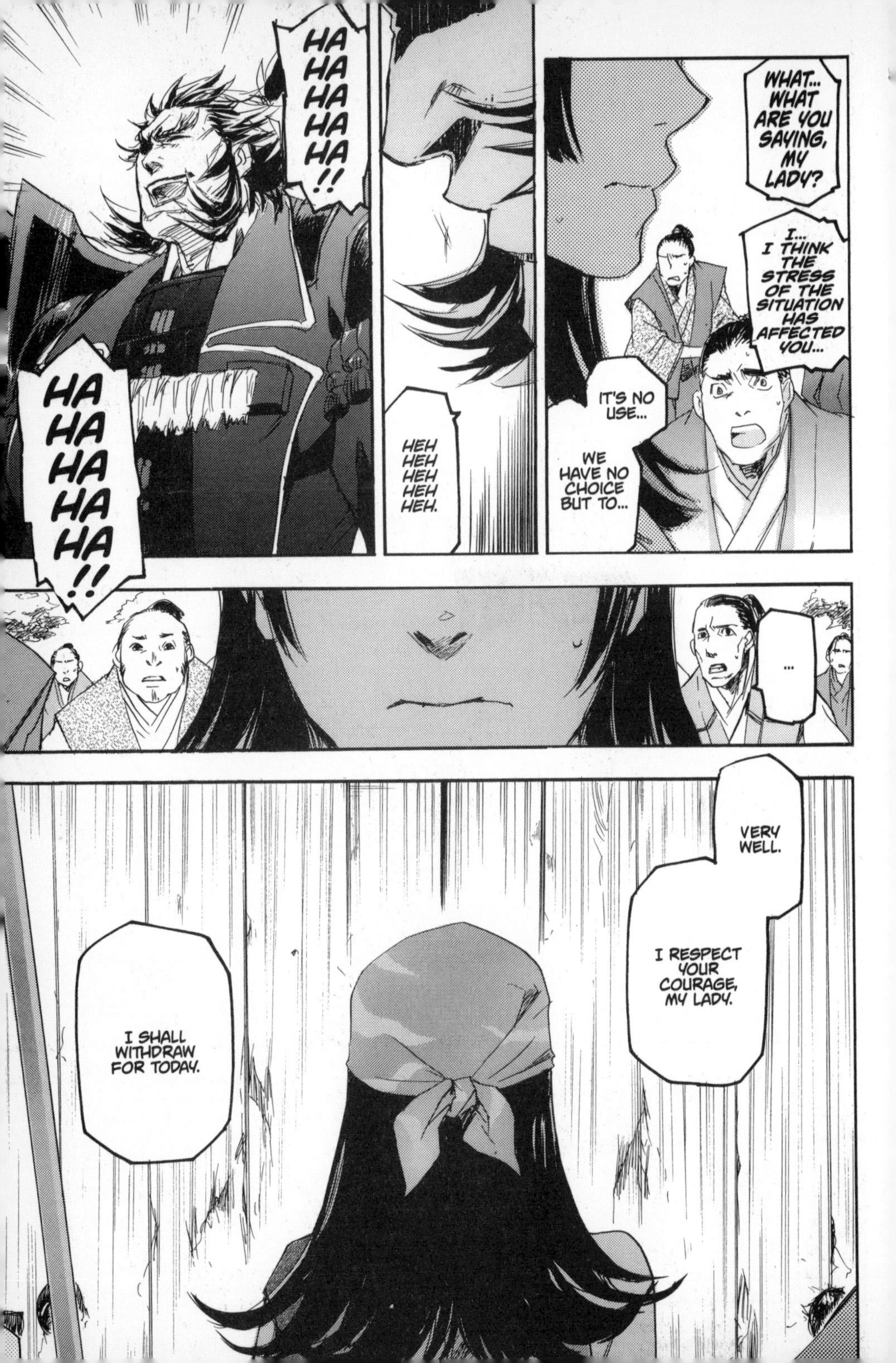
WHAT... WHAT ARE YOU SAYING, MY LADY?
I... I THINK THE STRESS OF THE SITUATION HAS AFFECTED YOU...
IT'S NO USE...
WE HAVE NO CHOICE BUT TO...
HEH HEH HEH HEH HEH.
HA HA HA HA HA!!
HA HA HA HA HA!!
...
VERY WELL.
I RESPECT YOUR COURAGE, MY LADY.
I SHALL WITHDRAW FOR TODAY.

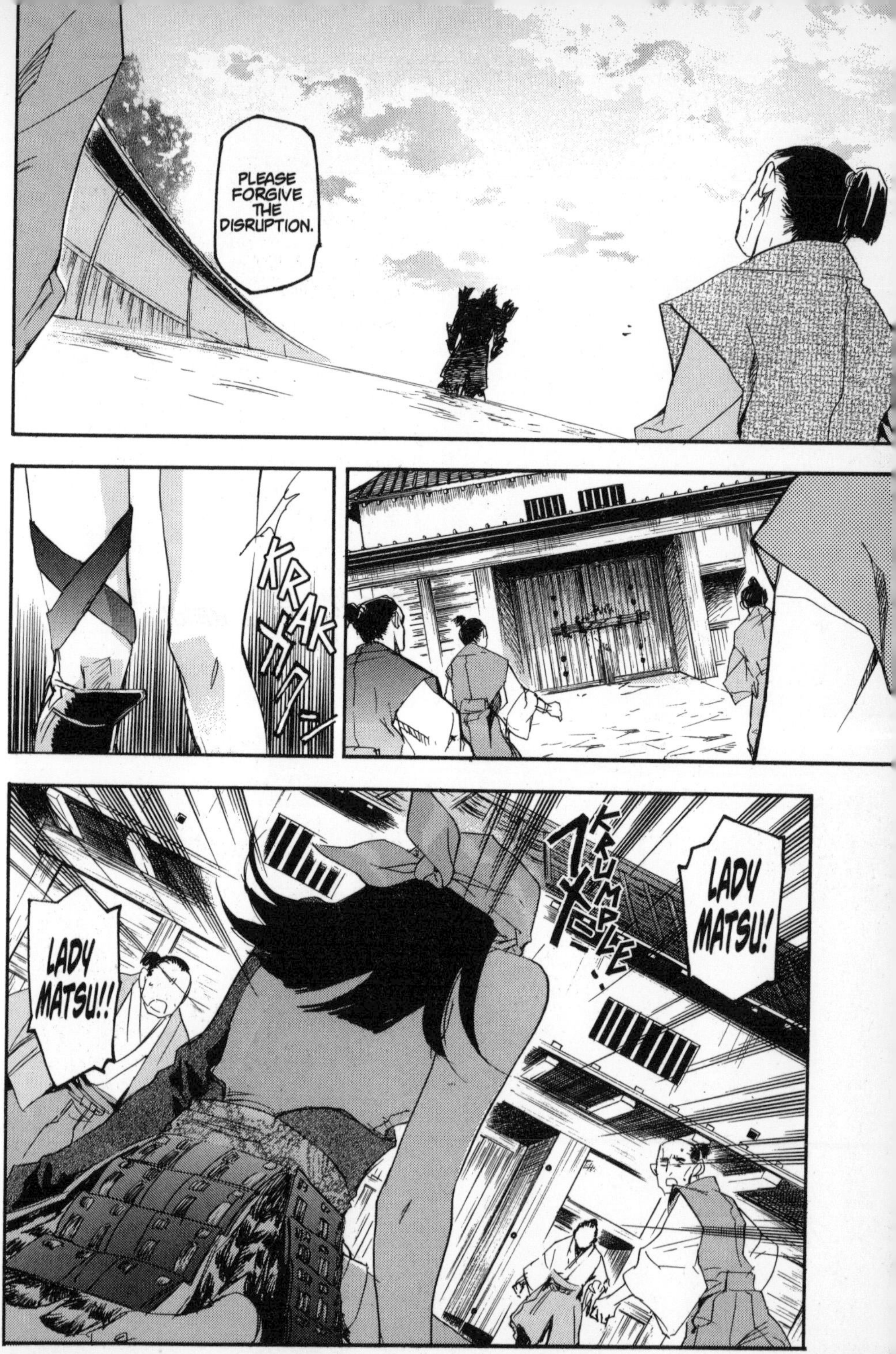

PLEASE FORGIVE THE DISRUPTION.
KRAK
LADY MATSU!
KRUMPLE
LADY MATSU!!

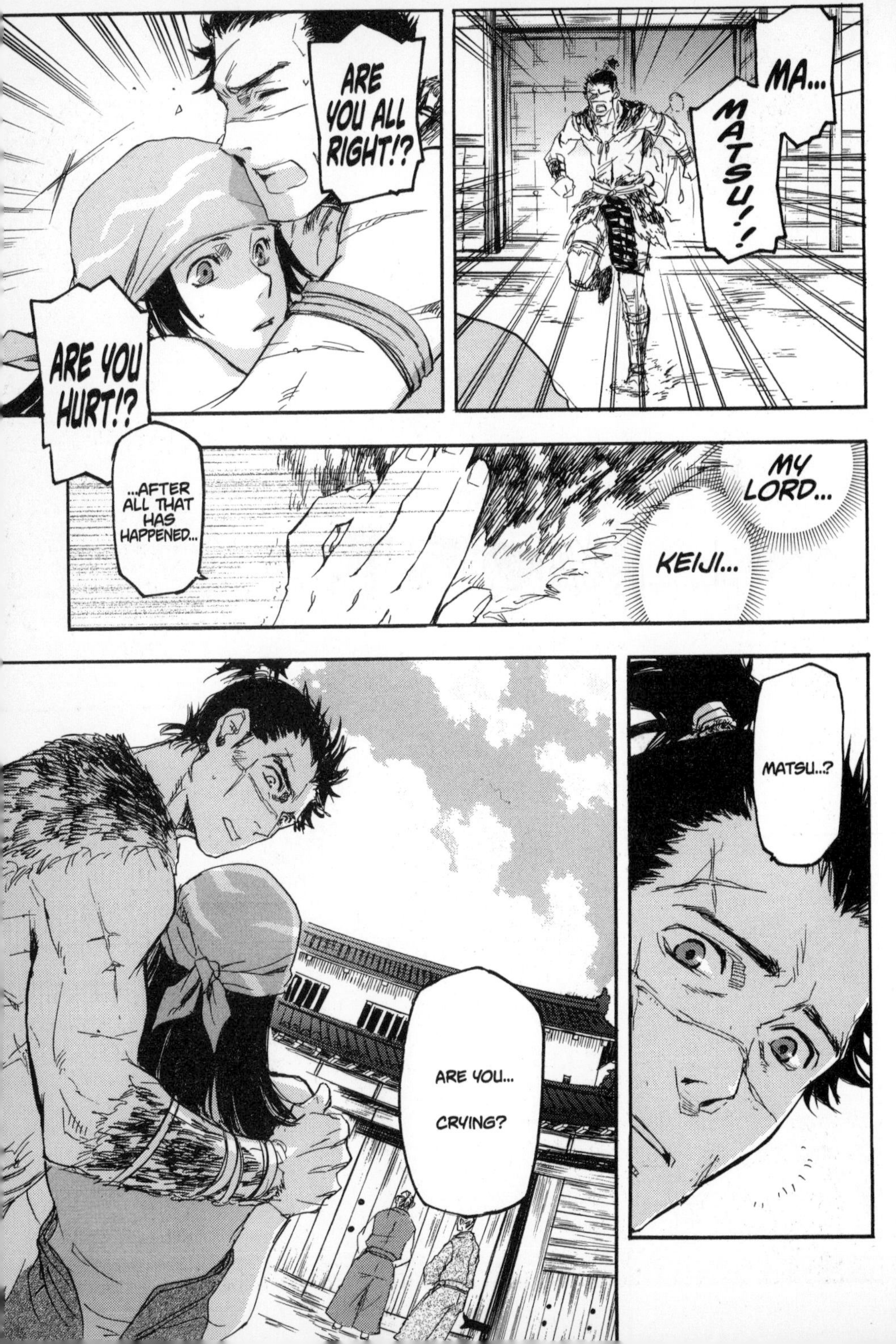
MA... MATSU!!
ARE YOU ALL RIGHT!?
ARE YOU HURT!?
MY LORD...
KEIJI...
...AFTER ALL THAT HAS HAPPENED...
MATSU...?
ARE YOU... CRYING?

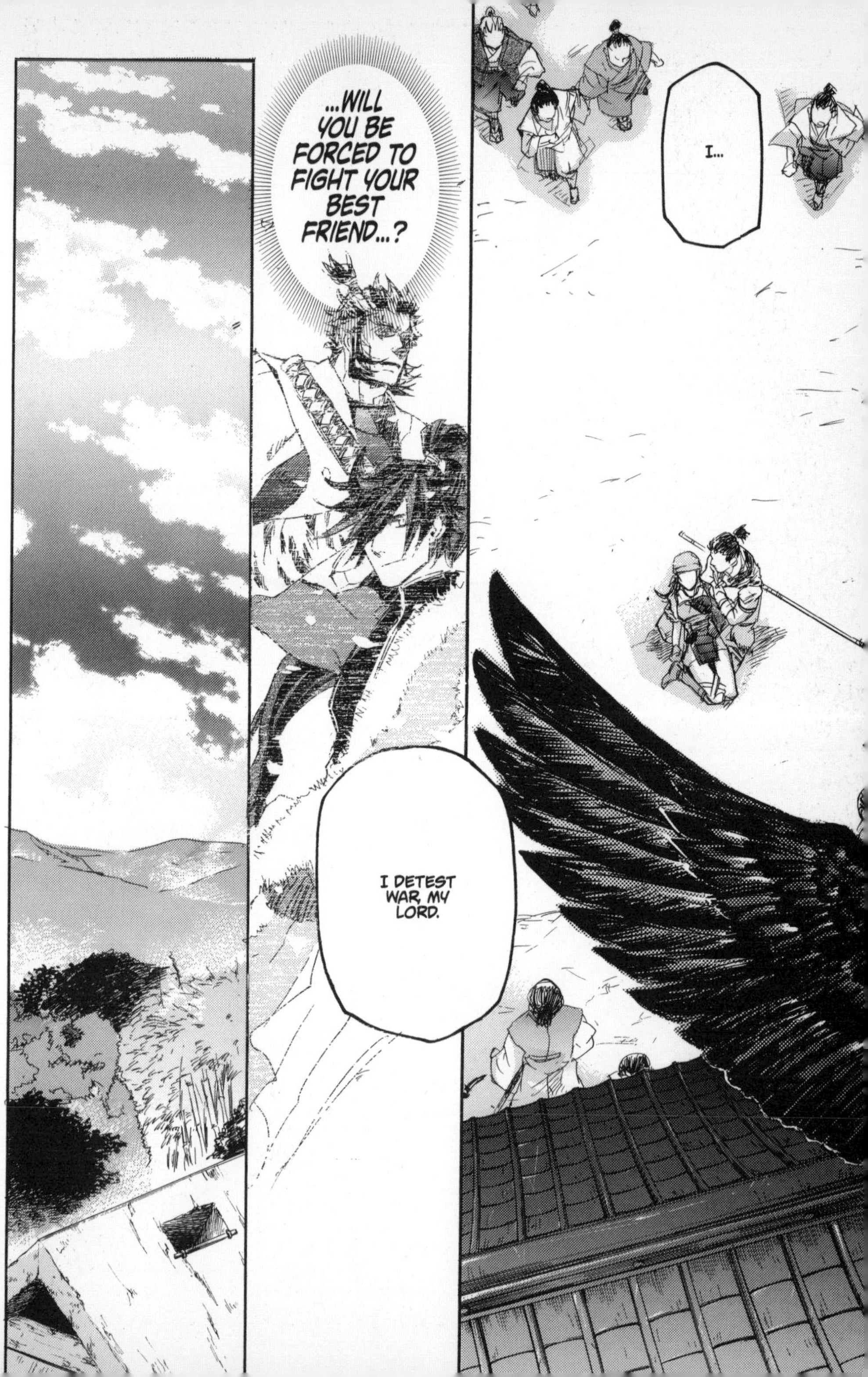
I...
I DETEST WAR, MY LORD.
...WILL YOU BE FORCED TO FIGHT YOUR BEST FRIEND...?

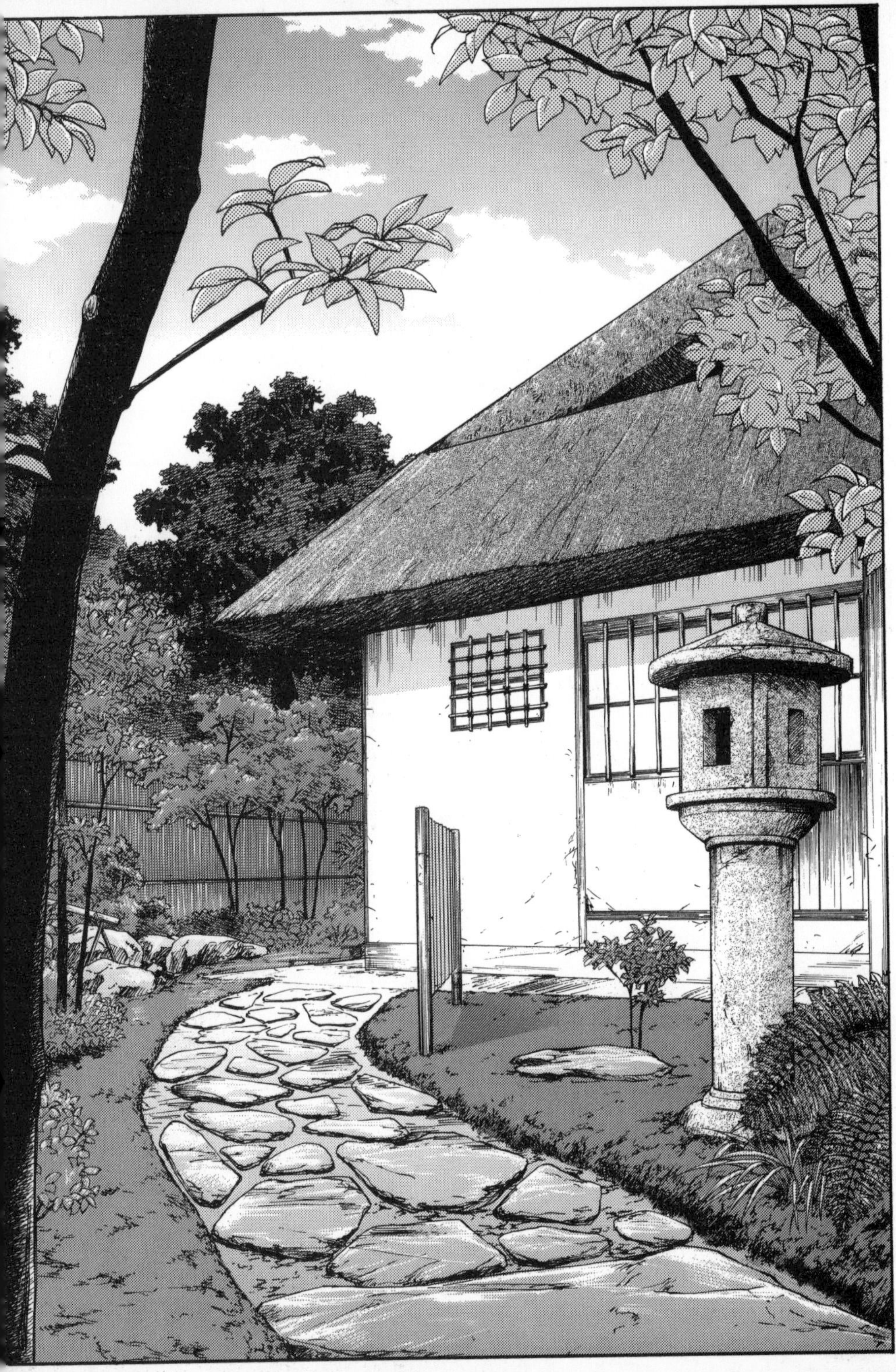

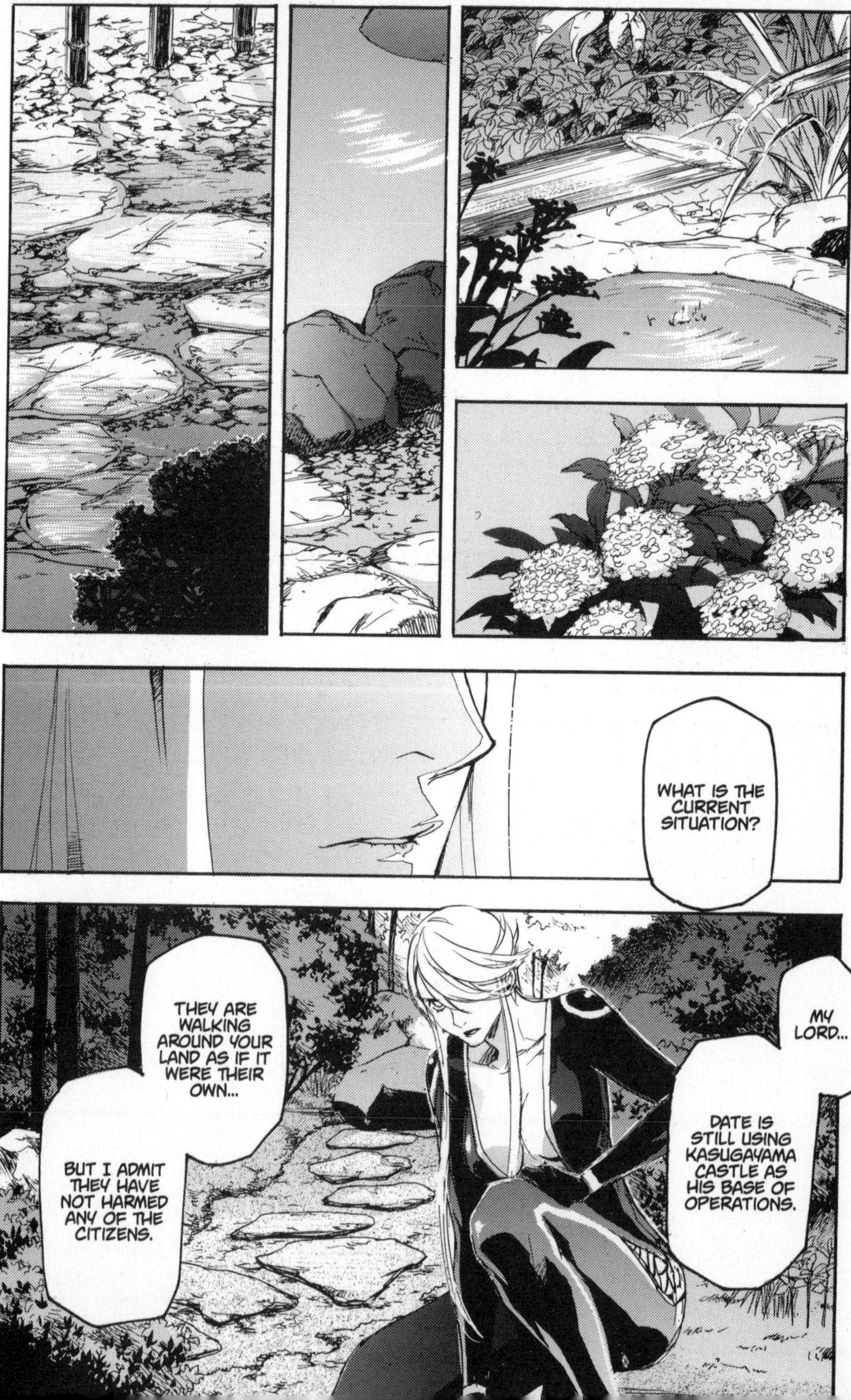
WHAT IS THE CURRENT SITUATION?
MY LORD...
DATE IS STILL USING KASUGAYAMA CASTLE AS HIS BASE OF OPERATIONS.
THEY ARE WALKING AROUND YOUR LAND AS IF IT WERE THEIR OWN...
BUT I ADMIT THEY HAVE NOT HARMED ANY OF THE CITIZENS.

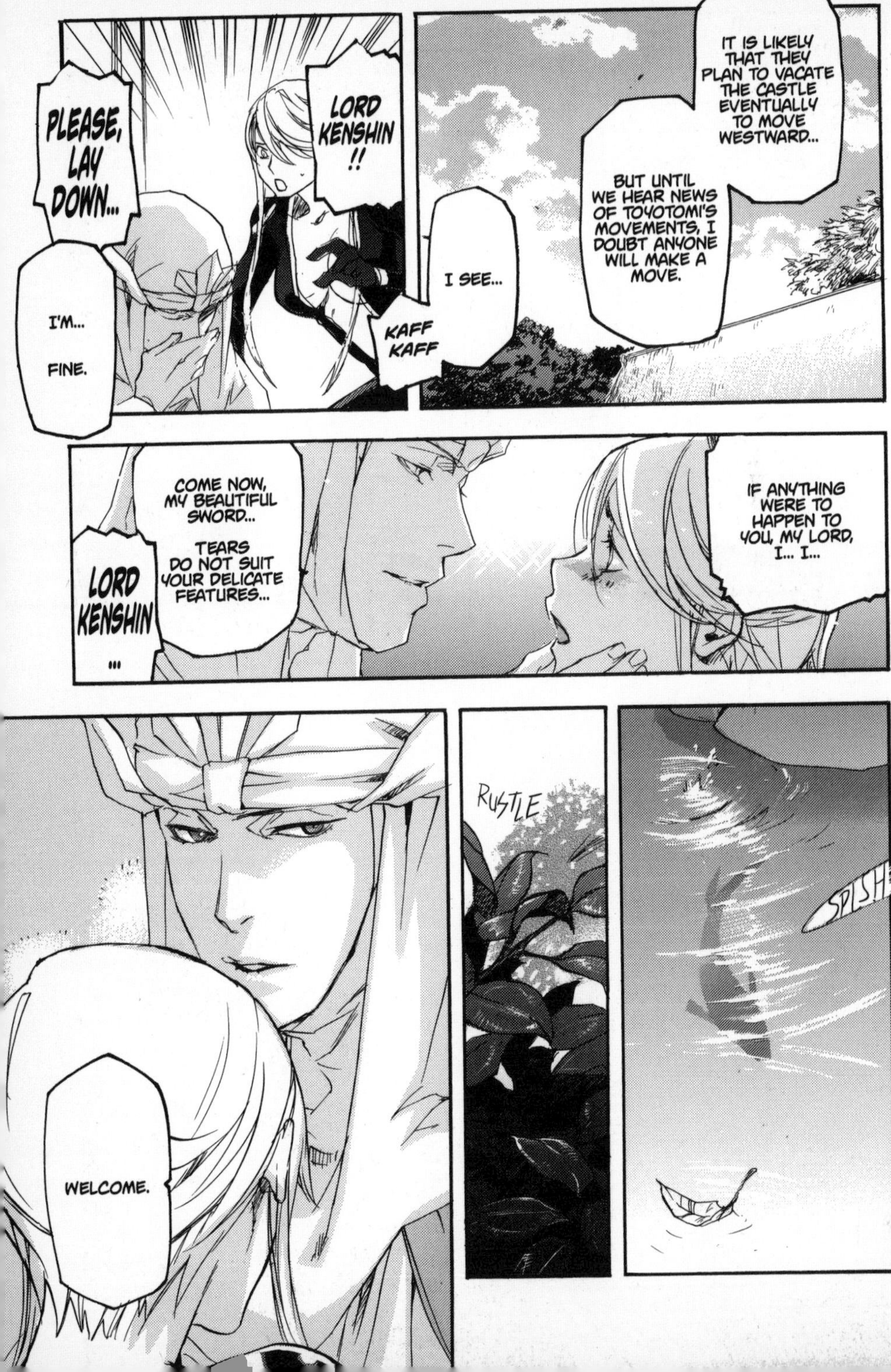

IT IS LIKELY THAT THEY PLAN TO VACATE THE CASTLE EVENTUALLY TO MOVE WESTWARD...
BUT UNTIL WE HEAR NEWS OF TOYOTOMI'S MOVEMENTS, I DOUBT ANYONE WILL MAKE A MOVE.
I SEE...
KAFF KAFF
LORD KENSHIN!!
PLEASE, LAY DOWN...
I'M... FINE.
IF ANYTHING WERE TO HAPPEN TO YOU, MY LORD, I... I...
COME NOW, MY BEAUTIFUL SWORD... TEARS DO NOT SUIT YOUR DELICATE FEATURES...
LORD KENSHIN...
SPLSH
RUSTLE
WELCOME.

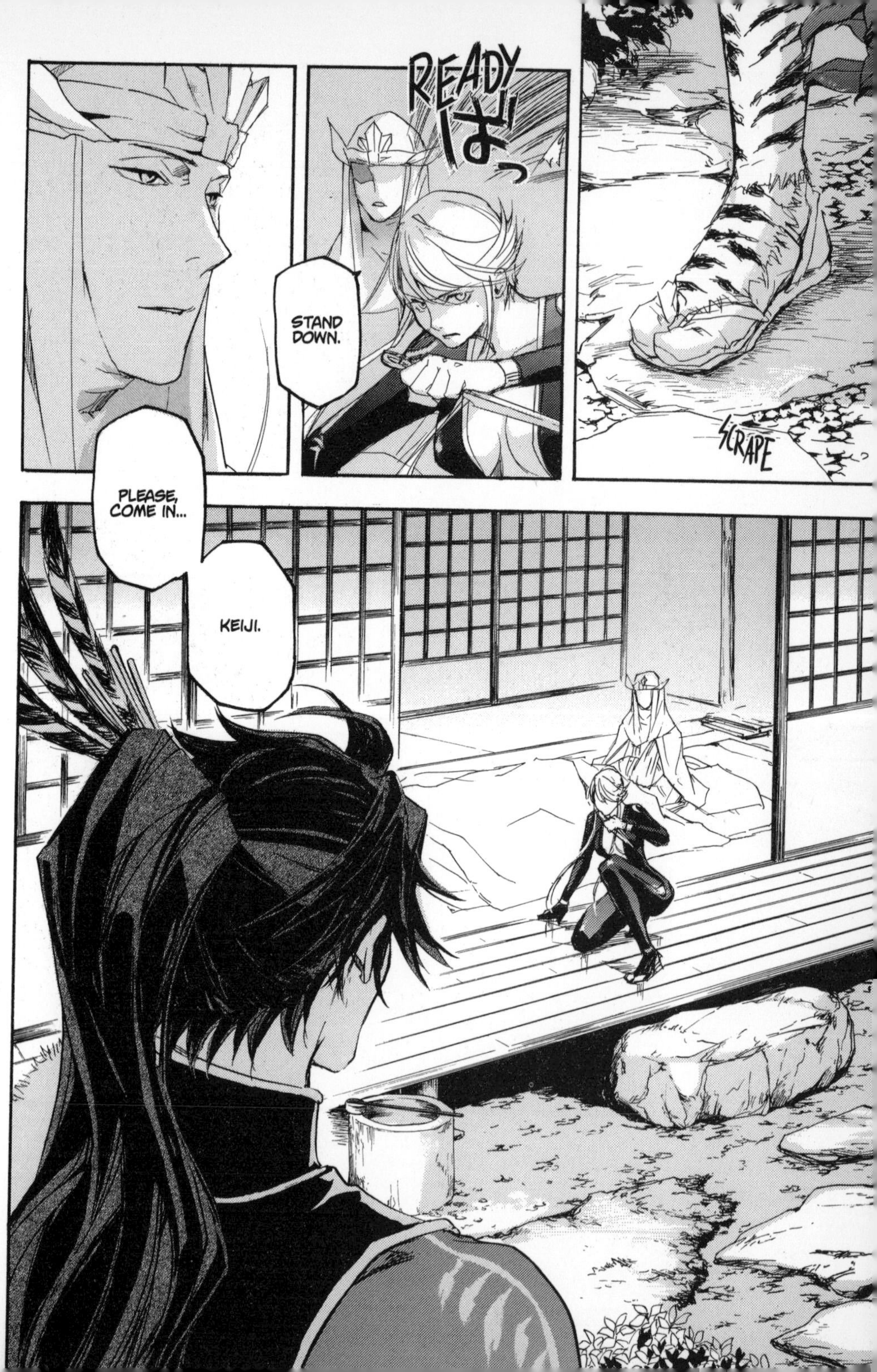
SCRAPE
READY
ぱっ
STAND DOWN.
PLEASE, COME IN...
KEIJI.

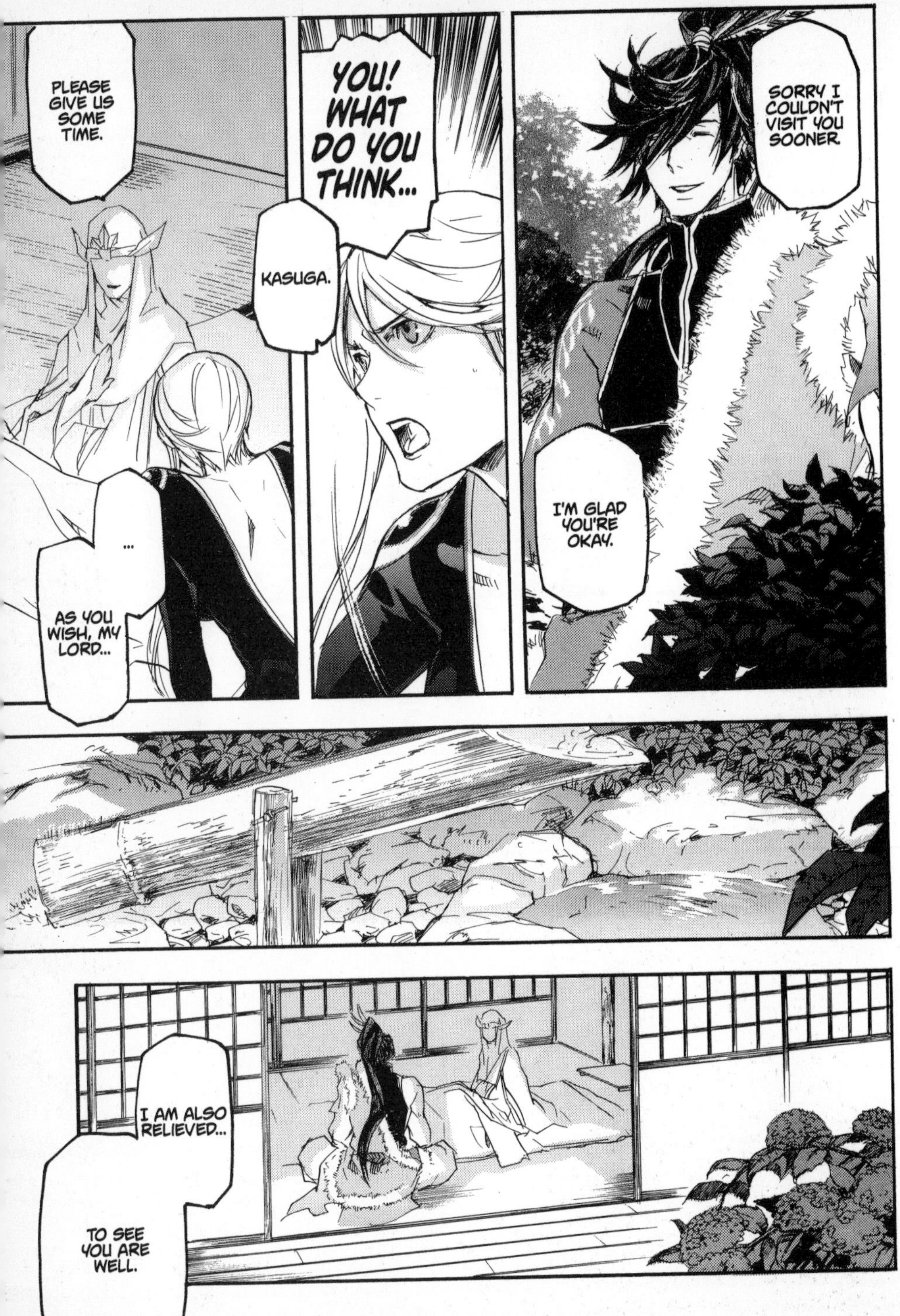
SORRY I COULDN'T VISIT YOU SOONER.
I'M GLAD YOU'RE OKAY.
YOU! WHAT DO YOU THINK...
KASUGA.
PLEASE GIVE US SOME TIME.
...
AS YOU WISH, MY LORD...
I AM ALSO RELIEVED...
TO SEE YOU ARE WELL.

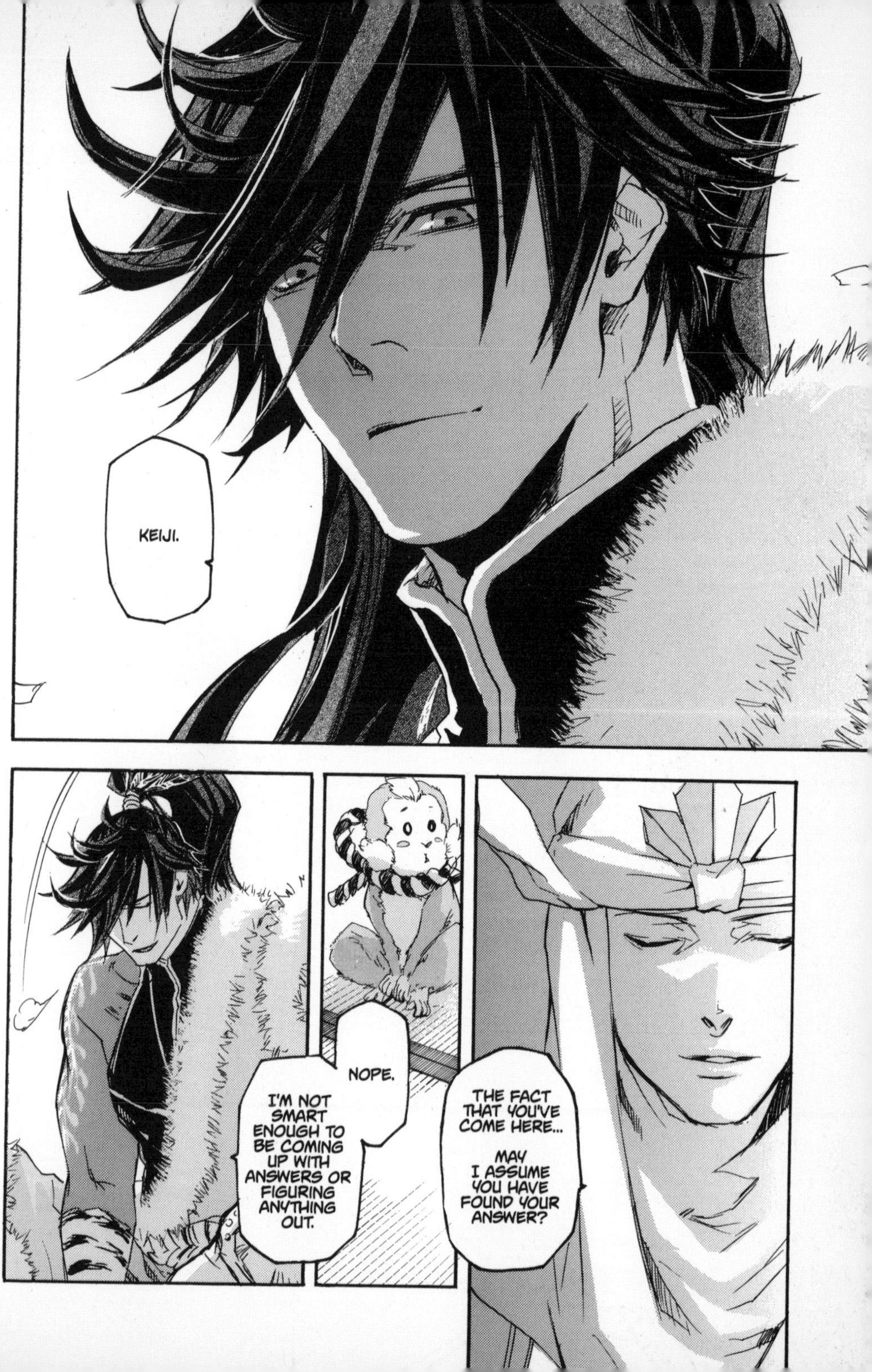
KEIJI.
THE FACT THAT YOU'VE COME HERE...
MAY I ASSUME YOU HAVE FOUND YOUR ANSWER?
NOPE.
I'M NOT SMART ENOUGH TO BE COMING UP WITH ANSWERS OR FIGURING ANYTHING OUT.

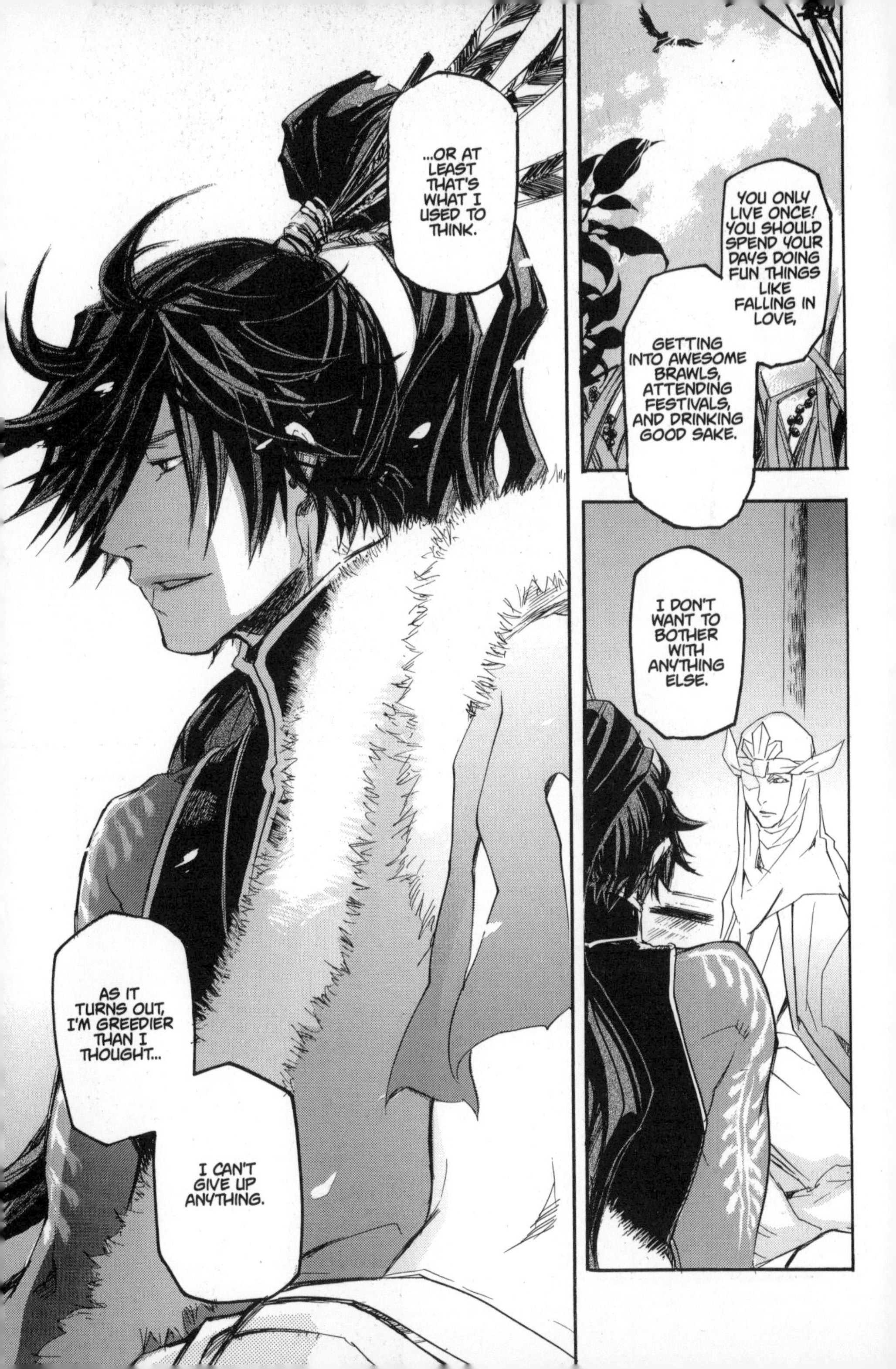
YOU ONLY LIVE ONCE! YOU SHOULD SPEND YOUR DAYS DOING FUN THINGS LIKE FALLING IN LOVE,
GETTING INTO AWESOME BRAWLS, ATTENDING FESTIVALS, AND DRINKING GOOD SAKE.
I DON'T WANT TO BOTHER WITH ANYTHING ELSE.
...OR AT LEAST THAT'S WHAT I USED TO THINK.
AS IT TURNS OUT, I'M GREEDIER THAN I THOUGHT...
I CAN'T GIVE UP ANYTHING.

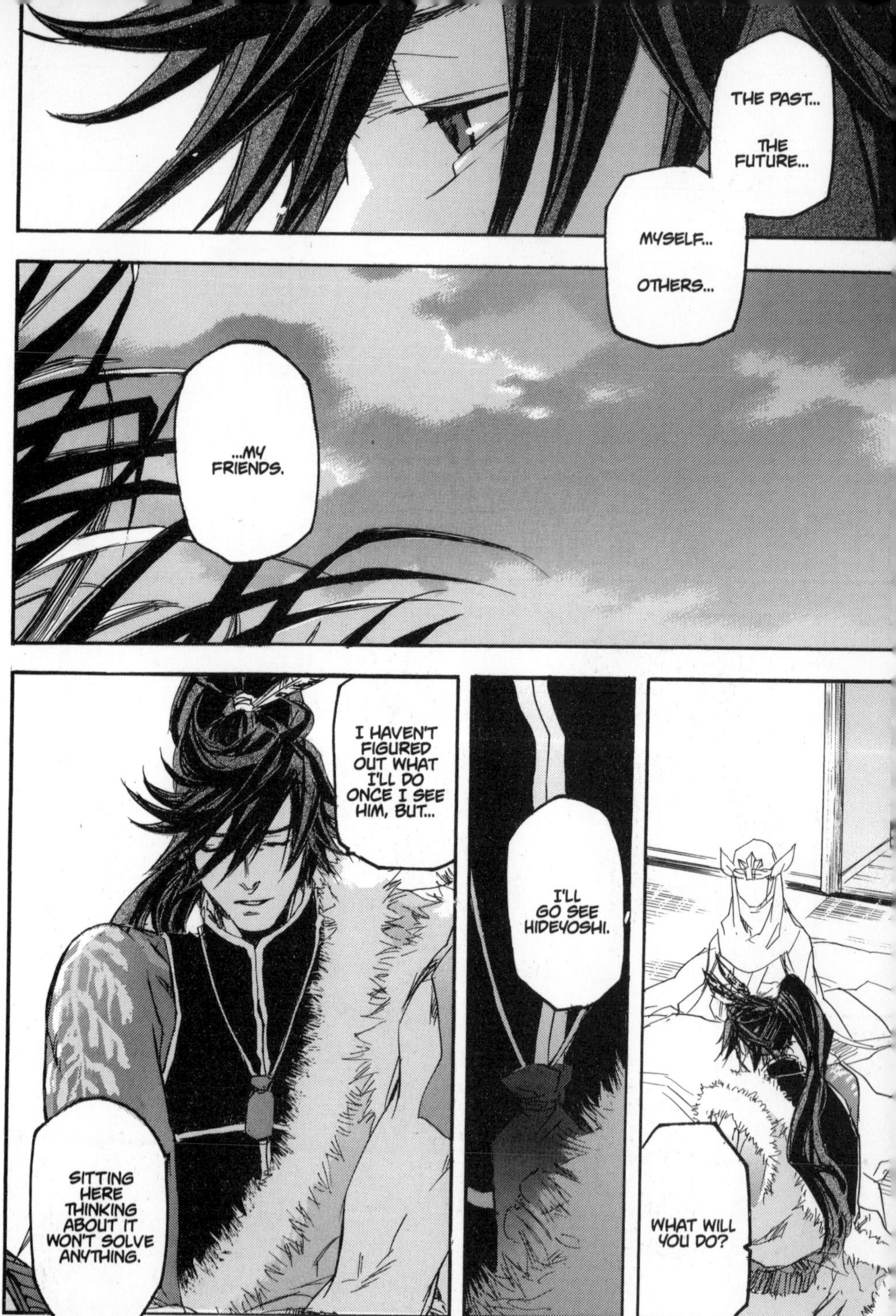
THE PAST... THE FUTURE...
MYSELF... OTHERS...
...MY FRIENDS.
WHAT WILL YOU DO?
I'LL GO SEE HIDEYOSHI.
I HAVEN'T FIGURED OUT WHAT I'LL DO ONCE I SEE HIM, BUT...
SITTING HERE THINKING ABOUT IT WON'T SOLVE ANYTHING.

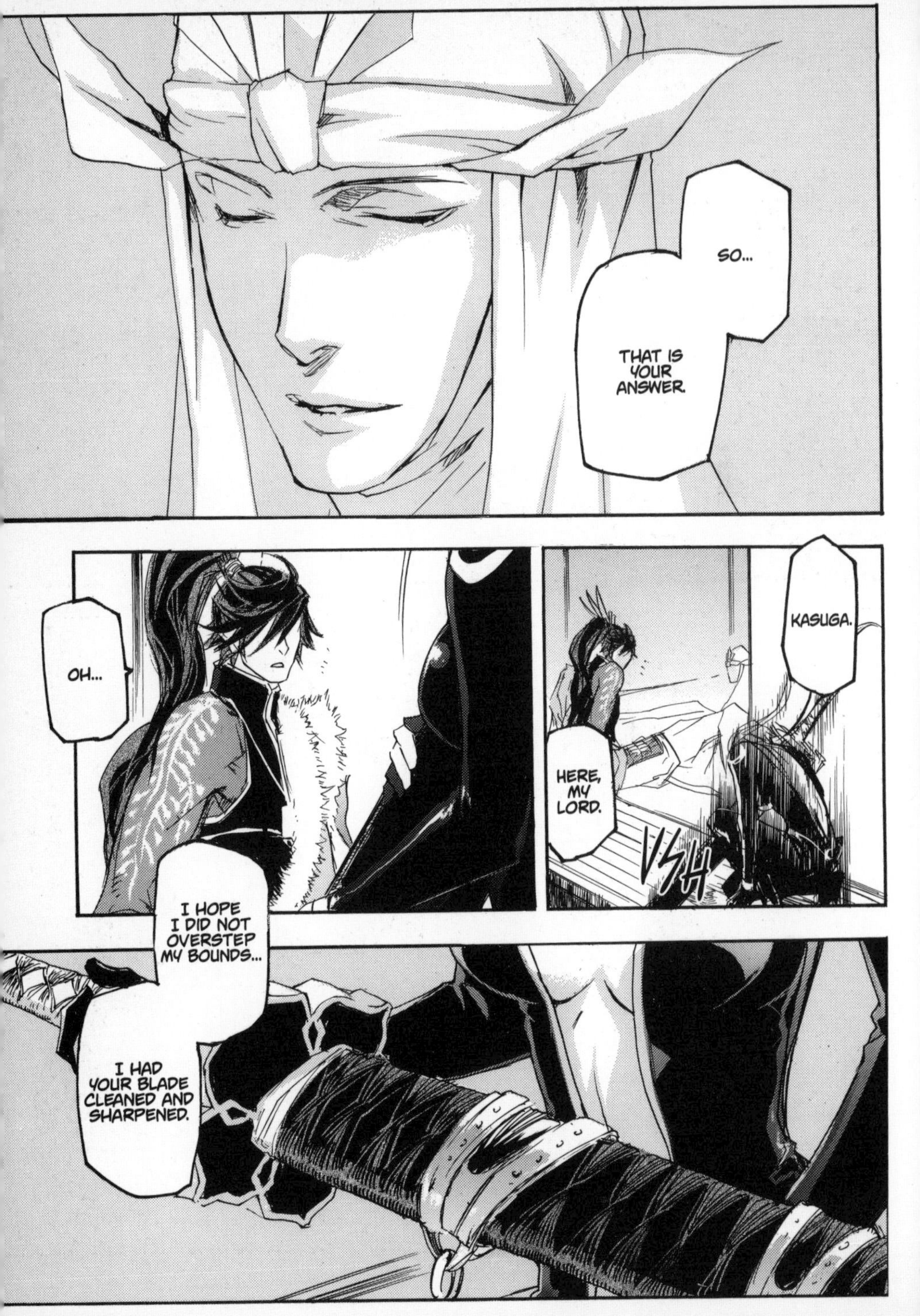
SO...
THAT IS YOUR ANSWER.
KASUGA.
HERE, MY LORD.
VSH
OH...
I HOPE I DID NOT OVERSTEP MY BOUNDS...
I HAD YOUR BLADE CLEANED AND SHARPENED.

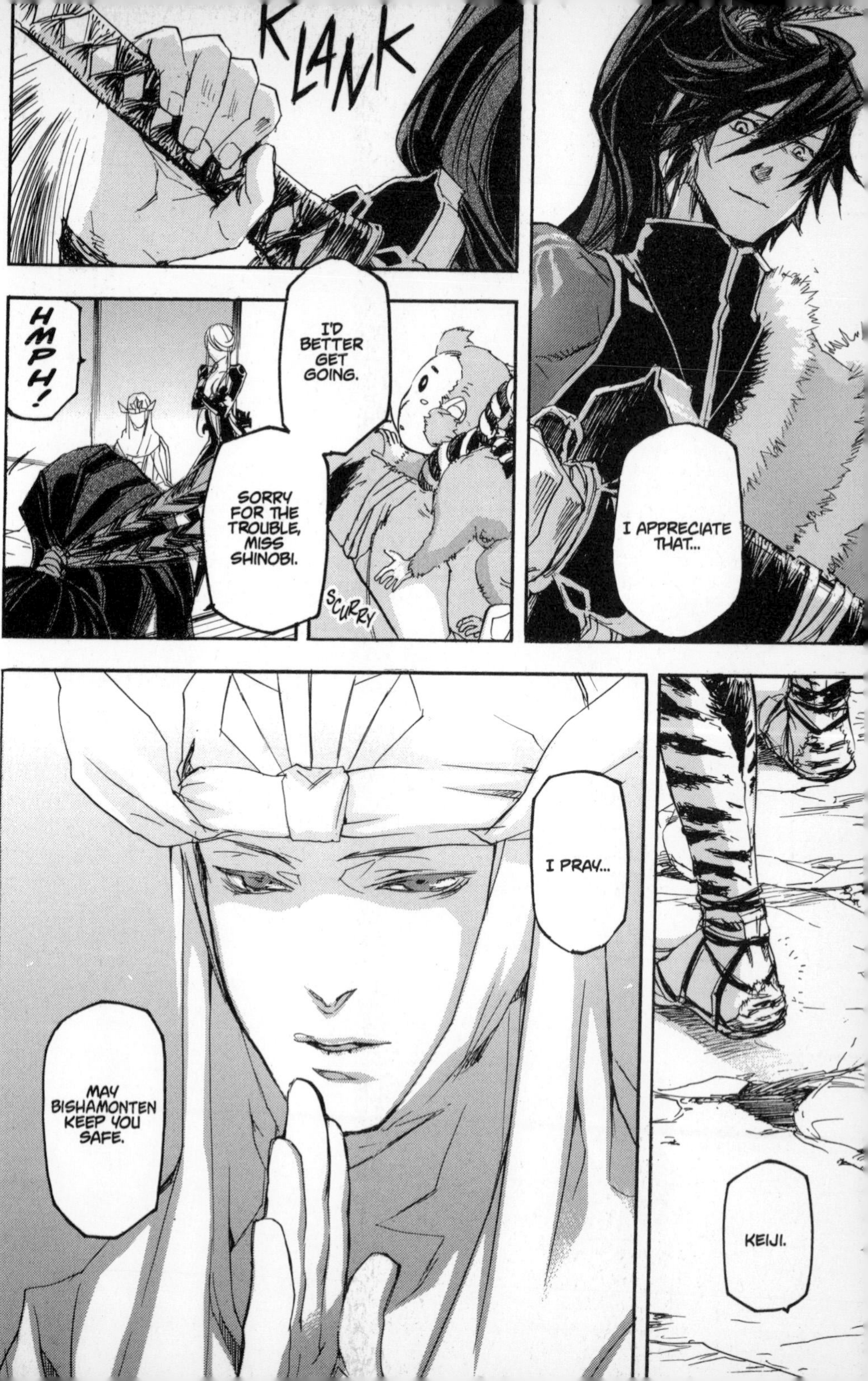
I APPRECIATE THAT...
KLANK
I'D BETTER GET GOING.
HMPH!
SORRY FOR THE TROUBLE, MISS SHINOBI.
SCURRY
KEIJI.
I PRAY...
MAY BISHAMONTEN KEEP YOU SAFE.

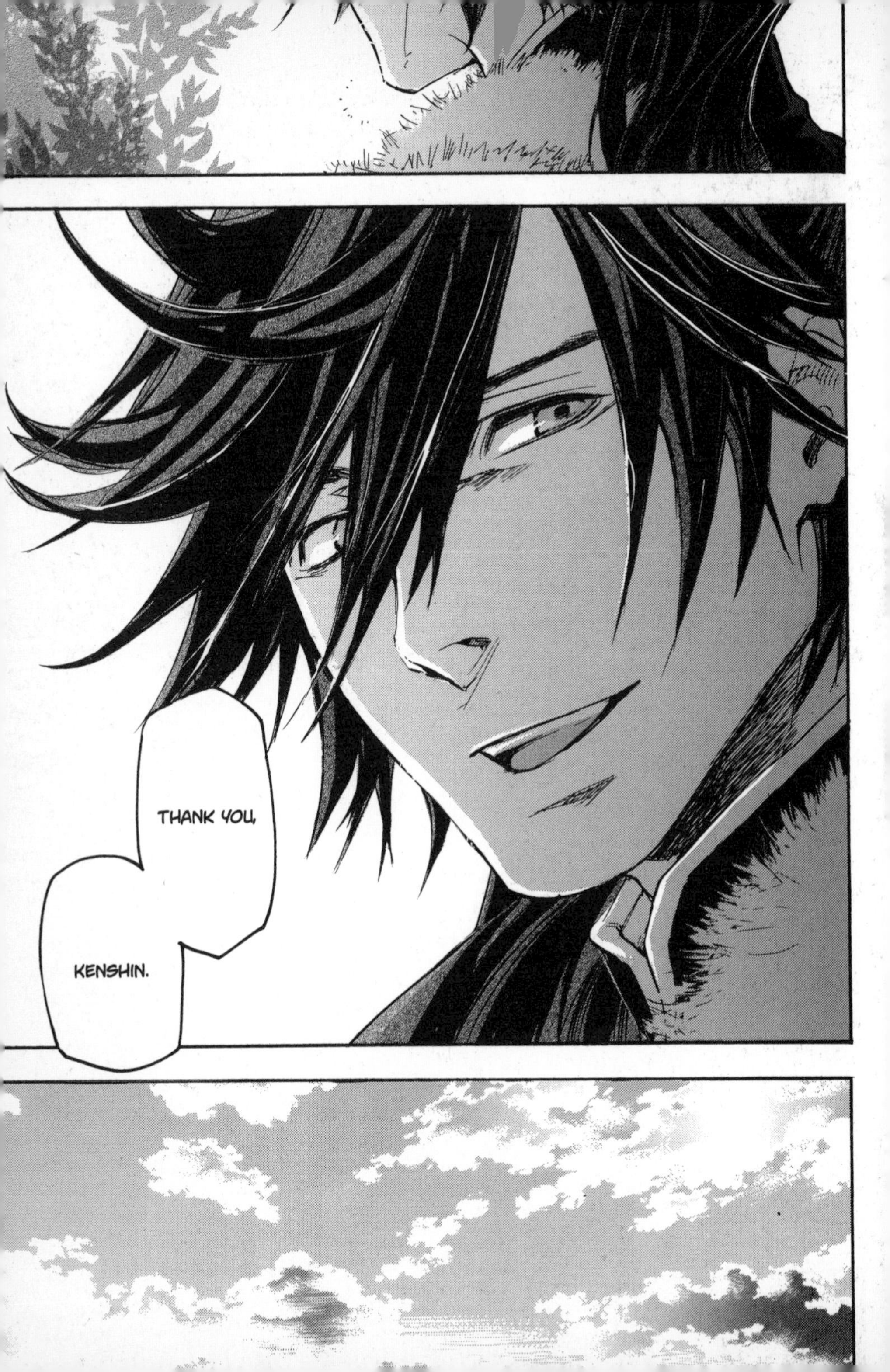
THANK YOU,
KENSHIN.

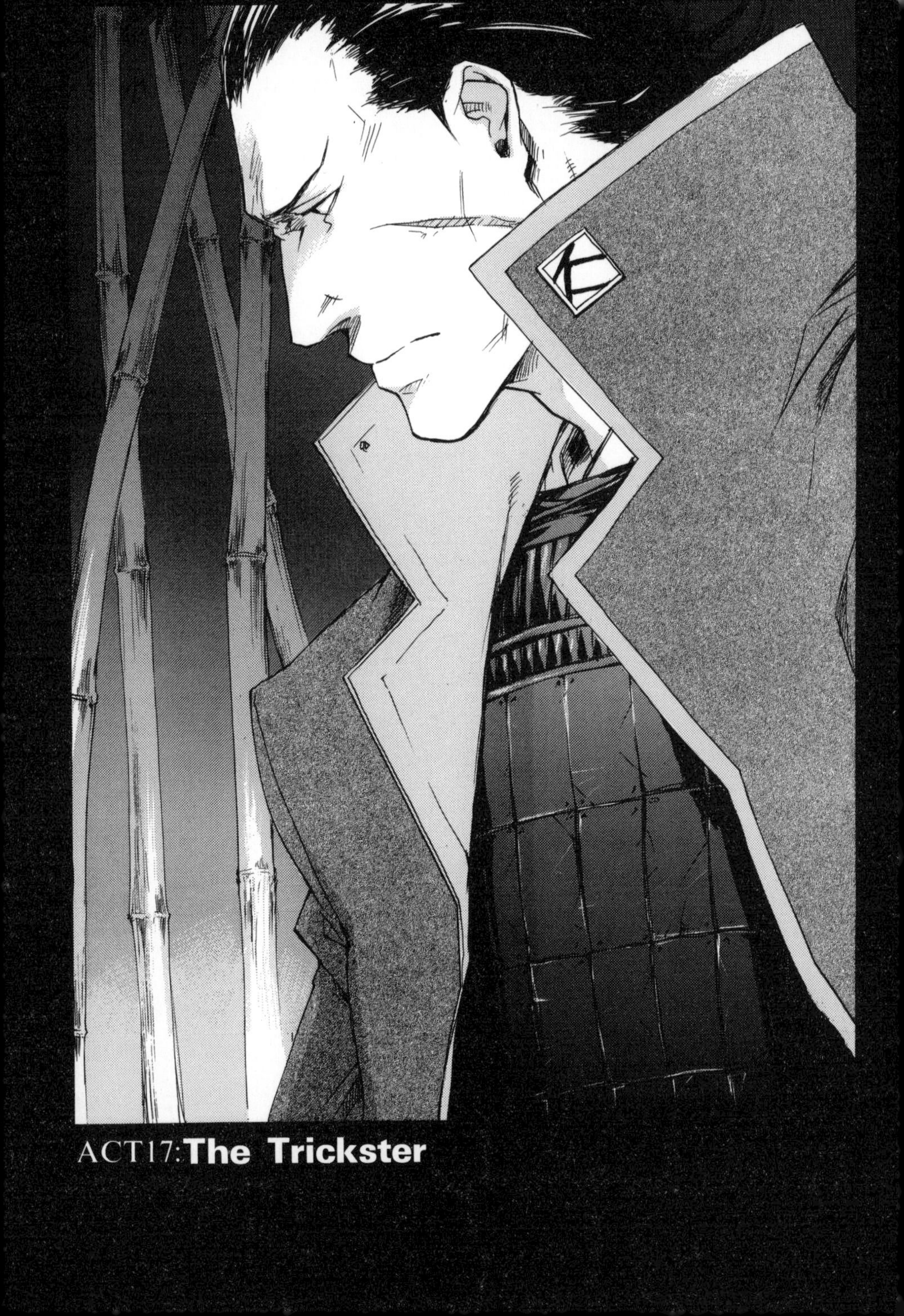
K

ACT17: **The Trickster**

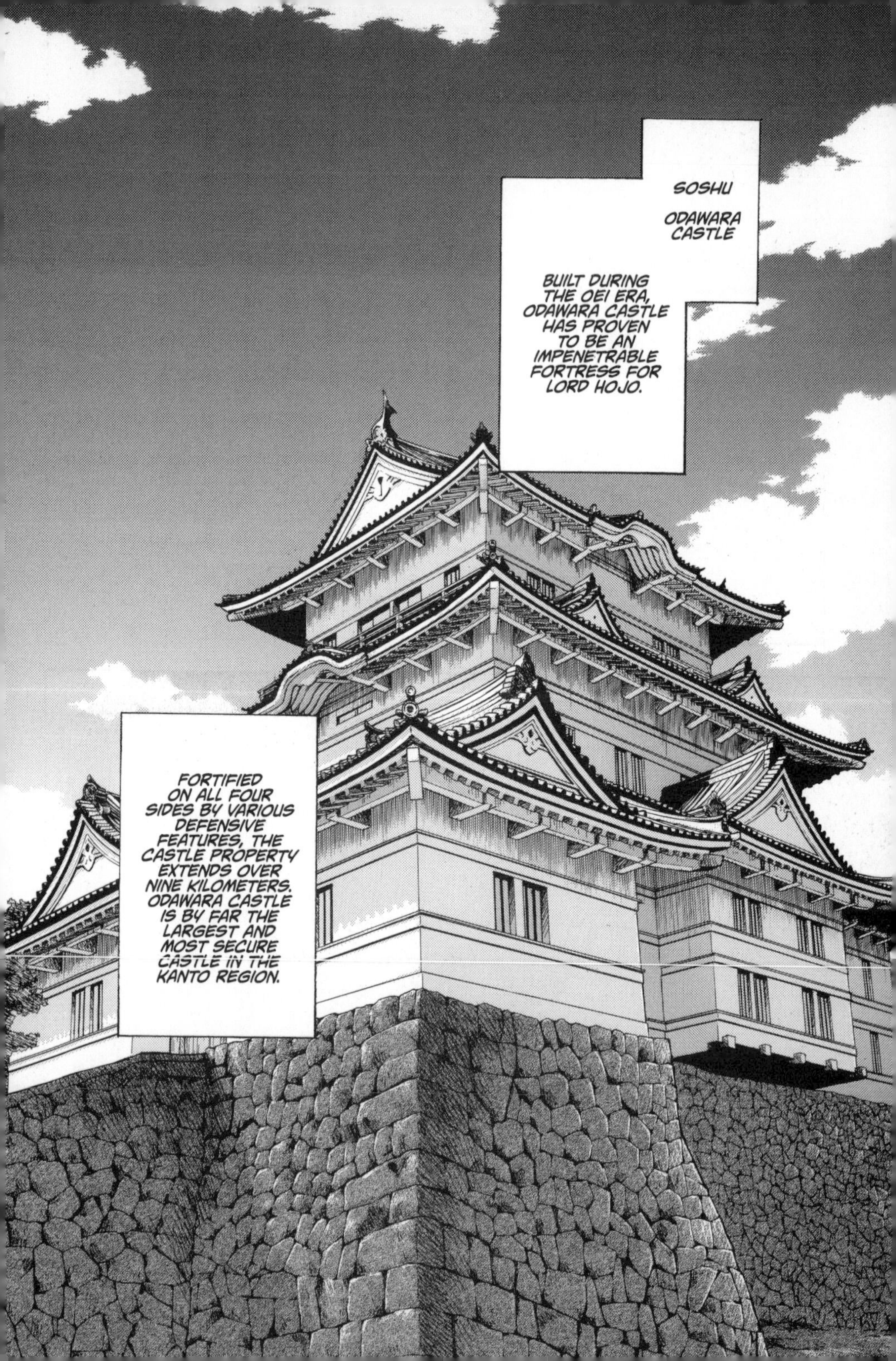
SOSHU
ODAWARA CASTLE
BUILT DURING THE OEI ERA, ODAWARA CASTLE HAS PROVEN TO BE AN IMPENETRABLE FORTRESS FOR LORD HOJO.
FORTIFIED ON ALL FOUR SIDES BY VARIOUS DEFENSIVE FEATURES, THE CASTLE PROPERTY EXTENDS OVER NINE KILOMETERS. ODAWARA CASTLE IS BY FAR THE LARGEST AND MOST SECURE CASTLE IN THE KANTO REGION.

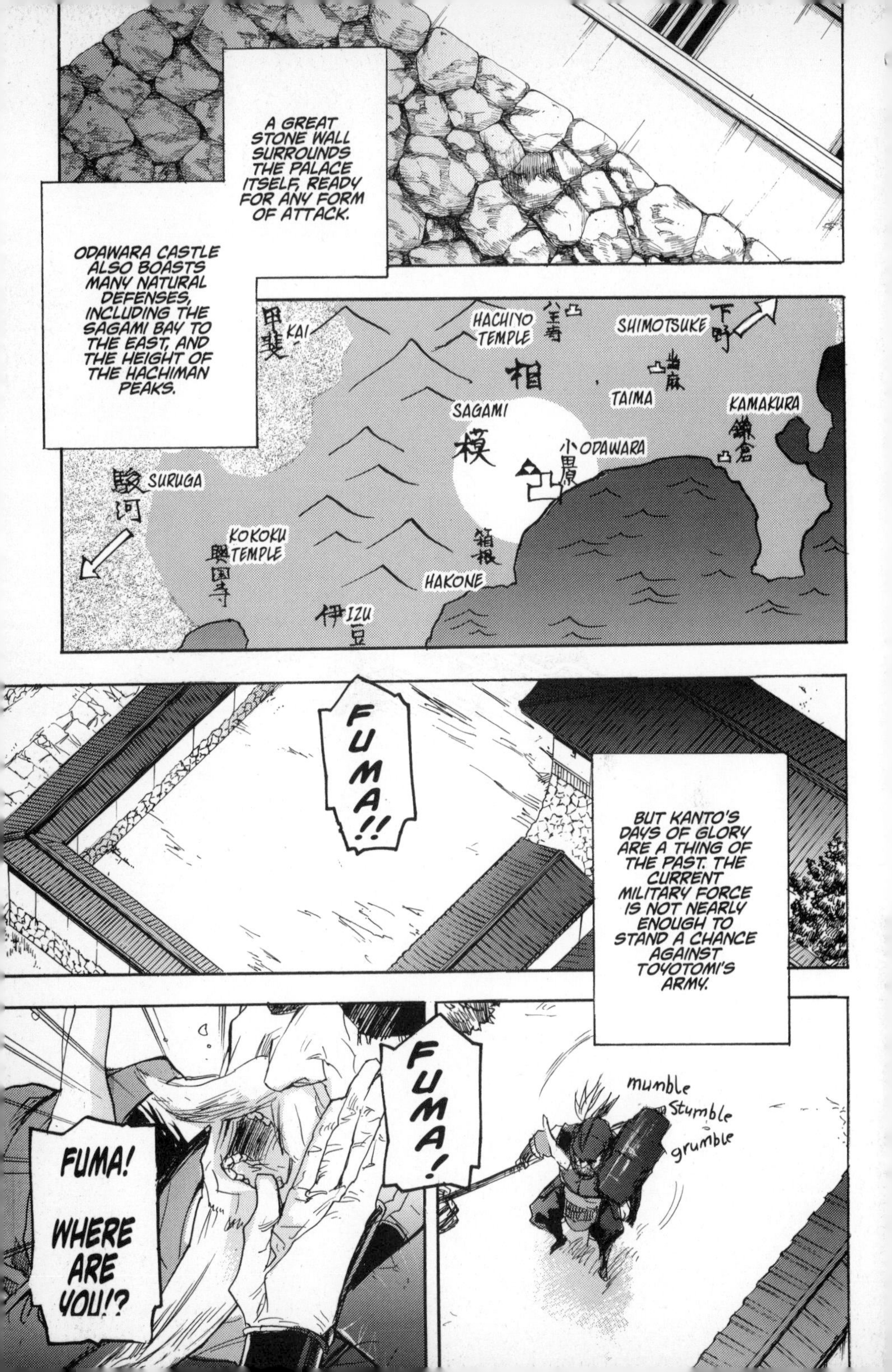
A GREAT STONE WALL SURROUNDS THE PALACE ITSELF, READY FOR ANY FORM OF ATTACK.
ODAWARA CASTLE ALSO BOASTS MANY NATURAL DEFENSES, INCLUDING THE SAGAMI BAY TO THE EAST, AND THE HEIGHT OF THE HACHIMAN PEAKS.
下野 SHIMOTSUKE
HACHIYO TEMPLE
甲斐 KAI
KAMAKURA 鎌倉
TAIMA
相模 SAGAMI
小田原 ODAWARA
駿河 SURUGA
箱根 HAKONE
KOKOKU TEMPLE
伊豆 IZU
BUT KANTO'S DAYS OF GLORY ARE A THING OF THE PAST. THE CURRENT MILITARY FORCE IS NOT NEARLY ENOUGH TO STAND A CHANCE AGAINST TOYOTOMI'S ARMY.
FUMA!!
mumble
stumble
grumble
FUMA!
FUMA!
WHERE ARE YOU!?

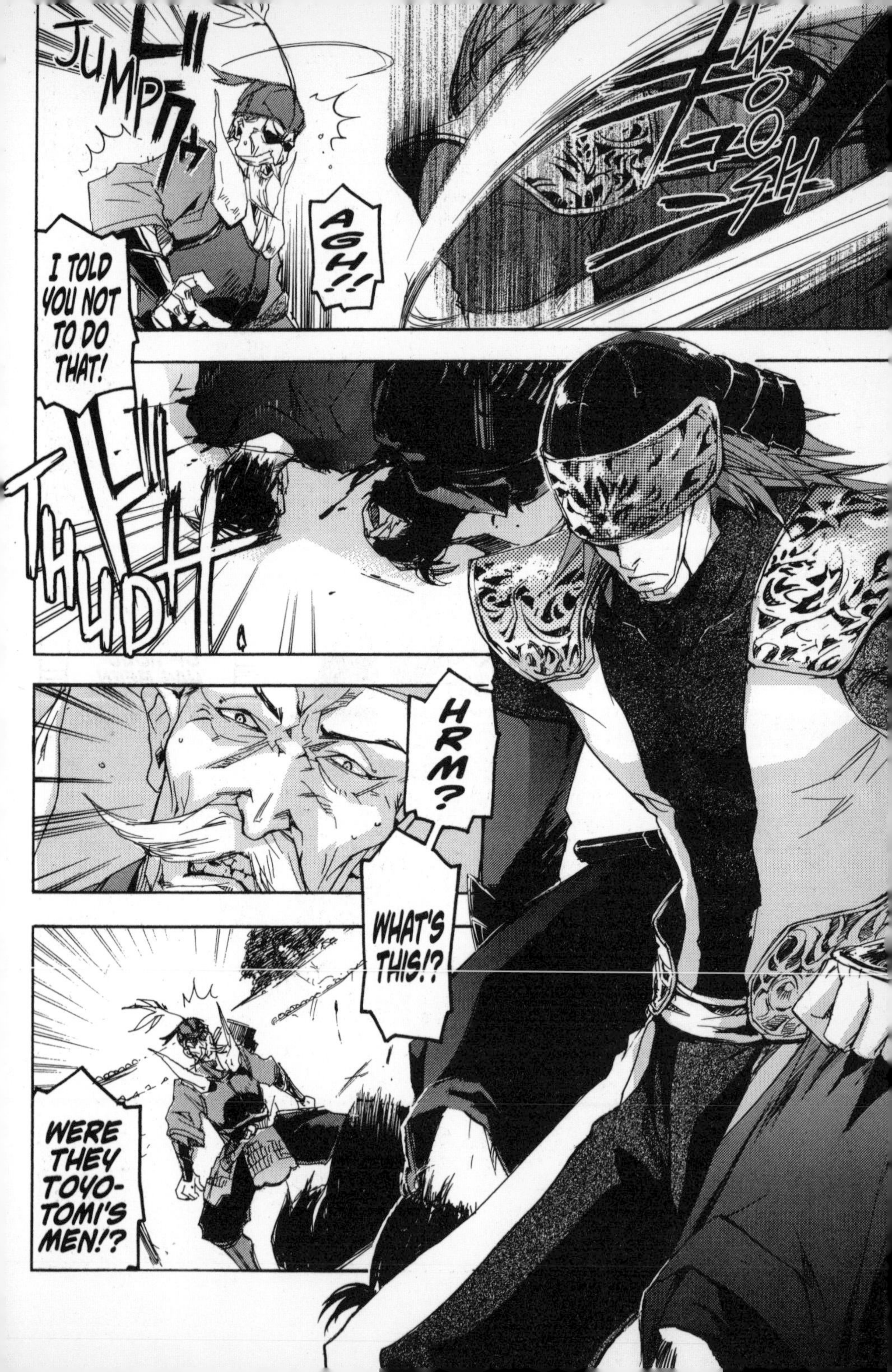
WOOSH
JUMP
AGH!!
I TOLD YOU NOT TO DO THAT!
HRM?
WHAT'S THIS!?
THUD
WERE THEY TOYO-TOMI'S MEN!?

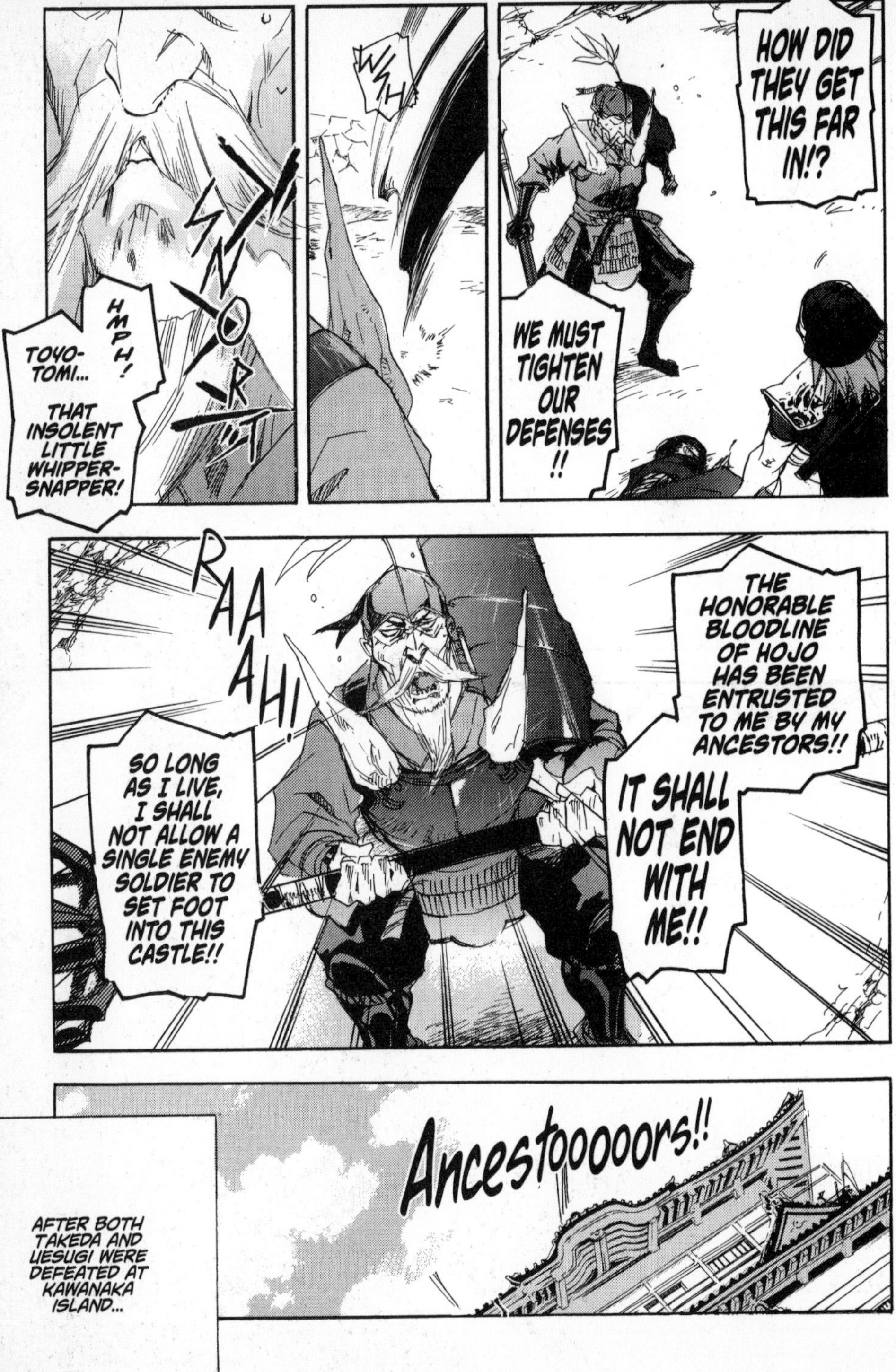
HOW DID THEY GET THIS FAR IN!?
WE MUST TIGHTEN OUR DEFENSES!!
WSH
SNORT
HMPH!
TOYO-TOMI...
THAT INSOLENT LITTLE WHIPPER-SNAPPER!
THE HONORABLE BLOODLINE OF HOJO HAS BEEN ENTRUSTED TO ME BY MY ANCESTORS!!
IT SHALL NOT END WITH ME!!
RAAAH!
SO LONG AS I LIVE, I SHALL NOT ALLOW A SINGLE ENEMY SOLDIER TO SET FOOT INTO THIS CASTLE!!
Ancestoooooors!!
AFTER BOTH TAKEDA AND UESUGI WERE DEFEATED AT KAWANAKA ISLAND...

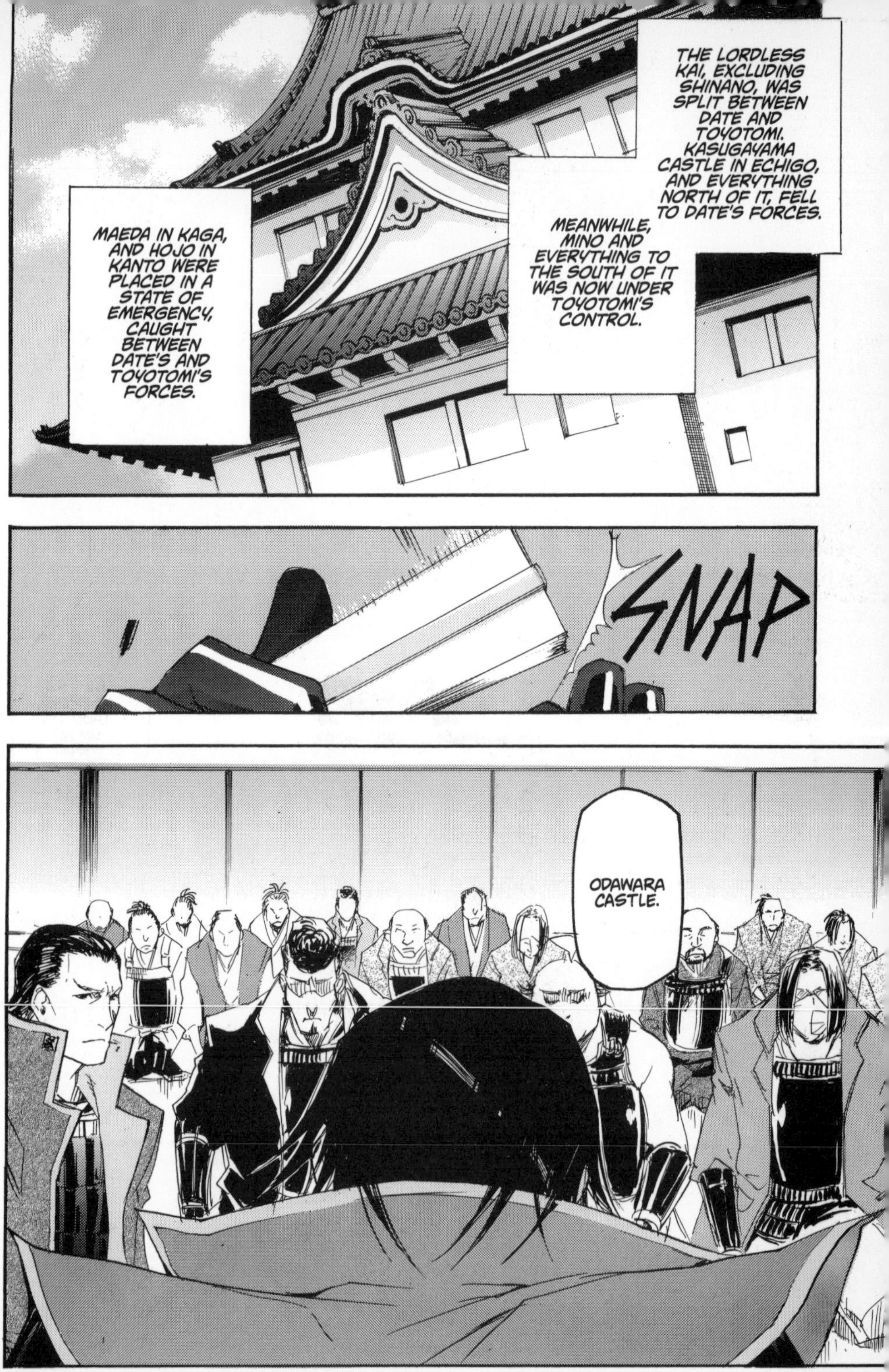
THE LORDLESS KAI, EXCLUDING SHINANO, WAS SPLIT BETWEEN DATE AND TOYOTOMI. KASUGAYAMA CASTLE IN ECHIGO, AND EVERYTHING NORTH OF IT, FELL TO DATE'S FORCES.
MEANWHILE, MINO AND EVERYTHING TO THE SOUTH OF IT WAS NOW UNDER TOYOTOMI'S CONTROL.
MAEDA IN KAGA, AND HOJO IN KANTO WERE PLACED IN A STATE OF EMERGENCY, CAUGHT BETWEEN DATE'S AND TOYOTOMI'S FORCES.
SNAP
ODAWARA CASTLE.

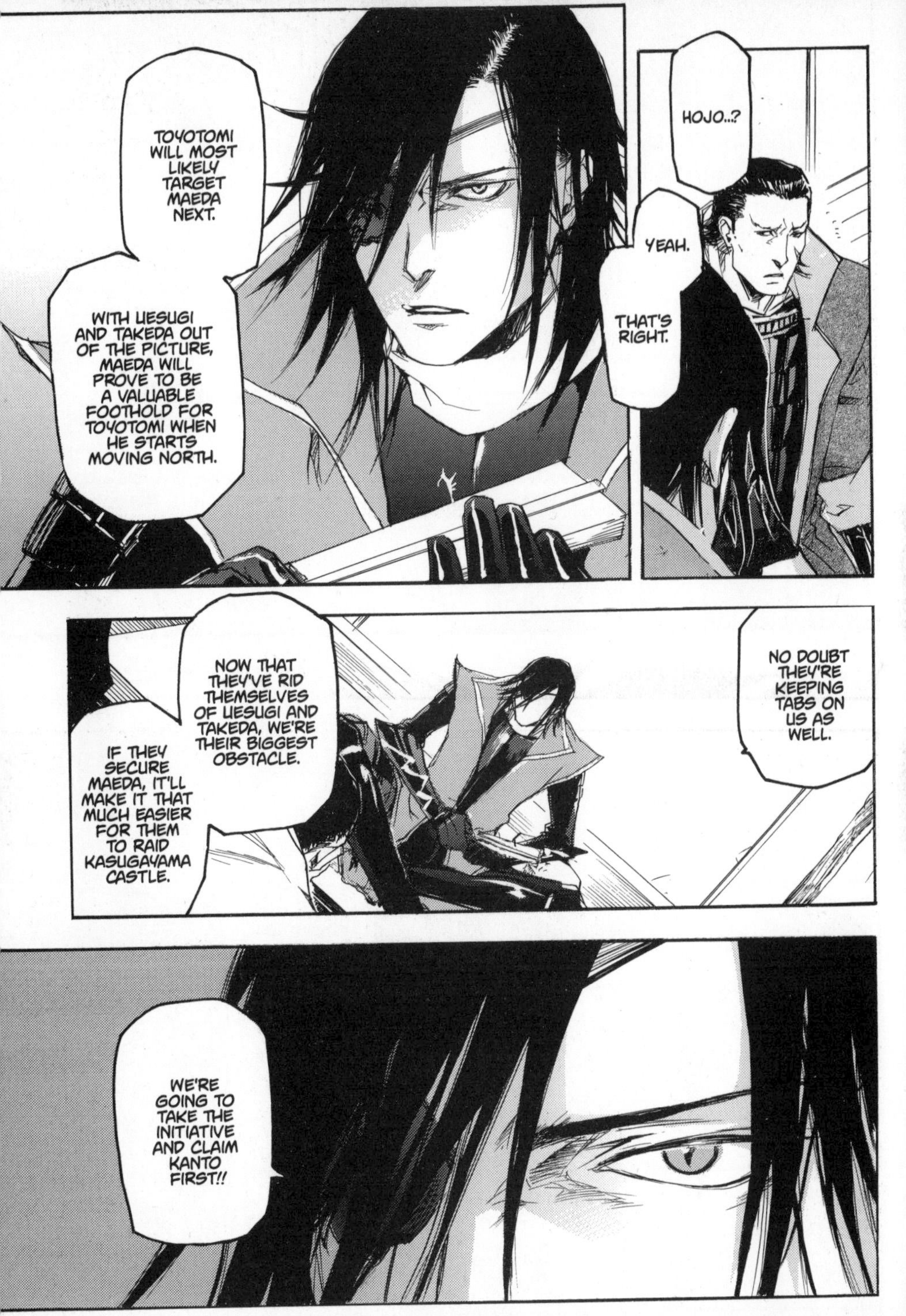
HOJO...?
YEAH.
THAT'S RIGHT.
TOYOTOMI WILL MOST LIKELY TARGET MAEDA NEXT.
WITH UESUGI AND TAKEDA OUT OF THE PICTURE, MAEDA WILL PROVE TO BE A VALUABLE FOOTHOLD FOR TOYOTOMI WHEN HE STARTS MOVING NORTH.
NO DOUBT THEY'RE KEEPING TABS ON US AS WELL.
NOW THAT THEY'VE RID THEMSELVES OF UESUGI AND TAKEDA, WE'RE THEIR BIGGEST OBSTACLE.
IF THEY SECURE MAEDA, IT'LL MAKE IT THAT MUCH EASIER FOR THEM TO RAID KASUGAYAMA CASTLE.
WE'RE GOING TO TAKE THE INITIATIVE AND CLAIM KANTO FIRST!!

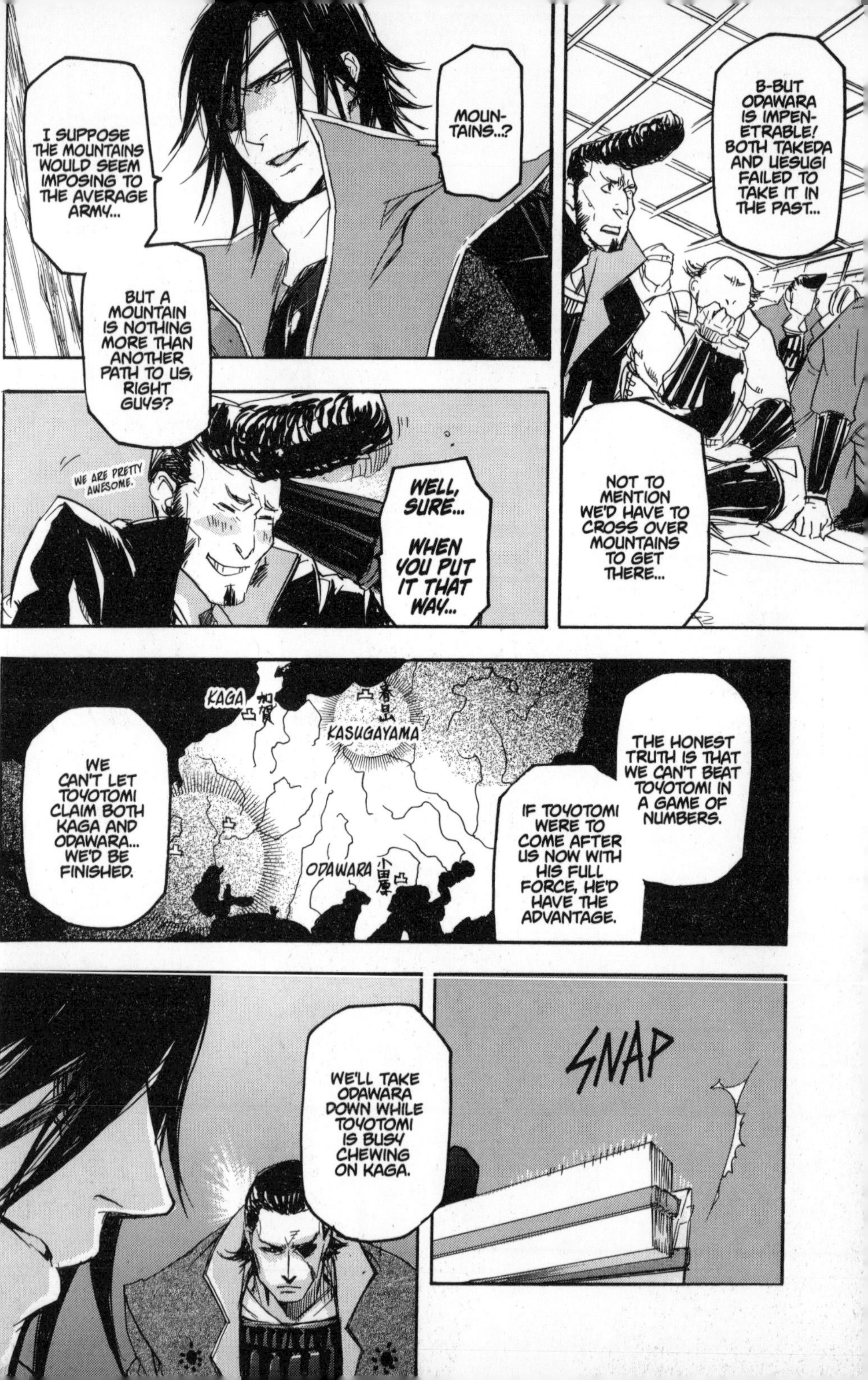
B-BUT ODAWARA IS IMPENETRABLE! BOTH TAKEDA AND UESUGI FAILED TO TAKE IT IN THE PAST...
NOT TO MENTION WE'D HAVE TO CROSS OVER MOUNTAINS TO GET THERE...
MOUNTAINS...?
I SUPPOSE THE MOUNTAINS WOULD SEEM IMPOSING TO THE AVERAGE ARMY...
BUT A MOUNTAIN IS NOTHING MORE THAN ANOTHER PATH TO US, RIGHT GUYS?
WELL, SURE... WHEN YOU PUT IT THAT WAY...
WE ARE PRETTY AWESOME.
KAGA 加賀
春日山 KASUGAYAMA
ODAWARA 小田原
THE HONEST TRUTH IS THAT WE CAN'T BEAT TOYOTOMI IN A GAME OF NUMBERS.
IF TOYOTOMI WERE TO COME AFTER US NOW WITH HIS FULL FORCE, HE'D HAVE THE ADVANTAGE.
WE CAN'T LET TOYOTOMI CLAIM BOTH KAGA AND ODAWARA... WE'D BE FINISHED.
SNAP
WE'LL TAKE ODAWARA DOWN WHILE TOYOTOMI IS BUSY CHEWING ON KAGA.

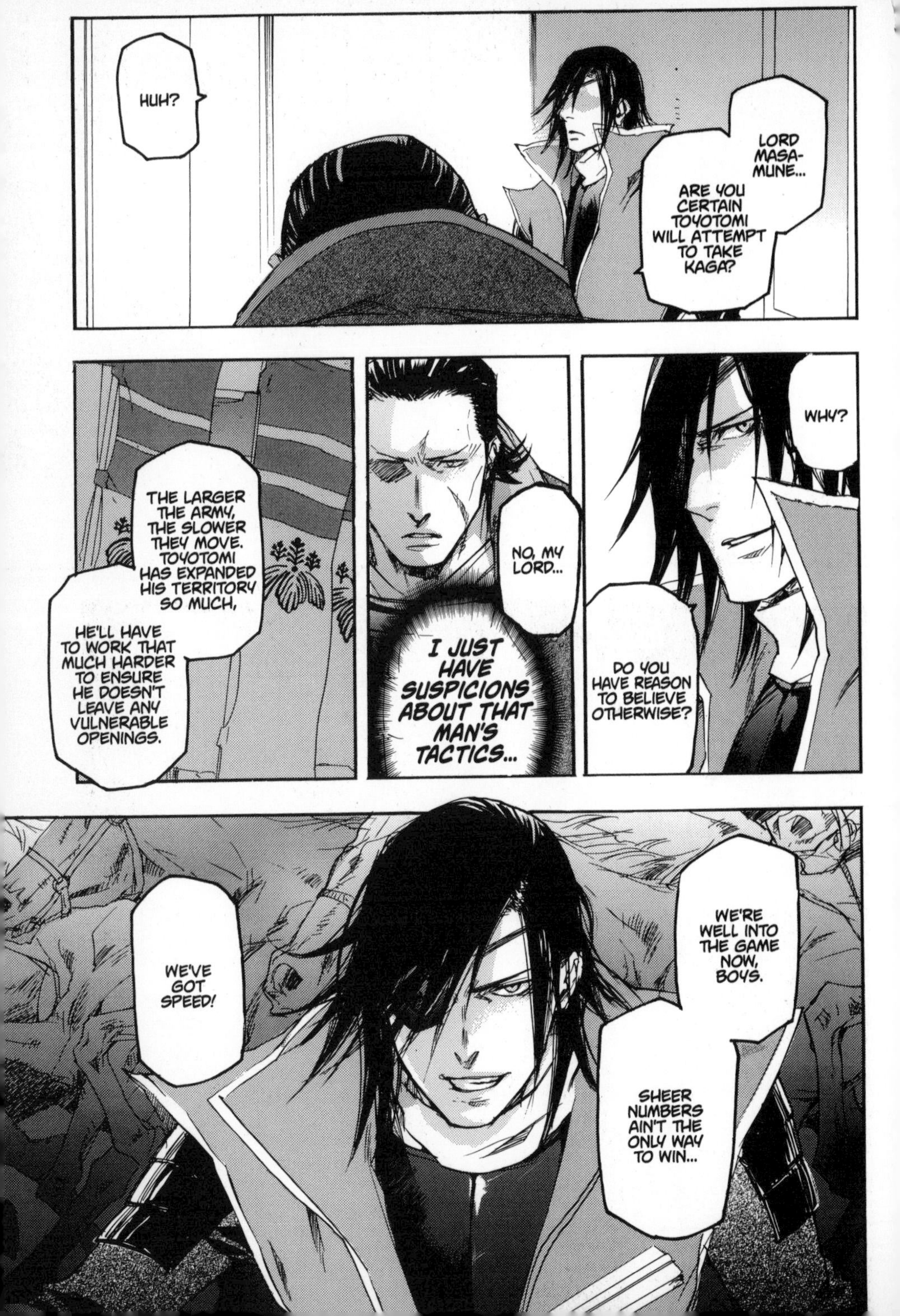
LORD MASAMUNE... ARE YOU CERTAIN TOYOTOMI WILL ATTEMPT TO TAKE KAGA?
HUH?
WHY?
DO YOU HAVE REASON TO BELIEVE OTHERWISE?
NO, MY LORD...
I JUST HAVE SUSPICIONS ABOUT THAT MAN'S TACTICS...
THE LARGER THE ARMY, THE SLOWER THEY MOVE. TOYOTOMI HAS EXPANDED HIS TERRITORY SO MUCH,
HE'LL HAVE TO WORK THAT MUCH HARDER TO ENSURE HE DOESN'T LEAVE ANY VULNERABLE OPENINGS.
WE'RE WELL INTO THE GAME NOW, BOYS.
SHEER NUMBERS AIN'T THE ONLY WAY TO WIN...
WE'VE GOT SPEED!

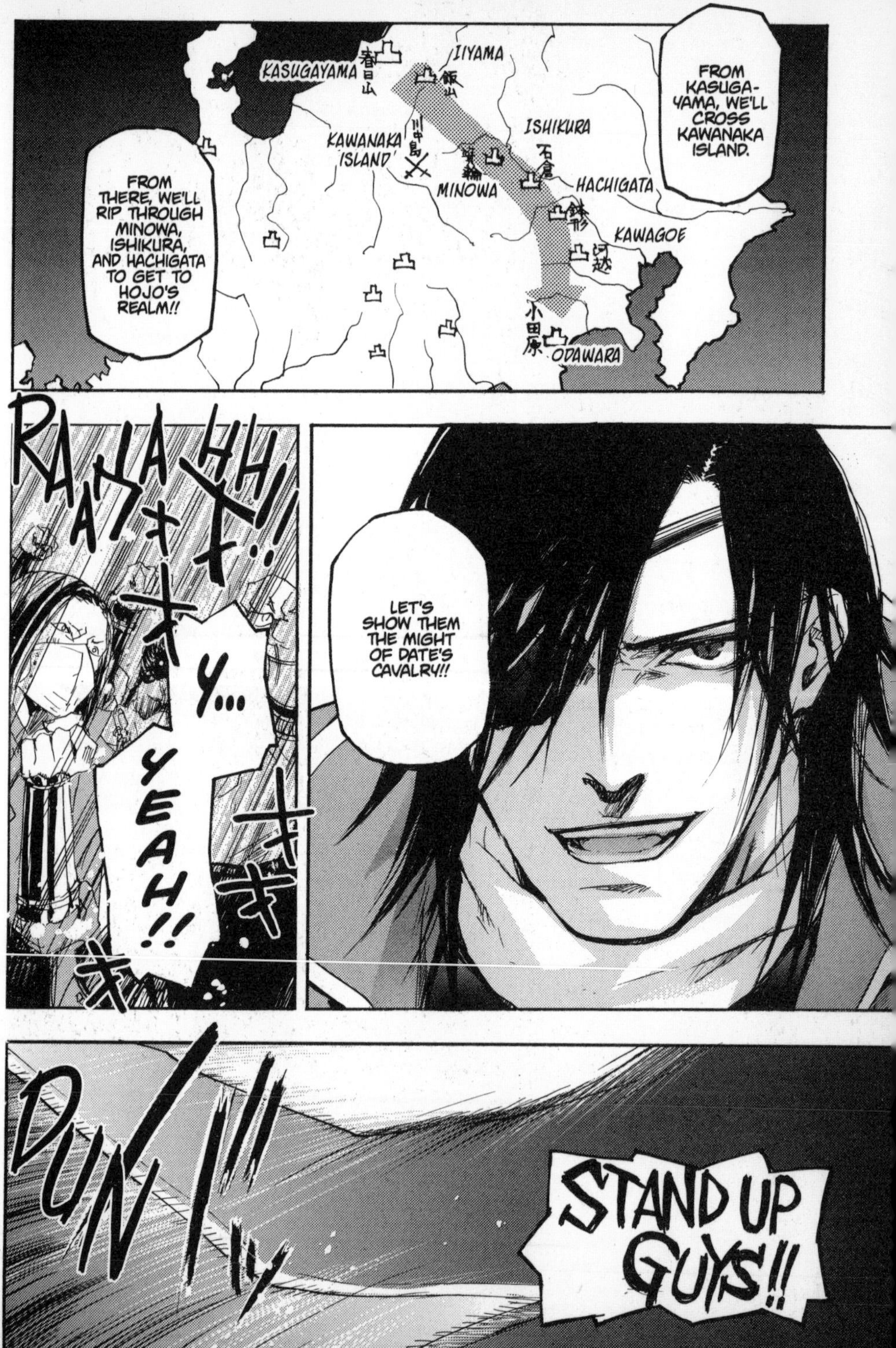
FROM KASUGA-YAMA, WE'LL CROSS KAWANAKA ISLAND.
FROM THERE, WE'LL RIP THROUGH MINOWA, ISHIKURA, AND HACHIGATA TO GET TO HOJO'S REALM!!
KASUGAYAMA
IIYAMA
KAWANAKA ISLAND
ISHIKURA
MINOWA
HACHIGATA
KAWAGOE
ODAWARA
LET'S SHOW THEM THE MIGHT OF DATE'S CAVALRY!!
RAAAAHHH!!
Y...
YEAH!!
STAND UP GUYS!!
DUN!!

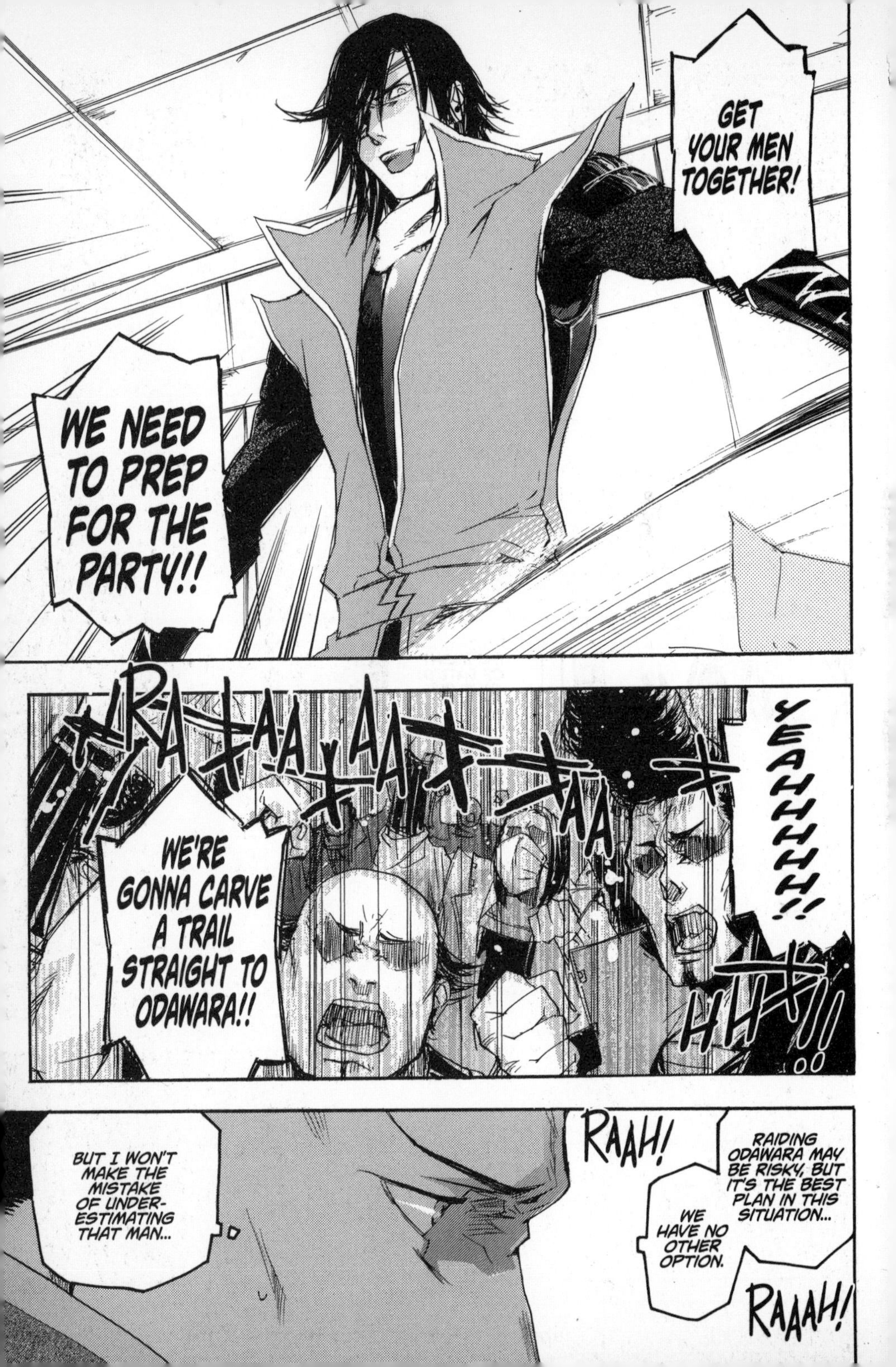
GET YOUR MEN TOGETHER!
WE NEED TO PREP FOR THE PARTY!!
YEAHHHHHH!!
RAAAAAAAAA
WE'RE GONNA CARVE A TRAIL STRAIGHT TO ODAWARA!!
HH!!
RAAH!
RAIDING ODAWARA MAY BE RISKY, BUT IT'S THE BEST PLAN IN THIS SITUATION...
WE HAVE NO OTHER OPTION.
RAAAH!
BUT I WON'T MAKE THE MISTAKE OF UNDER-ESTIMATING THAT MAN...

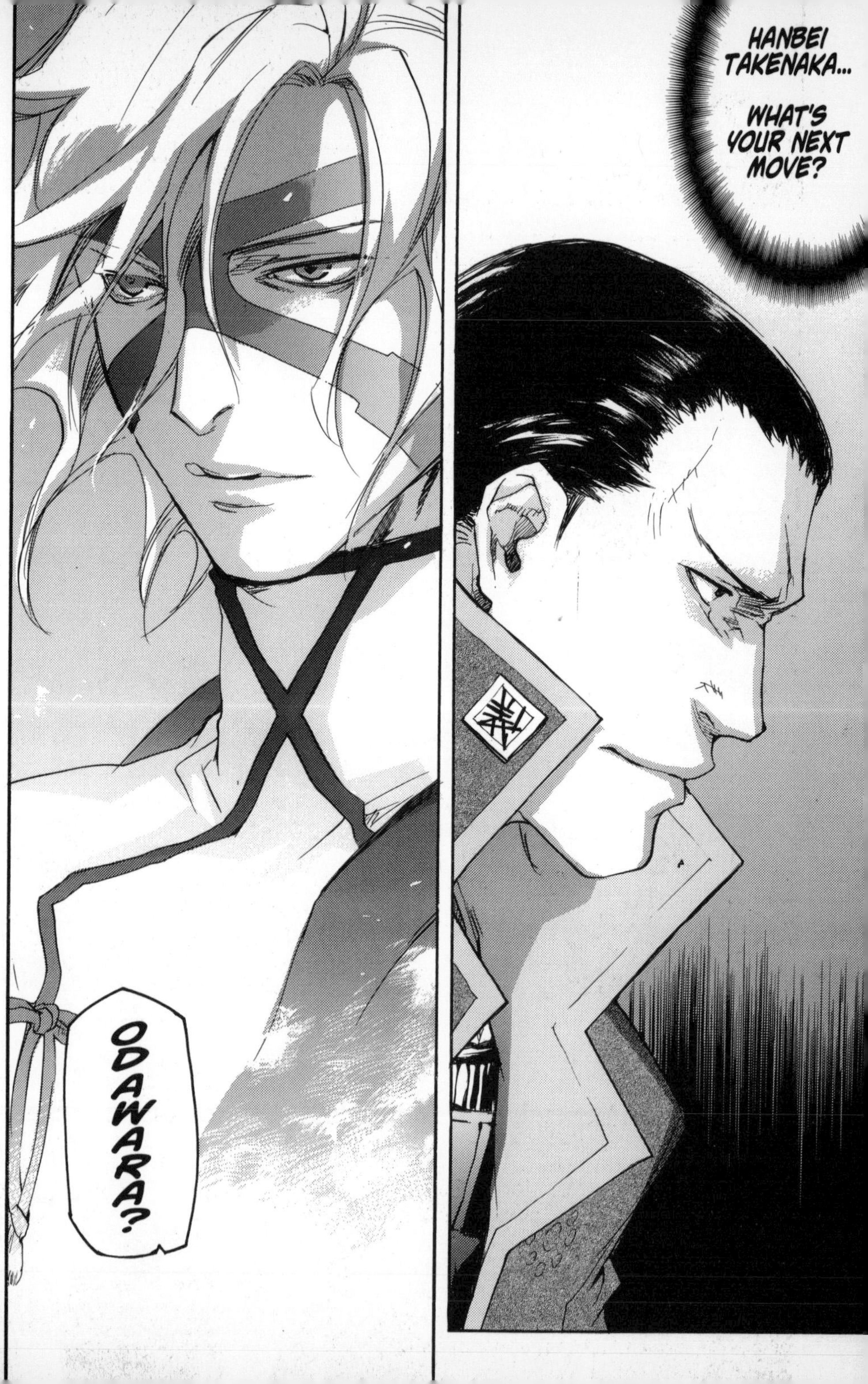
HANBEI TAKENAKA...
WHAT'S YOUR NEXT MOVE?
ODAWARA?

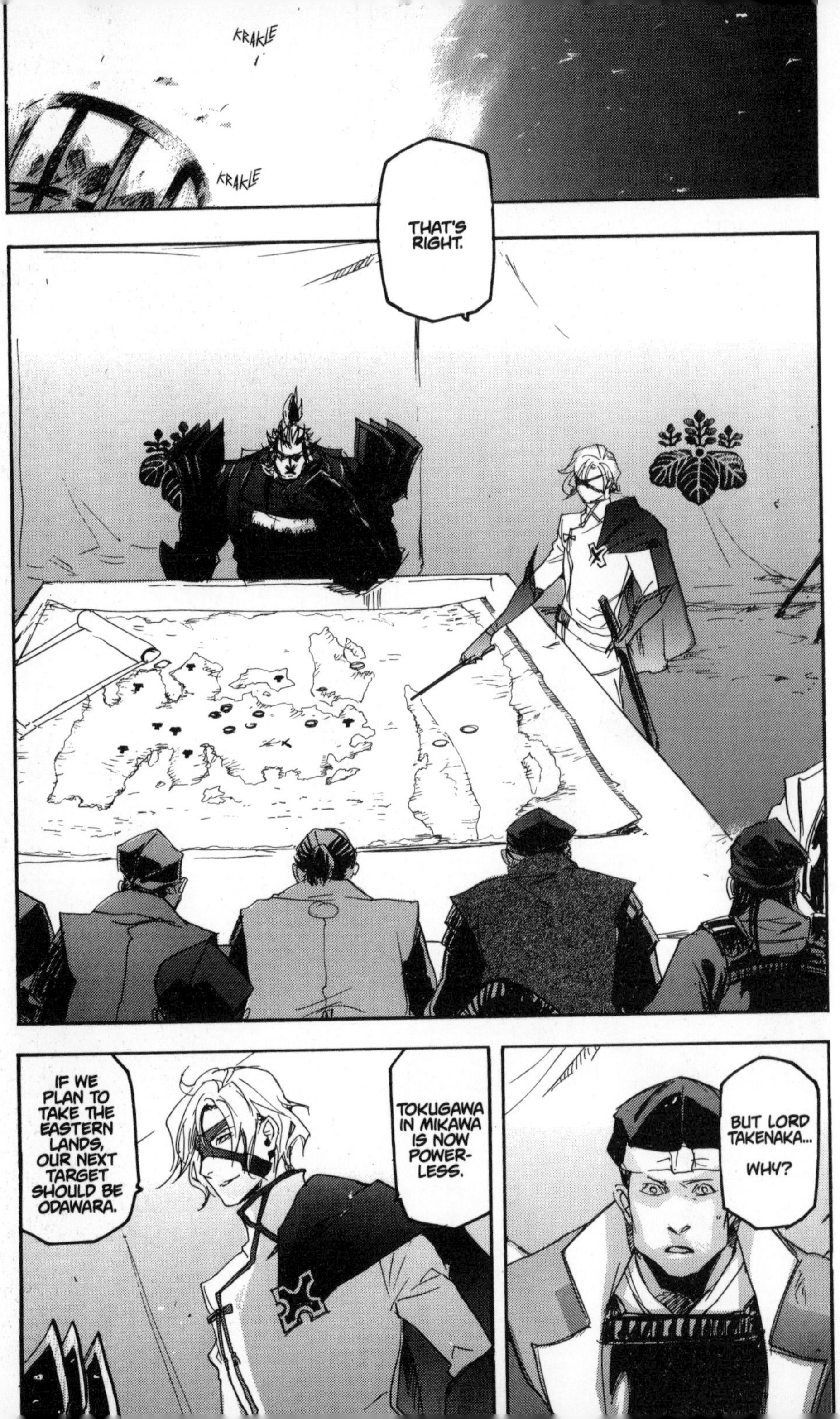
KRAKLE
KRAKLE
THAT'S RIGHT.
BUT LORD TAKENAKA... WHY?
TOKUGAWA IN MIKAWA IS NOW POWERLESS.
IF WE PLAN TO TAKE THE EASTERN LANDS, OUR NEXT TARGET SHOULD BE ODAWARA.

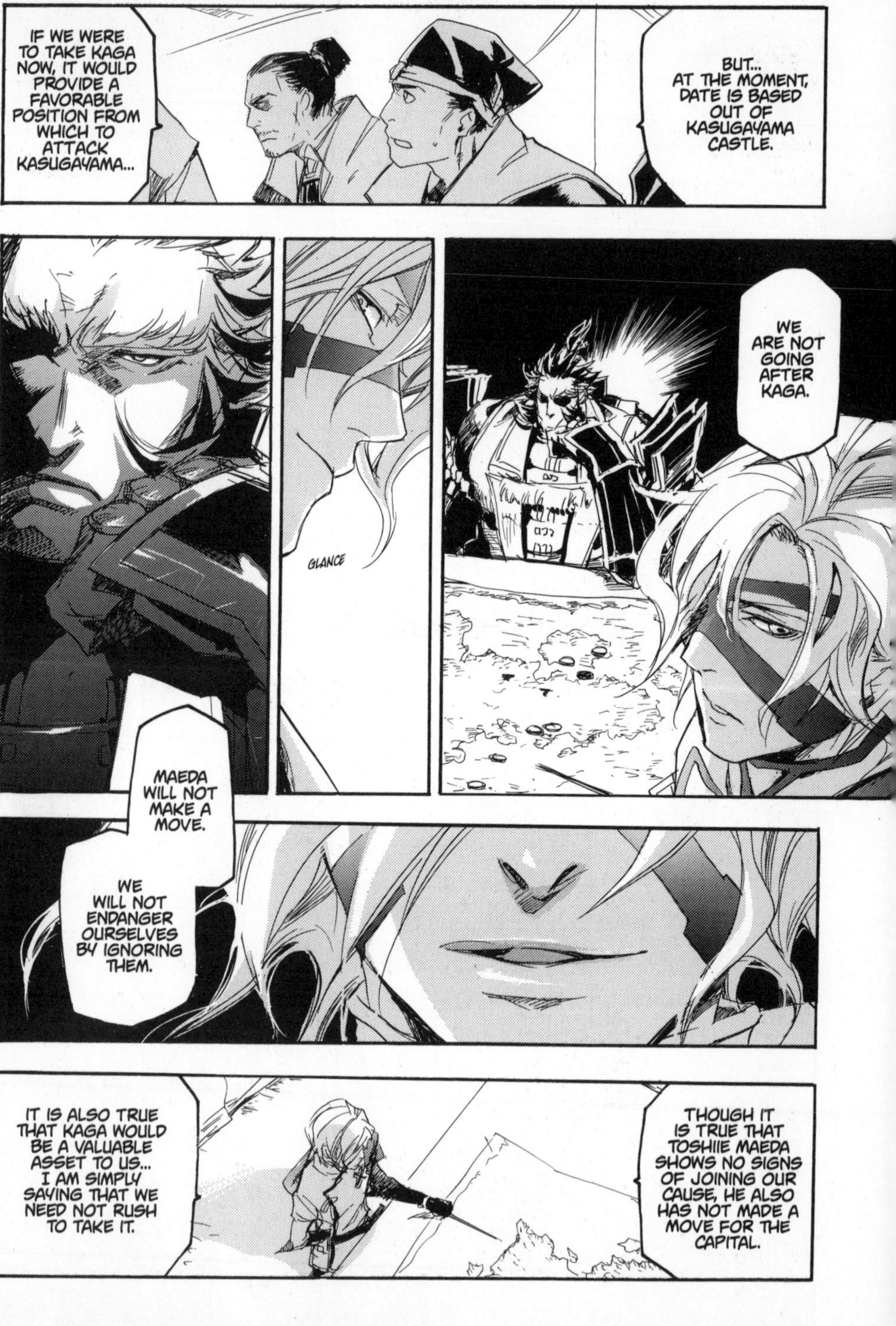
BUT... AT THE MOMENT, DATE IS BASED OUT OF KASUGAYAMA CASTLE.
IF WE WERE TO TAKE KAGA NOW, IT WOULD PROVIDE A FAVORABLE POSITION FROM WHICH TO ATTACK KASUGAYAMA...
WE ARE NOT GOING AFTER KAGA.
GLANCE
MAEDA WILL NOT MAKE A MOVE.
WE WILL NOT ENDANGER OURSELVES BY IGNORING THEM.
THOUGH IT IS TRUE THAT TOSHIIE MAEDA SHOWS NO SIGNS OF JOINING OUR CAUSE, HE ALSO HAS NOT MADE A MOVE FOR THE CAPITAL.
IT IS ALSO TRUE THAT KAGA WOULD BE A VALUABLE ASSET TO US... I AM SIMPLY SAYING THAT WE NEED NOT RUSH TO TAKE IT.

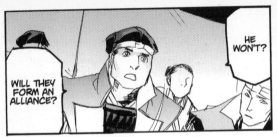

DATE WILL NOT ATTACK KAGA.
HE WON'T?
WILL THEY FORM AN ALLIANCE?
NO.
DATE WILL GO AFTER ODAWARA CASTLE, JUST AS WE WILL.
DATE IS CURRENTLY HOLED UP IN KASUG-AYAMA CASTLE.
KAGA IS JUST A STONE'S THROW AWAY, BUT HE WILL NOT BE TEMPTED BY IT. INSTEAD, HE WILL HEAD STRAIGHT SOUTH TO ODAWARA.
春日山
KASUGAYAMA CASTLE
加賀
KAGA
WHY..?
ODAWARA
小田原
BECAUSE HE WOULD NOT BE ABLE TO FIGHT FROM KAGA.
春日山
KASUGAYAMA
加賀
KAGA
信濃
SHINANO
INABAYAMA
IF DATE DID GO AFTER KAGA, HE'D BE SURROUNDED ONCE WE MOVED INTO SHINANO.

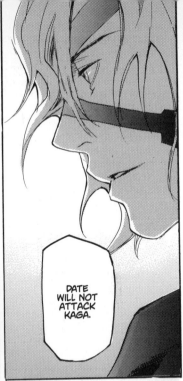

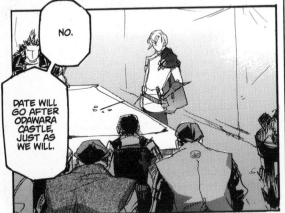

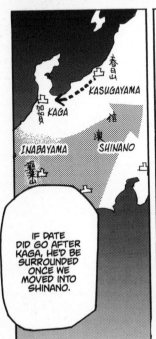

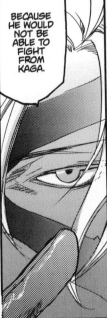

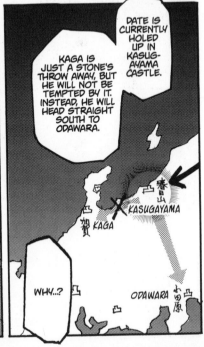

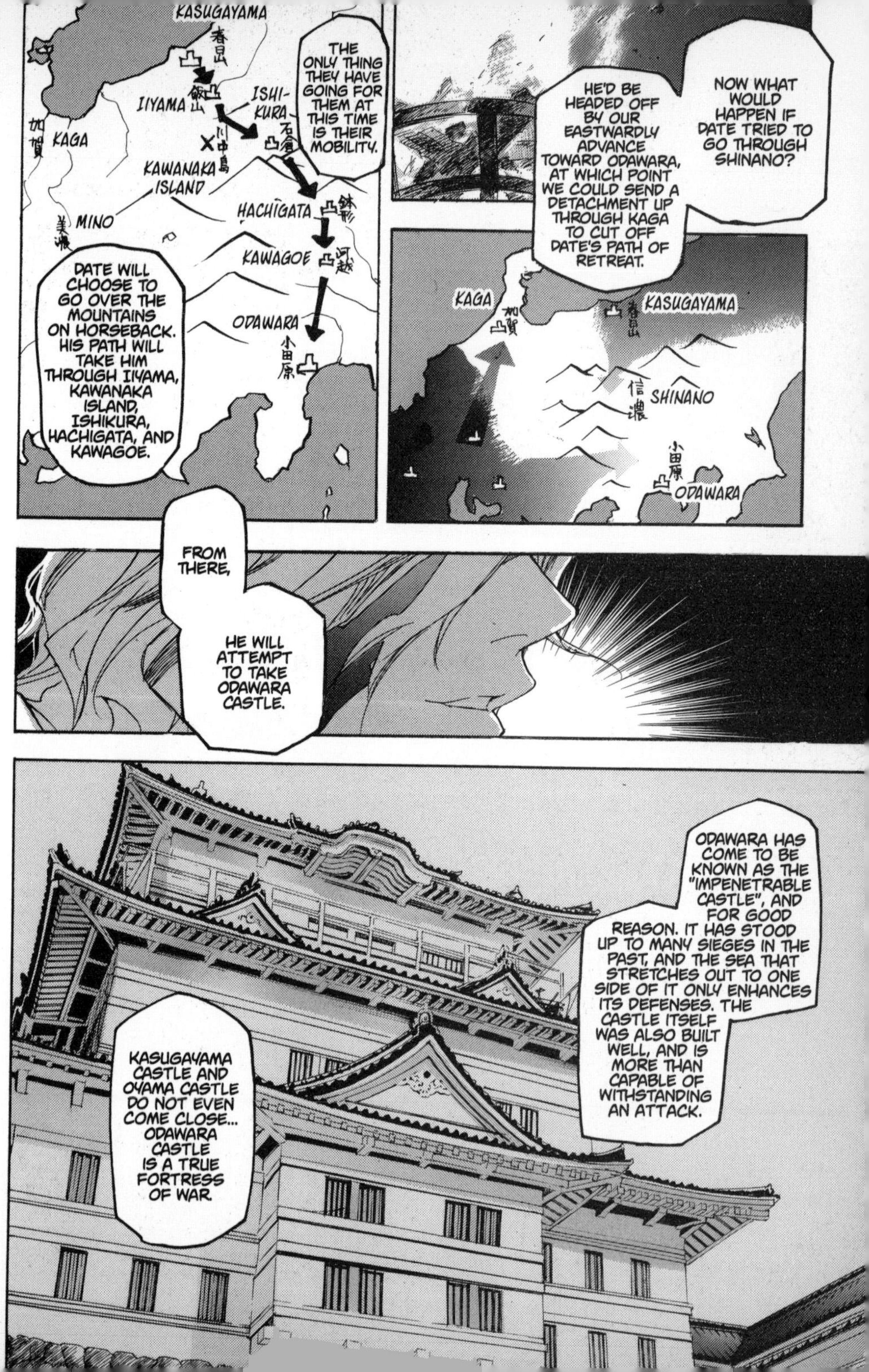
NOW WHAT WOULD HAPPEN IF DATE TRIED TO GO THROUGH SHINANO?
HE'D BE HEADED OFF BY OUR EASTWARDLY ADVANCE TOWARD ODAWARA, AT WHICH POINT WE COULD SEND A DETACHMENT UP THROUGH KAGA TO CUT OFF DATE'S PATH OF RETREAT.
KASUGAYAMA 春日山
KAGA 加賀
SHINANO 信濃
小田原 ODAWARA
THE ONLY THING THEY HAVE GOING FOR THEM AT THIS TIME IS THEIR MOBILITY.
KASUGAYAMA 春日山
ISHI-KURA 石倉
IIYAMA 飯山
加賀 KAGA
川中島 KAWANAKA ISLAND
美濃 MINO
HACHIGATA 鉢形
KAWAGOE 河越
ODAWARA 小田原
DATE WILL CHOOSE TO GO OVER THE MOUNTAINS ON HORSEBACK. HIS PATH WILL TAKE HIM THROUGH IIYAMA, KAWANAKA ISLAND, ISHIKURA, HACHIGATA, AND KAWAGOE.
FROM THERE,
HE WILL ATTEMPT TO TAKE ODAWARA CASTLE.
ODAWARA HAS COME TO BE KNOWN AS THE "IMPENETRABLE CASTLE", AND FOR GOOD REASON. IT HAS STOOD UP TO MANY SIEGES IN THE PAST, AND THE SEA THAT STRETCHES OUT TO ONE SIDE OF IT ONLY ENHANCES ITS DEFENSES. THE CASTLE ITSELF WAS ALSO BUILT WELL, AND IS MORE THAN CAPABLE OF WITHSTANDING AN ATTACK.
KASUGAYAMA CASTLE AND OYAMA CASTLE DO NOT EVEN COME CLOSE... ODAWARA CASTLE IS A TRUE FORTRESS OF WAR.

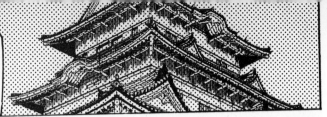

OLD MAN HOJO IS JUST BARELY CLINGING TO LIFE AS IT IS. THE POTENTIAL OF ODAWARA CASTLE IS WASTED ON THE OLD FOOL.

IF WE PLAN TO WAGE WAR IN THE KANTO REGION, ODAWARA CASTLE WILL BE OUR BASE OF OPERATIONS.

IN FACT, I WOULD DARE SAY

THE ONE WHO GAINS CONTROL OF ODAWARA CASTLE IS THE ONE WHO WILL TAKE ALL OF KANTO.

ALL OF KANTO...

THIS PLAN MAY SEEM A BIT RISKY AT FIRST GLANCE, BUT I...

...NAY, HE... WOULD HAVE IT NO OTHER WAY.

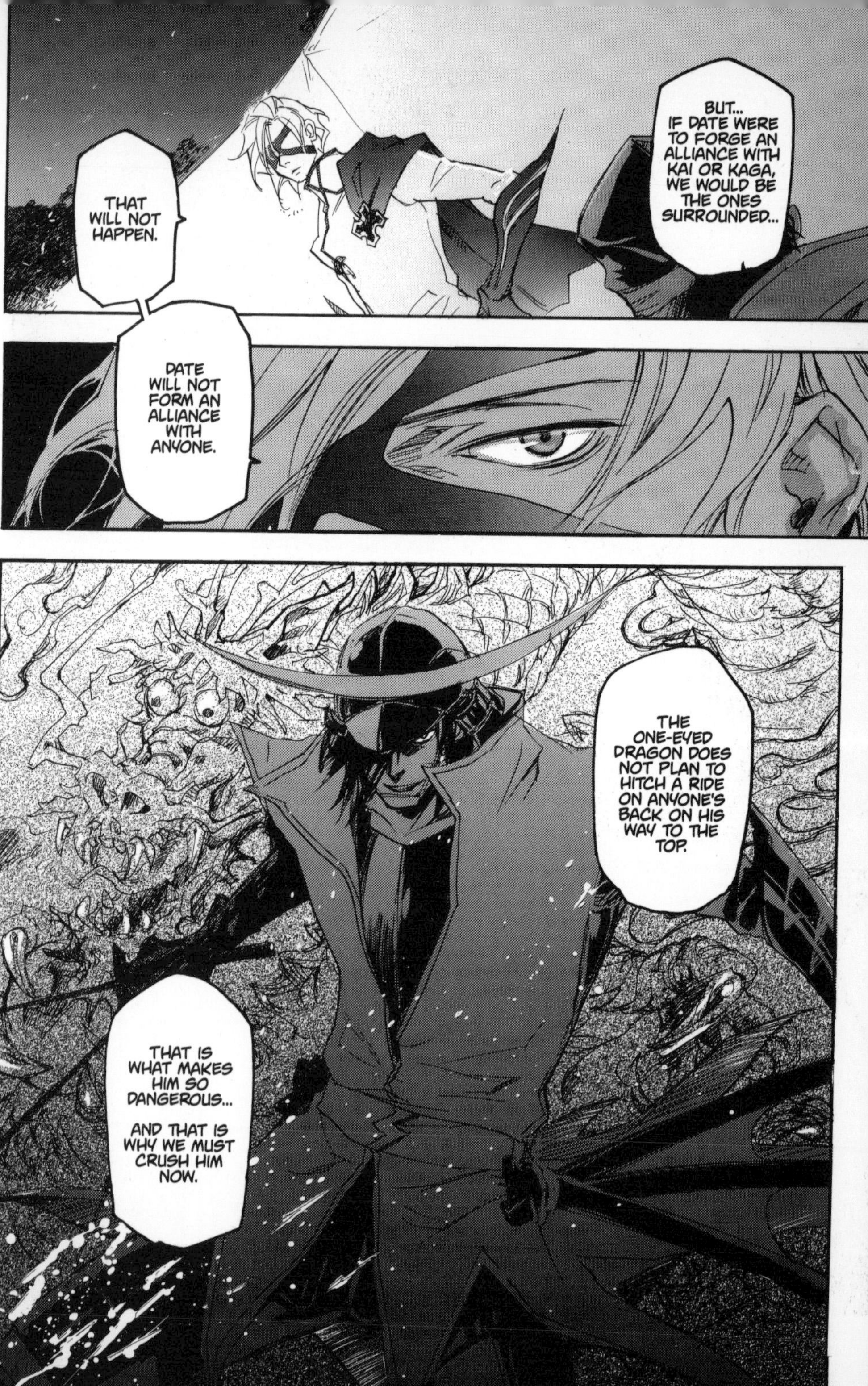
BUT... IF DATE WERE TO FORGE AN ALLIANCE WITH KAI OR KAGA, WE WOULD BE THE ONES SURROUNDED...
THAT WILL NOT HAPPEN.
DATE WILL NOT FORM AN ALLIANCE WITH ANYONE.
THE ONE-EYED DRAGON DOES NOT PLAN TO HITCH A RIDE ON ANYONE'S BACK ON HIS WAY TO THE TOP.
THAT IS WHAT MAKES HIM SO DANGEROUS...
AND THAT IS WHY WE MUST CRUSH HIM NOW.

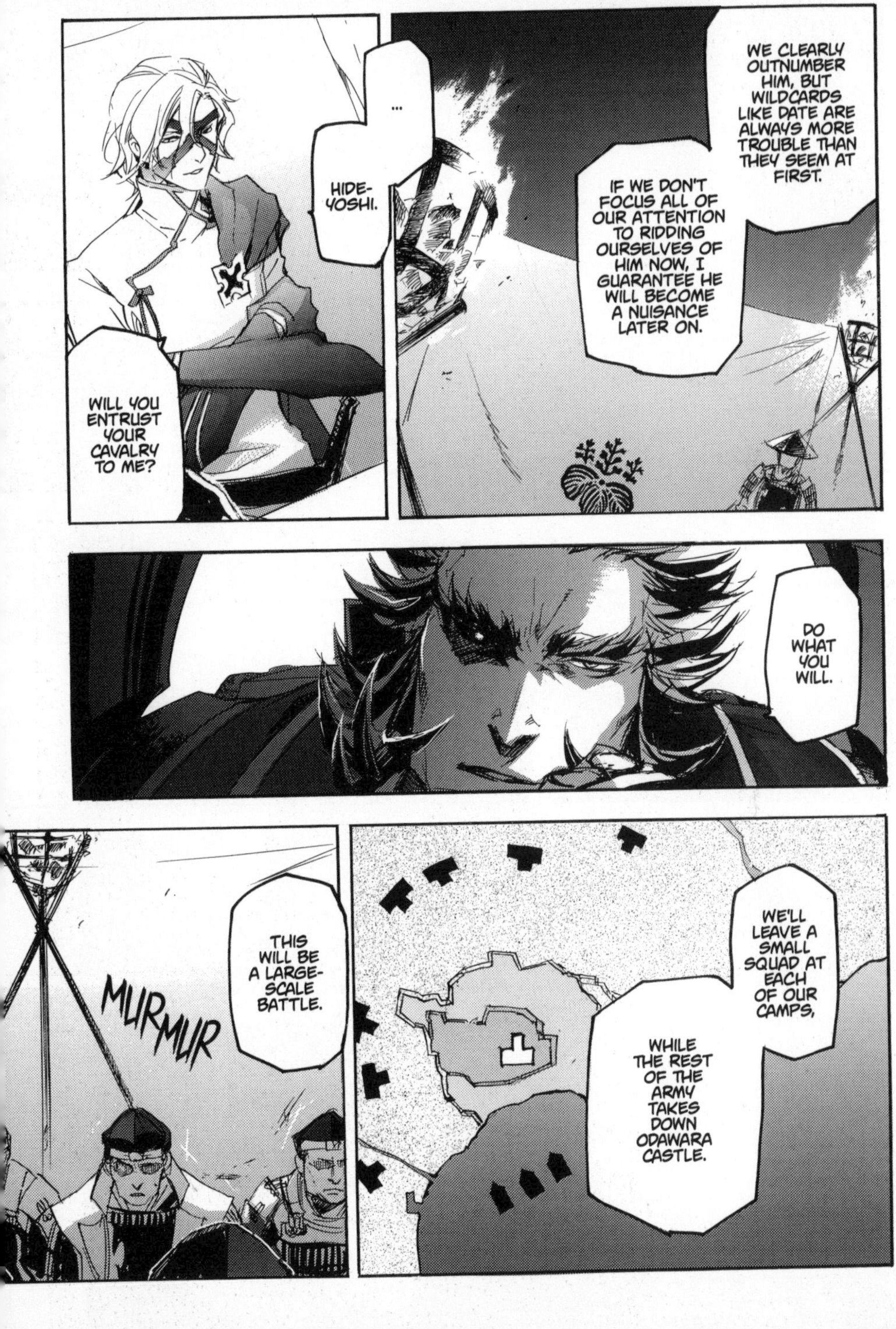
WE CLEARLY OUTNUMBER HIM, BUT WILDCARDS LIKE DATE ARE ALWAYS MORE TROUBLE THAN THEY SEEM AT FIRST.
IF WE DON'T FOCUS ALL OF OUR ATTENTION TO RIDDING OURSELVES OF HIM NOW, I GUARANTEE HE WILL BECOME A NUISANCE LATER ON.
...
HIDE-YOSHI.
WILL YOU ENTRUST YOUR CAVALRY TO ME?
DO WHAT YOU WILL.
WE'LL LEAVE A SMALL SQUAD AT EACH OF OUR CAMPS,
WHILE THE REST OF THE ARMY TAKES DOWN ODAWARA CASTLE.
THIS WILL BE A LARGE-SCALE BATTLE.
MURMUR

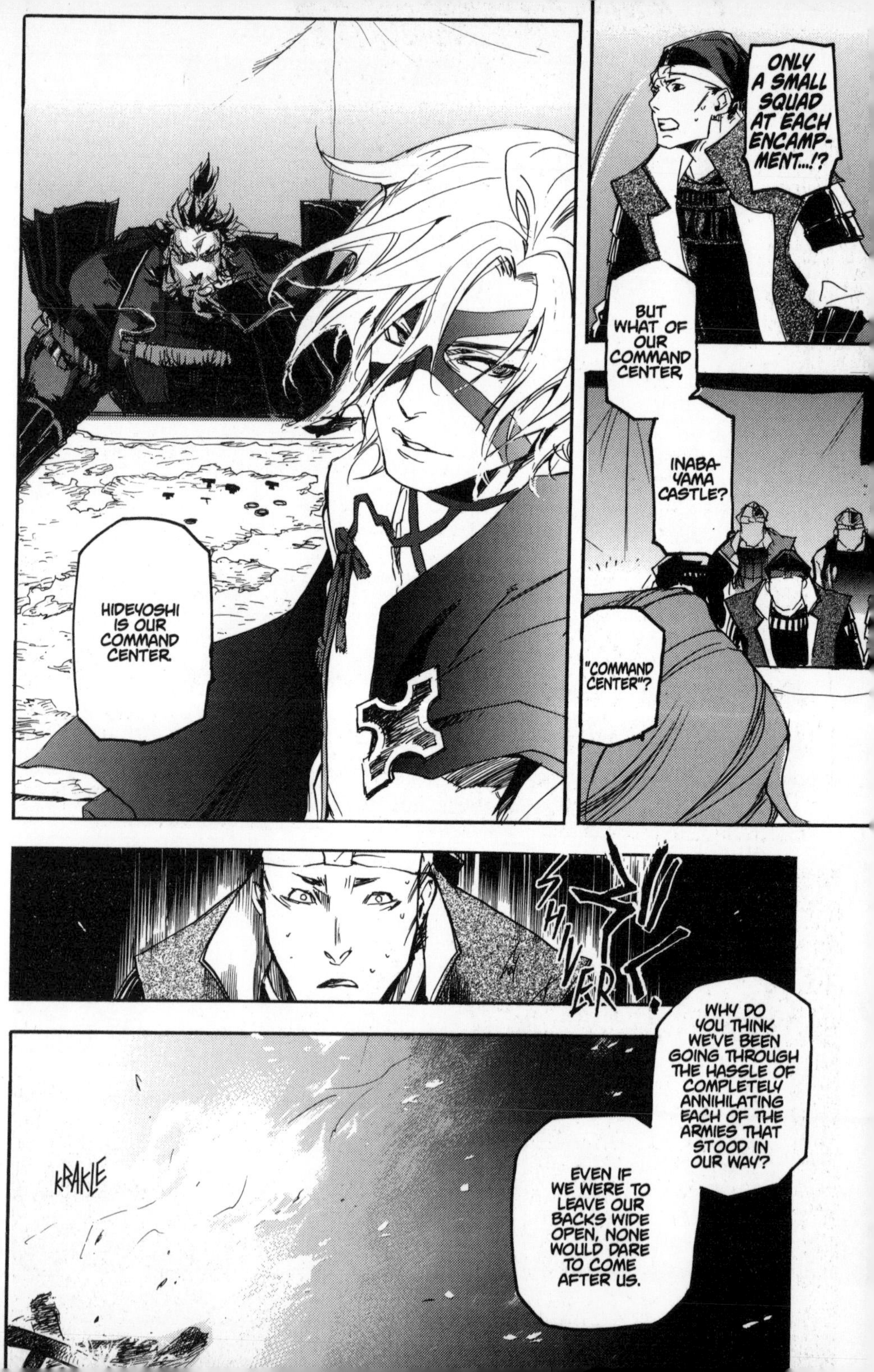
ONLY A SMALL SQUAD AT EACH ENCAMPMENT...!?
BUT WHAT OF OUR COMMAND CENTER,
INABA-YAMA CASTLE?
"COMMAND CENTER"?
HIDEYOSHI IS OUR COMMAND CENTER.
SHIVER
WHY DO YOU THINK WE'VE BEEN GOING THROUGH THE HASSLE OF COMPLETELY ANNIHILATING EACH OF THE ARMIES THAT STOOD IN OUR WAY?
EVEN IF WE WERE TO LEAVE OUR BACKS WIDE OPEN, NONE WOULD DARE TO COME AFTER US.
KRAKLE

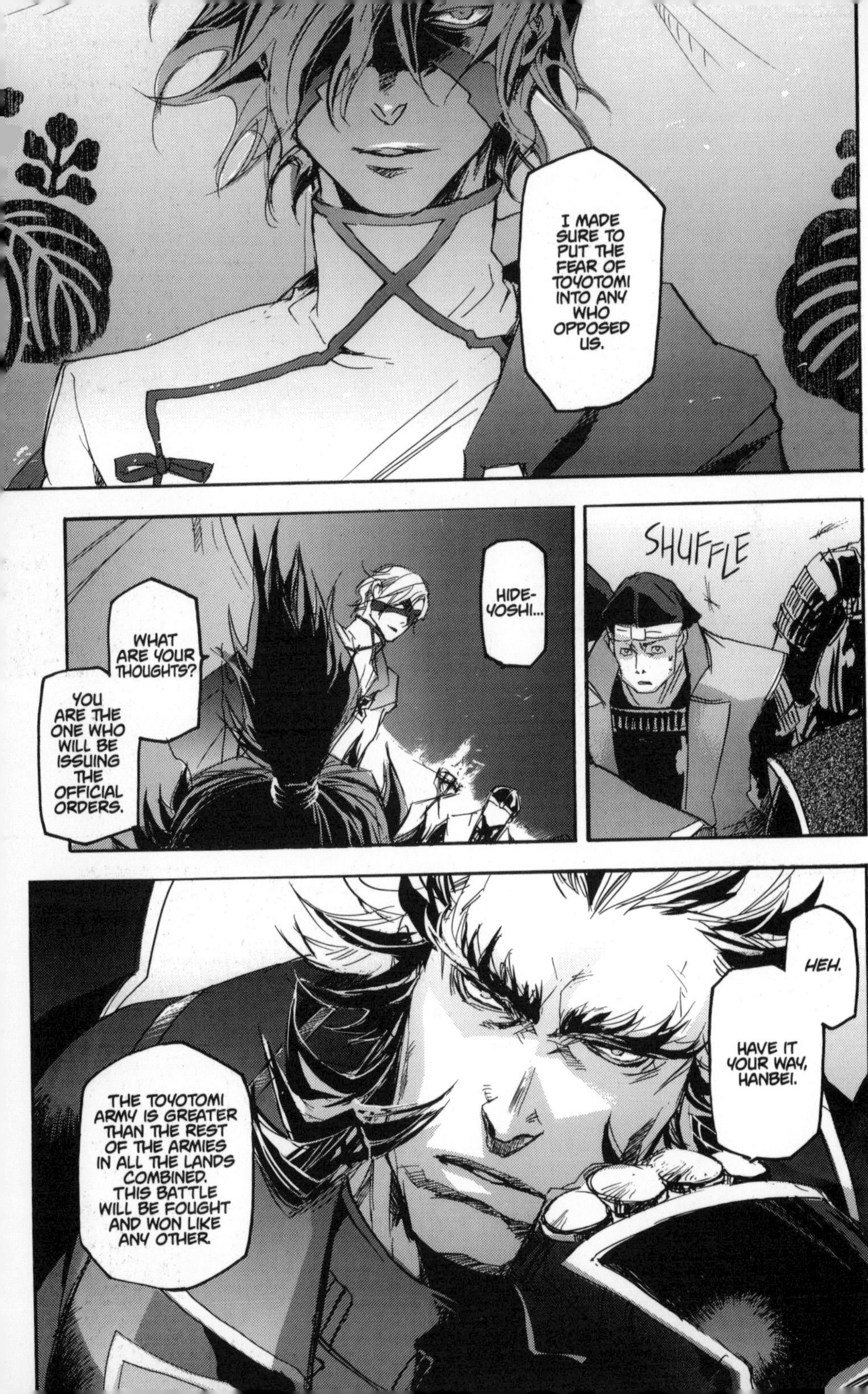
I MADE SURE TO PUT THE FEAR OF TOYOTOMI INTO ANY WHO OPPOSED US.
SHUFFLE
HIDE-YOSHI...
WHAT ARE YOUR THOUGHTS?
YOU ARE THE ONE WHO WILL BE ISSUING THE OFFICIAL ORDERS.
HEH.
HAVE IT YOUR WAY, HANBEI.
THE TOYOTOMI ARMY IS GREATER THAN THE REST OF THE ARMIES IN ALL THE LANDS COMBINED. THIS BATTLE WILL BE FOUGHT AND WON LIKE ANY OTHER.

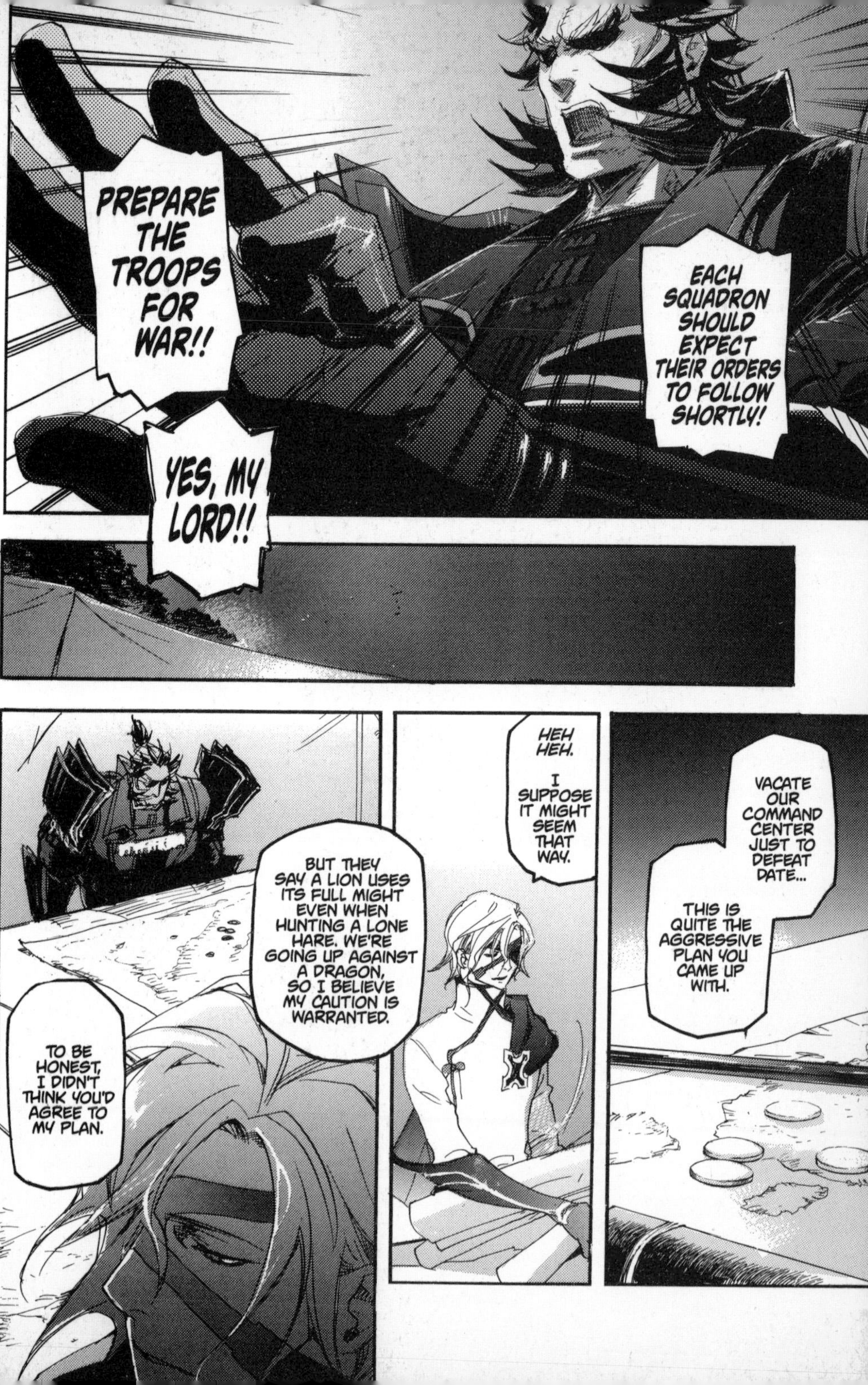
PREPARE THE TROOPS FOR WAR!!
EACH SQUADRON SHOULD EXPECT THEIR ORDERS TO FOLLOW SHORTLY!
YES, MY LORD!!
VACATE OUR COMMAND CENTER JUST TO DEFEAT DATE...
THIS IS QUITE THE AGGRESSIVE PLAN YOU CAME UP WITH.
HEH HEH.
I SUPPOSE IT MIGHT SEEM THAT WAY.
BUT THEY SAY A LION USES ITS FULL MIGHT EVEN WHEN HUNTING A LONE HARE. WE'RE GOING UP AGAINST A DRAGON, SO I BELIEVE MY CAUTION IS WARRANTED.
TO BE HONEST, I DIDN'T THINK YOU'D AGREE TO MY PLAN.

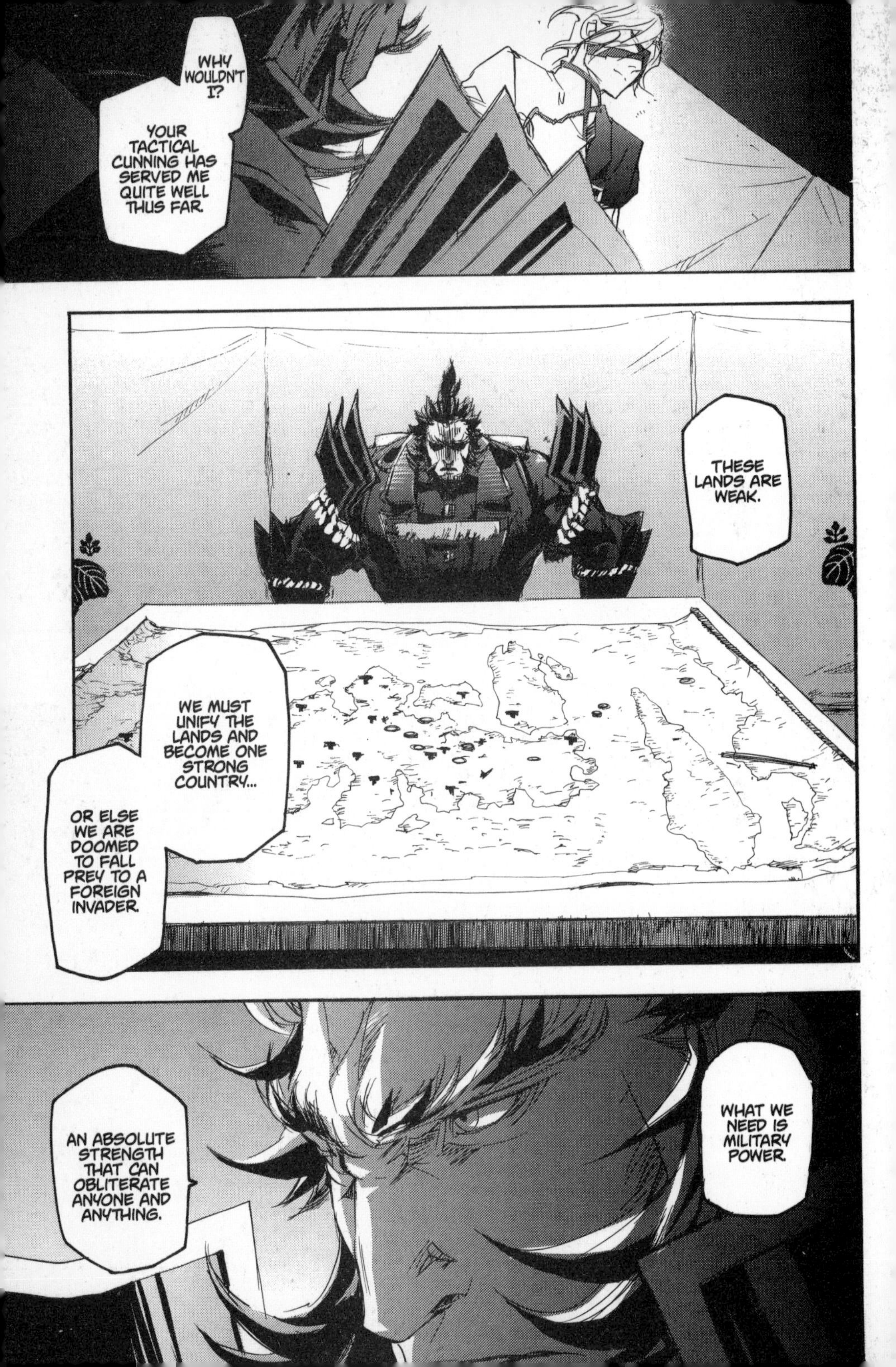
WHY WOULDN'T I?
YOUR TACTICAL CUNNING HAS SERVED ME QUITE WELL THUS FAR.
THESE LANDS ARE WEAK.
WE MUST UNIFY THE LANDS AND BECOME ONE STRONG COUNTRY...
OR ELSE WE ARE DOOMED TO FALL PREY TO A FOREIGN INVADER.
WHAT WE NEED IS MILITARY POWER.
AN ABSOLUTE STRENGTH THAT CAN OBLITERATE ANYONE AND ANYTHING.

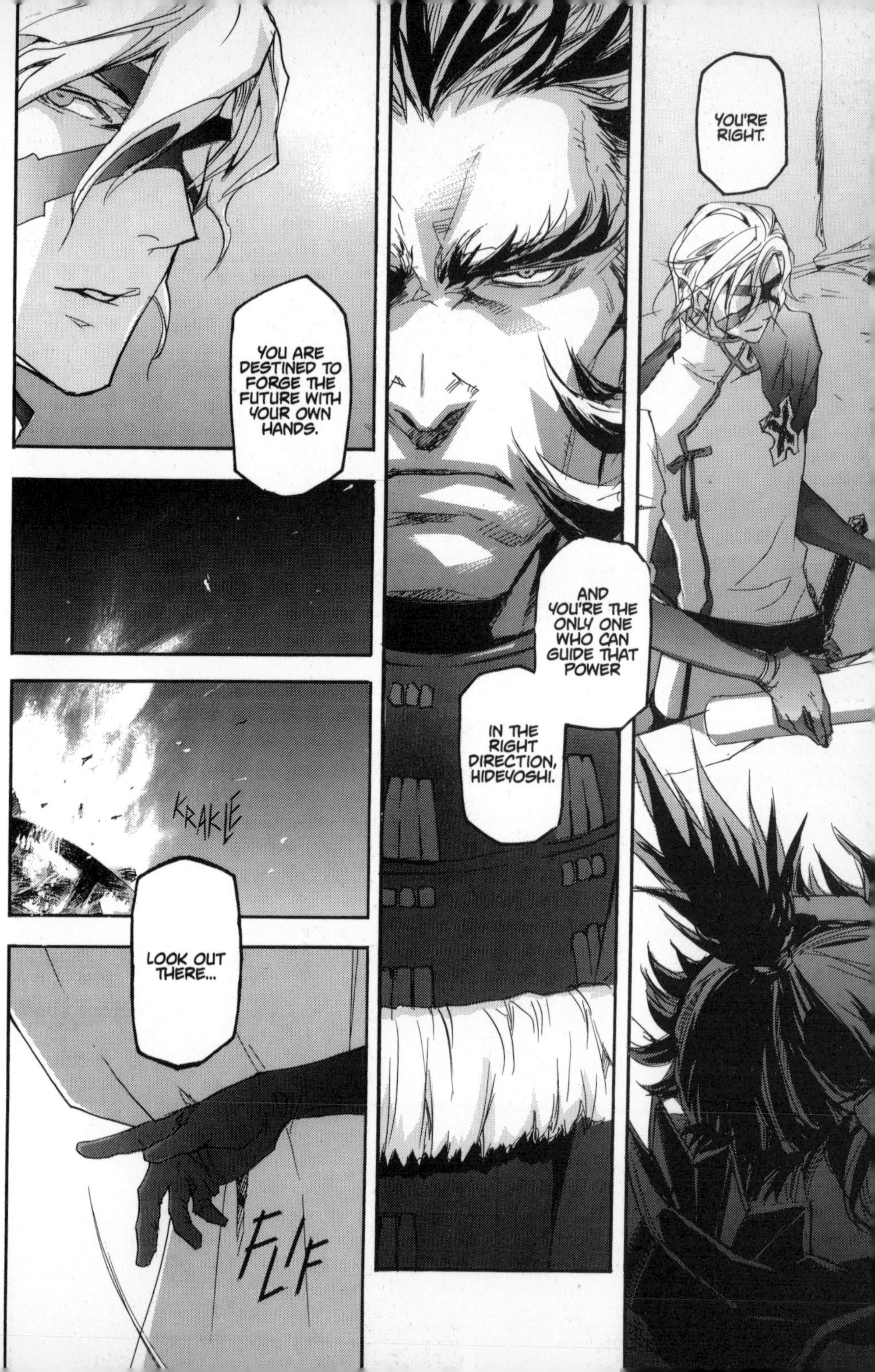
YOU'RE RIGHT.
AND YOU'RE THE ONLY ONE WHO CAN GUIDE THAT POWER
IN THE RIGHT DIRECTION, HIDEYOSHI.
YOU ARE DESTINED TO FORGE THE FUTURE WITH YOUR OWN HANDS.
KRAKLE
LOOK OUT THERE...
FLIF

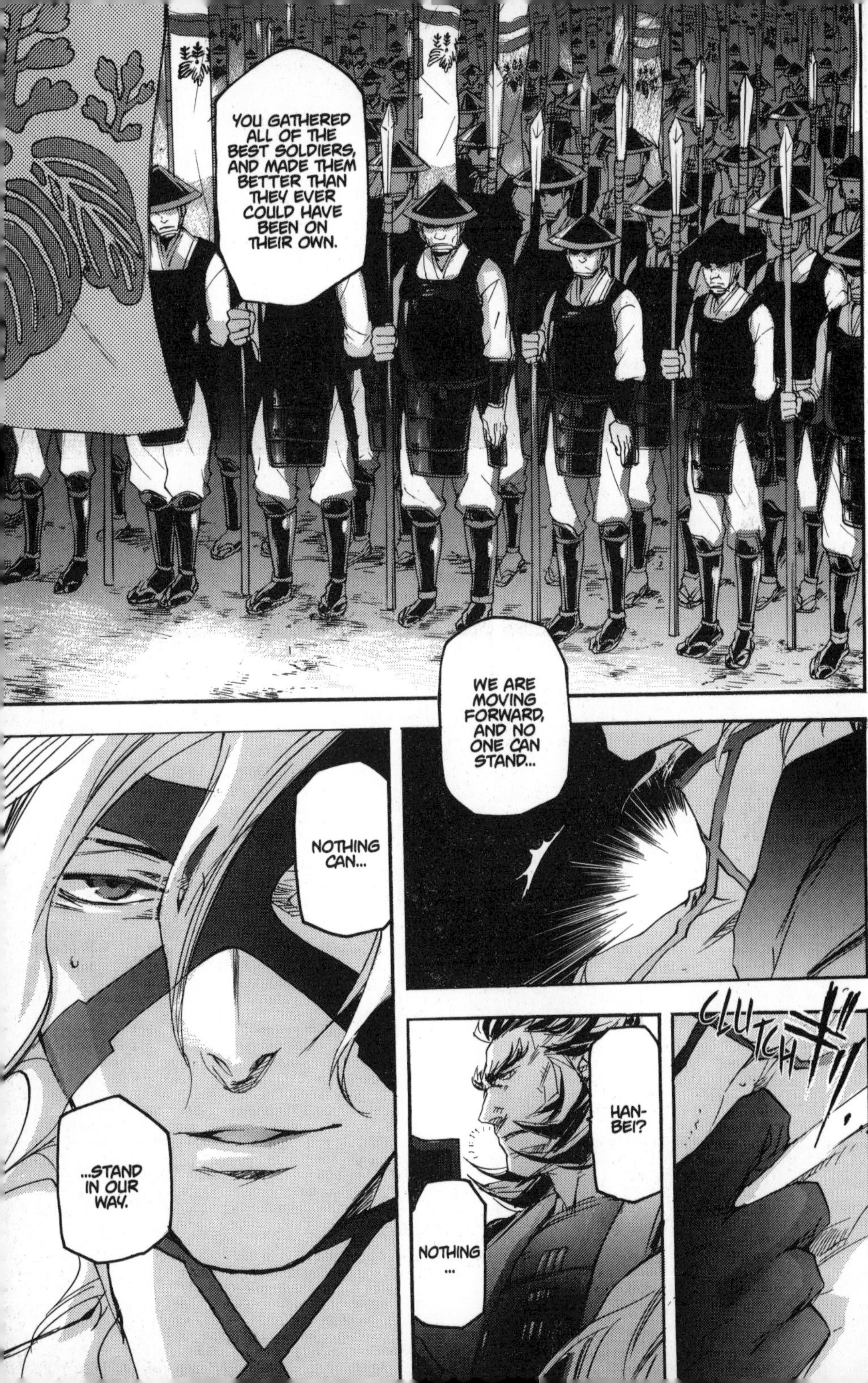
YOU GATHERED ALL OF THE BEST SOLDIERS, AND MADE THEM BETTER THAN THEY EVER COULD HAVE BEEN ON THEIR OWN.
WE ARE MOVING FORWARD, AND NO ONE CAN STAND...
NOTHING CAN...
...STAND IN OUR WAY.
CLUTCH!!
HAN-BEI?
NOTHING ...

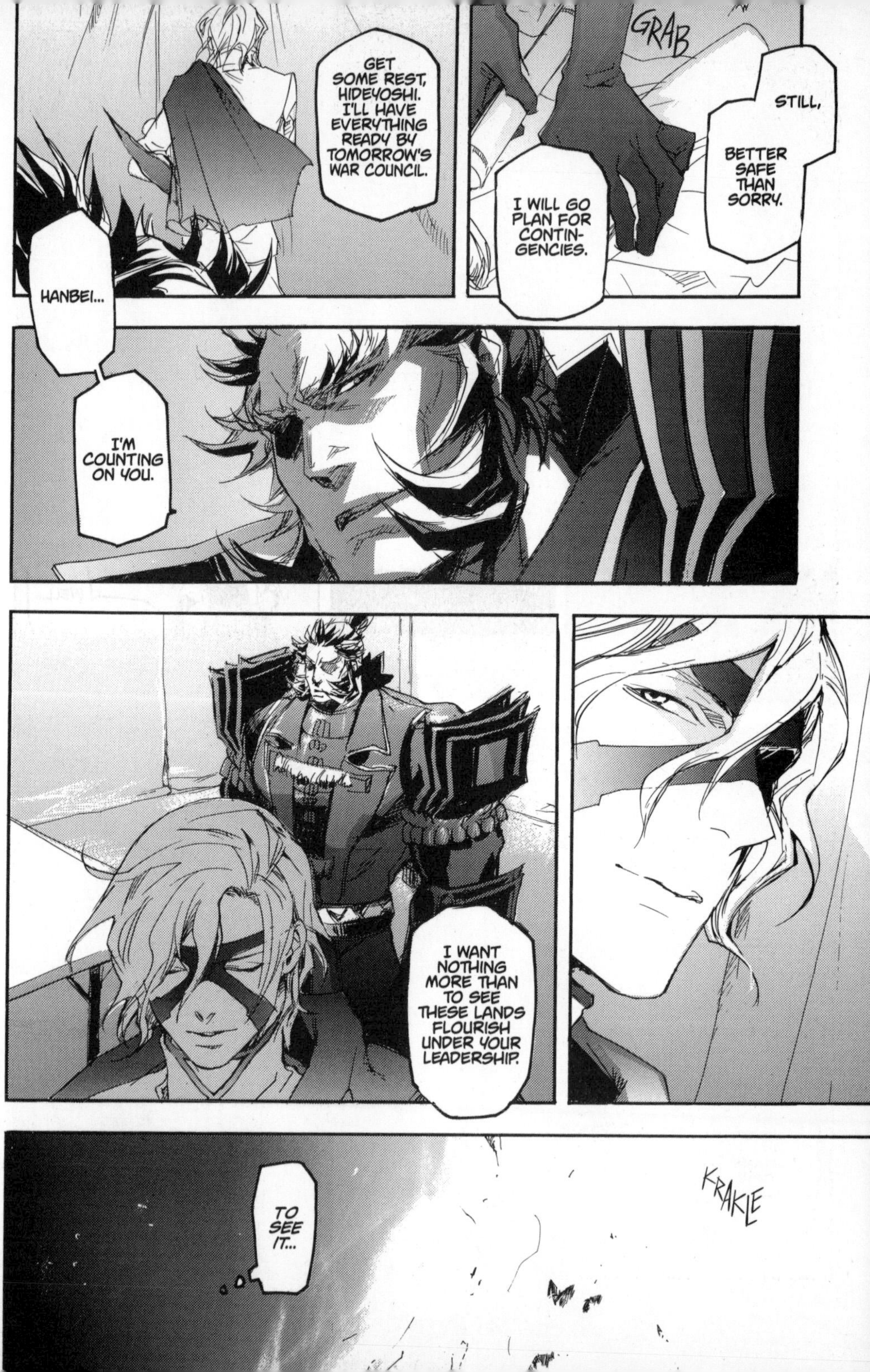
GRAB
STILL,
BETTER SAFE THAN SORRY.
I WILL GO PLAN FOR CONTIN-GENCIES.
GET SOME REST, HIDEYOSHI. I'LL HAVE EVERYTHING READY BY TOMORROW'S WAR COUNCIL.
HANBEI...
I'M COUNTING ON YOU.
I WANT NOTHING MORE THAN TO SEE THESE LANDS FLOURISH UNDER YOUR LEADERSHIP.
KRAKLE
TO SEE IT...

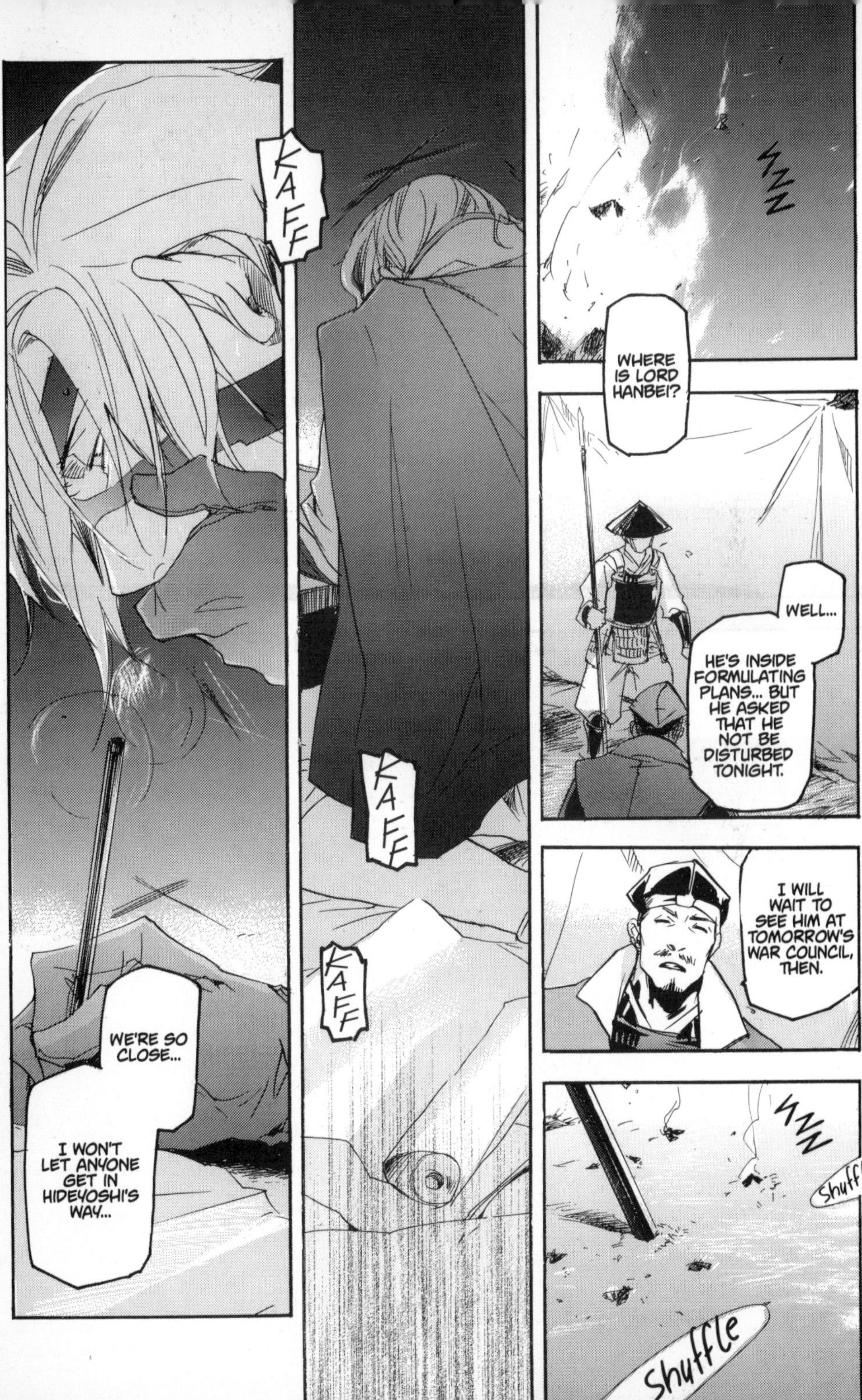
WHERE IS LORD HANBEI?
WELL...
HE'S INSIDE FORMULATING PLANS... BUT HE ASKED THAT HE NOT BE DISTURBED TONIGHT.
I WILL WAIT TO SEE HIM AT TOMORROW'S WAR COUNCIL, THEN.
Shuffle
Shuffle
KAFF
KAFF
KAFF
WE'RE SO CLOSE...
I WON'T LET ANYONE GET IN HIDEYOSHI'S WAY...

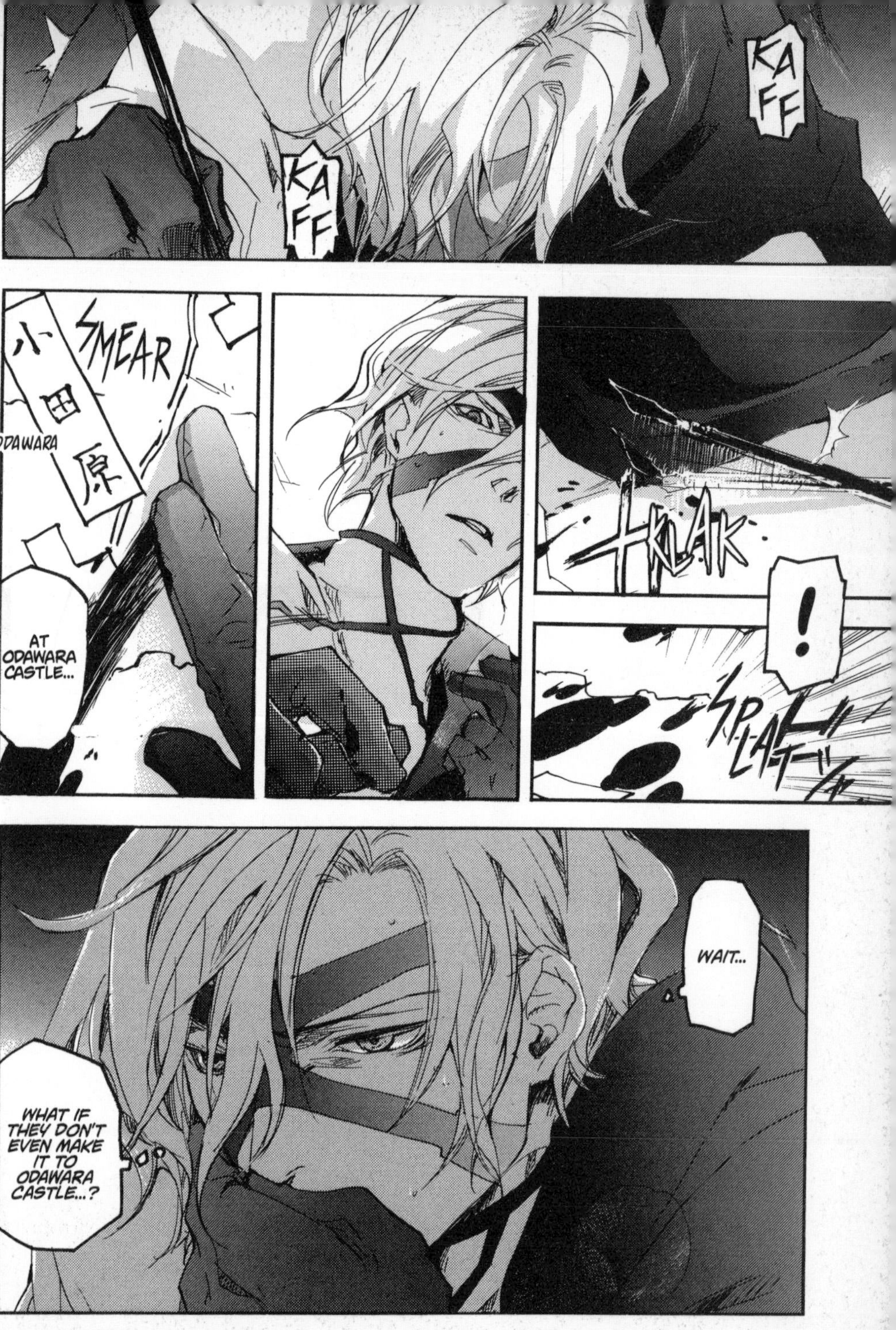
KAFF
KAFF
KLAK
!
SPLAT
SMEAR
小田原
ODAWARA
AT ODAWARA CASTLE...
WAIT...
WHAT IF THEY DON'T EVEN MAKE IT TO ODAWARA CASTLE...?

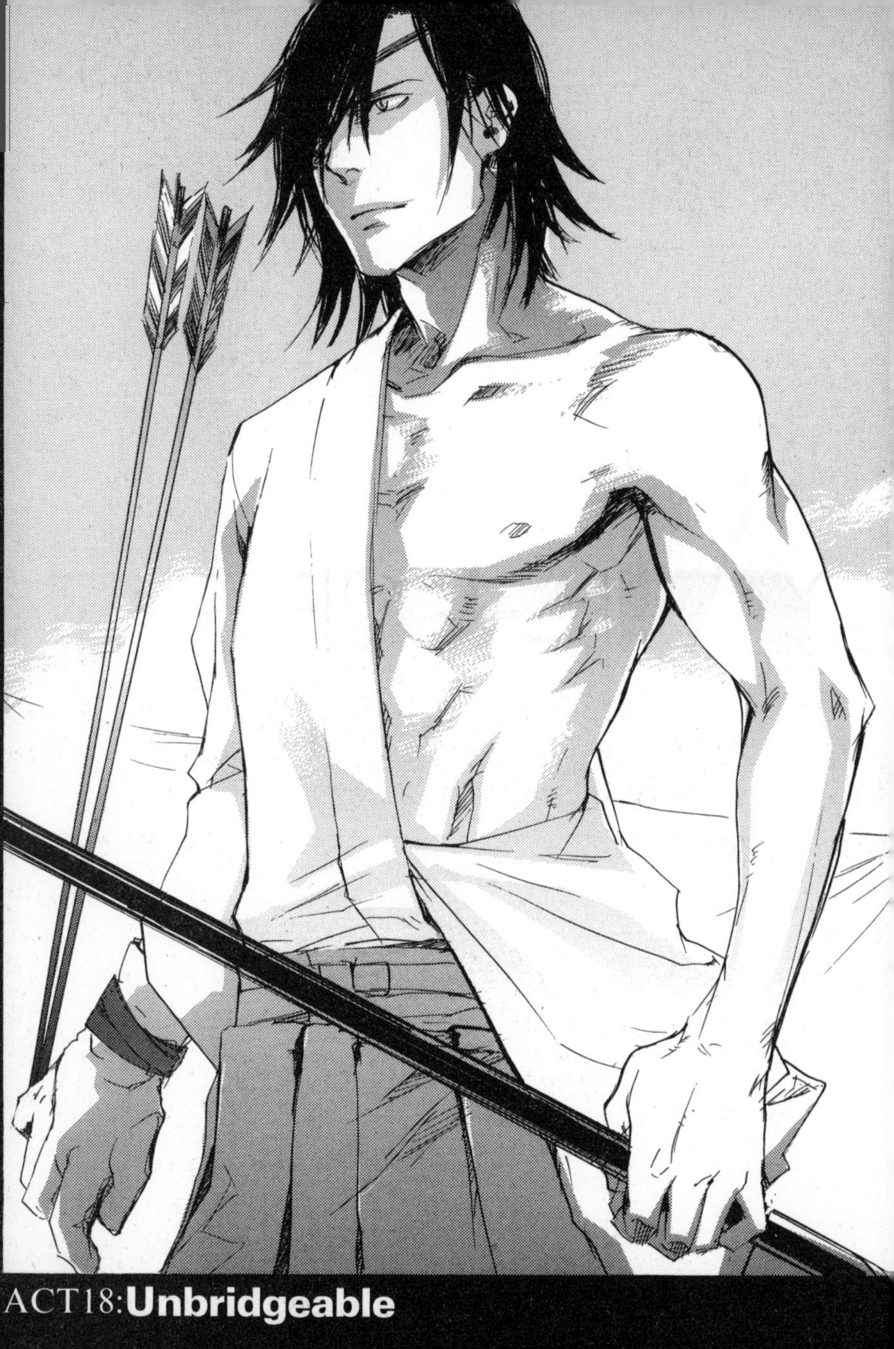

ACT18: **Unbridgeable**

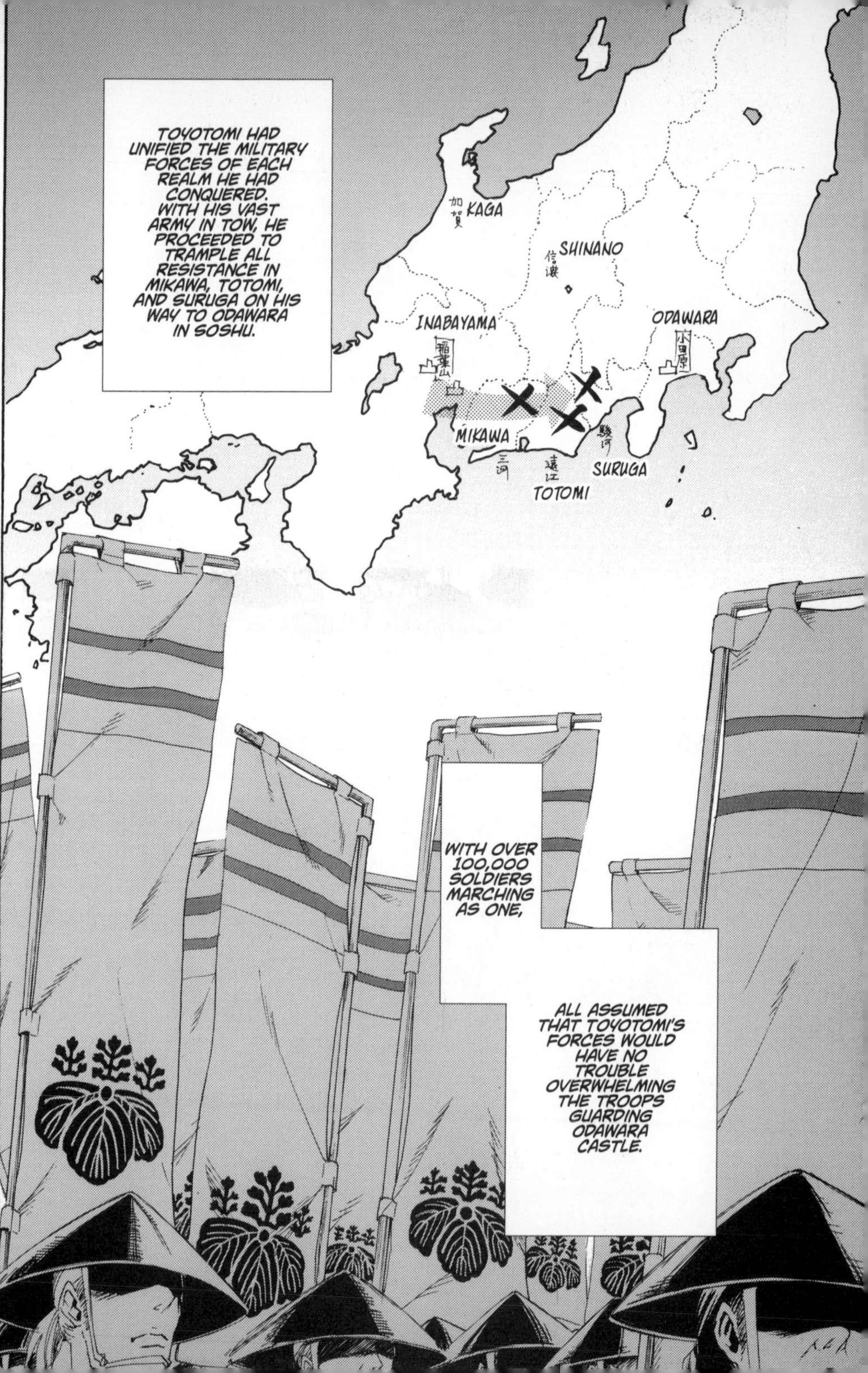
TOYOTOMI HAD UNIFIED THE MILITARY FORCES OF EACH REALM HE HAD CONQUERED. WITH HIS VAST ARMY IN TOW, HE PROCEEDED TO TRAMPLE ALL RESISTANCE IN MIKAWA, TOTOMI, AND SURUGA ON HIS WAY TO ODAWARA IN SOSHU.
加賀 KAGA
信濃 SHINANO
INABAYAMA 稲葉山
ODAWARA 小田原
MIKAWA 三河
遠江 TOTOMI
駿河 SURUGA
WITH OVER 100,000 SOLDIERS MARCHING AS ONE,
ALL ASSUMED THAT TOYOTOMI'S FORCES WOULD HAVE NO TROUBLE OVERWHELMING THE TROOPS GUARDING ODAWARA CASTLE.

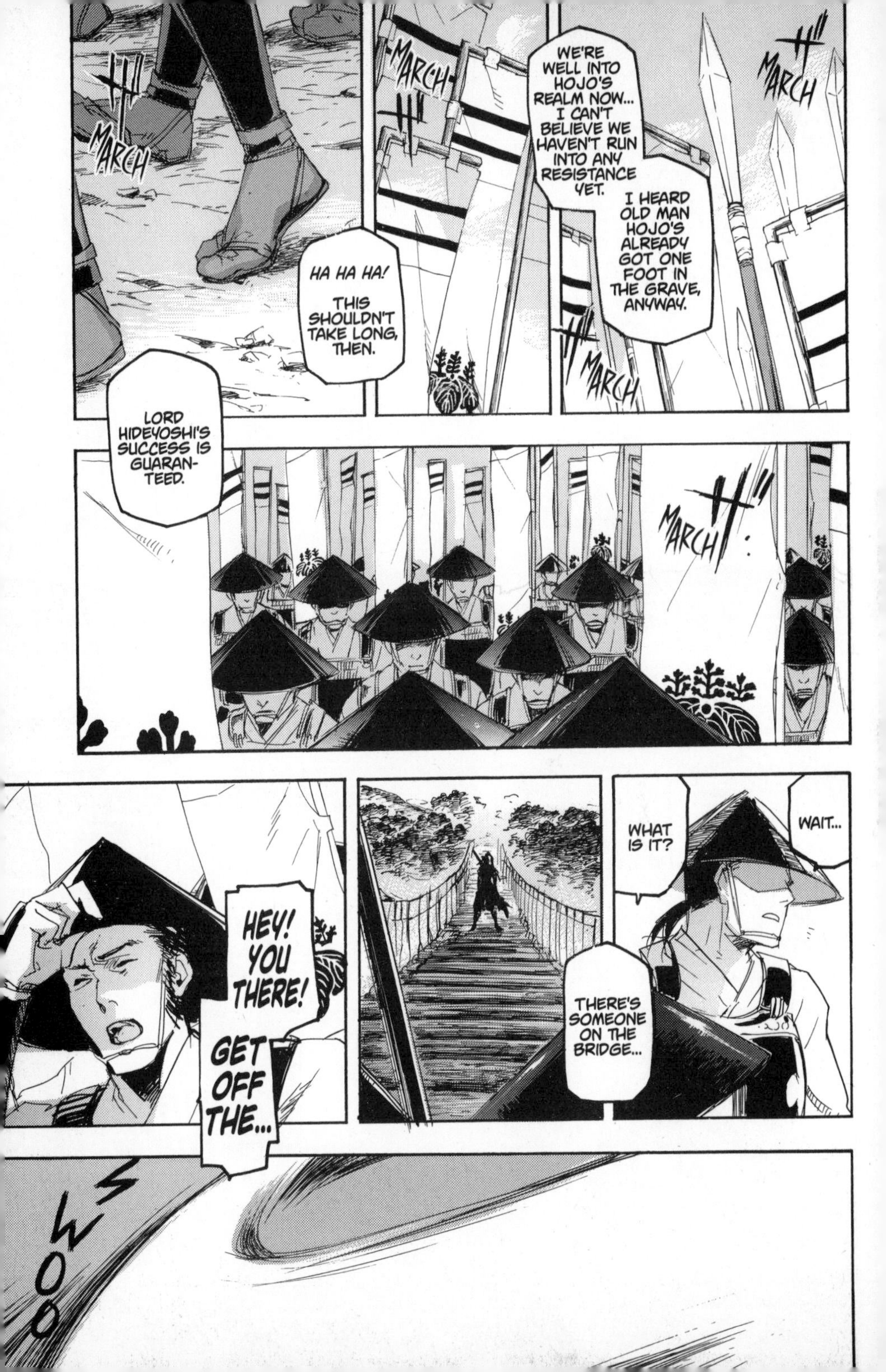
MARCH
WE'RE WELL INTO HOJO'S REALM NOW... I CAN'T BELIEVE WE HAVEN'T RUN INTO ANY RESISTANCE YET.
I HEARD OLD MAN HOJO'S ALREADY GOT ONE FOOT IN THE GRAVE, ANYWAY.
MARCH
MARCH
HA HA HA!
THIS SHOULDN'T TAKE LONG, THEN.
MARCH
MARCH
LORD HIDEYOSHI'S SUCCESS IS GUARAN-TEED.
WAIT...
WHAT IS IT?
THERE'S SOMEONE ON THE BRIDGE...
HEY! YOU THERE!
GET OFF THE...
SWOO

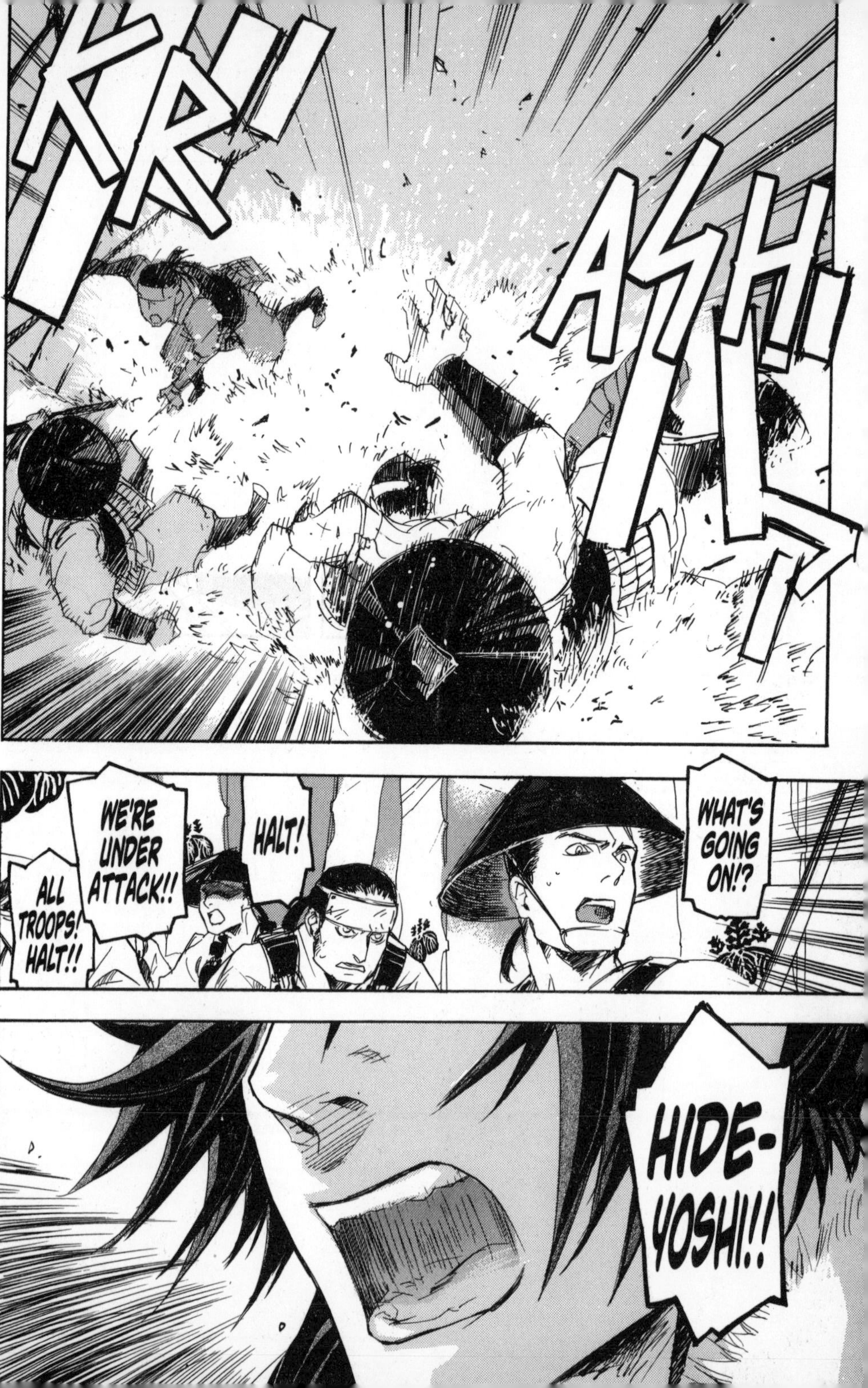
KRI-
ASH!!
WHAT'S GOING ON!?
HALT!
WE'RE UNDER ATTACK!!
ALL TROOPS! HALT!!
HIDE-YOSHI!!

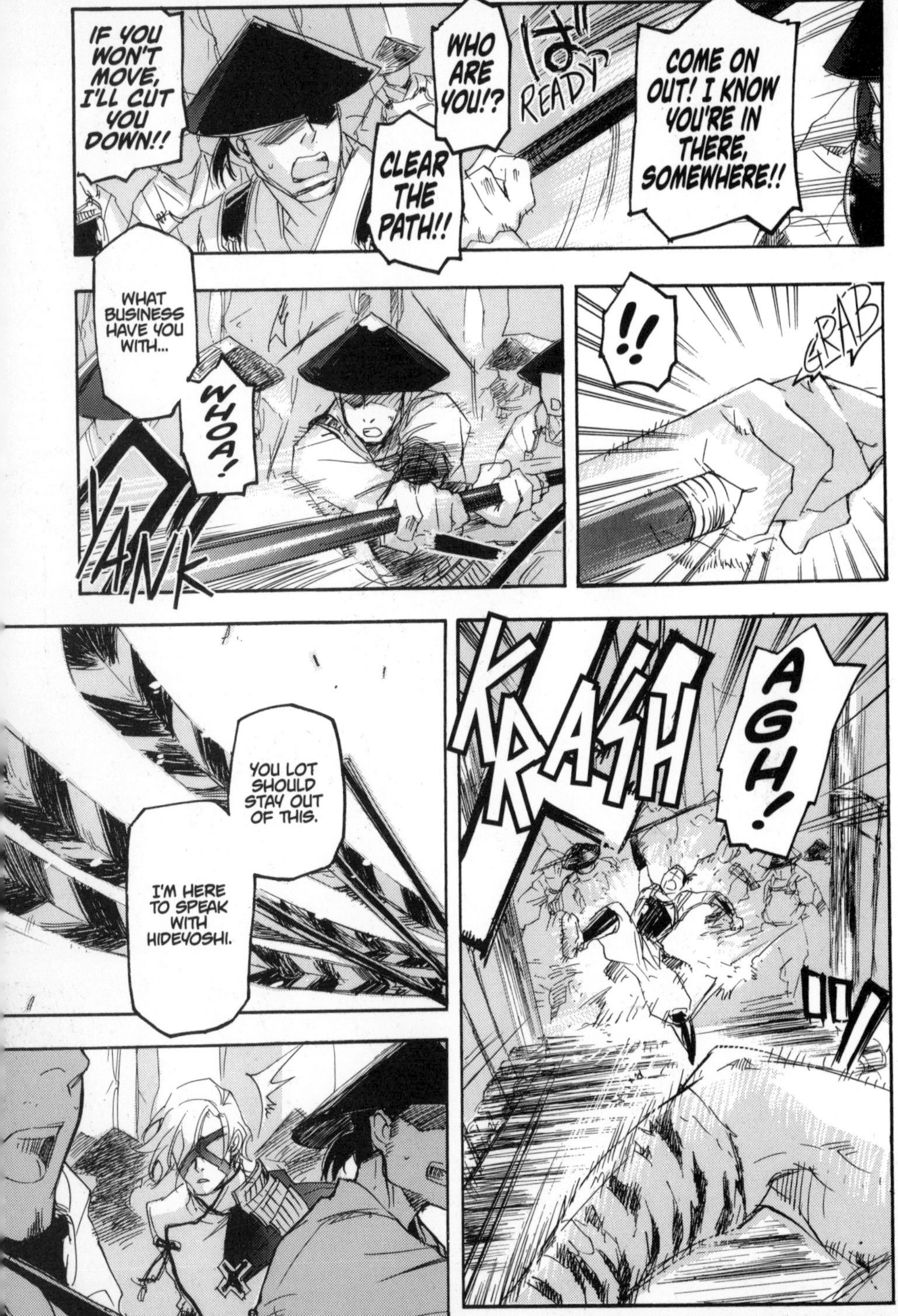
COME ON OUT! I KNOW YOU'RE IN THERE, SOMEWHERE!!
ばっ
READY
WHO ARE YOU!?
CLEAR THE PATH!!
IF YOU WON'T MOVE, I'LL CUT YOU DOWN!!
GRAB
!!
WHAT BUSINESS HAVE YOU WITH...
WHOA!
YANK
KRASH
AGH!
YOU LOT SHOULD STAY OUT OF THIS.
I'M HERE TO SPEAK WITH HIDEYOSHI.

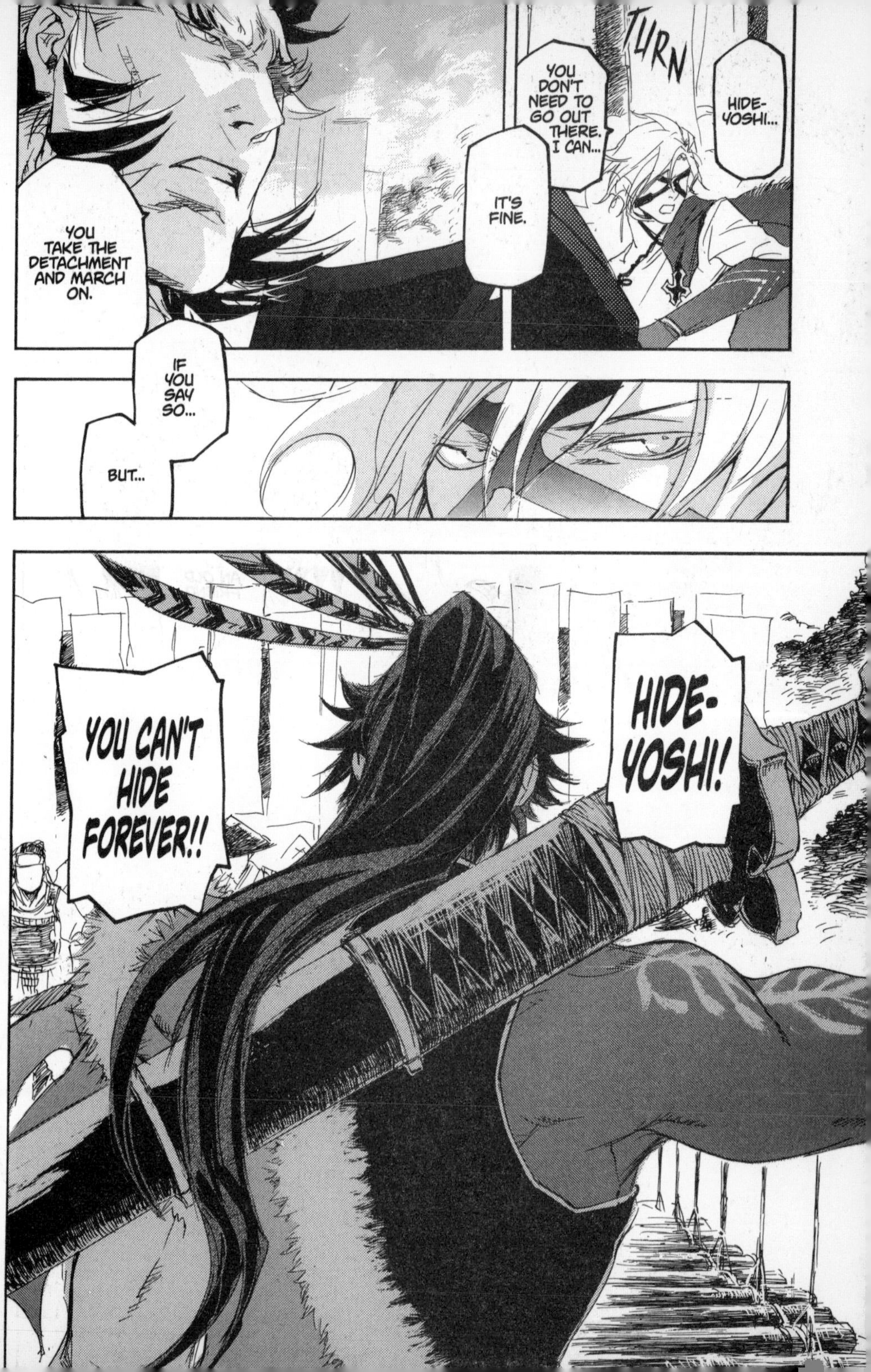
HIDE-YOSHI...
TURN
YOU DON'T NEED TO GO OUT THERE. I CAN...
IT'S FINE.
YOU TAKE THE DETACHMENT AND MARCH ON.
IF YOU SAY SO...
BUT...
HIDE-YOSHI!
YOU CAN'T HIDE FOREVER!!

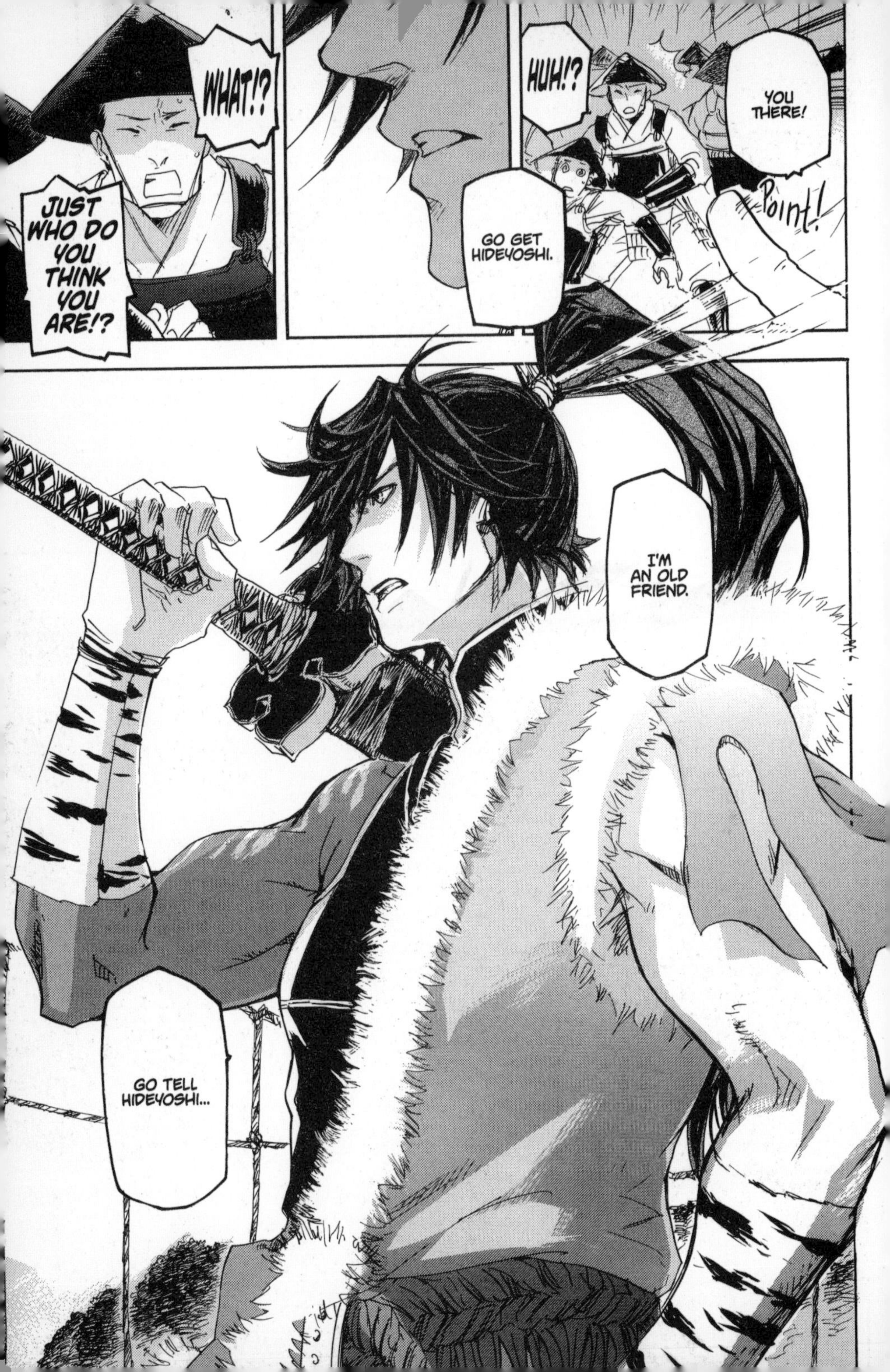
YOU THERE!
Point!
HUH!?
GO GET HIDEYOSHI.
WHAT!?
JUST WHO DO YOU THINK YOU ARE!?
I'M AN OLD FRIEND.
GO TELL HIDEYOSHI...

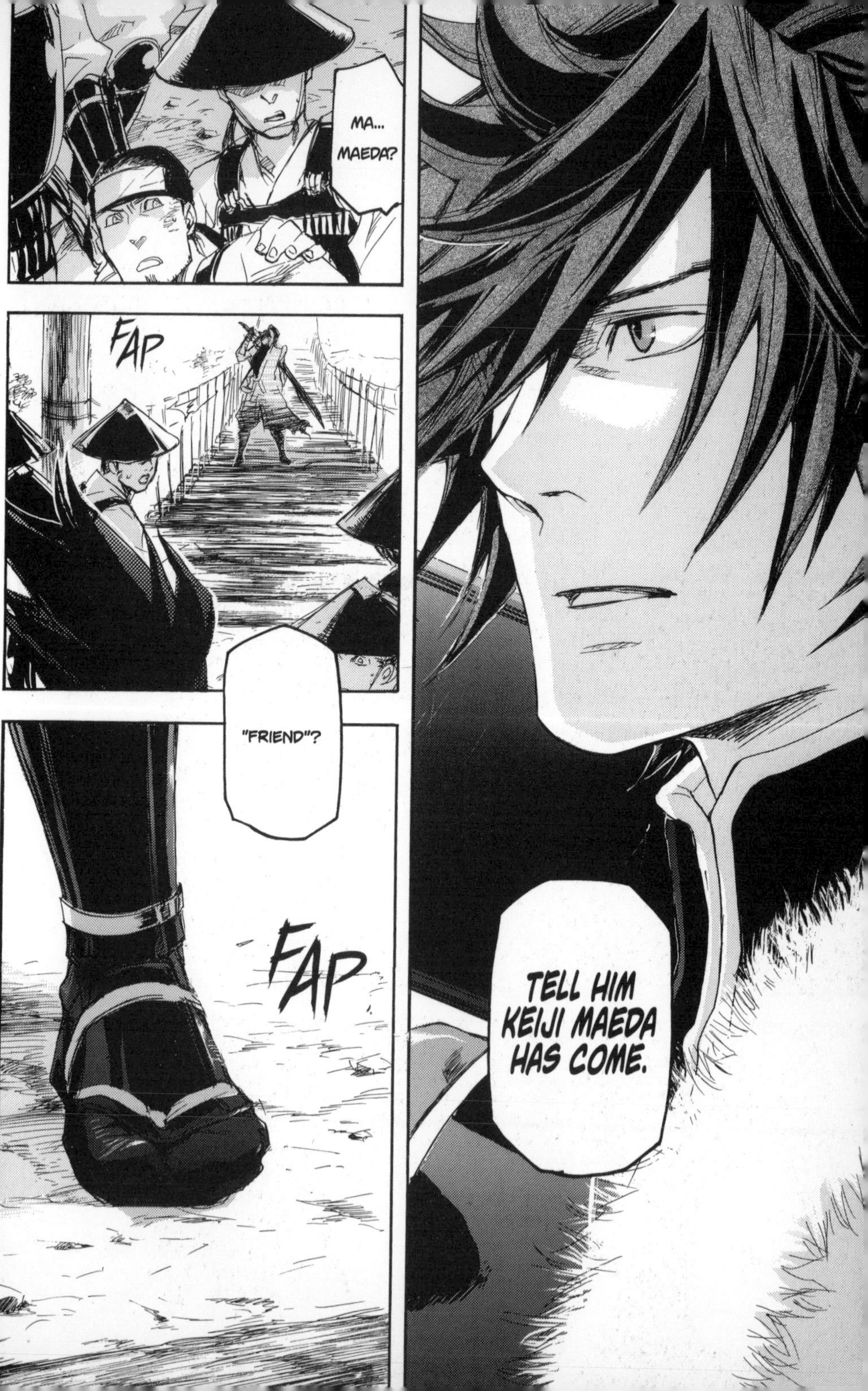
TELL HIM KEIJI MAEDA HAS COME.
MA... MAEDA?
FAP
"FRIEND"?
FAP

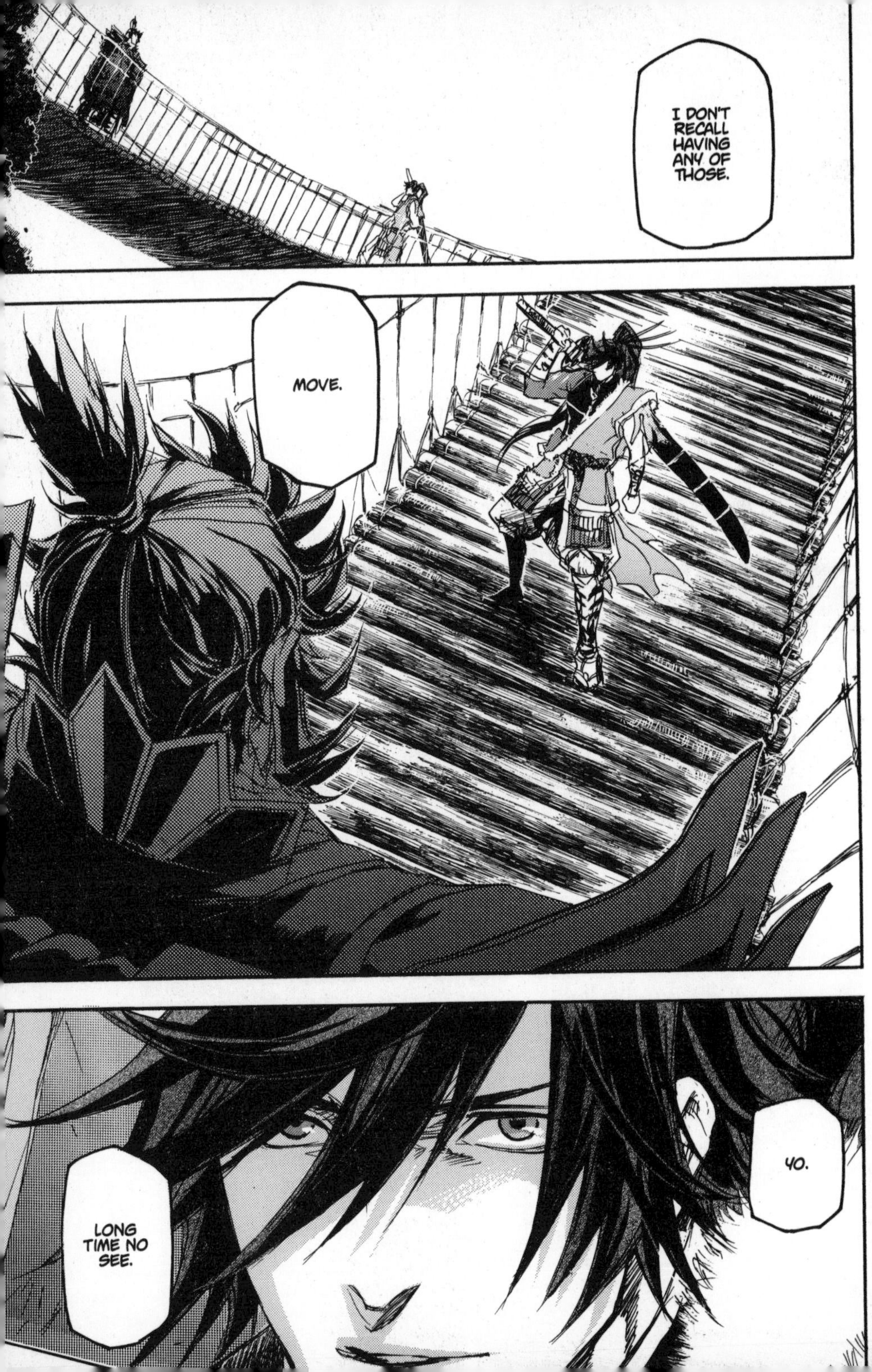
I DON'T RECALL HAVING ANY OF THOSE.
MOVE.
YO.
LONG TIME NO SEE.

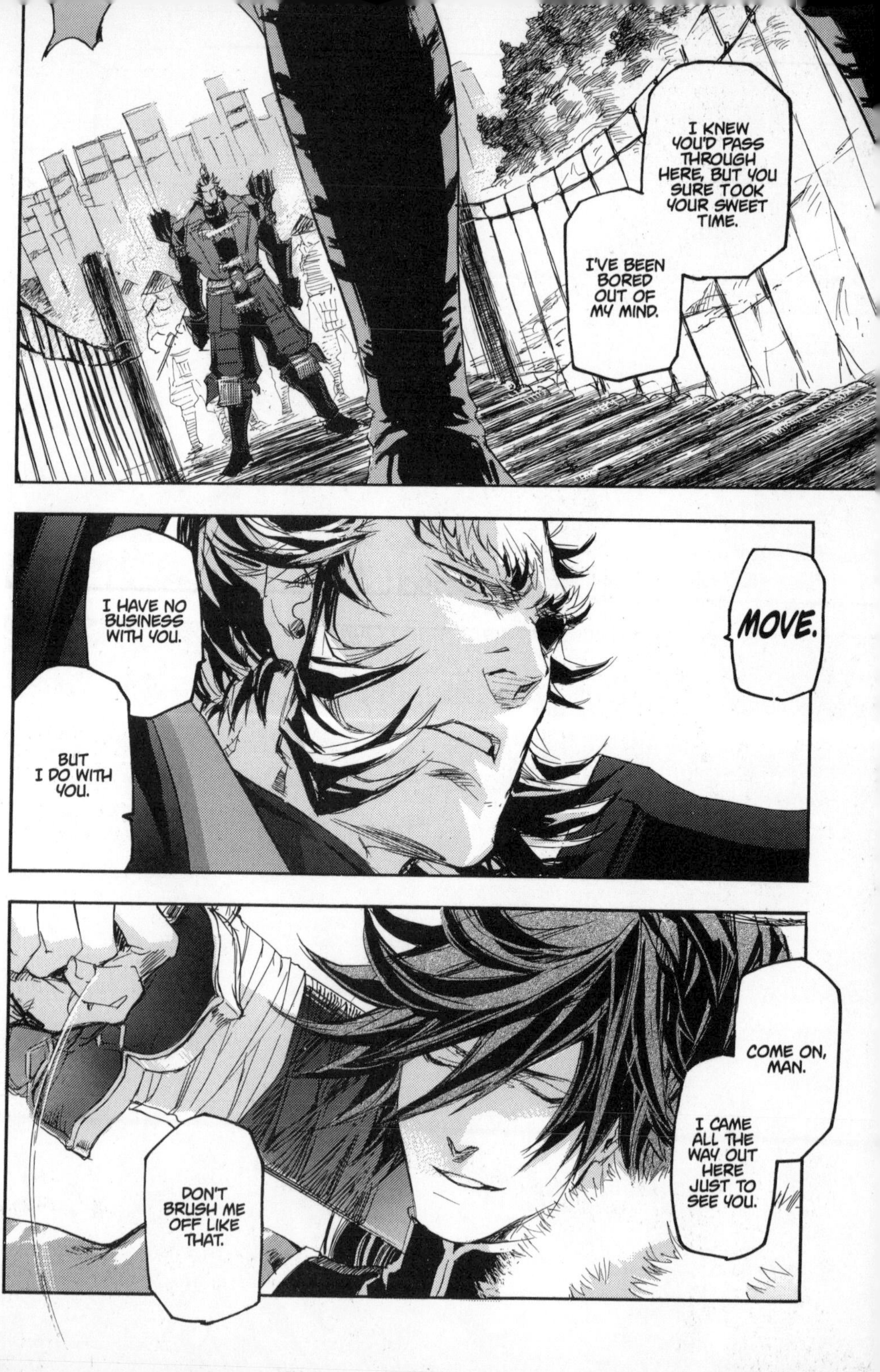
I KNEW YOU'D PASS THROUGH HERE, BUT YOU SURE TOOK YOUR SWEET TIME.
I'VE BEEN BORED OUT OF MY MIND.
I HAVE NO BUSINESS WITH YOU.
MOVE.
BUT I DO WITH YOU.
COME ON, MAN.
I CAME ALL THE WAY OUT HERE JUST TO SEE YOU.
DON'T BRUSH ME OFF LIKE THAT.

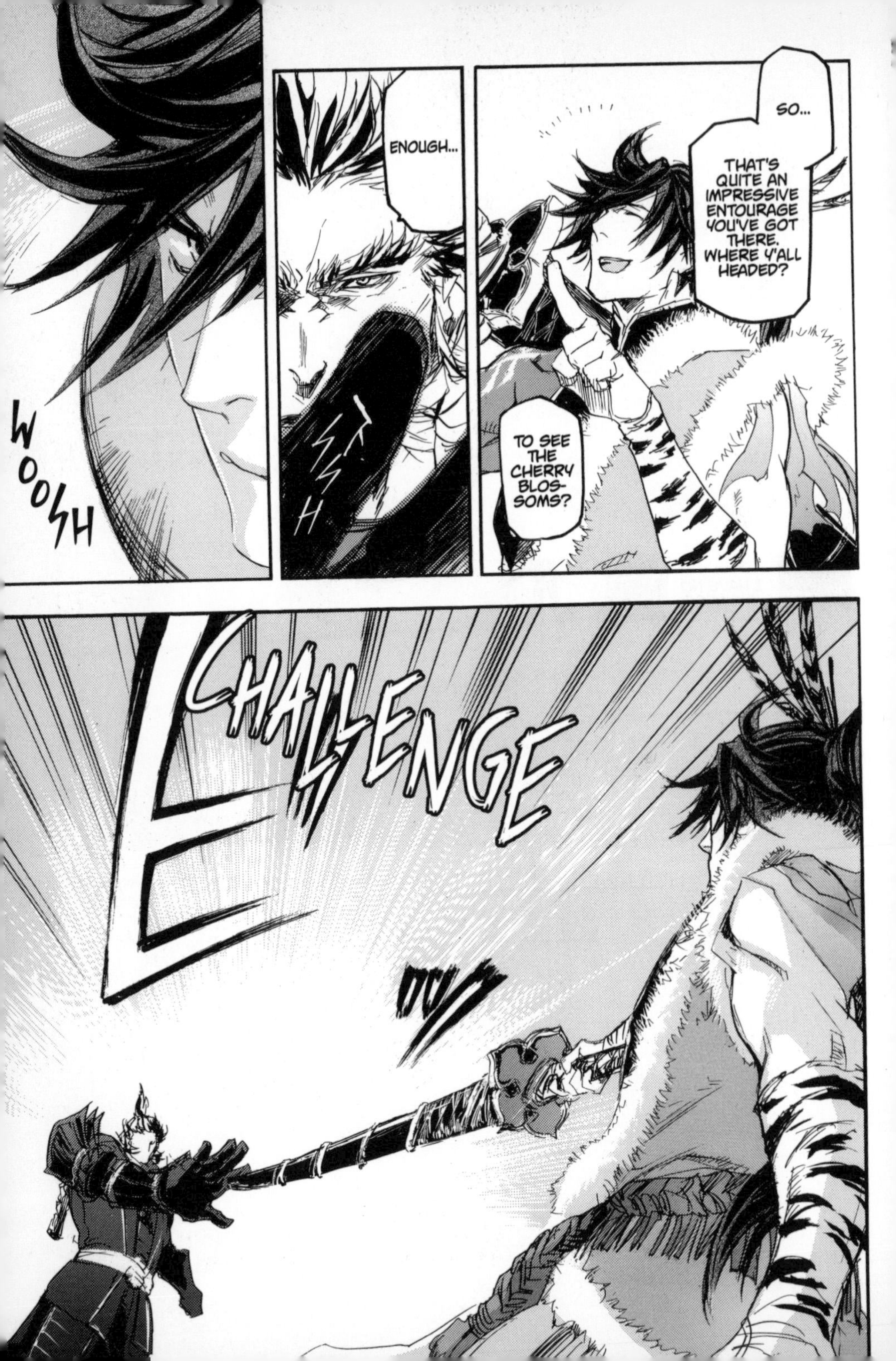
SO...
THAT'S QUITE AN IMPRESSIVE ENTOURAGE YOU'VE GOT THERE. WHERE Y'ALL HEADED?
TO SEE THE CHERRY BLOS-SOMS?
ENOUGH...
WOOSH
CHALLENGE

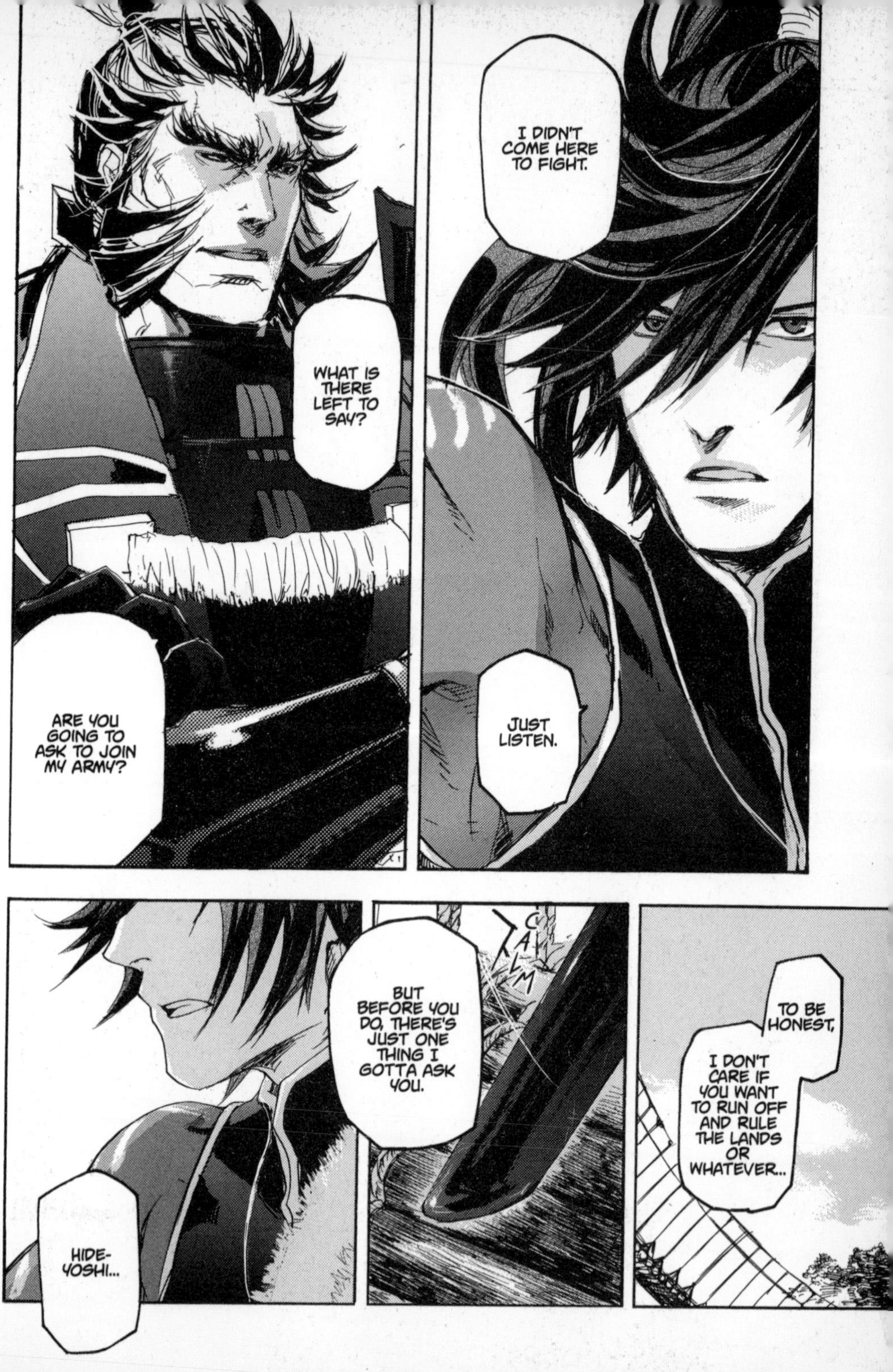
I DIDN'T COME HERE TO FIGHT.
JUST LISTEN.
WHAT IS THERE LEFT TO SAY?
ARE YOU GOING TO ASK TO JOIN MY ARMY?
TO BE HONEST,
I DON'T CARE IF YOU WANT TO RUN OFF AND RULE THE LANDS OR WHATEVER...
CALM
BUT BEFORE YOU DO, THERE'S JUST ONE THING I GOTTA ASK YOU.
HIDE-YOSHI...

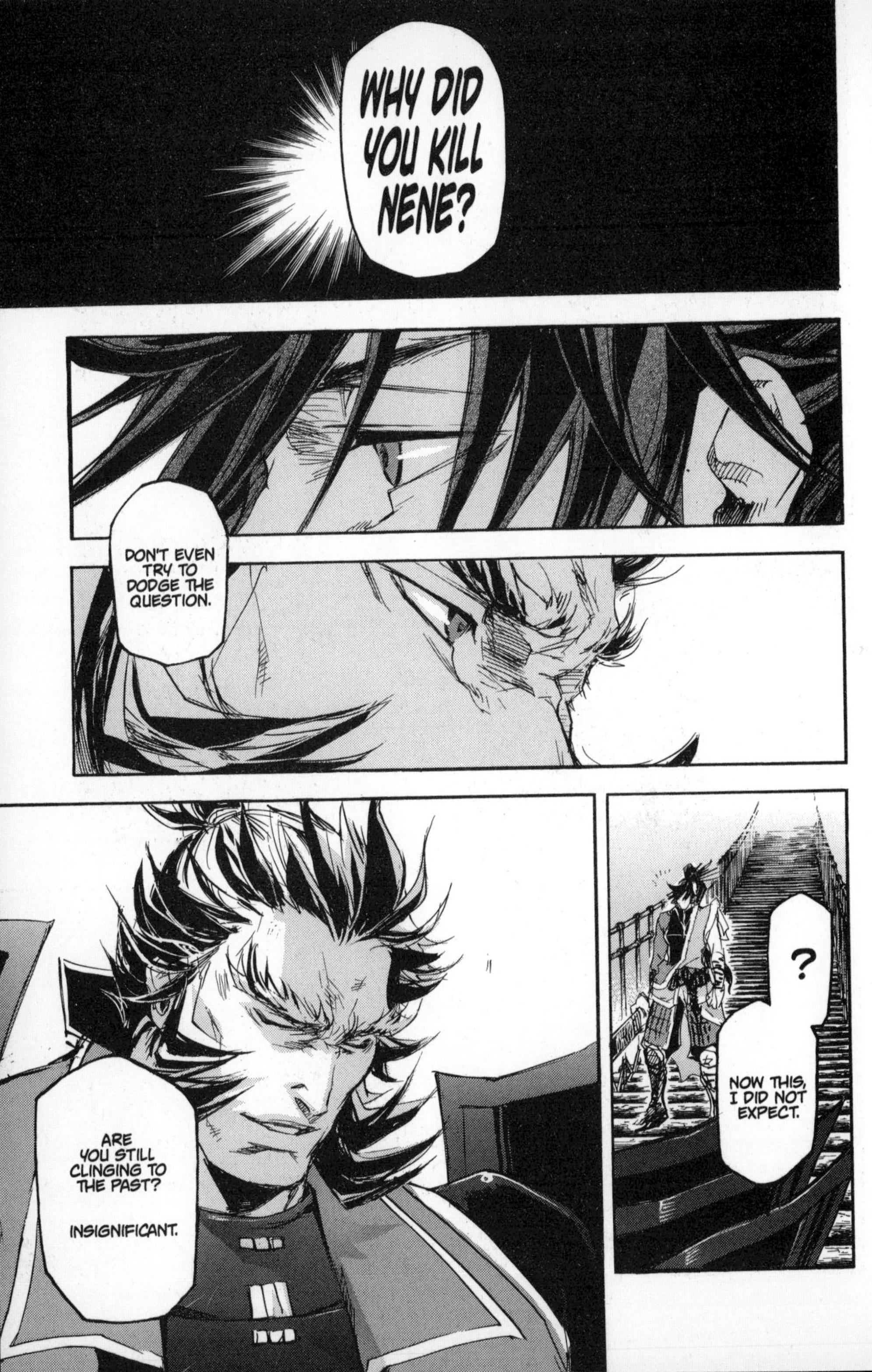
WHY DID YOU KILL NENE?
DON'T EVEN TRY TO DODGE THE QUESTION.
?
NOW THIS, I DID NOT EXPECT.
ARE YOU STILL CLINGING TO THE PAST?
INSIGNIFICANT.

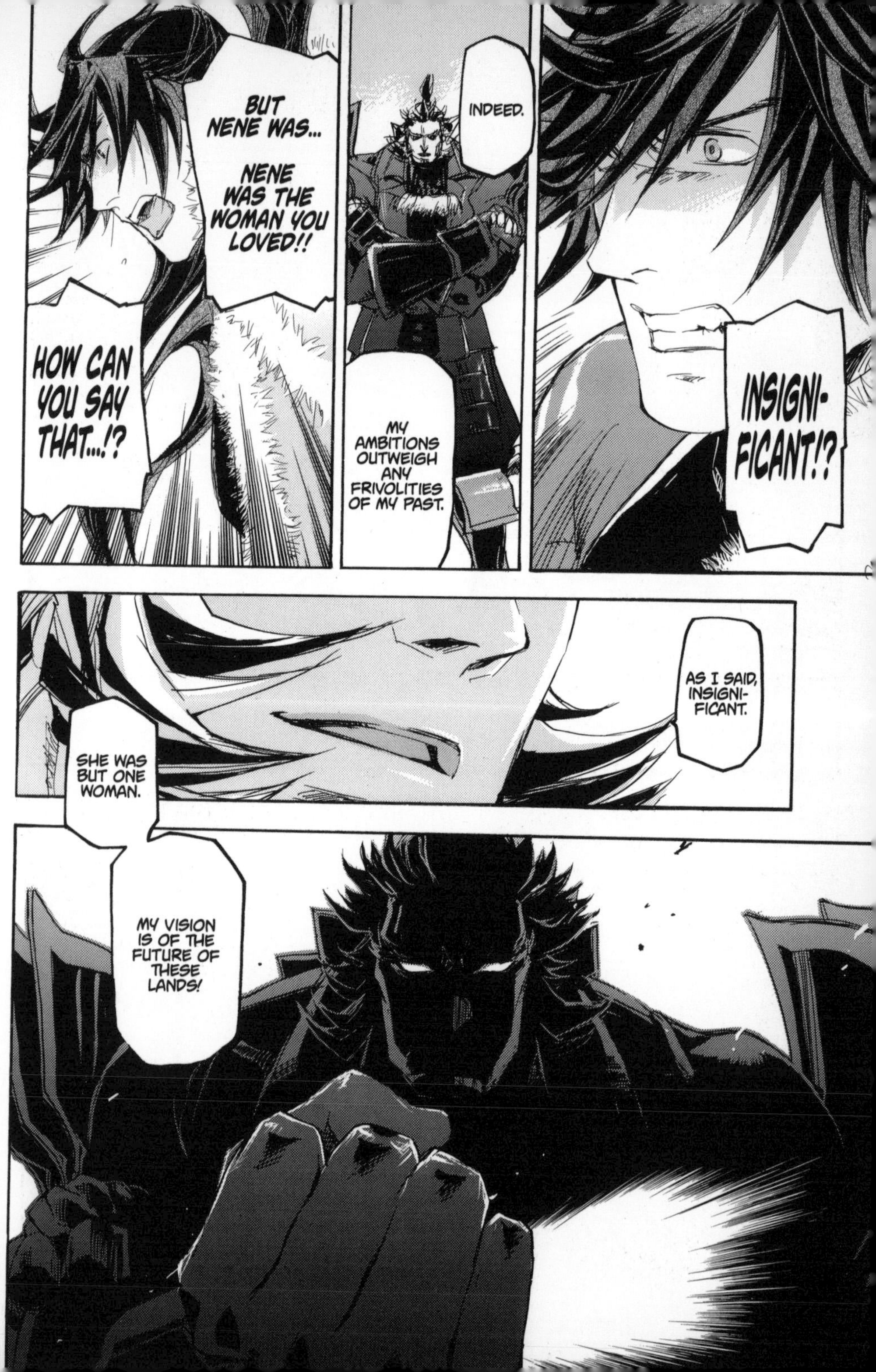
INSIGNI-FICANT!?
INDEED.
MY AMBITIONS OUTWEIGH ANY FRIVOLITIES OF MY PAST.
BUT NENE WAS...
NENE WAS THE WOMAN YOU LOVED!!
HOW CAN YOU SAY THAT...!?
AS I SAID, INSIGNI-FICANT.
SHE WAS BUT ONE WOMAN.
MY VISION IS OF THE FUTURE OF THESE LANDS!

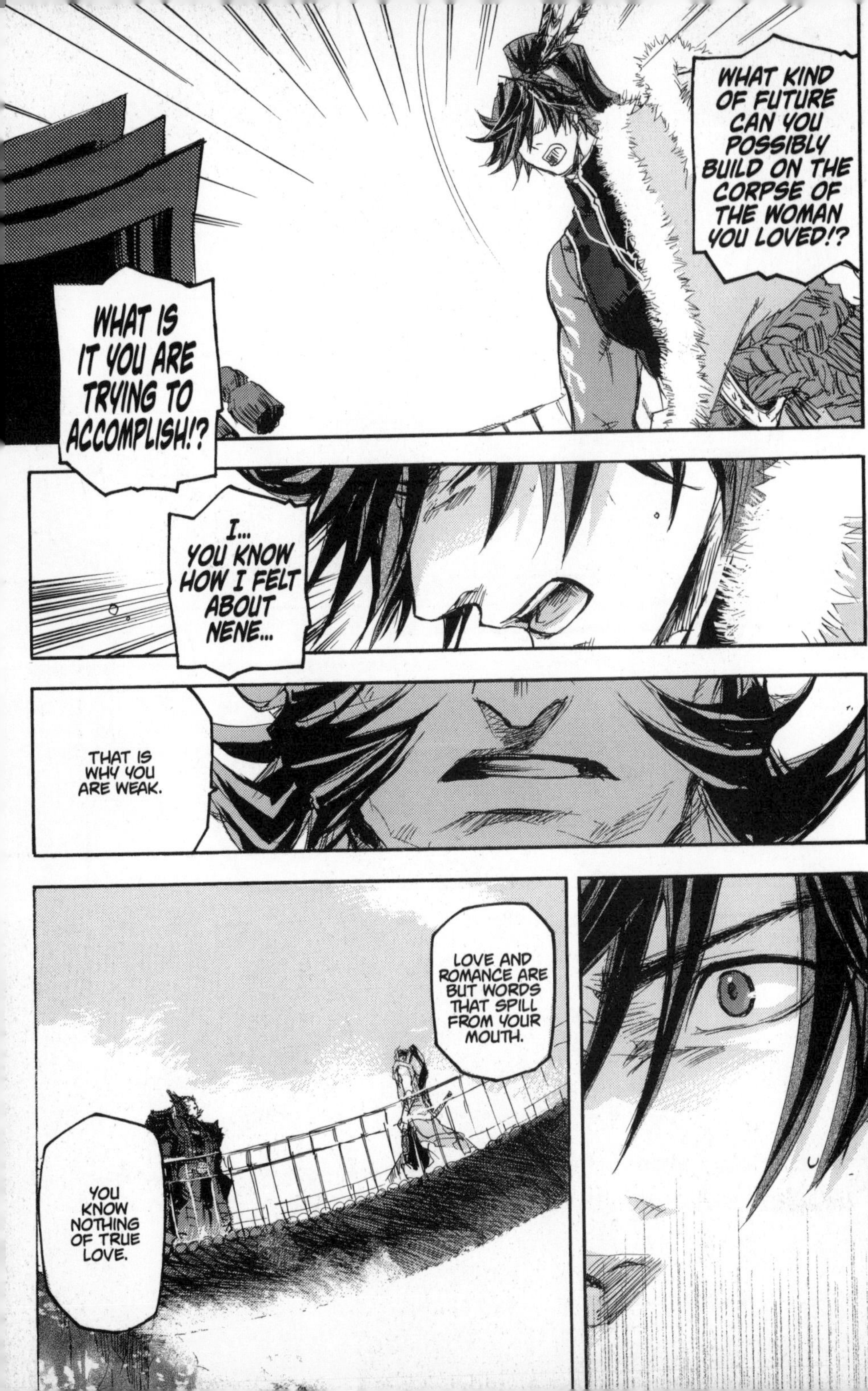
WHAT KIND OF FUTURE CAN YOU POSSIBLY BUILD ON THE CORPSE OF THE WOMAN YOU LOVED!?
WHAT IS IT YOU ARE TRYING TO ACCOMPLISH!?
I... YOU KNOW HOW I FELT ABOUT NENE...
THAT IS WHY YOU ARE WEAK.
LOVE AND ROMANCE ARE BUT WORDS THAT SPILL FROM YOUR MOUTH.
YOU KNOW NOTHING OF TRUE LOVE.

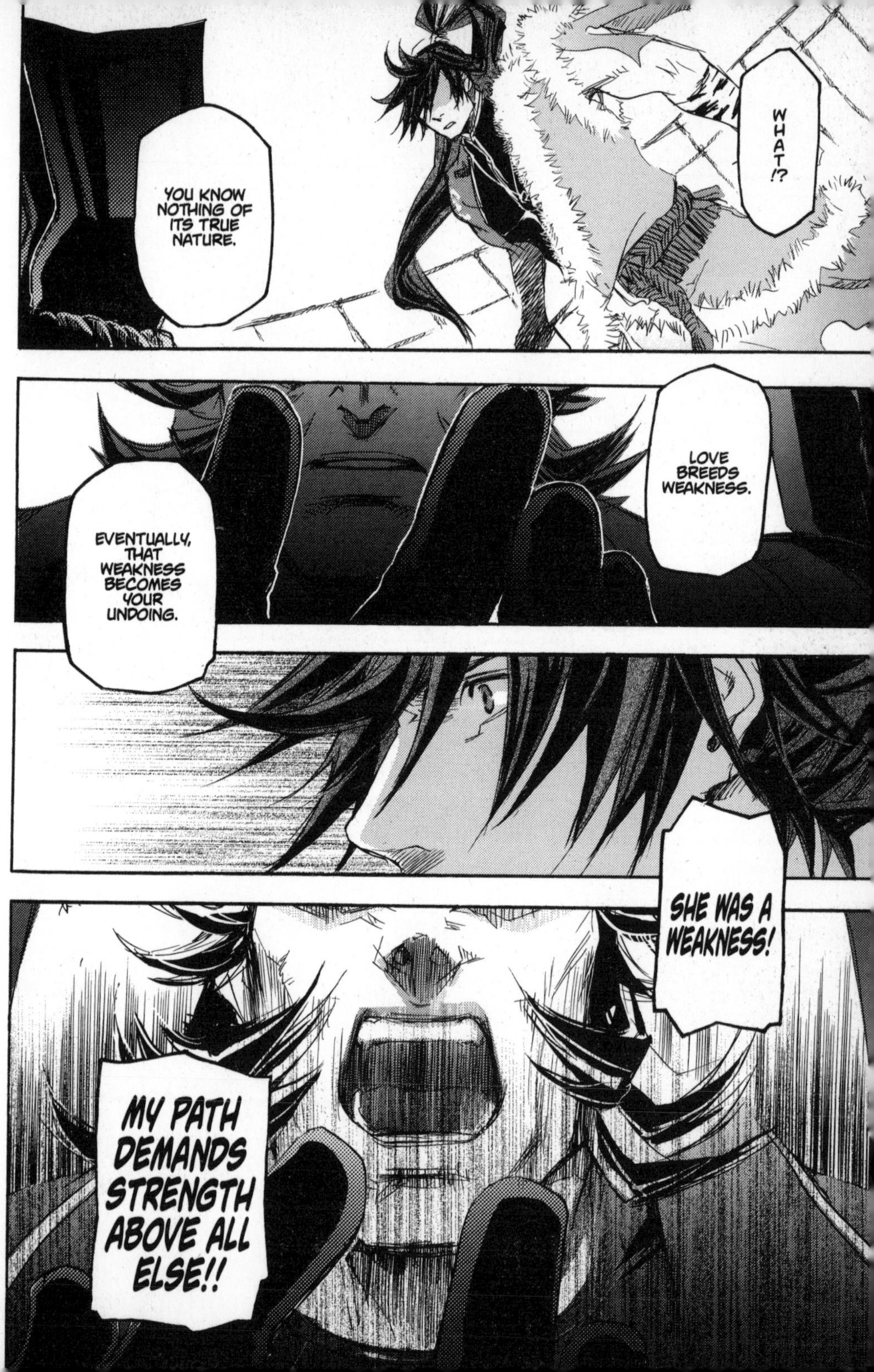
WHAT!?
YOU KNOW NOTHING OF ITS TRUE NATURE.
LOVE BREEDS WEAKNESS.
EVENTUALLY, THAT WEAKNESS BECOMES YOUR UNDOING.
SHE WAS A WEAKNESS!
MY PATH DEMANDS STRENGTH ABOVE ALL ELSE!!

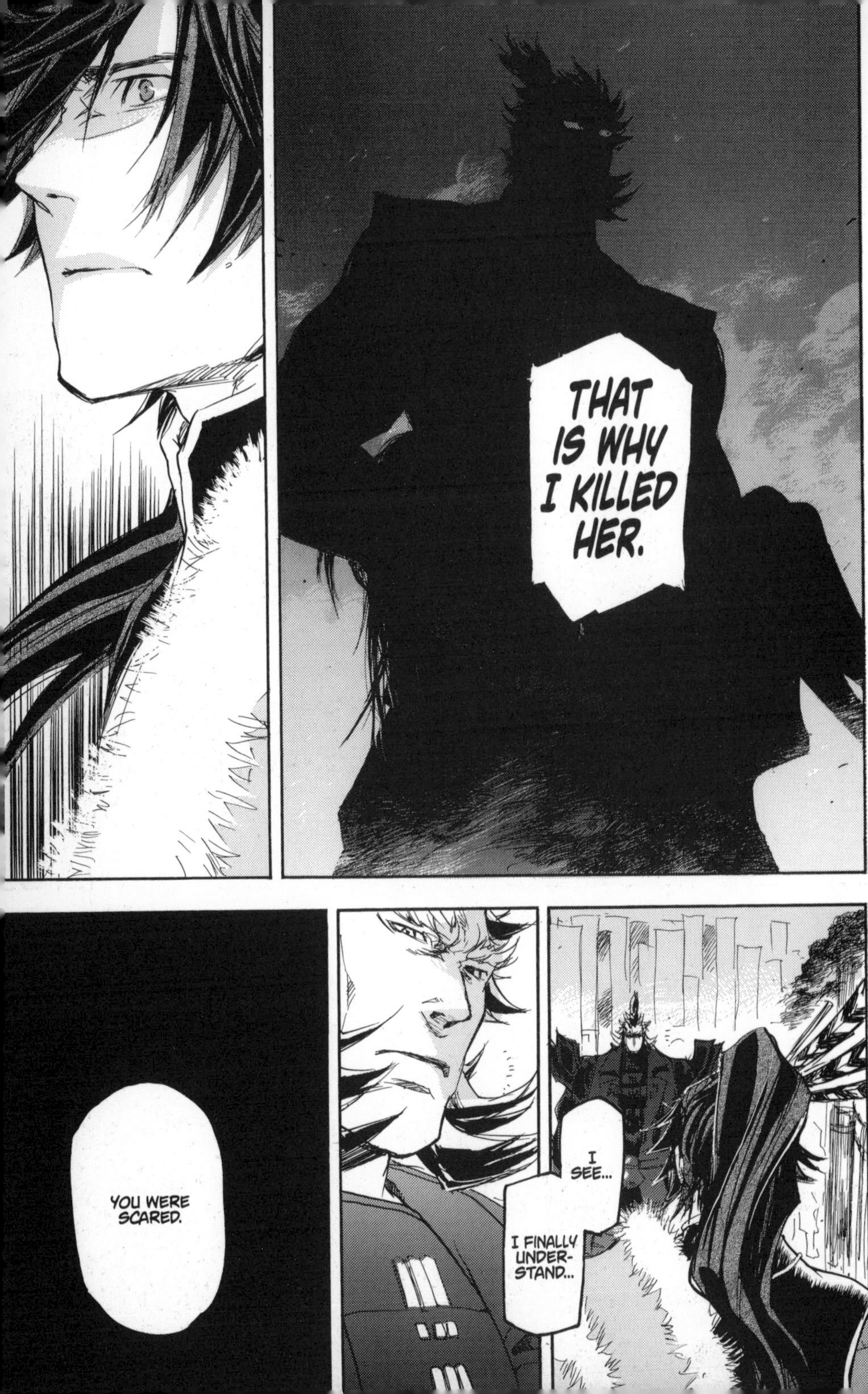
THAT IS WHY I KILLED HER.
I SEE...
I FINALLY UNDER-STAND...
YOU WERE SCARED.

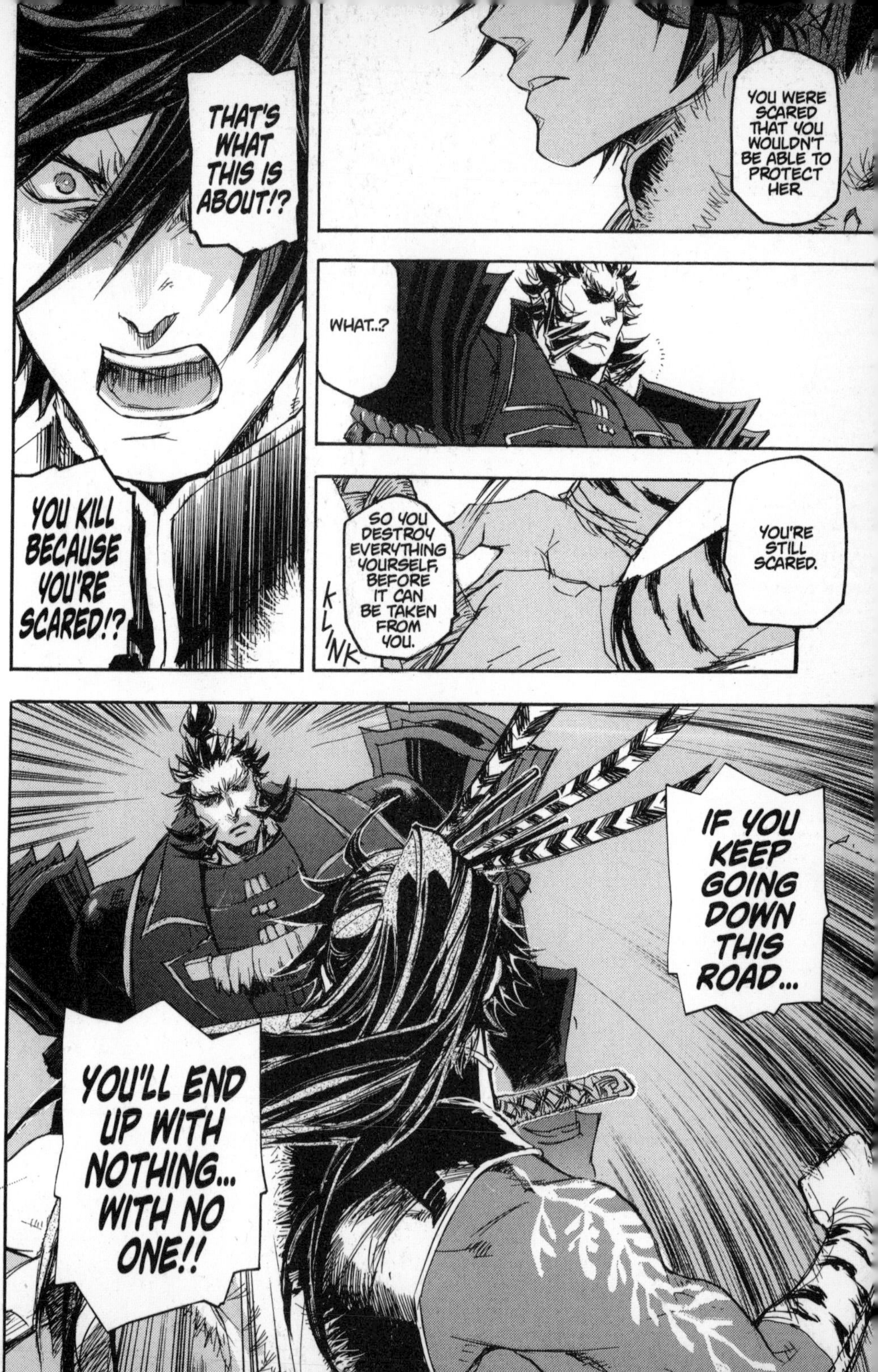
YOU WERE SCARED THAT YOU WOULDN'T BE ABLE TO PROTECT HER.
WHAT..?
THAT'S WHAT THIS IS ABOUT!?
YOU'RE STILL SCARED.
SO YOU DESTROY EVERYTHING YOURSELF, BEFORE IT CAN BE TAKEN FROM YOU.
KLINK
YOU KILL BECAUSE YOU'RE SCARED!?
IF YOU KEEP GOING DOWN THIS ROAD...
YOU'LL END UP WITH NOTHING... WITH NO ONE!!

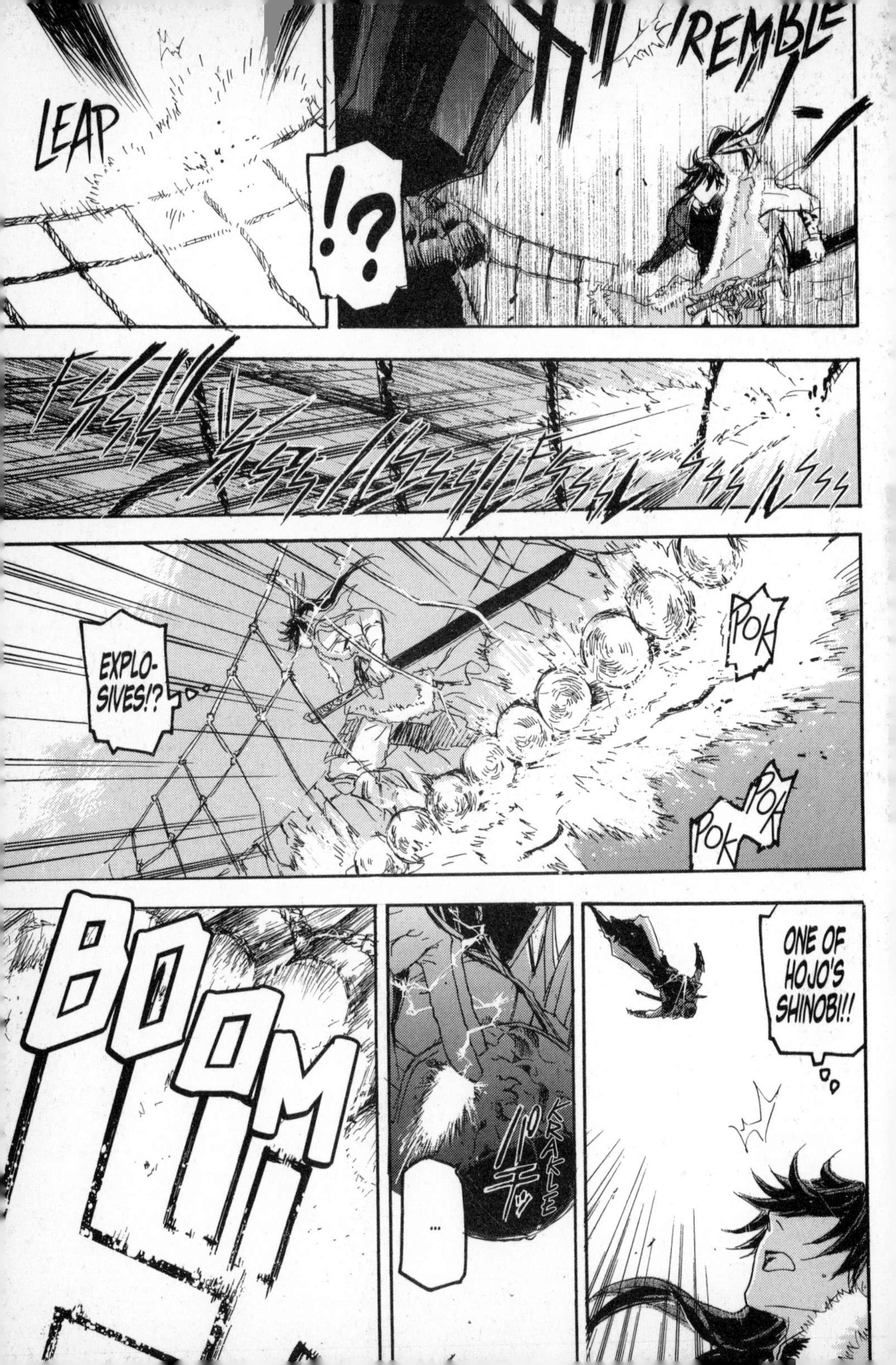
TREMBLE
!?
LEAP
EXPLOSIVES!?
POK
POK
POK
ONE OF HOJO'S SHINOBI!!
KRAKLE
...
BOOM!!

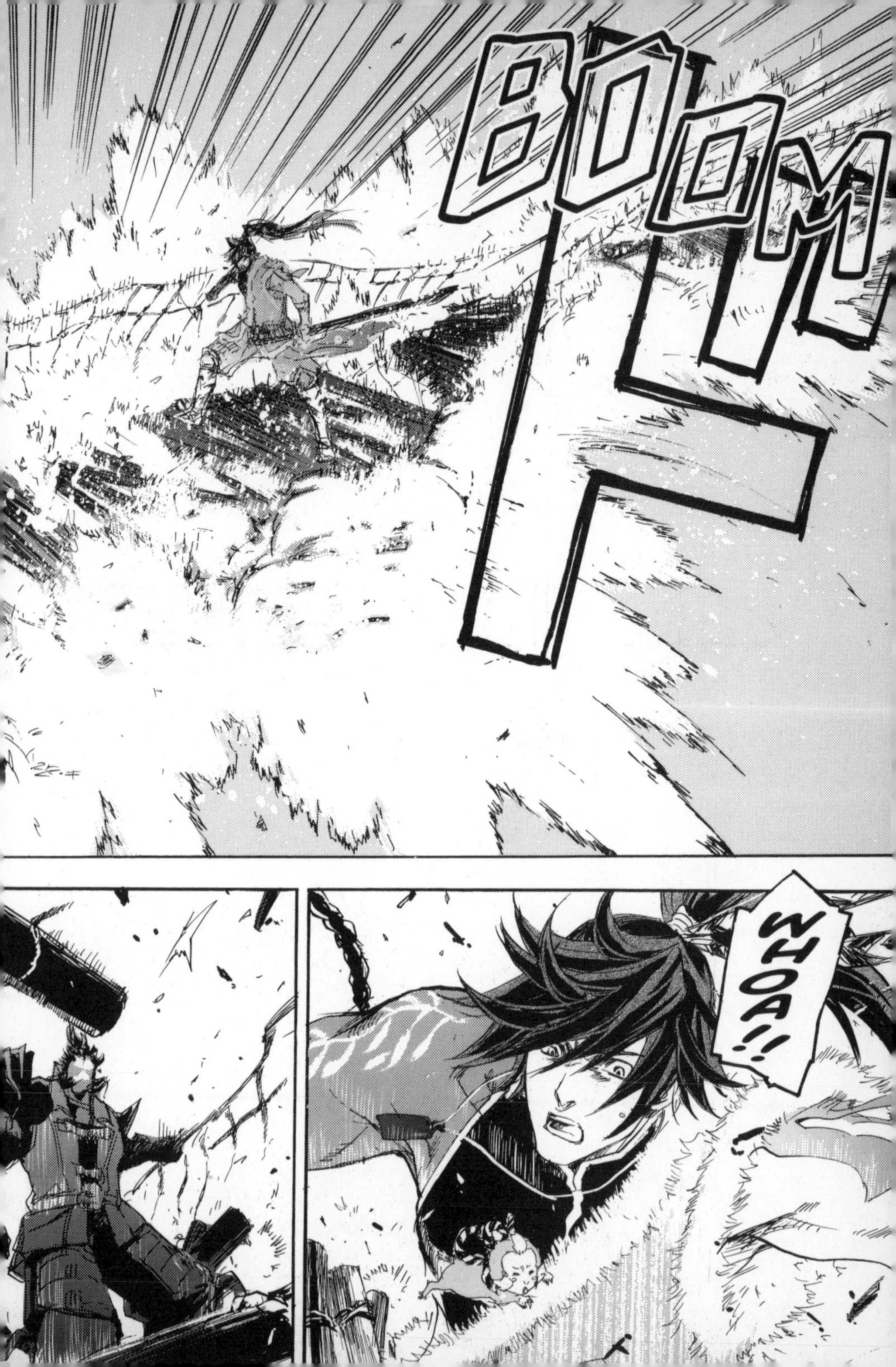
BOOM
WHOA!!

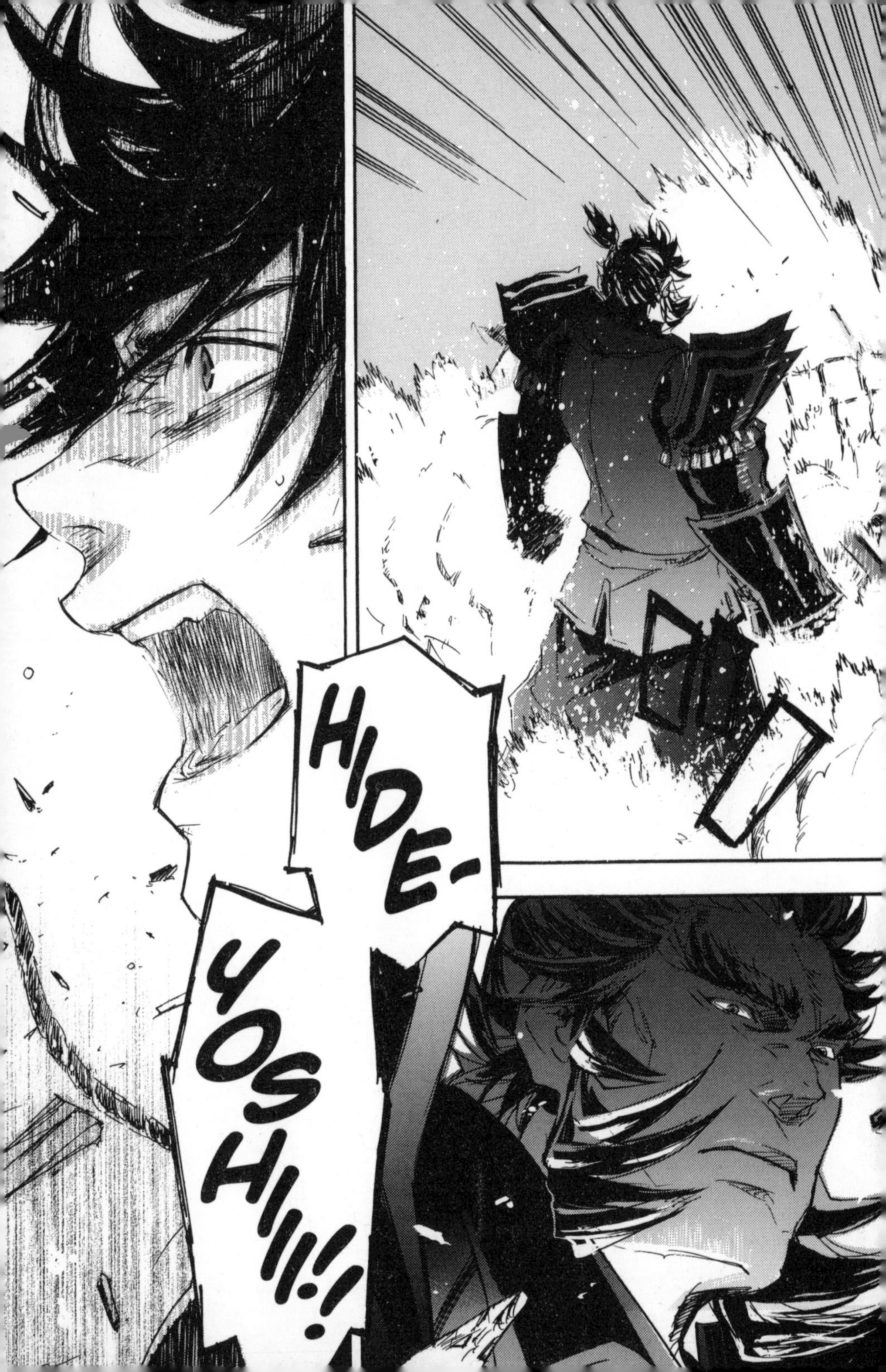
HIDE-YOSHIII!!

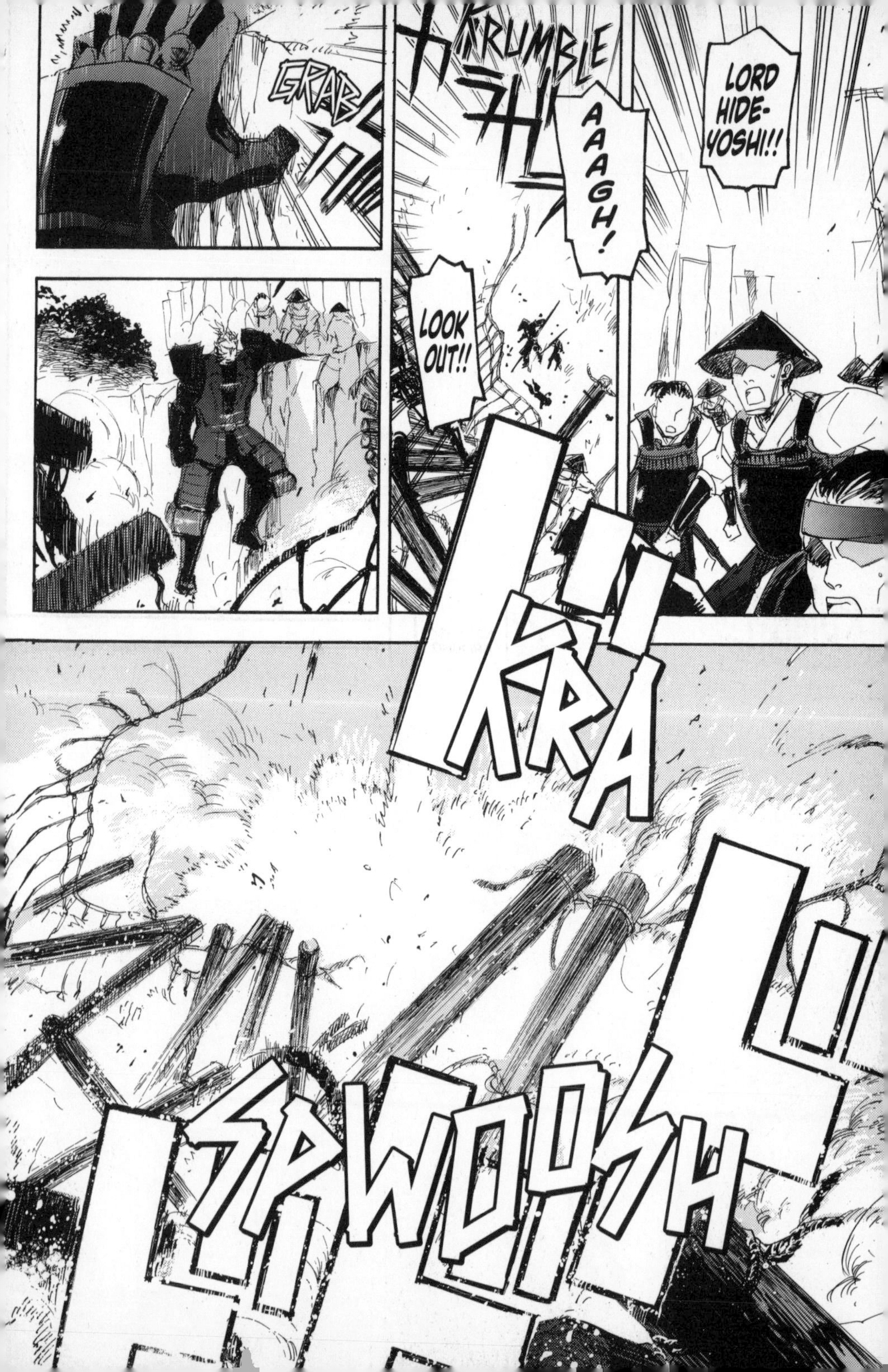

LORD HIDE-YOSHI!!
KRUMBLE
AAAAGH!
LOOK OUT!!
GRAB
KRA
SPWOOSH

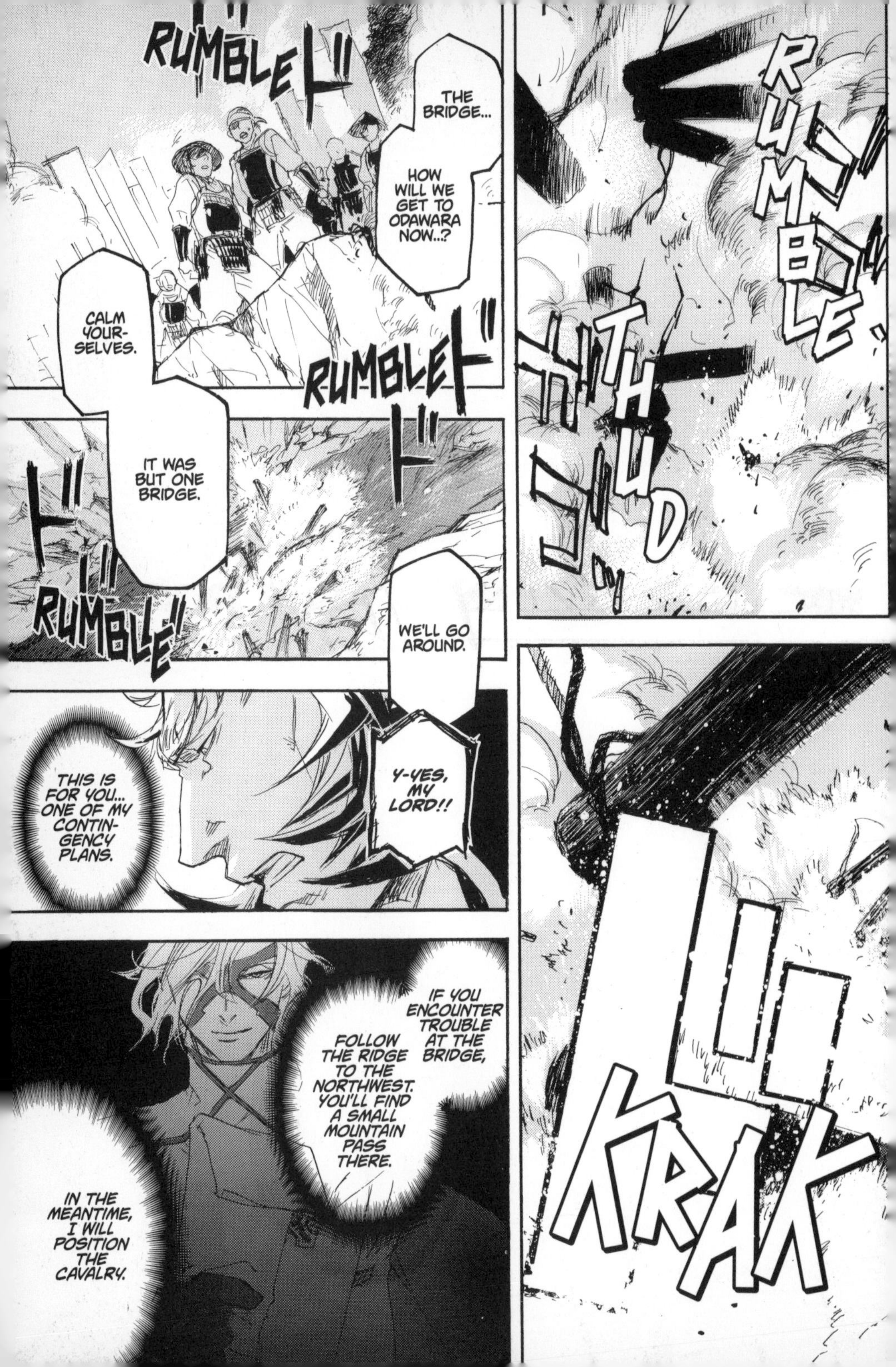

RUMBLE
THUD
RUMBLE
THE BRIDGE...
HOW WILL WE GET TO ODAWARA NOW..?
RUMBLE
CALM YOUR-SELVES.
IT WAS BUT ONE BRIDGE.
RUMBLE
KRAK
WE'LL GO AROUND.
Y-YES, MY LORD!!
THIS IS FOR YOU... ONE OF MY CONTIN-GENCY PLANS.
IF YOU ENCOUNTER TROUBLE AT THE BRIDGE,
FOLLOW THE RIDGE TO THE NORTHWEST. YOU'LL FIND A SMALL MOUNTAIN PASS THERE.
IN THE MEANTIME, I WILL POSITION THE CAVALRY.

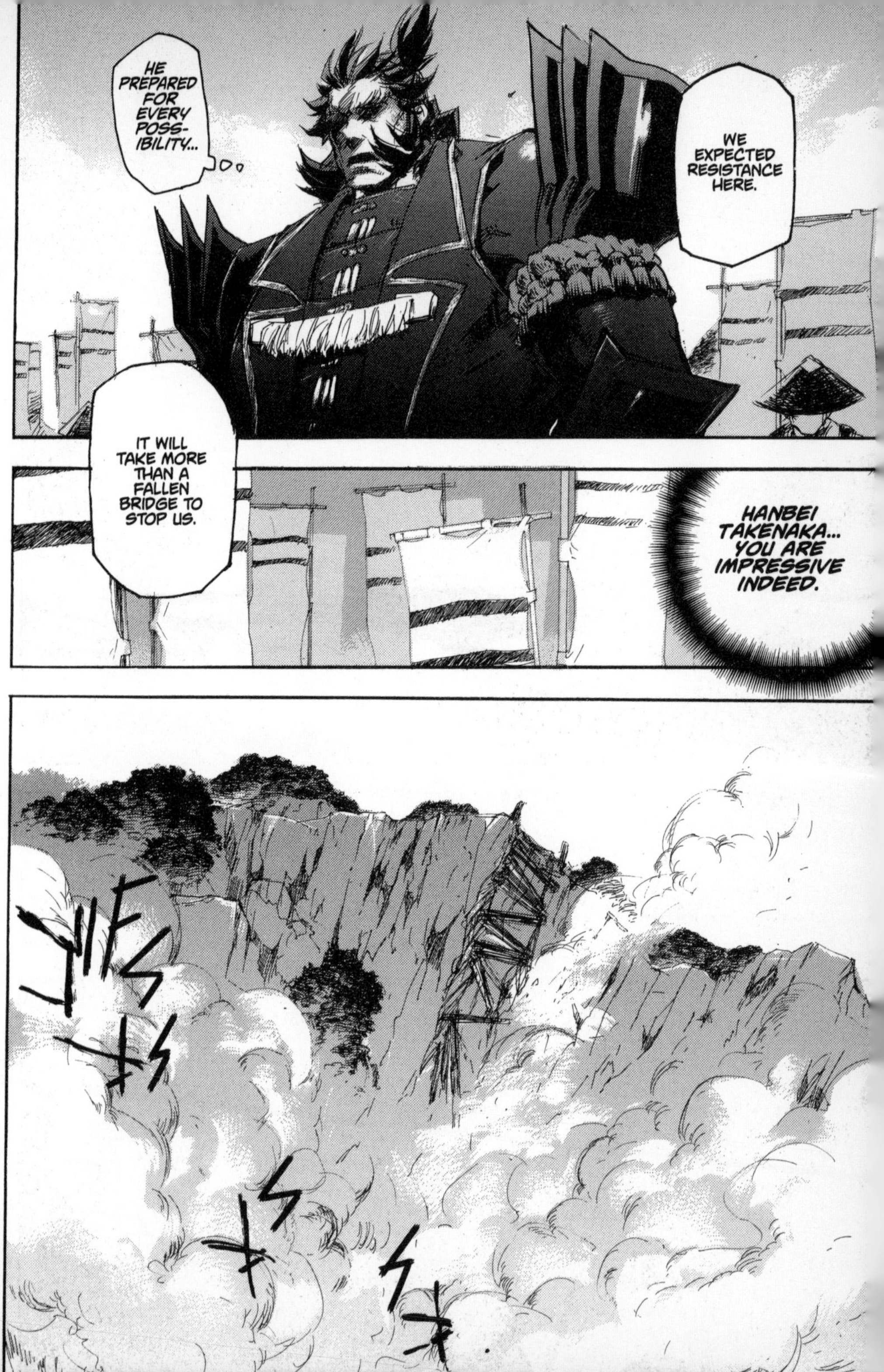
WE EXPECTED RESISTANCE HERE.
HE PREPARED FOR EVERY POSS-IBILITY...
IT WILL TAKE MORE THAN A FALLEN BRIDGE TO STOP US.
HANBEI TAKENAKA... YOU ARE IMPRESSIVE INDEED.

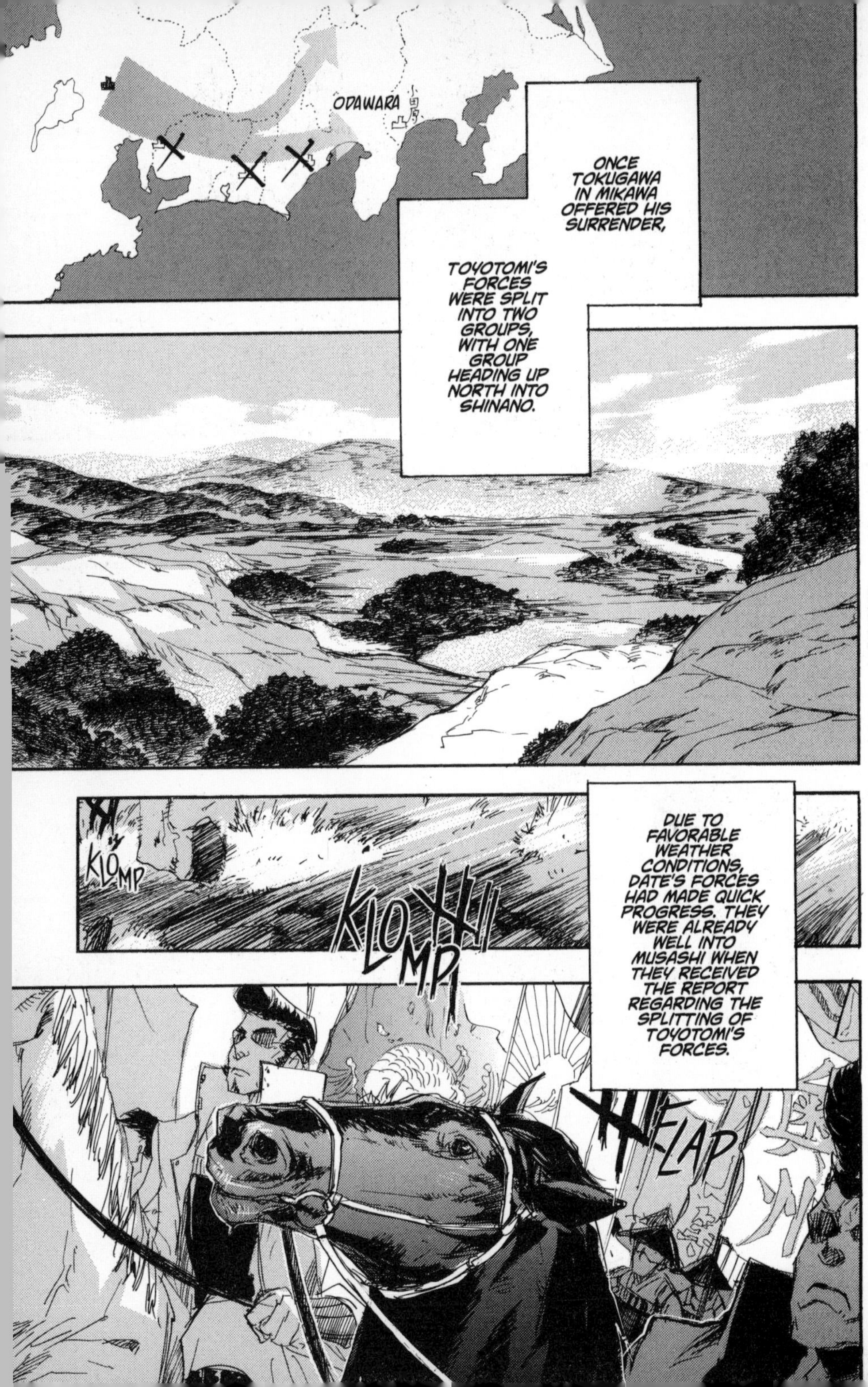
ODAWARA
ONCE TOKUGAWA IN MIKAWA OFFERED HIS SURRENDER,
TOYOTOMI'S FORCES WERE SPLIT INTO TWO GROUPS, WITH ONE GROUP HEADING UP NORTH INTO SHINANO.
KLOMP
KLOMP
DUE TO FAVORABLE WEATHER CONDITIONS, DATE'S FORCES HAD MADE QUICK PROGRESS. THEY WERE ALREADY WELL INTO MUSASHI WHEN THEY RECEIVED THE REPORT REGARDING THE SPLITTING OF TOYOTOMI'S FORCES.
FLAP

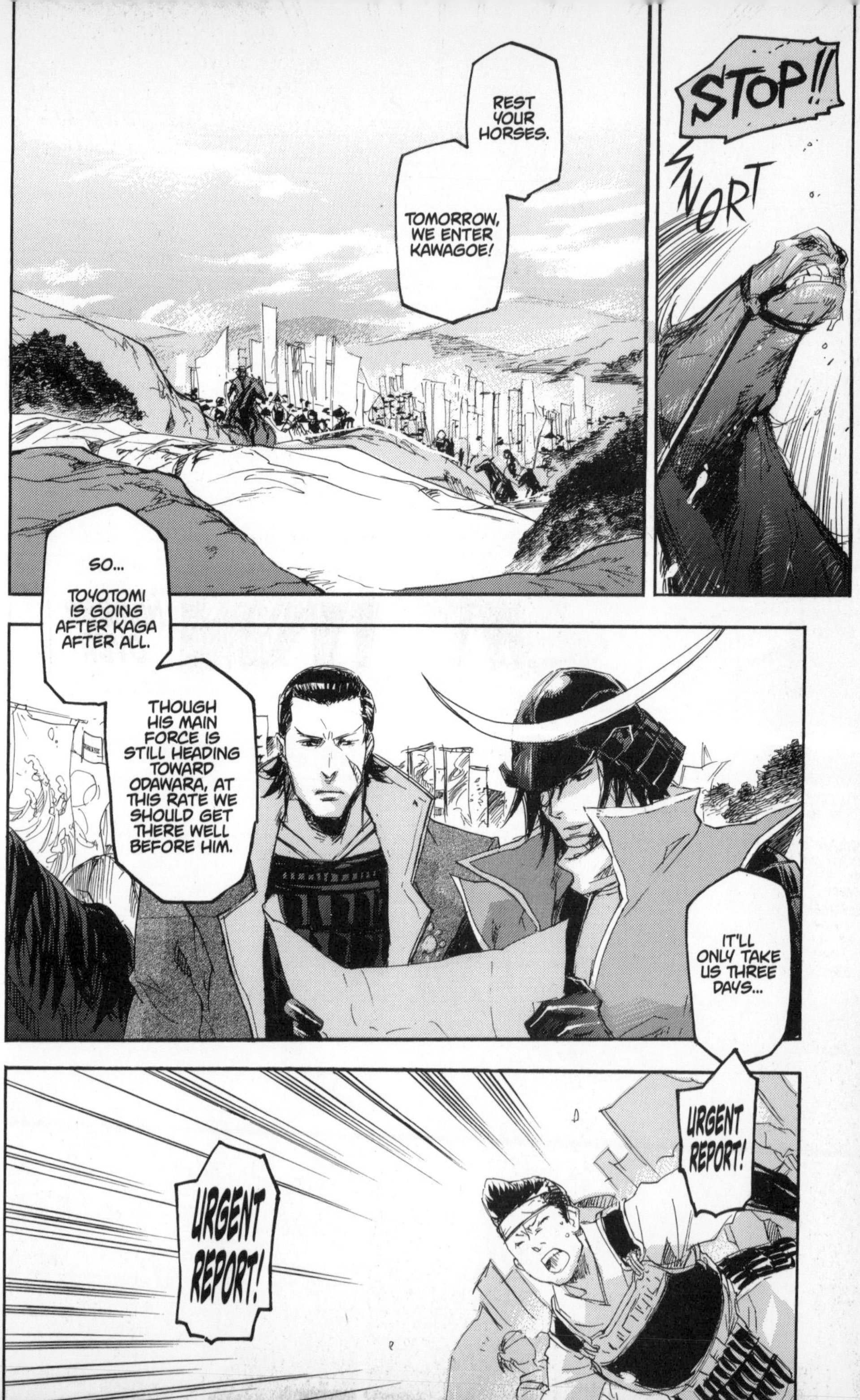
STOP!!
SNORT
REST YOUR HORSES.
TOMORROW, WE ENTER KAWAGOE!
SO...
TOYOTOMI IS GOING AFTER KAGA AFTER ALL.
THOUGH HIS MAIN FORCE IS STILL HEADING TOWARD ODAWARA, AT THIS RATE WE SHOULD GET THERE WELL BEFORE HIM.
IT'LL ONLY TAKE US THREE DAYS...
URGENT REPORT!
URGENT REPORT!

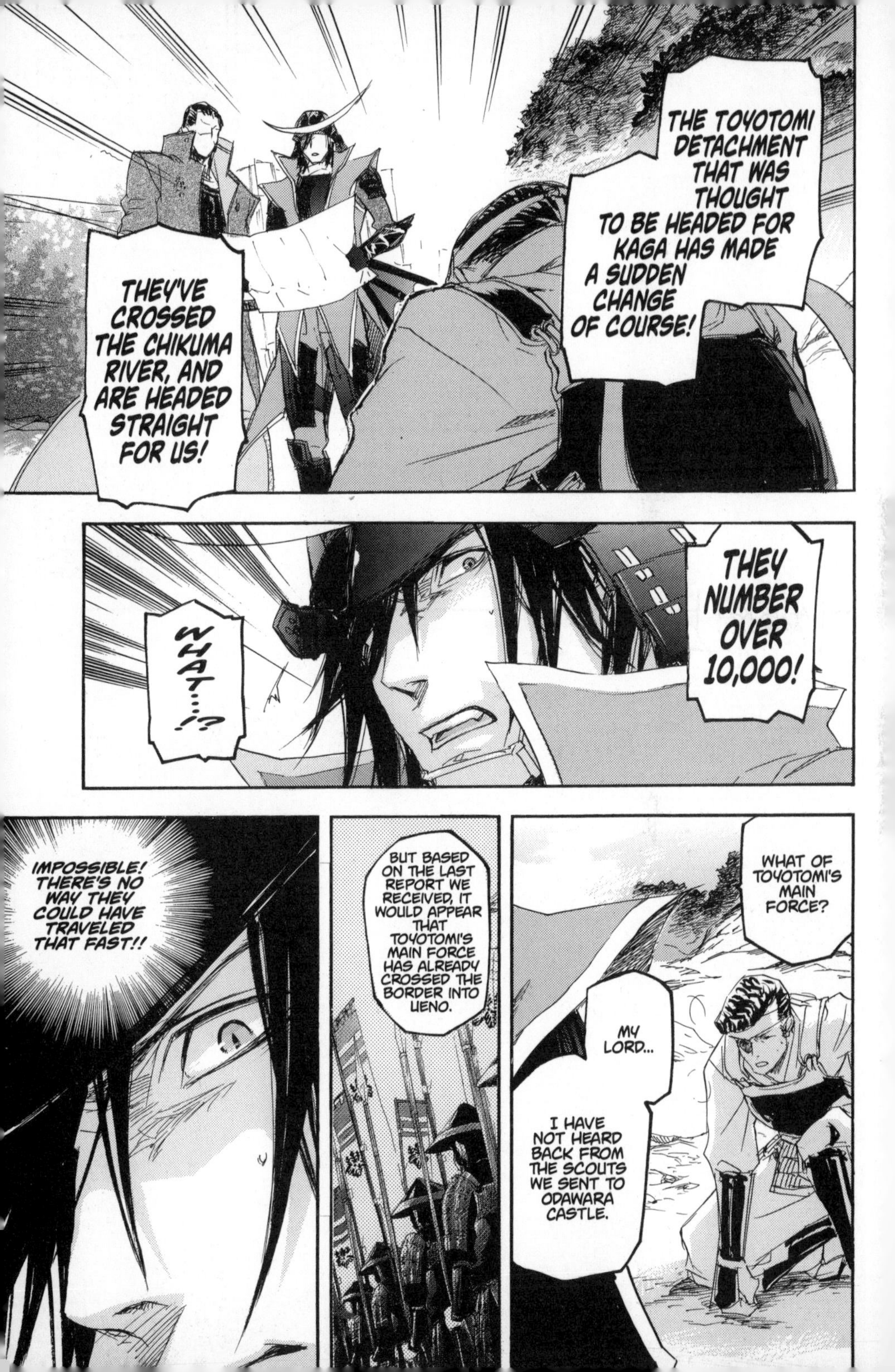
THE TOYOTOMI DETACHMENT THAT WAS THOUGHT TO BE HEADED FOR KAGA HAS MADE A SUDDEN CHANGE OF COURSE!
THEY'VE CROSSED THE CHIKUMA RIVER, AND ARE HEADED STRAIGHT FOR US!
THEY NUMBER OVER 10,000!
WHAT...!?
WHAT OF TOYOTOMI'S MAIN FORCE?
MY LORD...
I HAVE NOT HEARD BACK FROM THE SCOUTS WE SENT TO ODAWARA CASTLE.
BUT BASED ON THE LAST REPORT WE RECEIVED, IT WOULD APPEAR THAT TOYOTOMI'S MAIN FORCE HAS ALREADY CROSSED THE BORDER INTO UENO.
IMPOSSIBLE! THERE'S NO WAY THEY COULD HAVE TRAVELED THAT FAST!!

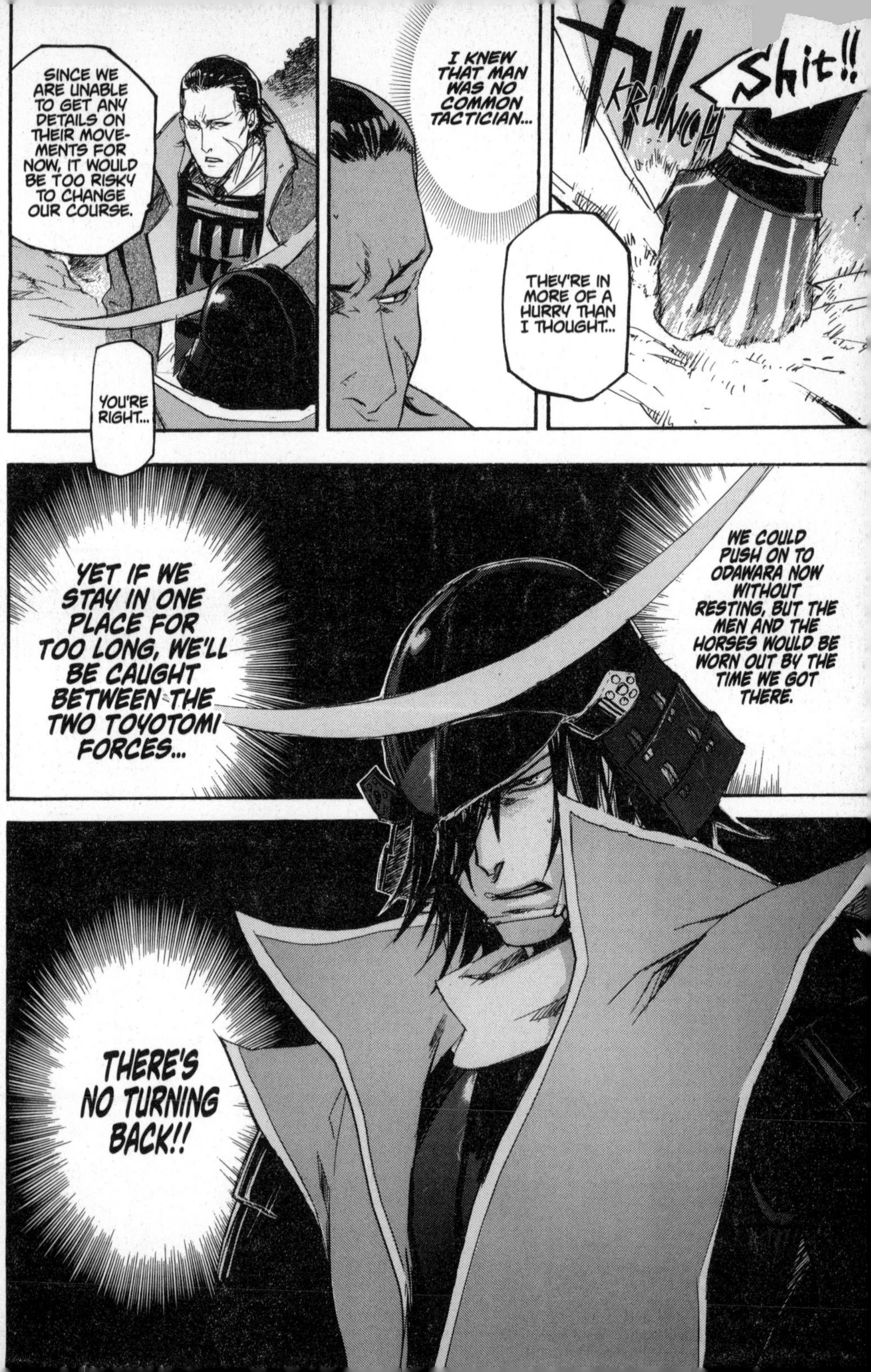
Shit!!
KRUNCH
THEY'RE IN MORE OF A HURRY THAN I THOUGHT...
I KNEW THAT MAN WAS NO COMMON TACTICIAN...
SINCE WE ARE UNABLE TO GET ANY DETAILS ON THEIR MOVEMENTS FOR NOW, IT WOULD BE TOO RISKY TO CHANGE OUR COURSE.
YOU'RE RIGHT...
WE COULD PUSH ON TO ODAWARA NOW WITHOUT RESTING, BUT THE MEN AND THE HORSES WOULD BE WORN OUT BY THE TIME WE GOT THERE.
YET IF WE STAY IN ONE PLACE FOR TOO LONG, WE'LL BE CAUGHT BETWEEN THE TWO TOYOTOMI FORCES...
THERE'S NO TURNING BACK!!

戦国BASARA2
SENGOKU BASARA2

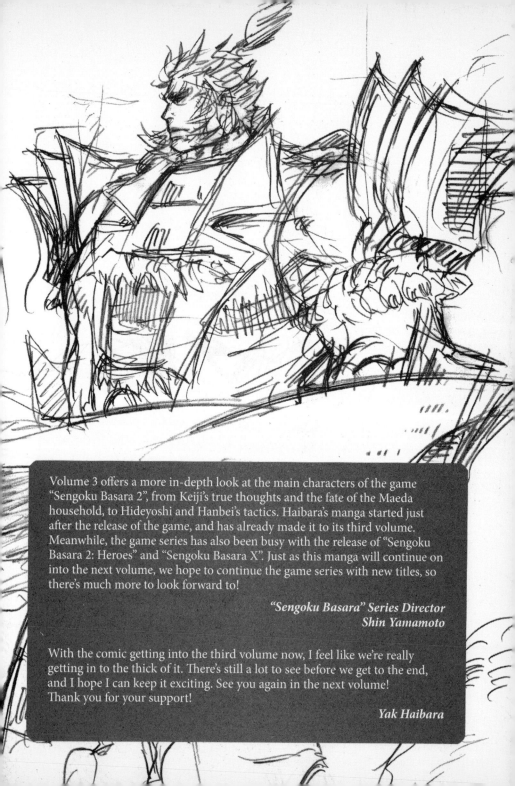

Volume 3 offers a more in-depth look at the main characters of the game "Sengoku Basara 2", from Keiji's true thoughts and the fate of the Maeda household, to Hideyoshi and Hanbei's tactics. Haibara's manga started just after the release of the game, and has already made it to its third volume. Meanwhile, the game series has also been busy with the release of "Sengoku Basara 2: Heroes" and "Sengoku Basara X". Just as this manga will continue on into the next volume, we hope to continue the game series with new titles, so there's much more to look forward to!

"Sengoku Basara" Series Director
Shin Yamamoto

With the comic getting into the third volume now, I feel like we're really getting in to the thick of it. There's still a lot to see before we get to the end, and I hope I can keep it exciting. See you again in the next volume! Thank you for your support!

Yak Haibara

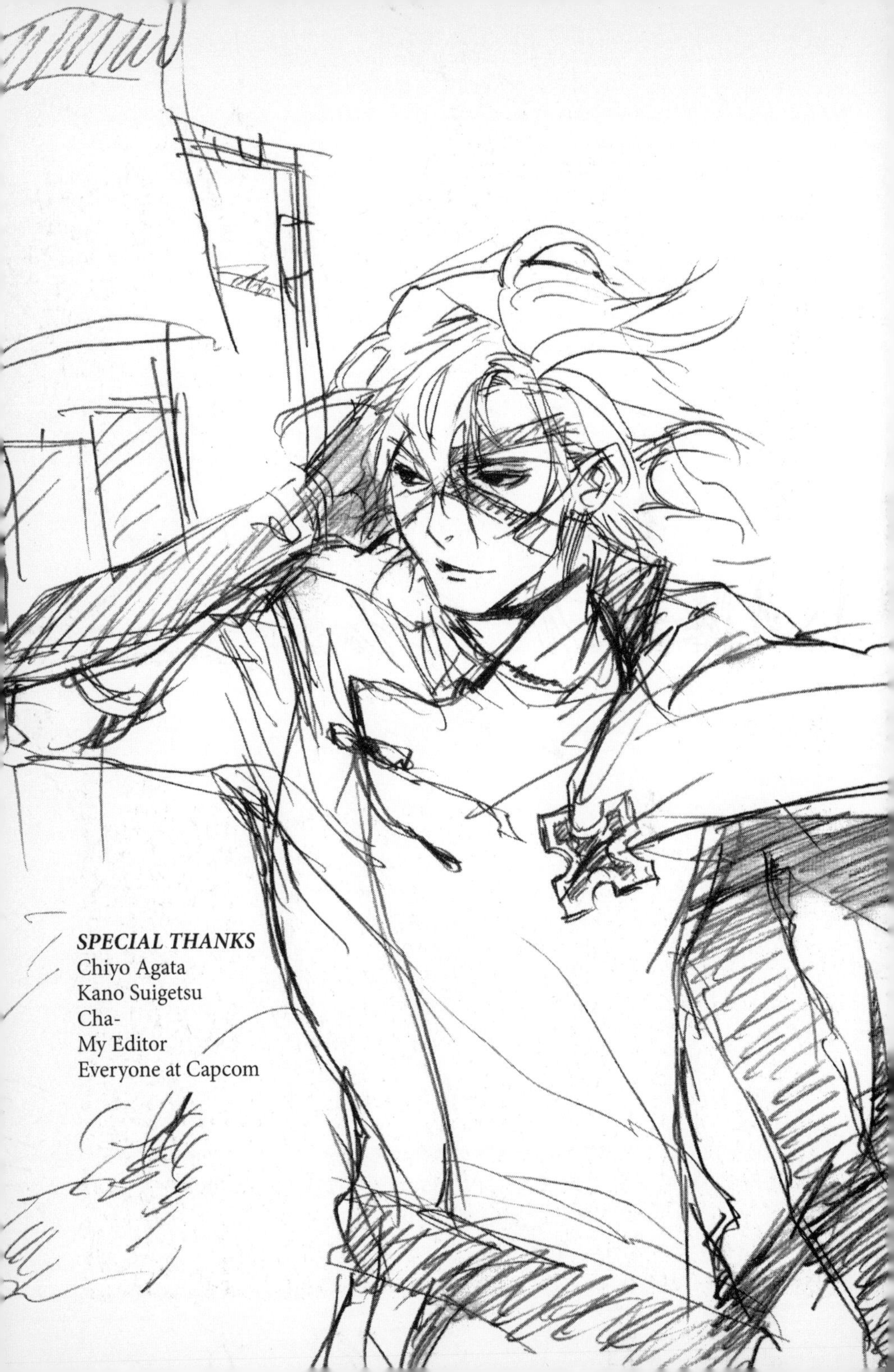

SPECIAL THANKS
Chiyo Agata
Kano Suigetsu
Cha-
My Editor
Everyone at Capcom

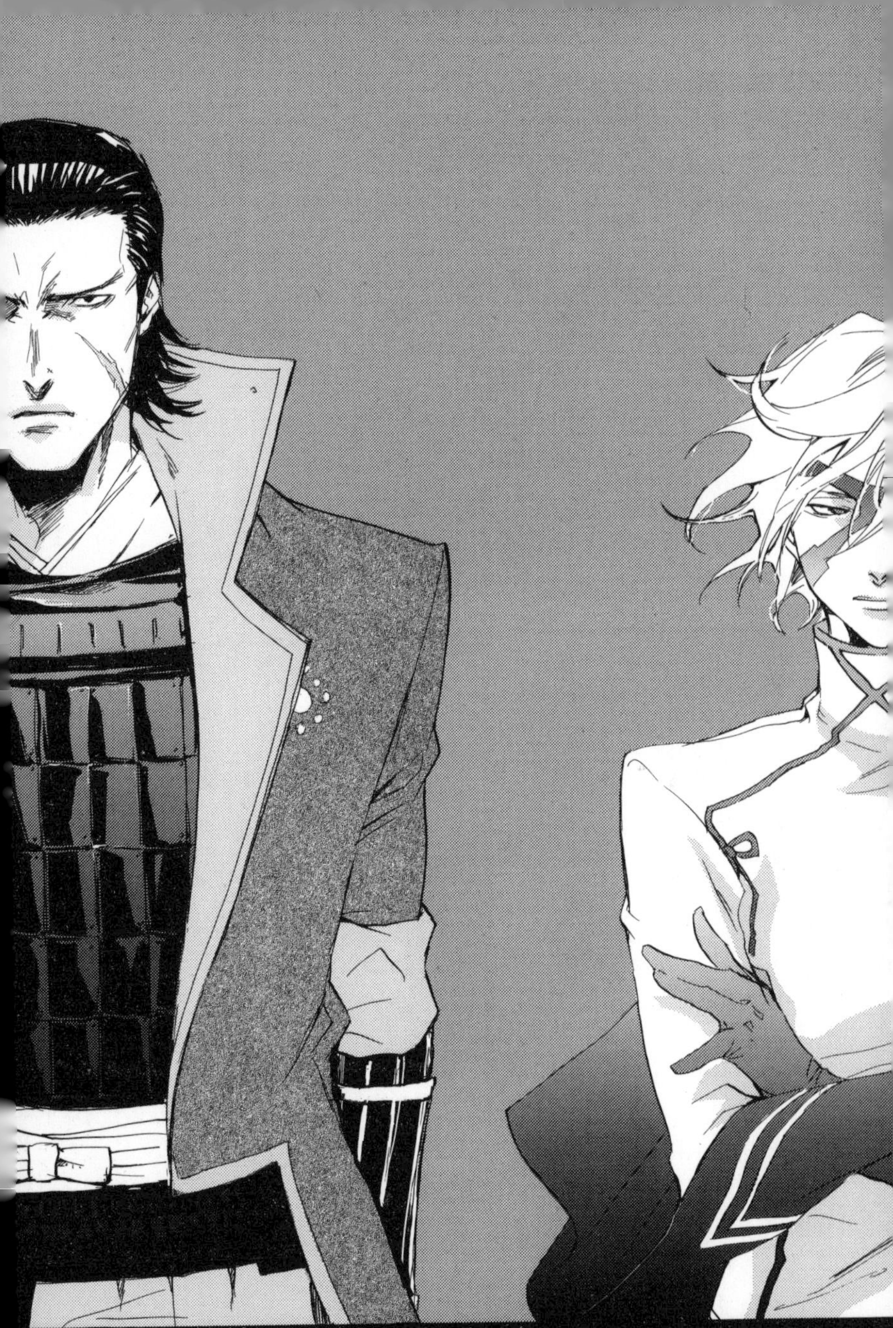

ACT19: Vengeance

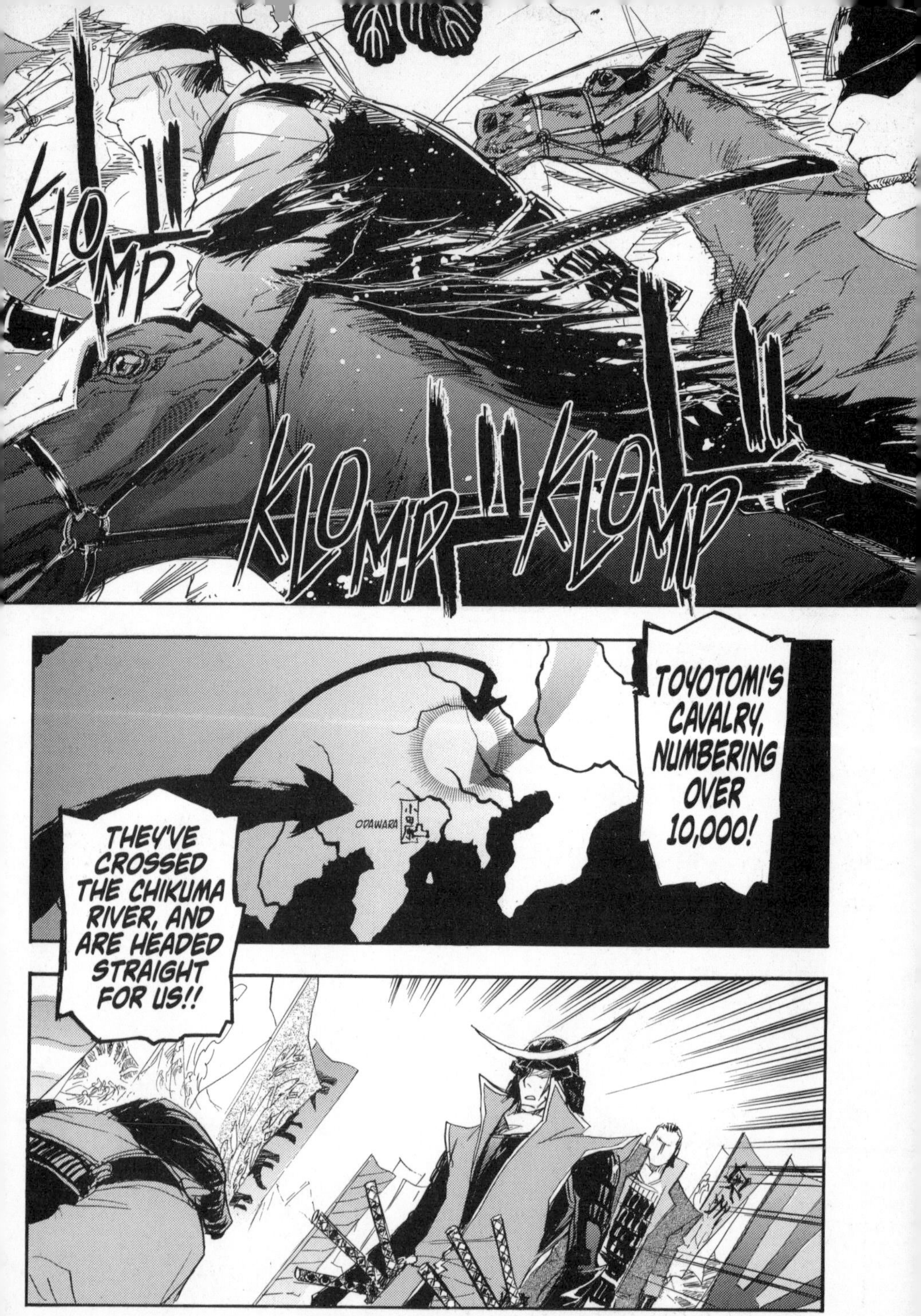
KLOMP
KLOMP
KLOMP
TOYOTOMI'S CAVALRY, NUMBERING OVER 10,000!
ODAWARA
小田原
THEY'VE CROSSED THE CHIKUMA RIVER, AND ARE HEADED STRAIGHT FOR US!!

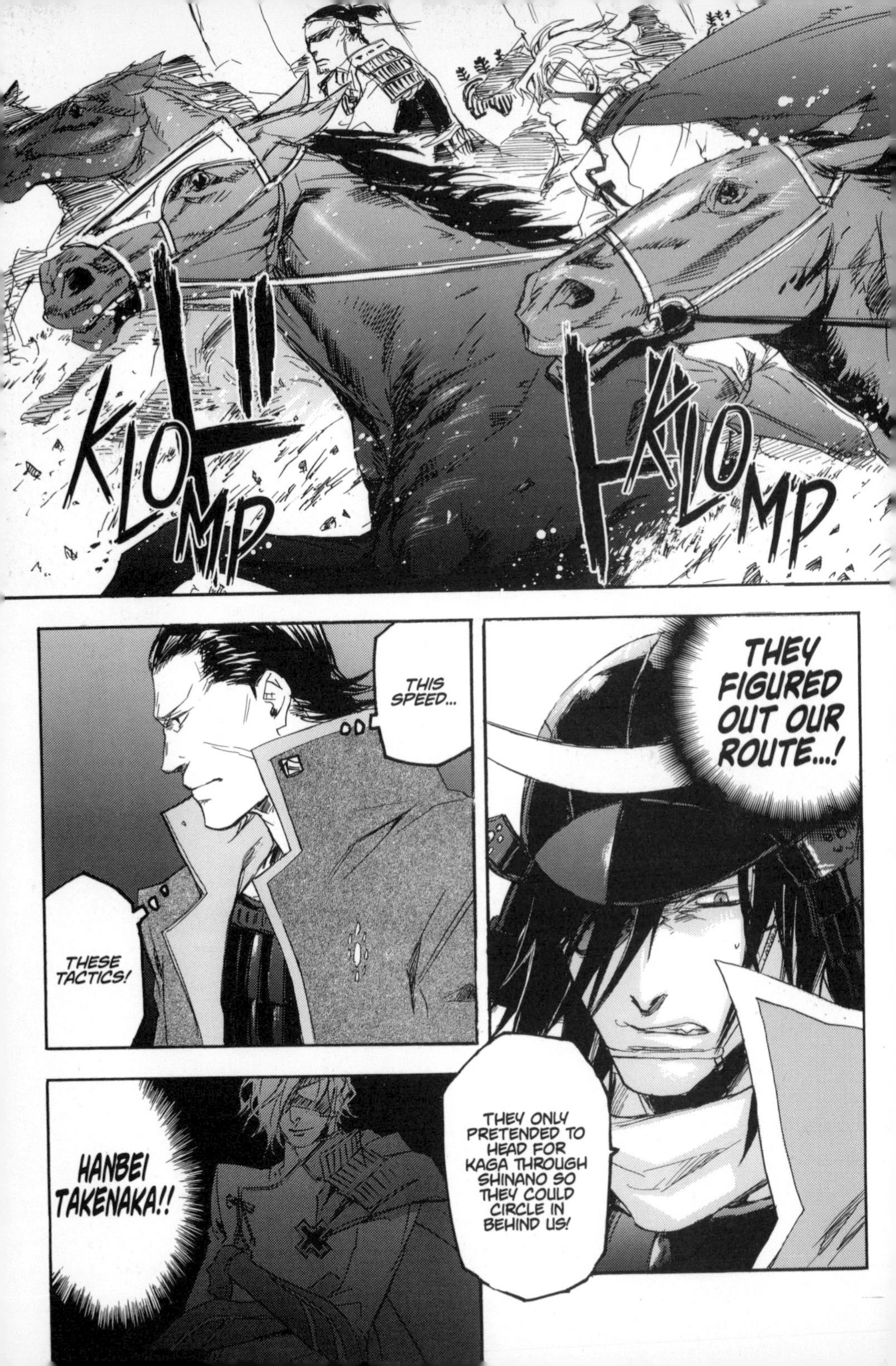
KLOMP
KLOMP
THEY FIGURED OUT OUR ROUTE...!
THEY ONLY PRETENDED TO HEAD FOR KAGA THROUGH SHINANO SO THEY COULD CIRCLE IN BEHIND US!
THIS SPEED...
THESE TACTICS!
HANBEI TAKENAKA!!

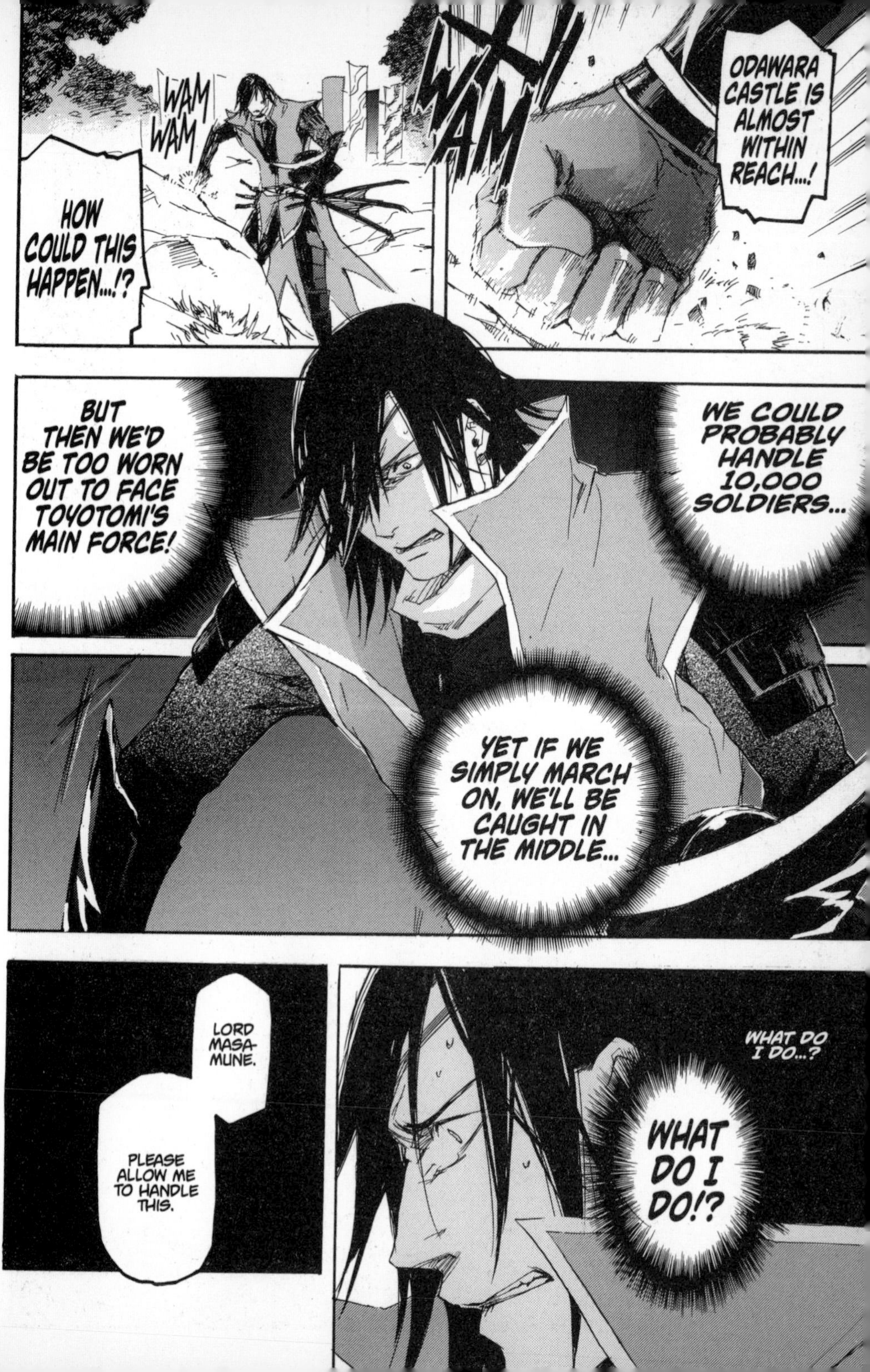
WHAM
ODAWARA CASTLE IS ALMOST WITHIN REACH...!
WAM WAM
HOW COULD THIS HAPPEN...!?
WE COULD PROBABLY HANDLE 10,000 SOLDIERS...
BUT THEN WE'D BE TOO WORN OUT TO FACE TOYOTOMI'S MAIN FORCE!
YET IF WE SIMPLY MARCH ON, WE'LL BE CAUGHT IN THE MIDDLE...
WHAT DO I DO...?
WHAT DO I DO!?
LORD MASAMUNE.
PLEASE ALLOW ME TO HANDLE THIS.

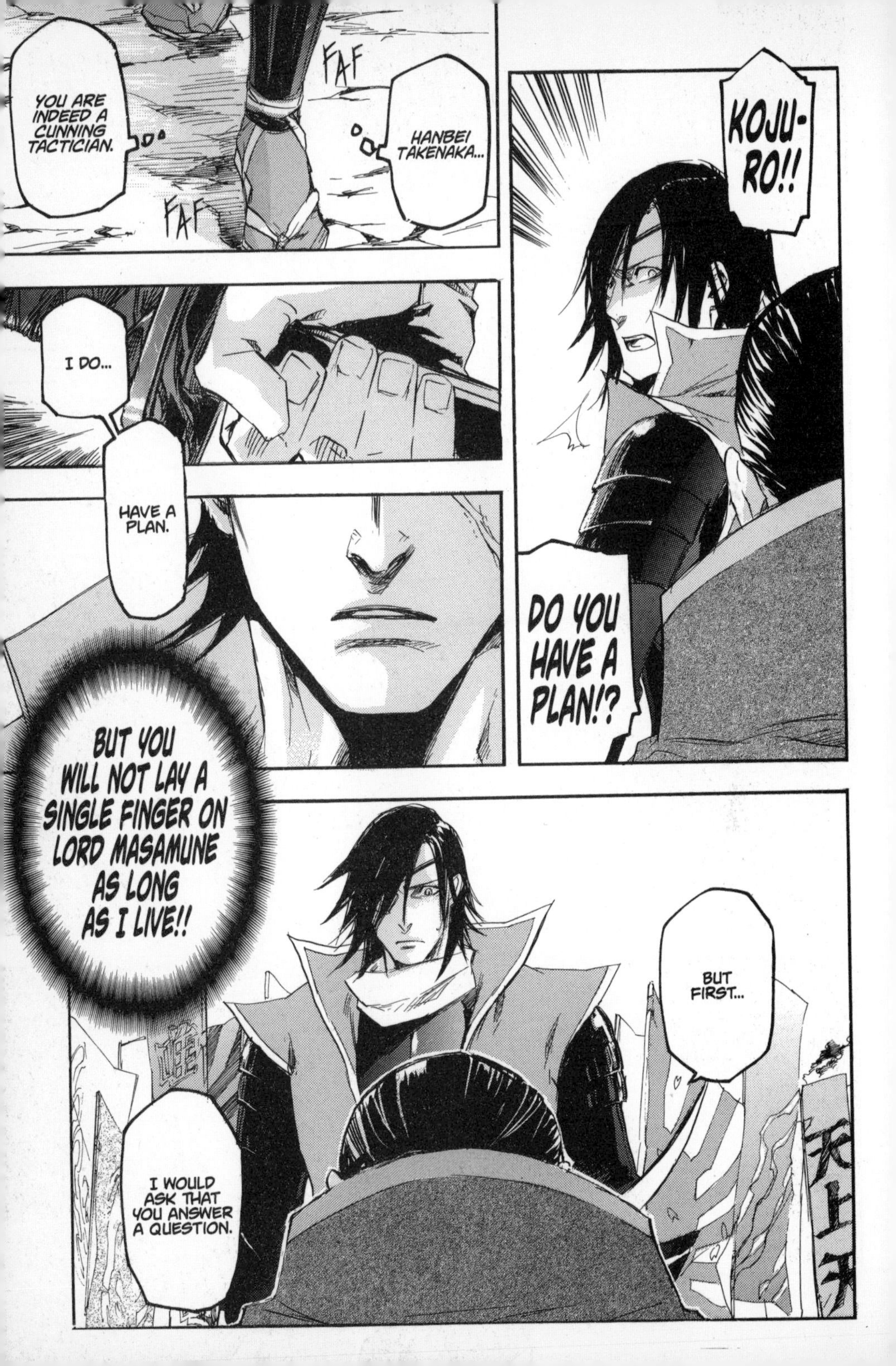

KOJU-RO!!
DO YOU HAVE A PLAN!?
HANBEI TAKENAKA...
FAF
FAF
YOU ARE INDEED A CUNNING TACTICIAN.
I DO...
HAVE A PLAN.
BUT YOU WILL NOT LAY A SINGLE FINGER ON LORD MASAMUNE AS LONG AS I LIVE!!
BUT FIRST...
I WOULD ASK THAT YOU ANSWER A QUESTION.

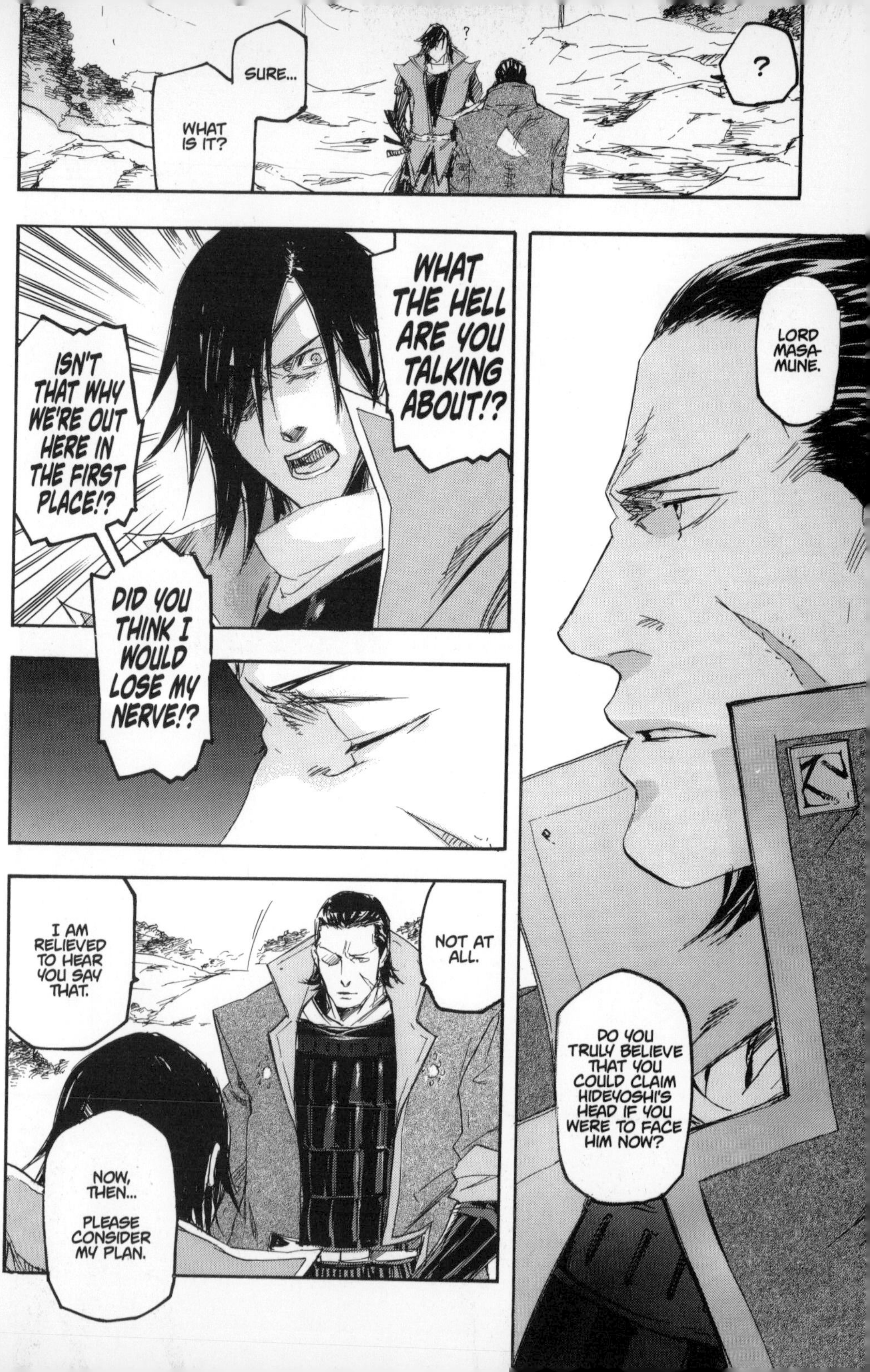
?
SURE...
WHAT IS IT?
LORD MASA-MUNE.
DO YOU TRULY BELIEVE THAT YOU COULD CLAIM HIDEYOSHI'S HEAD IF YOU WERE TO FACE HIM NOW?
WHAT THE HELL ARE YOU TALKING ABOUT!?
ISN'T THAT WHY WE'RE OUT HERE IN THE FIRST PLACE!?
DID YOU THINK I WOULD LOSE MY NERVE!?
NOT AT ALL.
I AM RELIEVED TO HEAR YOU SAY THAT.
NOW, THEN...
PLEASE CONSIDER MY PLAN.

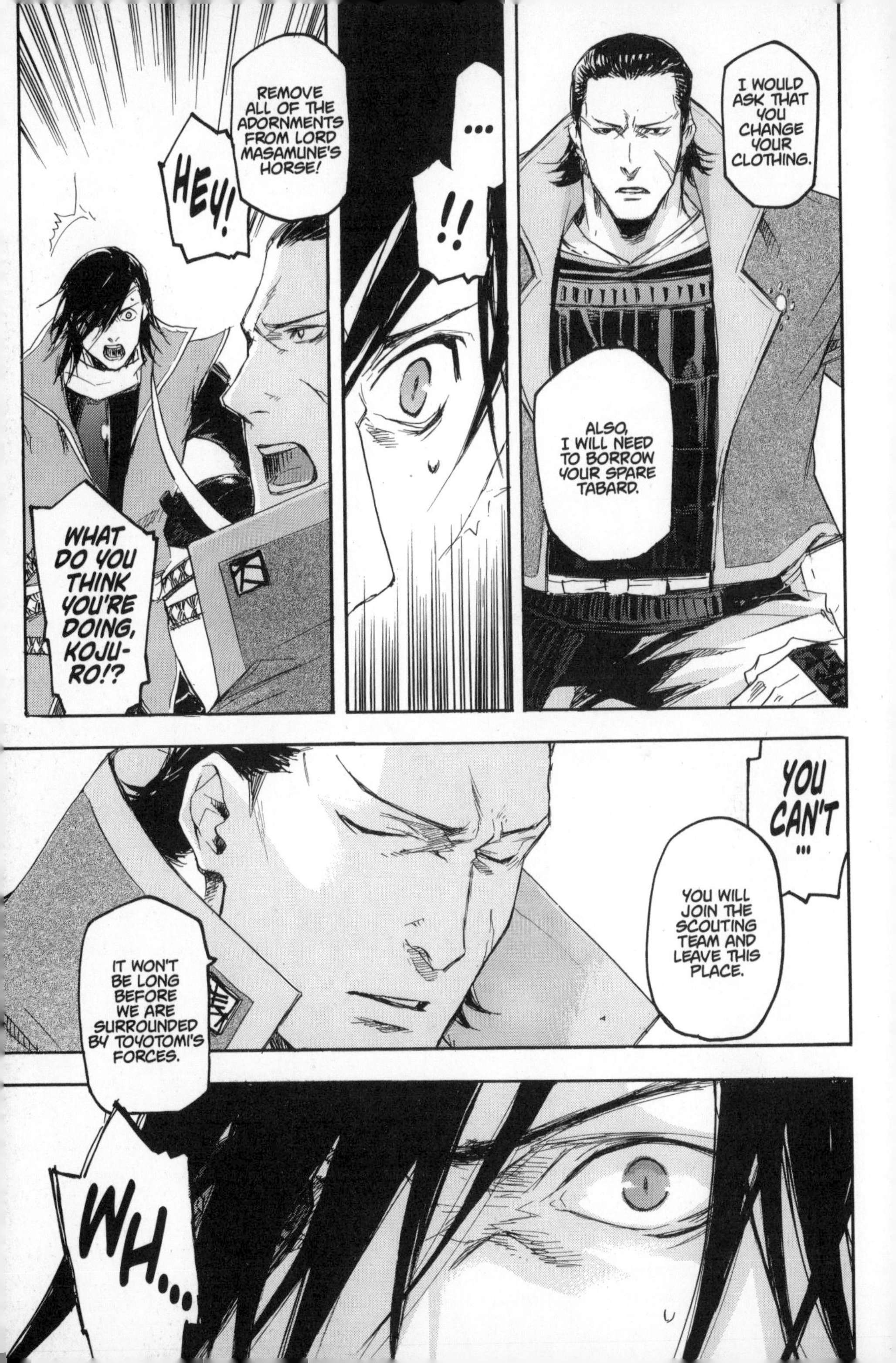
I WOULD ASK THAT YOU CHANGE YOUR CLOTHING.
ALSO, I WILL NEED TO BORROW YOUR SPARE TABARD.
...
!!
REMOVE ALL OF THE ADORNMENTS FROM LORD MASAMUNE'S HORSE!
HEY!
WHAT DO YOU THINK YOU'RE DOING, KOJURO!?
YOU CAN'T ...
YOU WILL JOIN THE SCOUTING TEAM AND LEAVE THIS PLACE.
IT WON'T BE LONG BEFORE WE ARE SURROUNDED BY TOYOTOMI'S FORCES.
WH...

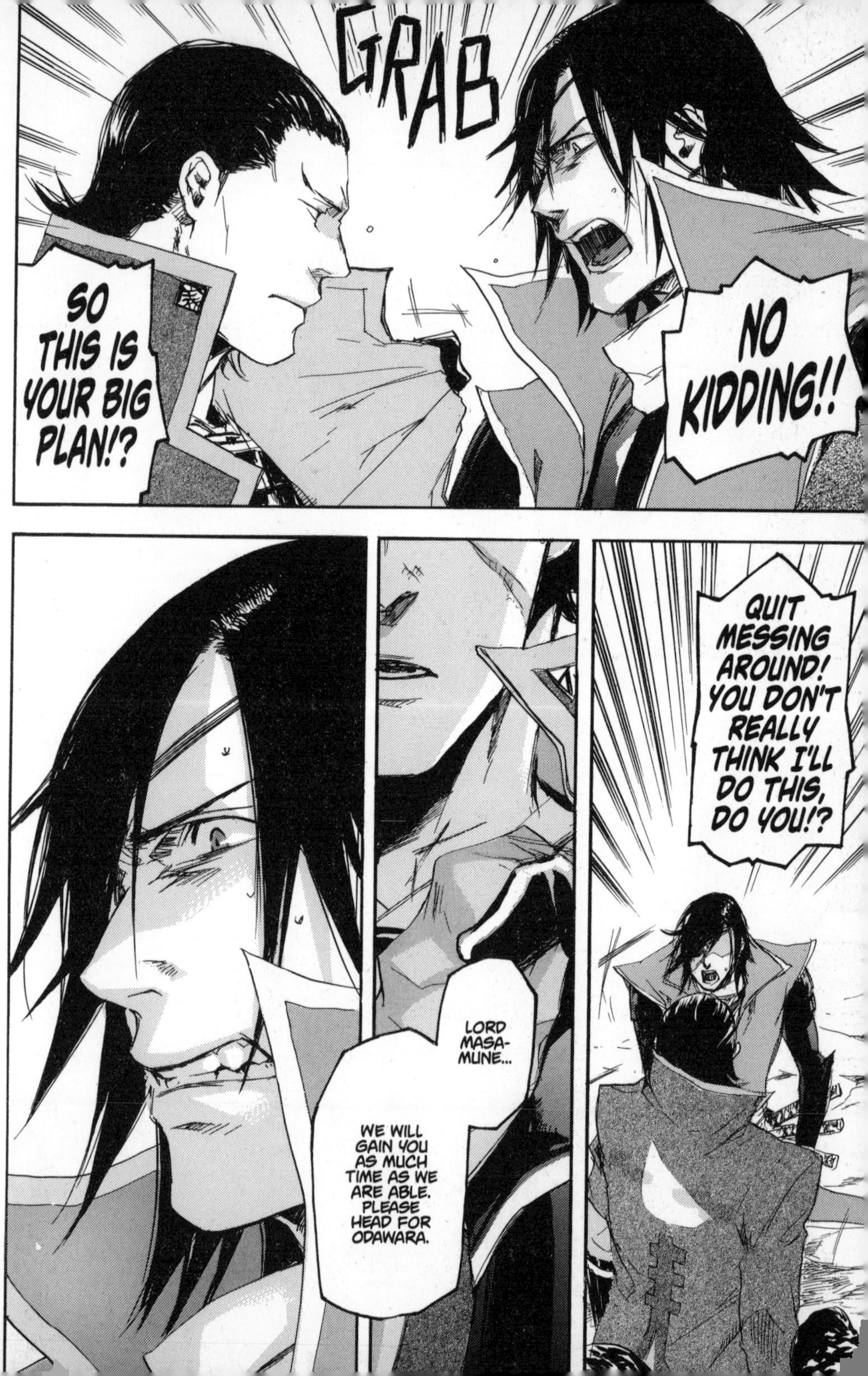
GRAB
NO KIDDING!!
SO THIS IS YOUR BIG PLAN!?
QUIT MESSING AROUND! YOU DON'T REALLY THINK I'LL DO THIS, DO YOU!?
LORD MASAMUNE...
WE WILL GAIN YOU AS MUCH TIME AS WE ARE ABLE. PLEASE HEAD FOR ODAWARA.

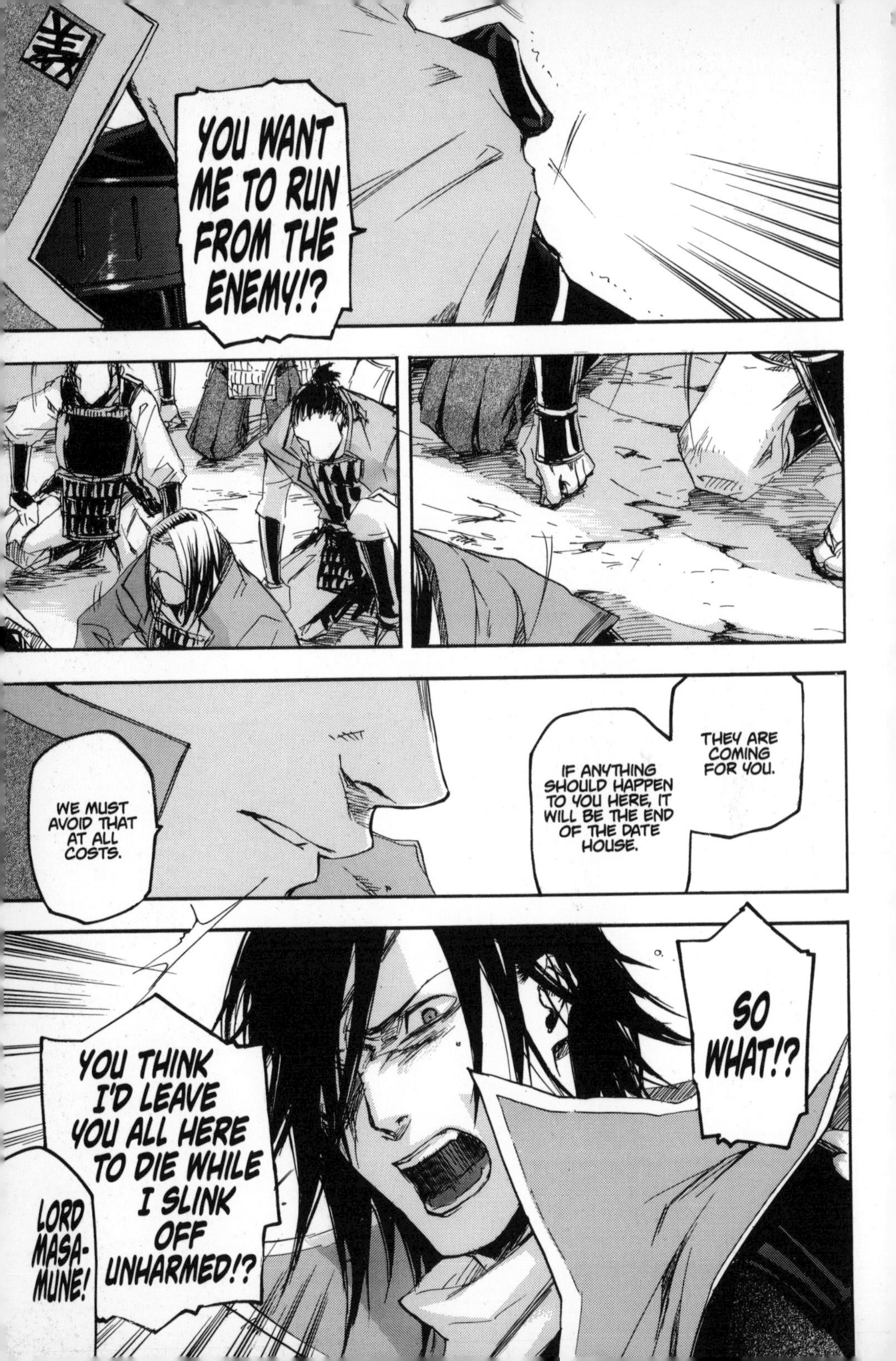
YOU WANT ME TO RUN FROM THE ENEMY!?
THEY ARE COMING FOR YOU.
IF ANYTHING SHOULD HAPPEN TO YOU HERE, IT WILL BE THE END OF THE DATE HOUSE.
WE MUST AVOID THAT AT ALL COSTS.
SO WHAT!?
YOU THINK I'D LEAVE YOU ALL HERE TO DIE WHILE I SLINK OFF UNHARMED!?
LORD MASA-MUNE!

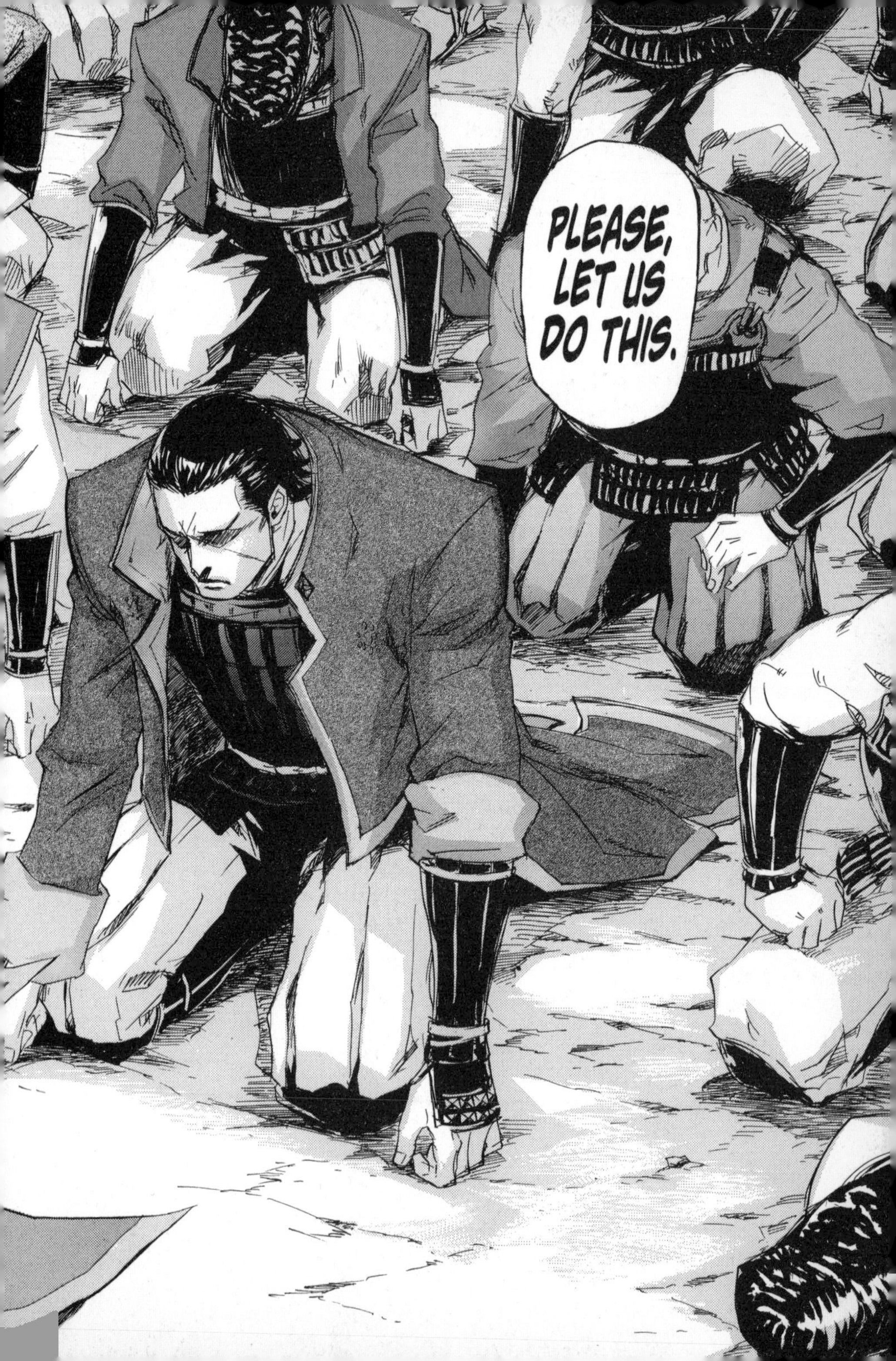
PLEASE, LET US DO THIS.

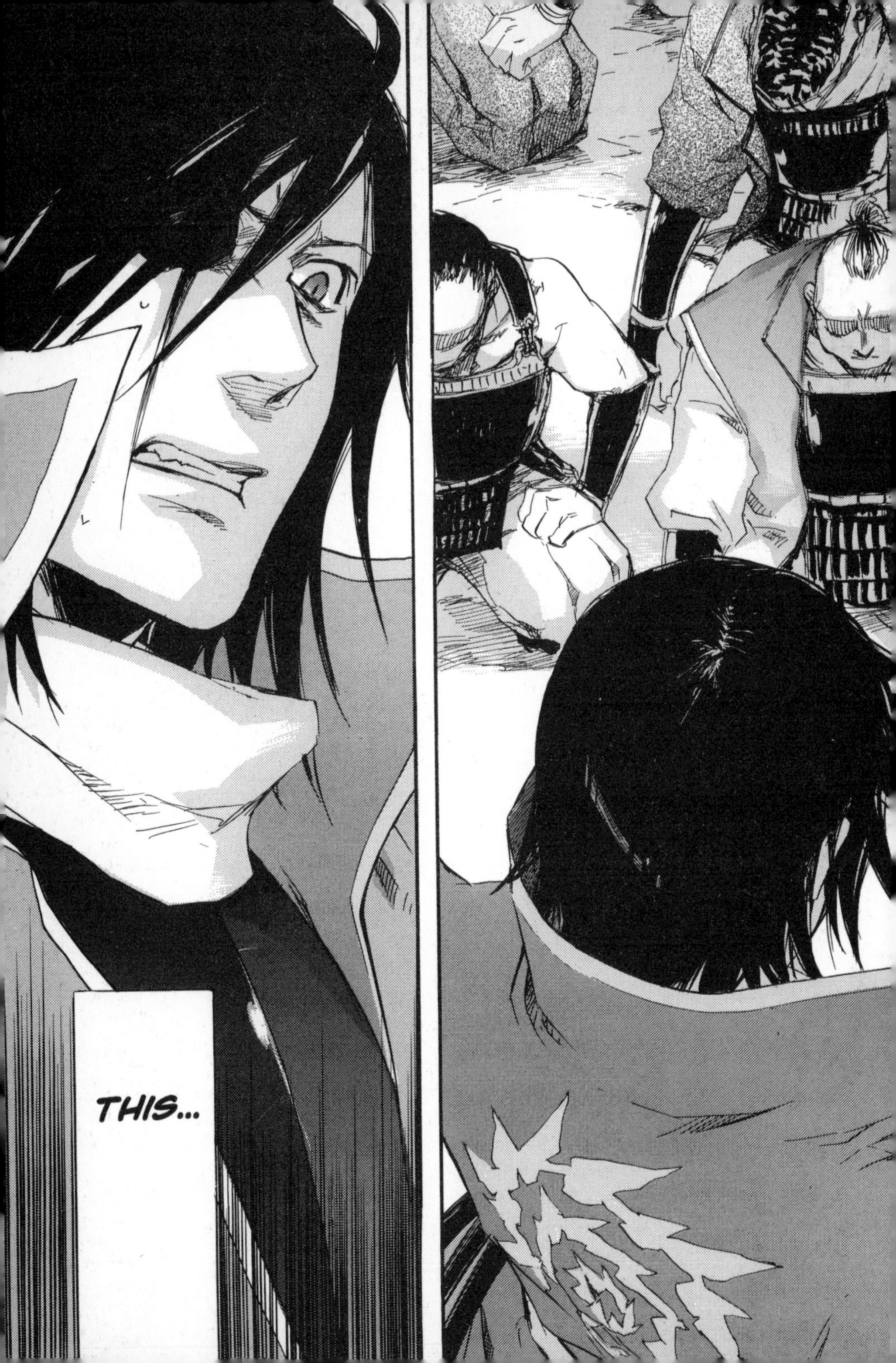
THIS...

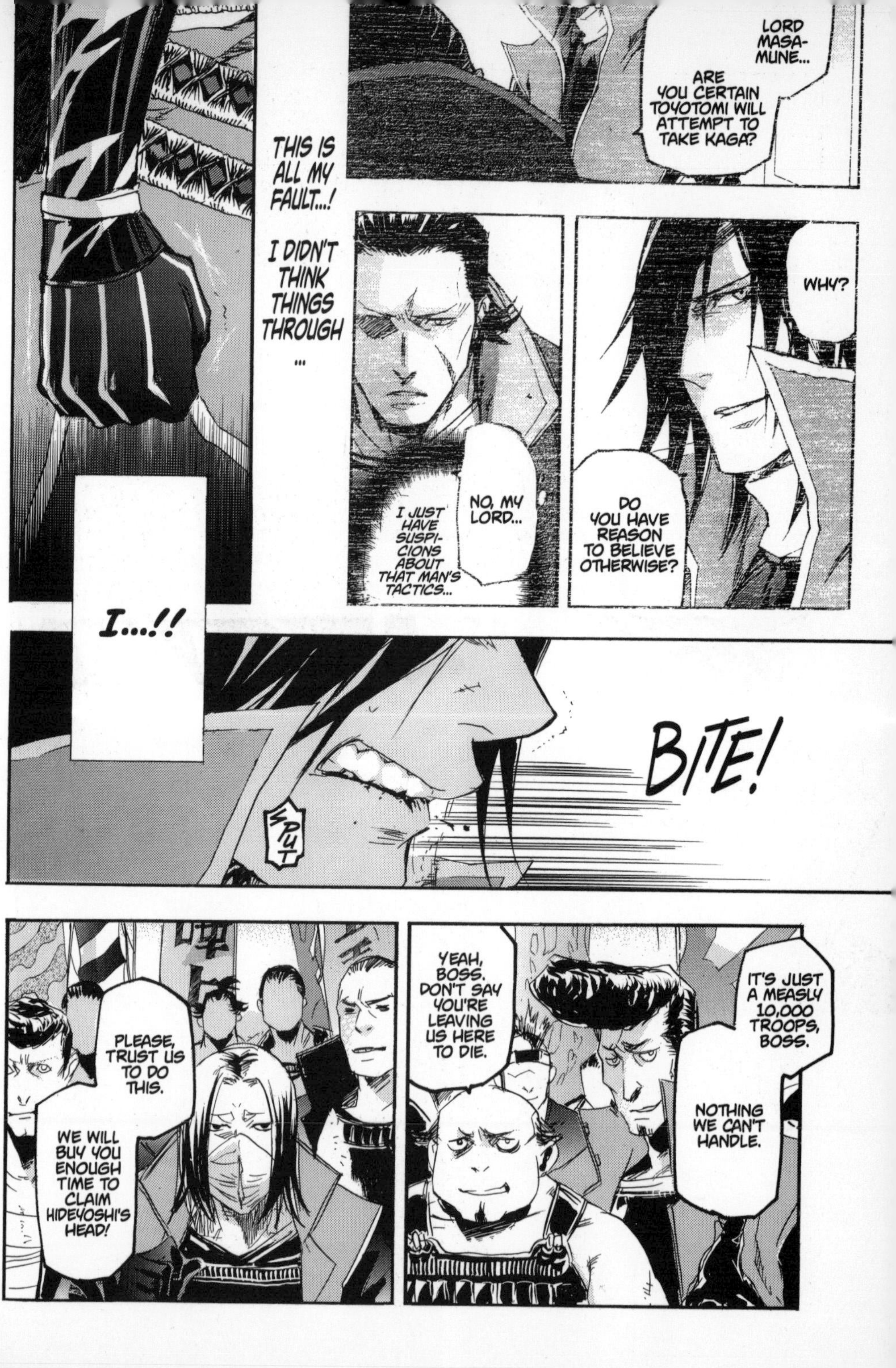
LORD MASAMUNE...
ARE YOU CERTAIN TOYOTOMI WILL ATTEMPT TO TAKE KAGA?
WHY?
DO YOU HAVE REASON TO BELIEVE OTHERWISE?
NO, MY LORD...
I JUST HAVE SUSPICIONS ABOUT THAT MAN'S TACTICS...
THIS IS ALL MY FAULT...!
I DIDN'T THINK THINGS THROUGH...
I...!!
BITE!
SPUT
IT'S JUST A MEASLY 10,000 TROOPS, BOSS.
NOTHING WE CAN'T HANDLE.
YEAH, BOSS. DON'T SAY YOU'RE LEAVING US HERE TO DIE.
PLEASE, TRUST US TO DO THIS.
WE WILL BUY YOU ENOUGH TIME TO CLAIM HIDEYOSHI'S HEAD!

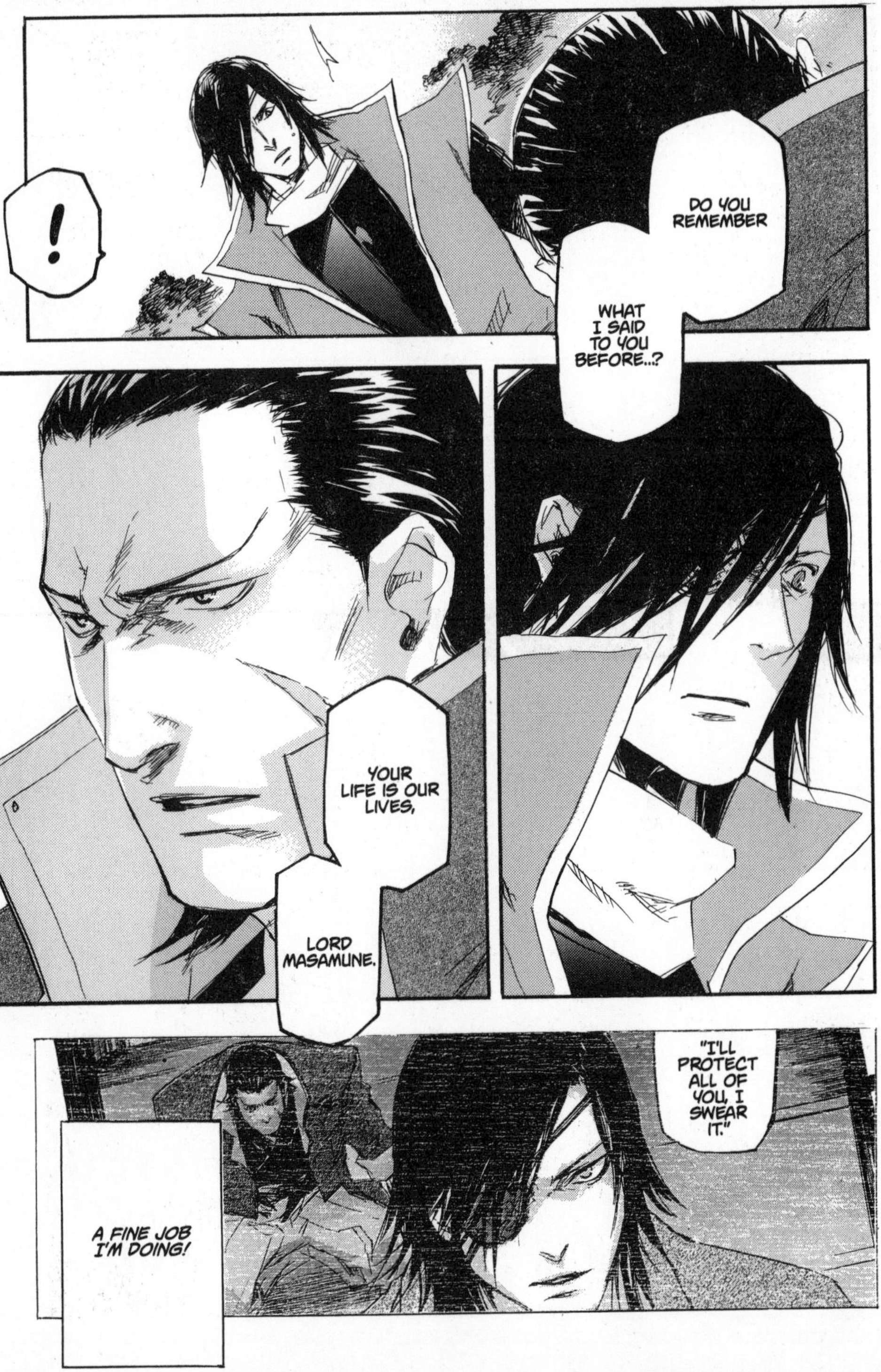
DO YOU REMEMBER
WHAT I SAID TO YOU BEFORE...?
!
YOUR LIFE IS OUR LIVES,
LORD MASAMUNE.
"I'LL PROTECT ALL OF YOU, I SWEAR IT."
A FINE JOB I'M DOING!

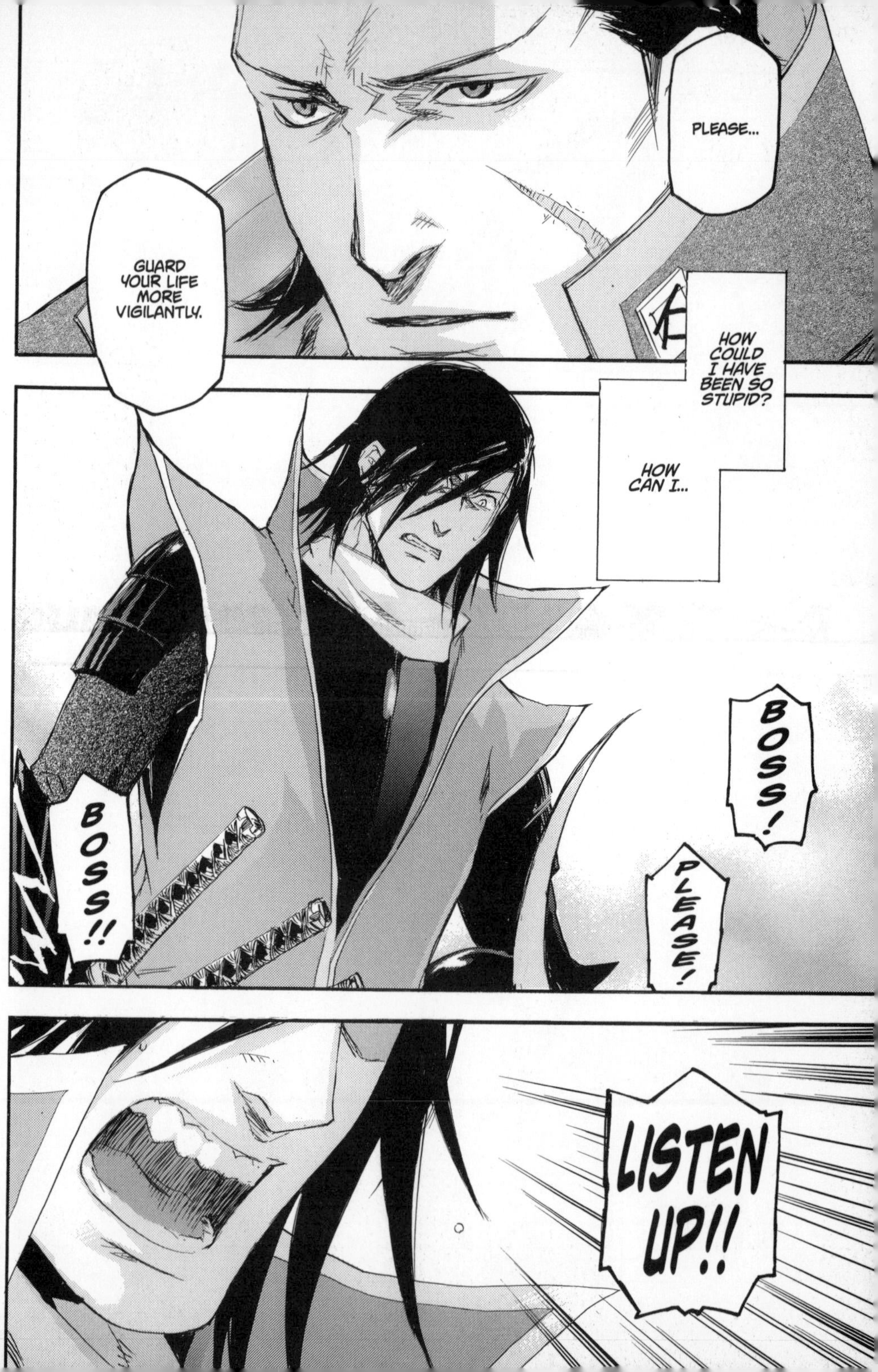
PLEASE...
GUARD YOUR LIFE MORE VIGILANTLY.
HOW COULD I HAVE BEEN SO STUPID?
HOW CAN I...
BOSS!
PLEASE!
BOSS!!
LISTEN UP!!

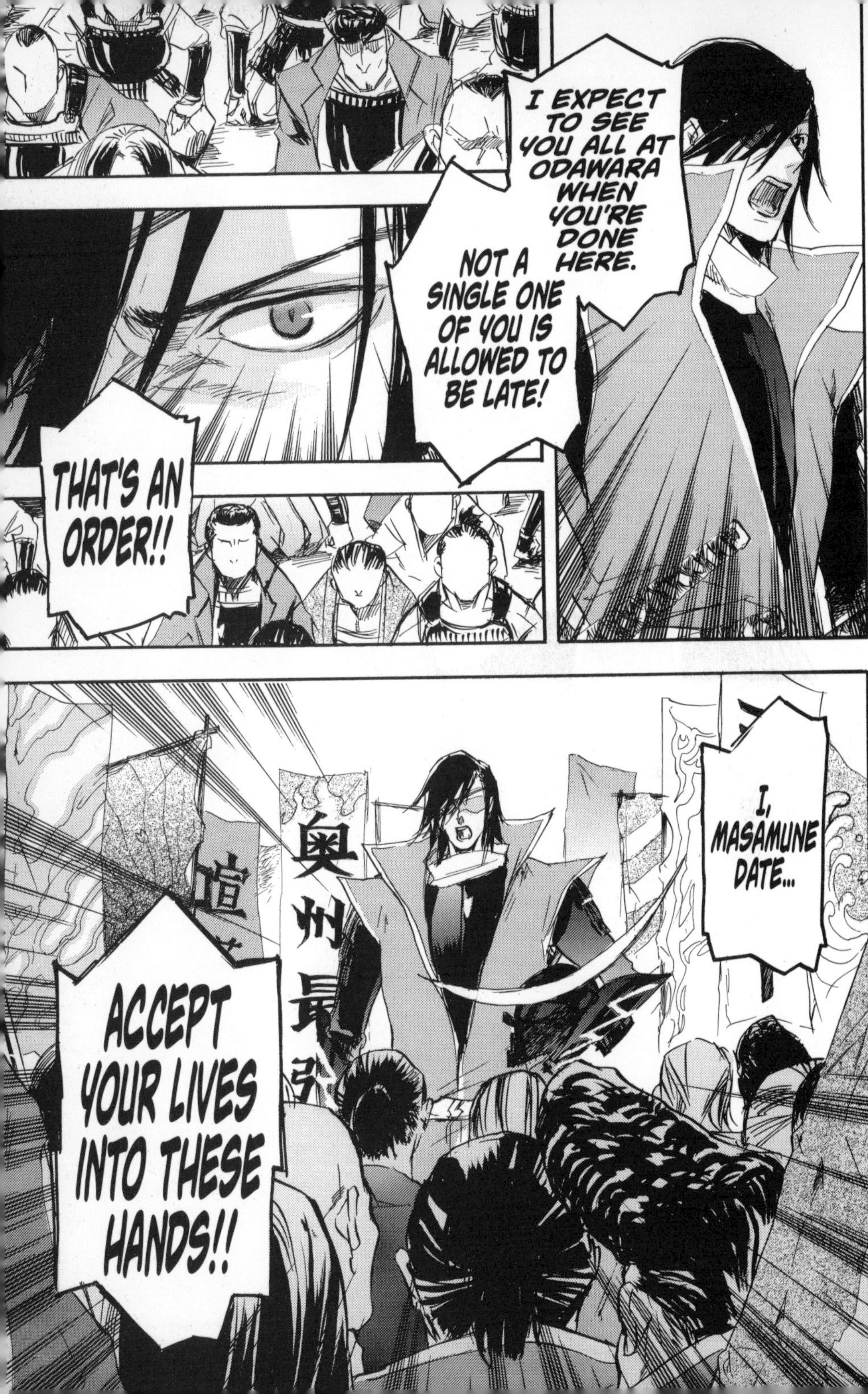
I EXPECT TO SEE YOU ALL AT ODAWARA WHEN YOU'RE DONE HERE.
NOT A SINGLE ONE OF YOU IS ALLOWED TO BE LATE!
THAT'S AN ORDER!!
I, MASAMUNE DATE...
ACCEPT YOUR LIVES INTO THESE HANDS!!

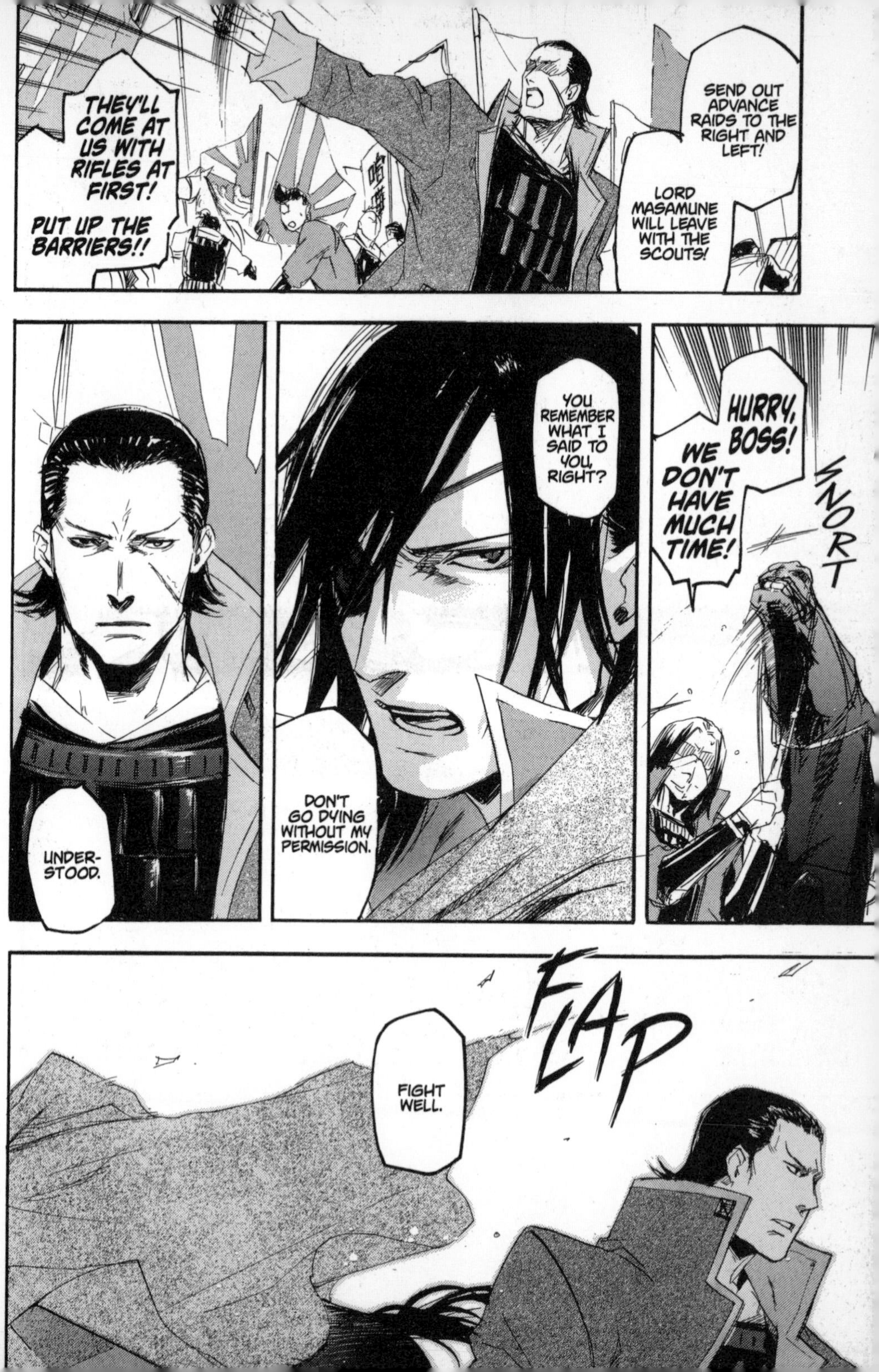

SEND OUT ADVANCE RAIDS TO THE RIGHT AND LEFT!
LORD MASAMUNE WILL LEAVE WITH THE SCOUTS!
THEY'LL COME AT US WITH RIFLES AT FIRST!
PUT UP THE BARRIERS!!
HURRY, BOSS!
WE DON'T HAVE MUCH TIME!
SNORT
YOU REMEMBER WHAT I SAID TO YOU, RIGHT?
DON'T GO DYING WITHOUT MY PERMISSION.
UNDER-STOOD.
FLAP
FIGHT WELL.

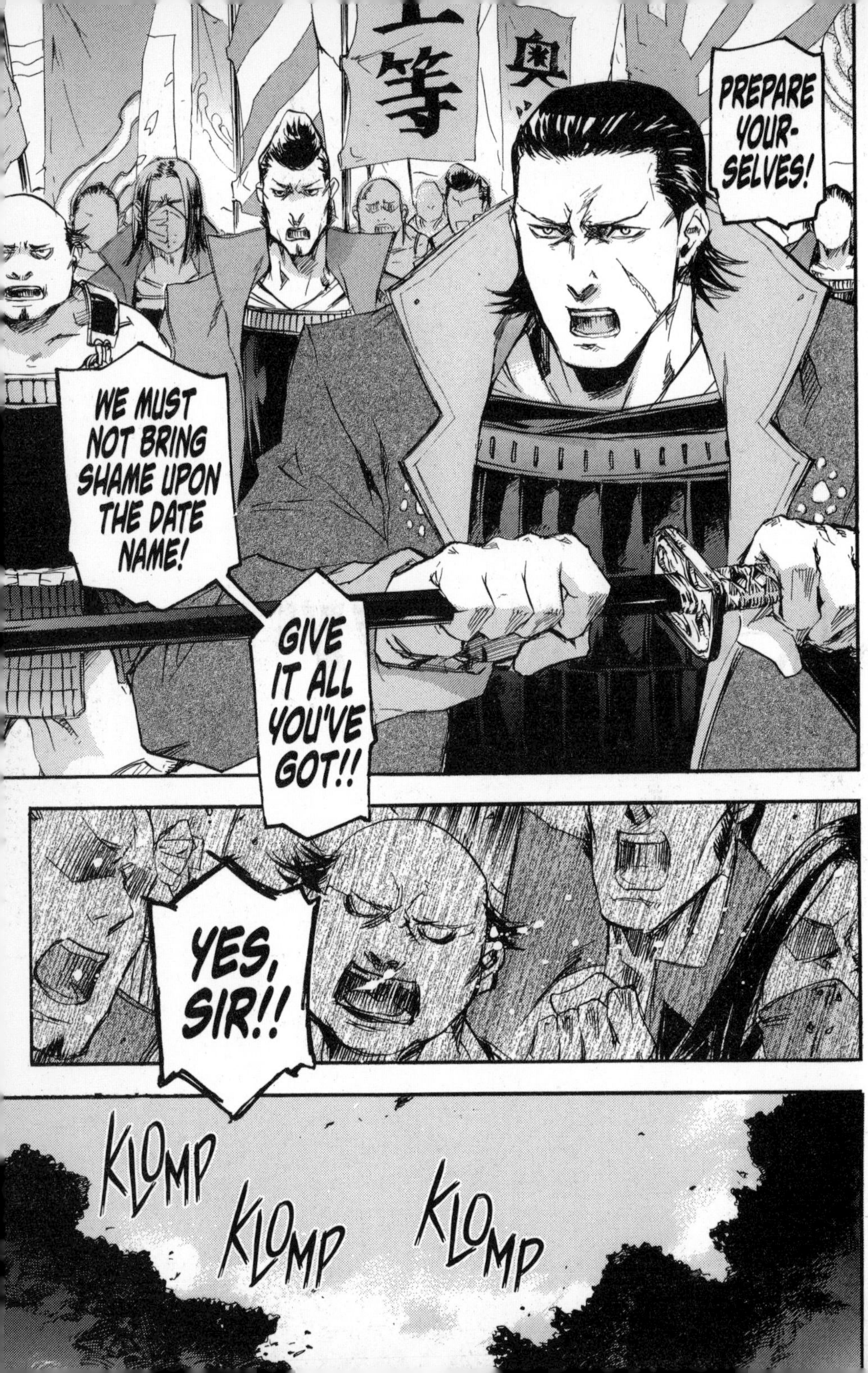
PREPARE YOUR-SELVES!
WE MUST NOT BRING SHAME UPON THE DATE NAME!
GIVE IT ALL YOU'VE GOT!!
YES, SIR!!
KLOMP
KLOMP
KLOMP

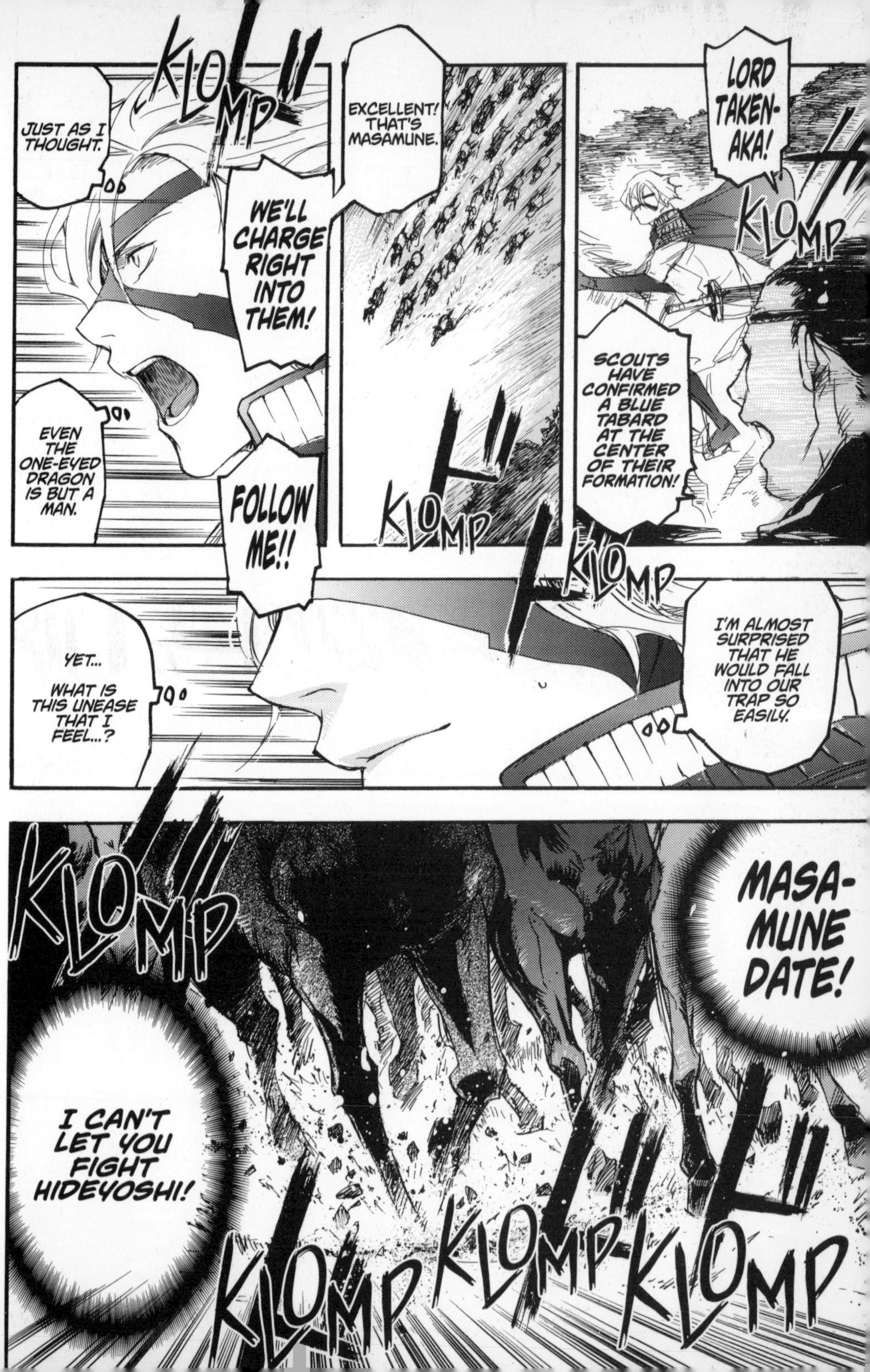
LORD TAKEN-AKA!
KLOMP
SCOUTS HAVE CONFIRMED A BLUE TABARD AT THE CENTER OF THEIR FORMATION!
EXCELLENT! THAT'S MASAMUNE.
KLOMP
KLOMP!!
JUST AS I THOUGHT.
WE'LL CHARGE RIGHT INTO THEM!
EVEN THE ONE-EYED DRAGON IS BUT A MAN.
FOLLOW ME!!
KLOMP
I'M ALMOST SURPRISED THAT HE WOULD FALL INTO OUR TRAP SO EASILY.
YET... WHAT IS THIS UNEASE THAT I FEEL...?
MASA-MUNE DATE!
KLOMP
I CAN'T LET YOU FIGHT HIDEYOSHI!
KLOMP
KLOMP
KLOMP

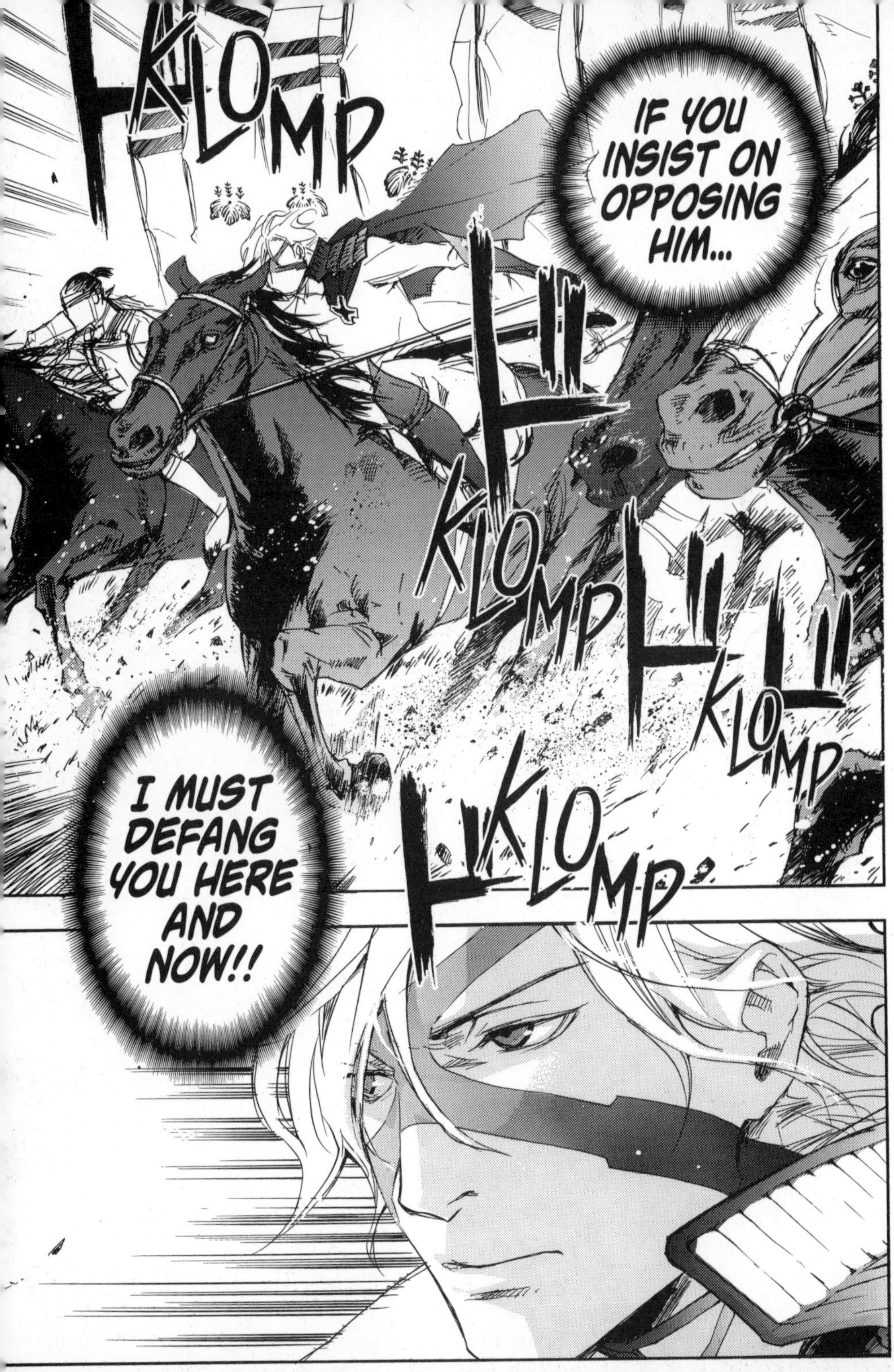
IF YOU INSIST ON OPPOSING HIM...
KLOMP
KLOMP
KLOMP
KLOMP
I MUST DEFANG YOU HERE AND NOW!!

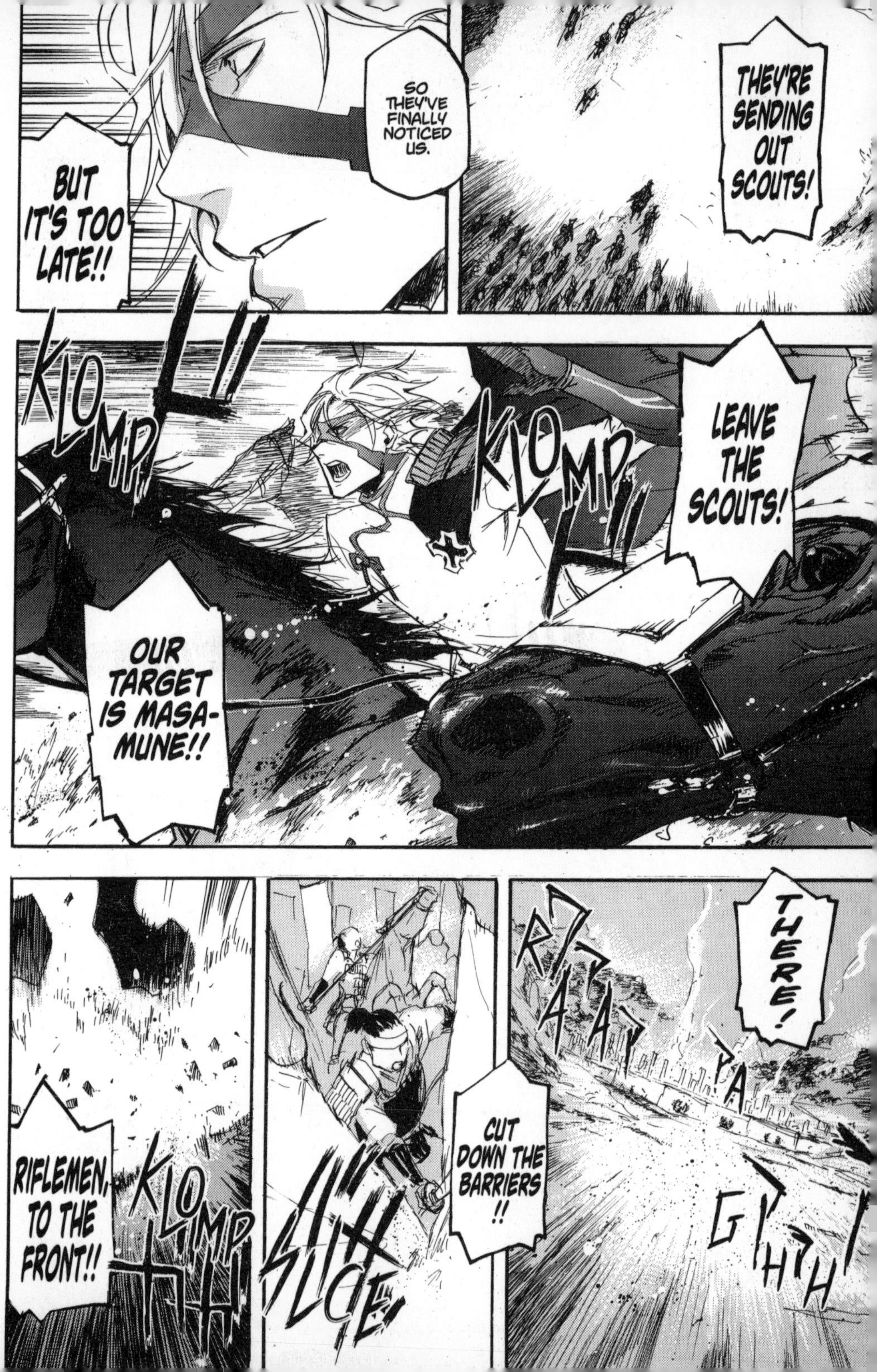
THEY'RE SENDING OUT SCOUTS!
SO THEY'VE FINALLY NOTICED US.
BUT IT'S TOO LATE!!
KLOMP
LEAVE THE SCOUTS!
KLOMP
OUR TARGET IS MASAMUNE!!
THERE!
CUT DOWN THE BARRIERS!!
SLICE
RIFLEMEN, TO THE FRONT!!
KLOMP

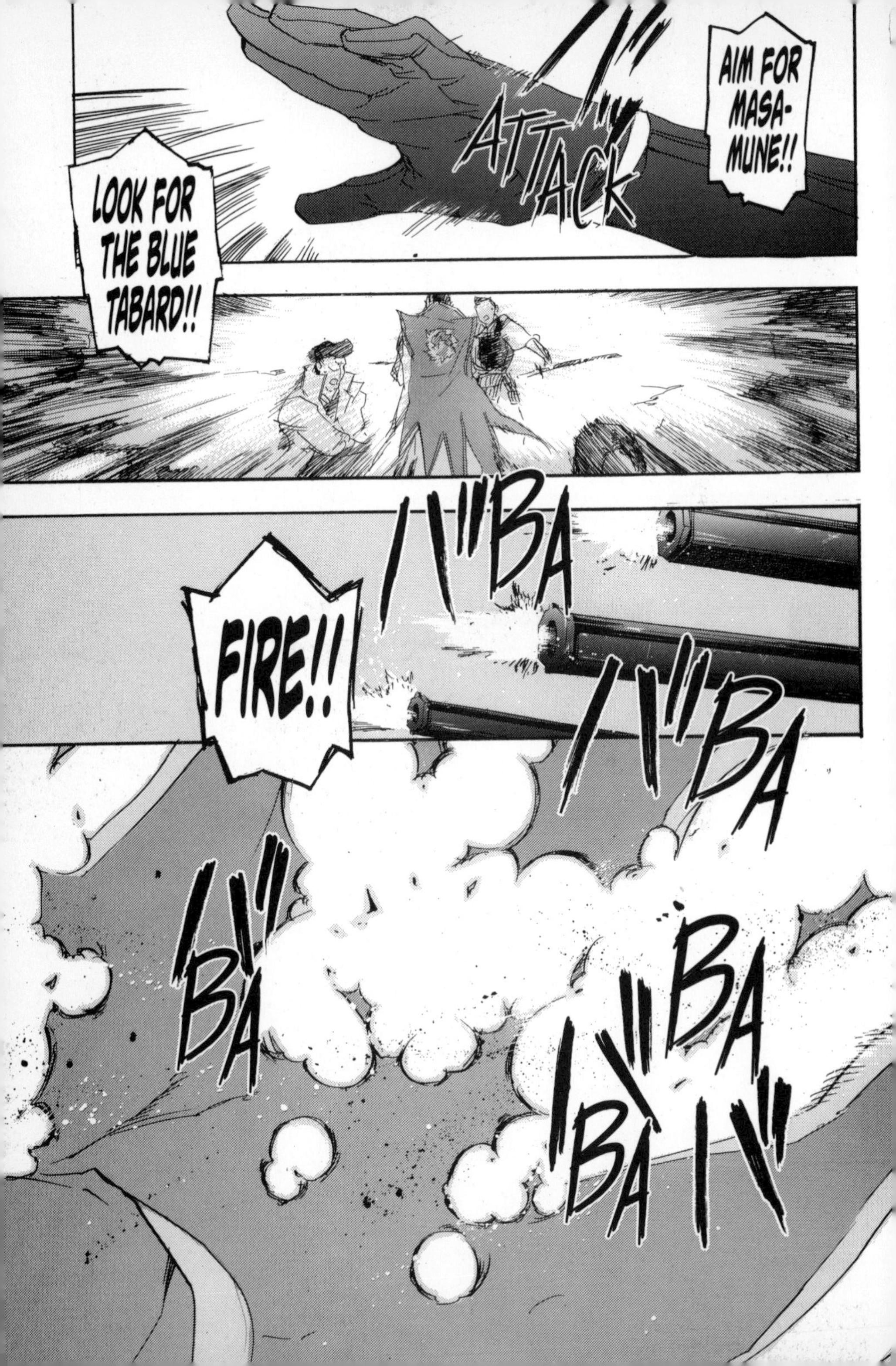
AIM FOR MASA-MUNE!!
ATTACK
LOOK FOR THE BLUE TABARD!!
BA
BA
FIRE!!
BA
BA
BA
BA

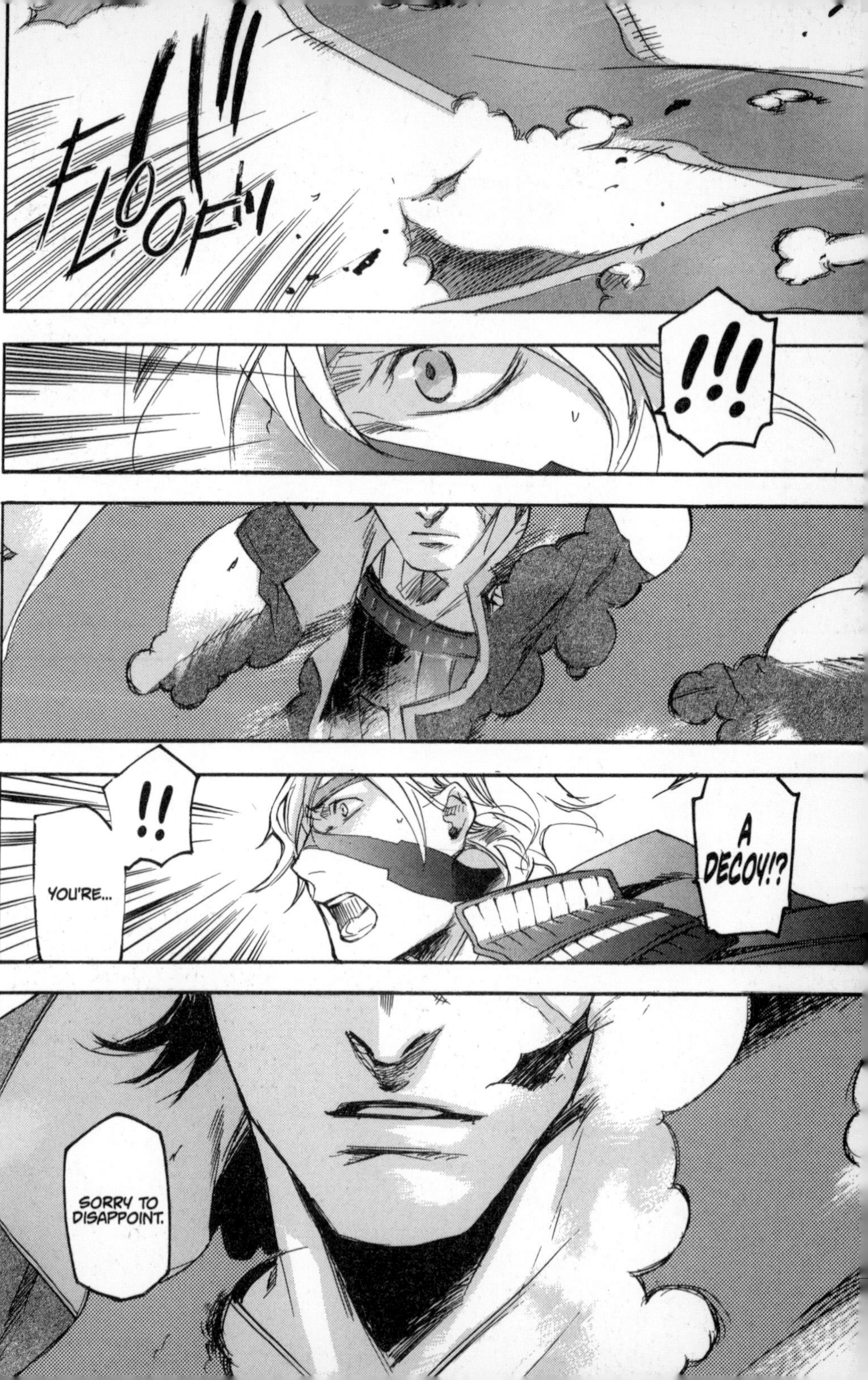
FLOOF!!
!!!
A DECOY!?
!!
YOU'RE...
SORRY TO DISAPPOINT.

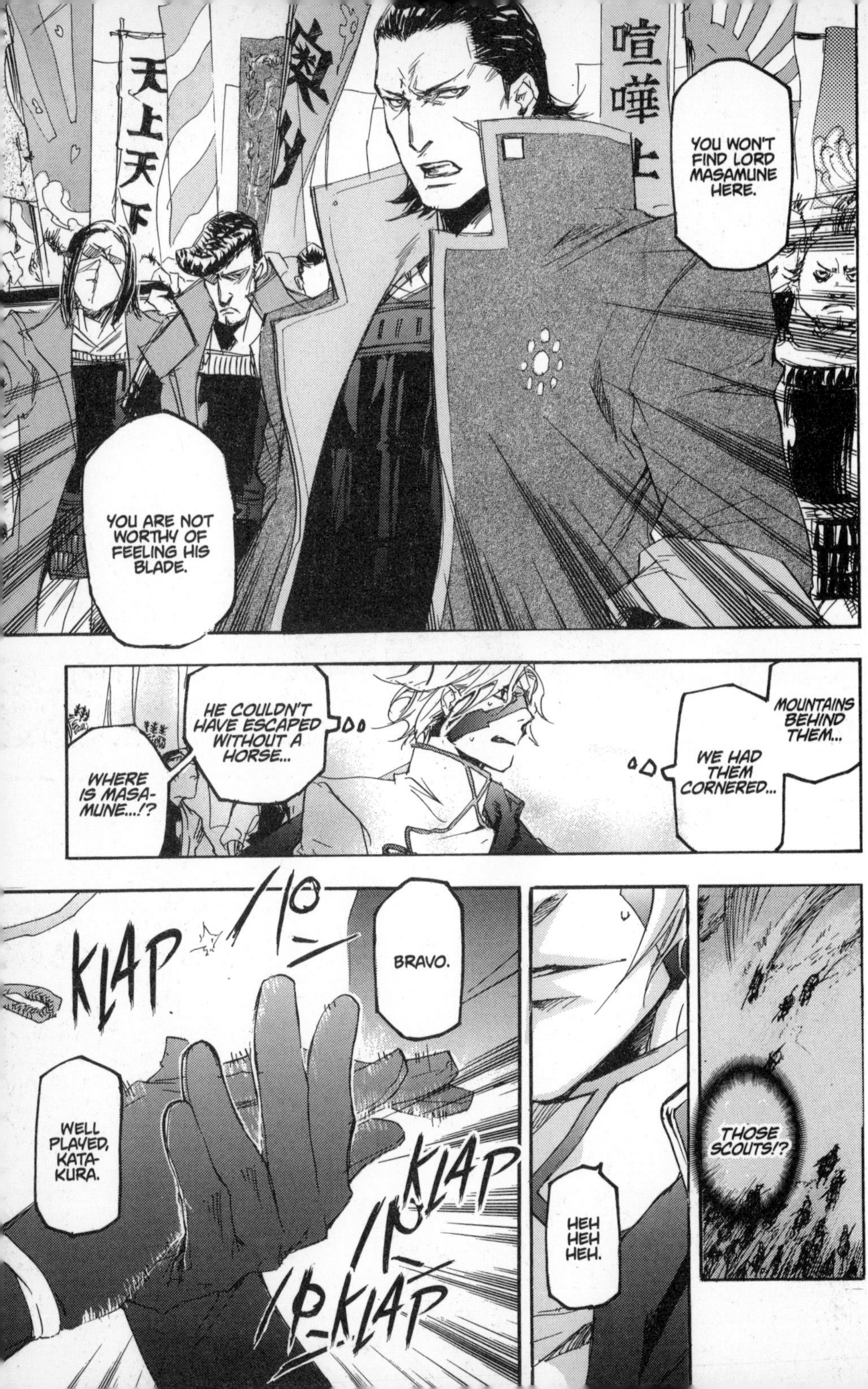
喧嘩上
天上天下
YOU WON'T FIND LORD MASAMUNE HERE.
YOU ARE NOT WORTHY OF FEELING HIS BLADE.
MOUNTAINS BEHIND THEM...
WE HAD THEM CORNERED...
HE COULDN'T HAVE ESCAPED WITHOUT A HORSE...
WHERE IS MASA-MUNE...!?
THOSE SCOUTS!?
HEH HEH HEH.
BRAVO.
KLAP
WELL PLAYED, KATA-KURA.
KLAP
P-KLAP

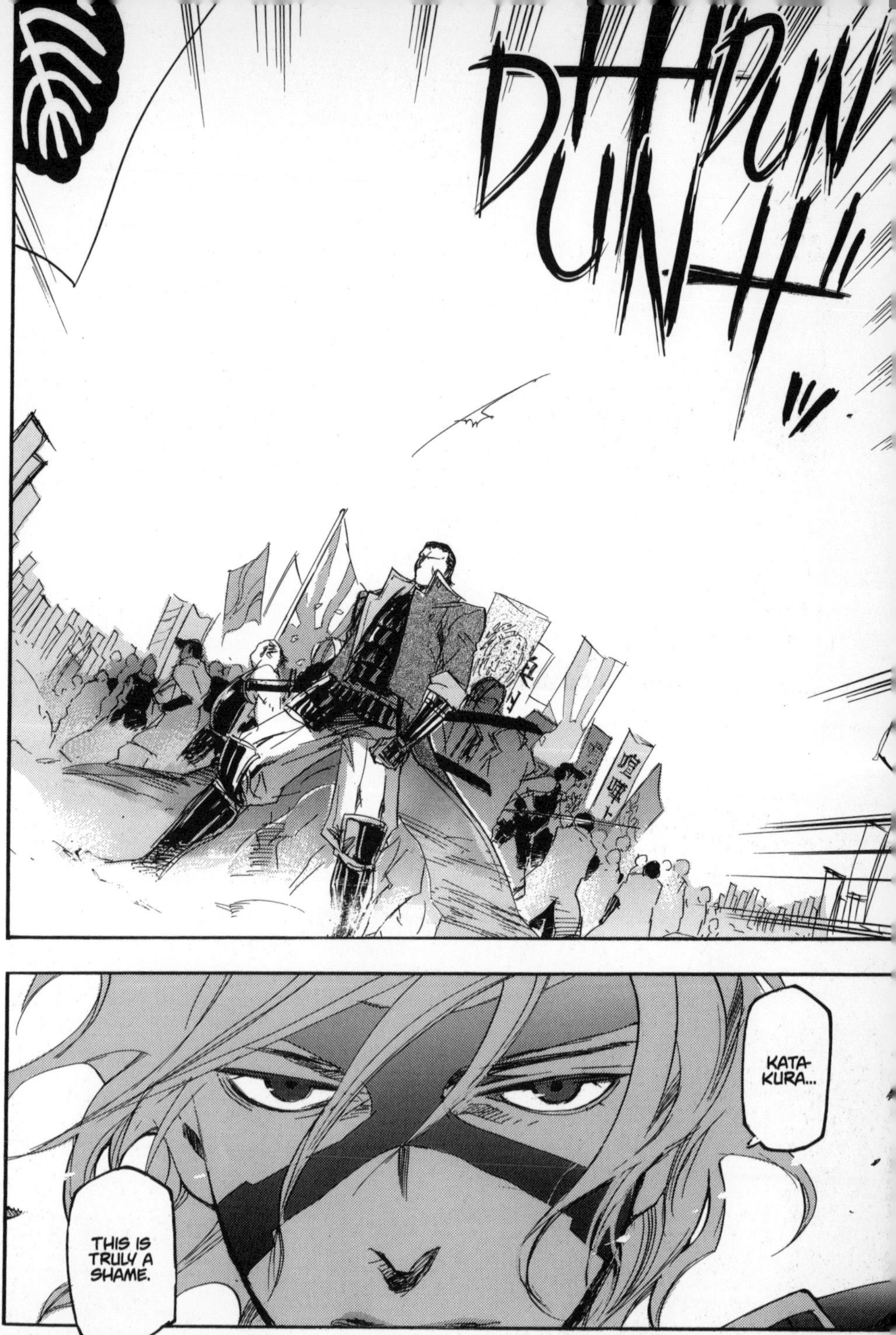
DHHDUN UN-H
KATA-KURA...
THIS IS TRULY A SHAME.

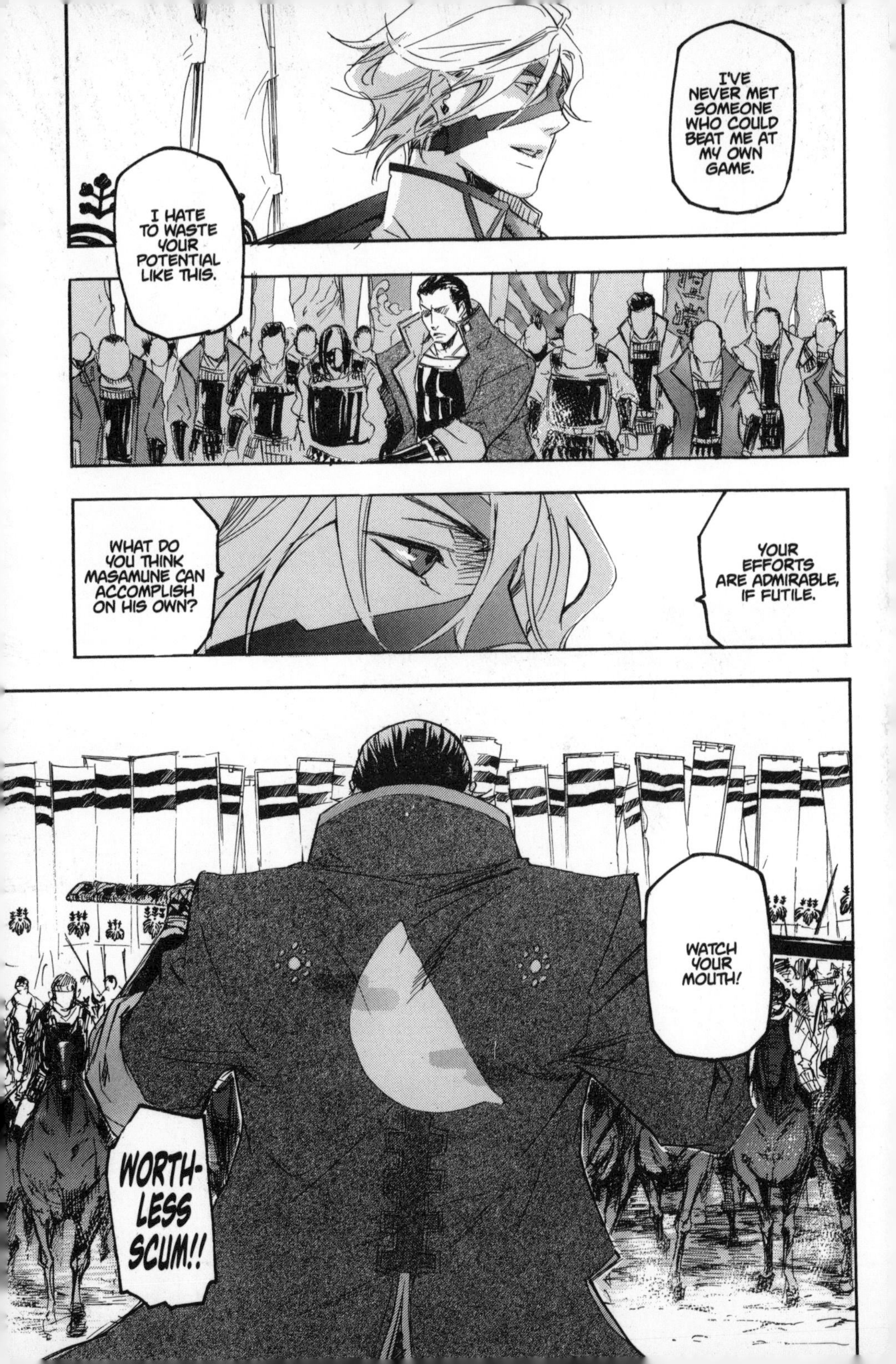
I'VE NEVER MET SOMEONE WHO COULD BEAT ME AT MY OWN GAME.
I HATE TO WASTE YOUR POTENTIAL LIKE THIS.
YOUR EFFORTS ARE ADMIRABLE, IF FUTILE.
WHAT DO YOU THINK MASAMUNE CAN ACCOMPLISH ON HIS OWN?
WATCH YOUR MOUTH!
WORTH-LESS SCUM!!

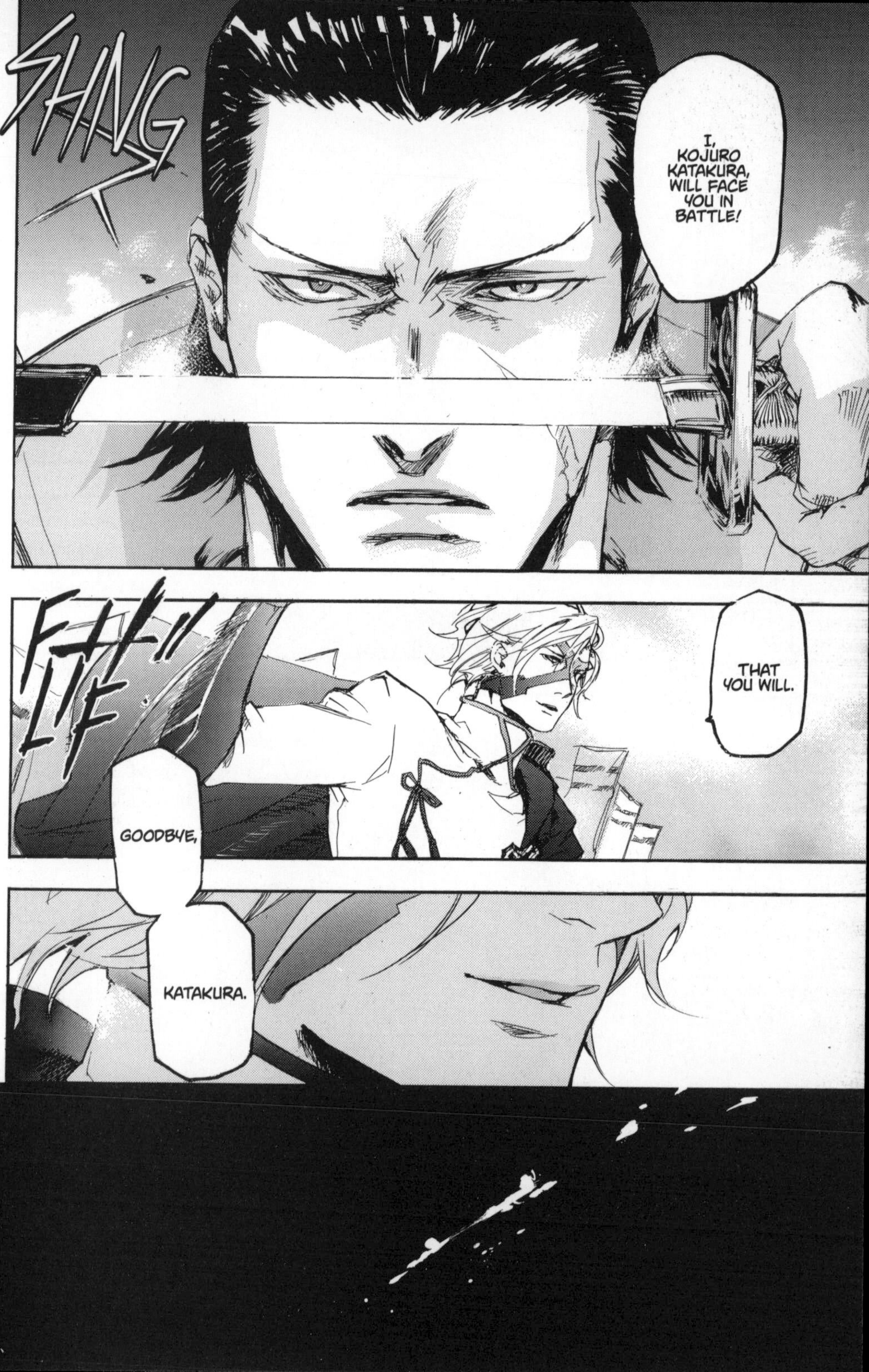
I, KOJURO KATAKURA, WILL FACE YOU IN BATTLE!
SHNG
THAT YOU WILL.
GOODBYE,
KATAKURA.

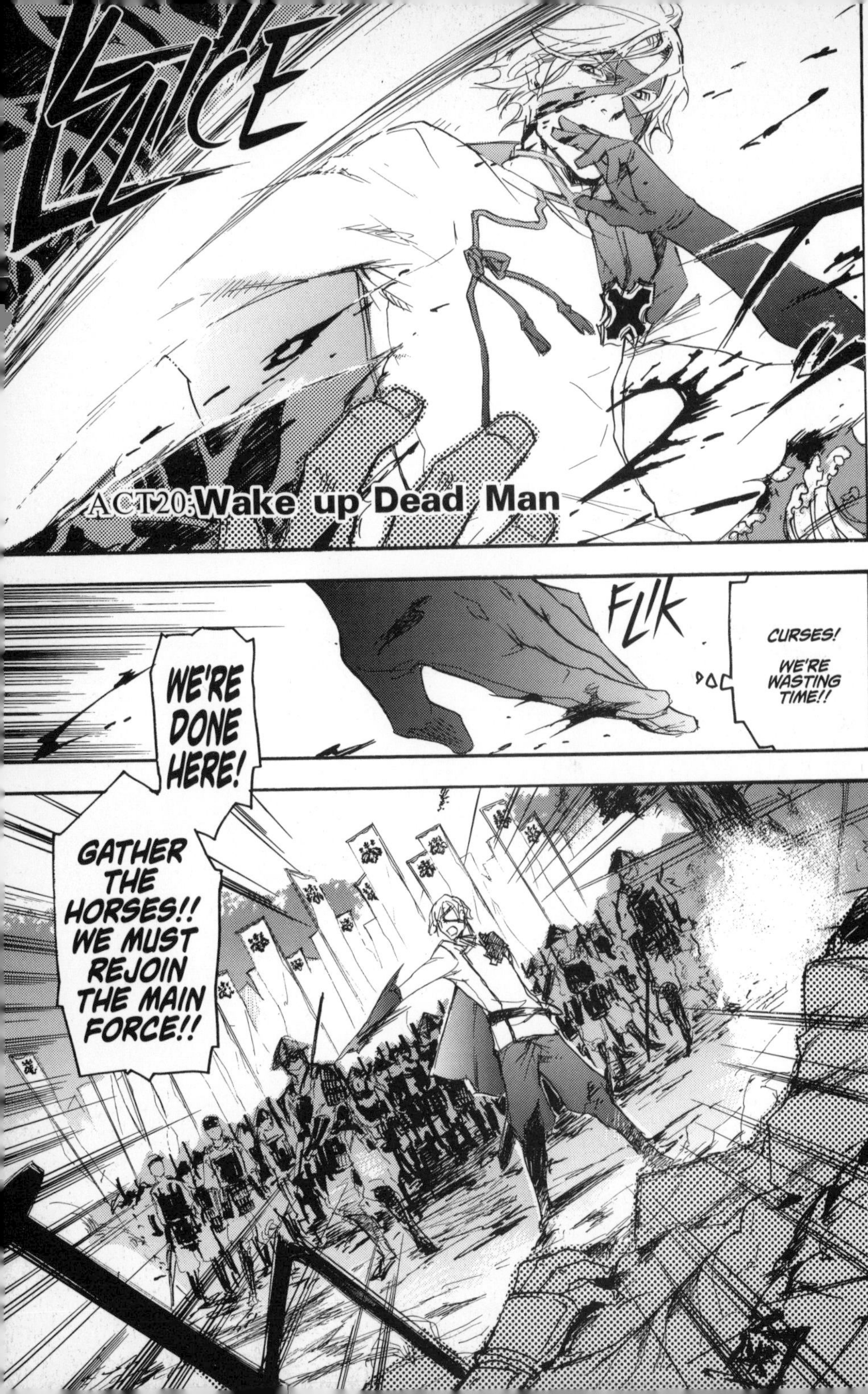
SLICE
ACT20: Wake up Dead Man
CURSES! WE'RE WASTING TIME!!
FLIK
WE'RE DONE HERE!
GATHER THE HORSES!! WE MUST REJOIN THE MAIN FORCE!!

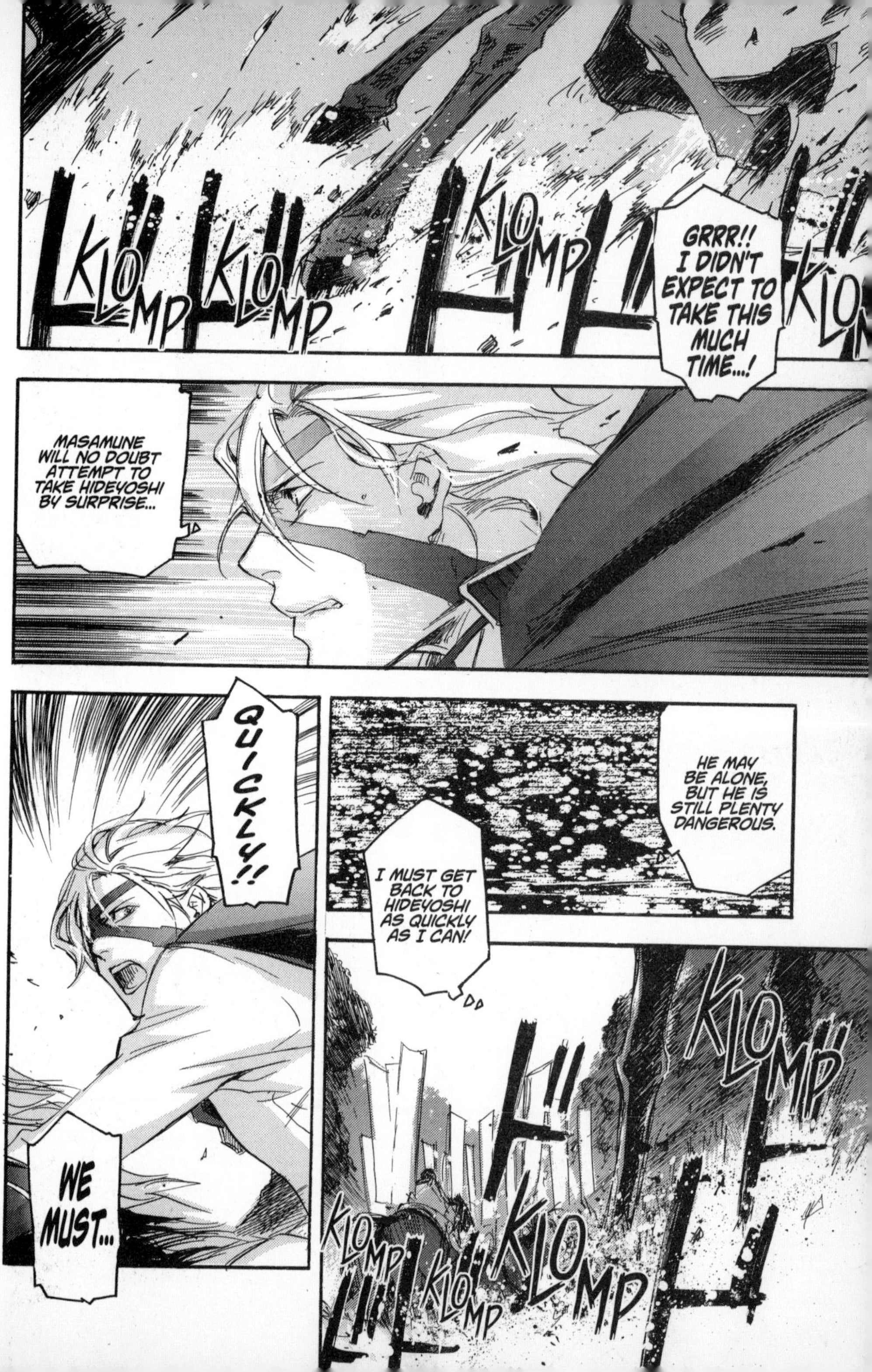
GRRR!! I DIDN'T EXPECT TO TAKE THIS MUCH TIME...!
KLO
KLOMP
KLOMP
KLOMP
MASAMUNE WILL NO DOUBT ATTEMPT TO TAKE HIDEYOSHI BY SURPRISE...
HE MAY BE ALONE, BUT HE IS STILL PLENTY DANGEROUS.
I MUST GET BACK TO HIDEYOSHI AS QUICKLY AS I CAN!
KLOMP
KLOMP
KLOMP
KLOMP
QUICKLY!!
WE MUST...

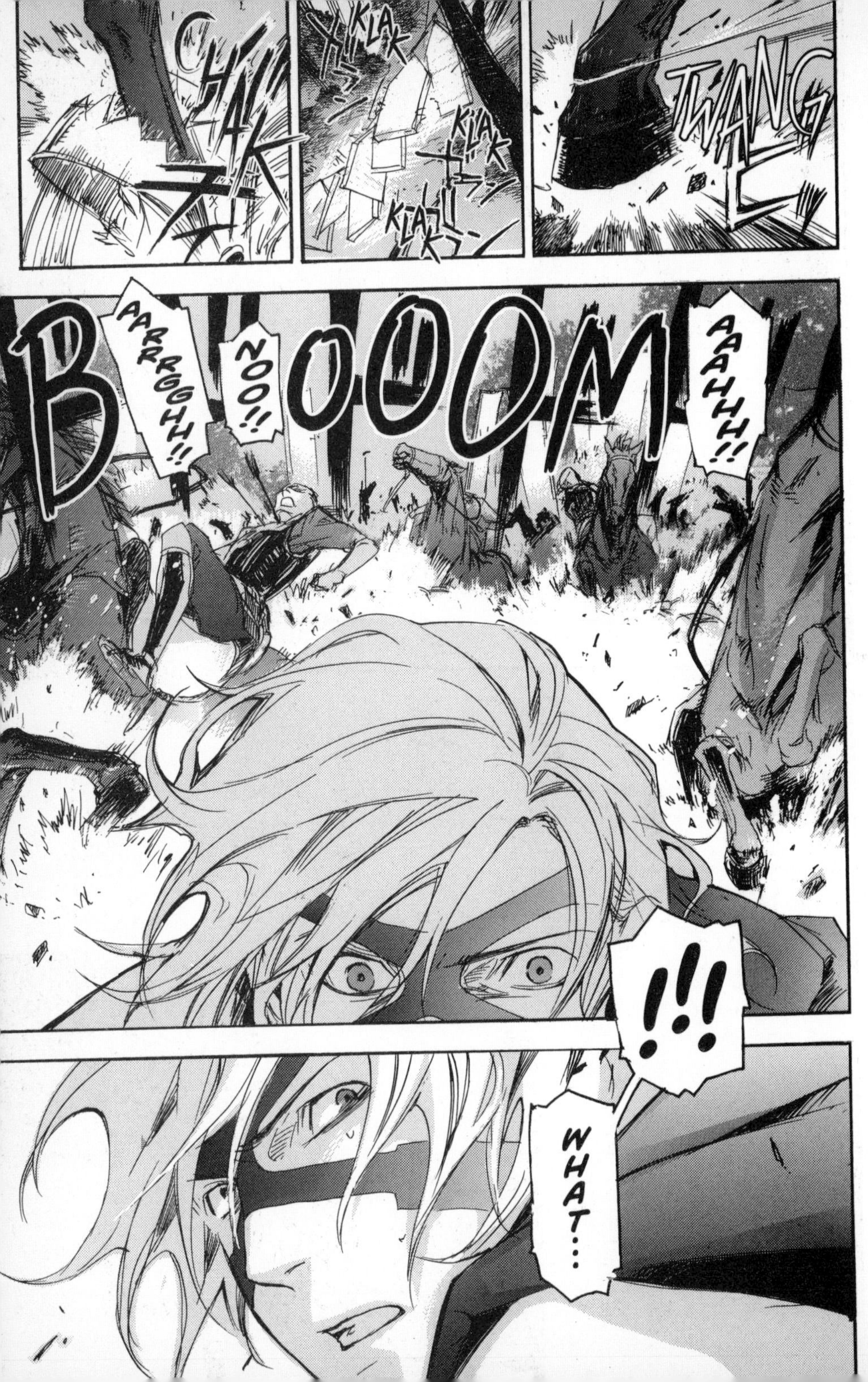
TWANG
KLAK
KLAK
KLAK
CHAK
AAAHHH!!
BOOOM
NOO!!
AARRGGHH!!
!!!
WHAT...

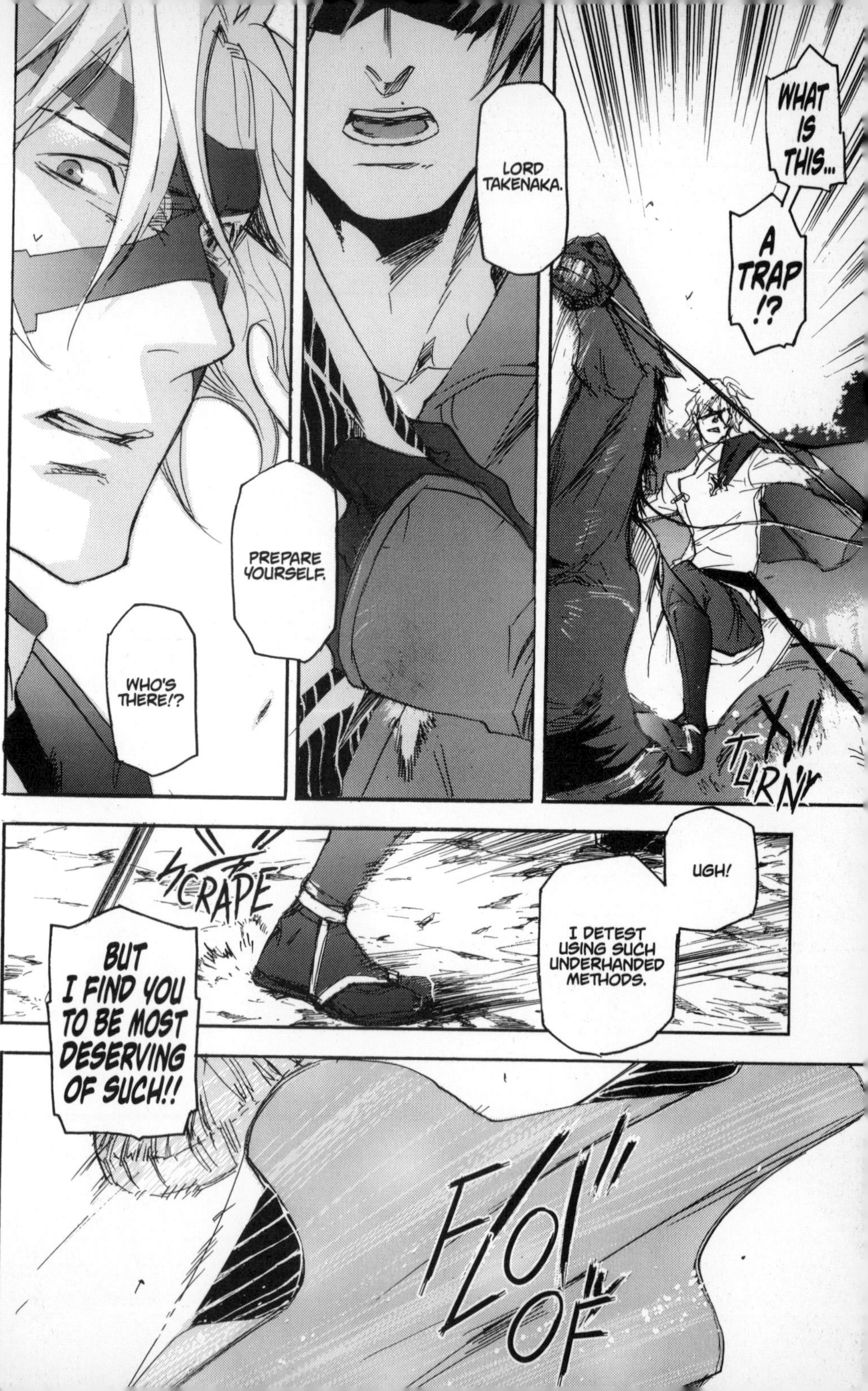
WHAT IS THIS...
A TRAP!?
TURN
LORD TAKENAKA.
PREPARE YOURSELF.
WHO'S THERE!?
UGH!
I DETEST USING SUCH UNDERHANDED METHODS.
SCRAPE
BUT I FIND YOU TO BE MOST DESERVING OF SUCH!!
FLOOF

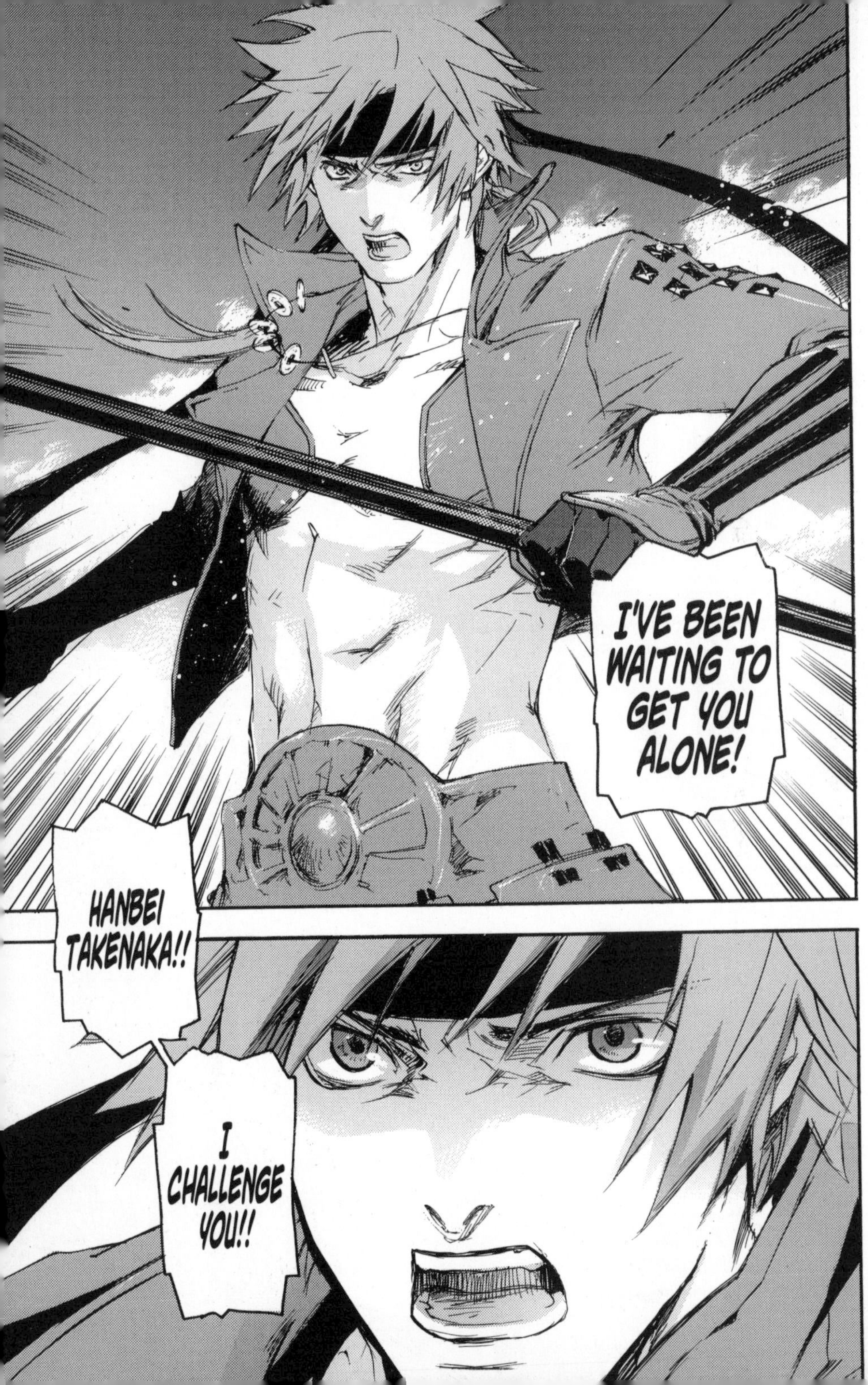
I'VE BEEN WAITING TO GET YOU ALONE!
HANBEI TAKENAKA!!
I CHALLENGE YOU!!

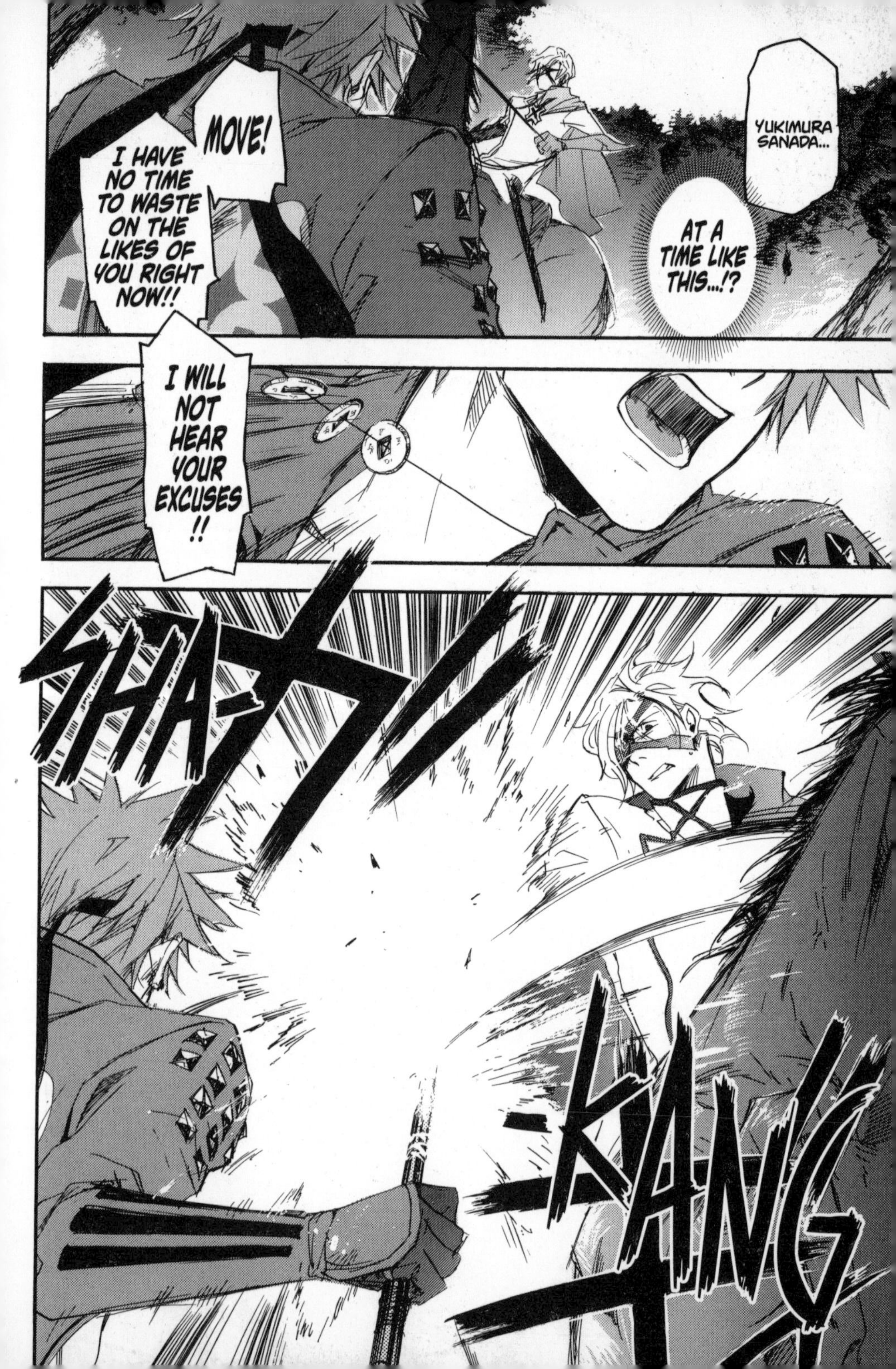
YUKIMURA SANADA...
AT A TIME LIKE THIS...!?
MOVE!
I HAVE NO TIME TO WASTE ON THE LIKES OF YOU RIGHT NOW!!
I WILL NOT HEAR YOUR EXCUSES!!
SHAK
KANG

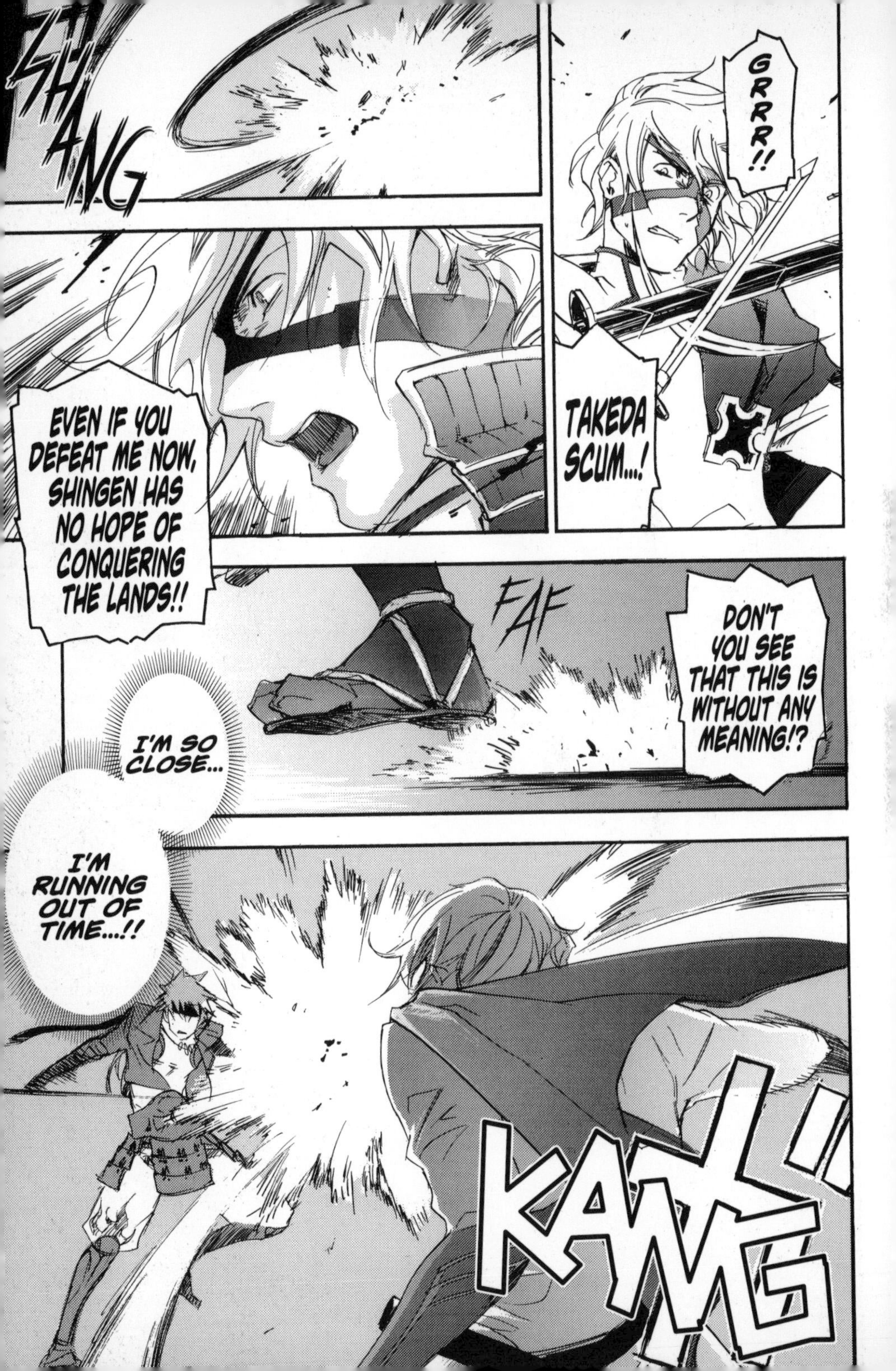
GRRR!!
TAKEDA SCUM...!
SHANG
EVEN IF YOU DEFEAT ME NOW, SHINGEN HAS NO HOPE OF CONQUERING THE LANDS!!
DON'T YOU SEE THAT THIS IS WITHOUT ANY MEANING!?
FAF
I'M SO CLOSE...
I'M RUNNING OUT OF TIME...!!
KANG

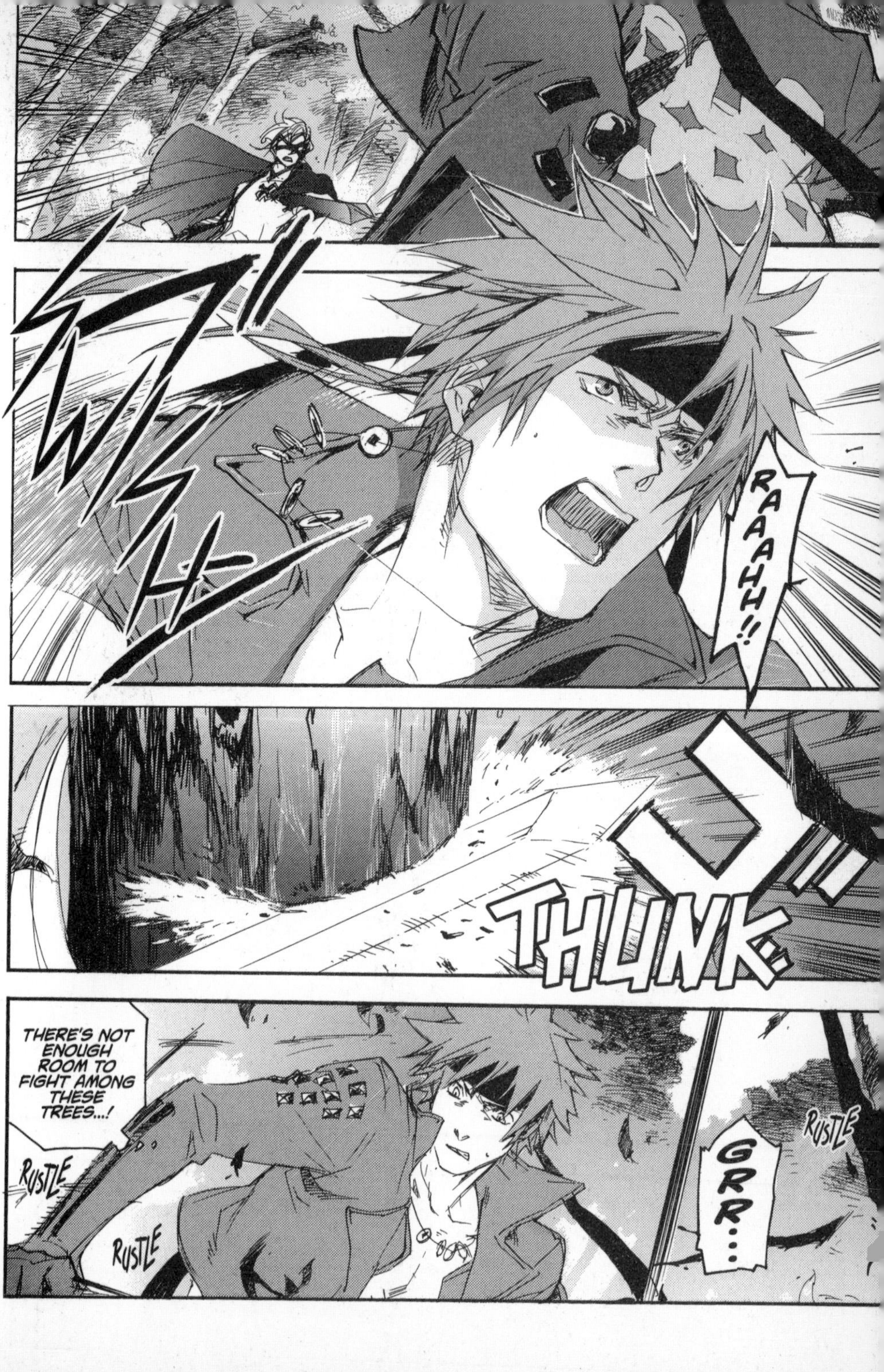

WHSSH
RAAAHH!!
THUNK
THERE'S NOT ENOUGH ROOM TO FIGHT AMONG THESE TREES...!
RUSTLE
GRR...
RUSTLE
RUSTLE

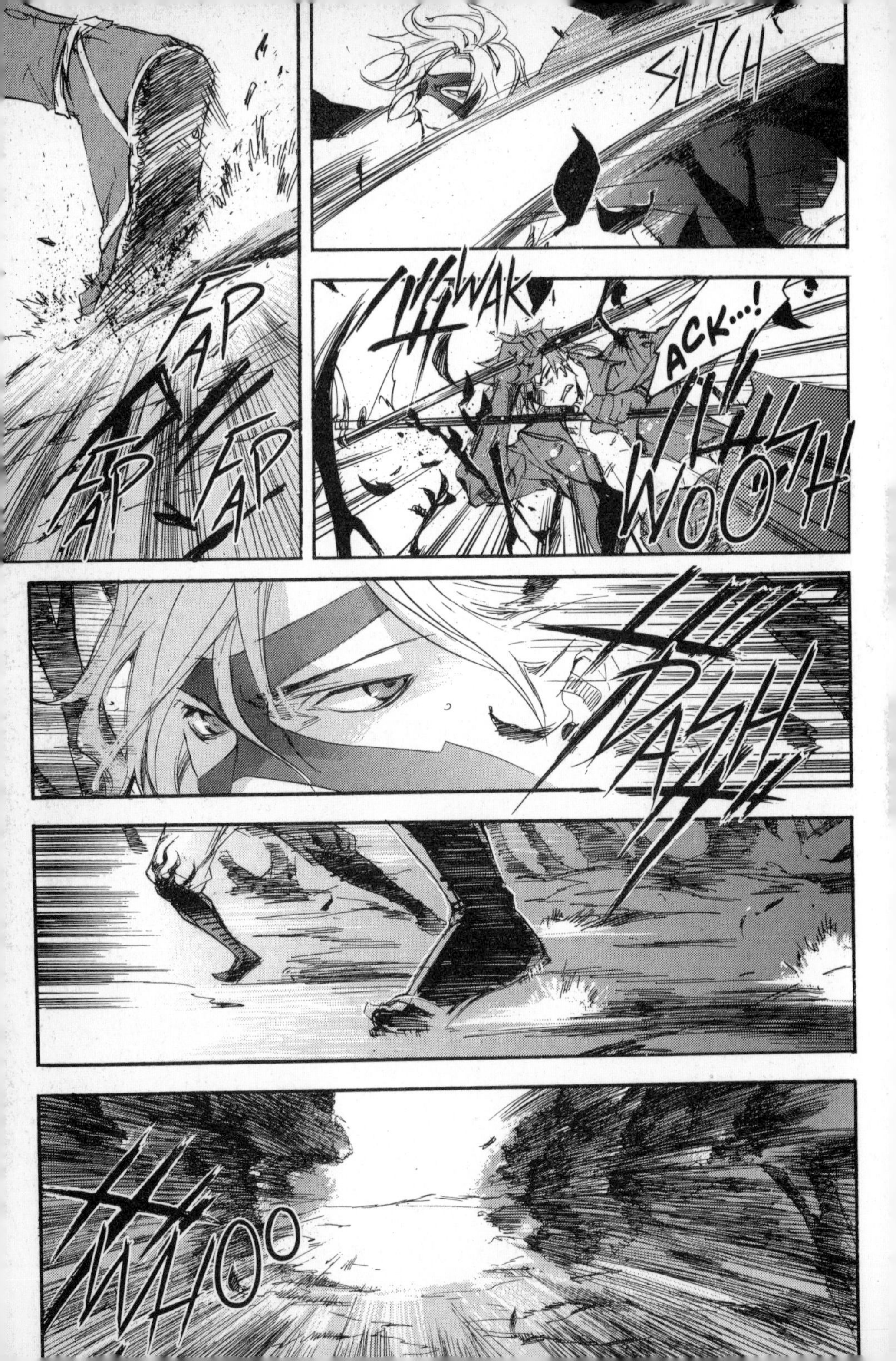
SLITCH
THWAK
ACK...!
WHOOSH
FAP FAP FAP
DASH
WHOO

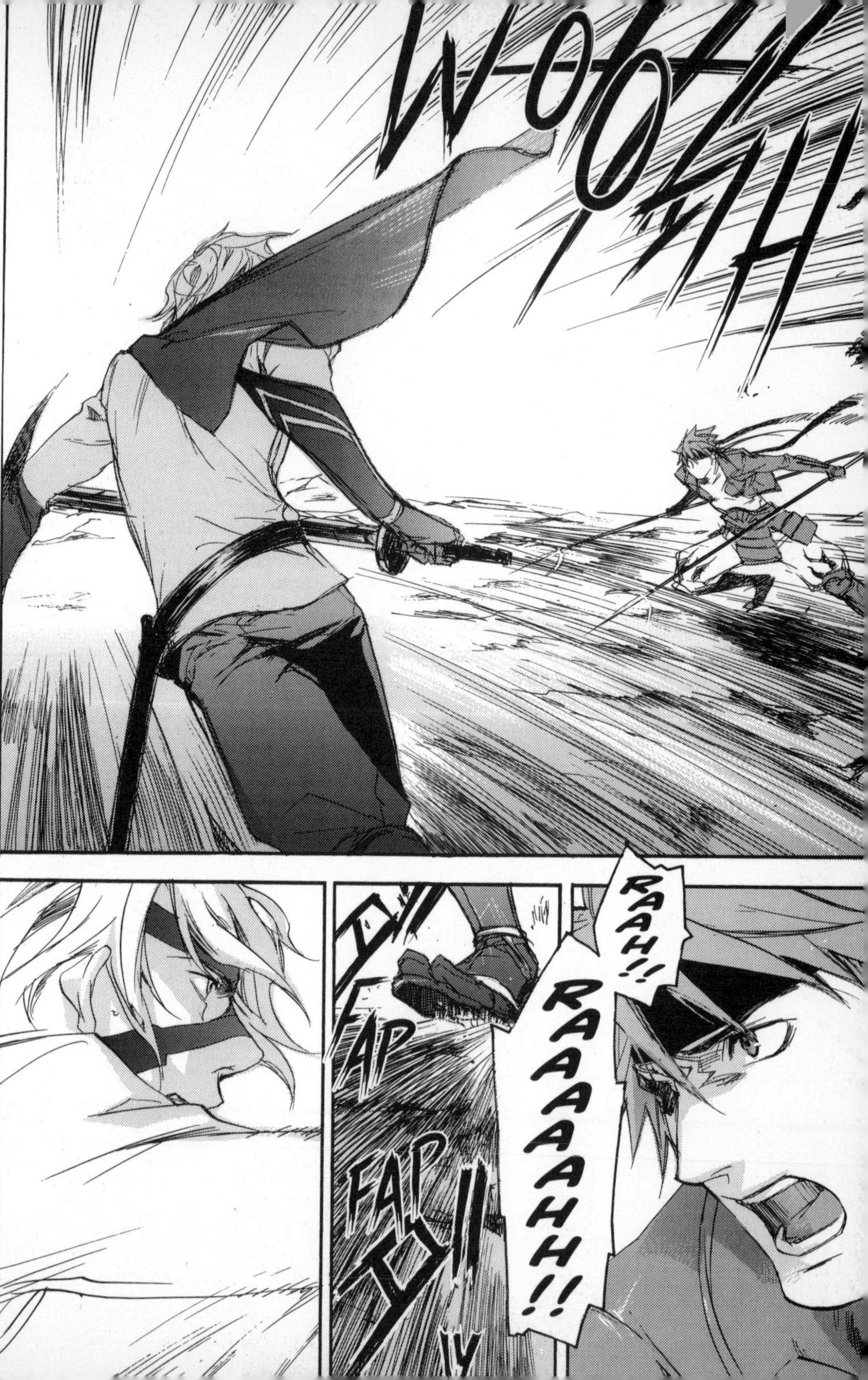
WOOSH
RAAH!!
RAAAAAHH!!
FAP
FAP

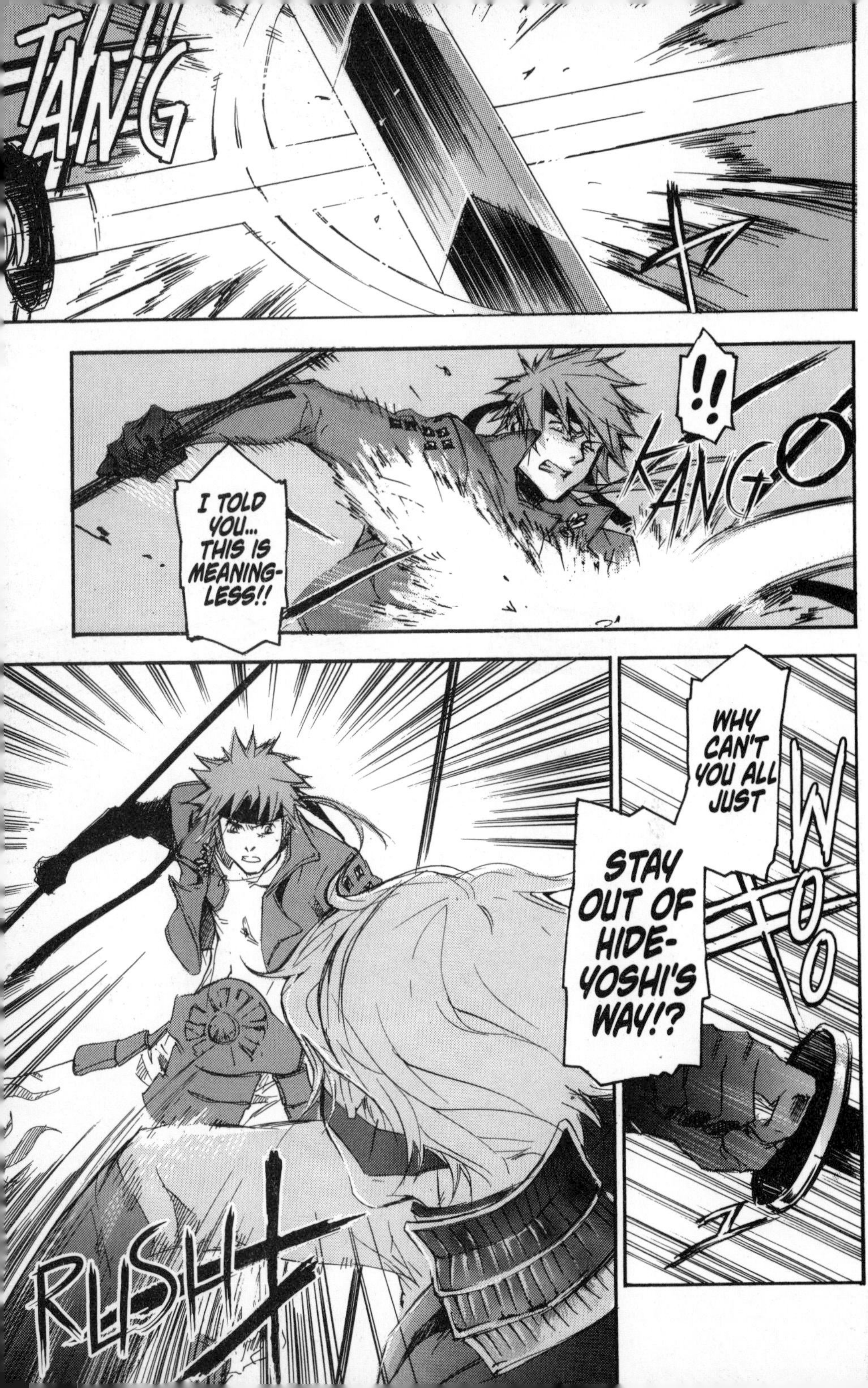
TANG
!!
KANG
I TOLD YOU... THIS IS MEANING-LESS!!
WOO
WHY CAN'T YOU ALL JUST
STAY OUT OF HIDE-YOSHI'S WAY!?
RUSH

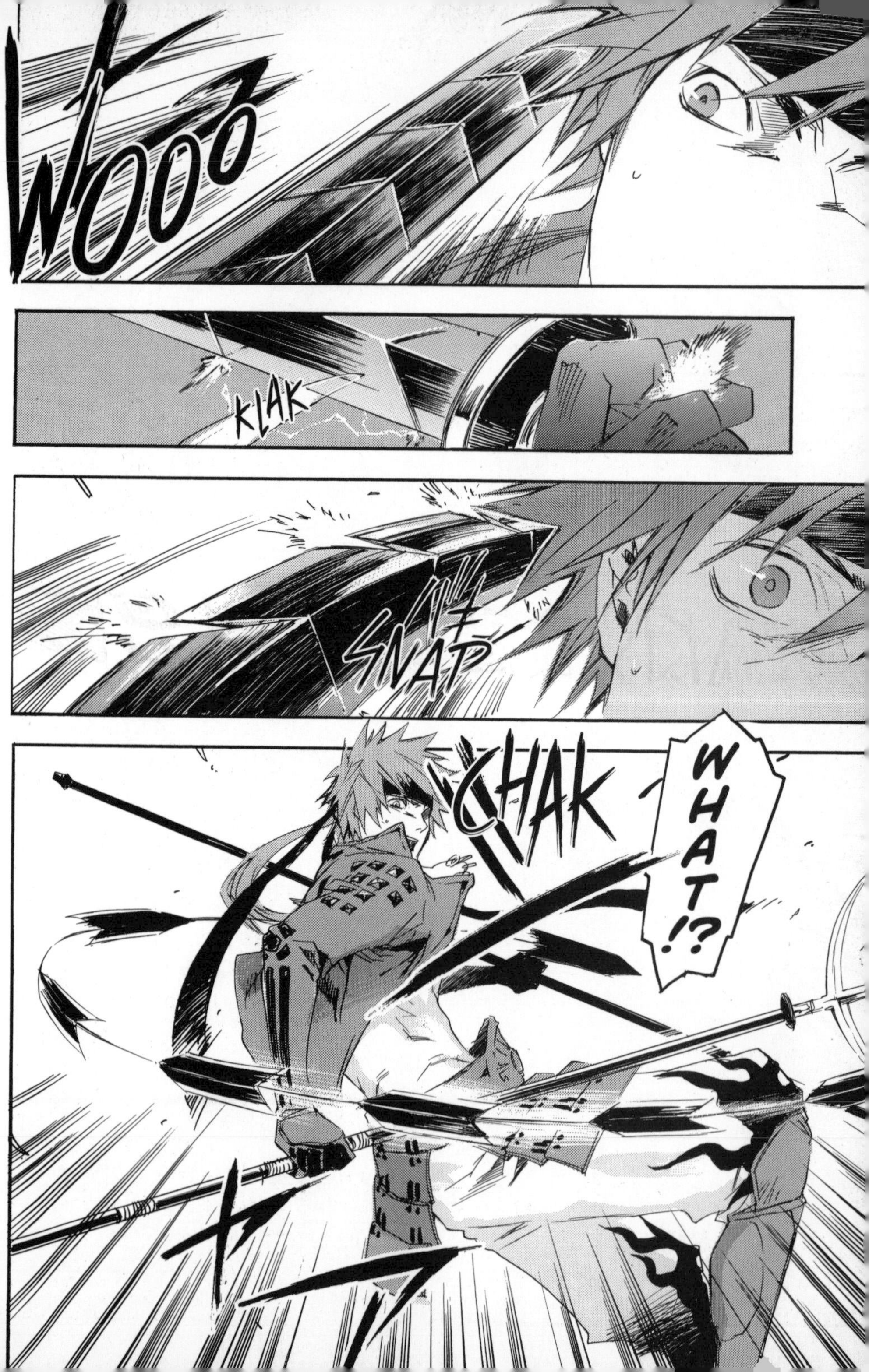
WOOO
KLAK
SNAP
WHAT!?
CHAK

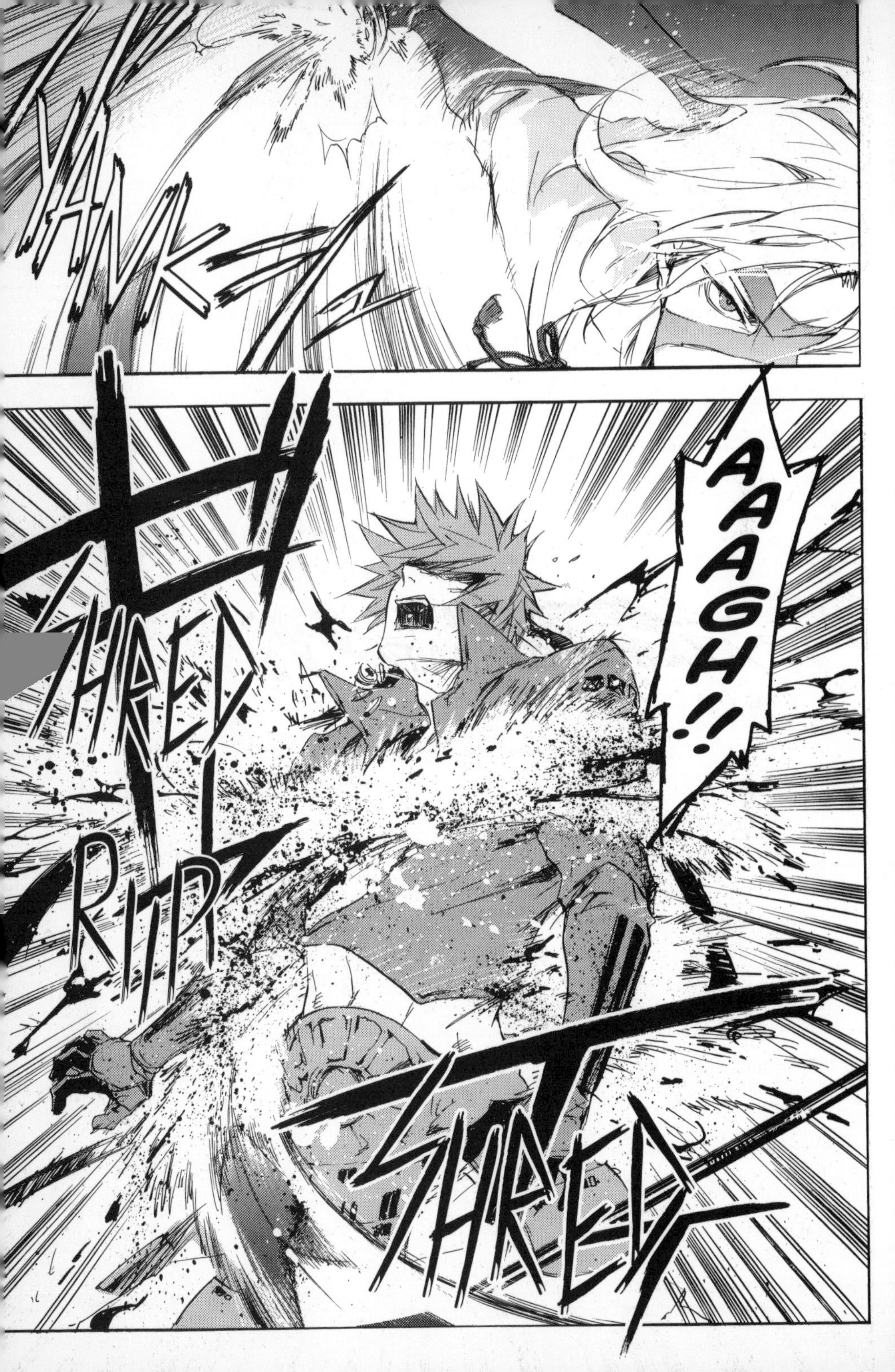
YANK
AAAAGH!!!
SHRED
RIP
SHRED

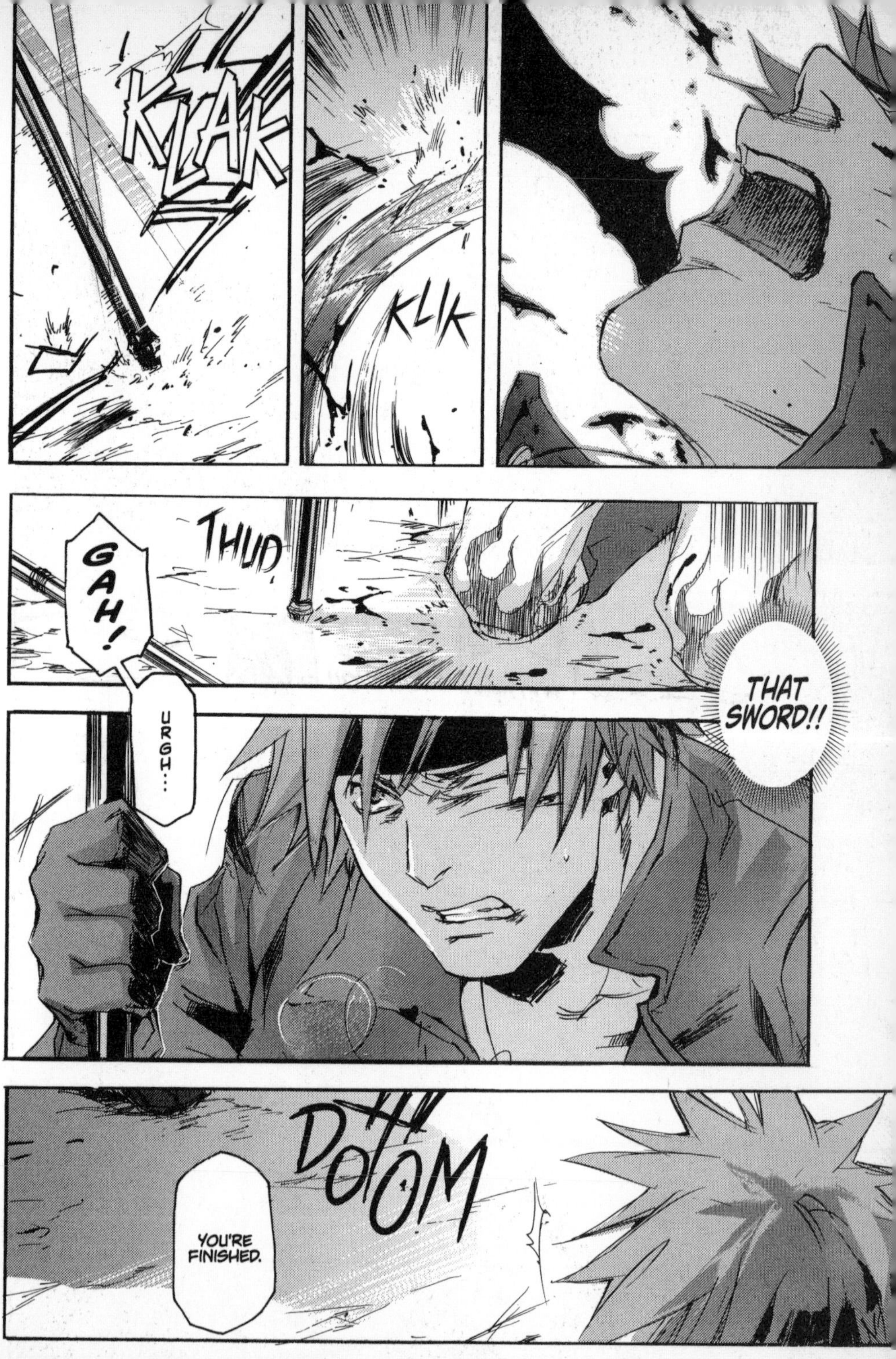
KLIK
KLAK
THUD
GAH!
THAT SWORD!!
URGH...
DOOM
YOU'RE FINISHED.

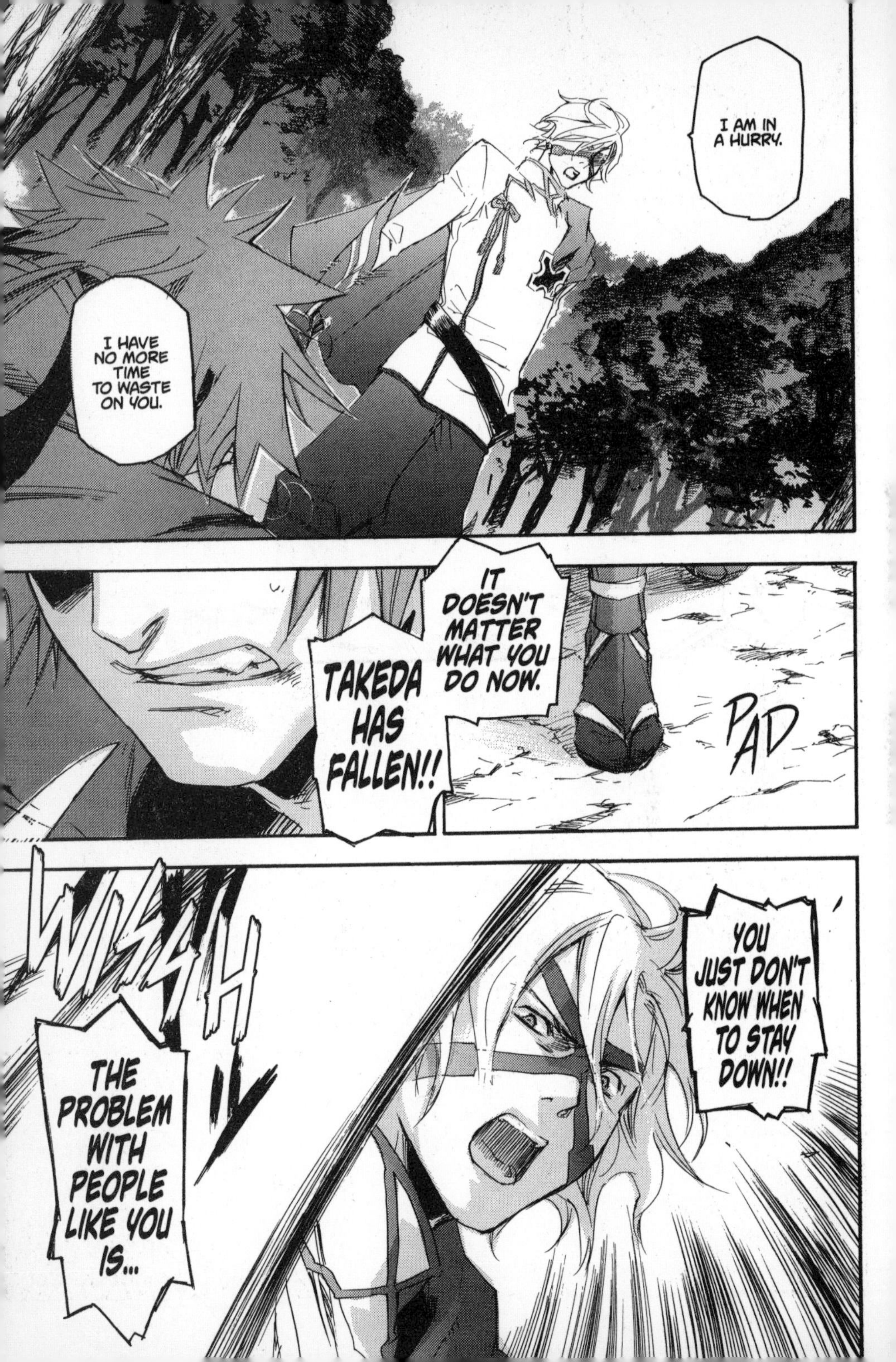
I AM IN A HURRY.
I HAVE NO MORE TIME TO WASTE ON YOU.
PAD
IT DOESN'T MATTER WHAT YOU DO NOW.
TAKEDA HAS FALLEN!!
YOU JUST DON'T KNOW WHEN TO STAY DOWN!!
WISSH
THE PROBLEM WITH PEOPLE LIKE YOU IS...

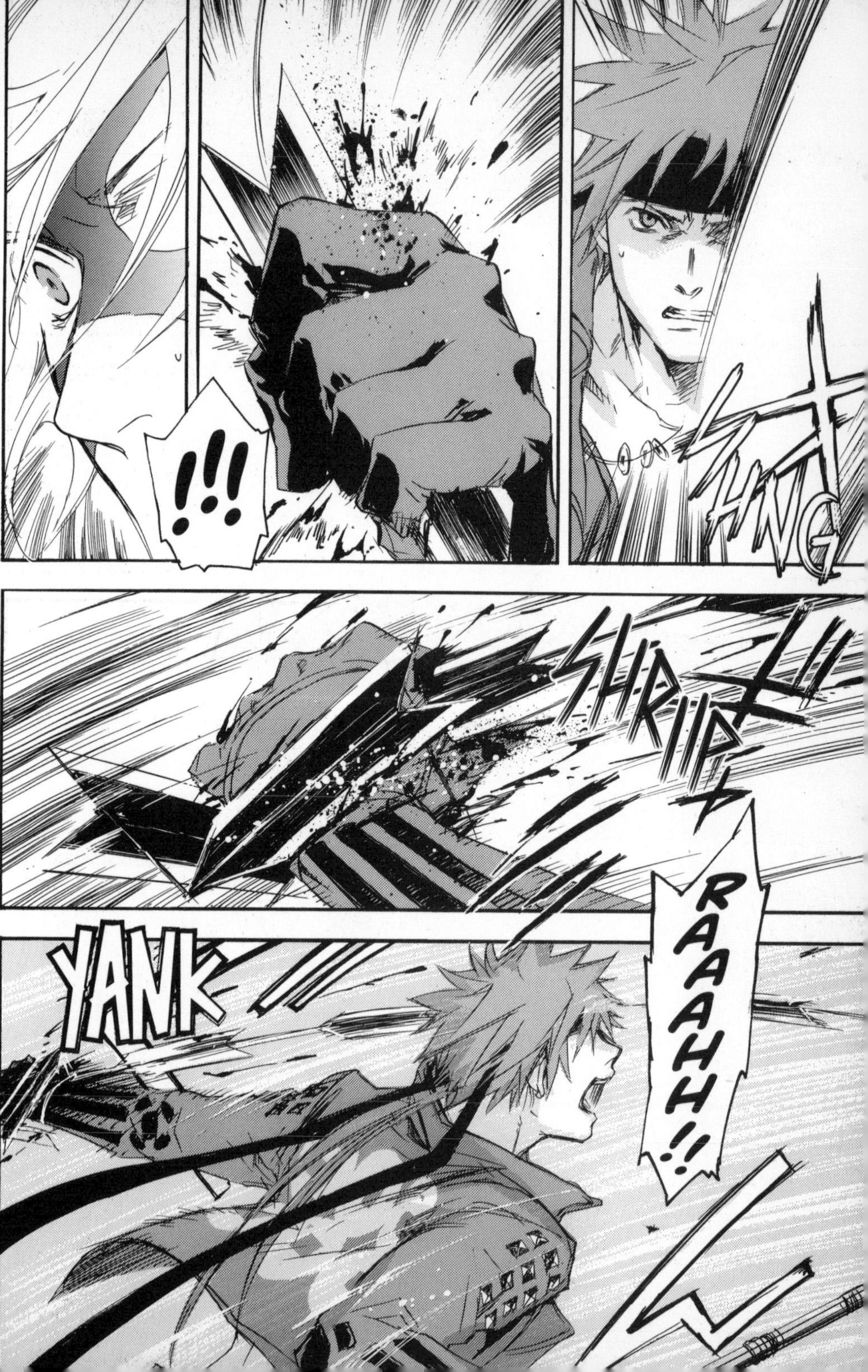
SHING
!!!
SHRIIP
RAAAAHH!!
YANK

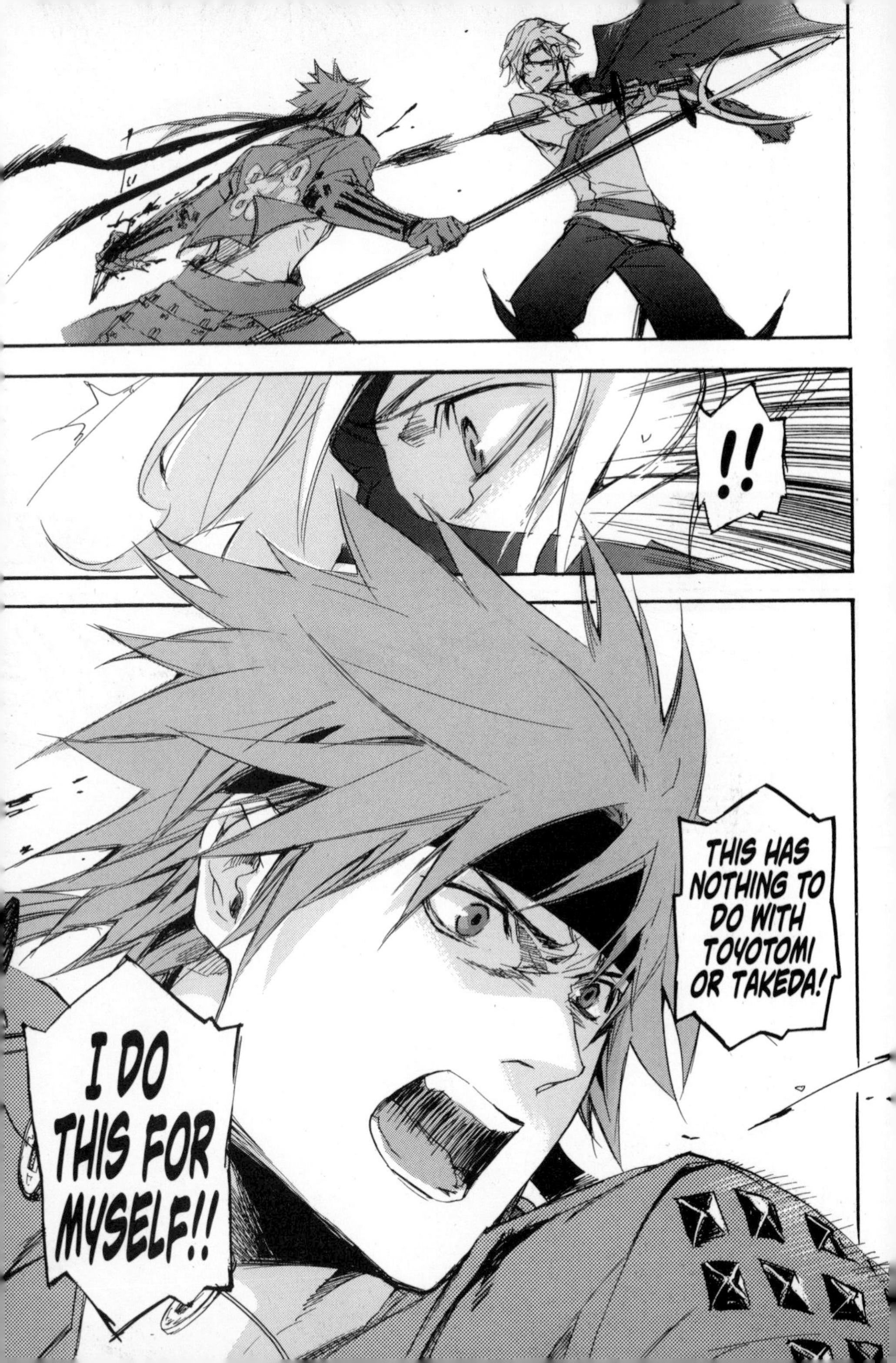
!!
THIS HAS NOTHING TO DO WITH TOYOTOMI OR TAKEDA!
I DO THIS FOR MYSELF!!

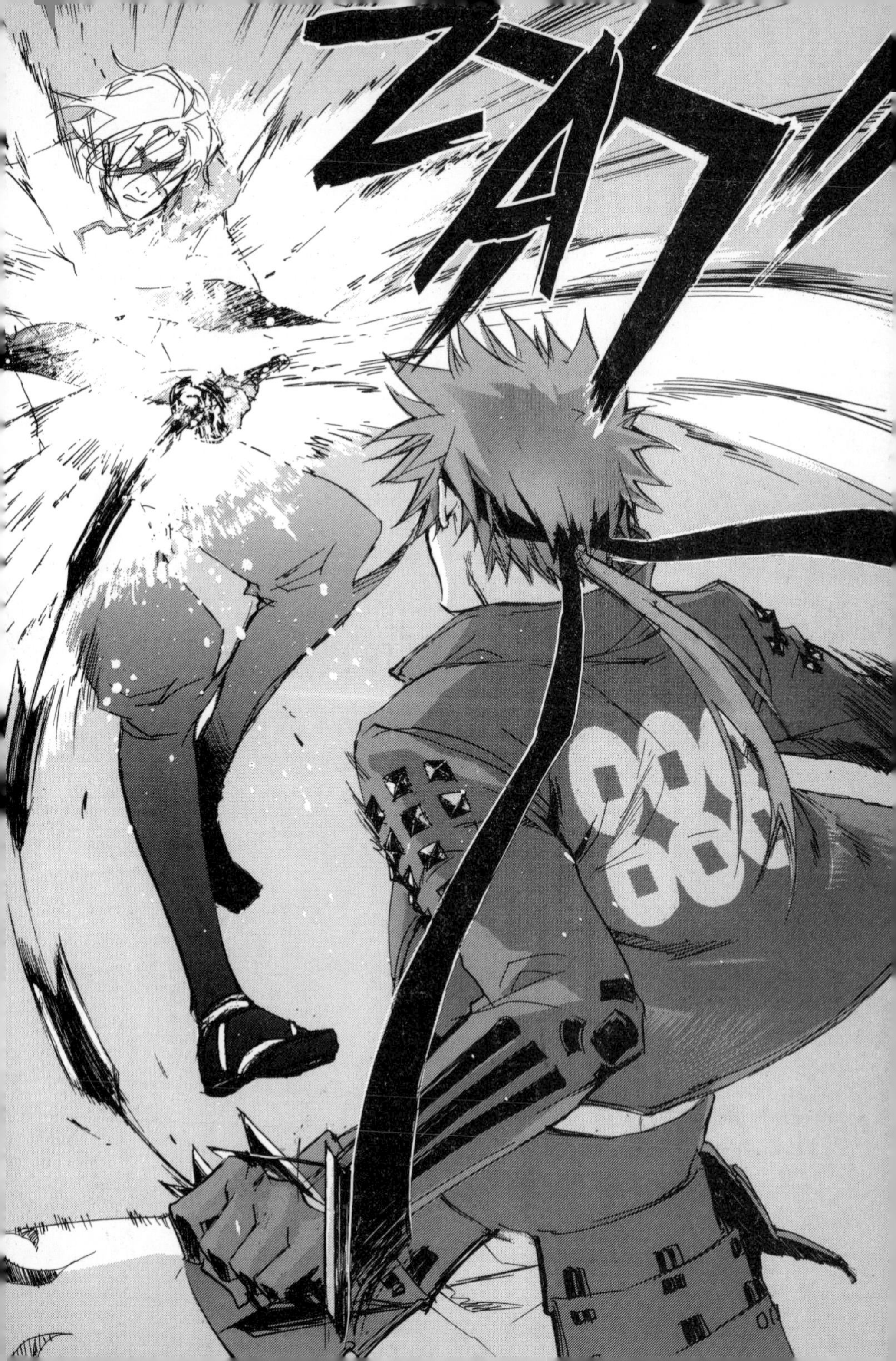
ZAK!

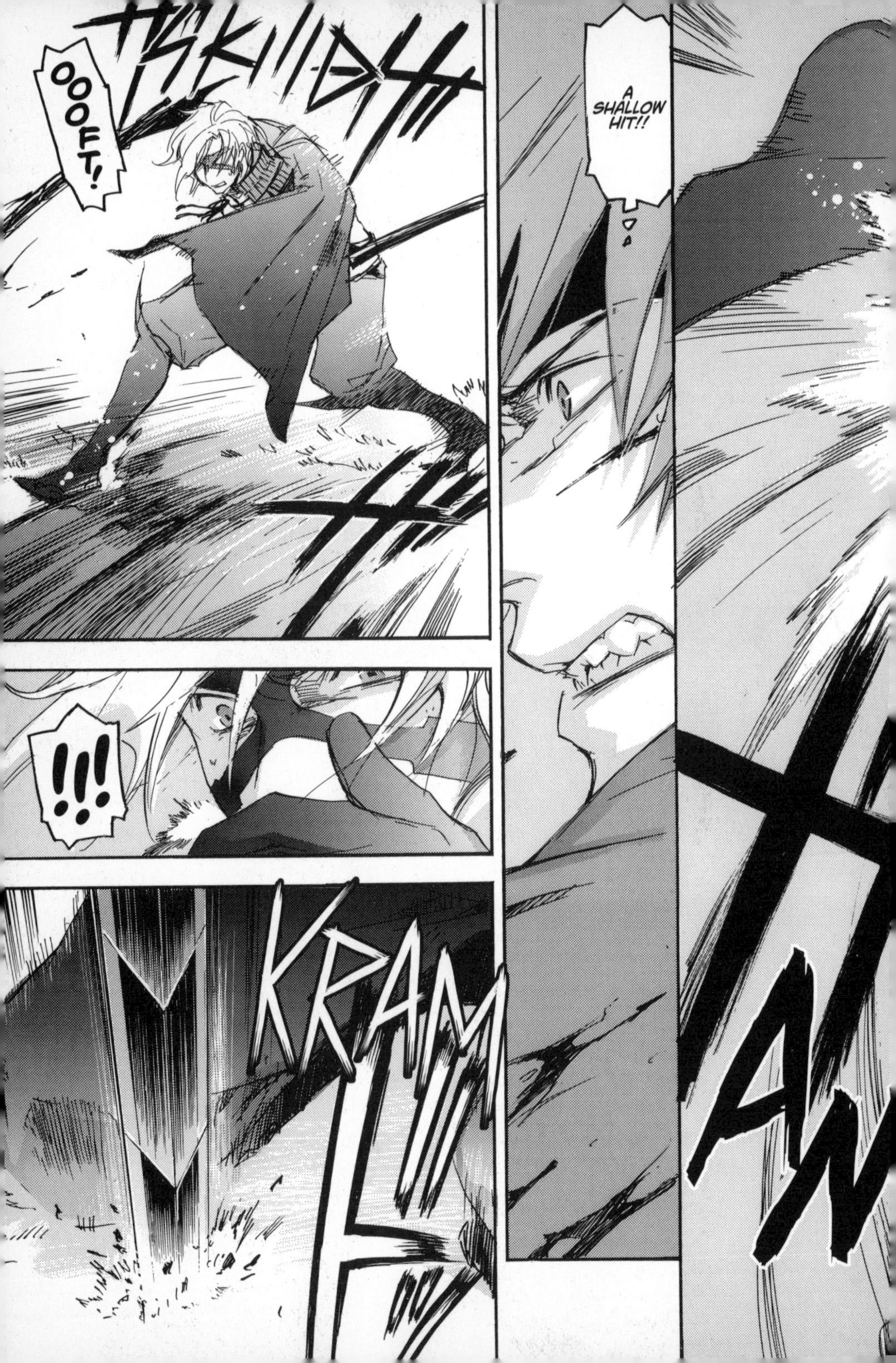

A SHALLOW HIT!!
OOOFT!
!!!
KRAM

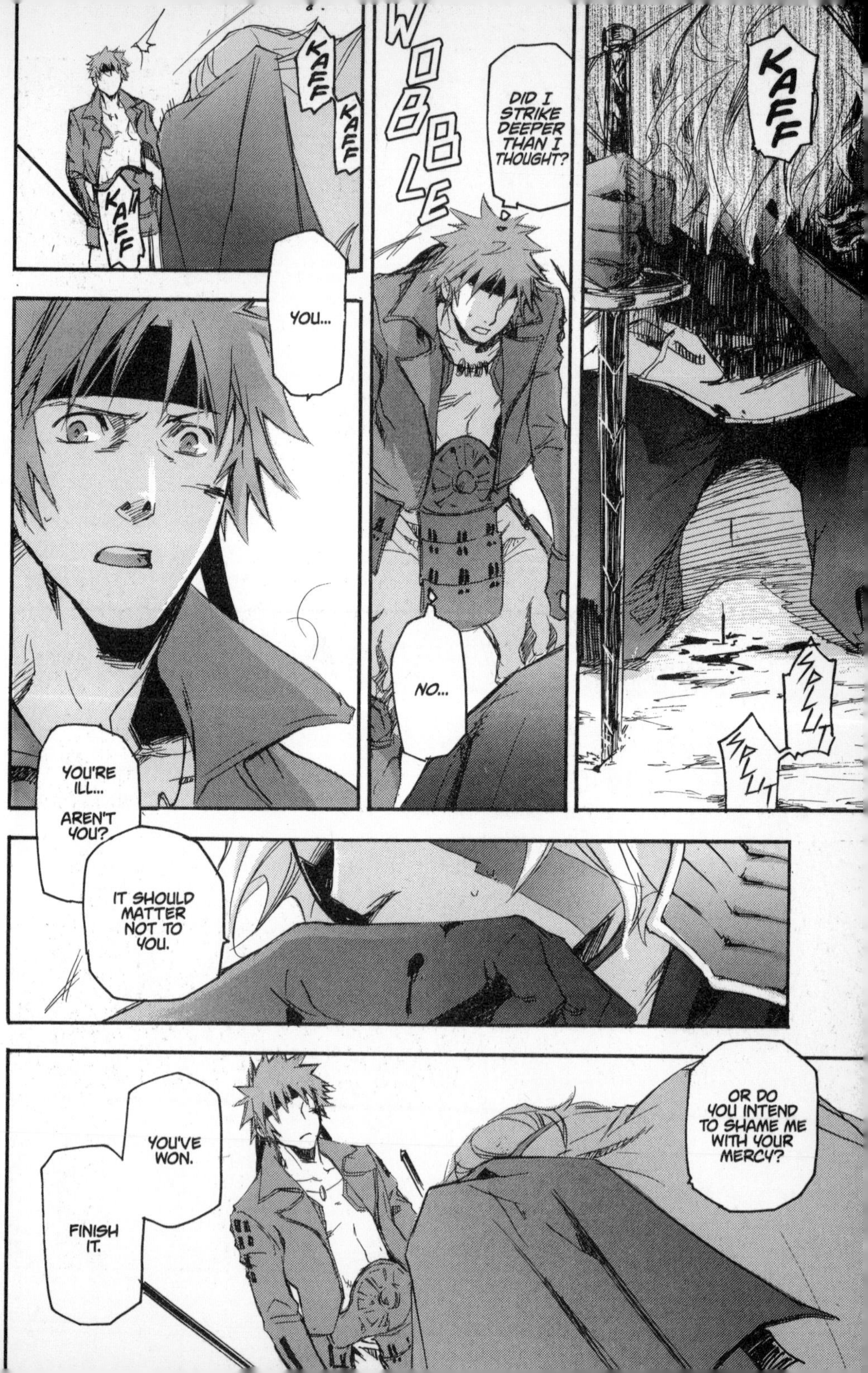
KAFF
SPLUT
SPLUT
WOBBLE
DID I STRIKE DEEPER THAN I THOUGHT?
NO...
KAFF
KAFF
KAFF
KAFF
YOU...
YOU'RE ILL...
AREN'T YOU?
IT SHOULD MATTER NOT TO YOU.
OR DO YOU INTEND TO SHAME ME WITH YOUR MERCY?
YOU'VE WON.
FINISH IT.

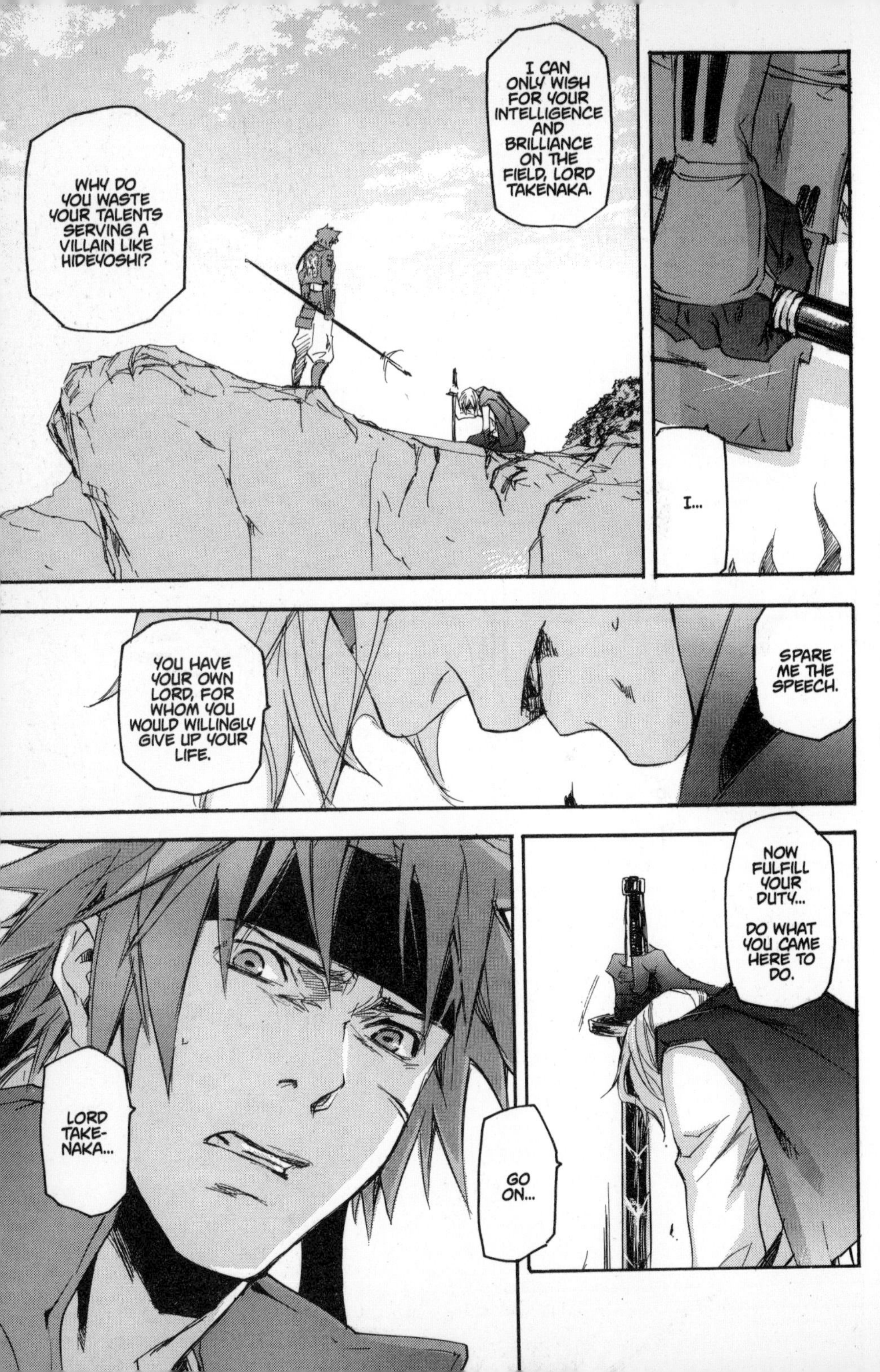
I...
I CAN ONLY WISH FOR YOUR INTELLIGENCE AND BRILLIANCE ON THE FIELD, LORD TAKENAKA.
WHY DO YOU WASTE YOUR TALENTS SERVING A VILLAIN LIKE HIDEYOSHI?
SPARE ME THE SPEECH.
YOU HAVE YOUR OWN LORD, FOR WHOM YOU WOULD WILLINGLY GIVE UP YOUR LIFE.
NOW FULFILL YOUR DUTY...
DO WHAT YOU CAME HERE TO DO.
GO ON...
LORD TAKE-NAKA...

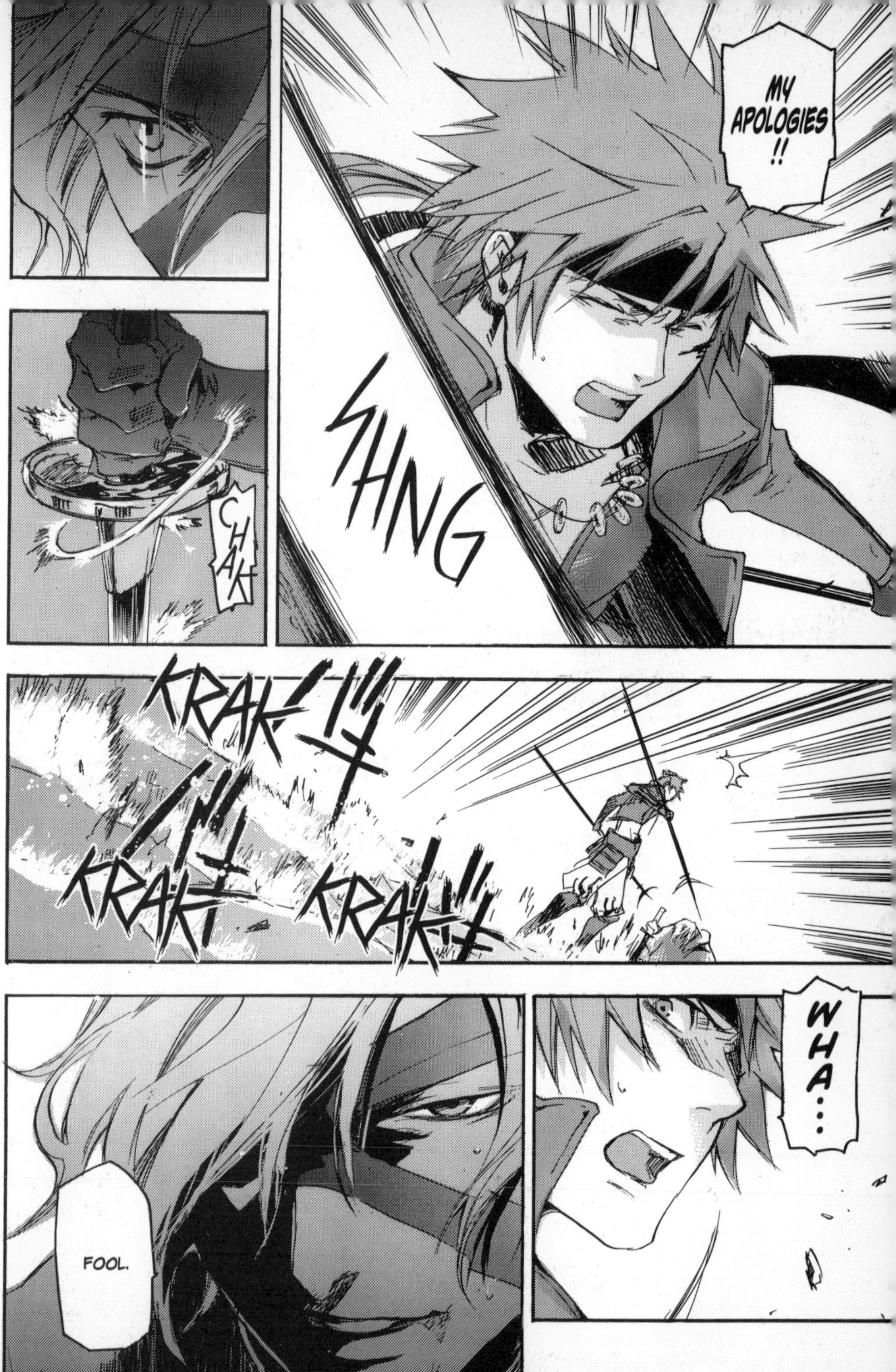
MY APOLOGIES !!
SHNG
CHAK
KRAK!!
KRAK!!
KRAK!!
WHA...
FOOL.

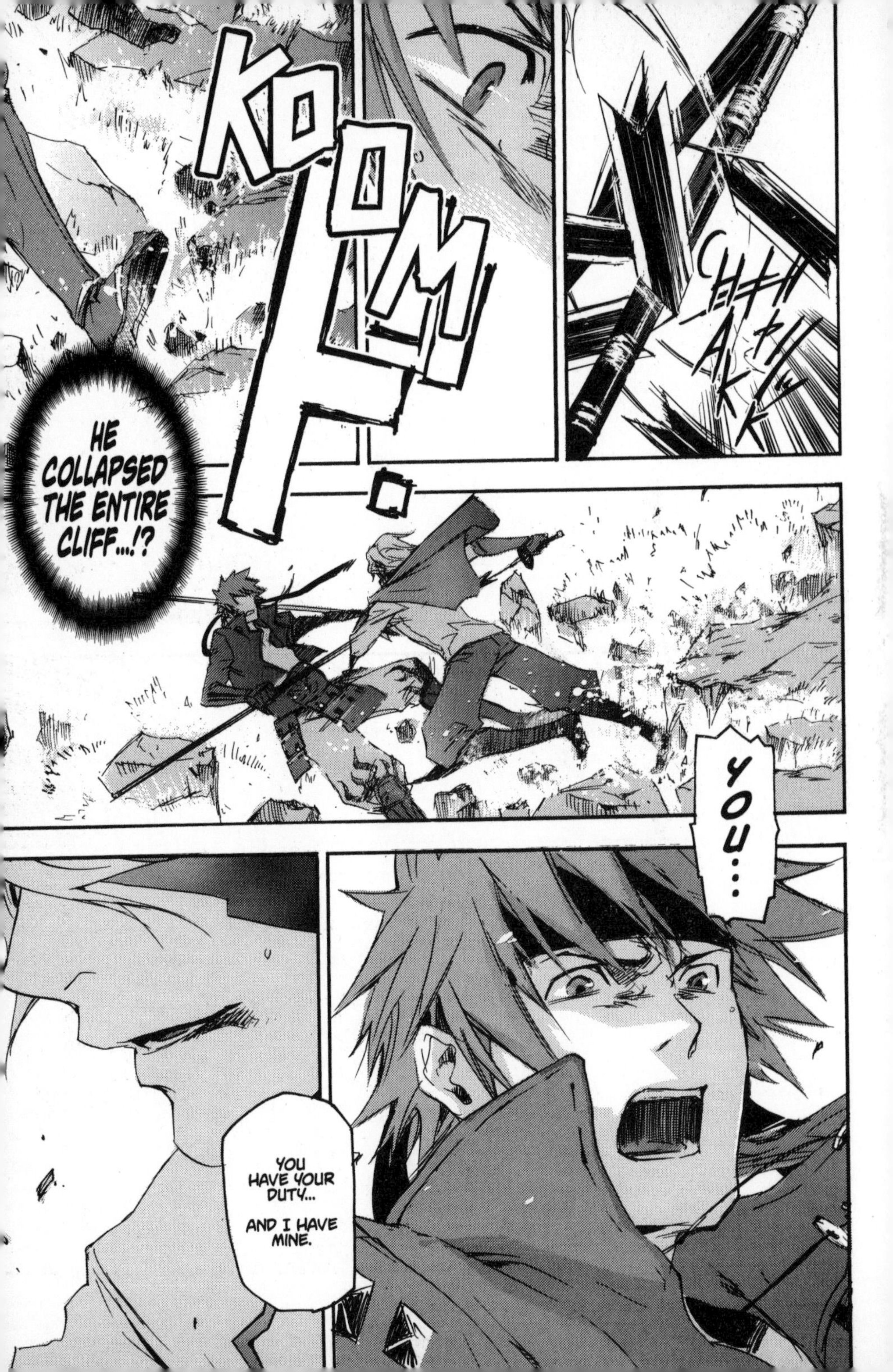
CHHHAKK
KOOM
HE COLLAPSED THE ENTIRE CLIFF...!?
YOU...
YOU HAVE YOUR DUTY...
AND I HAVE MINE.

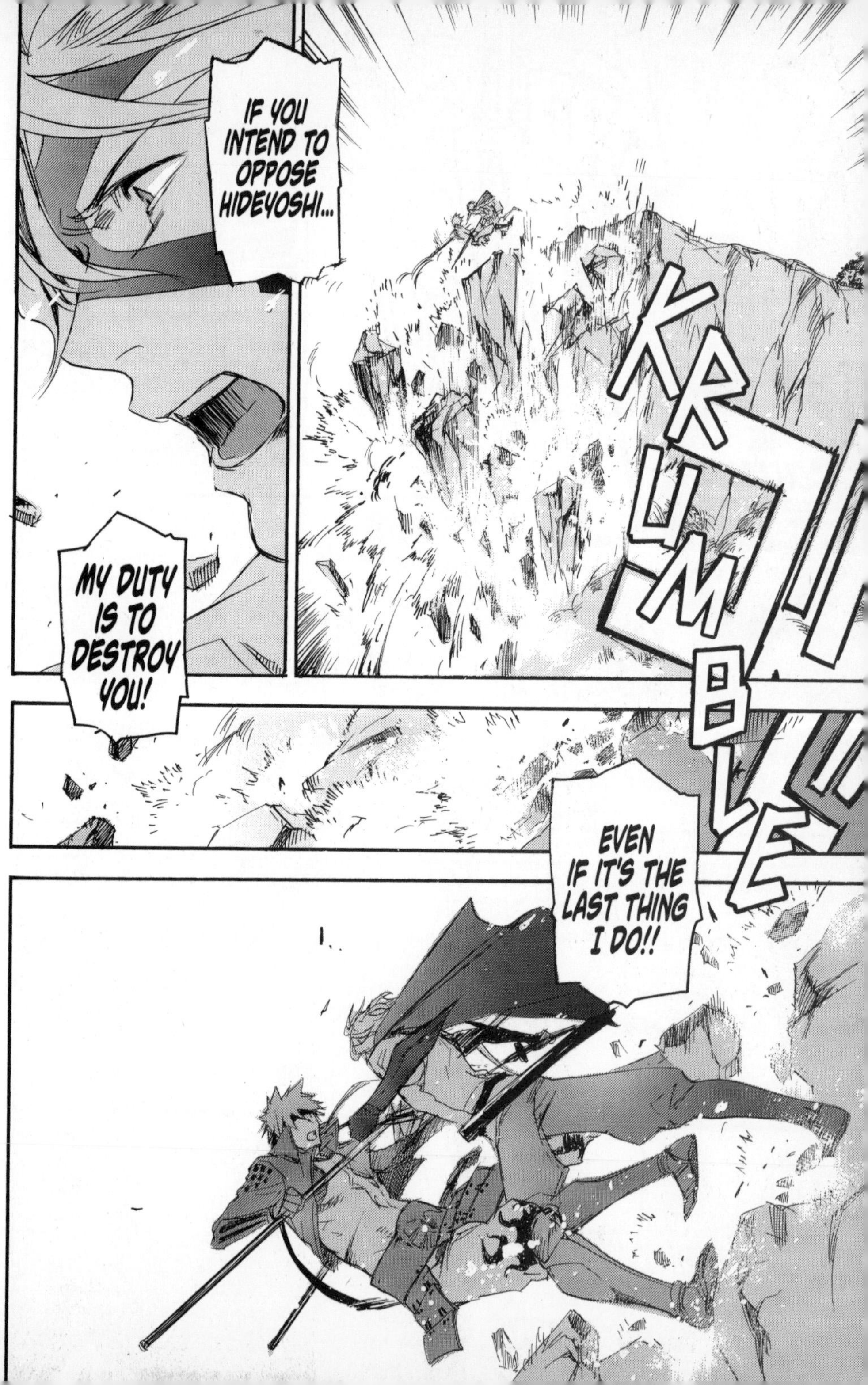
KRUMBLE
IF YOU INTEND TO OPPOSE HIDEYOSHI...
MY DUTY IS TO DESTROY YOU!
EVEN IF IT'S THE LAST THING I DO!!

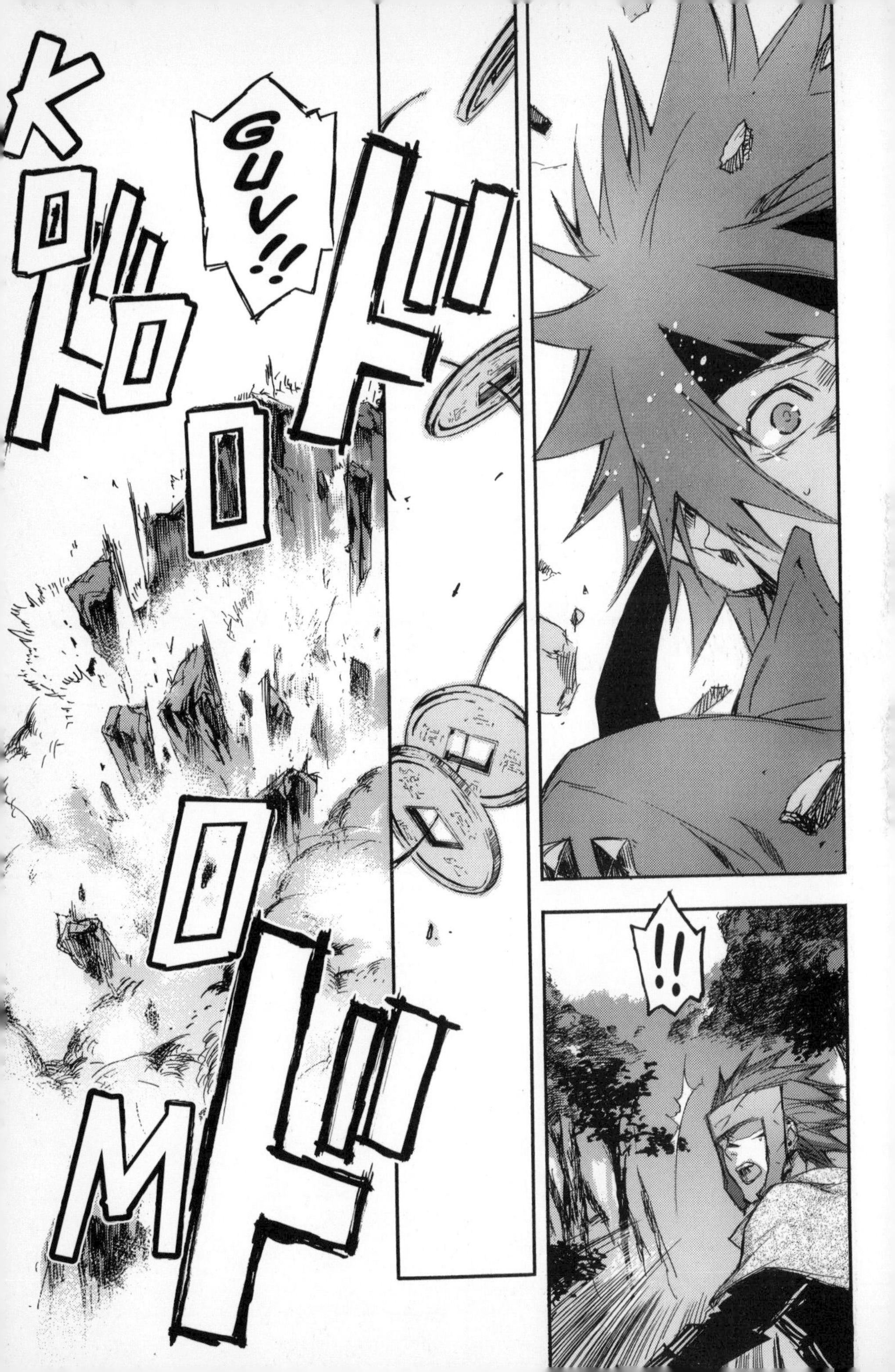
!!
GUV!!

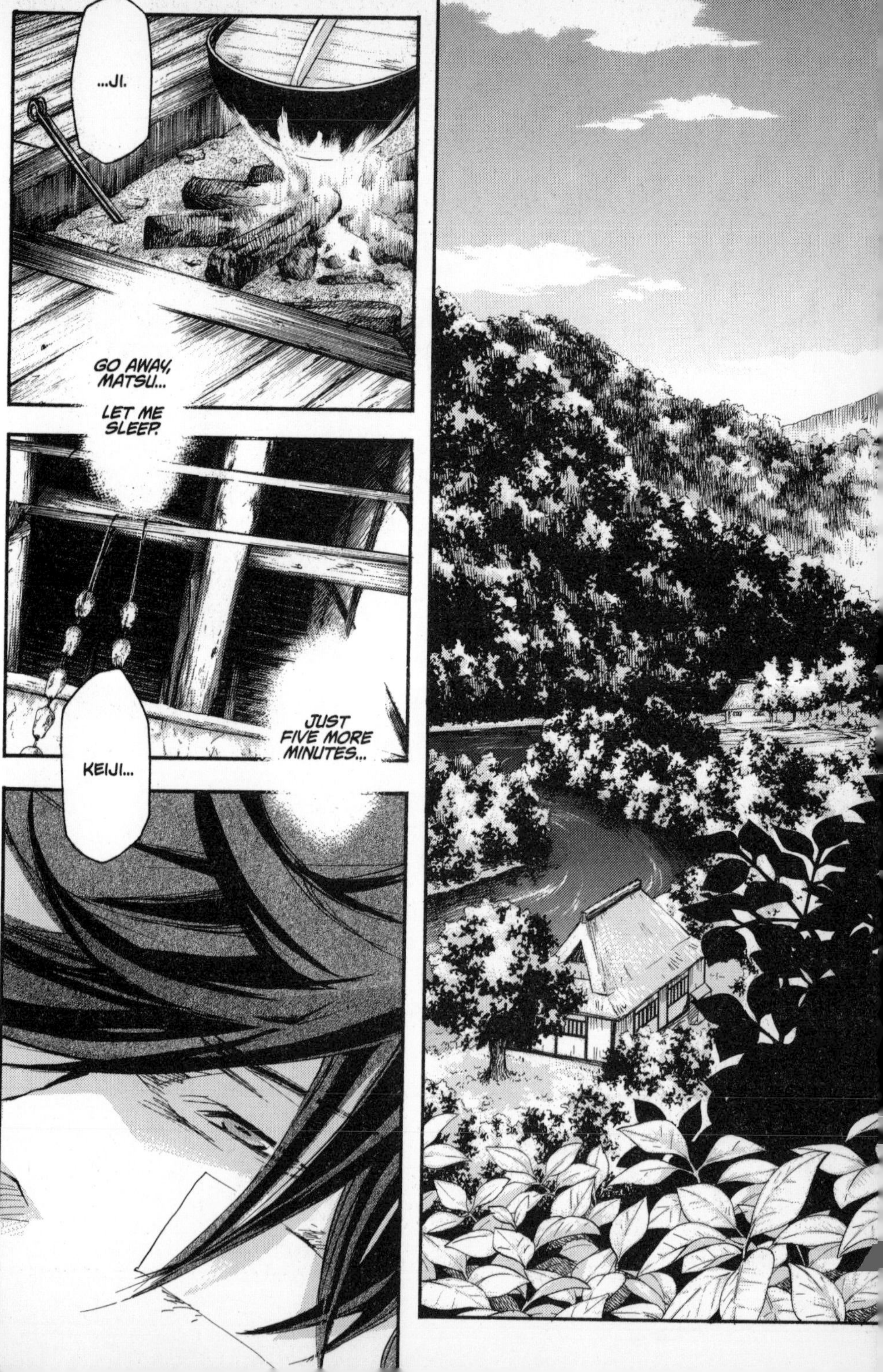
...JI.
GO AWAY, MATSU...
LET ME SLEEP.
JUST FIVE MORE MINUTES...
KEIJI...

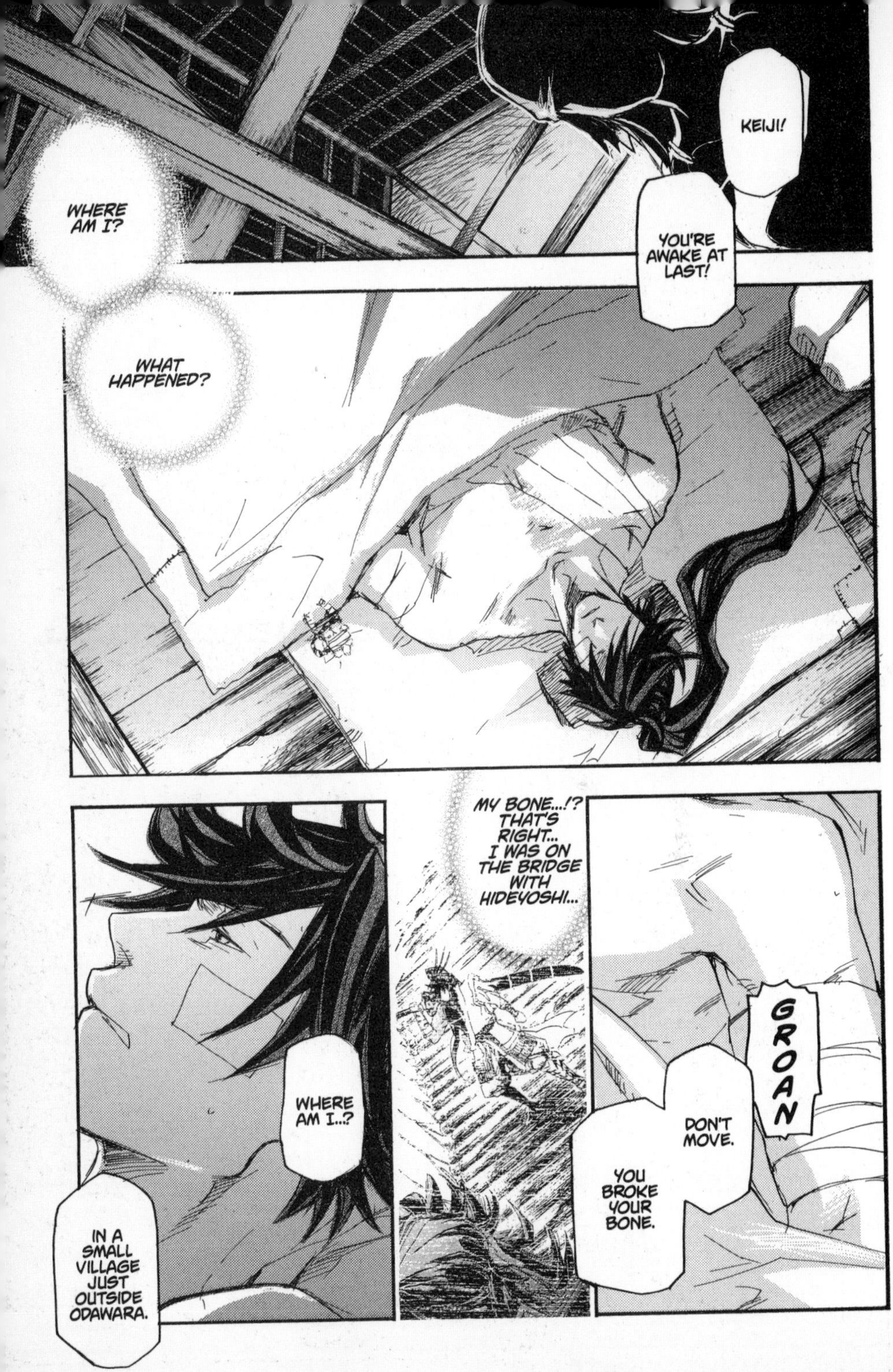
KEIJI!
YOU'RE AWAKE AT LAST!
WHERE AM I?
WHAT HAPPENED?
GROAN
DON'T MOVE.
YOU BROKE YOUR BONE.
MY BONE...!? THAT'S RIGHT... I WAS ON THE BRIDGE WITH HIDEYOSHI...
WHERE AM I..?
IN A SMALL VILLAGE JUST OUTSIDE ODAWARA.

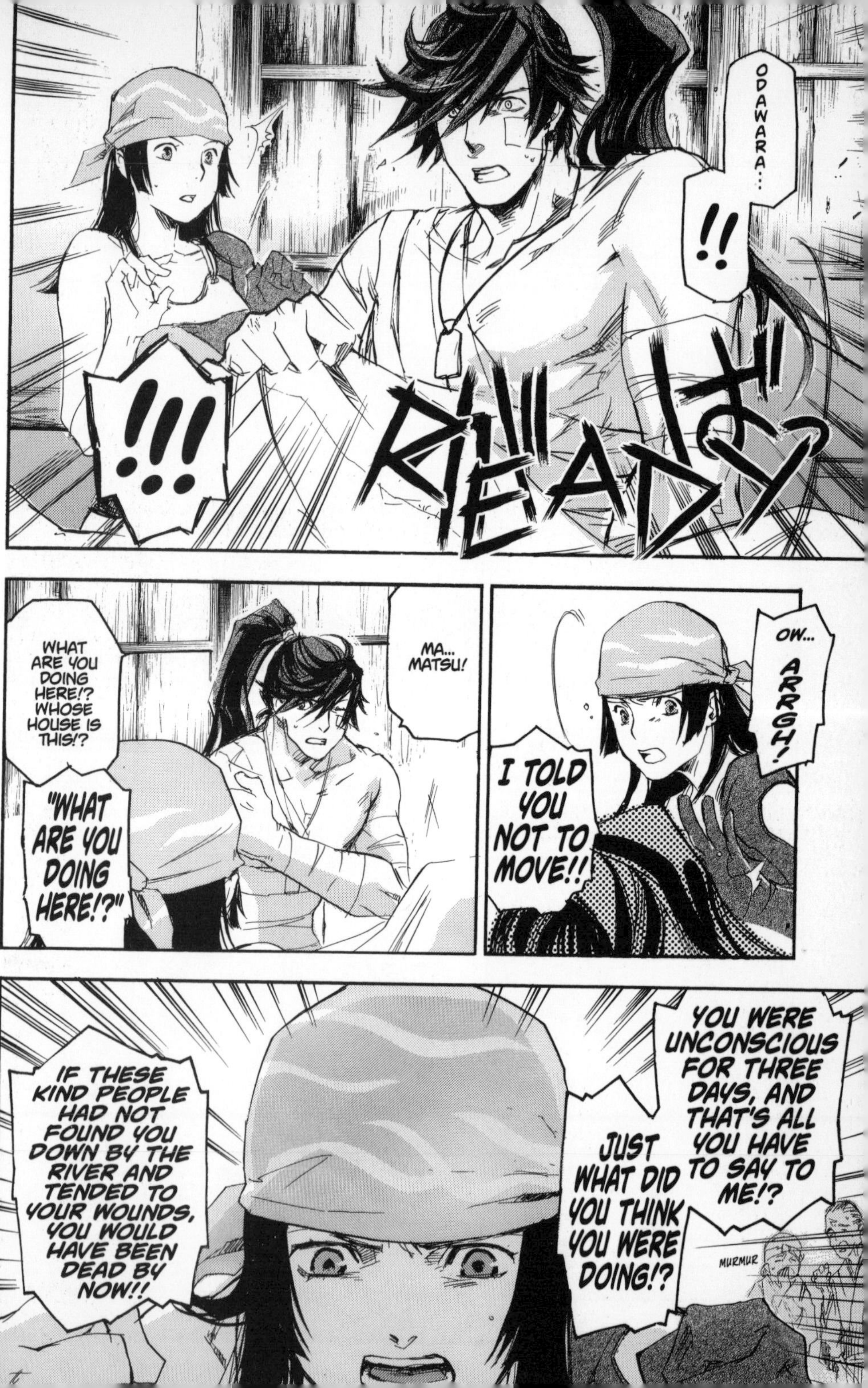
ODAWARA...
!!
!!!
OW... ARRGH!
I TOLD YOU NOT TO MOVE!!
MA... MATSU!
WHAT ARE YOU DOING HERE!? WHOSE HOUSE IS THIS!?
"WHAT ARE YOU DOING HERE!?"
YOU WERE UNCONSCIOUS FOR THREE DAYS, AND THAT'S ALL YOU HAVE TO SAY TO ME!?
JUST WHAT DID YOU THINK YOU WERE DOING!?
IF THESE KIND PEOPLE HAD NOT FOUND YOU DOWN BY THE RIVER AND TENDED TO YOUR WOUNDS, YOU WOULD HAVE BEEN DEAD BY NOW!!
MURMUR

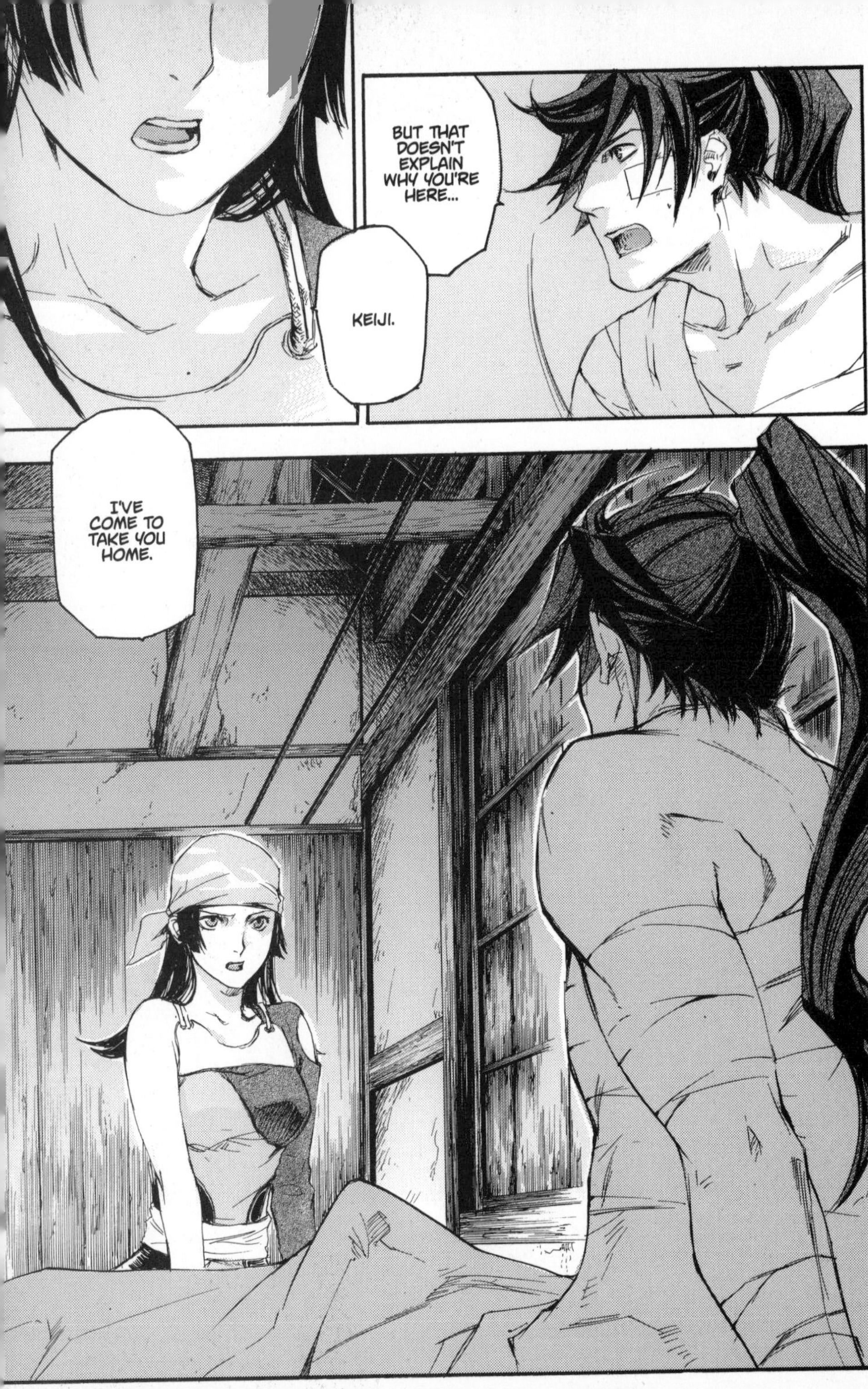
BUT THAT DOESN'T EXPLAIN WHY YOU'RE HERE...
KEIJI.
I'VE COME TO TAKE YOU HOME.

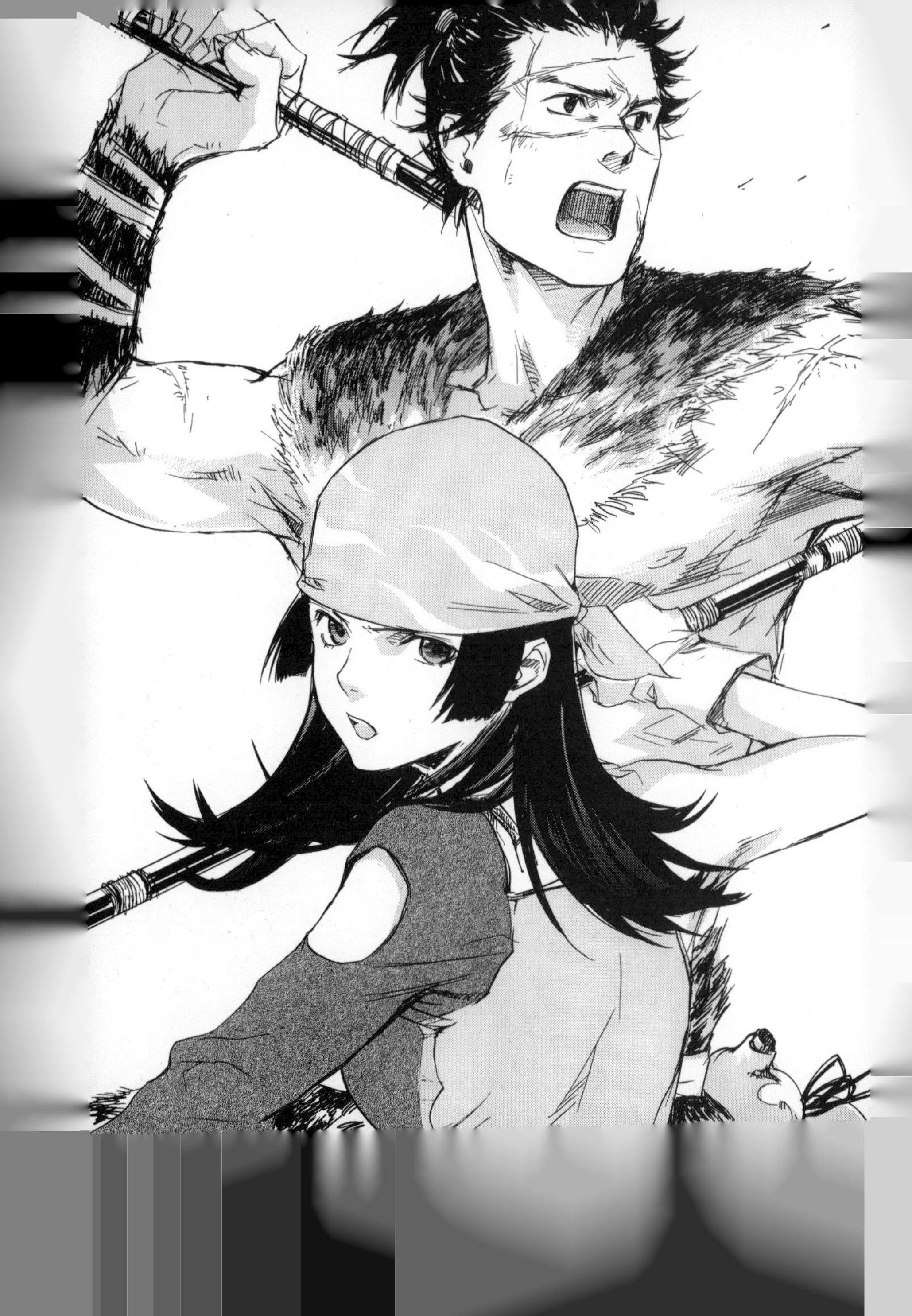

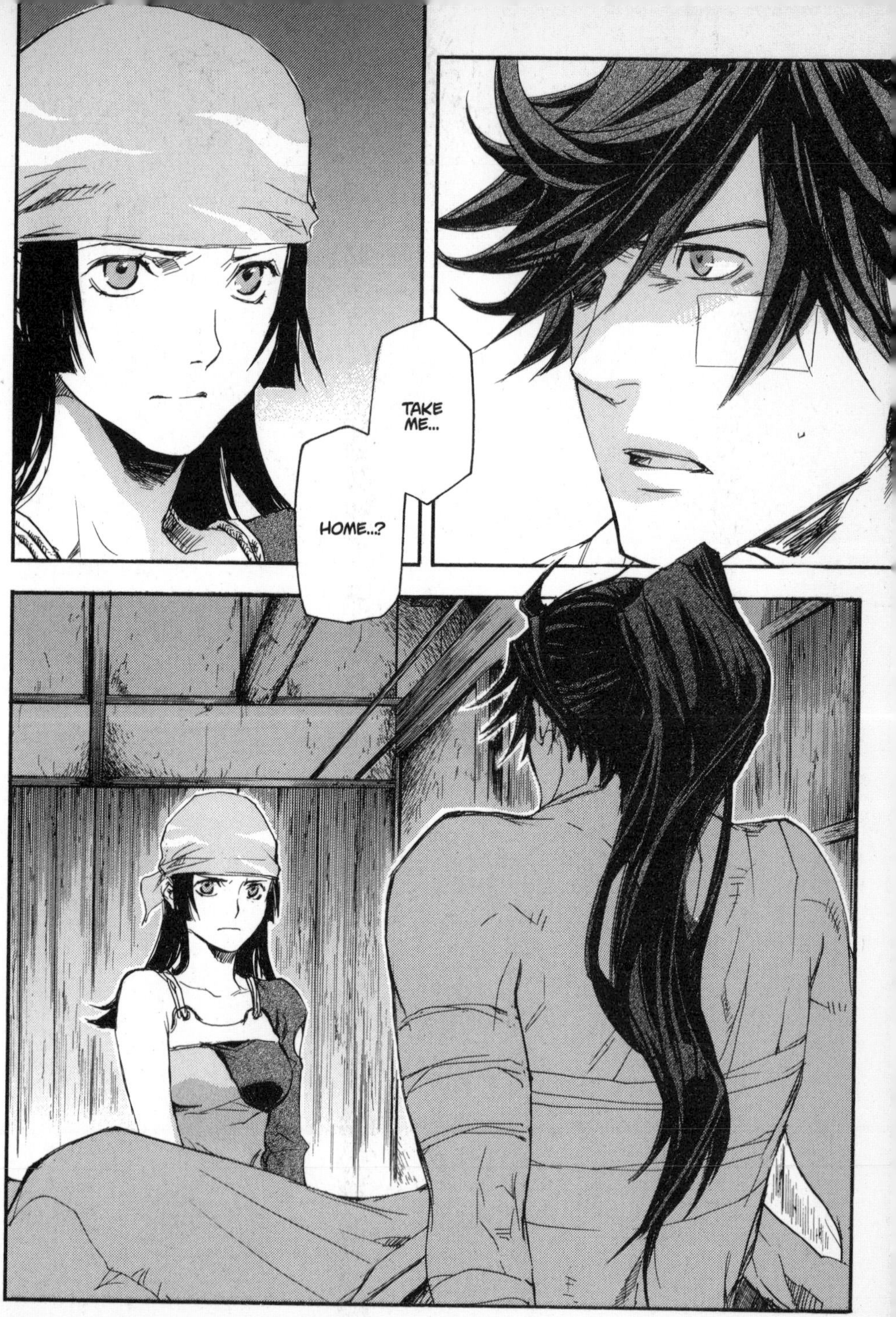
TAKE ME...
HOME...?

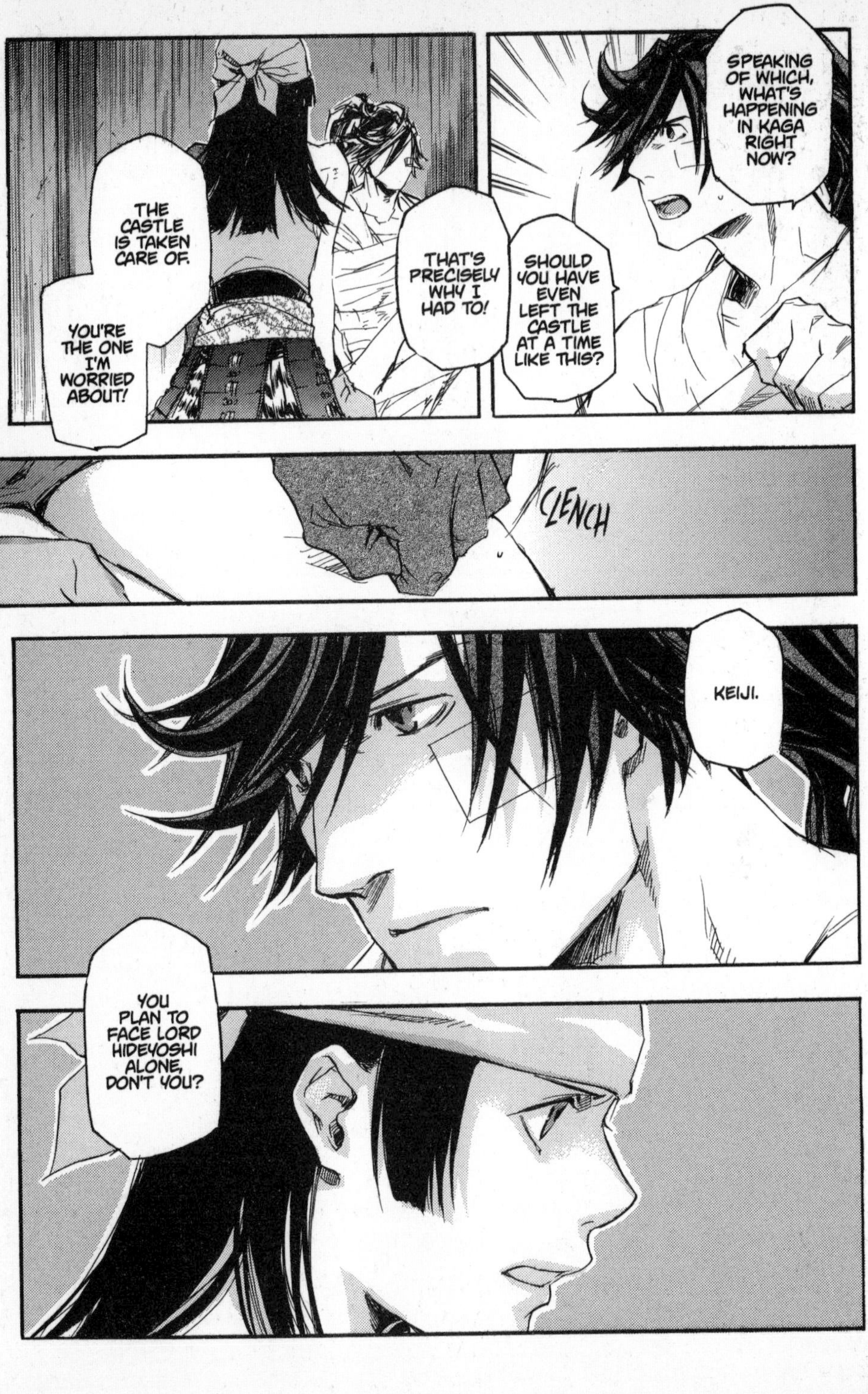
SPEAKING OF WHICH, WHAT'S HAPPENING IN KAGA RIGHT NOW?
SHOULD YOU HAVE EVEN LEFT THE CASTLE AT A TIME LIKE THIS?
THAT'S PRECISELY WHY I HAD TO!
THE CASTLE IS TAKEN CARE OF.
YOU'RE THE ONE I'M WORRIED ABOUT!
CLENCH
KEIJI.
YOU PLAN TO FACE LORD HIDEYOSHI ALONE, DON'T YOU?

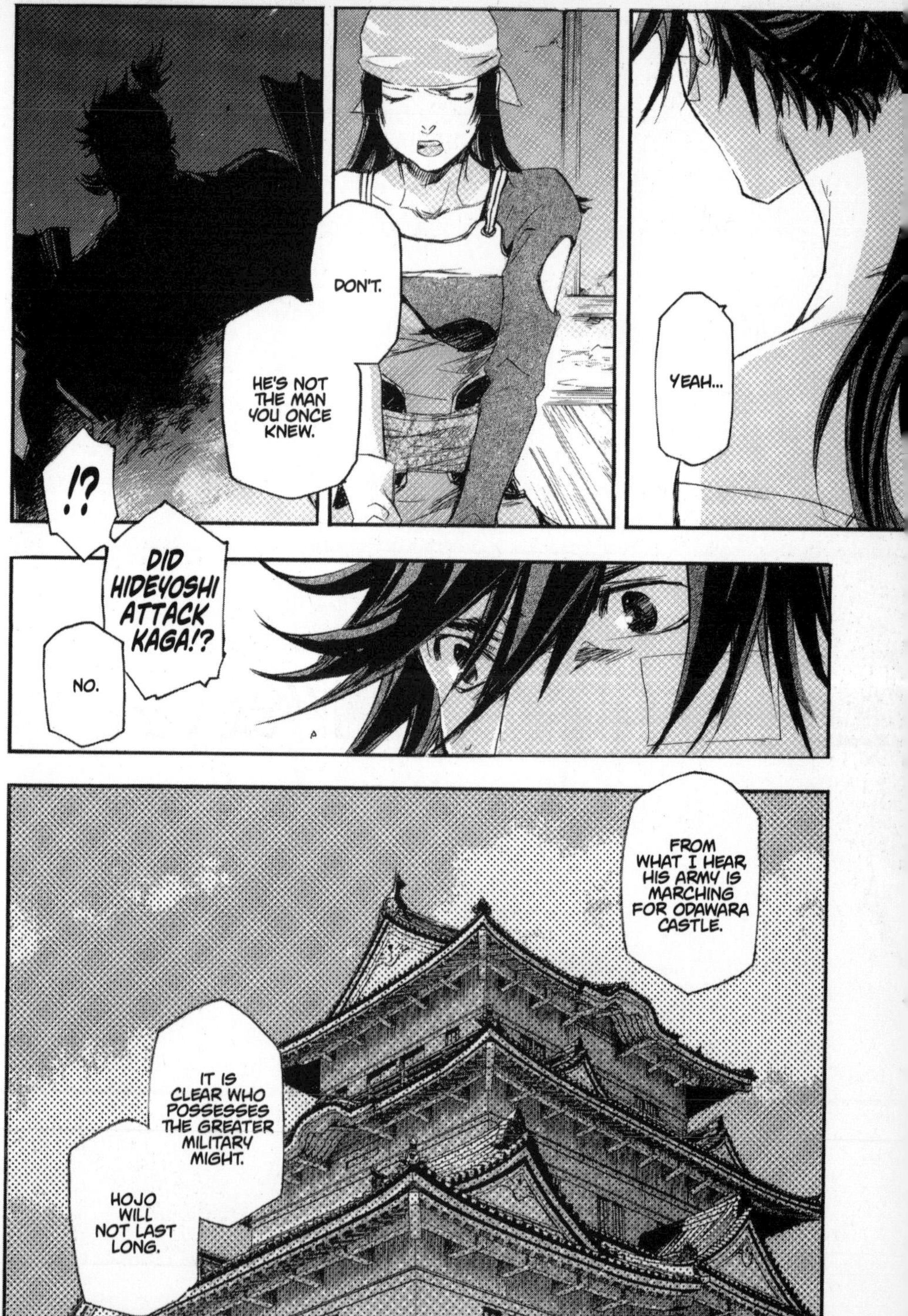
YEAH...
DON'T.
HE'S NOT THE MAN YOU ONCE KNEW.
!?
DID HIDEYOSHI ATTACK KAGA!?
NO.
FROM WHAT I HEAR, HIS ARMY IS MARCHING FOR ODAWARA CASTLE.
IT IS CLEAR WHO POSSESSES THE GREATER MILITARY MIGHT.
HOJO WILL NOT LAST LONG.

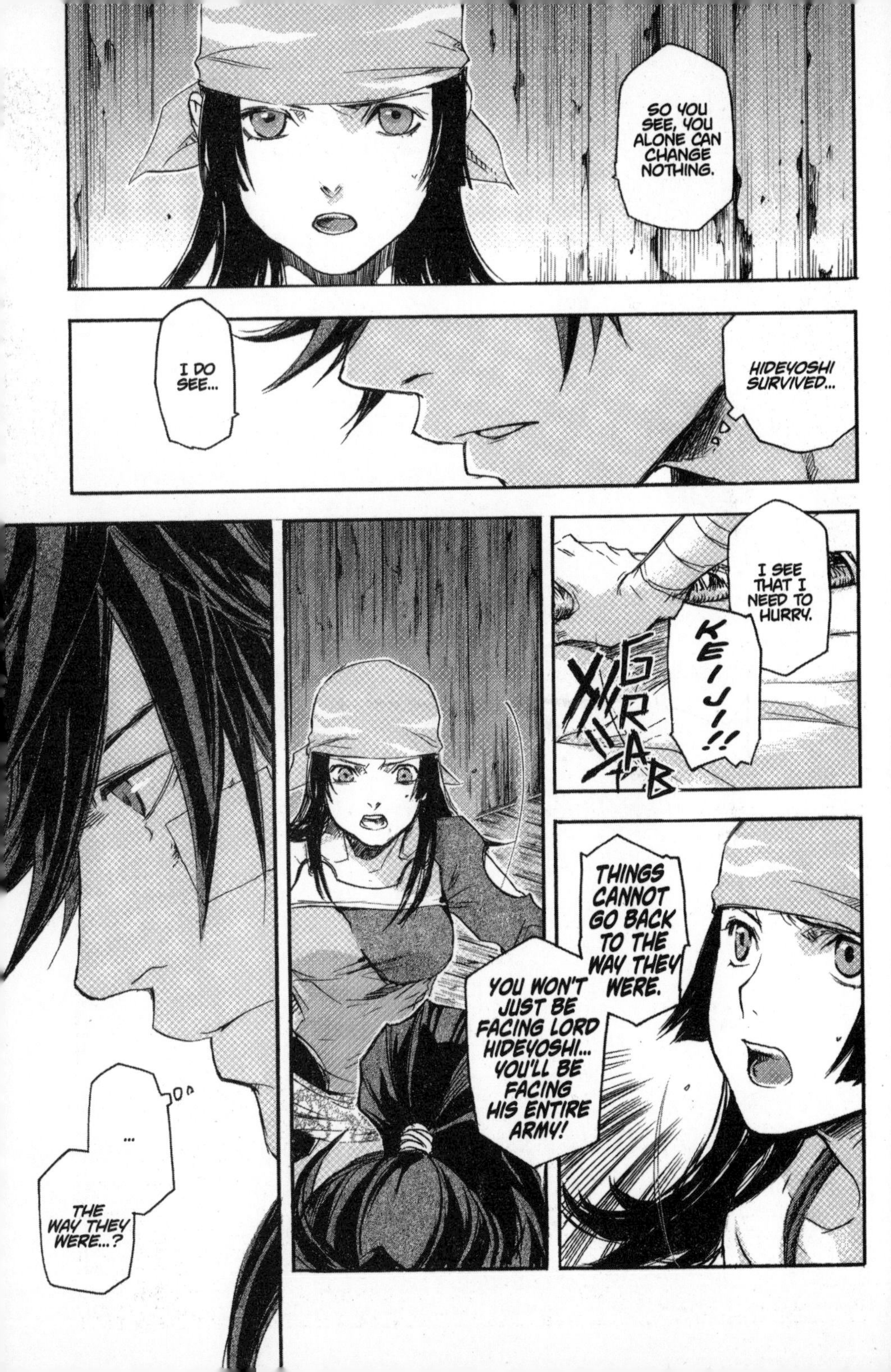
SO YOU SEE, YOU ALONE CAN CHANGE NOTHING.
HIDEYOSHI SURVIVED...
I DO SEE...
I SEE THAT I NEED TO HURRY.
KEIJI!!
GRAB
THINGS CANNOT GO BACK TO THE WAY THEY WERE.
YOU WON'T JUST BE FACING LORD HIDEYOSHI... YOU'LL BE FACING HIS ENTIRE ARMY!
...
THE WAY THEY WERE...?

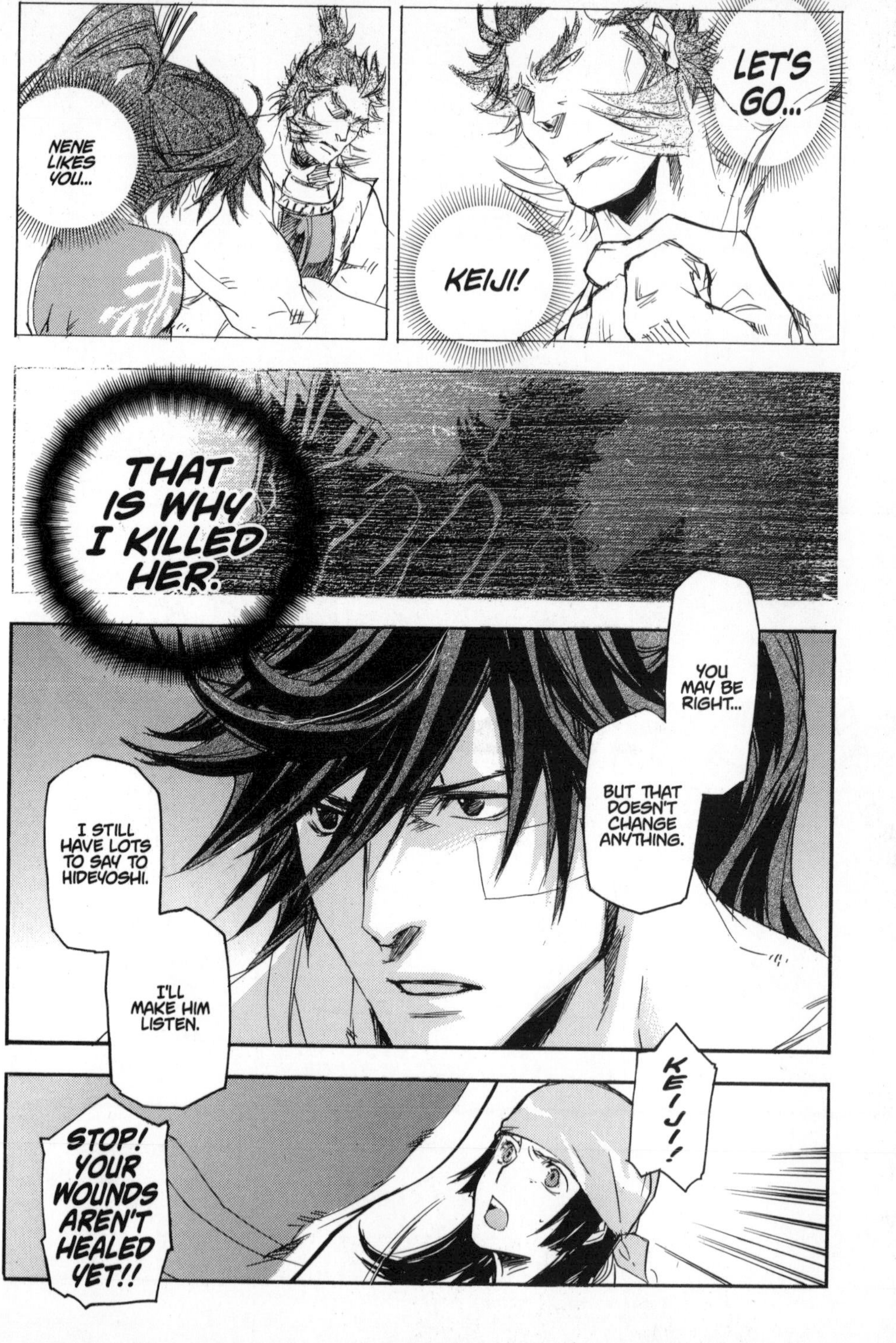
LET'S GO...
KEIJI!
NENE LIKES YOU...
THAT IS WHY I KILLED HER.
YOU MAY BE RIGHT...
BUT THAT DOESN'T CHANGE ANYTHING.
I STILL HAVE LOTS TO SAY TO HIDEYOSHI.
I'LL MAKE HIM LISTEN.
KEIJI!!
STOP! YOUR WOUNDS AREN'T HEALED YET!!

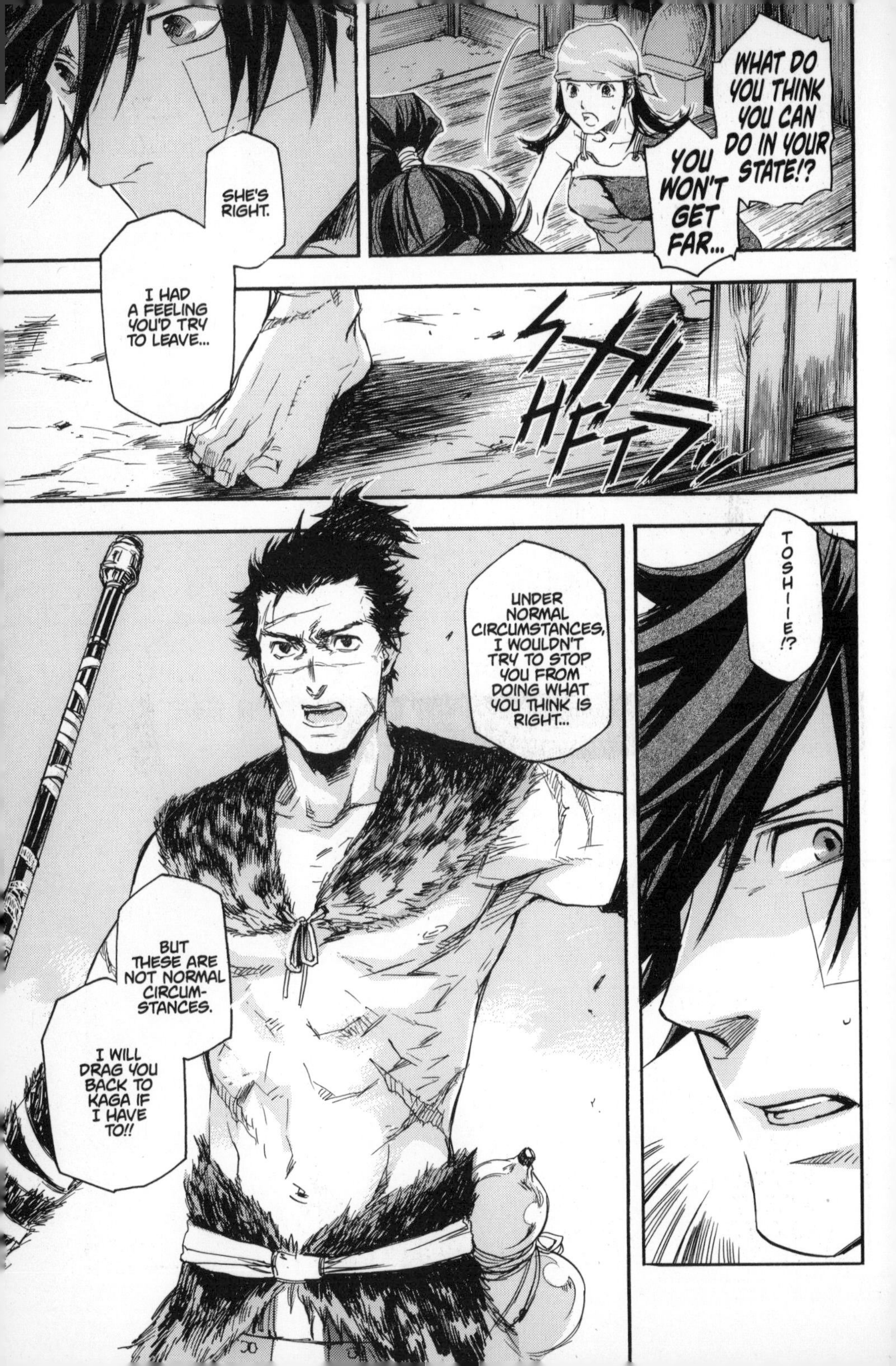
WHAT DO YOU THINK YOU CAN DO IN YOUR STATE!?
YOU WON'T GET FAR...
SHE'S RIGHT.
I HAD A FEELING YOU'D TRY TO LEAVE...
SHHFT
TOSHIIE!?
UNDER NORMAL CIRCUMSTANCES, I WOULDN'T TRY TO STOP YOU FROM DOING WHAT YOU THINK IS RIGHT...
BUT THESE ARE NOT NORMAL CIRCUM-STANCES.
I WILL DRAG YOU BACK TO KAGA IF I HAVE TO!!

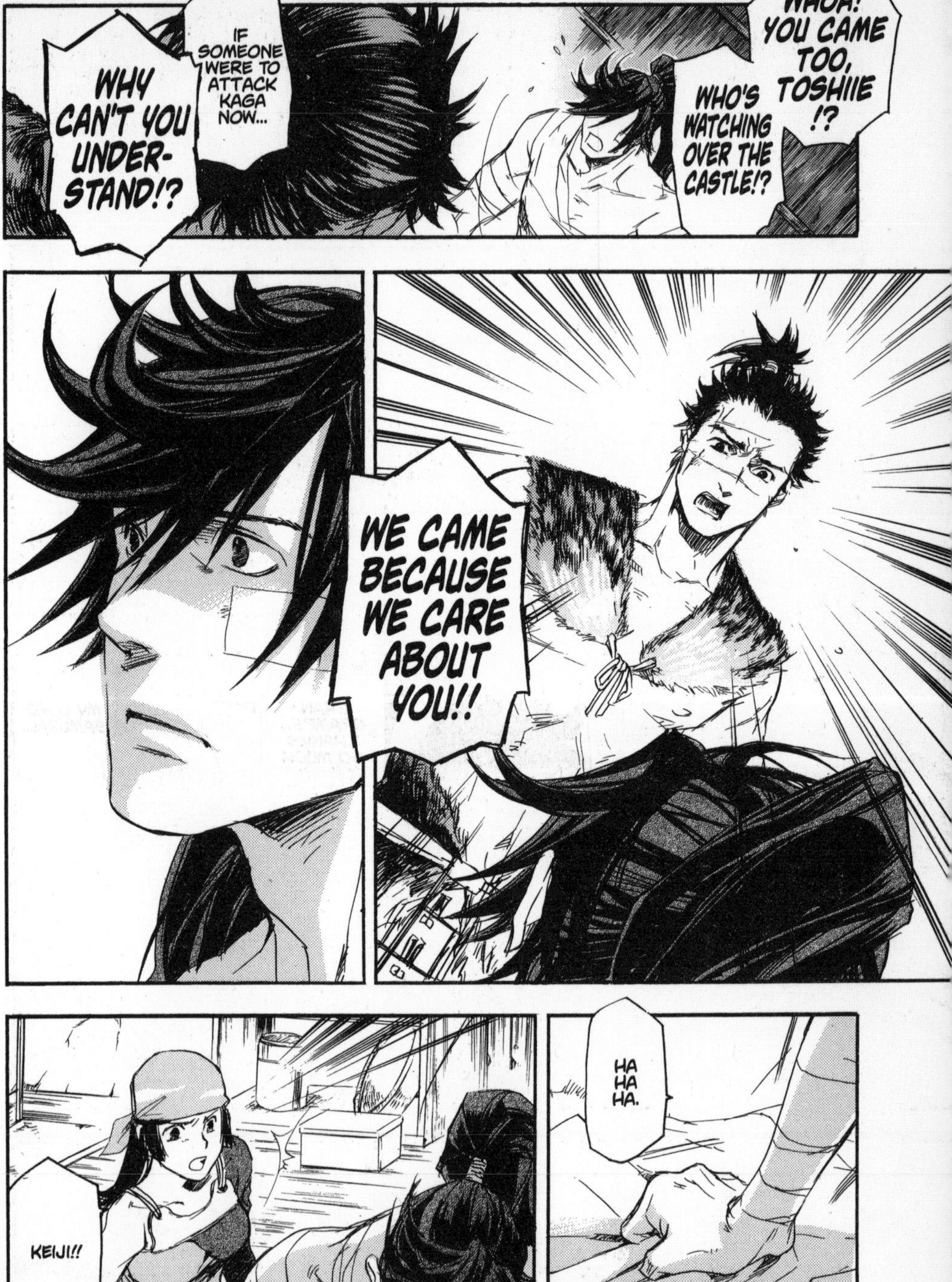
WHOA! YOU CAME TOO, TOSHIIE!?
WHO'S WATCHING OVER THE CASTLE!?
IF SOMEONE WERE TO ATTACK KAGA NOW...
WHY CAN'T YOU UNDER-STAND!?
WE CAME BECAUSE WE CARE ABOUT YOU!!
HA HA HA.
KEIJI!!

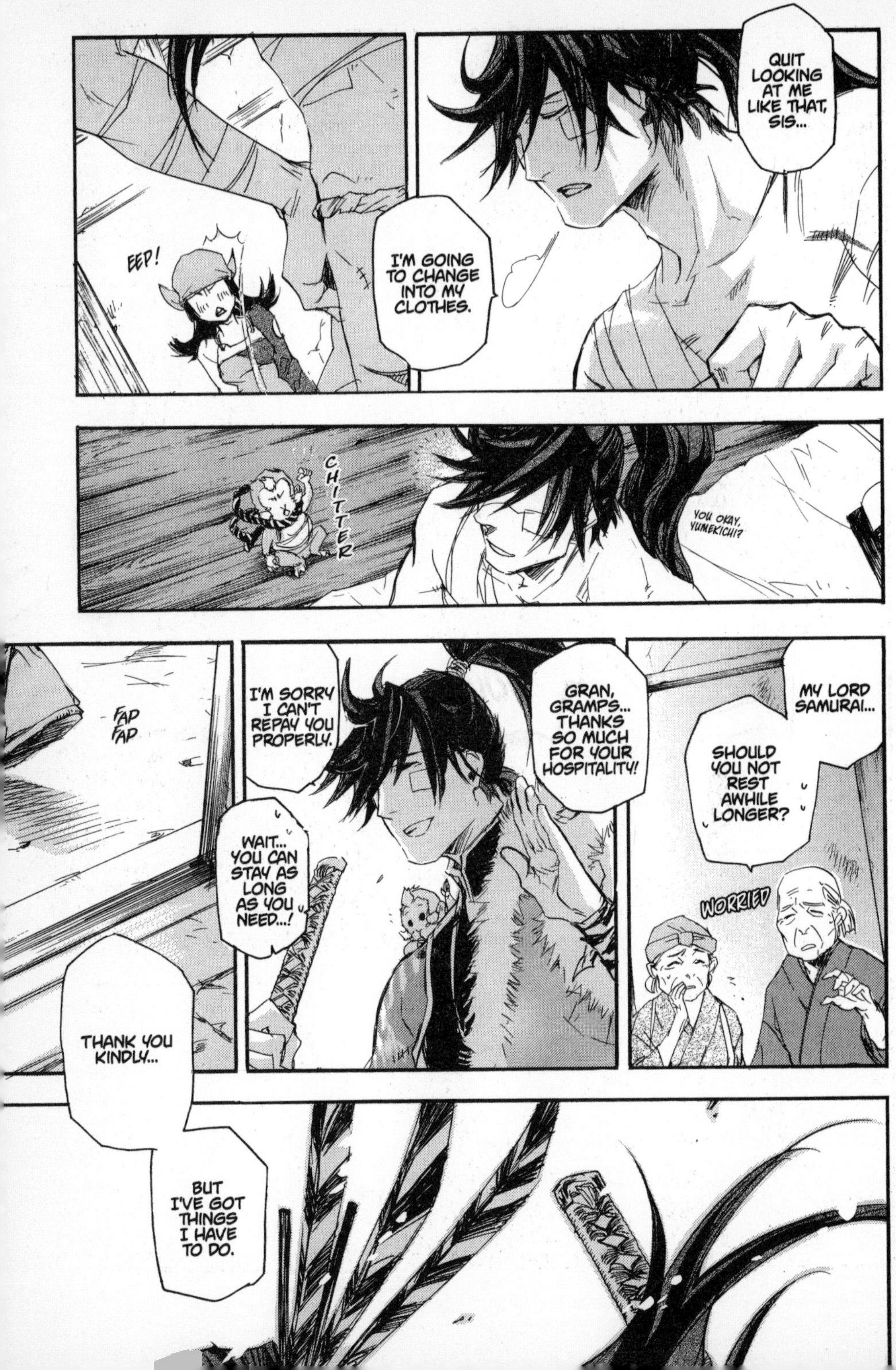
QUIT LOOKING AT ME LIKE THAT, SIS...
I'M GOING TO CHANGE INTO MY CLOTHES.
EEP!
YOU OKAY, YUMEKICHI?
CHITTER
MY LORD SAMURAI...
SHOULD YOU NOT REST AWHILE LONGER?
WORRIED
GRAN, GRAMPS... THANKS SO MUCH FOR YOUR HOSPITALITY!
I'M SORRY I CAN'T REPAY YOU PROPERLY.
WAIT... YOU CAN STAY AS LONG AS YOU NEED...!
FAP FAP
THANK YOU KINDLY...
BUT I'VE GOT THINGS I HAVE TO DO.

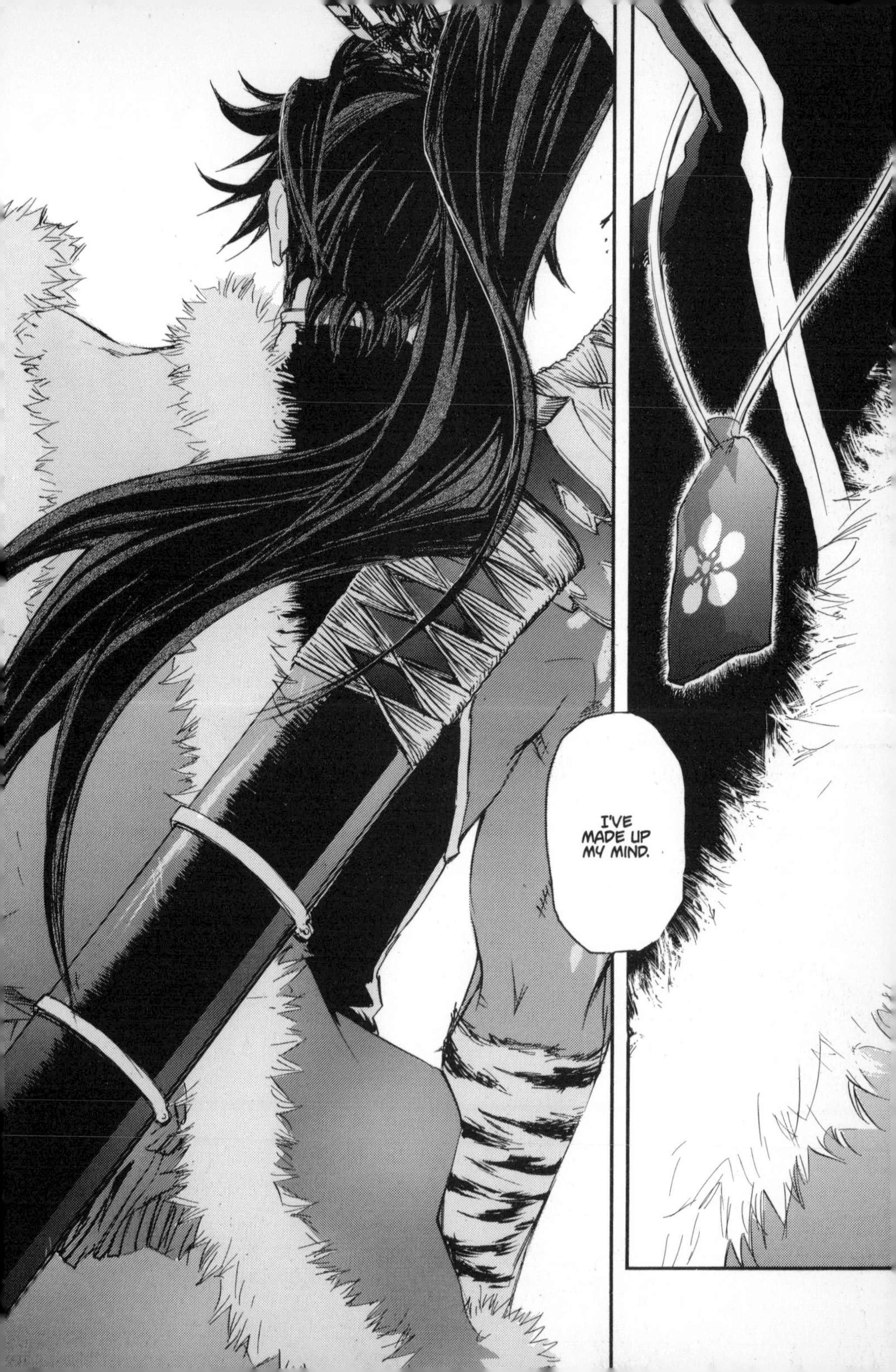
I'VE MADE UP MY MIND.

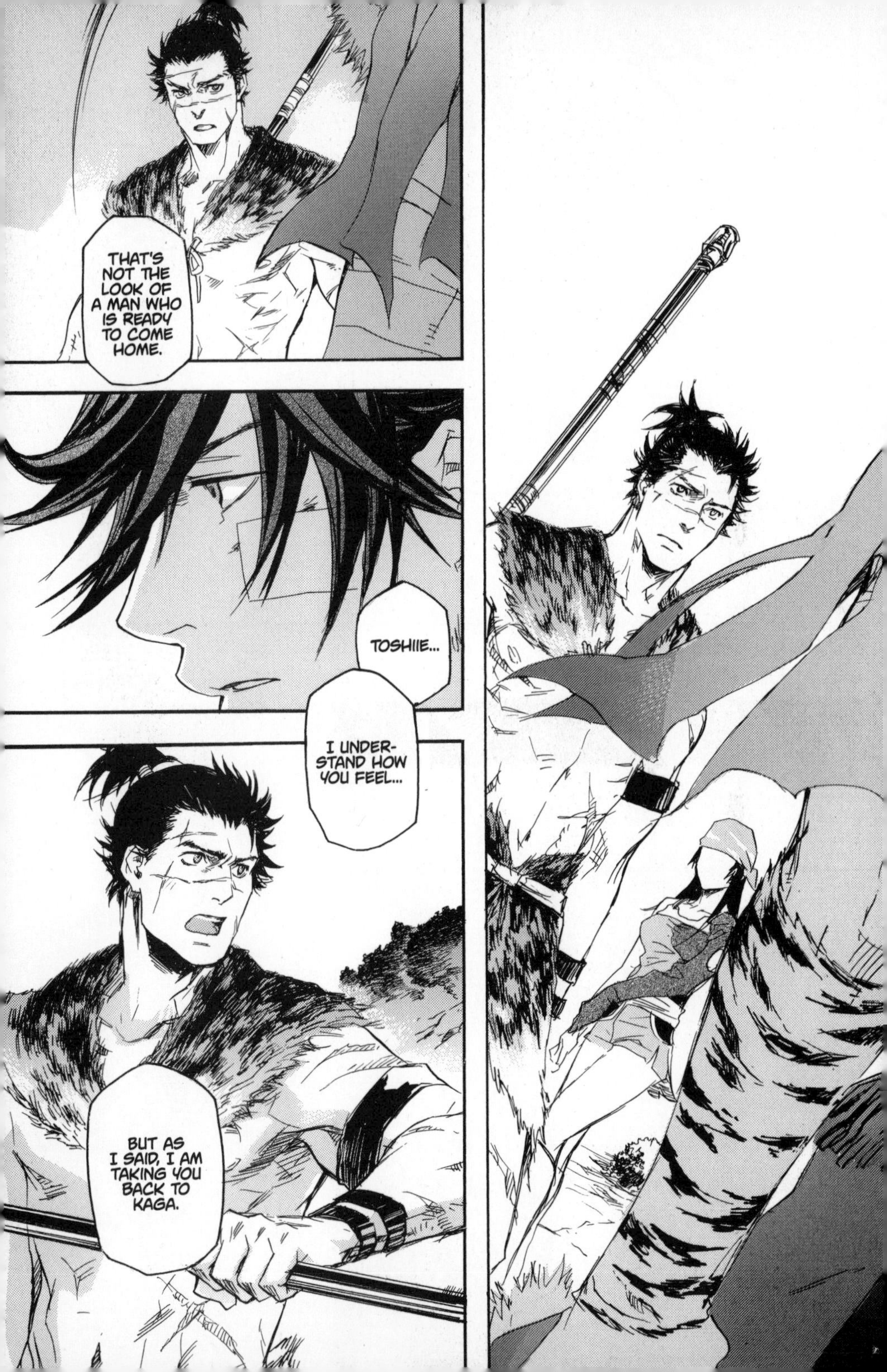
THAT'S NOT THE LOOK OF A MAN WHO IS READY TO COME HOME.
TOSHIIE...
I UNDER-STAND HOW YOU FEEL...
BUT AS I SAID, I AM TAKING YOU BACK TO KAGA.

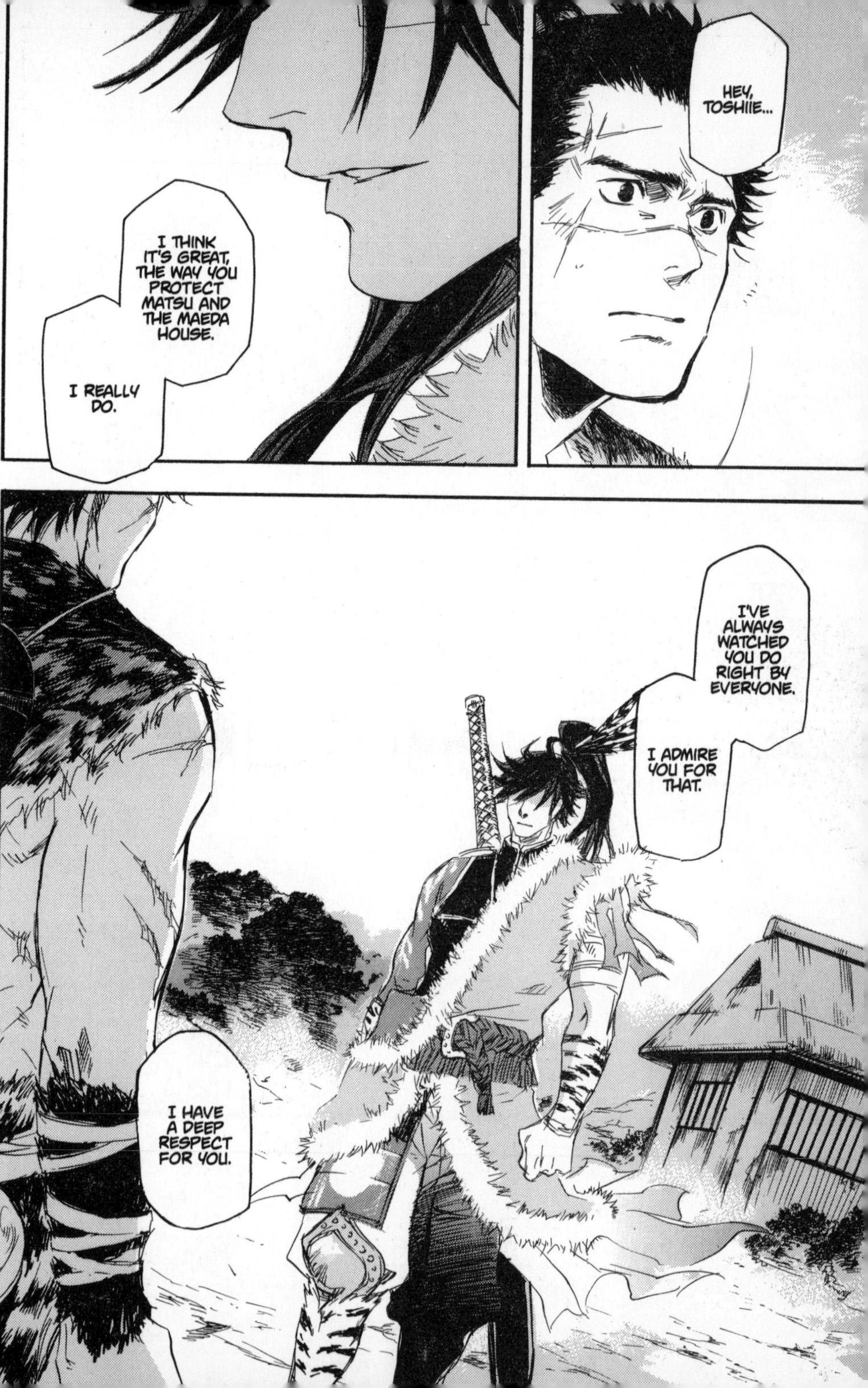
HEY, TOSHIIE...
I THINK IT'S GREAT, THE WAY YOU PROTECT MATSU AND THE MAEDA HOUSE.
I REALLY DO.
I'VE ALWAYS WATCHED YOU DO RIGHT BY EVERYONE.
I ADMIRE YOU FOR THAT.
I HAVE A DEEP RESPECT FOR YOU.

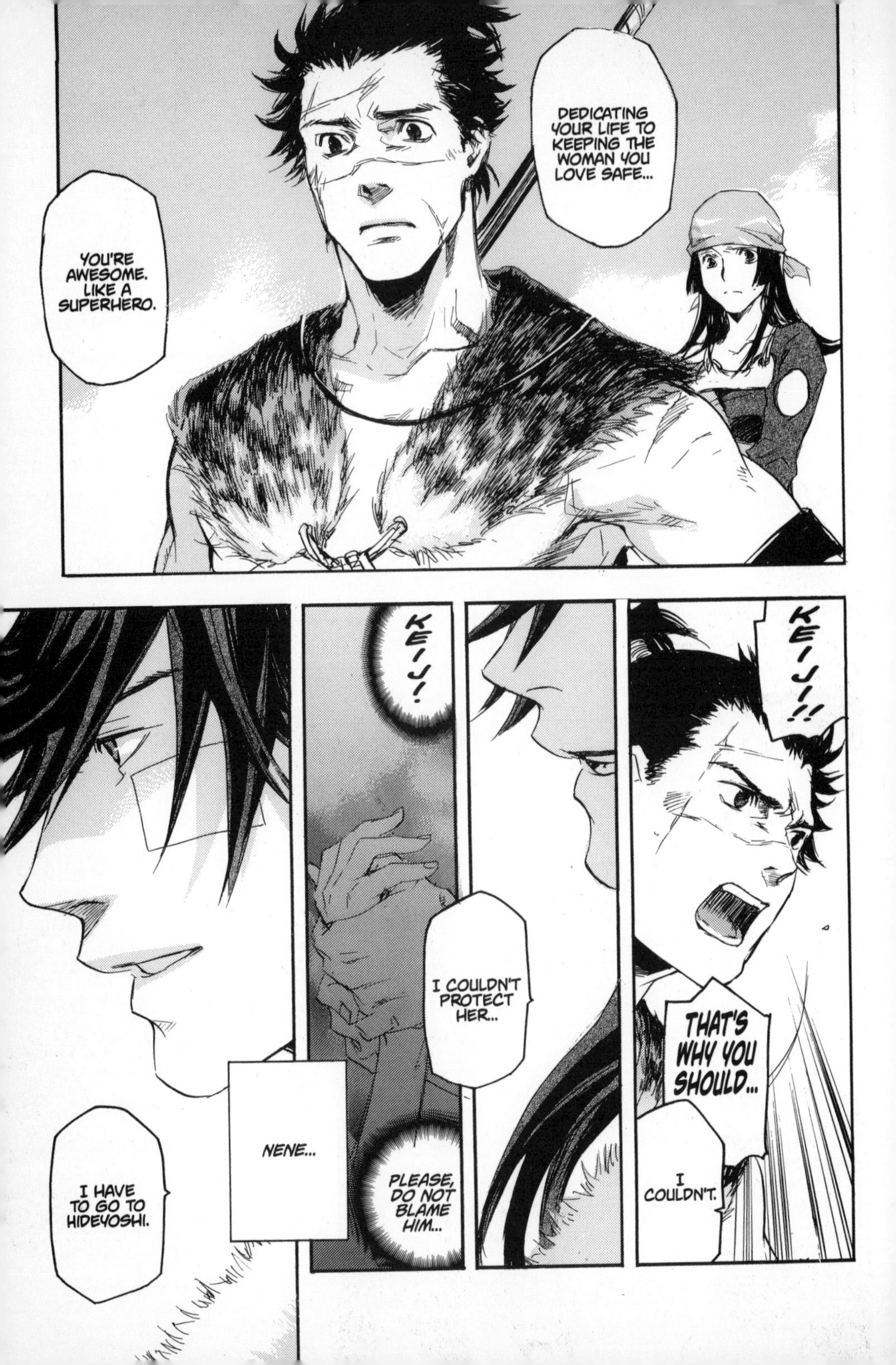
DEDICATING YOUR LIFE TO KEEPING THE WOMAN YOU LOVE SAFE...
YOU'RE AWESOME. LIKE A SUPERHERO.
KEIJI!!
THAT'S WHY YOU SHOULD...
I COULDN'T.
I COULDN'T PROTECT HER...
KEIJI!
PLEASE, DO NOT BLAME HIM...
NENE...
I HAVE TO GO TO HIDEYOSHI.

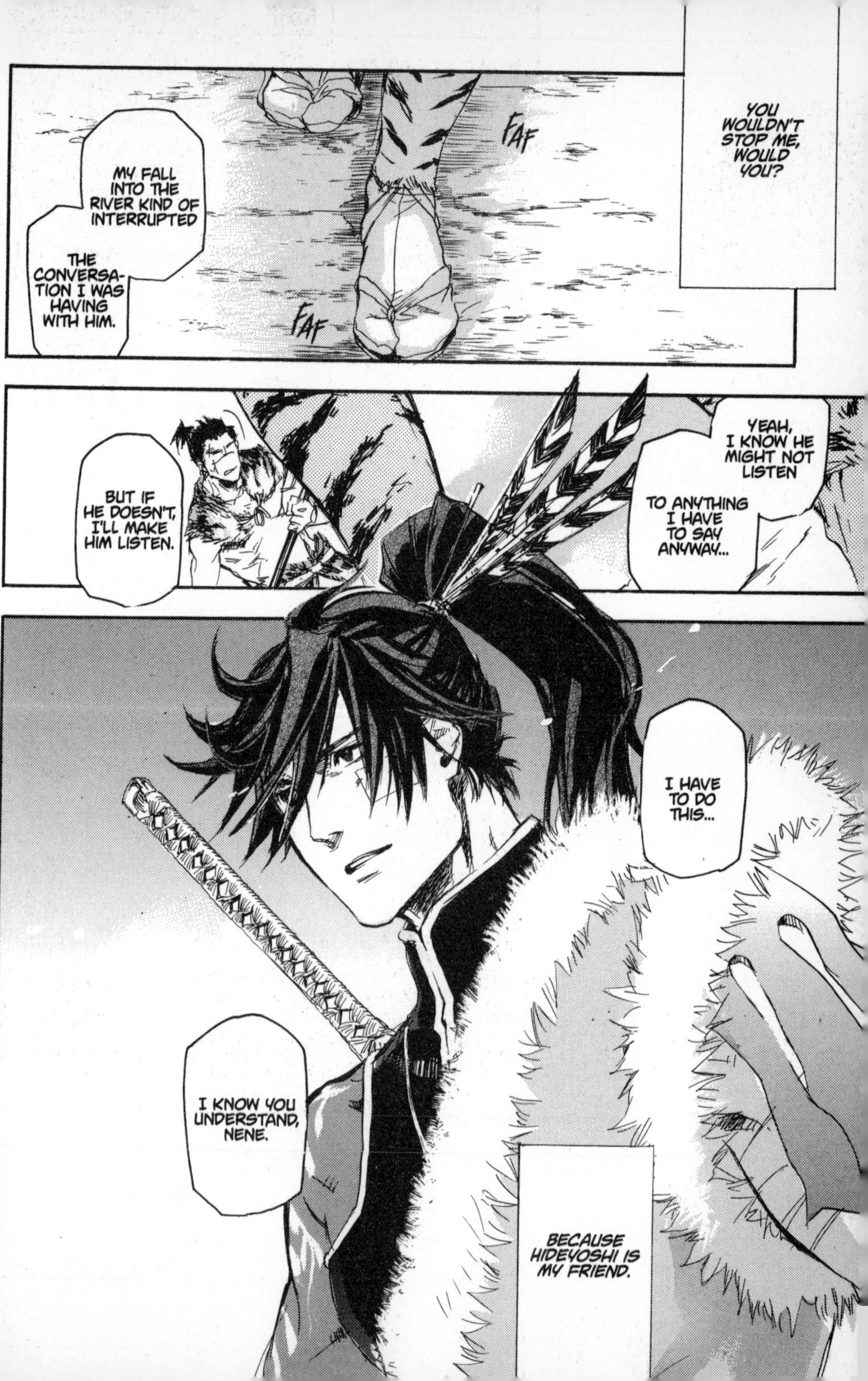
YOU WOULDN'T STOP ME, WOULD YOU?
MY FALL INTO THE RIVER KIND OF INTERRUPTED
THE CONVERSATION I WAS HAVING WITH HIM.
FAF
FAF
YEAH, I KNOW HE MIGHT NOT LISTEN
TO ANYTHING I HAVE TO SAY ANYWAY...
BUT IF HE DOESN'T, I'LL MAKE HIM LISTEN.
I HAVE TO DO THIS...
I KNOW YOU UNDERSTAND, NENE.
BECAUSE HIDEYOSHI IS MY FRIEND.

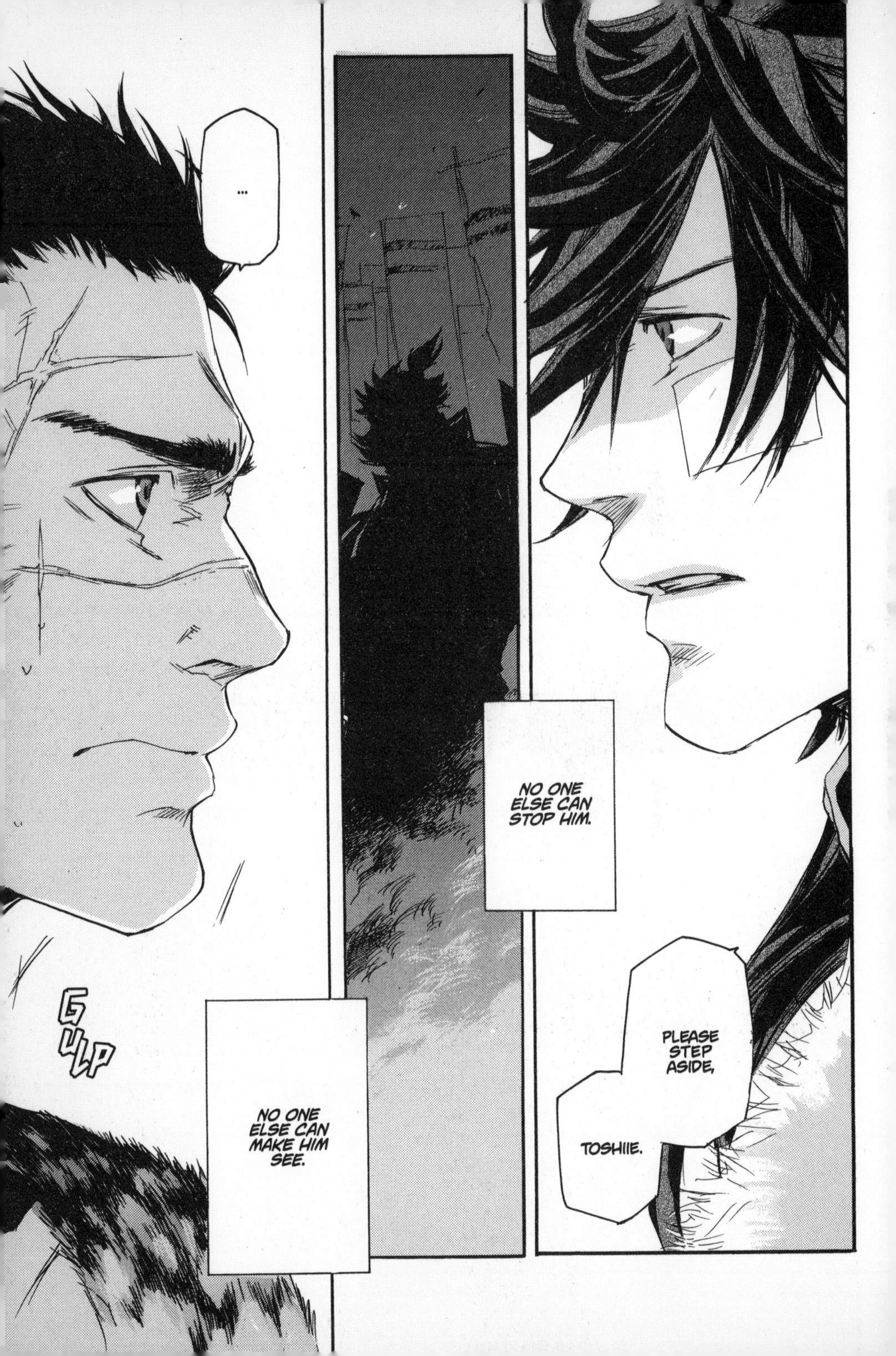
...
NO ONE ELSE CAN STOP HIM.
PLEASE STEP ASIDE,
TOSHIIE.
GULP
NO ONE ELSE CAN MAKE HIM SEE.

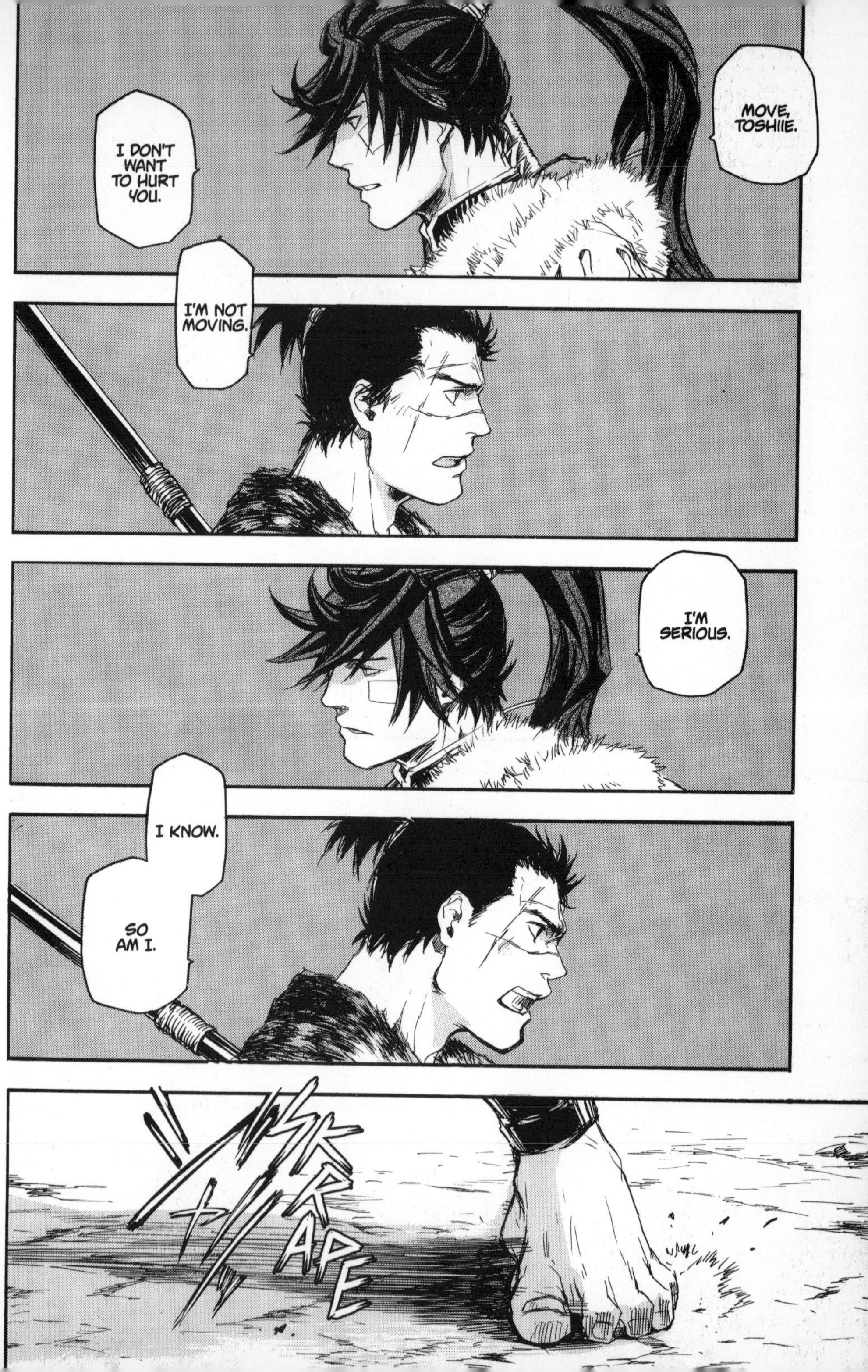
MOVE, TOSHIIE.
I DON'T WANT TO HURT YOU.
I'M NOT MOVING.
I'M SERIOUS.
I KNOW.
SO AM I.
SKRAPE

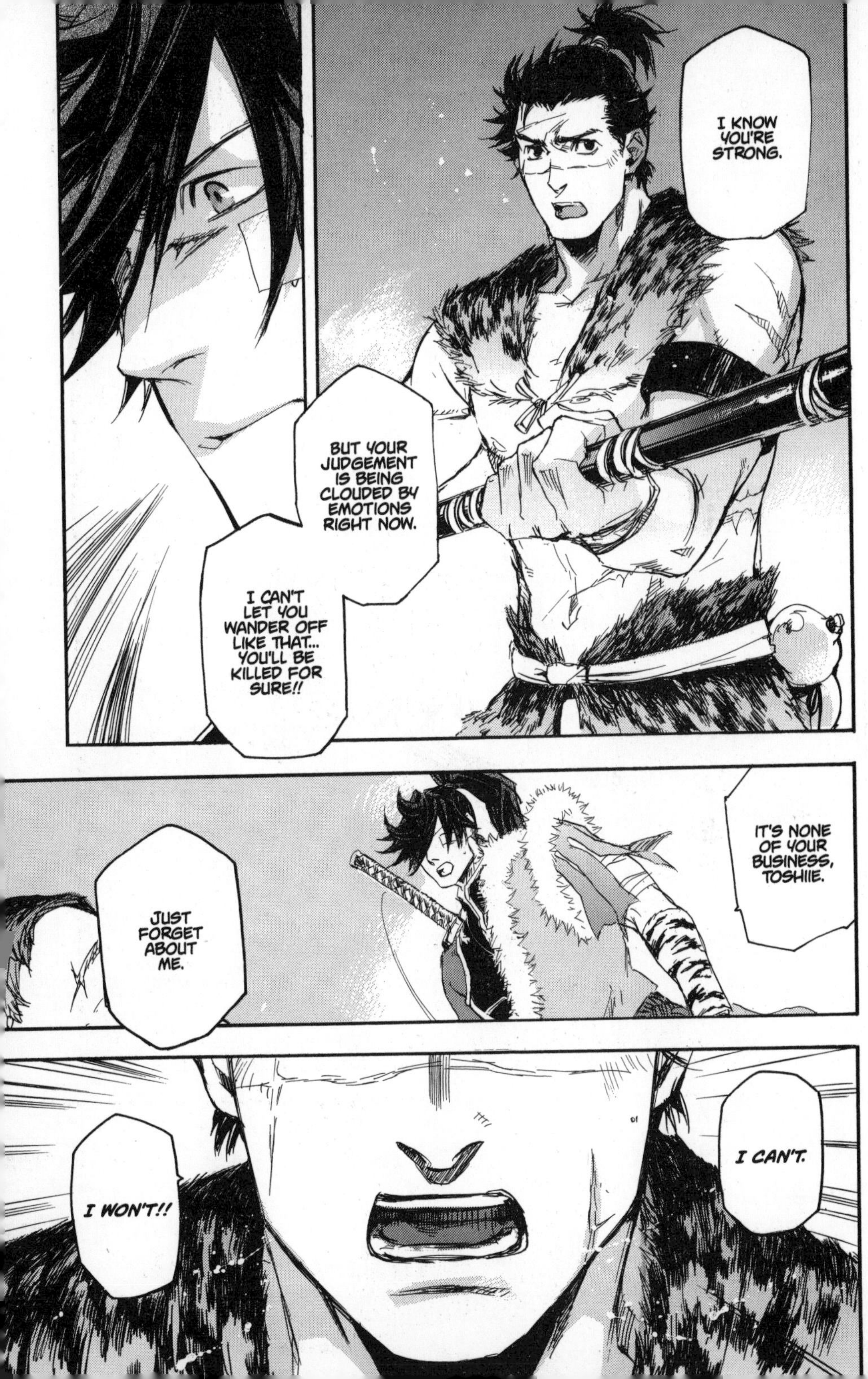
I KNOW YOU'RE STRONG.
BUT YOUR JUDGEMENT IS BEING CLOUDED BY EMOTIONS RIGHT NOW.
I CAN'T LET YOU WANDER OFF LIKE THAT... YOU'LL BE KILLED FOR SURE!!
IT'S NONE OF YOUR BUSINESS, TOSHIIE.
JUST FORGET ABOUT ME.
I CAN'T.
I WON'T!!

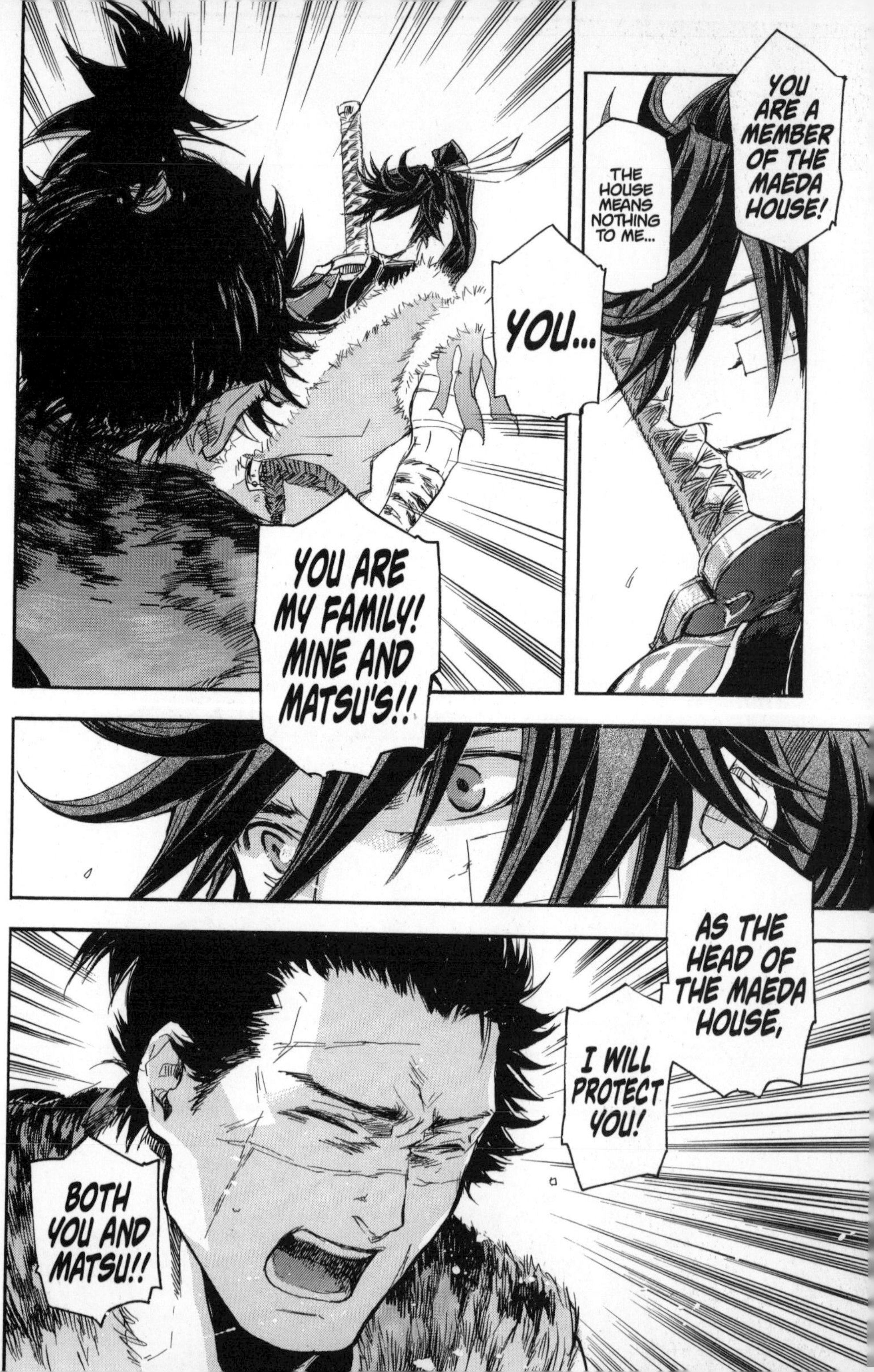
YOU ARE A MEMBER OF THE MAEDA HOUSE!
THE HOUSE MEANS NOTHING TO ME...
YOU...
YOU ARE MY FAMILY! MINE AND MATSU'S!!
AS THE HEAD OF THE MAEDA HOUSE,
I WILL PROTECT YOU!
BOTH YOU AND MATSU!!

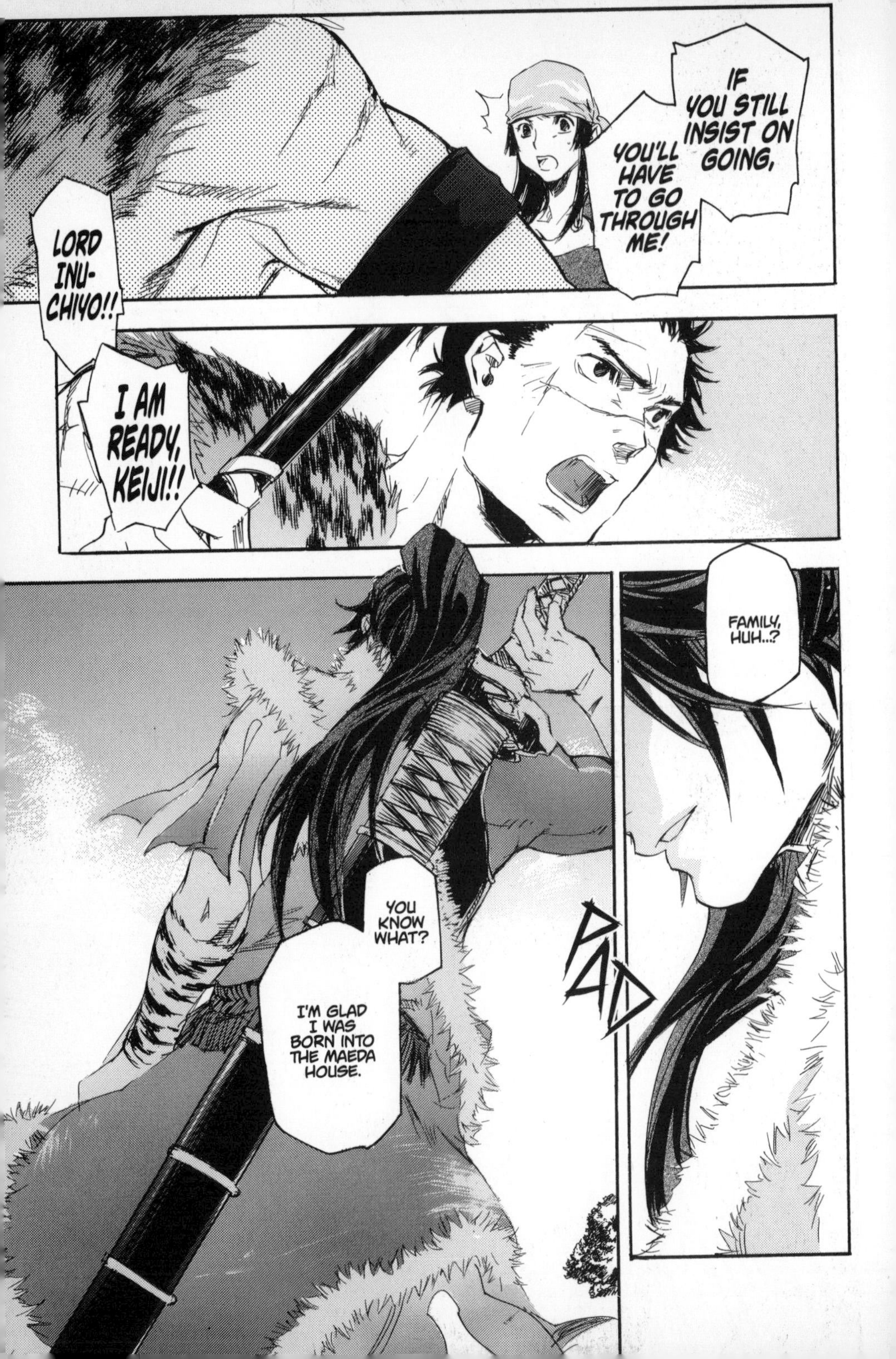
IF YOU STILL INSIST ON GOING,
YOU'LL HAVE TO GO THROUGH ME!
LORD INU-CHIYO!!
I AM READY, KEIJI!!
FAMILY, HUH...?
PAD
YOU KNOW WHAT?
I'M GLAD I WAS BORN INTO THE MAEDA HOUSE.

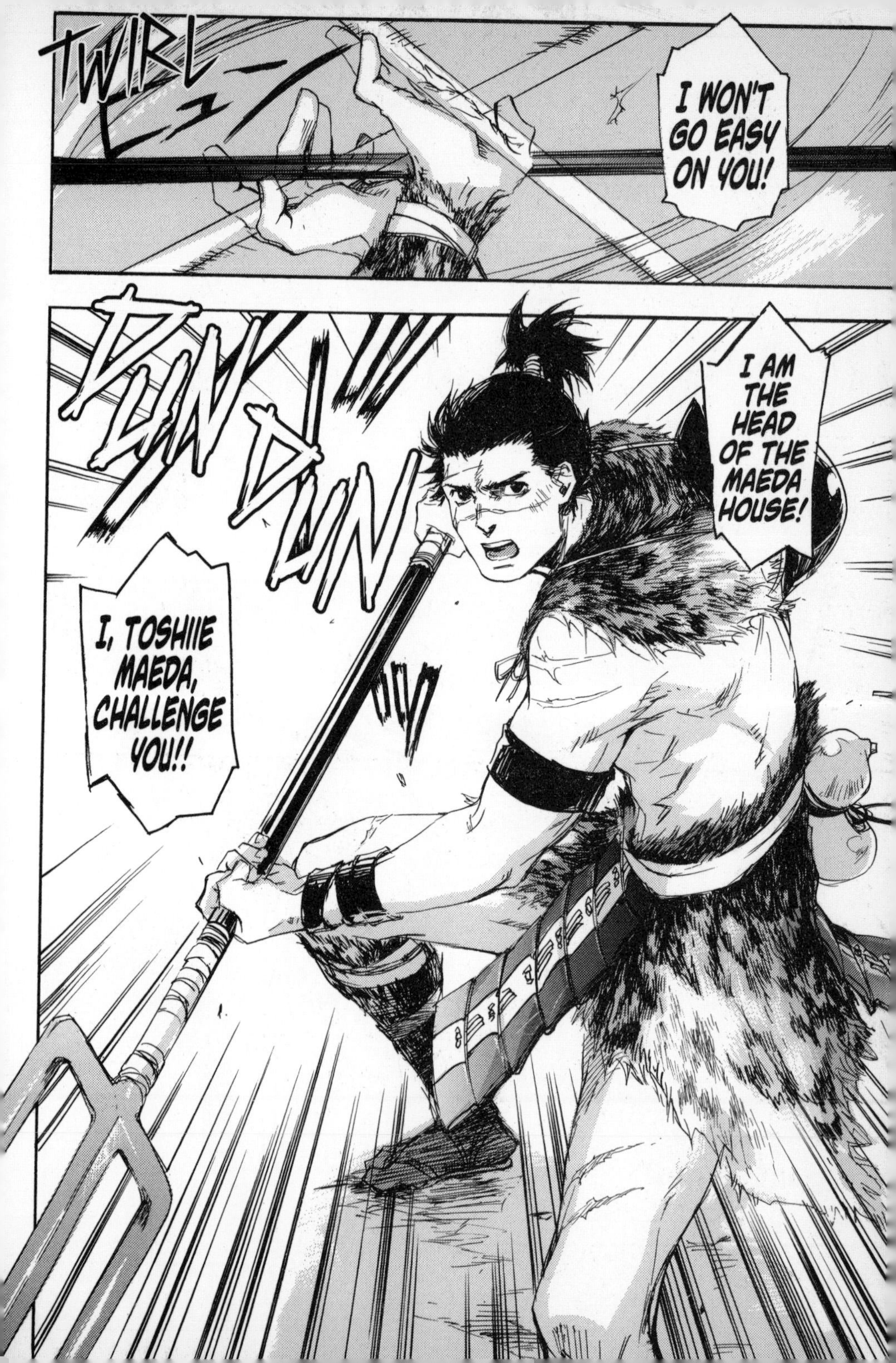
I WON'T GO EASY ON YOU!
TWIRL
ヒュー
I AM THE HEAD OF THE MAEDA HOUSE!
DUN DUN DUN
I, TOSHIIE MAEDA, CHALLENGE YOU!!

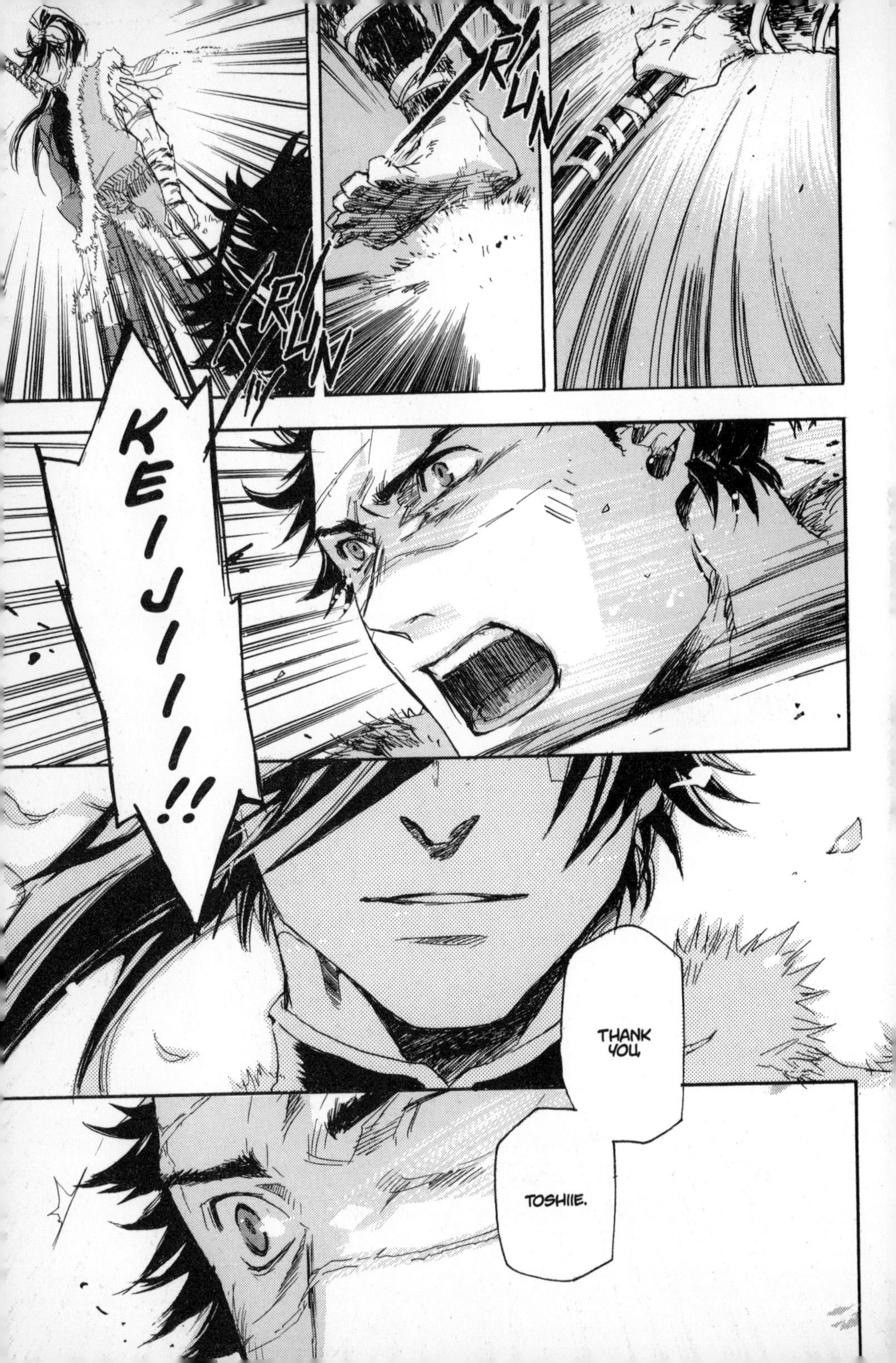
FRUN
FRUN
KEIJIII!!
THANK YOU,
TOSHIIE.

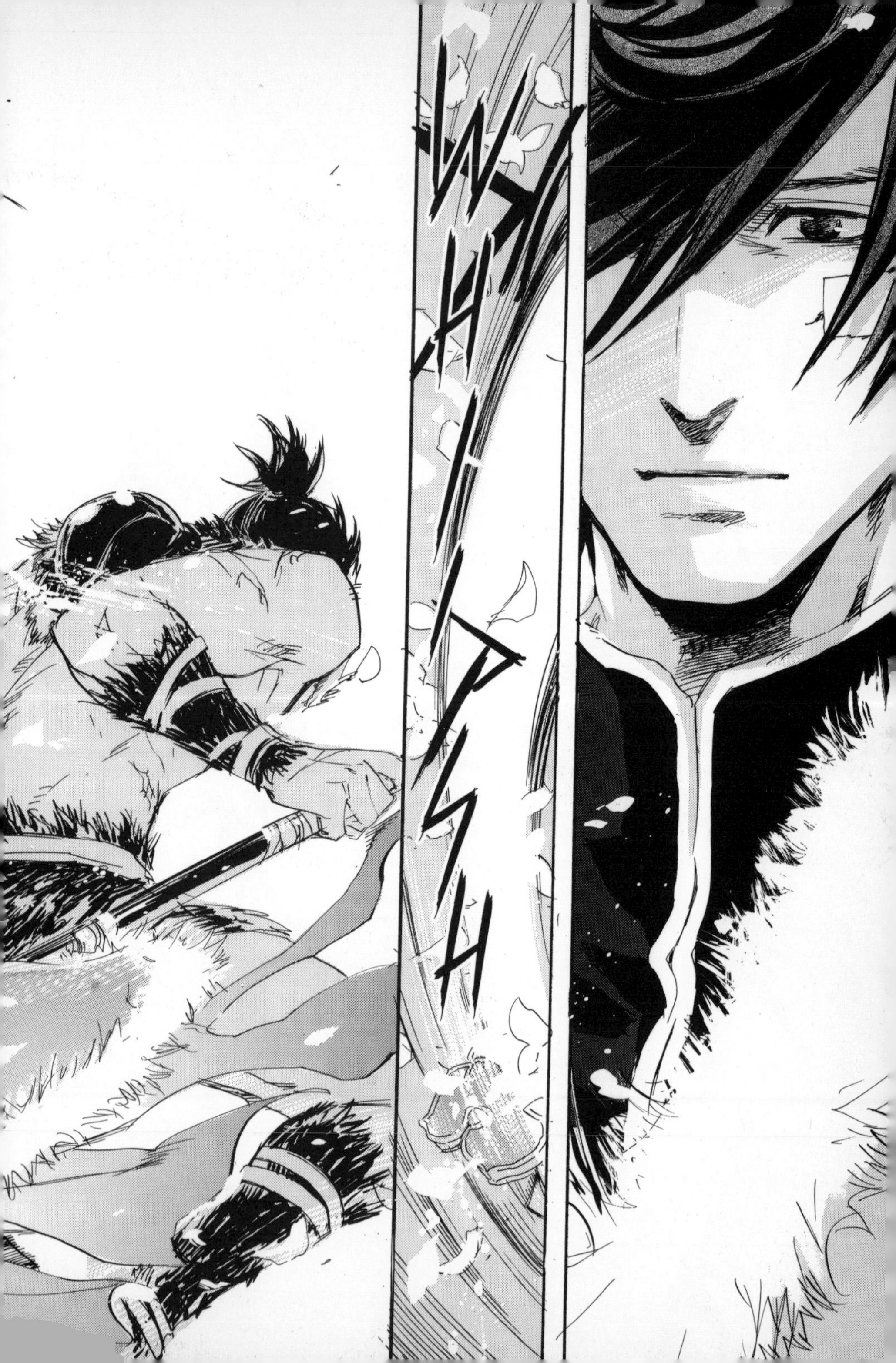
WHIIASH

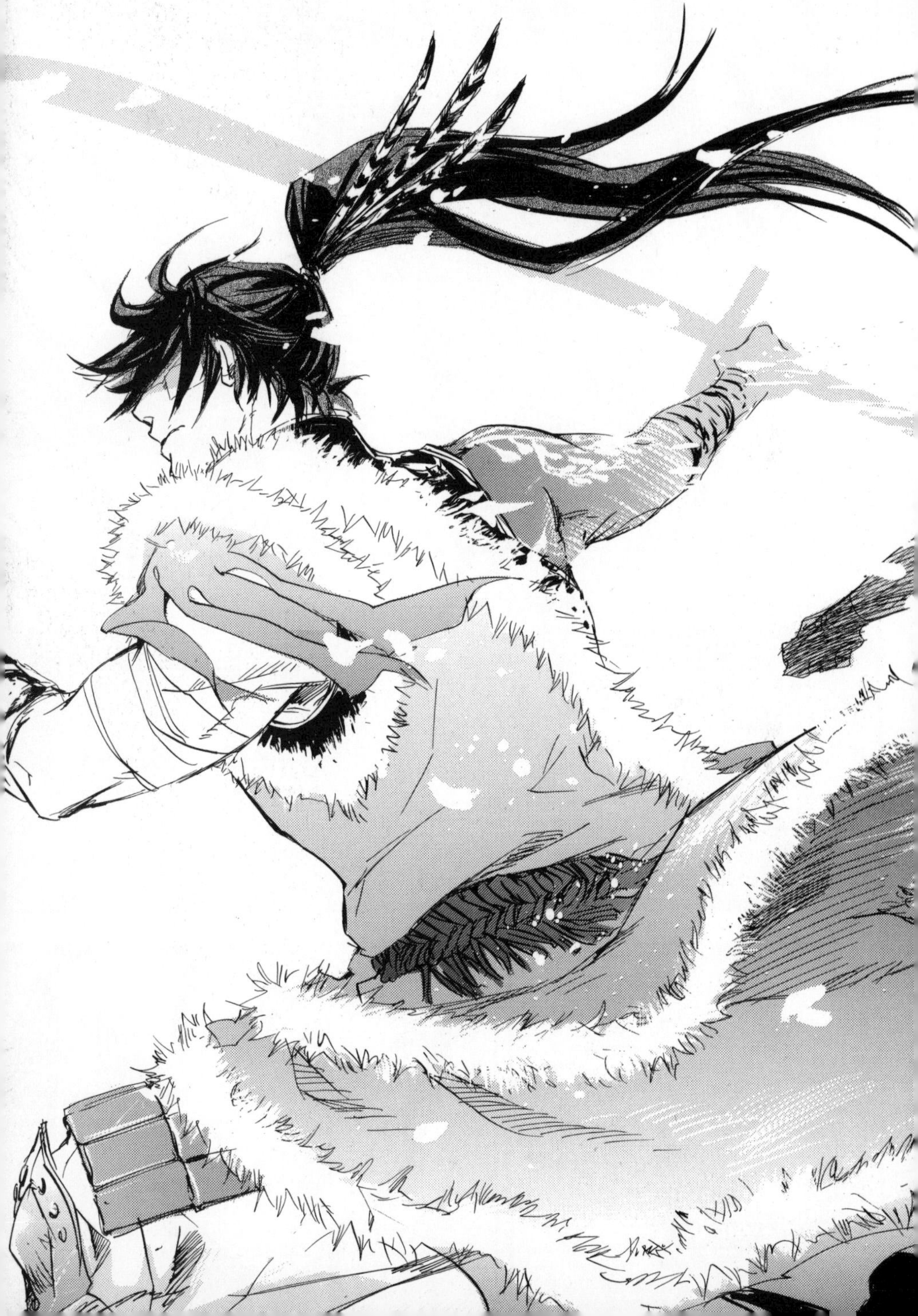

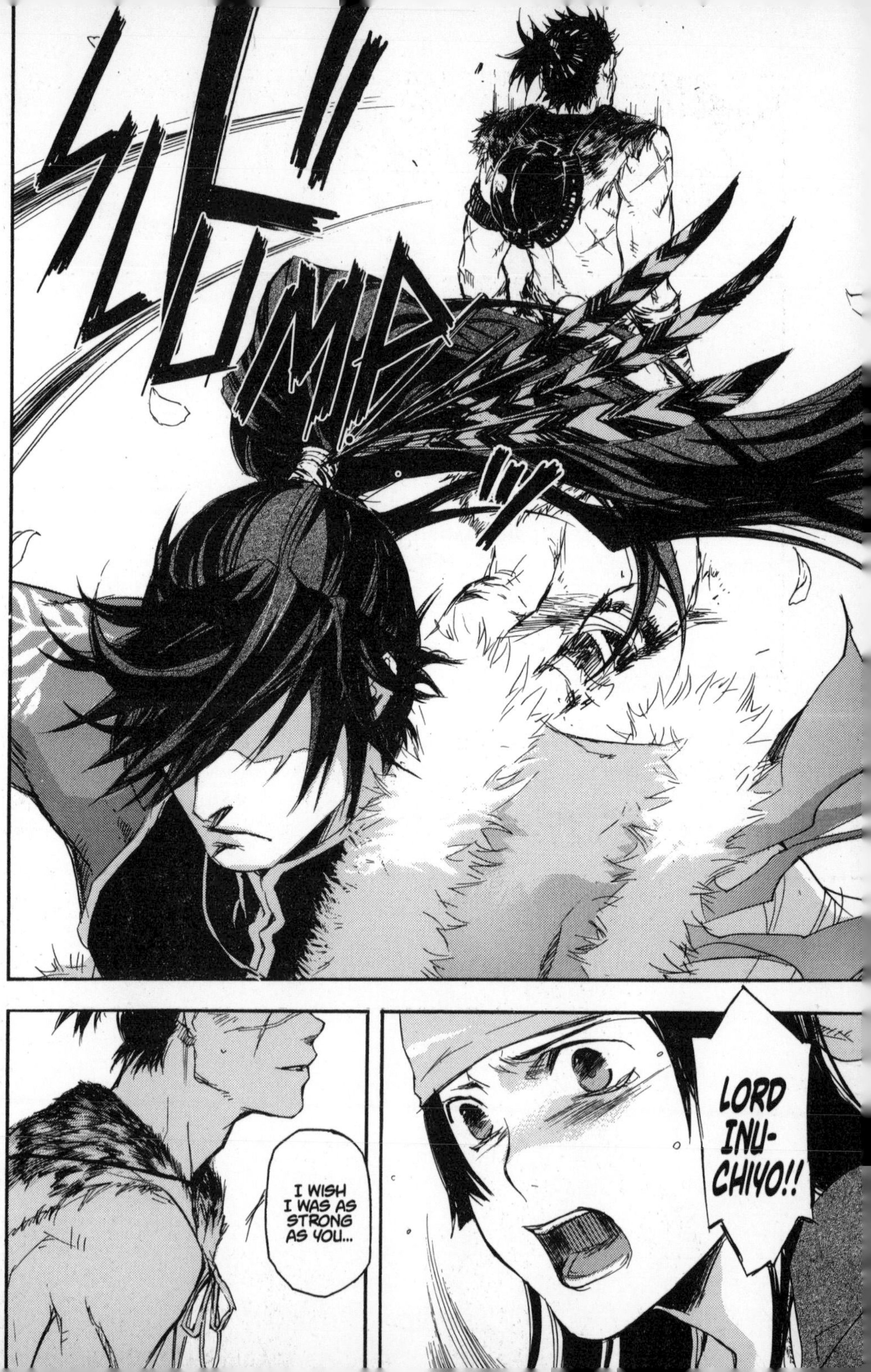
SLUMP
LORD INU-CHIYO!!
I WISH I WAS AS STRONG AS YOU...

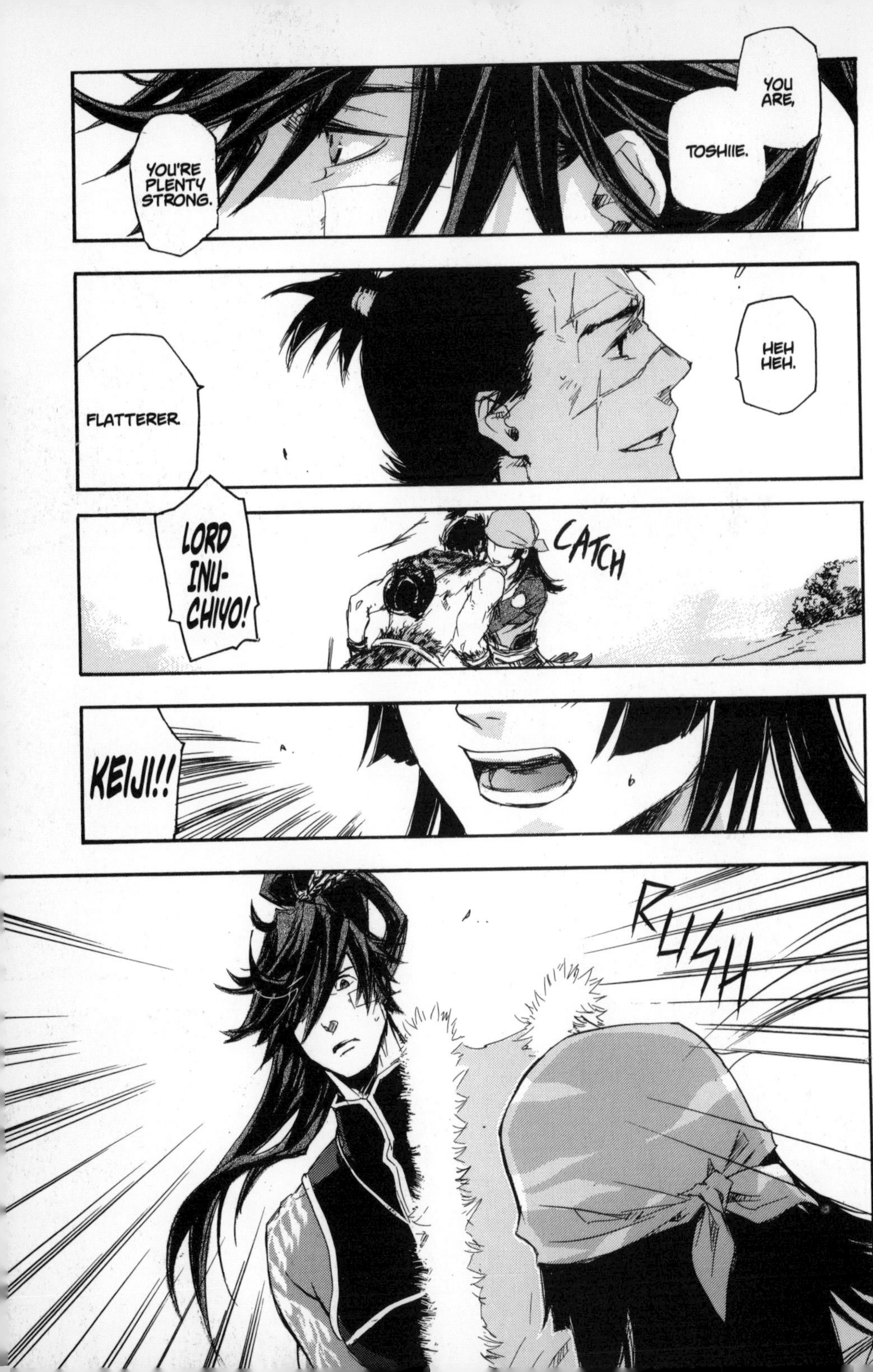
YOU ARE,
TOSHIIE.
YOU'RE PLENTY STRONG.
HEH HEH.
FLATTERER.
CATCH
LORD INU-CHIYO!
KEIJI!!
RUSH

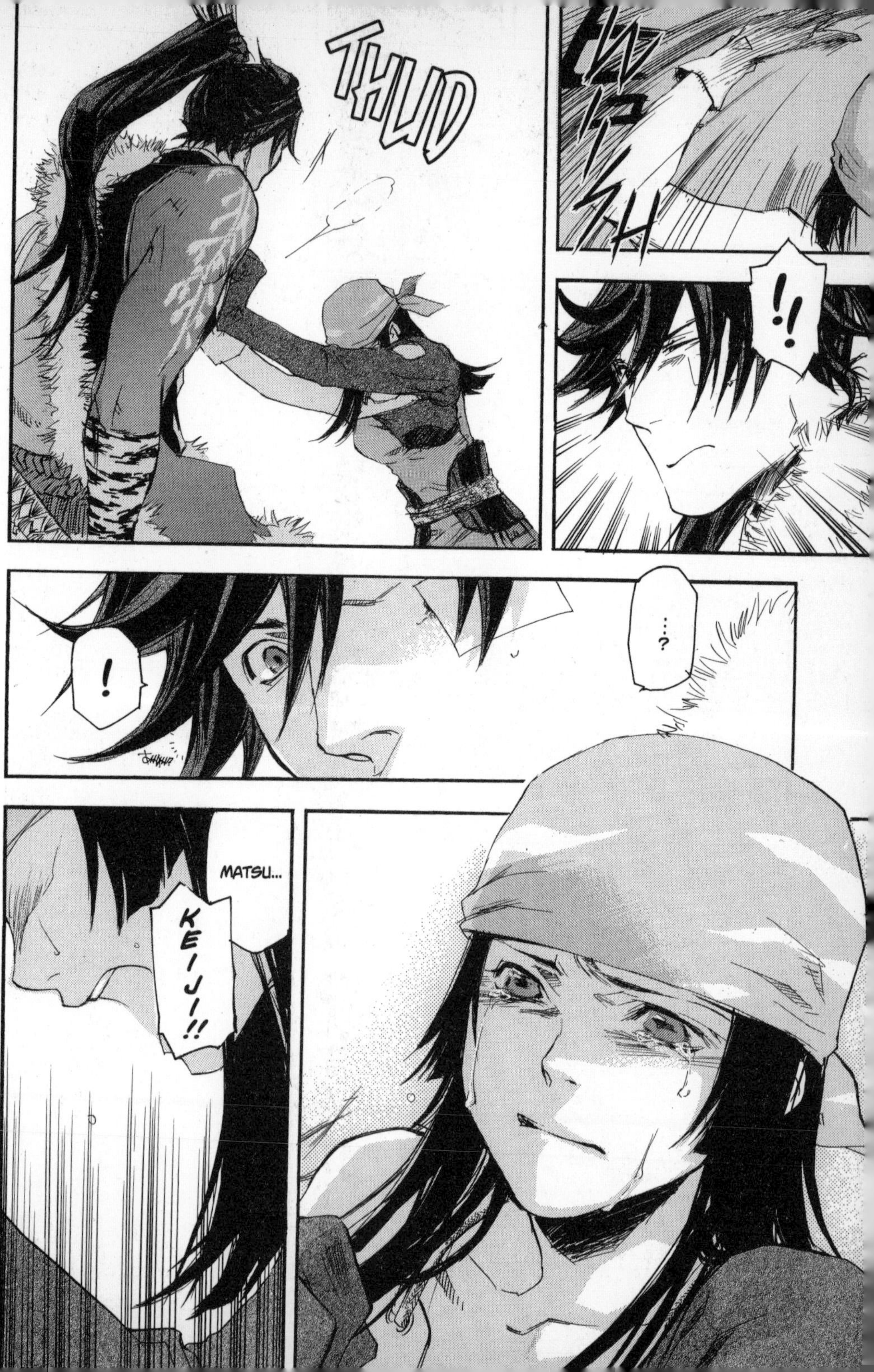
!!
THUD
...?
!
MATSU...
KEIJI!!

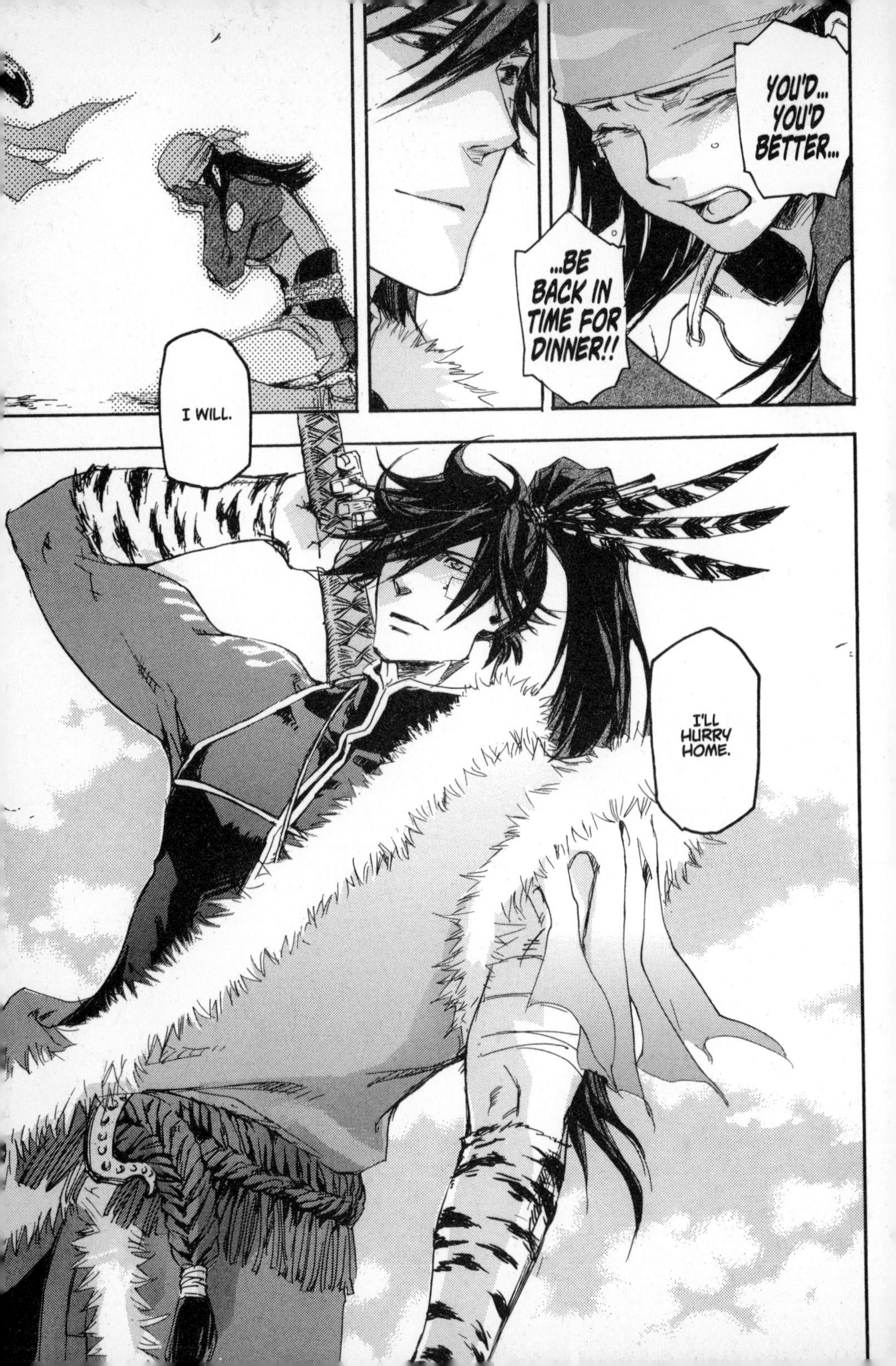
YOU'D... YOU'D BETTER...
...BE BACK IN TIME FOR DINNER!!
I WILL.
I'LL HURRY HOME.

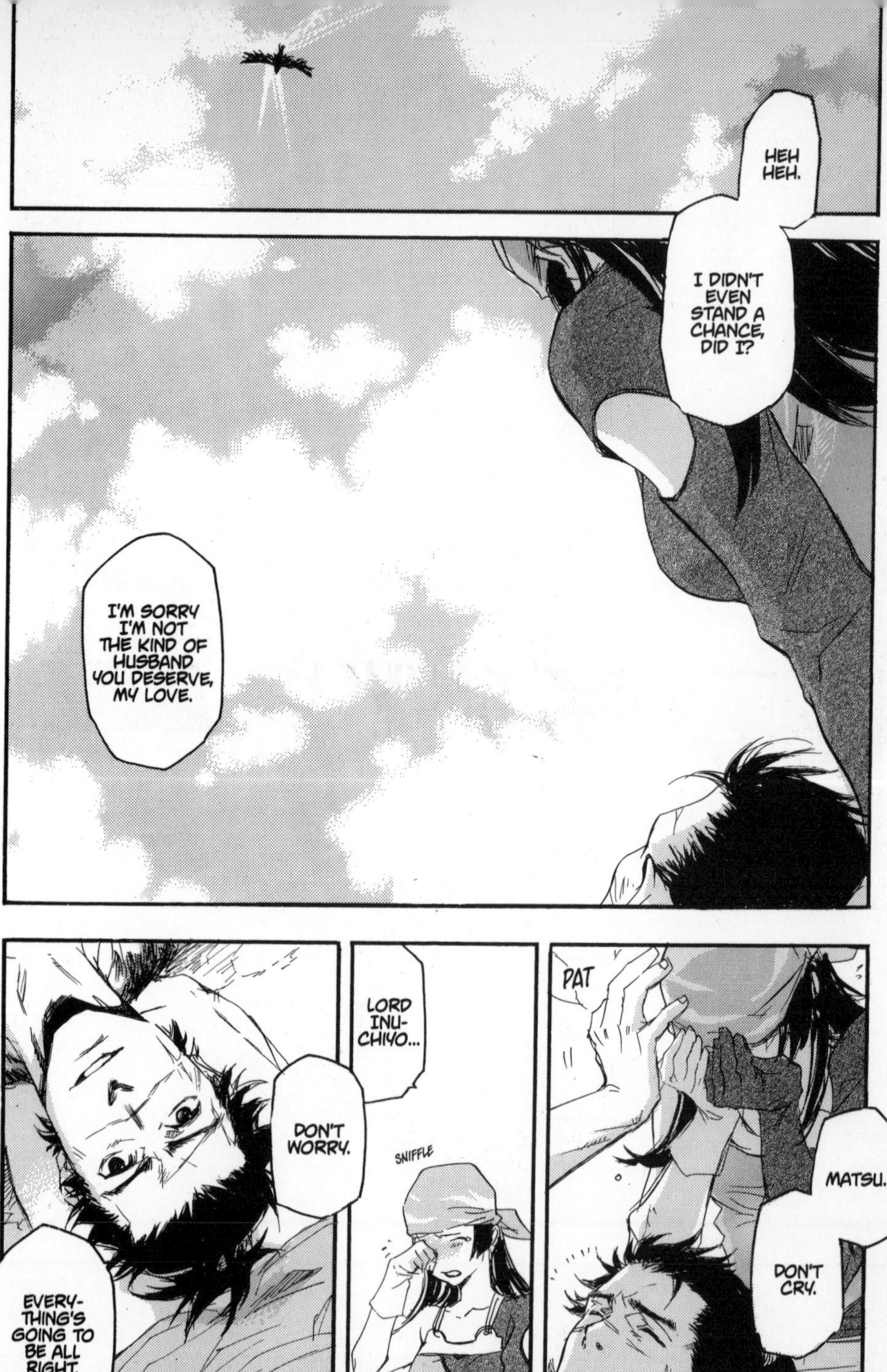
HEH HEH.
I DIDN'T EVEN STAND A CHANCE, DID I?
I'M SORRY I'M NOT THE KIND OF HUSBAND YOU DESERVE, MY LOVE.
PAT
MATSU...
DON'T CRY.
LORD INU-CHIYO...
SNIFFLE
DON'T WORRY.
EVERY-THING'S GOING TO BE ALL RIGHT.

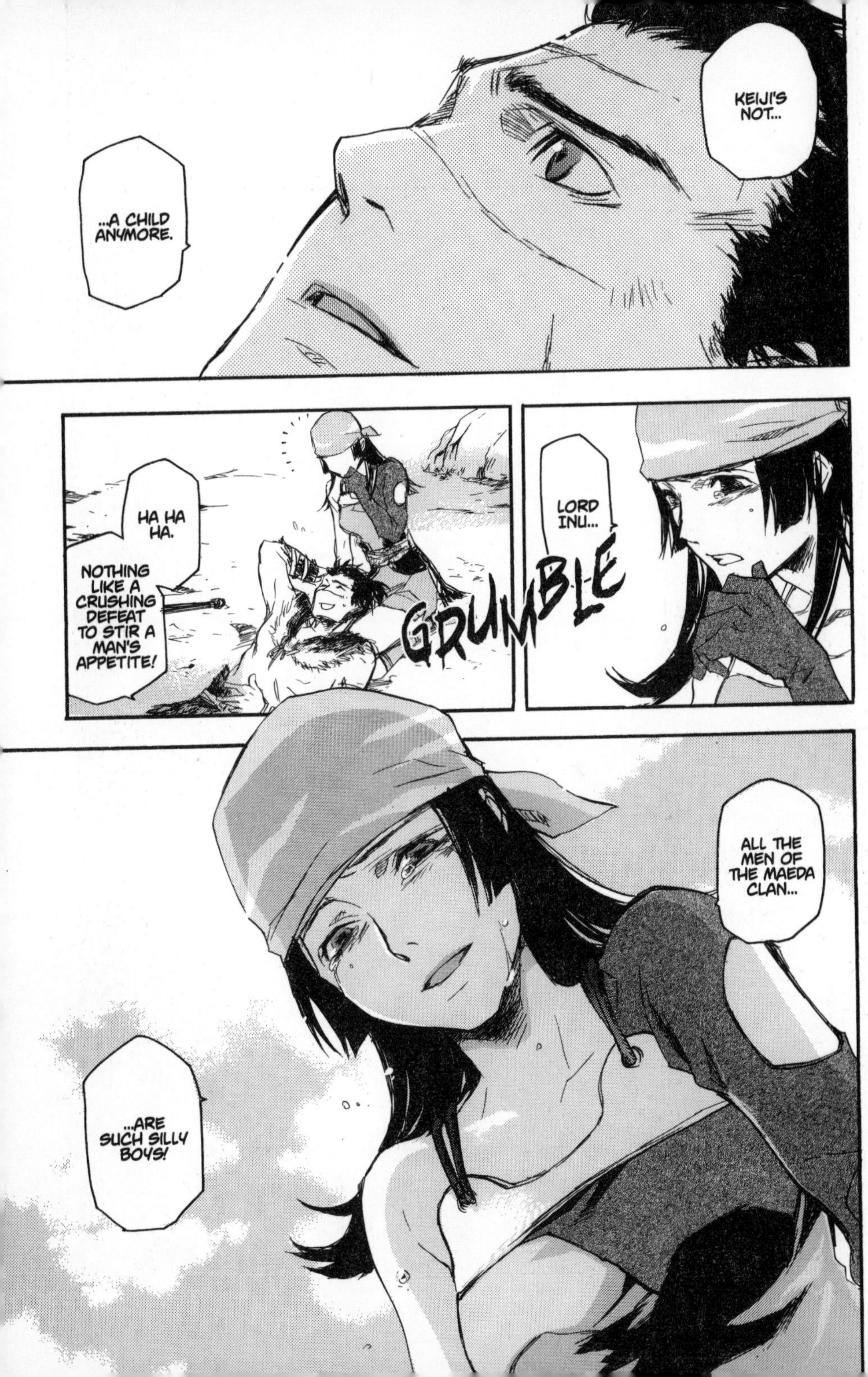
KEIJI'S NOT...
...A CHILD ANYMORE.
LORD INU...
GRUMBLE
HA HA HA.
NOTHING LIKE A CRUSHING DEFEAT TO STIR A MAN'S APPETITE!
ALL THE MEN OF THE MAEDA CLAN...
...ARE SUCH SILLY BOYS!

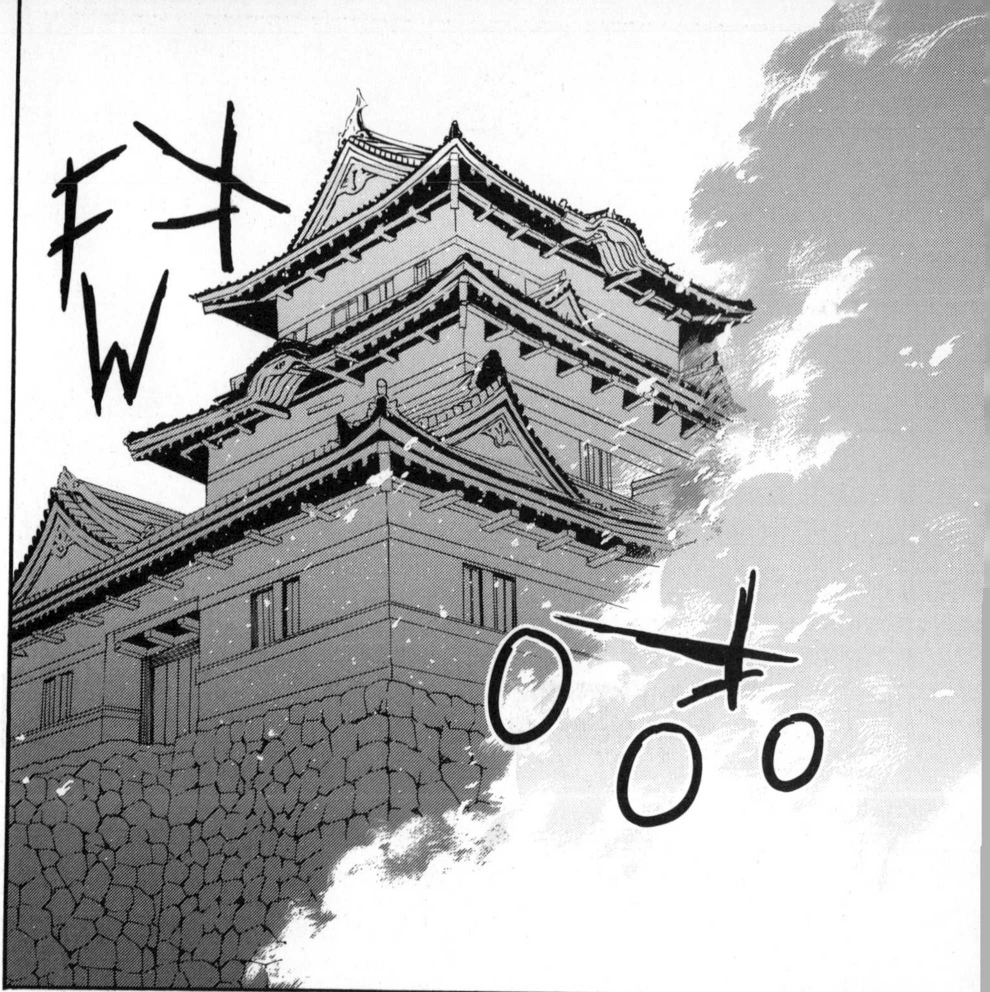
FW
OOO
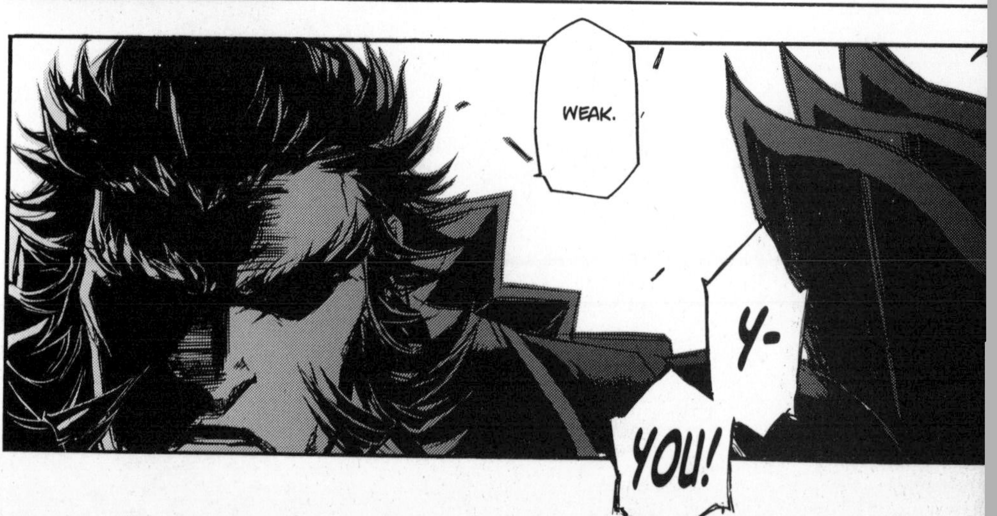
WEAK.
Y- YOU!

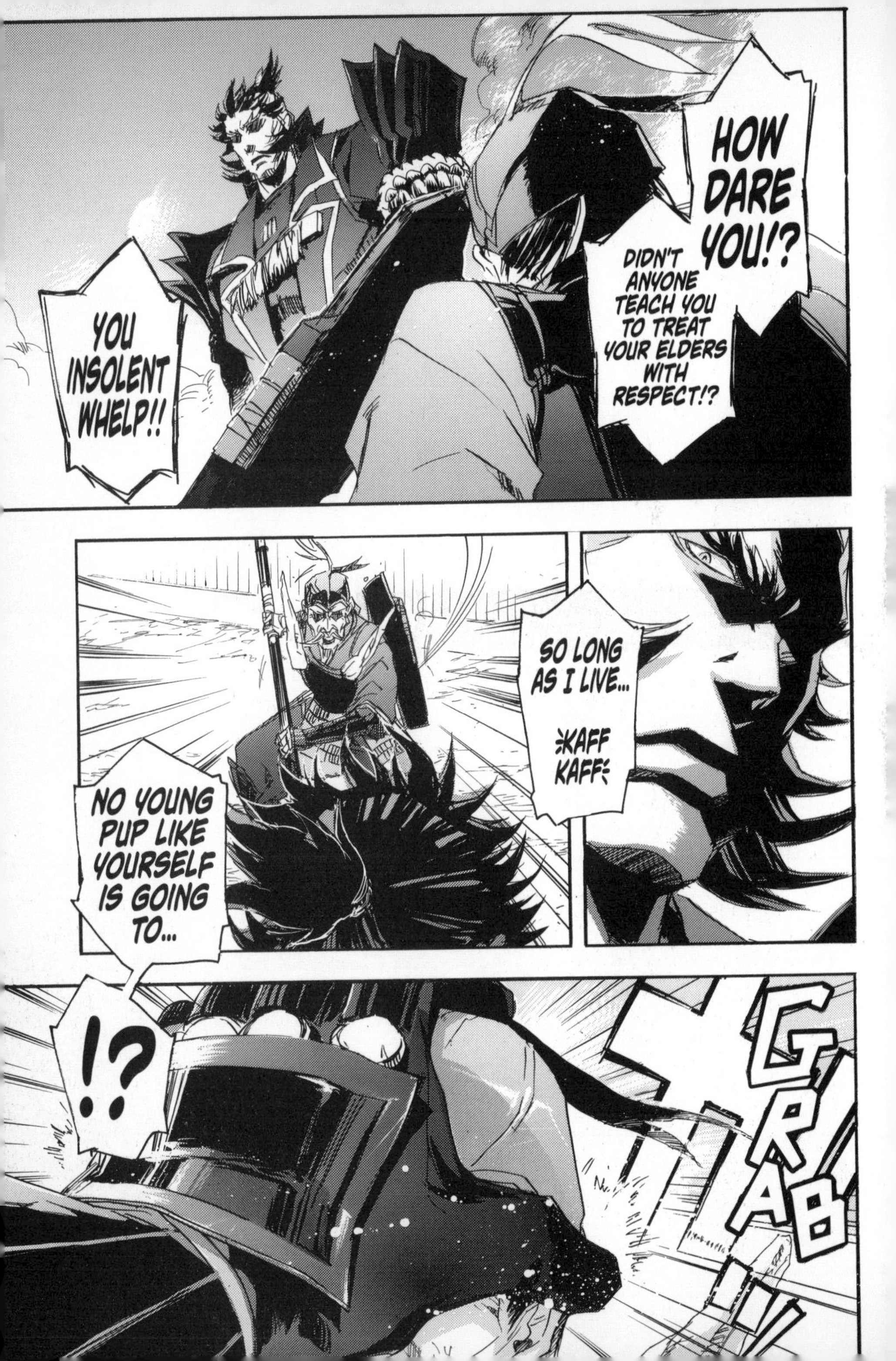
HOW DARE YOU!?
DIDN'T ANYONE TEACH YOU TO TREAT YOUR ELDERS WITH RESPECT!?
YOU INSOLENT WHELP!!
SO LONG AS I LIVE...
KAFF KAFF
NO YOUNG PUP LIKE YOURSELF IS GOING TO...
GRAB!!
!?

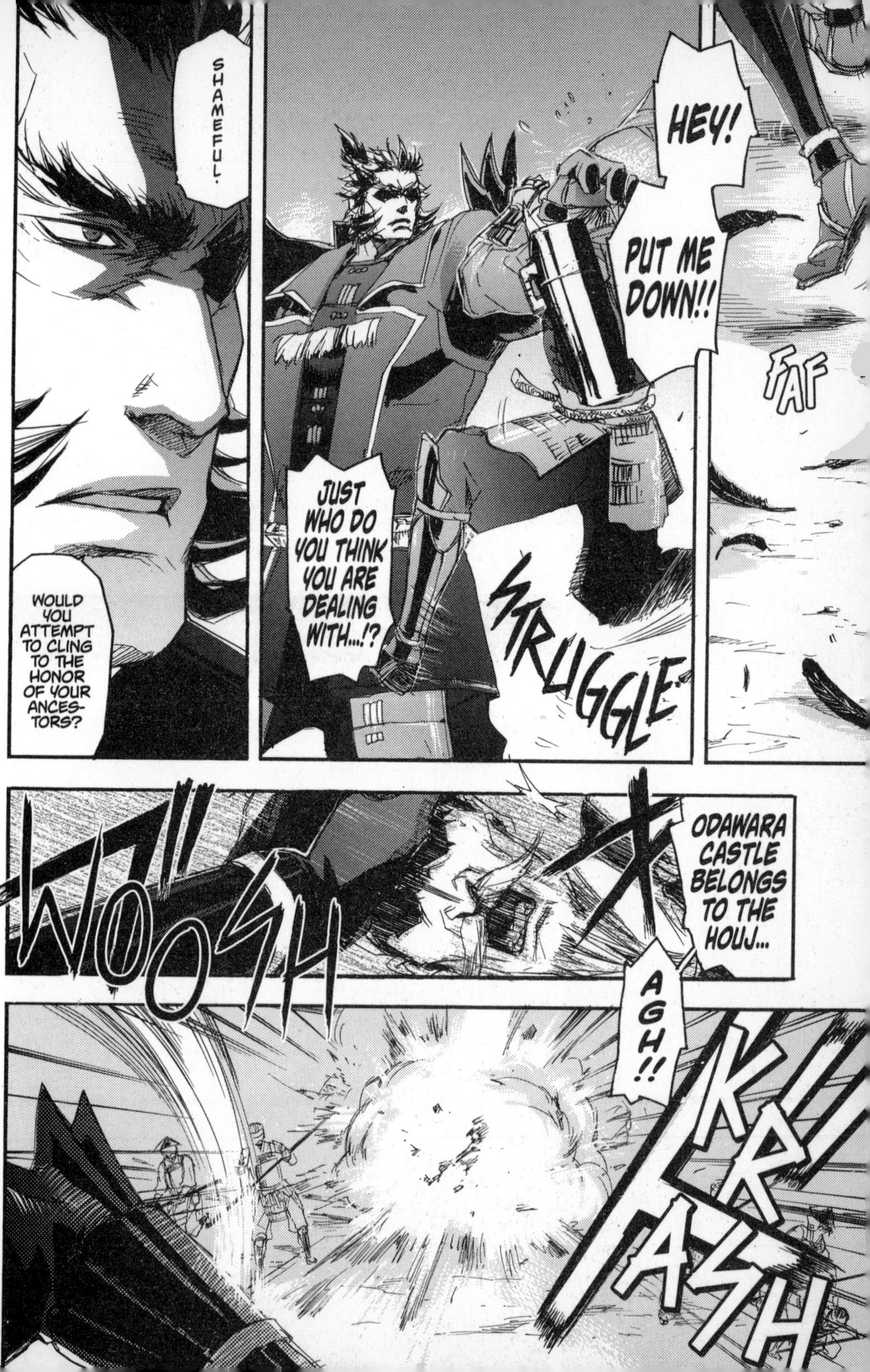
HEY!
PUT ME DOWN!!
FAF
JUST WHO DO YOU THINK YOU ARE DEALING WITH...!?
STRUGGLE
SHAMEFUL.
WOULD YOU ATTEMPT TO CLING TO THE HONOR OF YOUR ANCES-TORS?
ODAWARA CASTLE BELONGS TO THE HOUJ...
WOOSH
AGH!!
KRASH

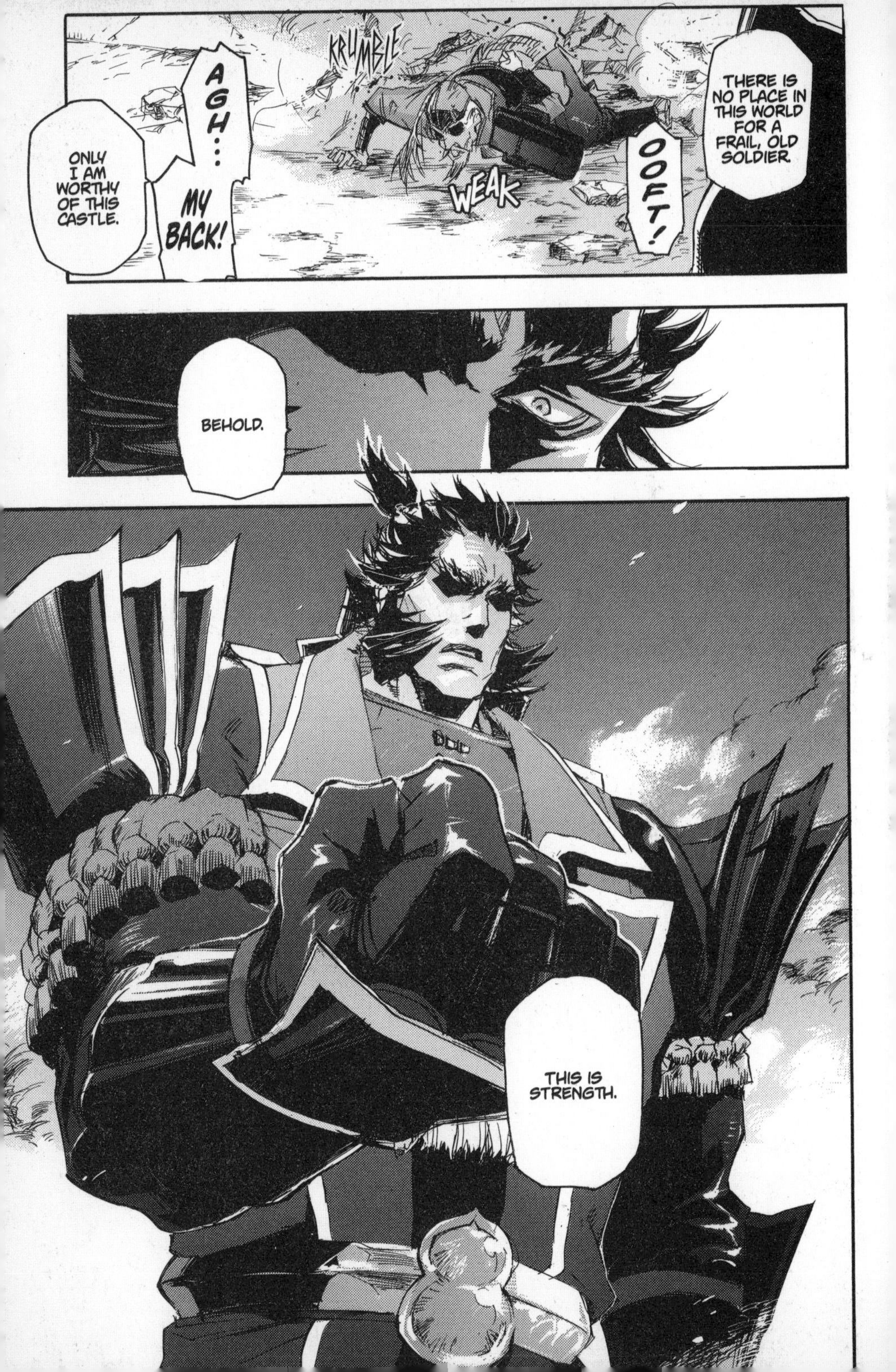
THERE IS NO PLACE IN THIS WORLD FOR A FRAIL, OLD SOLDIER.
OOFT!
WEAK
KRUMBLE
AGH... MY BACK!
ONLY I AM WORTHY OF THIS CASTLE.
BEHOLD.
THIS IS STRENGTH.

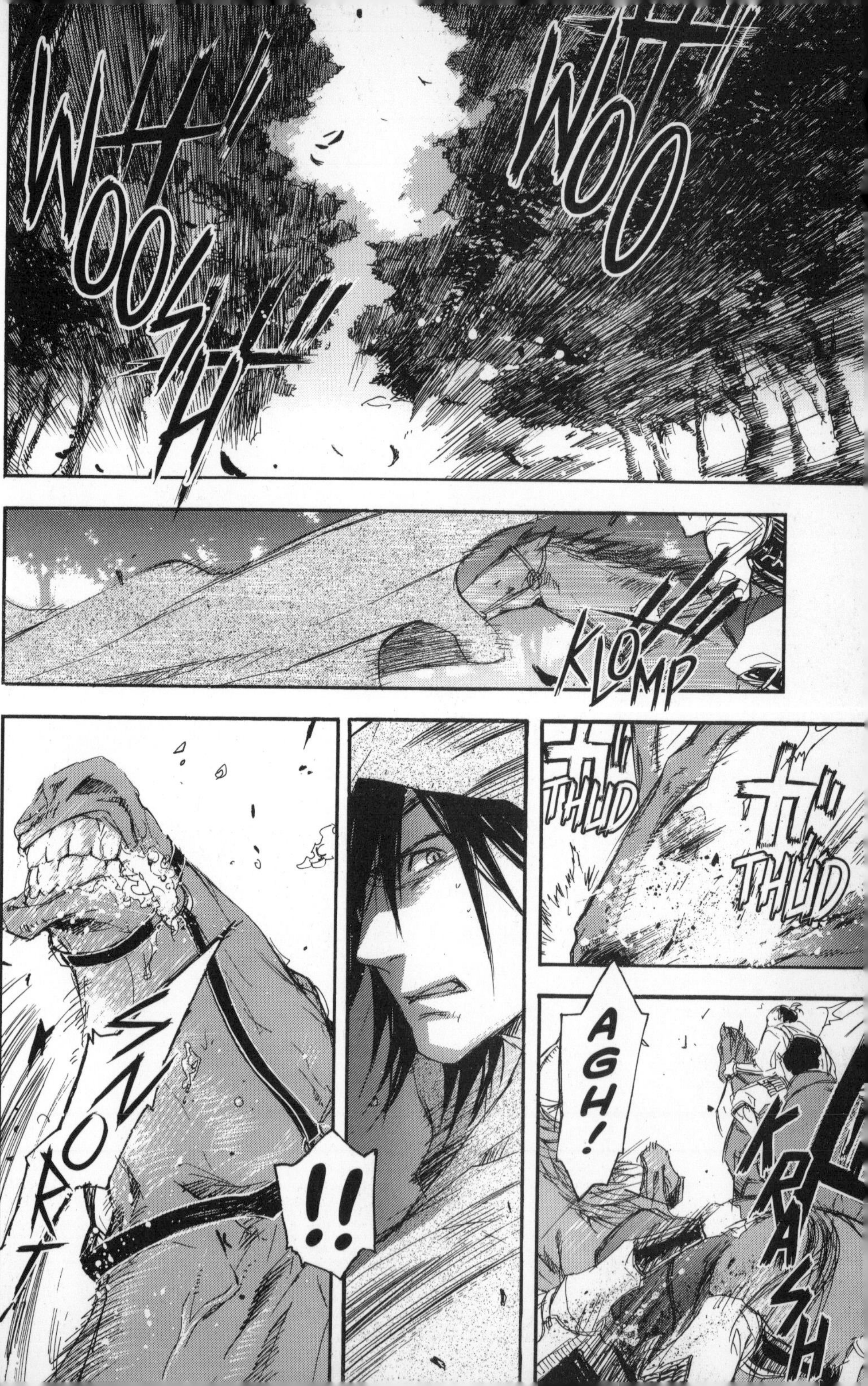
WOO
WHOOSH
KLOMP
THUD
THUD
AGH!
KRASH
!!
SNORT

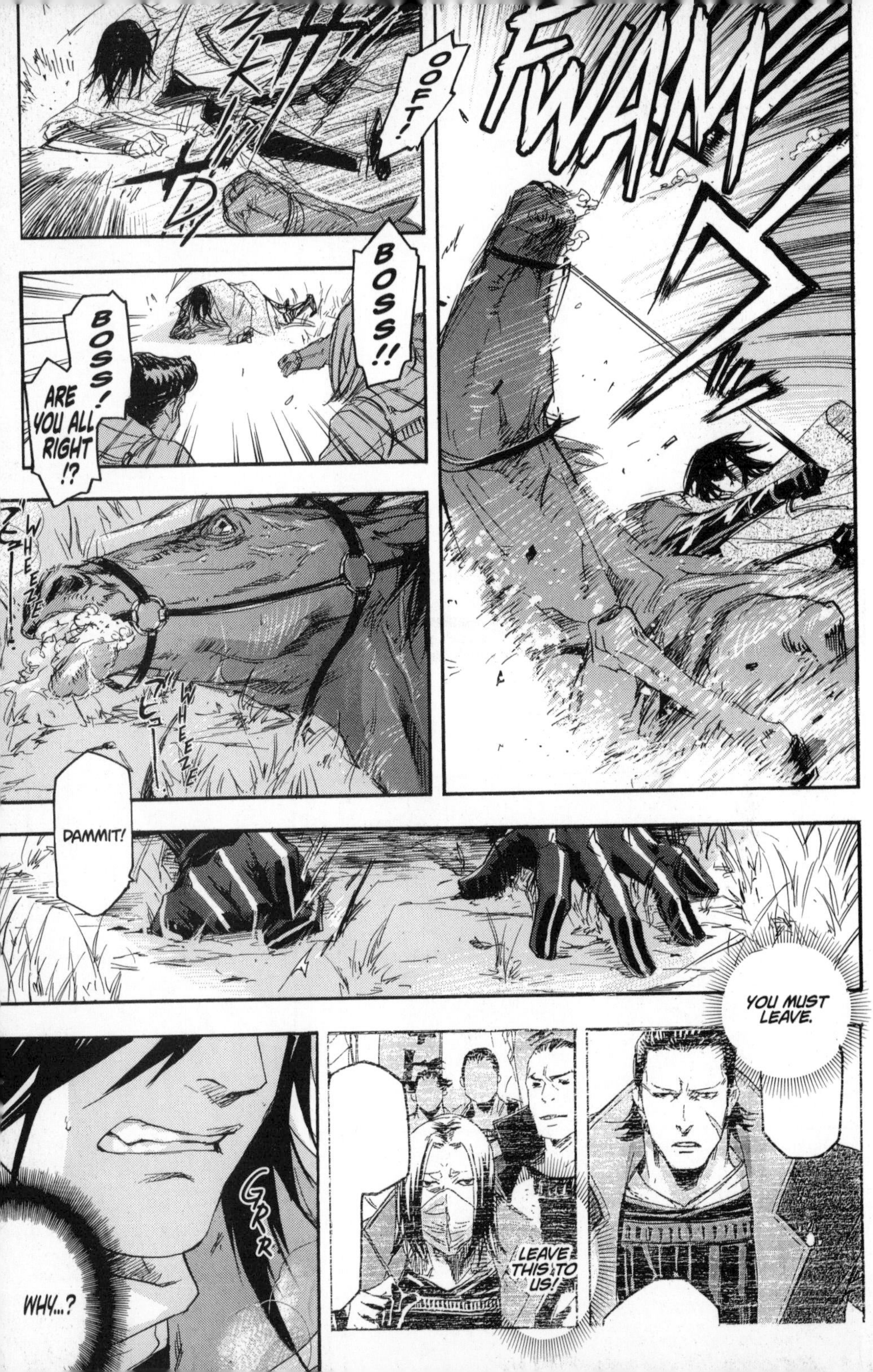
FWAM
OOFT!
SKID
BOSS!!
BOSS! ARE YOU ALL RIGHT!?
WHEEZE
WHEEZE
DAMMIT!
YOU MUST LEAVE.
LEAVE THIS TO US!
GRR
WHY...?

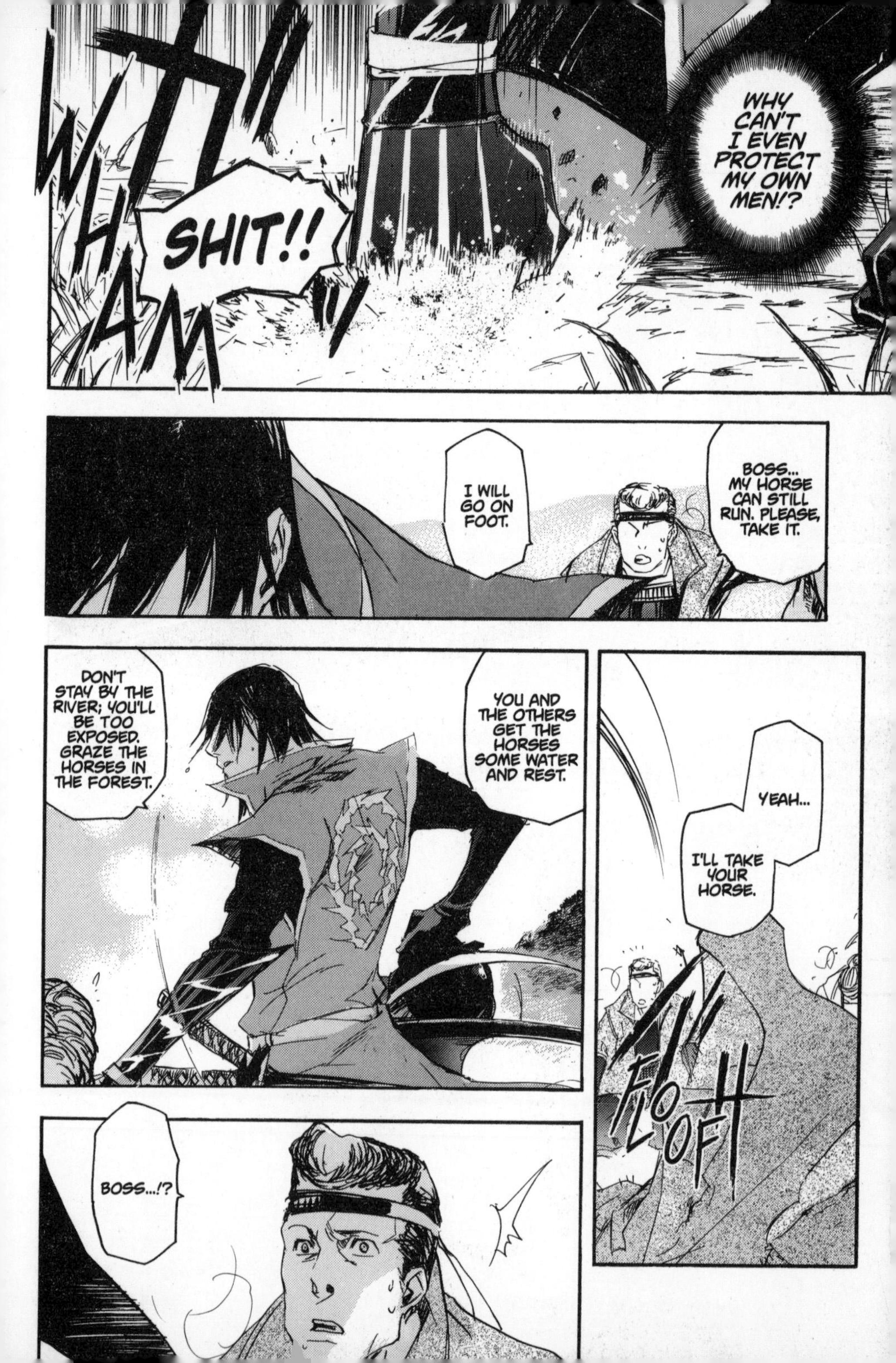
WHY CAN'T I EVEN PROTECT MY OWN MEN!?
SHIT!!
WHAM
BOSS... MY HORSE CAN STILL RUN. PLEASE, TAKE IT.
I WILL GO ON FOOT.
YEAH...
I'LL TAKE YOUR HORSE.
FLOOF
YOU AND THE OTHERS GET THE HORSES SOME WATER AND REST.
DON'T STAY BY THE RIVER; YOU'LL BE TOO EXPOSED. GRAZE THE HORSES IN THE FOREST.
BOSS...!?

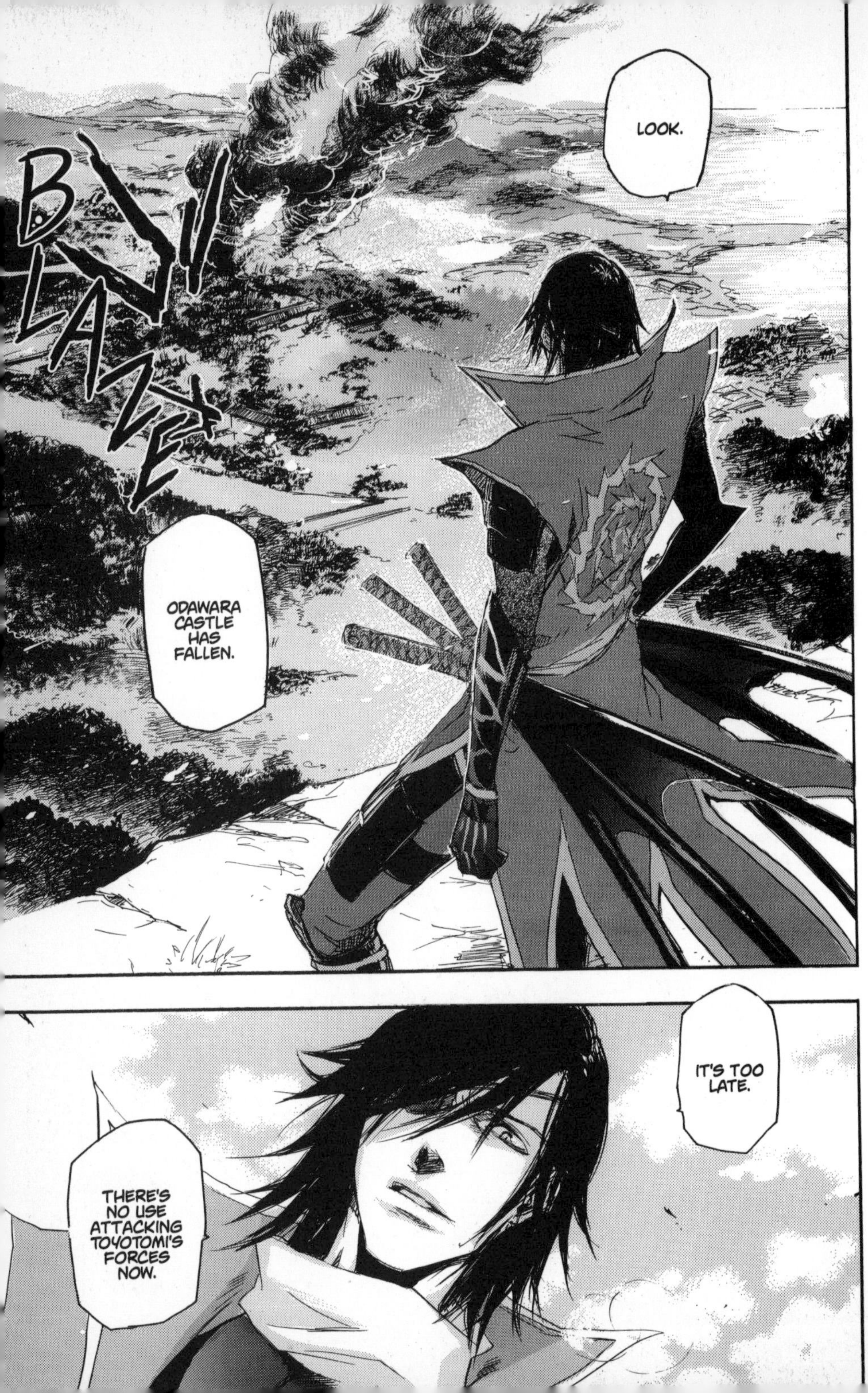
LOOK.
BLAZE
ODAWARA CASTLE HAS FALLEN.
IT'S TOO LATE.
THERE'S NO USE ATTACKING TOYOTOMI'S FORCES NOW.

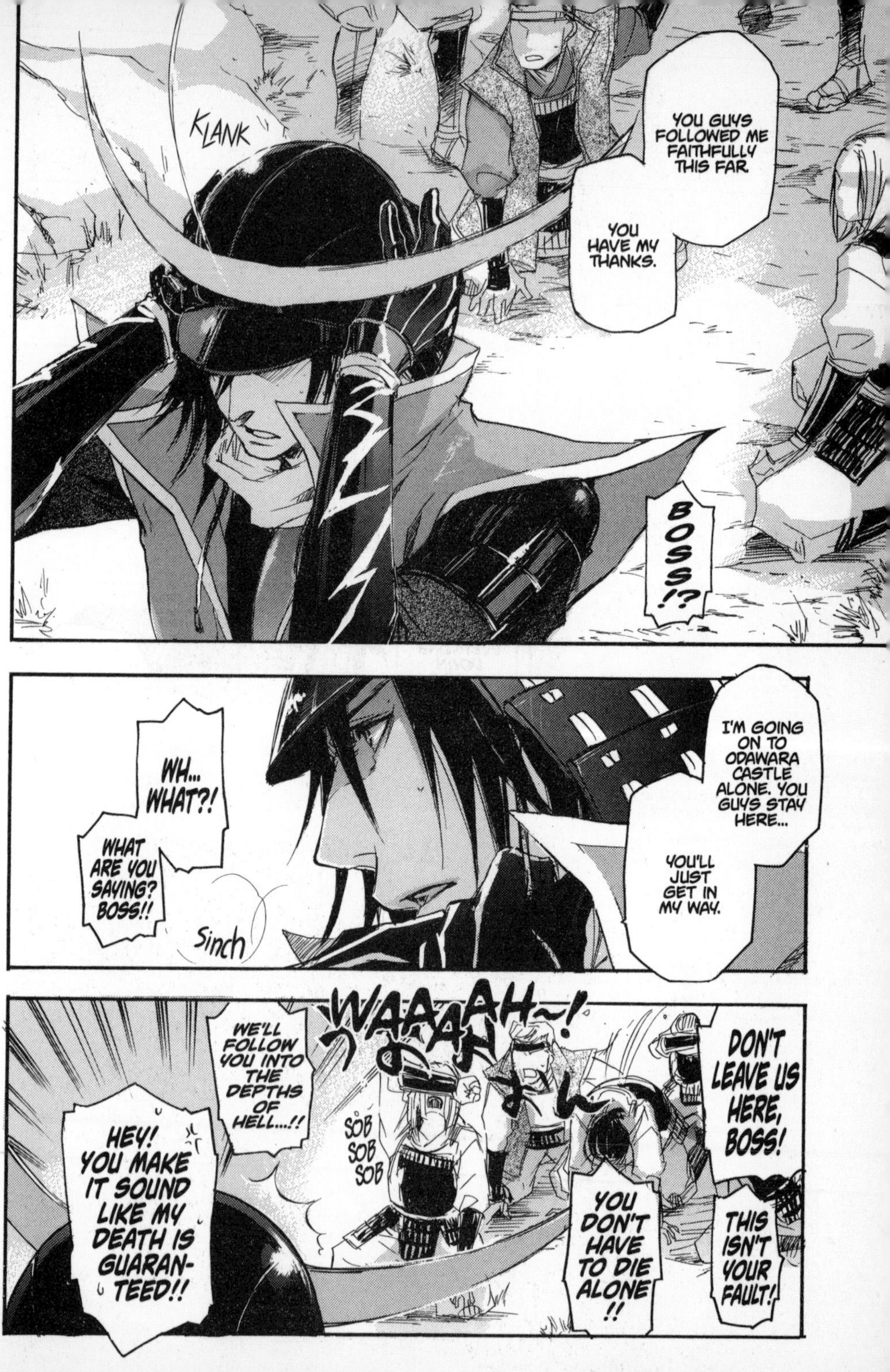
YOU GUYS FOLLOWED ME FAITHFULLY THIS FAR.
YOU HAVE MY THANKS.
KLANK
BOSS!?
I'M GOING ON TO ODAWARA CASTLE ALONE. YOU GUYS STAY HERE...
YOU'LL JUST GET IN MY WAY.
WH... WHAT?!
WHAT ARE YOU SAYING? BOSS!!
Sinch
DON'T LEAVE US HERE, BOSS!
WAAAAH~!
THIS ISN'T YOUR FAULT!
YOU DON'T HAVE TO DIE ALONE!!
WE'LL FOLLOW YOU INTO THE DEPTHS OF HELL...!!
SOB SOB SOB
HEY! YOU MAKE IT SOUND LIKE MY DEATH IS GUARANTEED!!

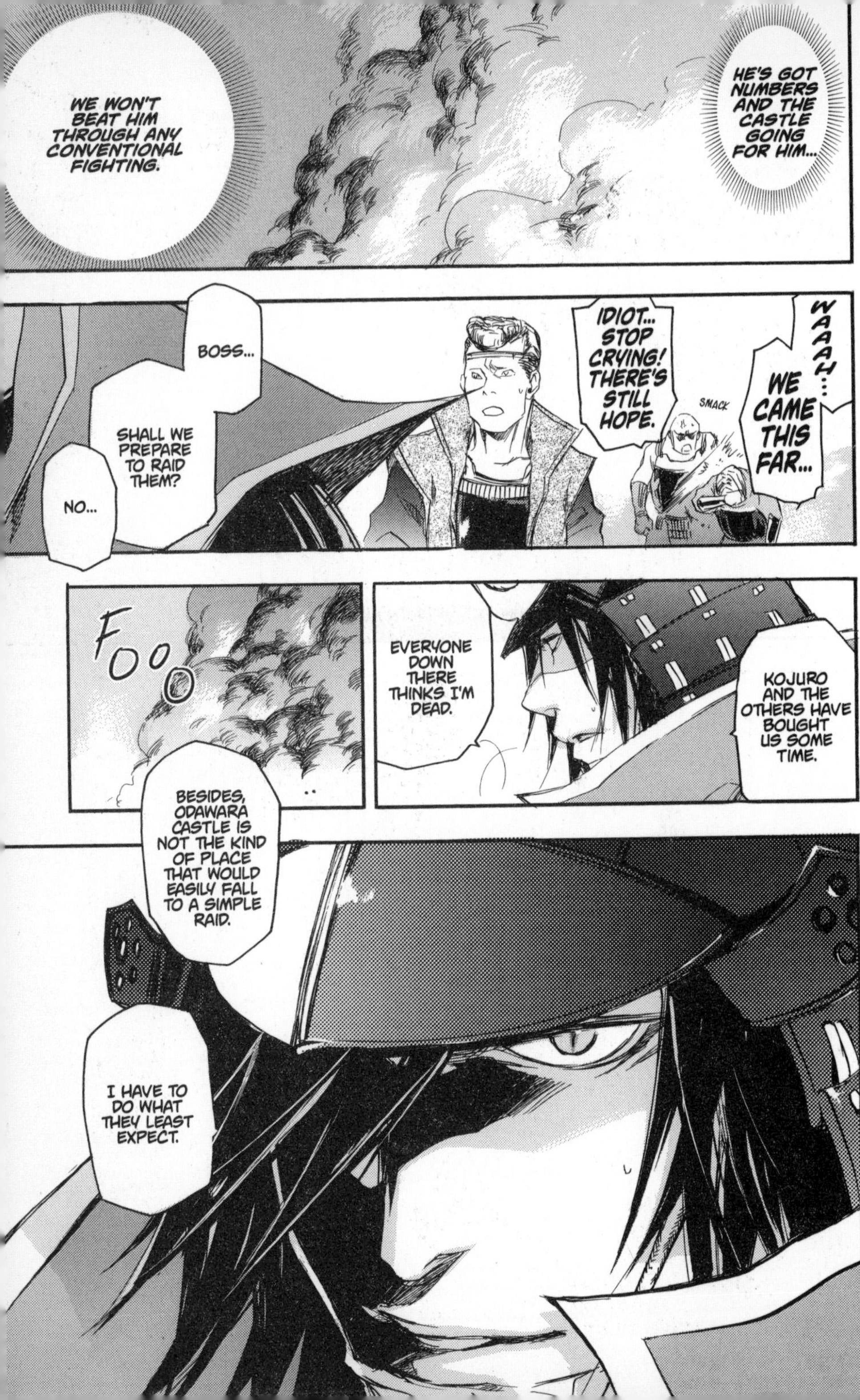
HE'S GOT NUMBERS AND THE CASTLE GOING FOR HIM...
WE WON'T BEAT HIM THROUGH ANY CONVENTIONAL FIGHTING.
WAAAAH... WE CAME THIS FAR...
SMACK
IDIOT... STOP CRYING! THERE'S STILL HOPE.
BOSS...
SHALL WE PREPARE TO RAID THEM?
NO...
KOJURO AND THE OTHERS HAVE BOUGHT US SOME TIME.
EVERYONE DOWN THERE THINKS I'M DEAD.
FOOO
..
BESIDES, ODAWARA CASTLE IS NOT THE KIND OF PLACE THAT WOULD EASILY FALL TO A SIMPLE RAID.
I HAVE TO DO WHAT THEY LEAST EXPECT.

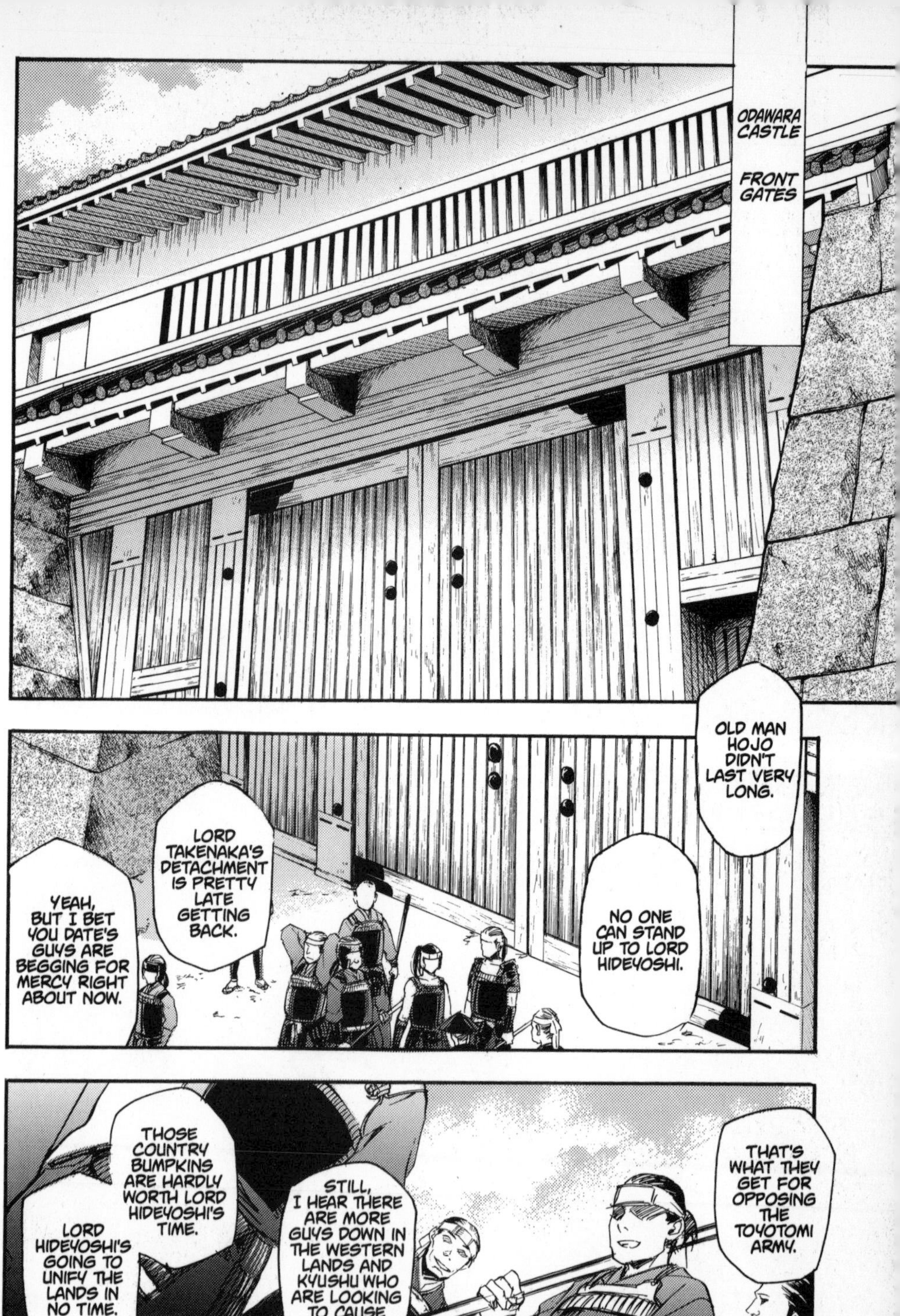
ODAWARA CASTLE
FRONT GATES
OLD MAN HOJO DIDN'T LAST VERY LONG.
NO ONE CAN STAND UP TO LORD HIDEYOSHI.
LORD TAKENAKA'S DETACHMENT IS PRETTY LATE GETTING BACK.
YEAH, BUT I BET YOU DATE'S GUYS ARE BEGGING FOR MERCY RIGHT ABOUT NOW.
THAT'S WHAT THEY GET FOR OPPOSING THE TOYOTOMI ARMY.
STILL, I HEAR THERE ARE MORE GUYS DOWN IN THE WESTERN LANDS AND KYUSHU WHO ARE LOOKING TO CAUSE TROUBLE.
THOSE COUNTRY BUMPKINS ARE HARDLY WORTH LORD HIDEYOSHI'S TIME.
LORD HIDEYOSHI'S GOING TO UNIFY THE LANDS IN NO TIME.

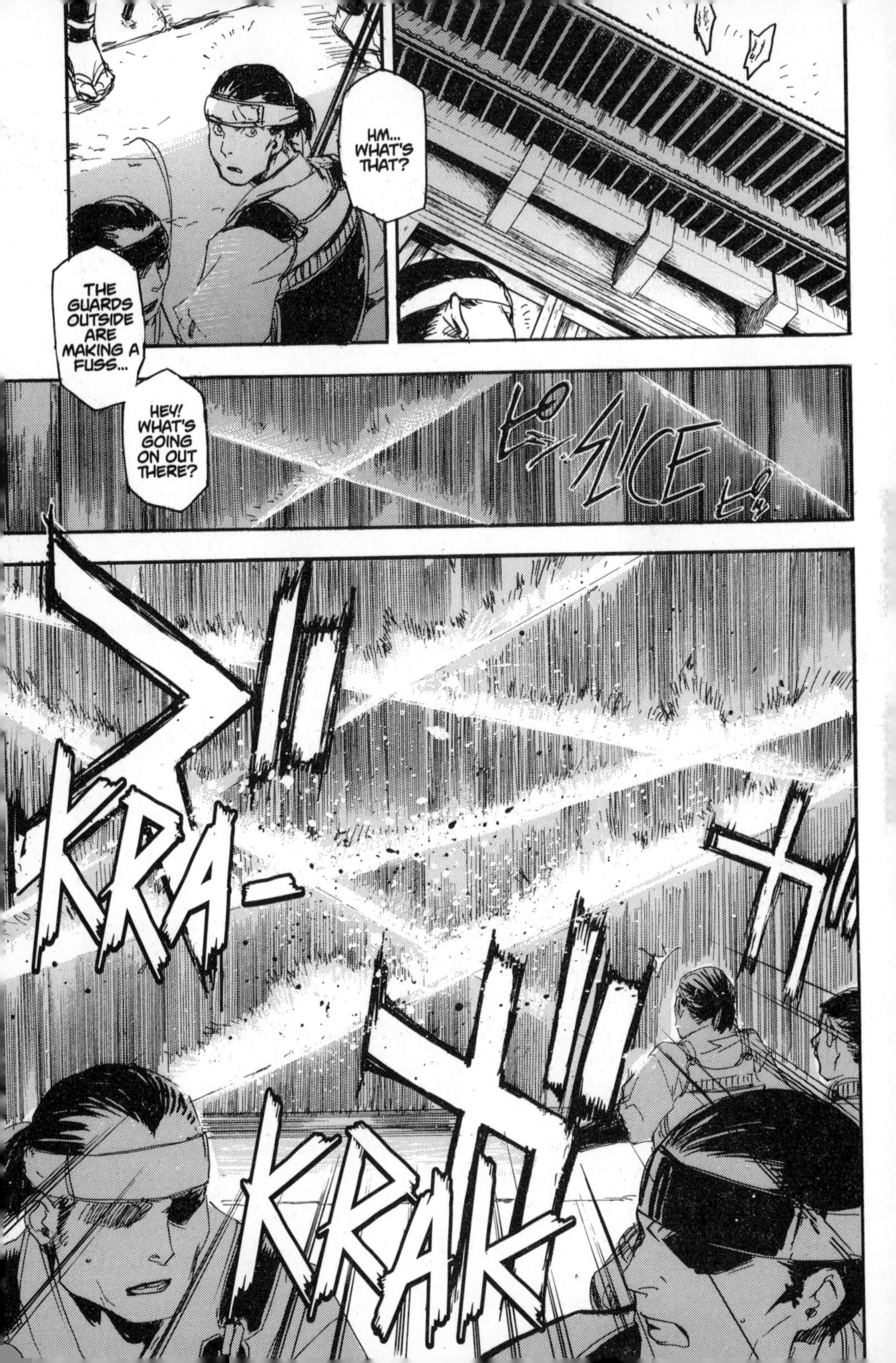
HM... WHAT'S THAT?
THE GUARDS OUTSIDE ARE MAKING A FUSS...
HEY! WHAT'S GOING ON OUT THERE?
SLICE
KRA-
KRAK

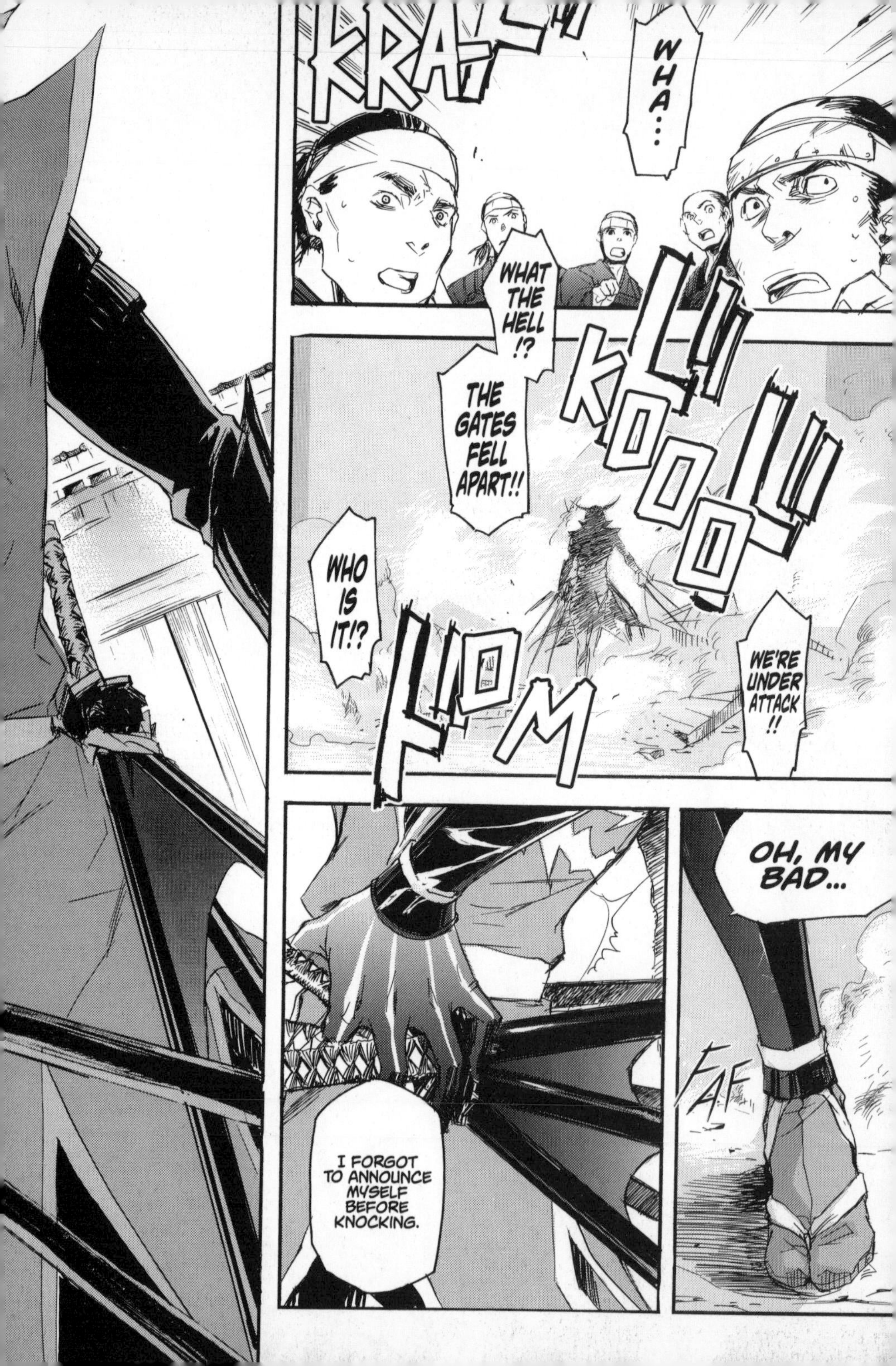
KRA
WHA...
WHAT THE HELL!?
KOOOO
THE GATES FELL APART!!
WE'RE UNDER ATTACK!!
WHO IS IT!?
DOM
OH, MY BAD...
FAF
I FORGOT TO ANNOUNCE MYSELF BEFORE KNOCKING.

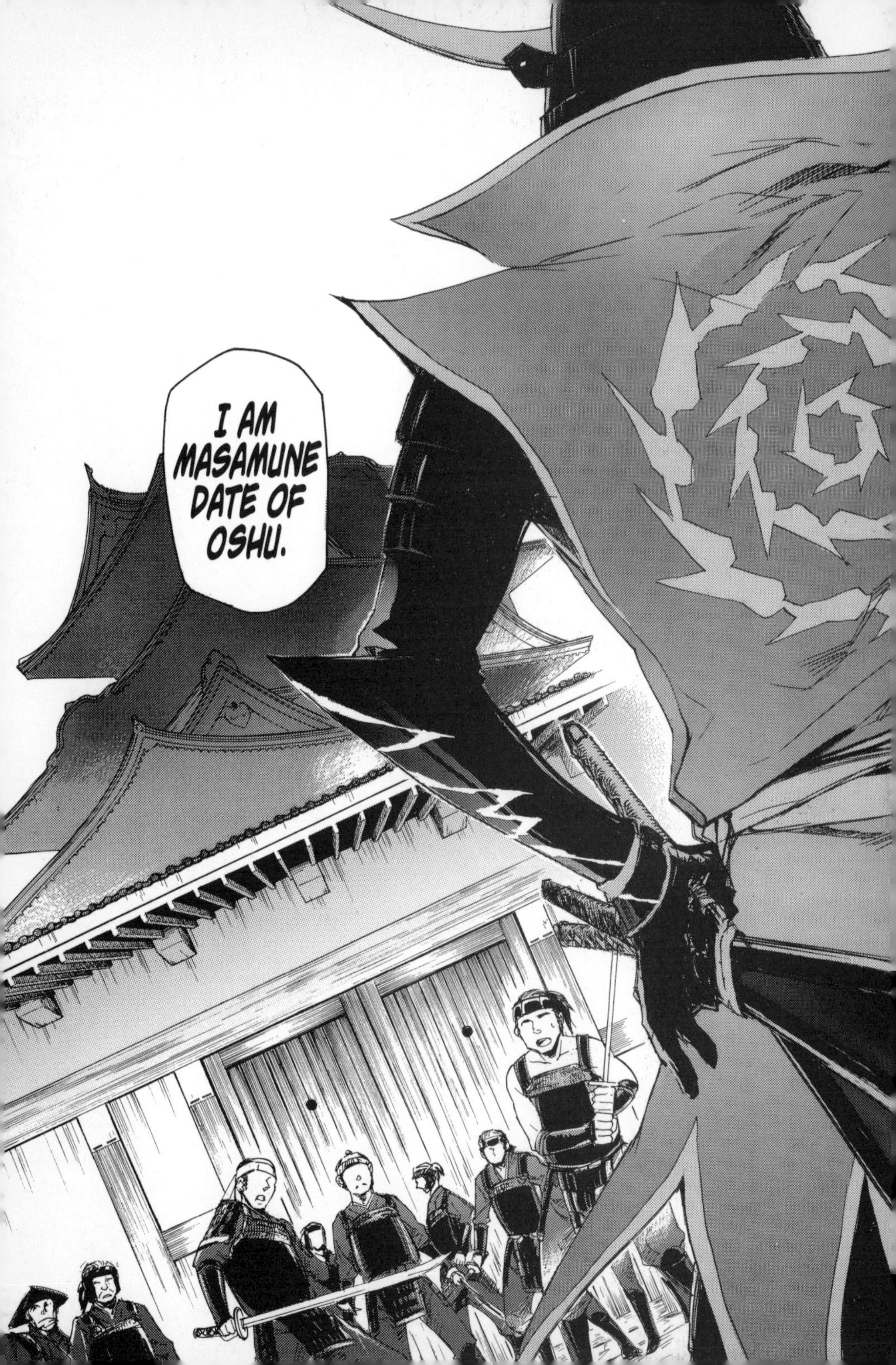
I AM MASAMUNE DATE OF OSHU.

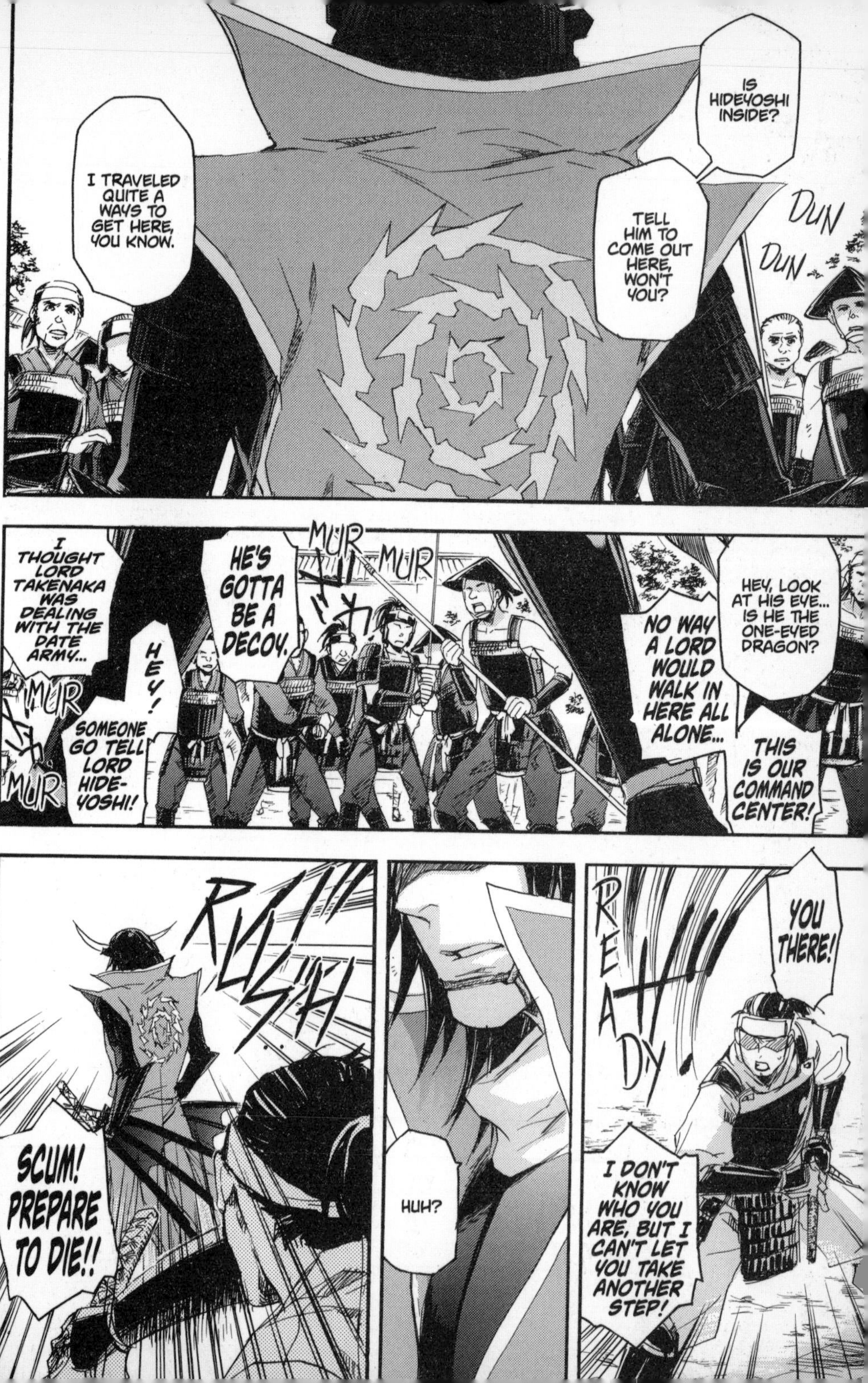
IS HIDEYOSHI INSIDE?
TELL HIM TO COME OUT HERE, WON'T YOU?
DUN DUN
I TRAVELED QUITE A WAYS TO GET HERE, YOU KNOW.
HEY, LOOK AT HIS EYE... IS HE THE ONE-EYED DRAGON?
NO WAY A LORD WOULD WALK IN HERE ALL ALONE...
THIS IS OUR COMMAND CENTER!
MUR MUR
HE'S GOTTA BE A DECOY.
I THOUGHT LORD TAKENAKA WAS DEALING WITH THE DATE ARMY...
HEY!
SOMEONE GO TELL LORD HIDE-YOSHI!
MUR
MUR
YOU THERE!
I DON'T KNOW WHO YOU ARE, BUT I CAN'T LET YOU TAKE ANOTHER STEP!
HUH?
RUSH
SCUM! PREPARE TO DIE!!

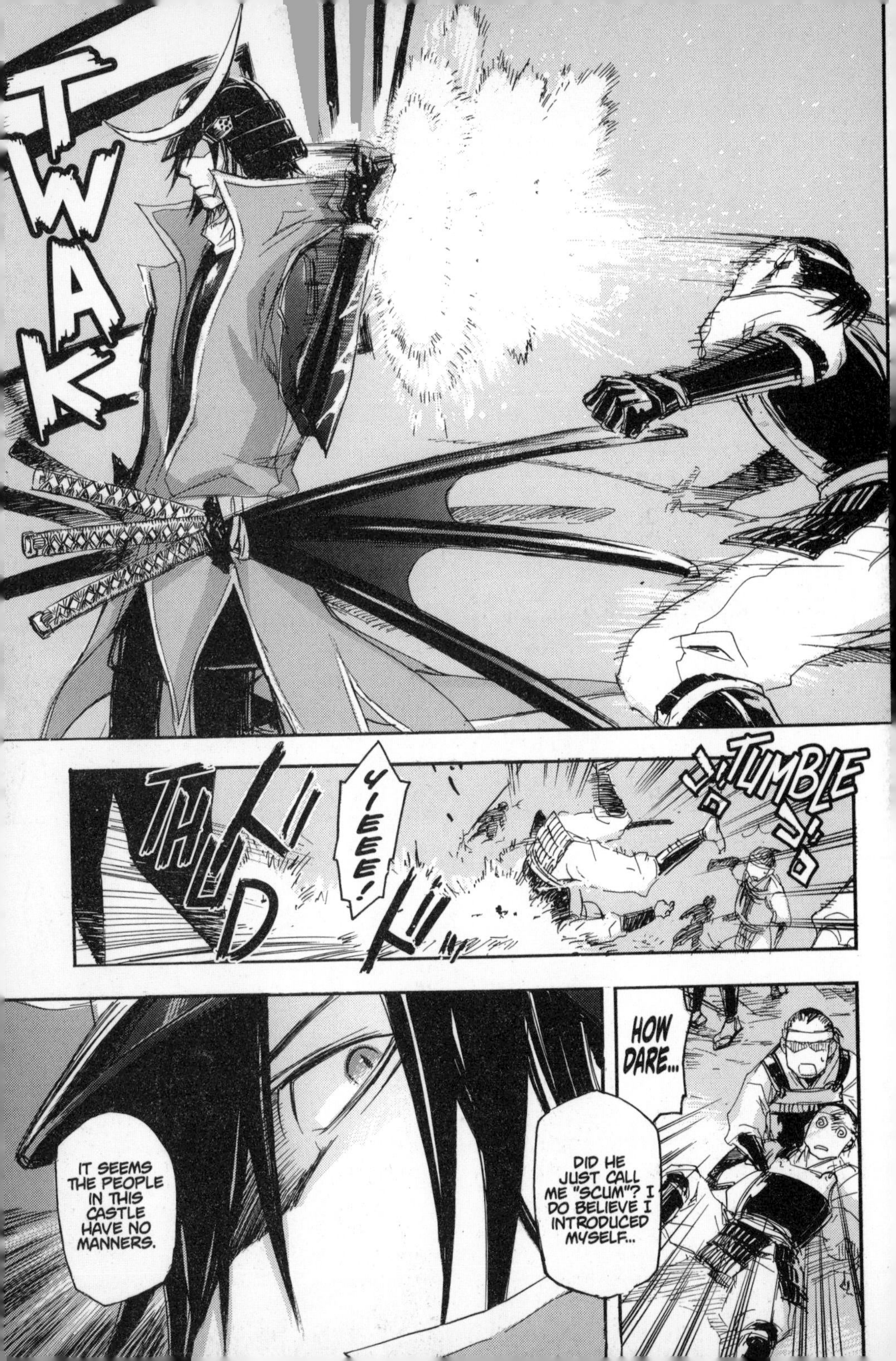
TWAK
TUMBLE
YIEEE!
THUD
HOW DARE...
DID HE JUST CALL ME "SCUM"? I DO BELIEVE I INTRODUCED MYSELF...
IT SEEMS THE PEOPLE IN THIS CASTLE HAVE NO MANNERS.

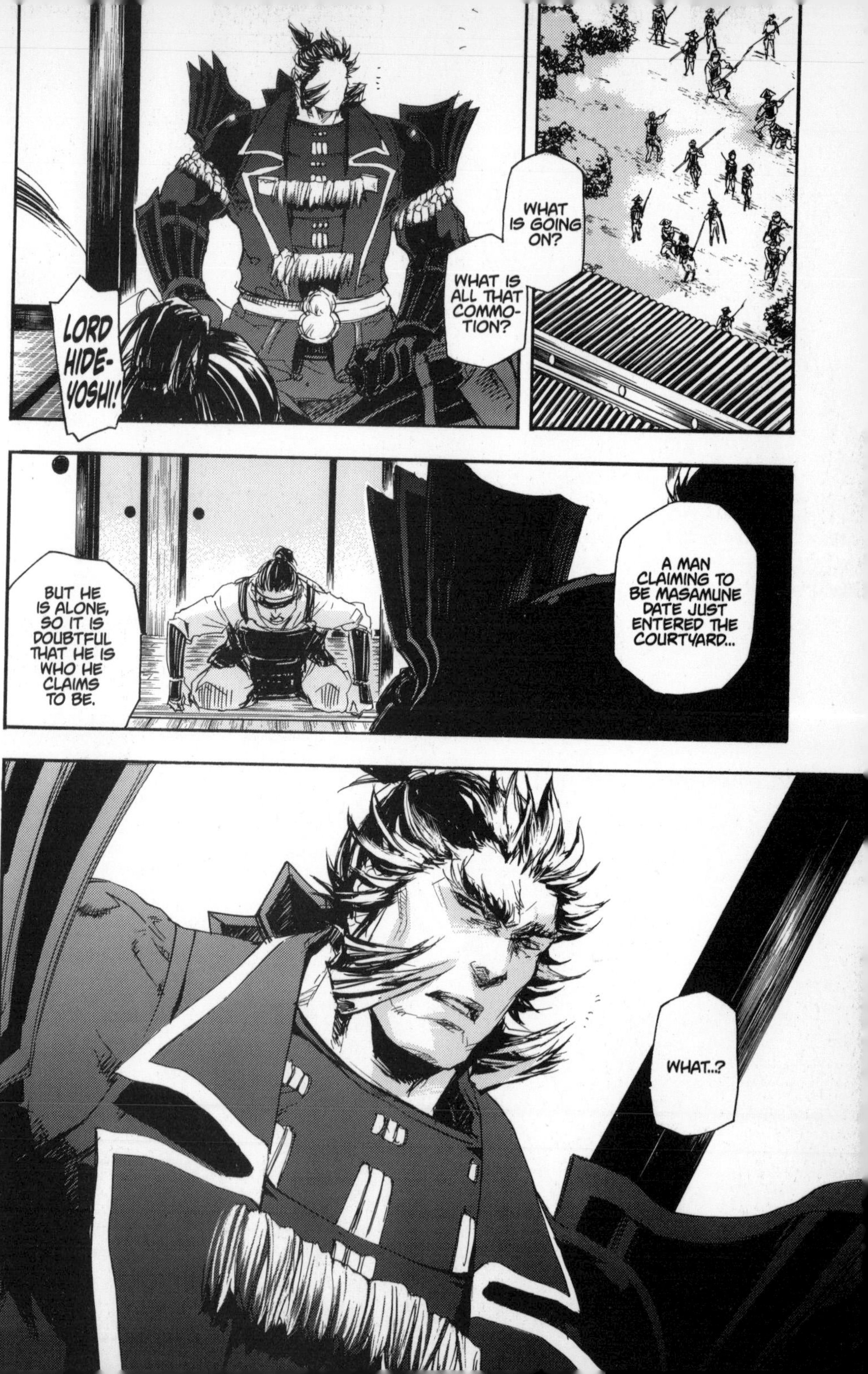
WHAT IS GOING ON?
WHAT IS ALL THAT COMMOTION?
LORD HIDE-YOSHI!
A MAN CLAIMING TO BE MASAMUNE DATE JUST ENTERED THE COURTYARD...
BUT HE IS ALONE, SO IT IS DOUBTFUL THAT HE IS WHO HE CLAIMS TO BE.
WHAT..?

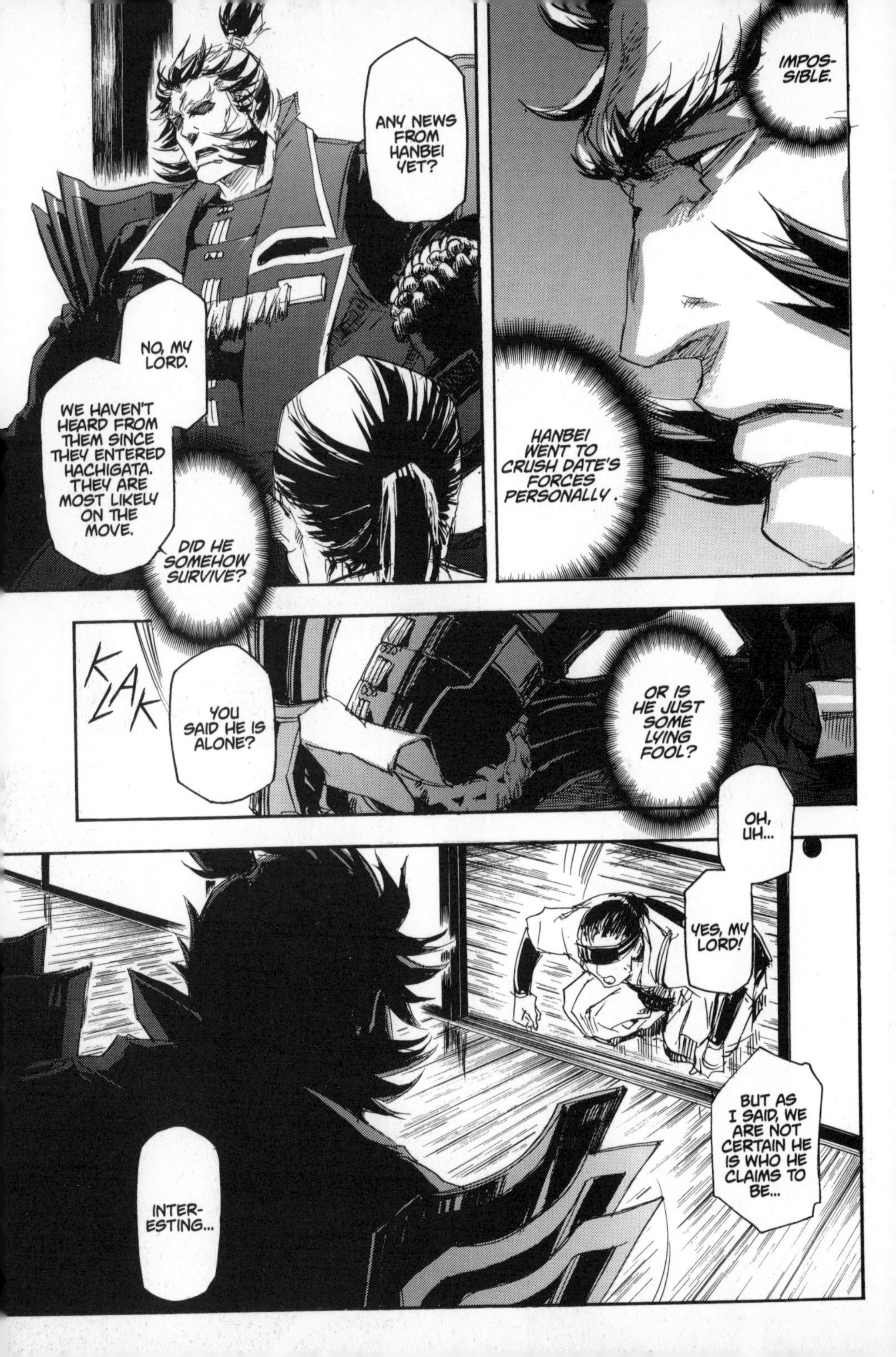

IMPOSSIBLE.
HANBEI WENT TO CRUSH DATE'S FORCES PERSONALLY.
ANY NEWS FROM HANBEI YET?
NO, MY LORD.
WE HAVEN'T HEARD FROM THEM SINCE THEY ENTERED HACHIGATA. THEY ARE MOST LIKELY ON THE MOVE.
DID HE SOMEHOW SURVIVE?
OR IS HE JUST SOME LYING FOOL?
YOU SAID HE IS ALONE?
KLAK
OH, UH...
YES, MY LORD!
BUT AS I SAID, WE ARE NOT CERTAIN HE IS WHO HE CLAIMS TO BE...
INTERESTING...

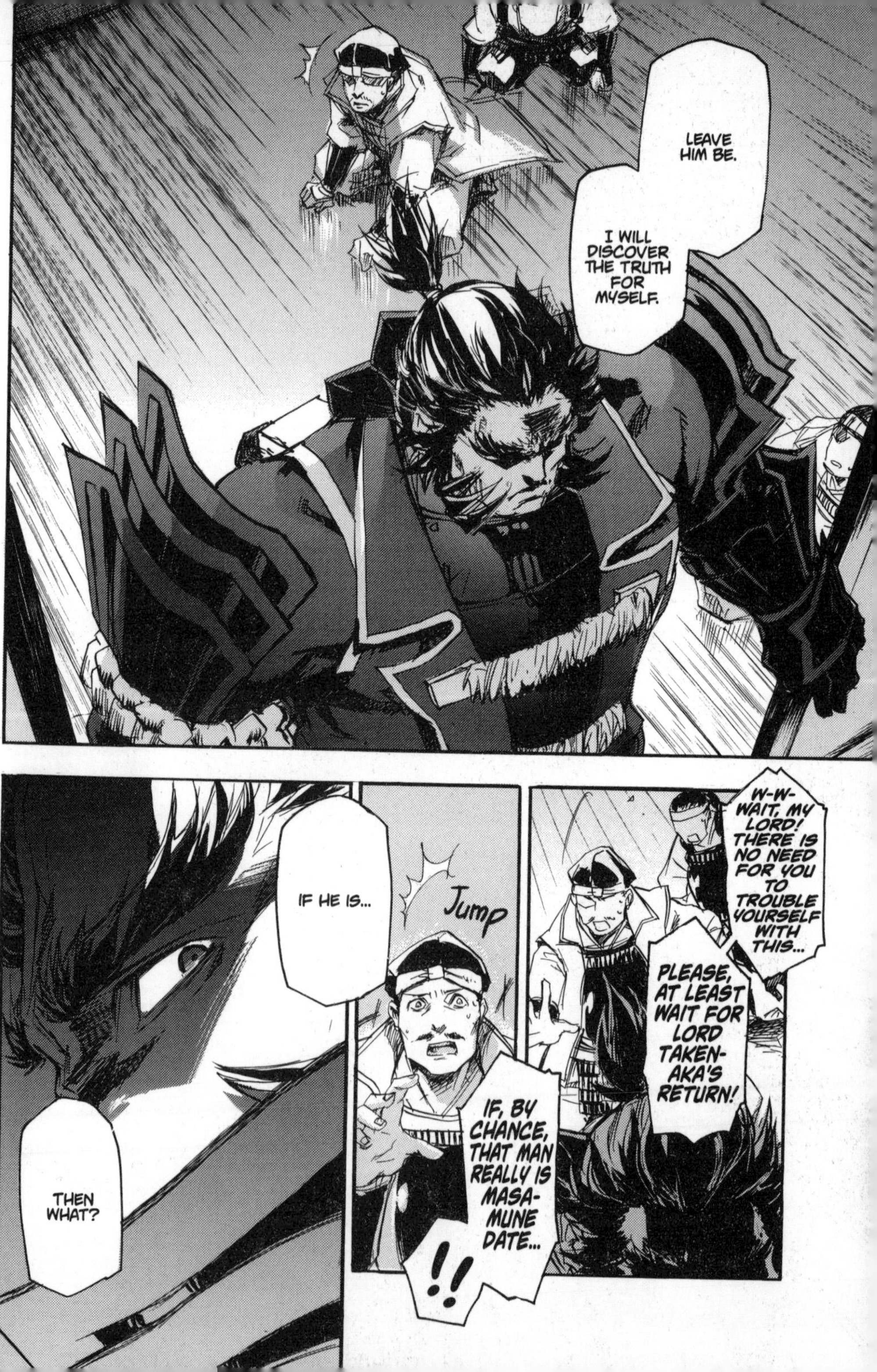
LEAVE HIM BE.
I WILL DISCOVER THE TRUTH FOR MYSELF.
W-W-WAIT, MY LORD! THERE IS NO NEED FOR YOU TO TROUBLE YOURSELF WITH THIS...
PLEASE, AT LEAST WAIT FOR LORD TAKEN-AKA'S RETURN!
IF, BY CHANCE, THAT MAN REALLY IS MASA-MUNE DATE...
Jump
!!
IF HE IS...
THEN WHAT?

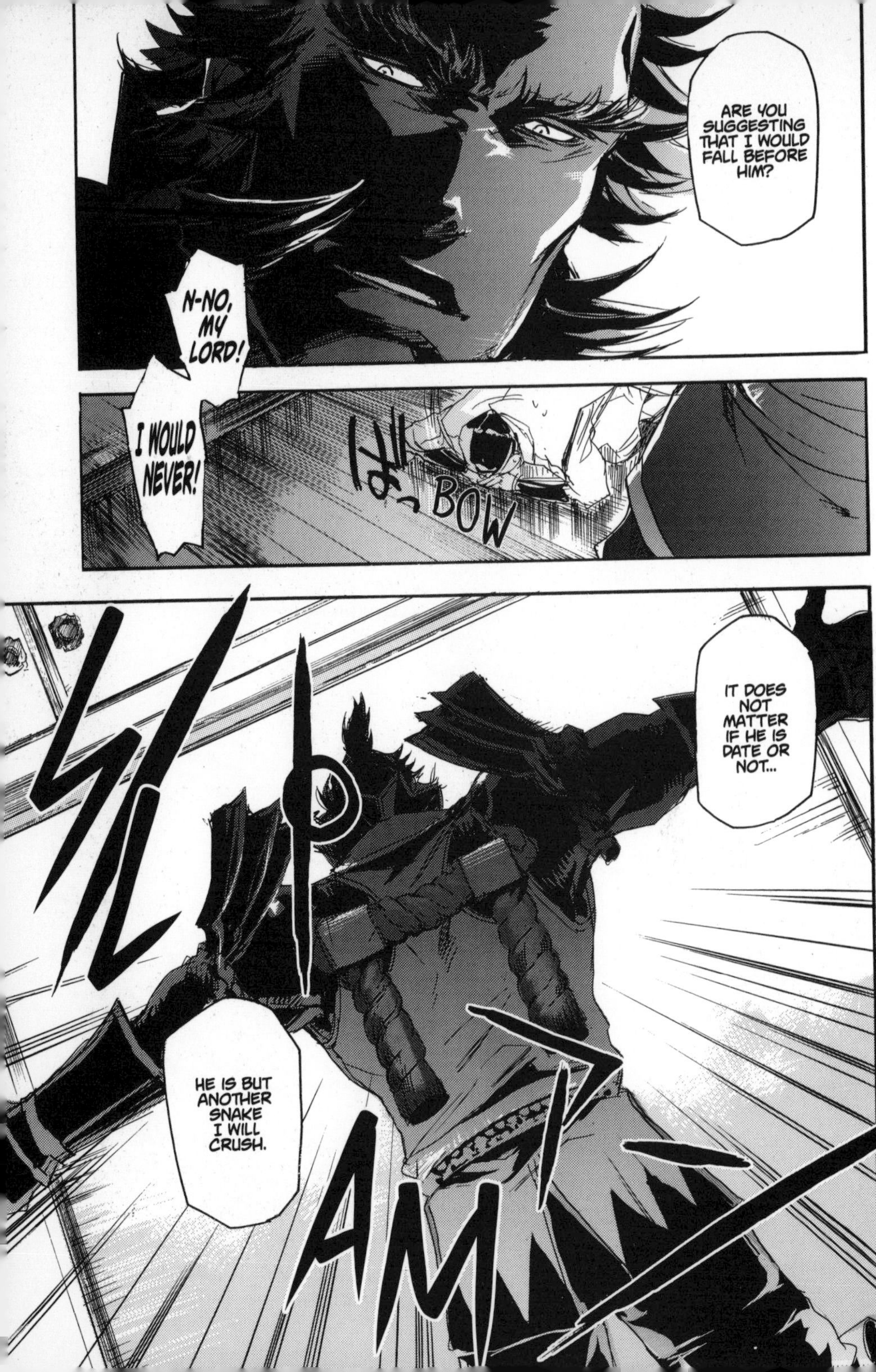
ARE YOU SUGGESTING THAT I WOULD FALL BEFORE HIM?
N-NO, MY LORD!
I WOULD NEVER!
ばっ
BOW
IT DOES NOT MATTER IF HE IS DATE OR NOT...
HE IS BUT ANOTHER SNAKE I WILL CRUSH.
SLAM

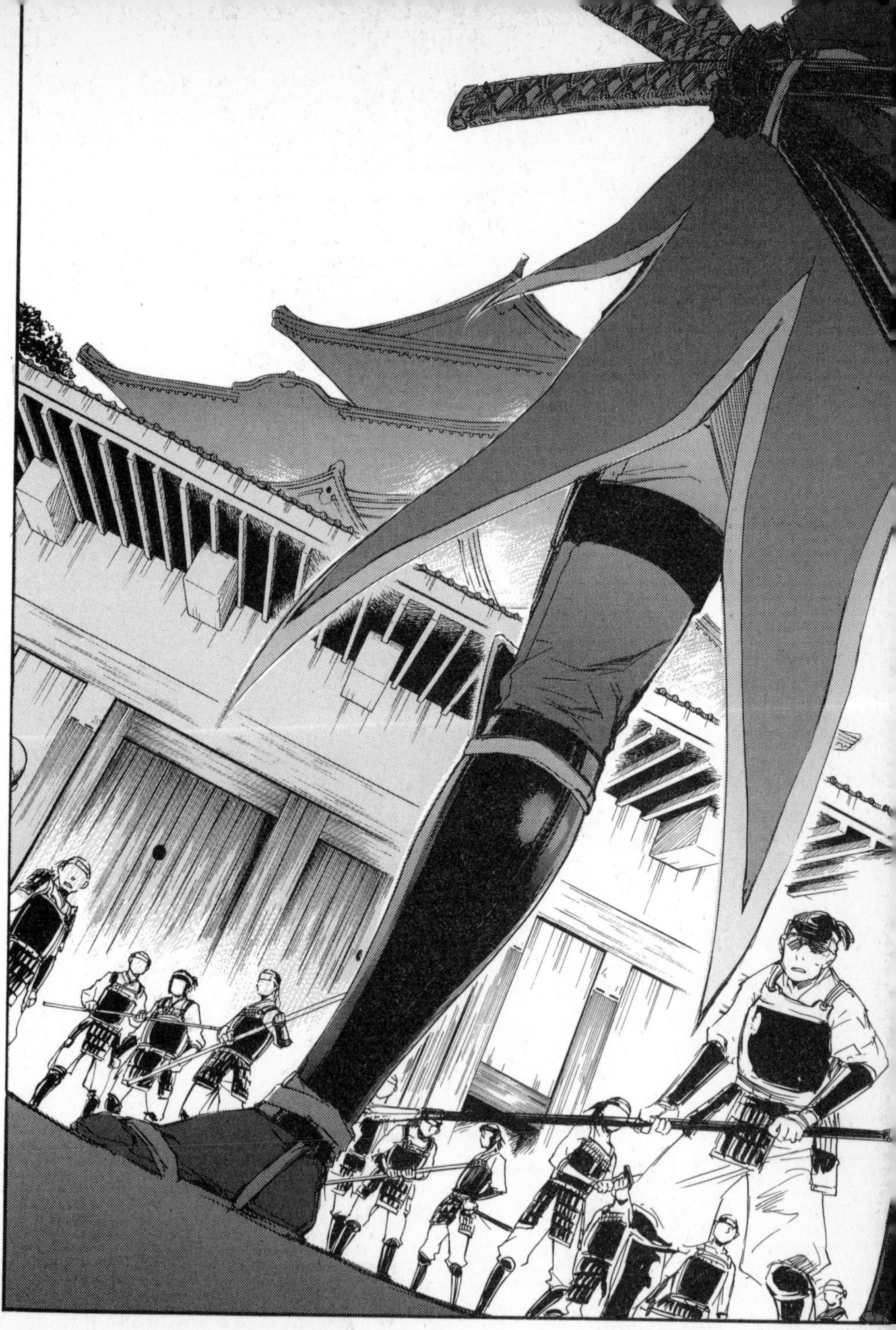

ACT22:**Yom Kippur**

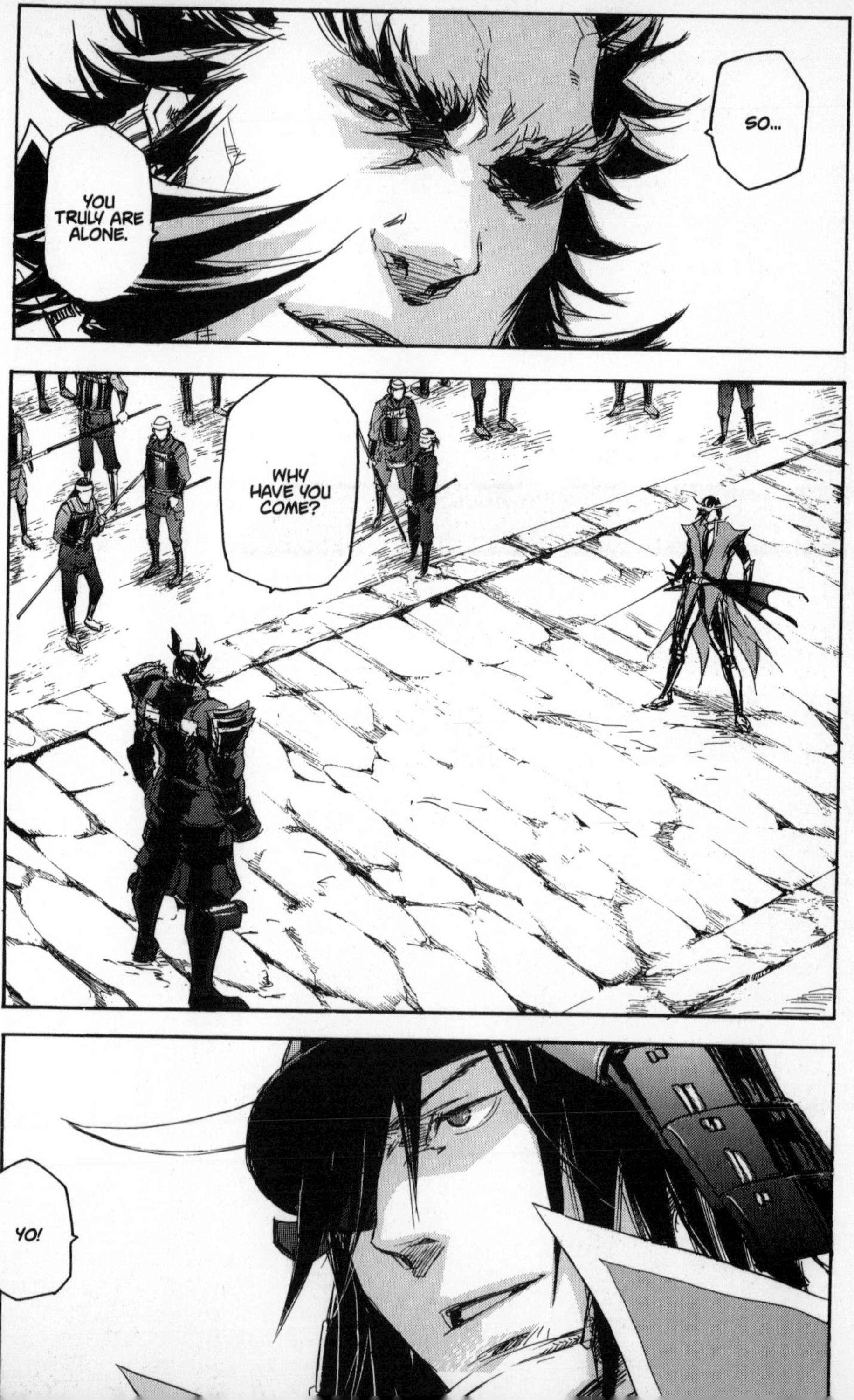
SO...
YOU TRULY ARE ALONE.
WHY HAVE YOU COME?
YO!

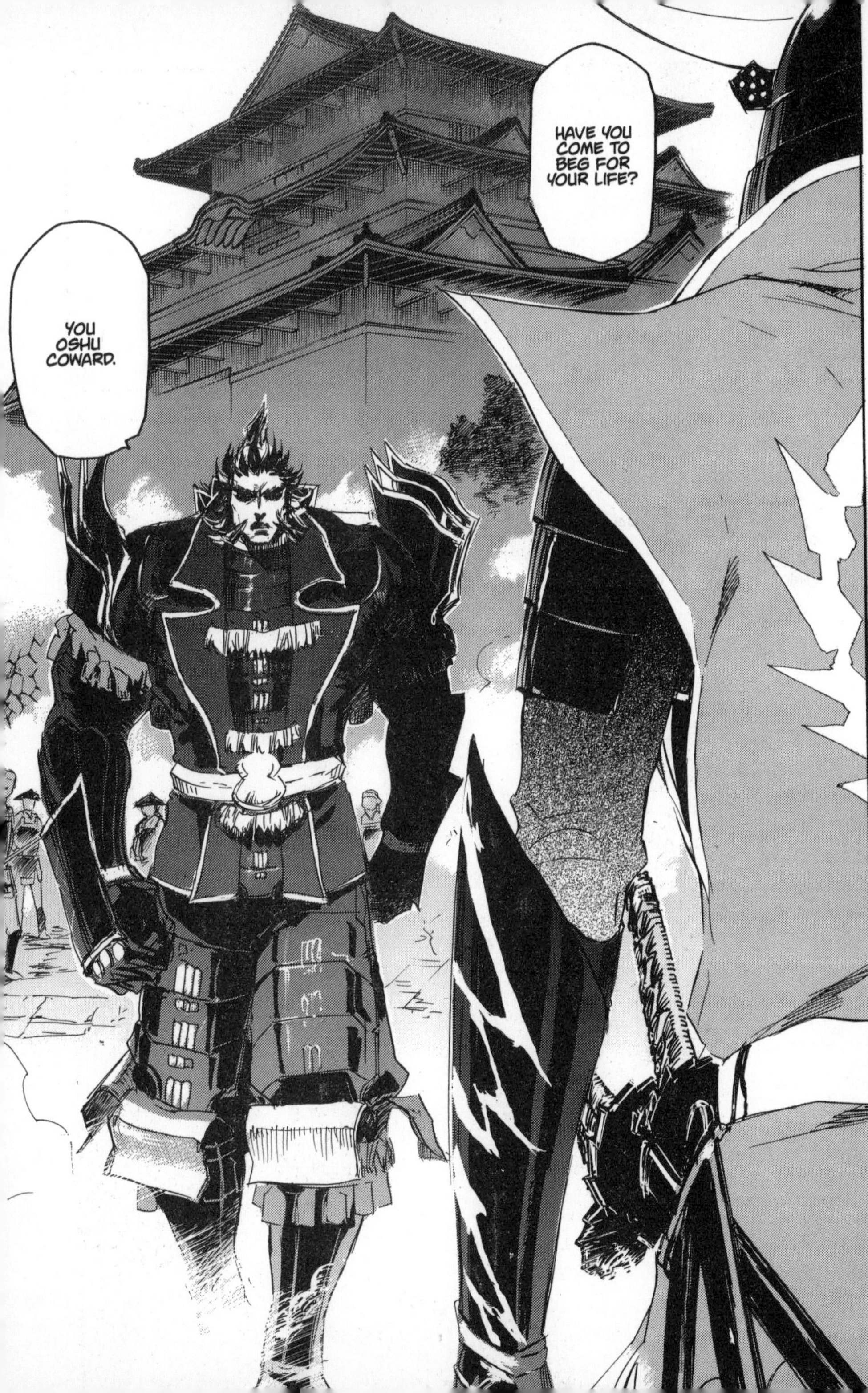
HAVE YOU COME TO BEG FOR YOUR LIFE?
YOU OSHU COWARD.

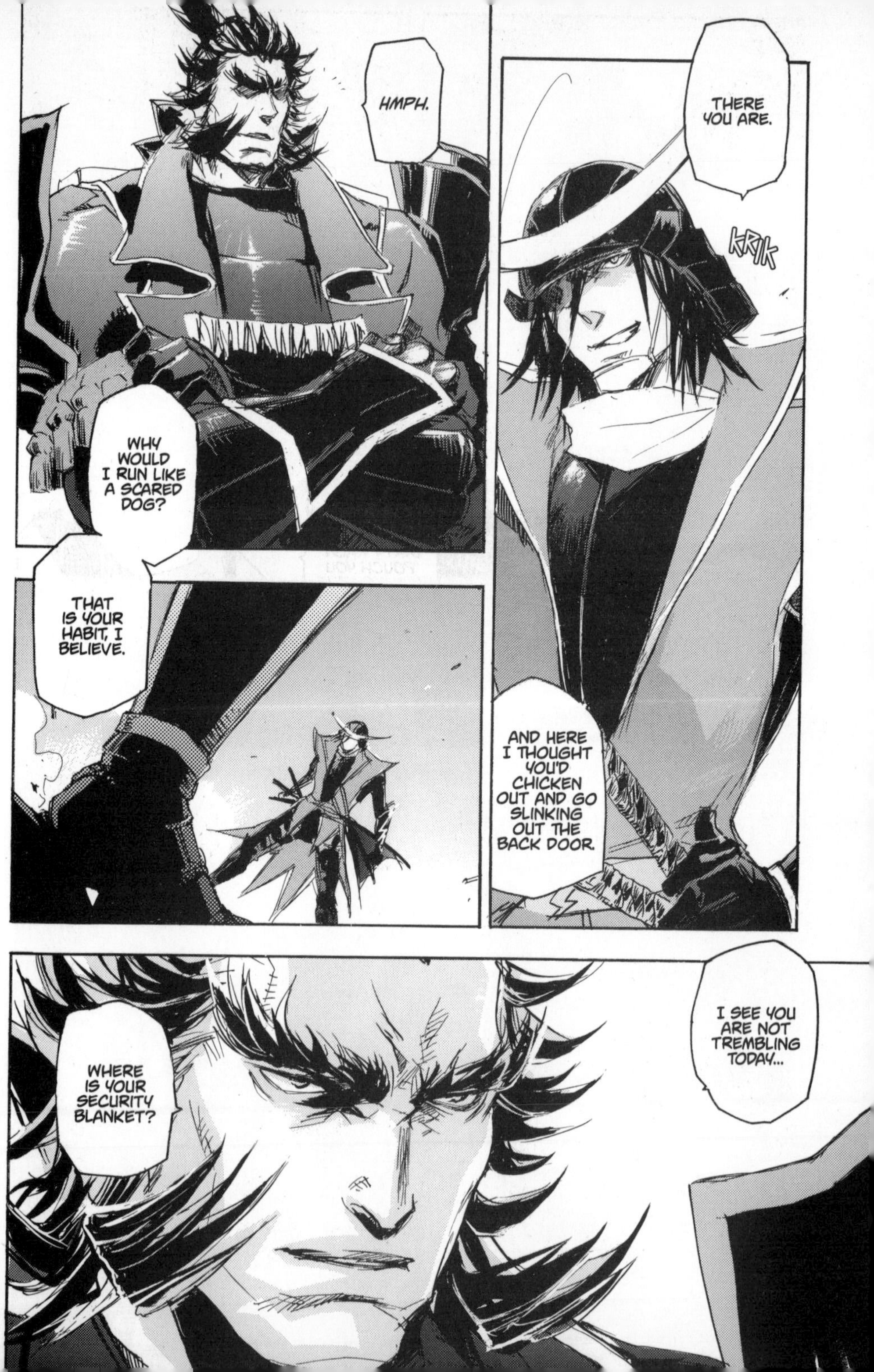
THERE YOU ARE.
KRIK
AND HERE I THOUGHT YOU'D CHICKEN OUT AND GO SLINKING OUT THE BACK DOOR.
HMPH.
WHY WOULD I RUN LIKE A SCARED DOG?
THAT IS YOUR HABIT, I BELIEVE.
I SEE YOU ARE NOT TREMBLING TODAY...
WHERE IS YOUR SECURITY BLANKET?

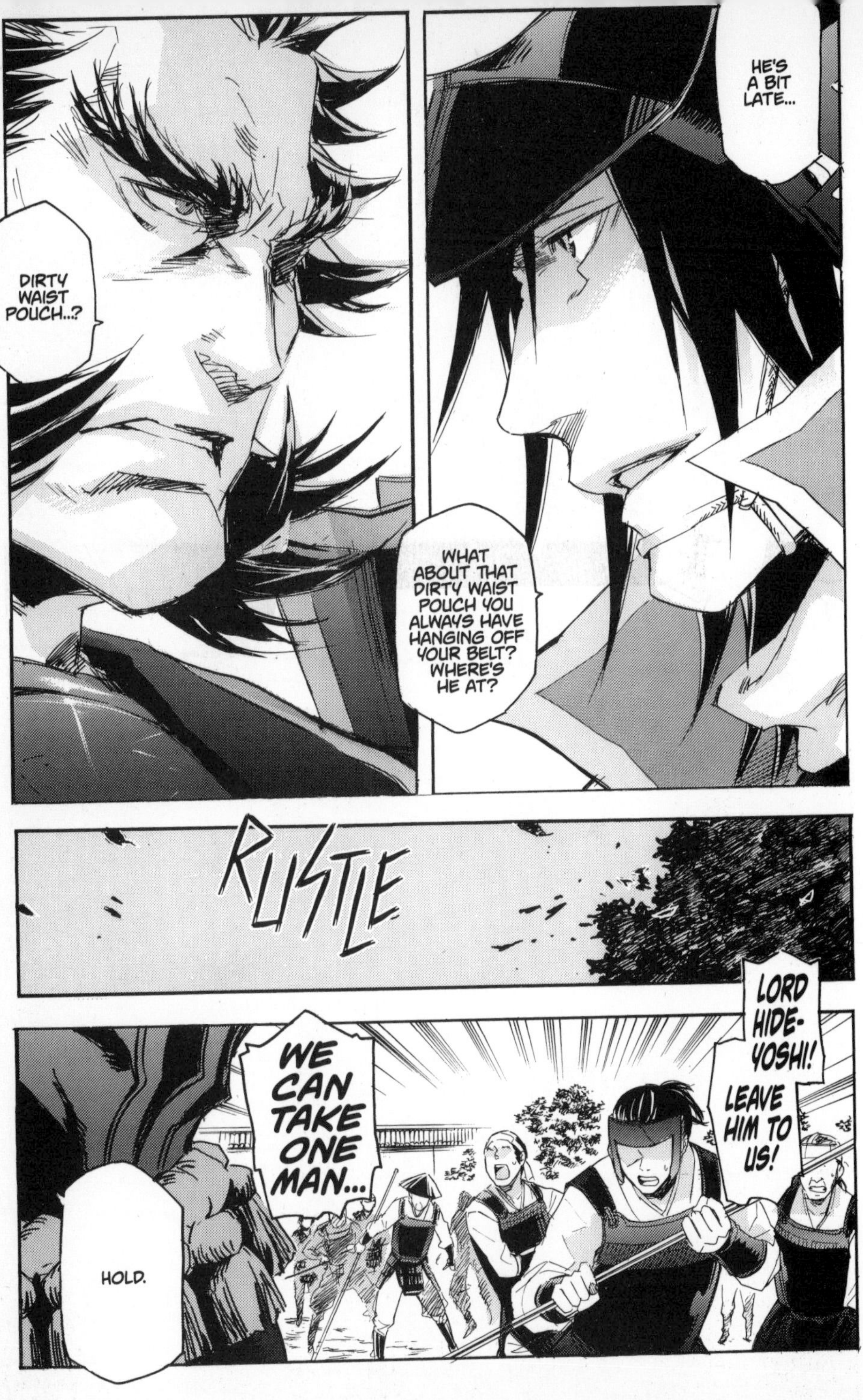
HE'S A BIT LATE...
WHAT ABOUT THAT DIRTY WAIST POUCH YOU ALWAYS HAVE HANGING OFF YOUR BELT? WHERE'S HE AT?
DIRTY WAIST POUCH..?
RUSTLE
LORD HIDE-YOSHI!
LEAVE HIM TO US!
WE CAN TAKE ONE MAN...
HOLD.

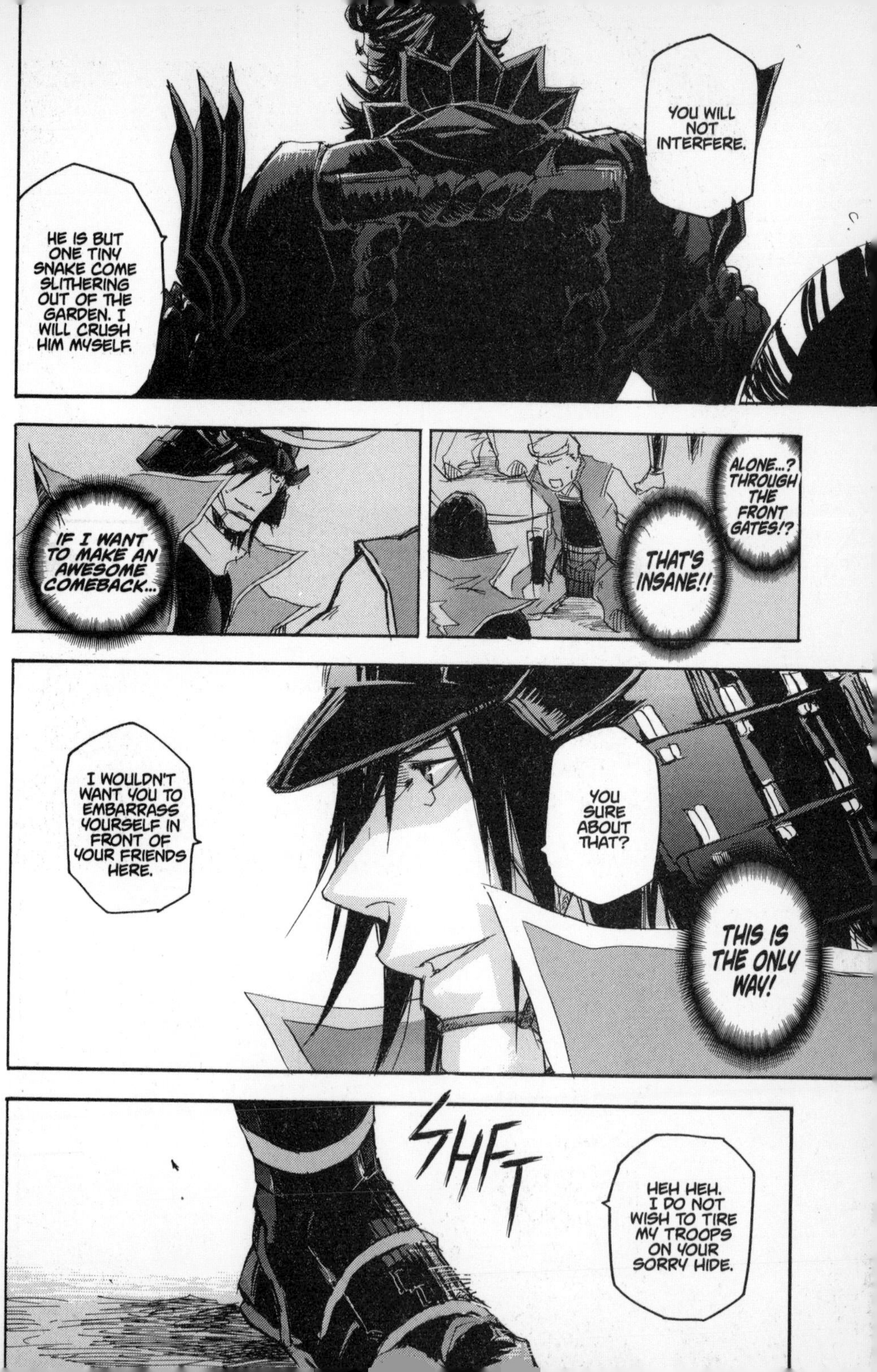
YOU WILL NOT INTERFERE.
HE IS BUT ONE TINY SNAKE COME SLITHERING OUT OF THE GARDEN. I WILL CRUSH HIM MYSELF.
ALONE...? THROUGH THE FRONT GATES!?
THAT'S INSANE!!
IF I WANT TO MAKE AN AWESOME COMEBACK...
YOU SURE ABOUT THAT?
THIS IS THE ONLY WAY!
I WOULDN'T WANT YOU TO EMBARRASS YOURSELF IN FRONT OF YOUR FRIENDS HERE.
SHFT
HEH HEH. I DO NOT WISH TO TIRE MY TROOPS ON YOUR SORRY HIDE.

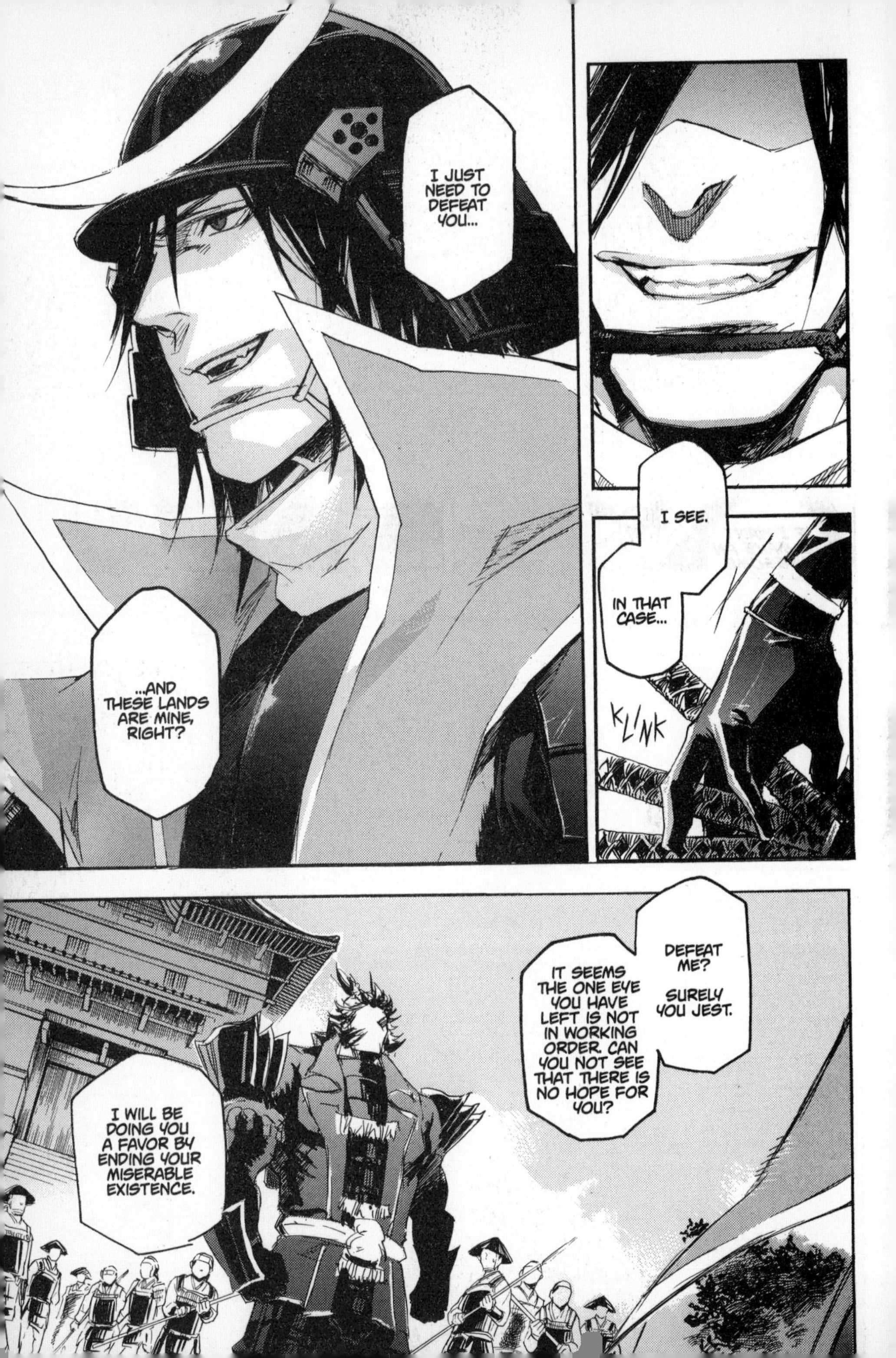
I SEE.
IN THAT CASE...
KLINK
I JUST NEED TO DEFEAT YOU...
...AND THESE LANDS ARE MINE, RIGHT?
DEFEAT ME? SURELY YOU JEST.
IT SEEMS THE ONE EYE YOU HAVE LEFT IS NOT IN WORKING ORDER. CAN YOU NOT SEE THAT THERE IS NO HOPE FOR YOU?
I WILL BE DOING YOU A FAVOR BY ENDING YOUR MISERABLE EXISTENCE.

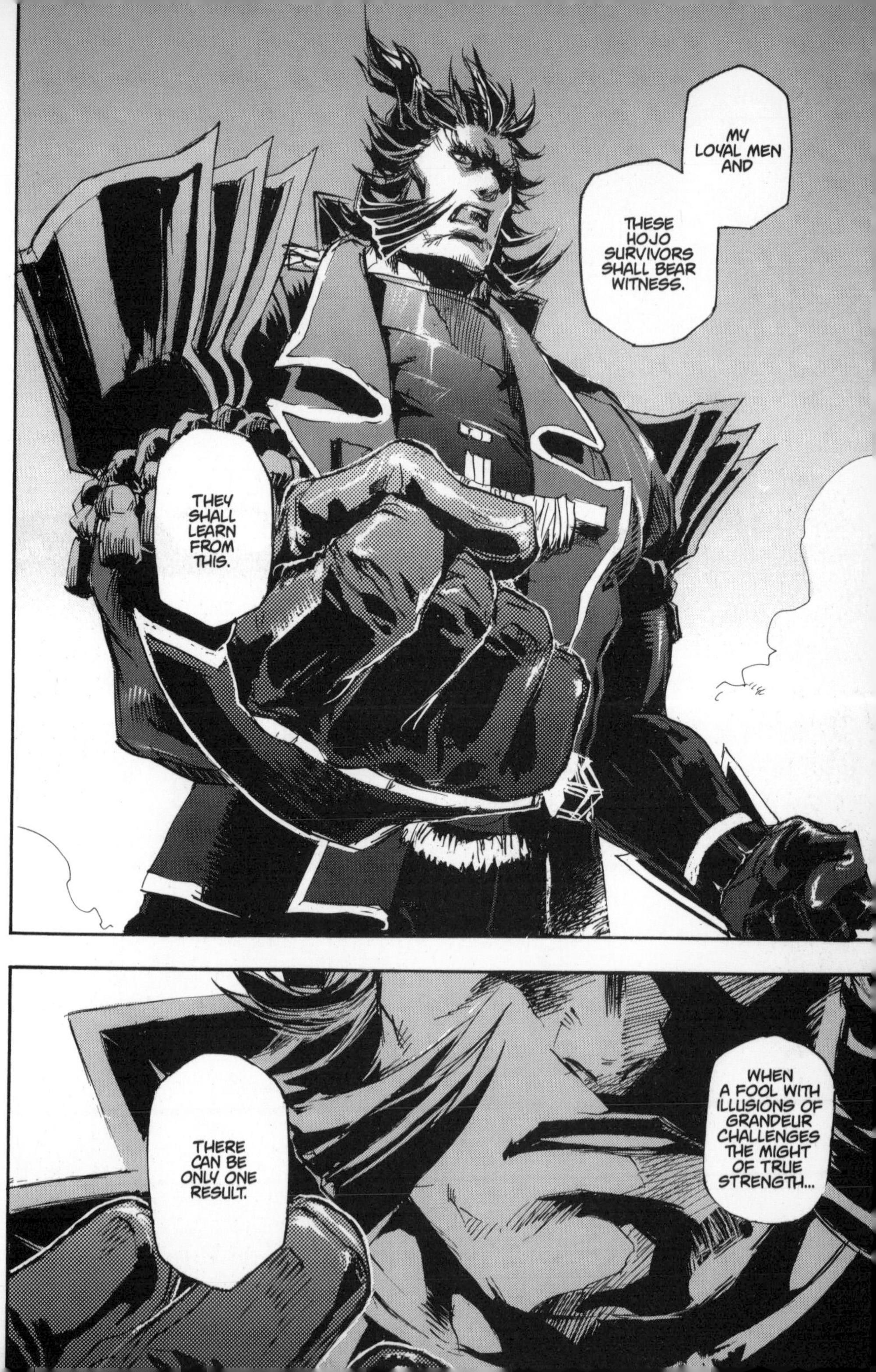
MY LOYAL MEN AND
THESE HOJO SURVIVORS SHALL BEAR WITNESS.
THEY SHALL LEARN FROM THIS.
WHEN A FOOL WITH ILLUSIONS OF GRANDEUR CHALLENGES THE MIGHT OF TRUE STRENGTH...
THERE CAN BE ONLY ONE RESULT.

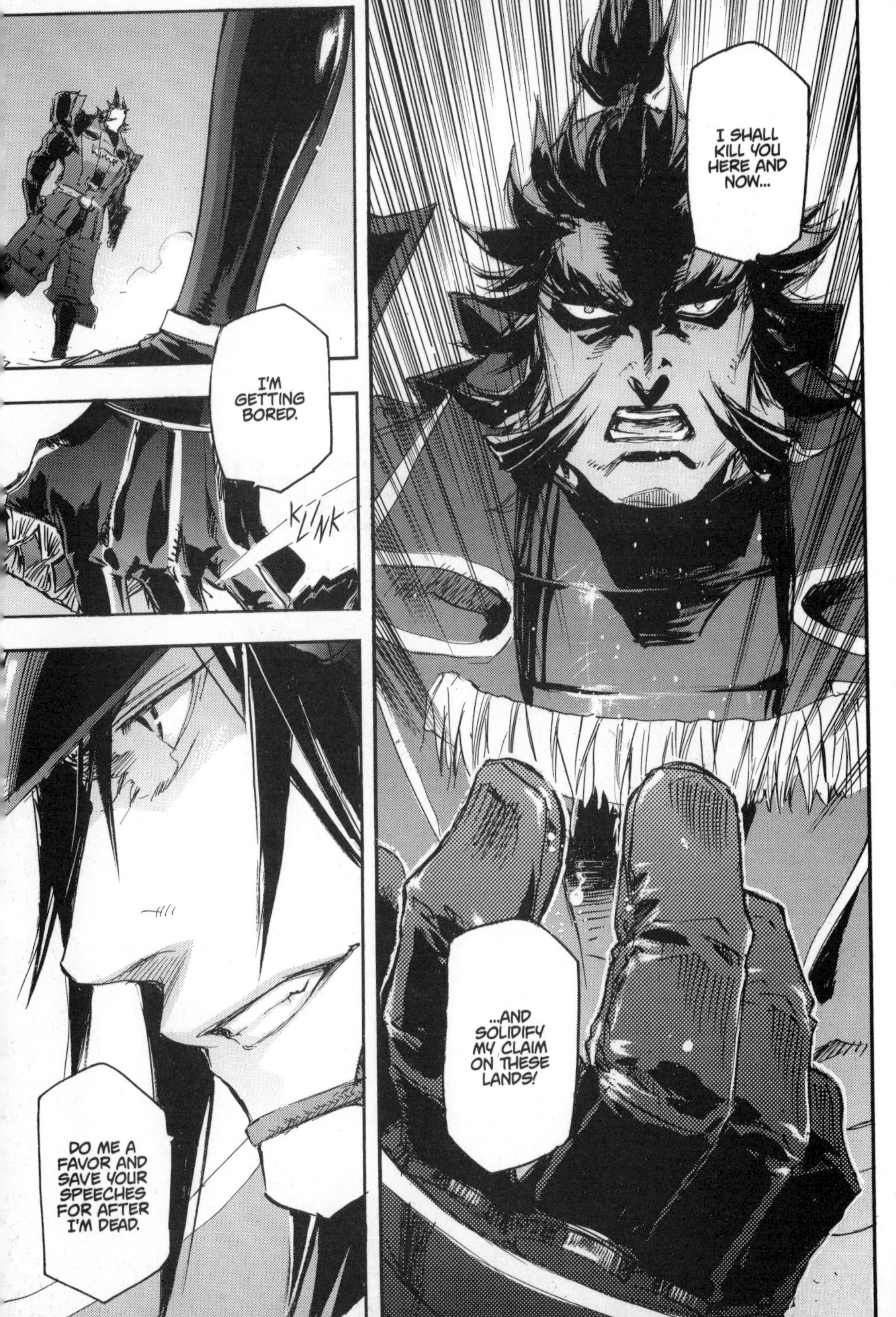
I SHALL KILL YOU HERE AND NOW...
...AND SOLIDIFY MY CLAIM ON THESE LANDS!
I'M GETTING BORED.
KLINK
DO ME A FAVOR AND SAVE YOUR SPEECHES FOR AFTER I'M DEAD.

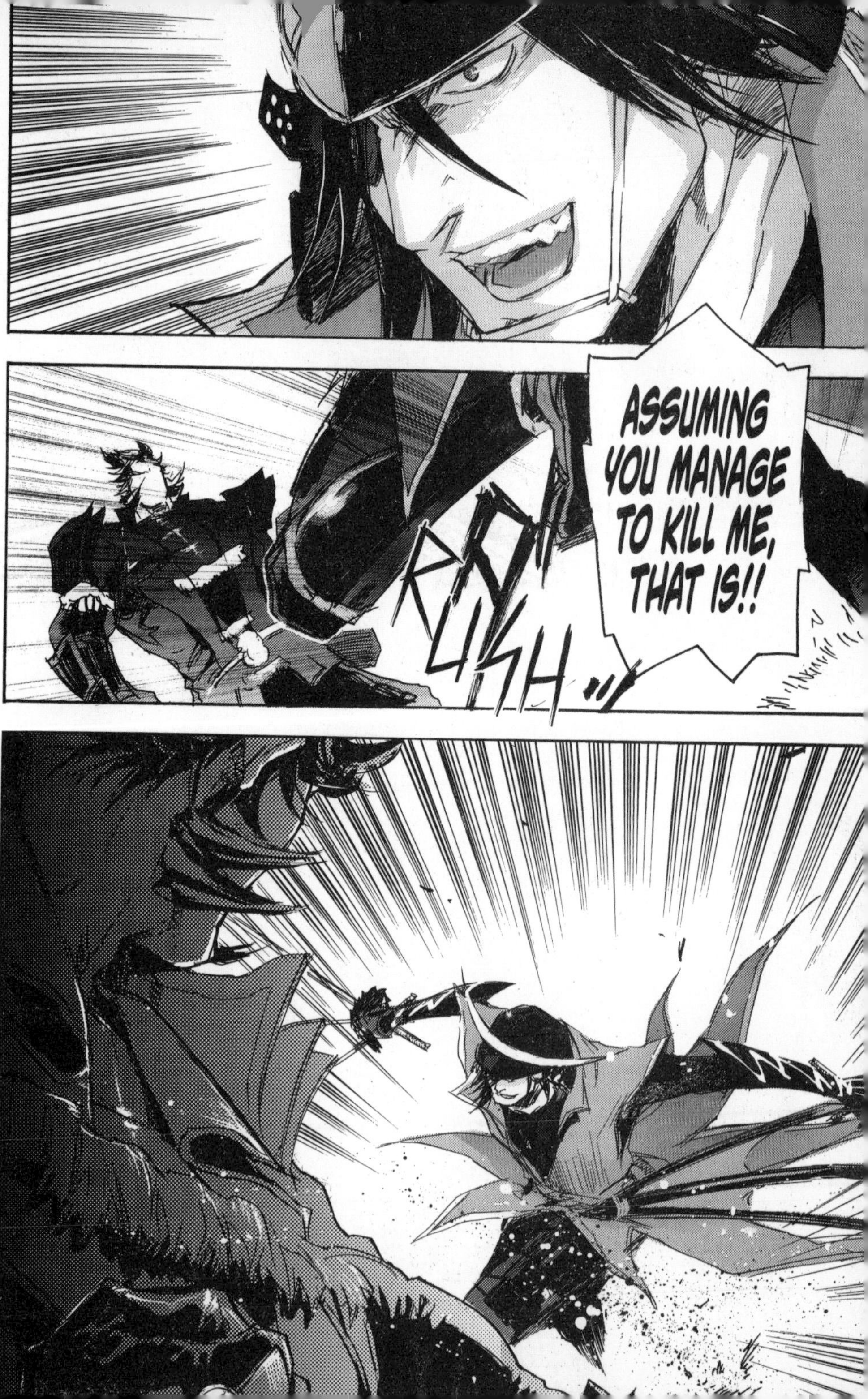
ASSUMING YOU MANAGE TO KILL ME, THAT IS!!
RRRUSH

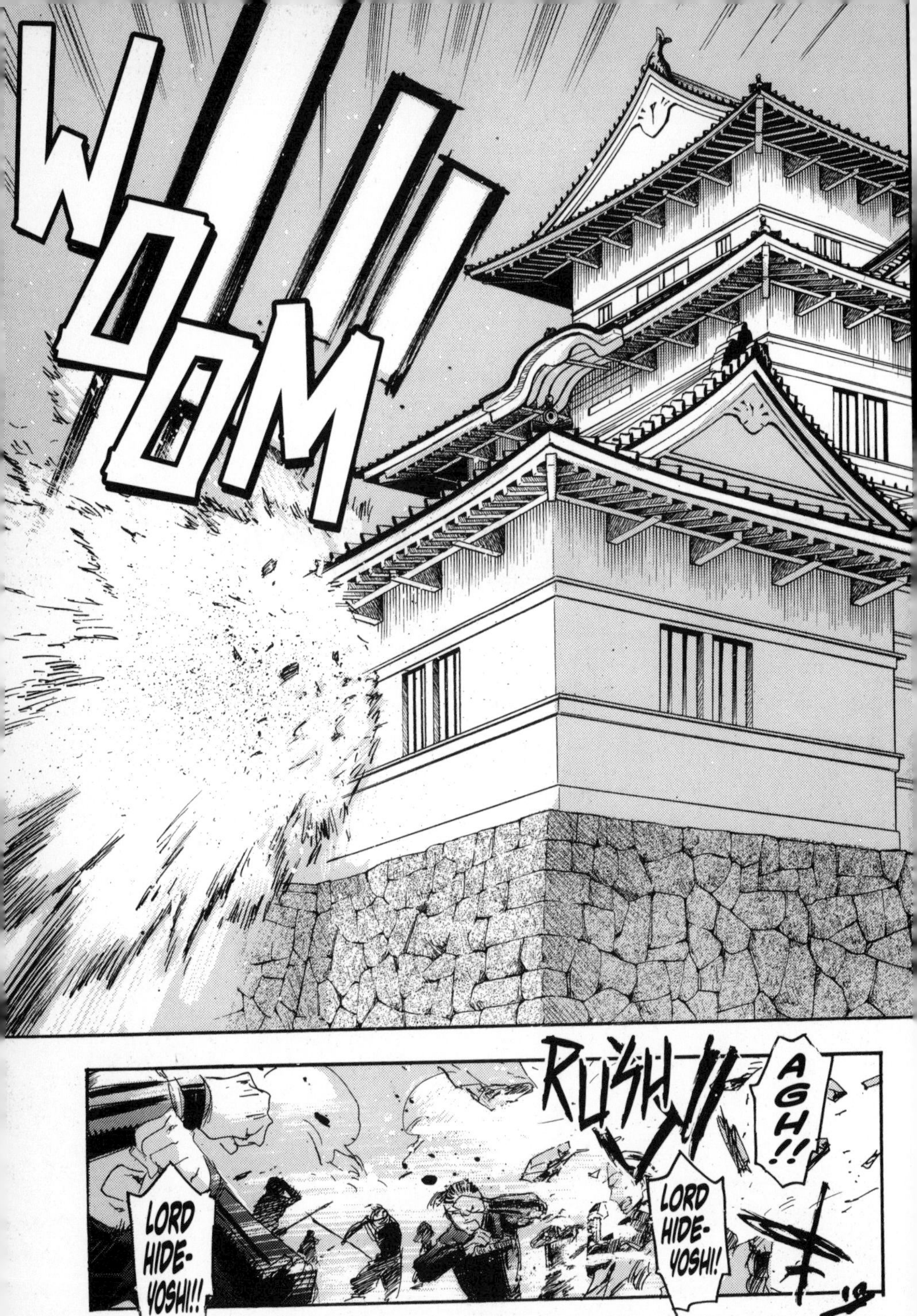
WOOM
AGH!!
RUSH!!
LORD HIDE-YOSHI!
LORD HIDE-YOSHI!!

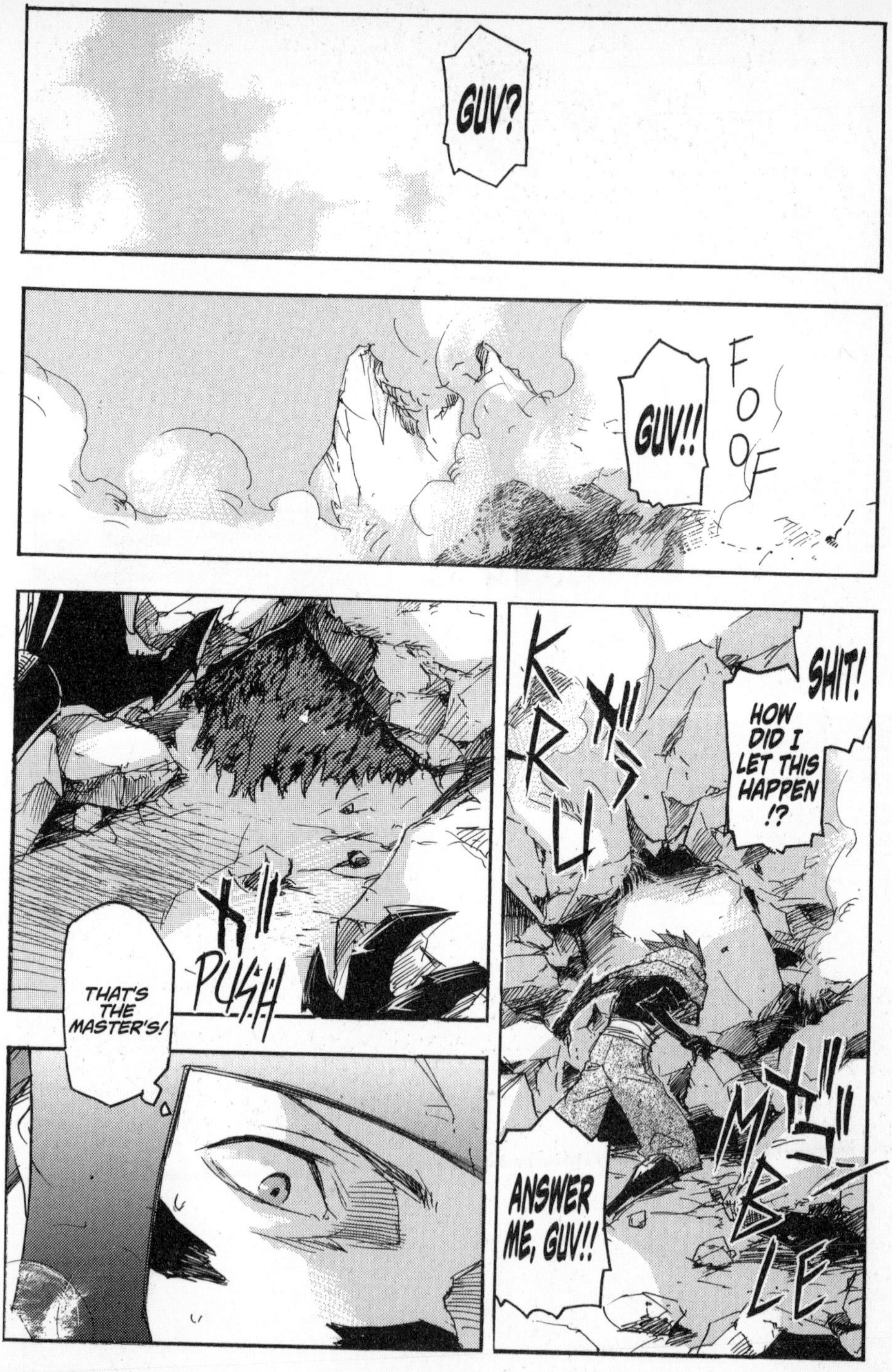
GUV?
GUV!!
FOOF
KRU
SHIT!
HOW DID I LET THIS HAPPEN!?
ANSWER ME, GUV!!
MBLE
PUSH
THAT'S THE MASTER'S!

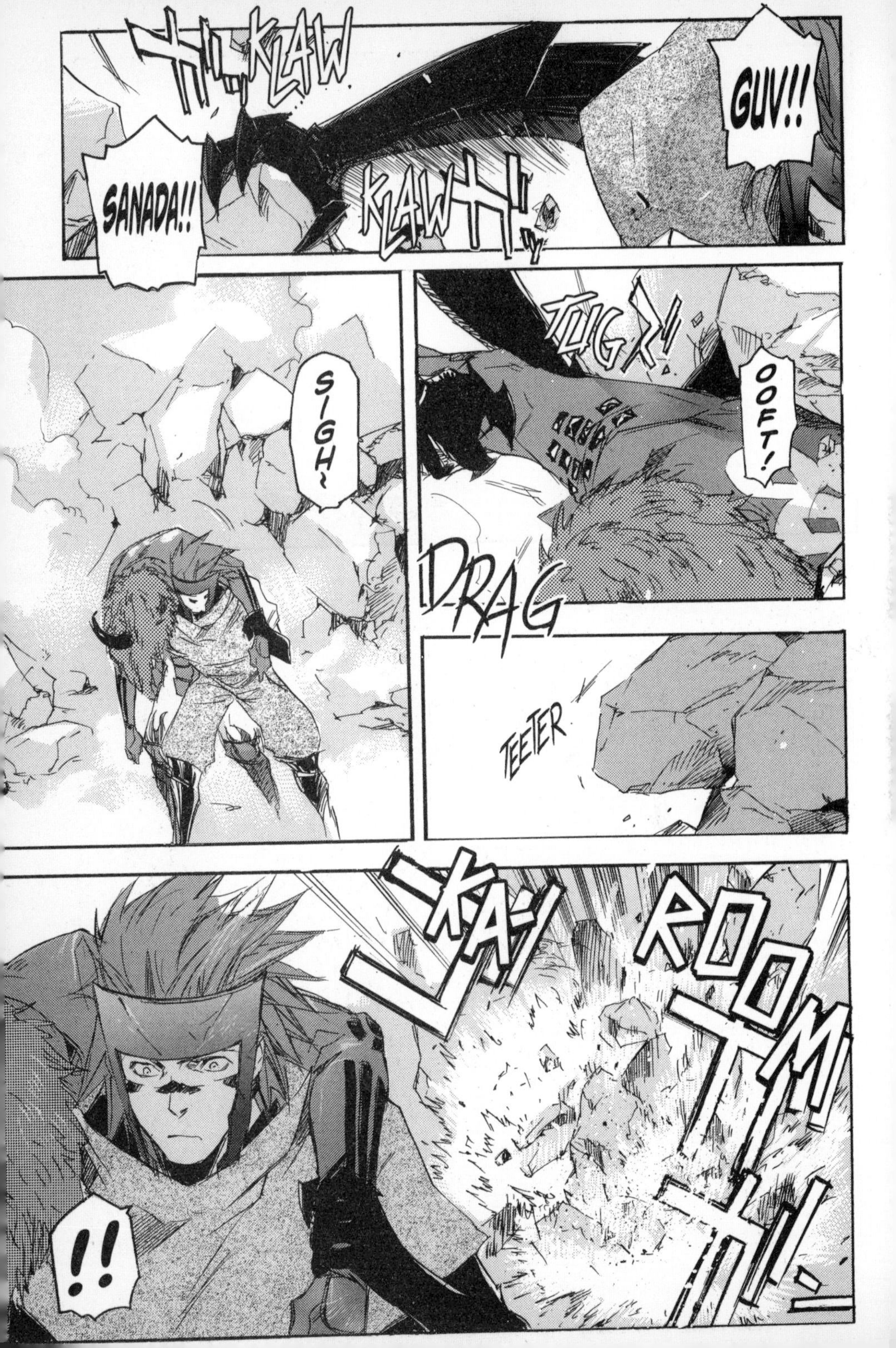
GUV!!
KLAW
KLAW
SANADA!!
TUG
OOFT!
DRAG
TEETER
SIGH~
KA-Y
ROOM
!!

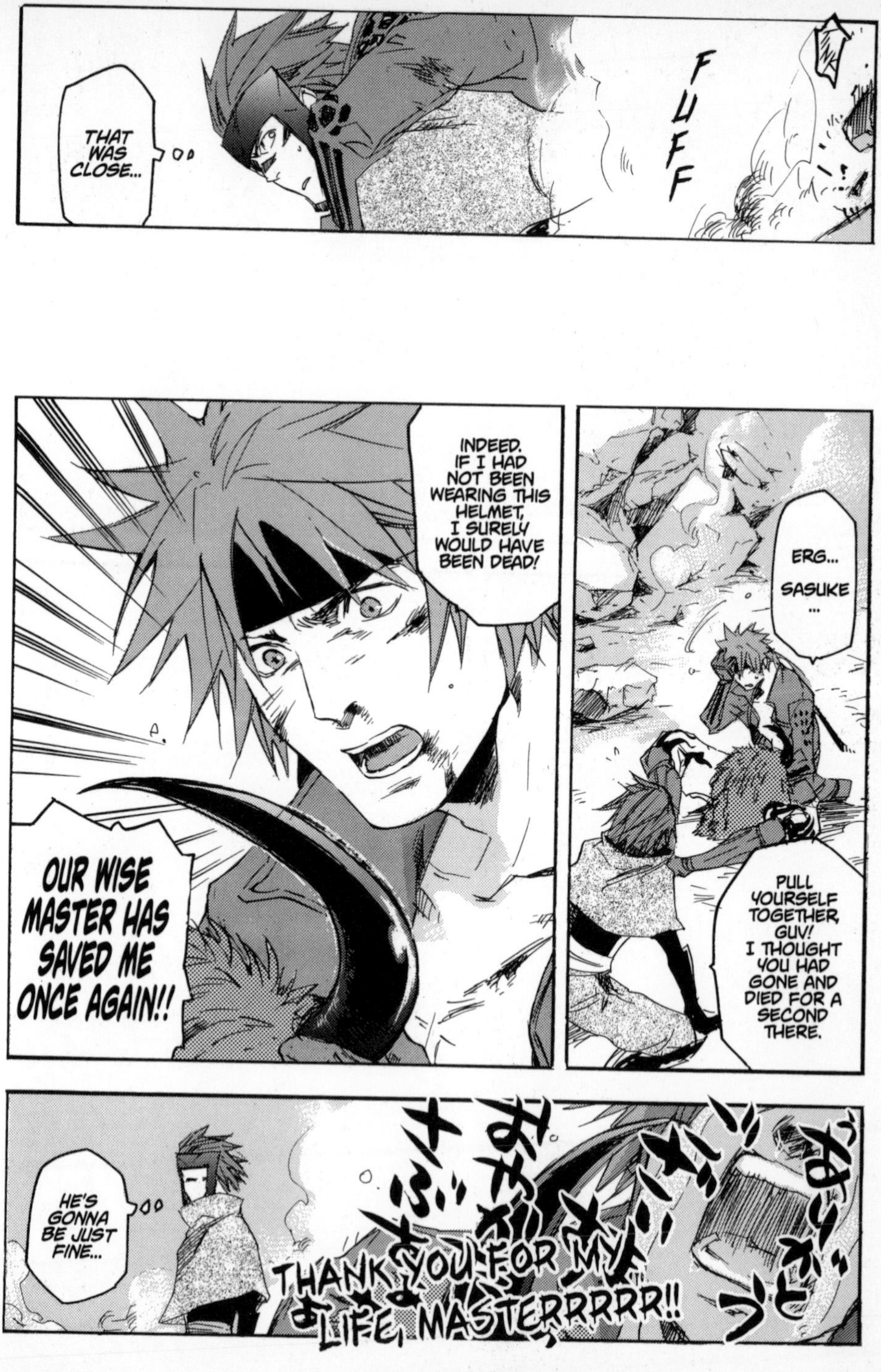
FUFF
THAT WAS CLOSE...
ERG... SASUKE ...
PULL YOURSELF TOGETHER, GUV! I THOUGHT YOU HAD GONE AND DIED FOR A SECOND THERE.
INDEED. IF I HAD NOT BEEN WEARING THIS HELMET, I SURELY WOULD HAVE BEEN DEAD!
OUR WISE MASTER HAS SAVED ME ONCE AGAIN!!
THANK YOU FOR MY LIFE, MASTERRRRR!!
HE'S GONNA BE JUST FINE...

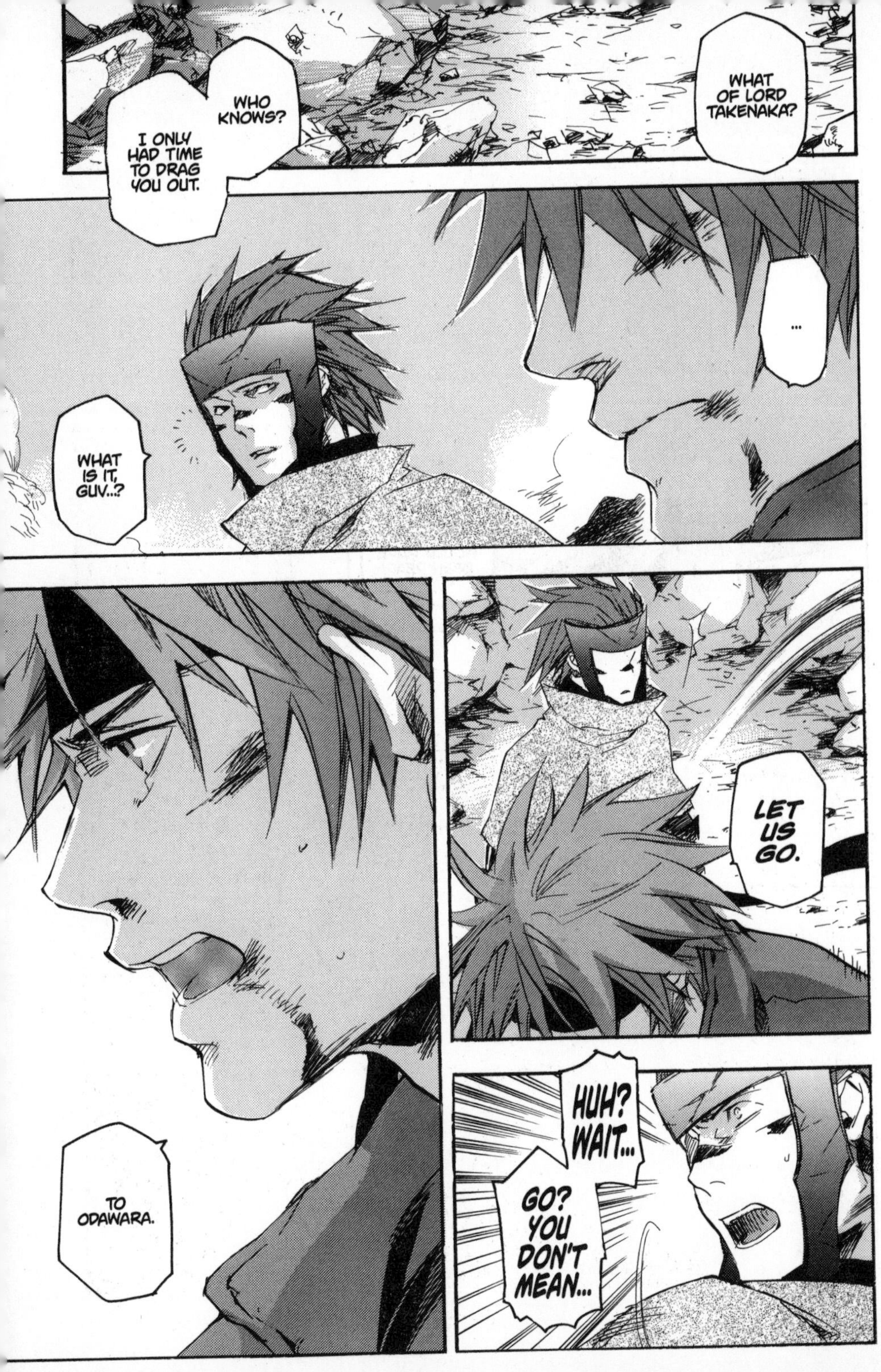
WHAT OF LORD TAKENAKA?
WHO KNOWS?
I ONLY HAD TIME TO DRAG YOU OUT.
...
WHAT IS IT, GUV...?
LET US GO.
HUH? WAIT...
GO? YOU DON'T MEAN...
TO ODAWARA.

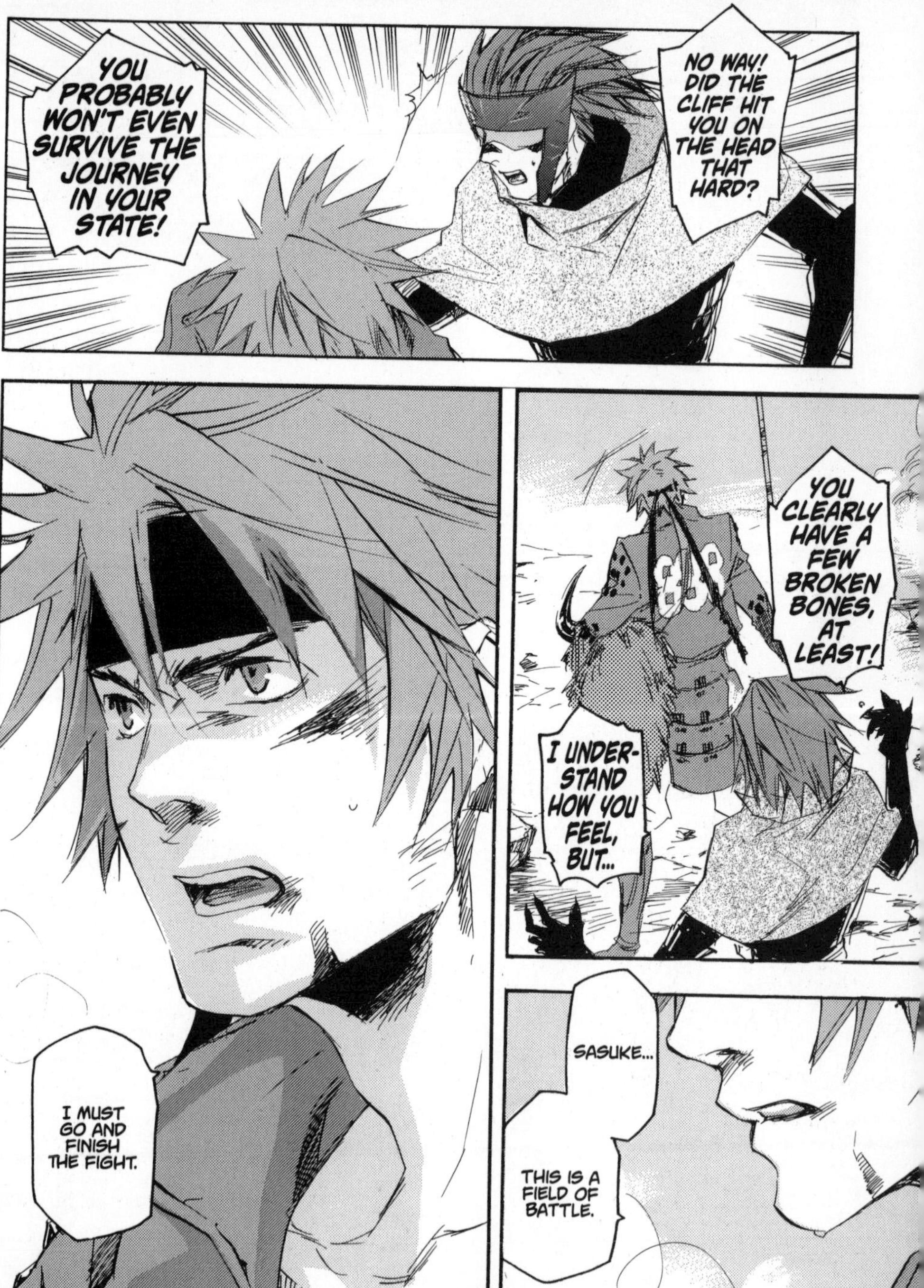
NO WAY! DID THE CLIFF HIT YOU ON THE HEAD THAT HARD?
YOU PROBABLY WON'T EVEN SURVIVE THE JOURNEY IN YOUR STATE!
YOU CLEARLY HAVE A FEW BROKEN BONES, AT LEAST!
I UNDER-STAND HOW YOU FEEL, BUT...
SASUKE...
THIS IS A FIELD OF BATTLE.
I MUST GO AND FINISH THE FIGHT.

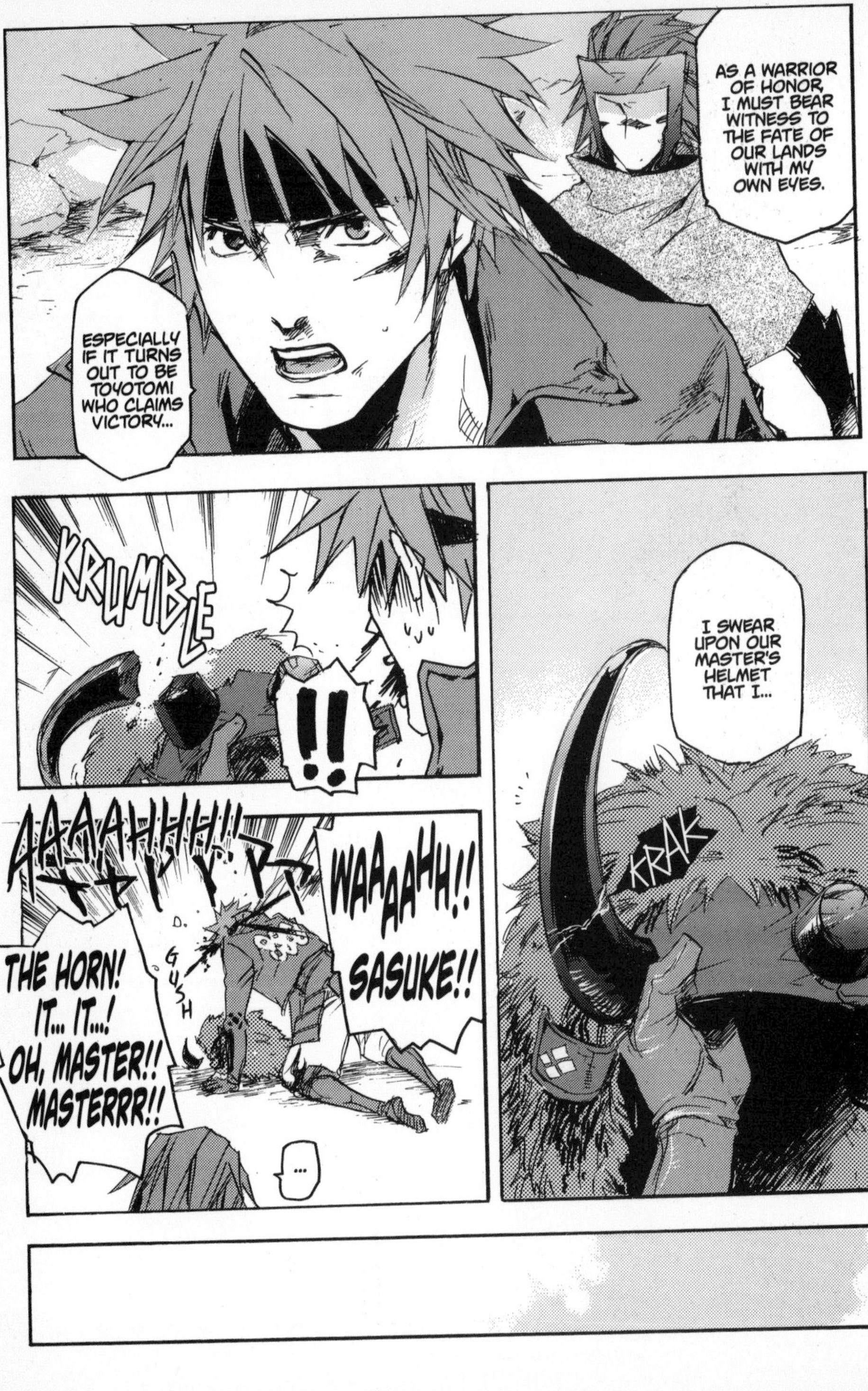

AS A WARRIOR OF HONOR, I MUST BEAR WITNESS TO THE FATE OF OUR LANDS WITH MY OWN EYES.
ESPECIALLY IF IT TURNS OUT TO BE TOYOTOMI WHO CLAIMS VICTORY...
I SWEAR UPON OUR MASTER'S HELMET THAT I...
KRAK
KRUMBLE
!!
WAAAAHH!!
SASUKE!!
AAAAHHH!!
GUSH
THE HORN! IT... IT...! OH, MASTER!! MASTERRR!!
...

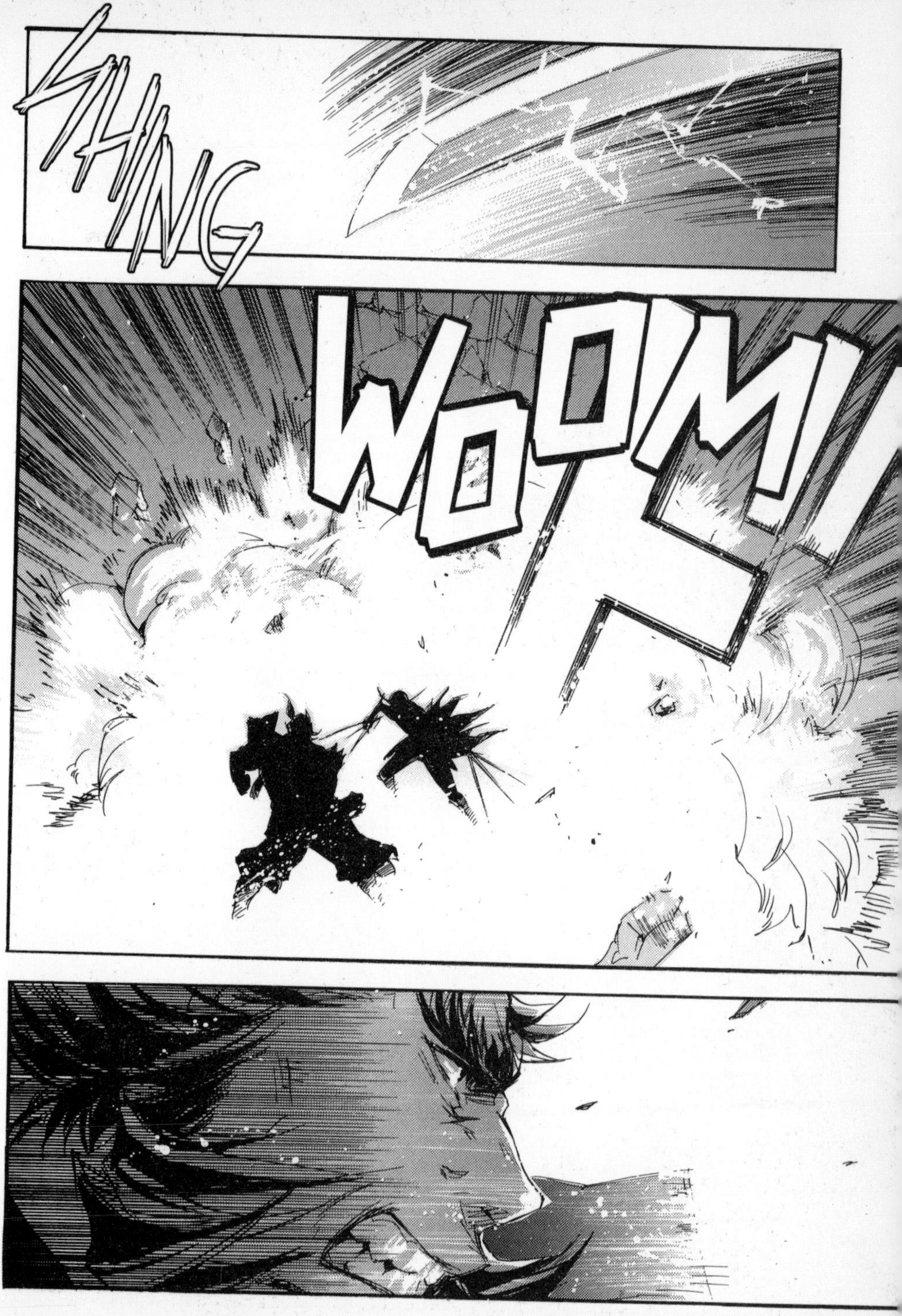

SHING
WOOM!

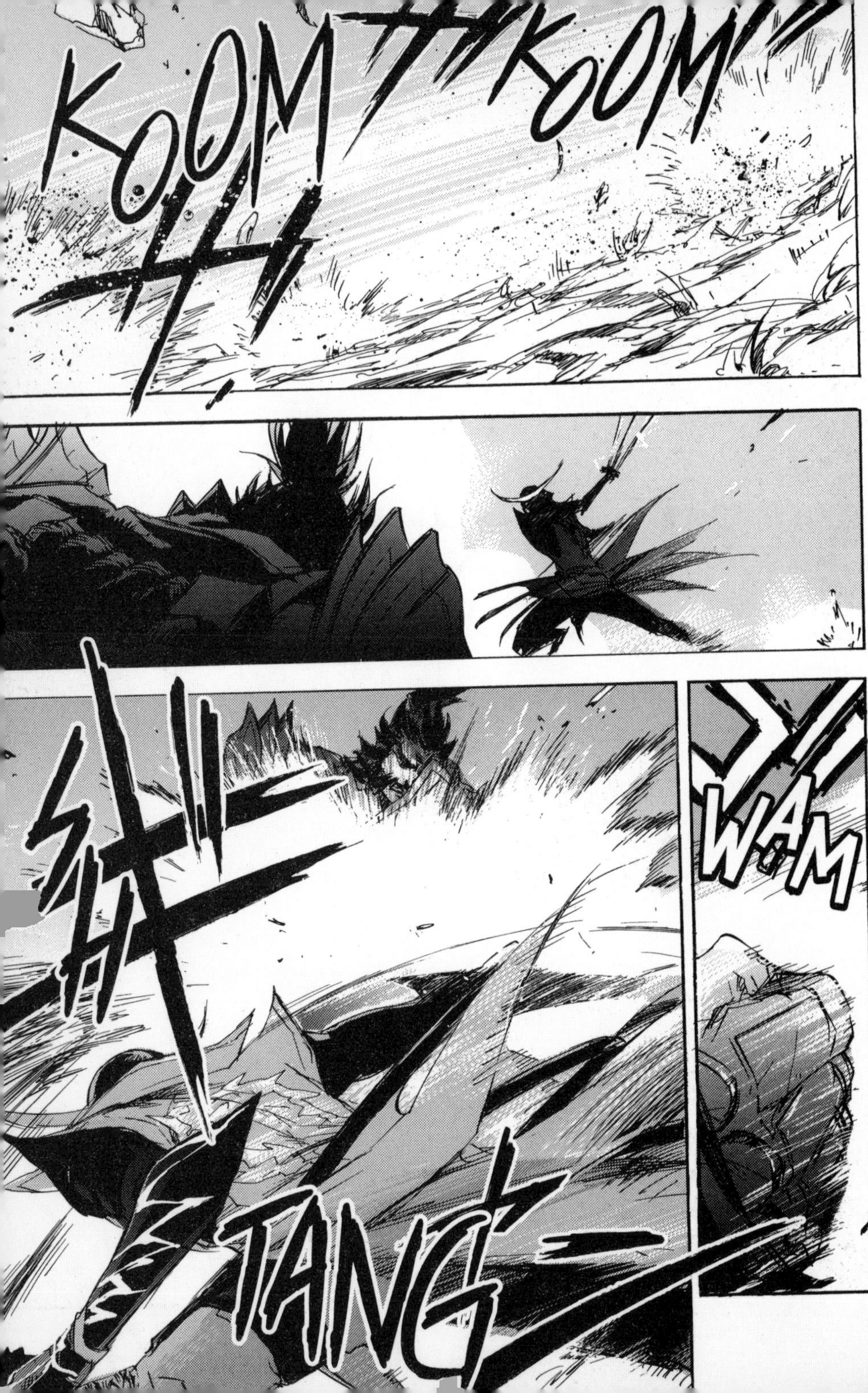
KOOM
KOOM
WAM
SHH
TANG

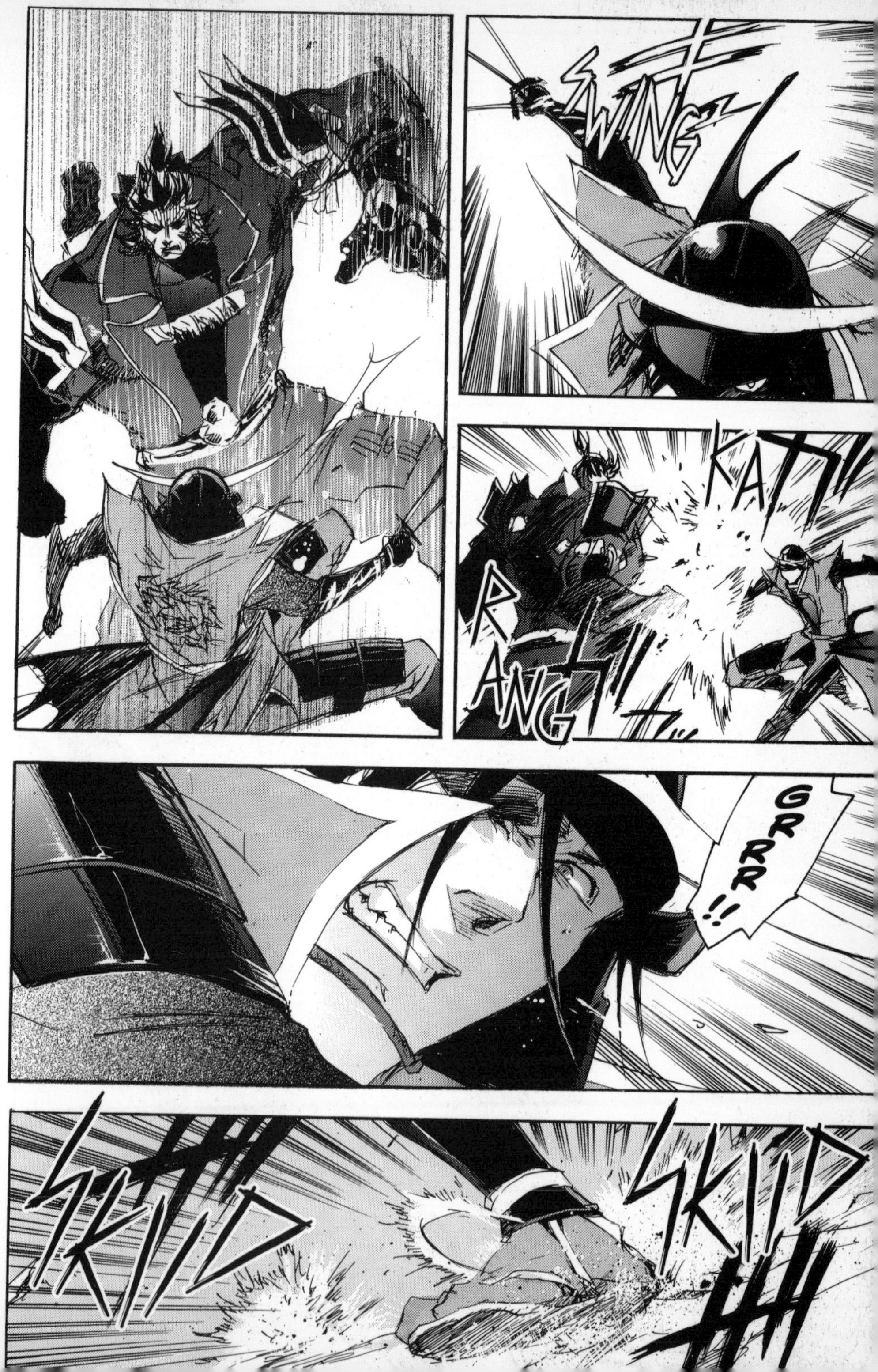
SWING
KA-RANG
GRRR!!
SKID
SKRID

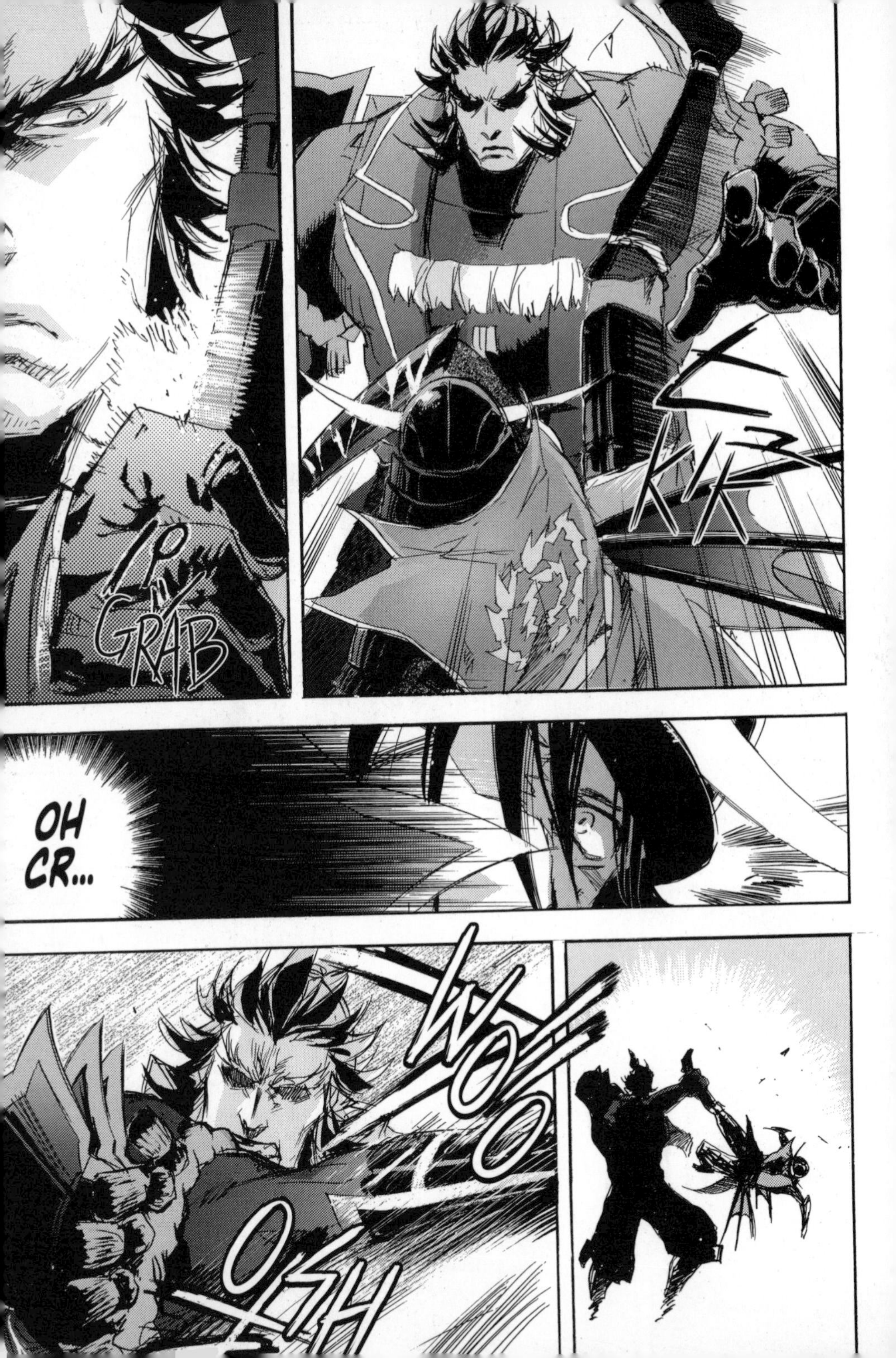
KLIK
GRAB
OH CR...
WOOOSH

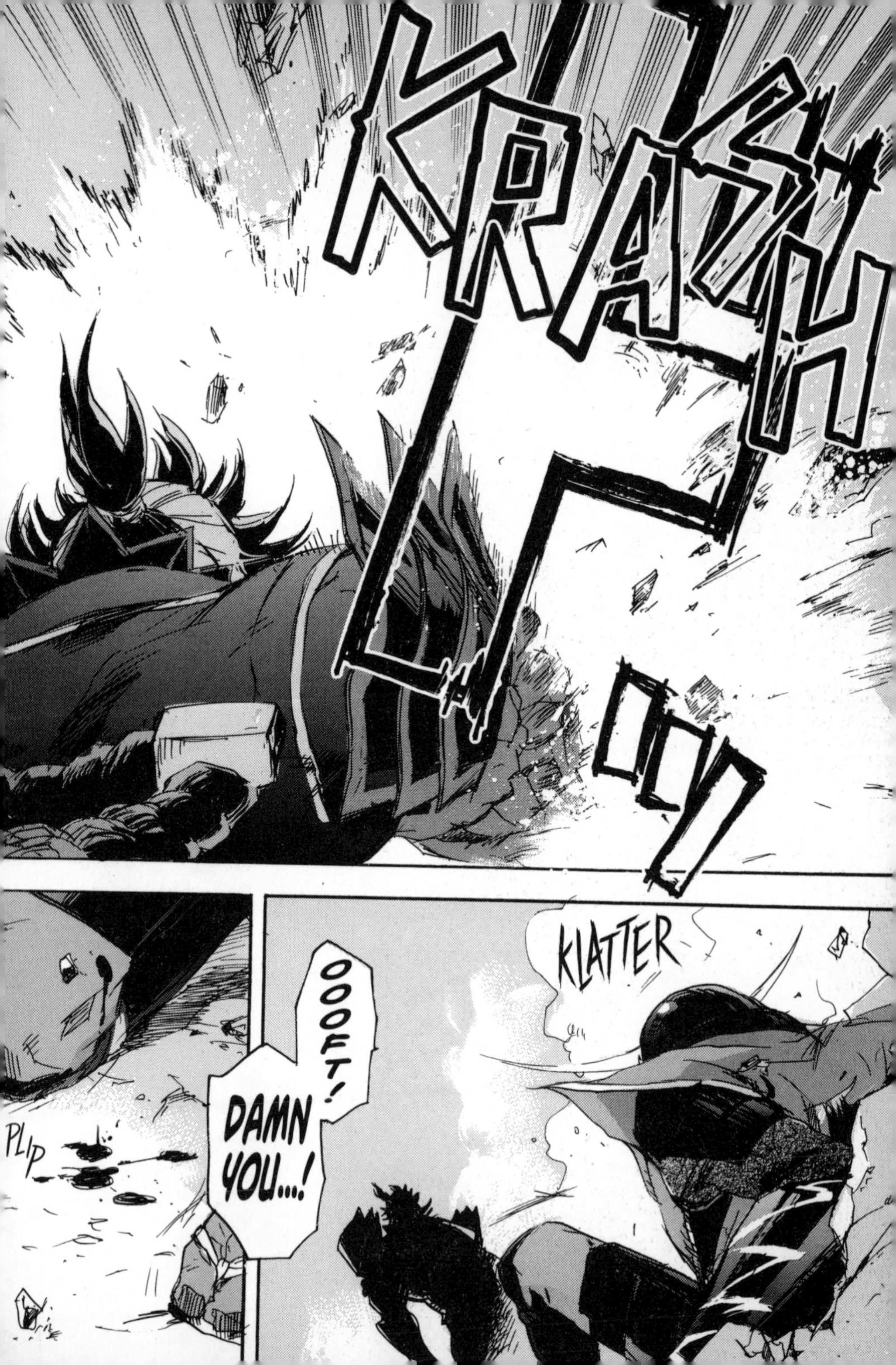
KRASH
KLATTER
OOOOFT!
DAMN YOU...!
PLIP

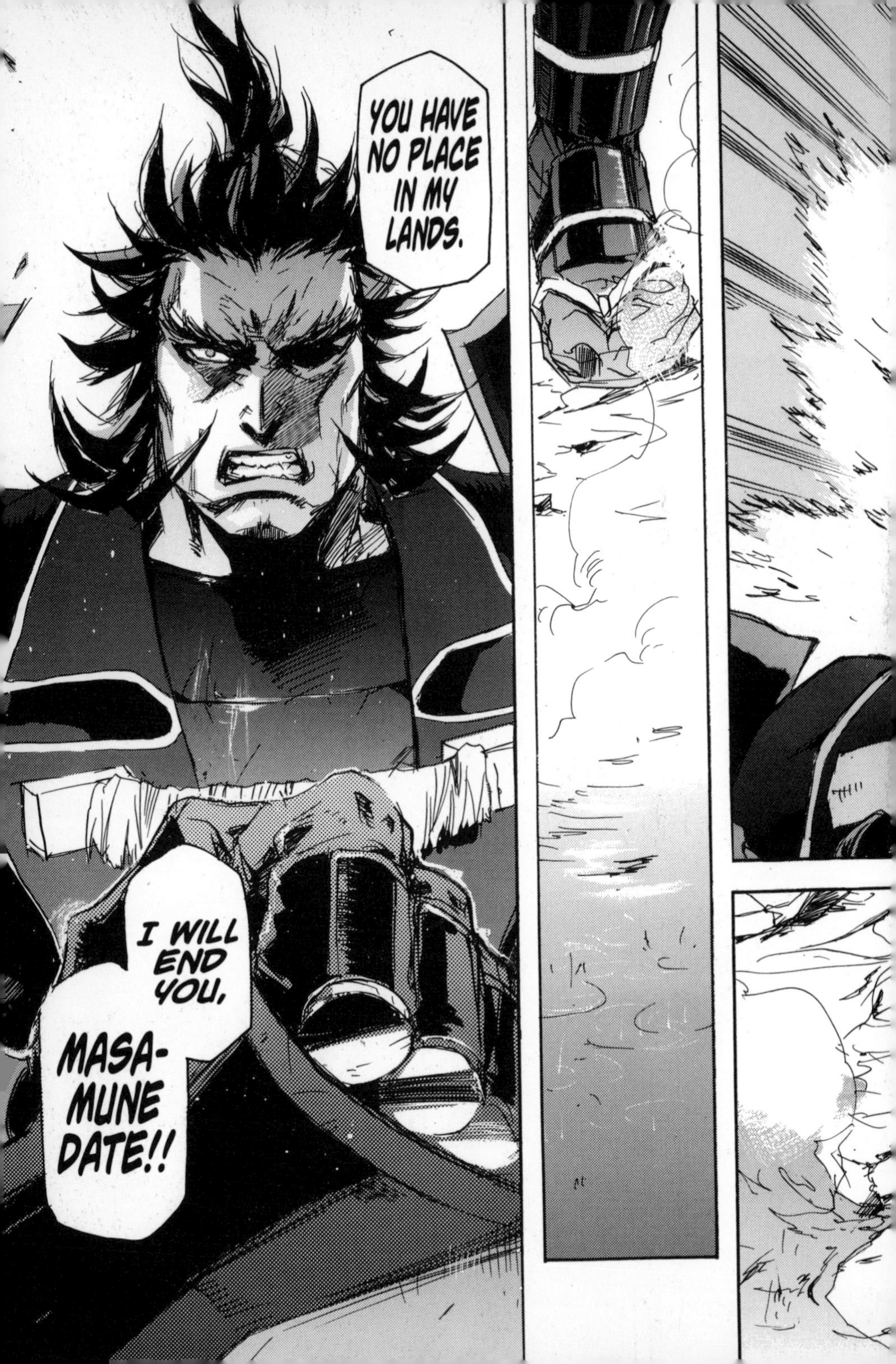
YOU HAVE NO PLACE IN MY LANDS.
I WILL END YOU,
MASA-MUNE DATE!!

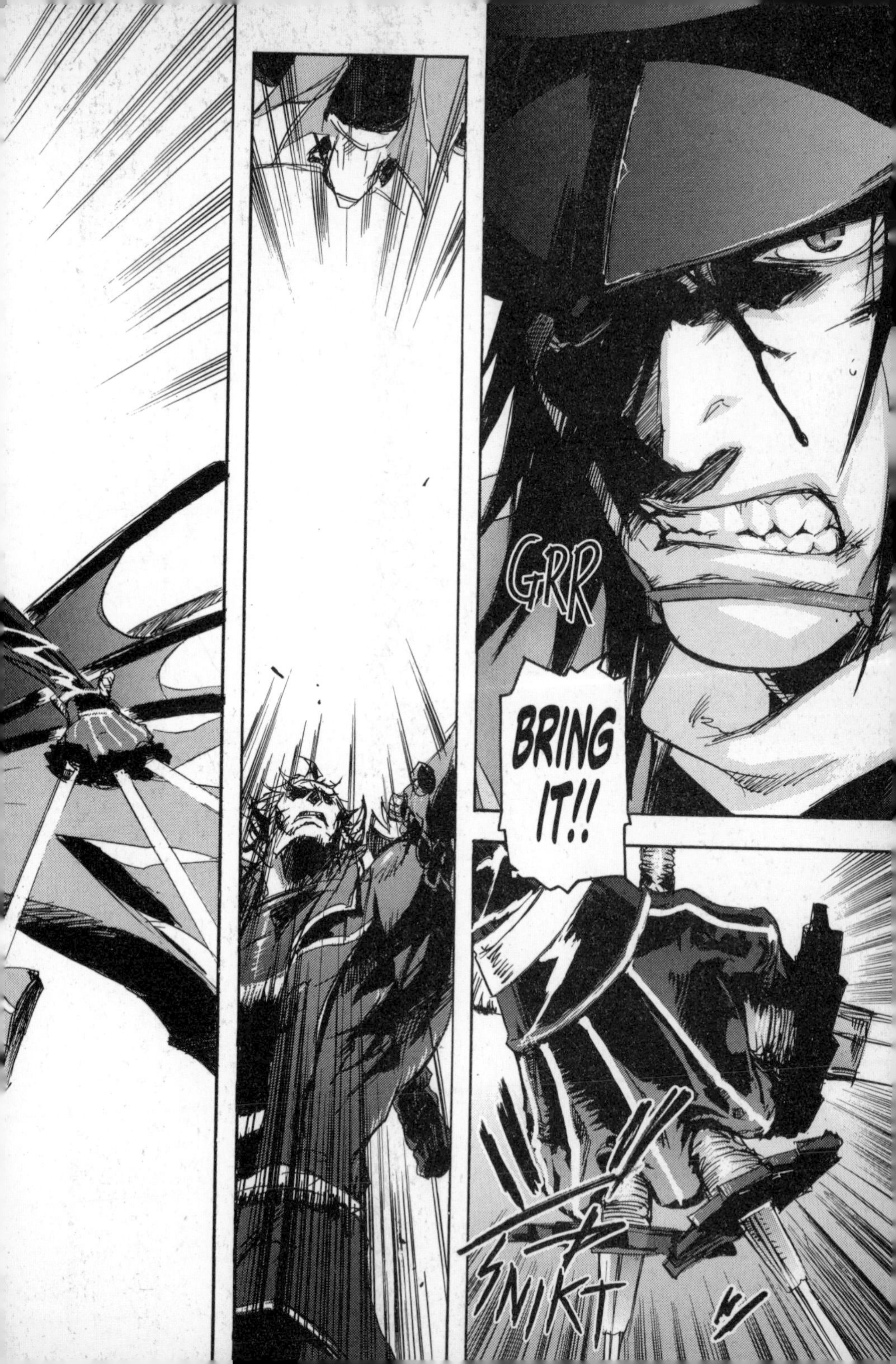
GRR
BRING IT!!
SNIKT

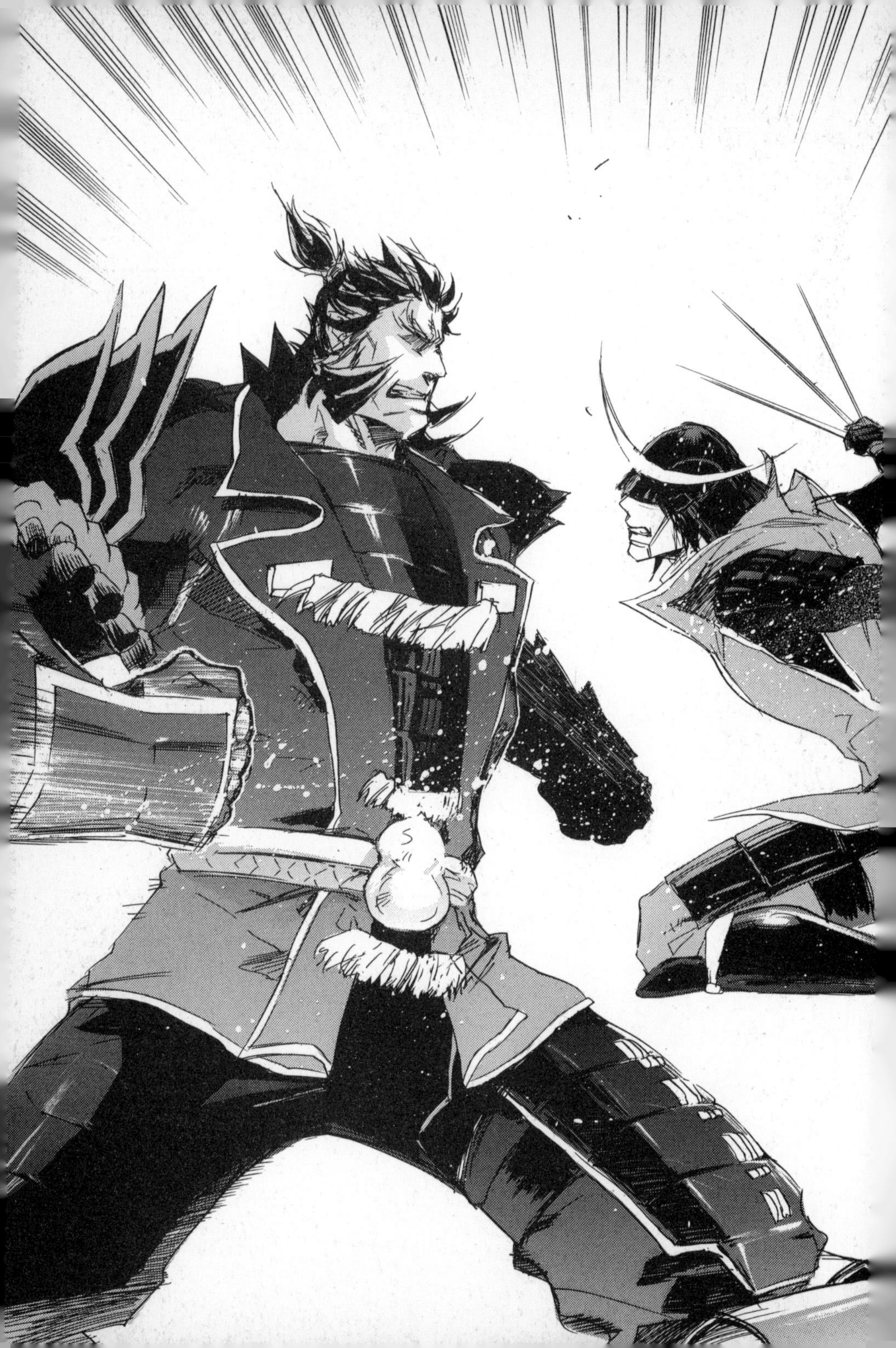

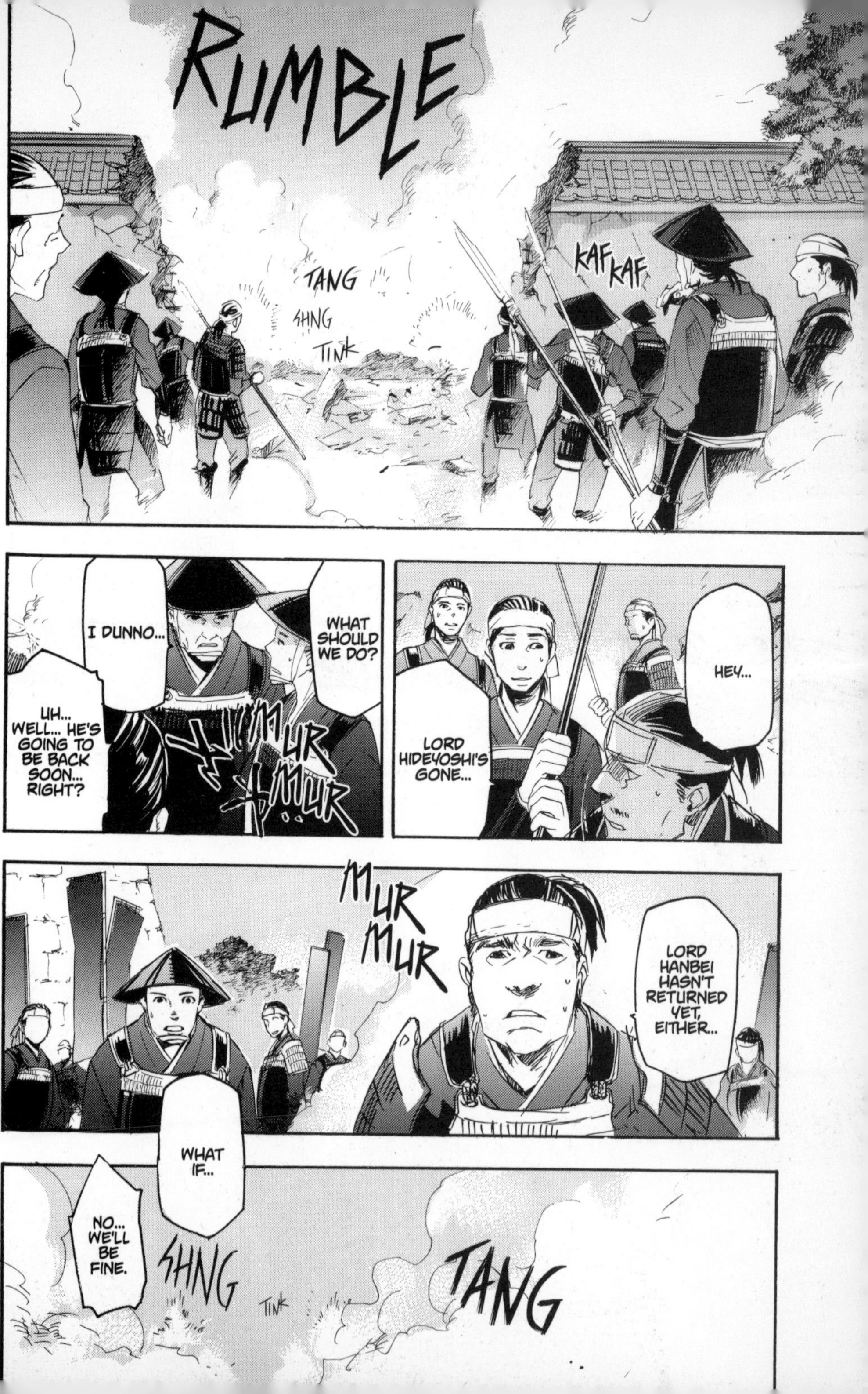
RUMBLE
KAF KAF
TANG
SHNG
TINK
HEY...
LORD HIDEYOSHI'S GONE...
WHAT SHOULD WE DO?
I DUNNO...
MUR MUR
UH... WELL... HE'S GOING TO BE BACK SOON... RIGHT?
LORD HANBEI HASN'T RETURNED YET, EITHER...
MUR MUR
WHAT IF...
NO... WE'LL BE FINE.
TANG
TINK
SHNG

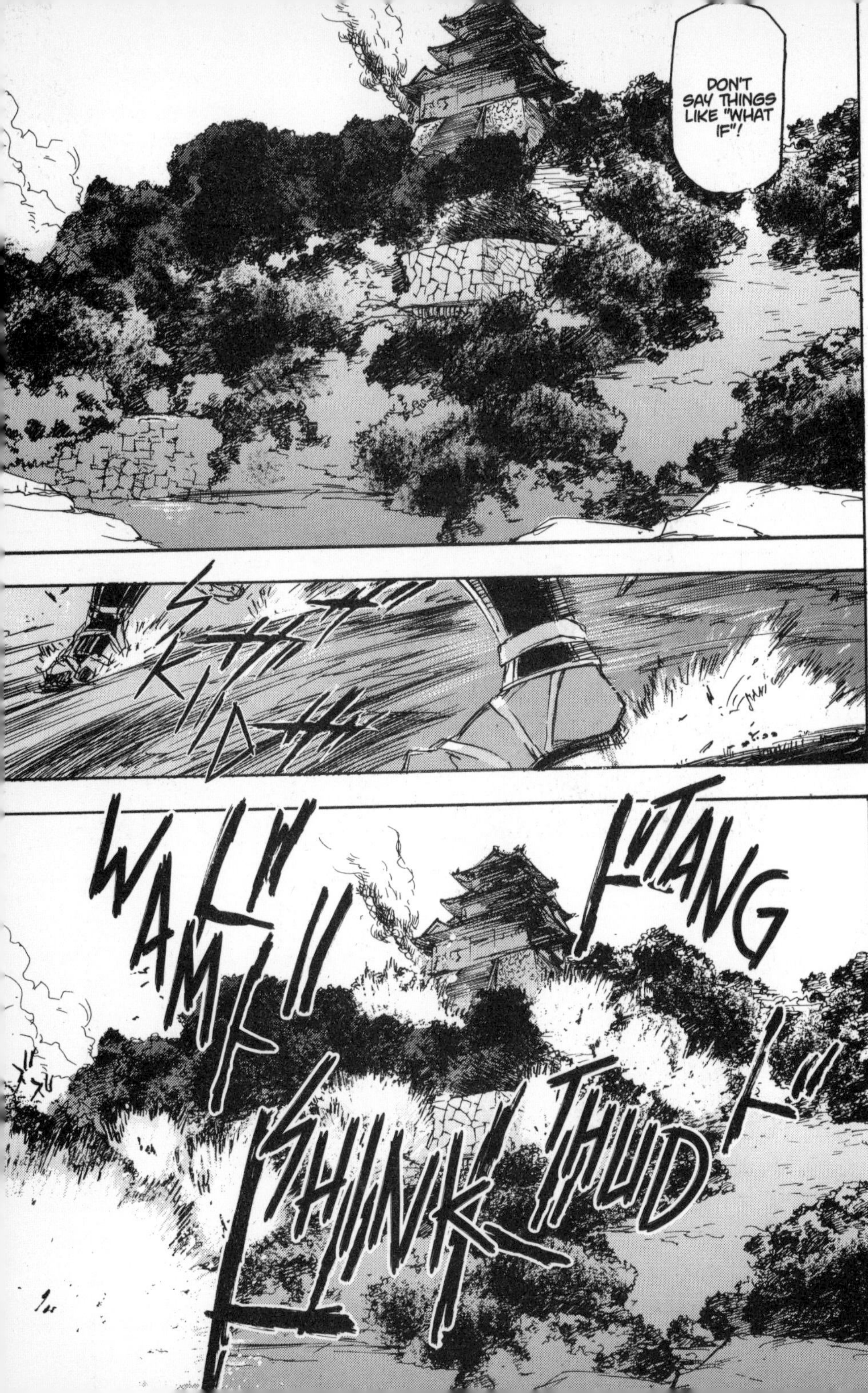
DON'T SAY THINGS LIKE "WHAT IF"!
SKID
THUD!!
SHINK
WAM!!

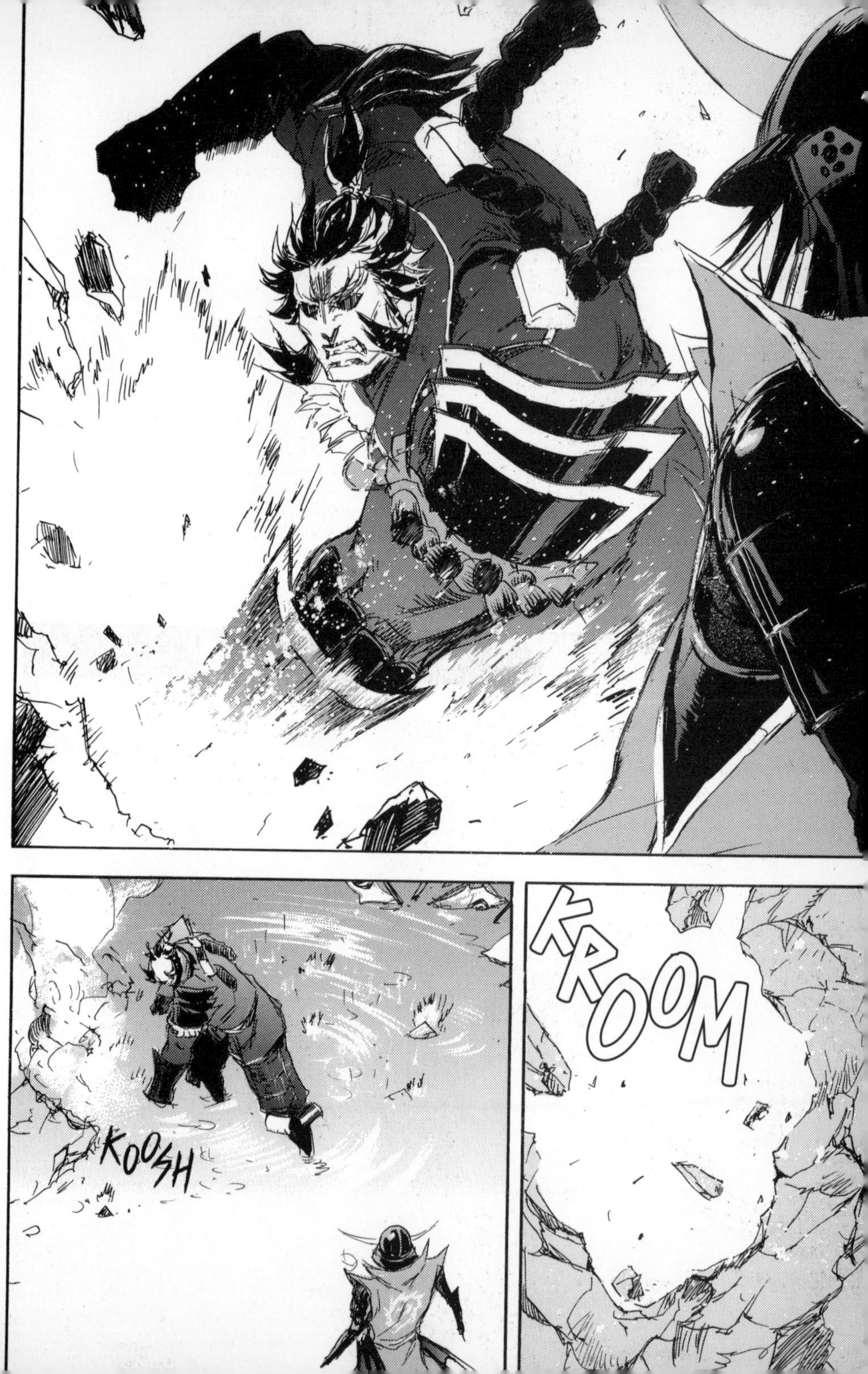
KROOM
KOOSH

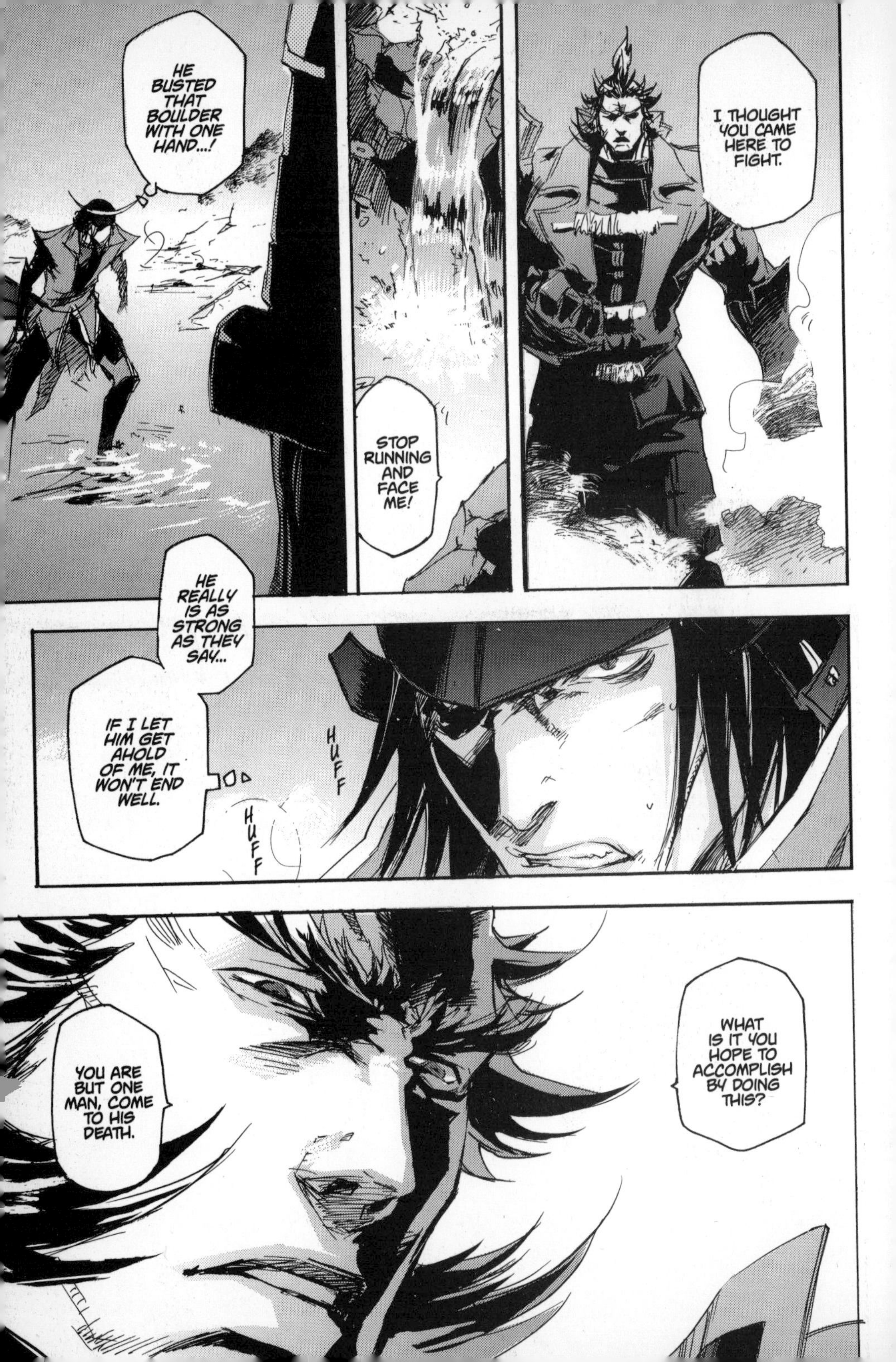
I THOUGHT YOU CAME HERE TO FIGHT.
STOP RUNNING AND FACE ME!
HE BUSTED THAT BOULDER WITH ONE HAND...!
HE REALLY IS AS STRONG AS THEY SAY...
IF I LET HIM GET AHOLD OF ME, IT WON'T END WELL.
HUFF
HUFF
WHAT IS IT YOU HOPE TO ACCOMPLISH BY DOING THIS?
YOU ARE BUT ONE MAN, COME TO HIS DEATH.

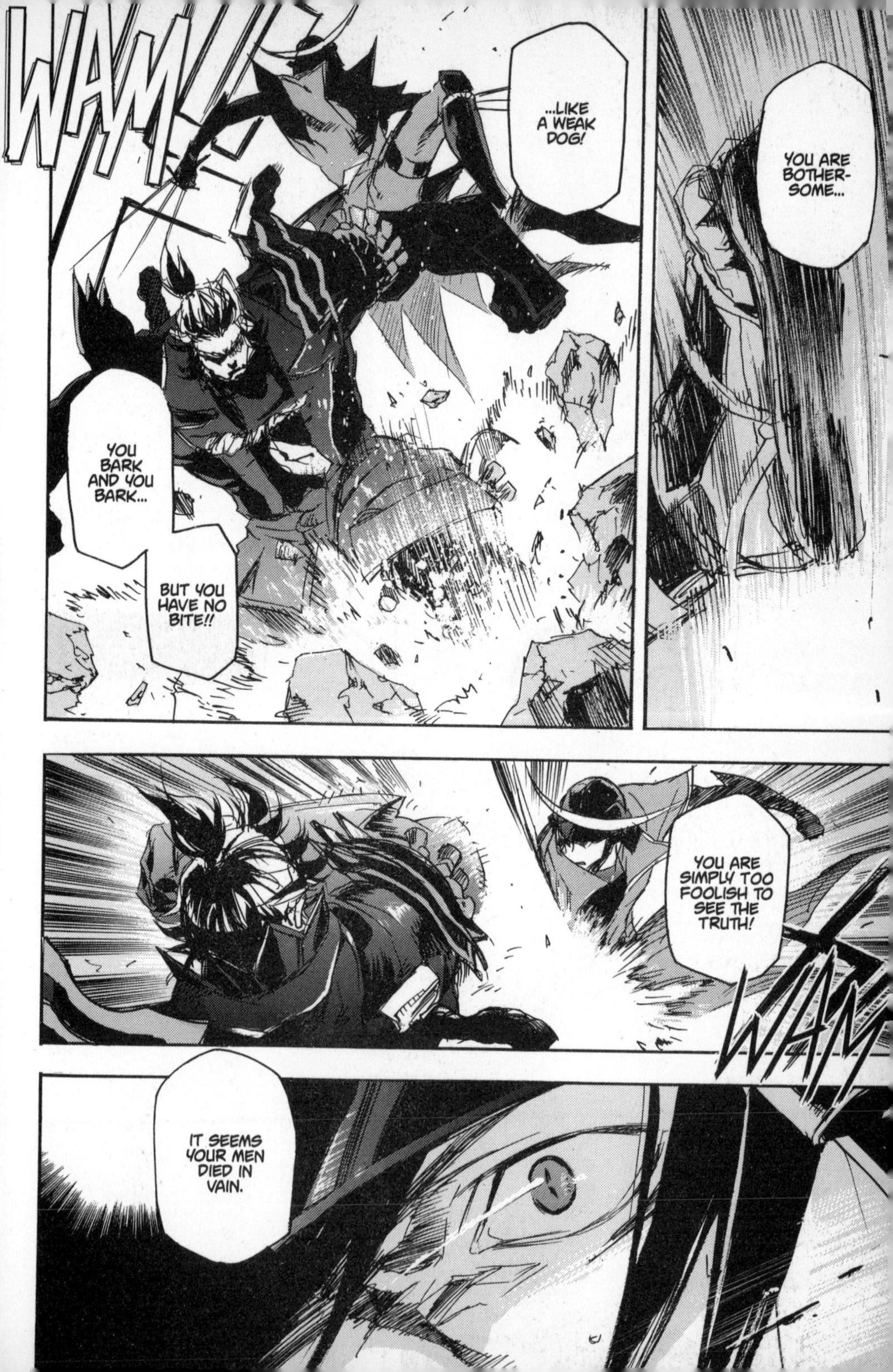
YOU ARE BOTHER-SOME...
...LIKE A WEAK DOG!
WAM!!
YOU BARK AND YOU BARK...
BUT YOU HAVE NO BITE!!
YOU ARE SIMPLY TOO FOOLISH TO SEE THE TRUTH!
WAM
IT SEEMS YOUR MEN DIED IN VAIN.

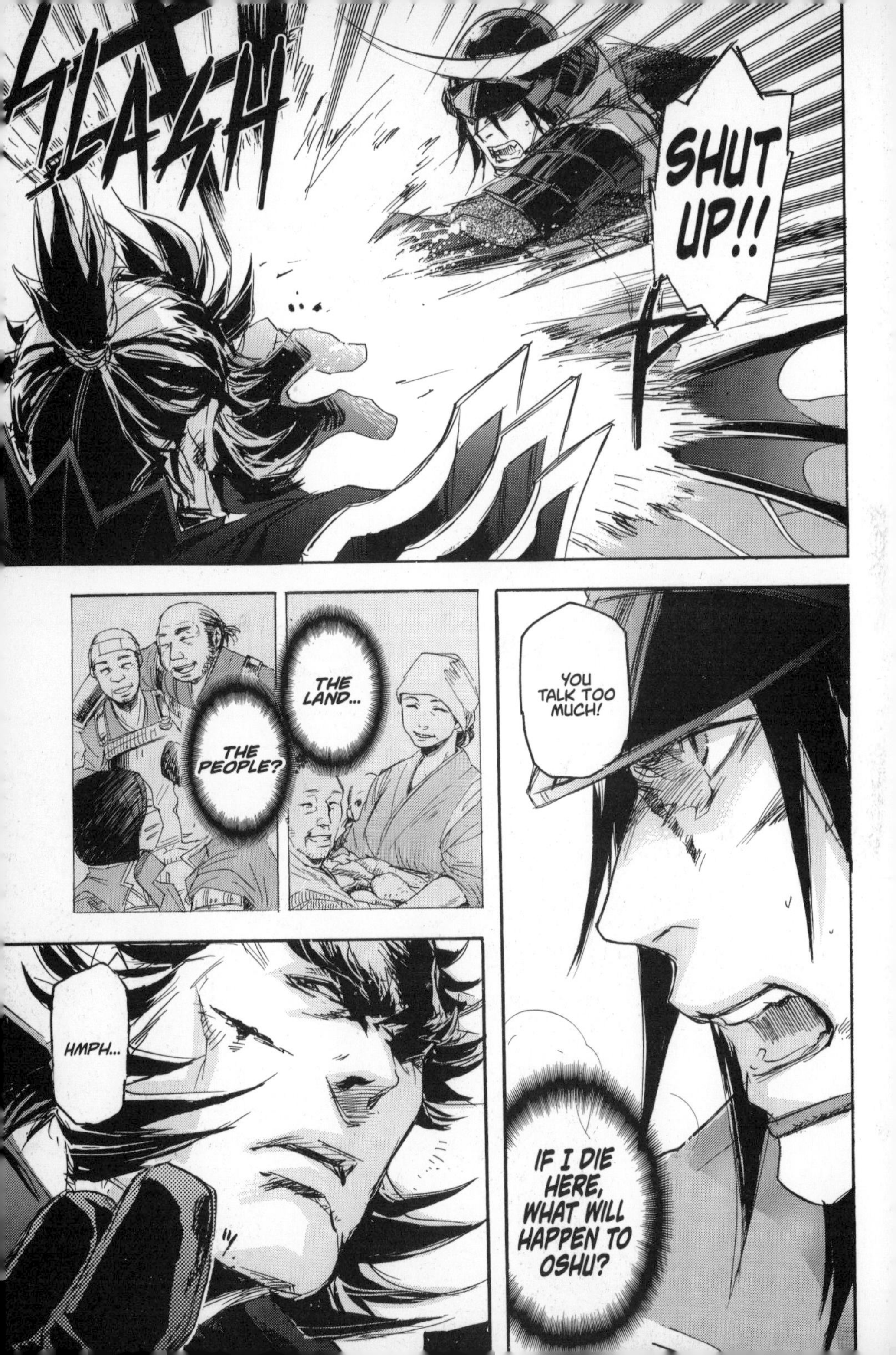
SHUT UP!!
SLASH
YOU TALK TOO MUCH!
IF I DIE HERE, WHAT WILL HAPPEN TO OSHU?
THE LAND...
THE PEOPLE?
HMPH...

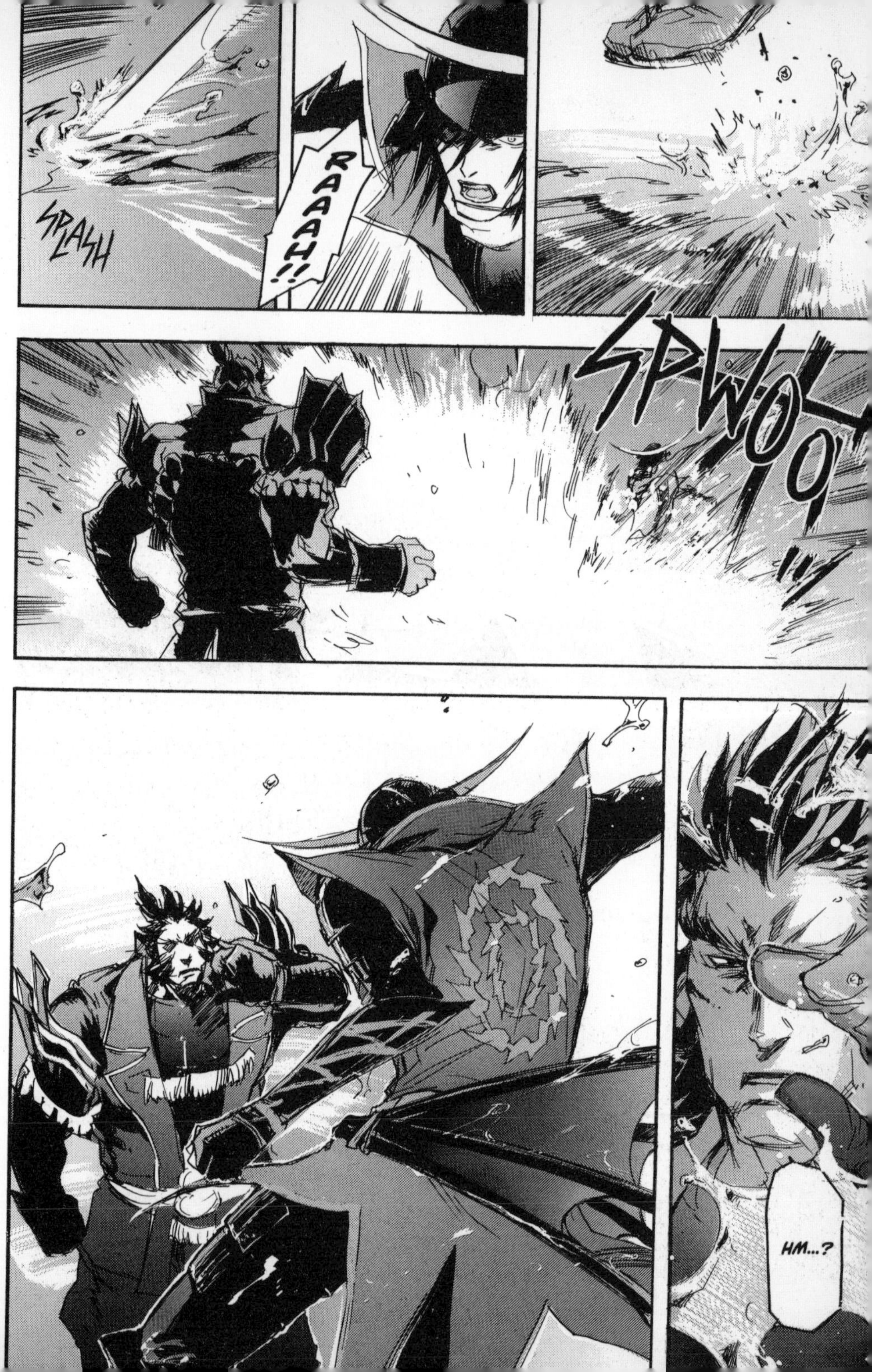
RAAAAH!!
SPLASH
SPWOOOO!!
HM...?

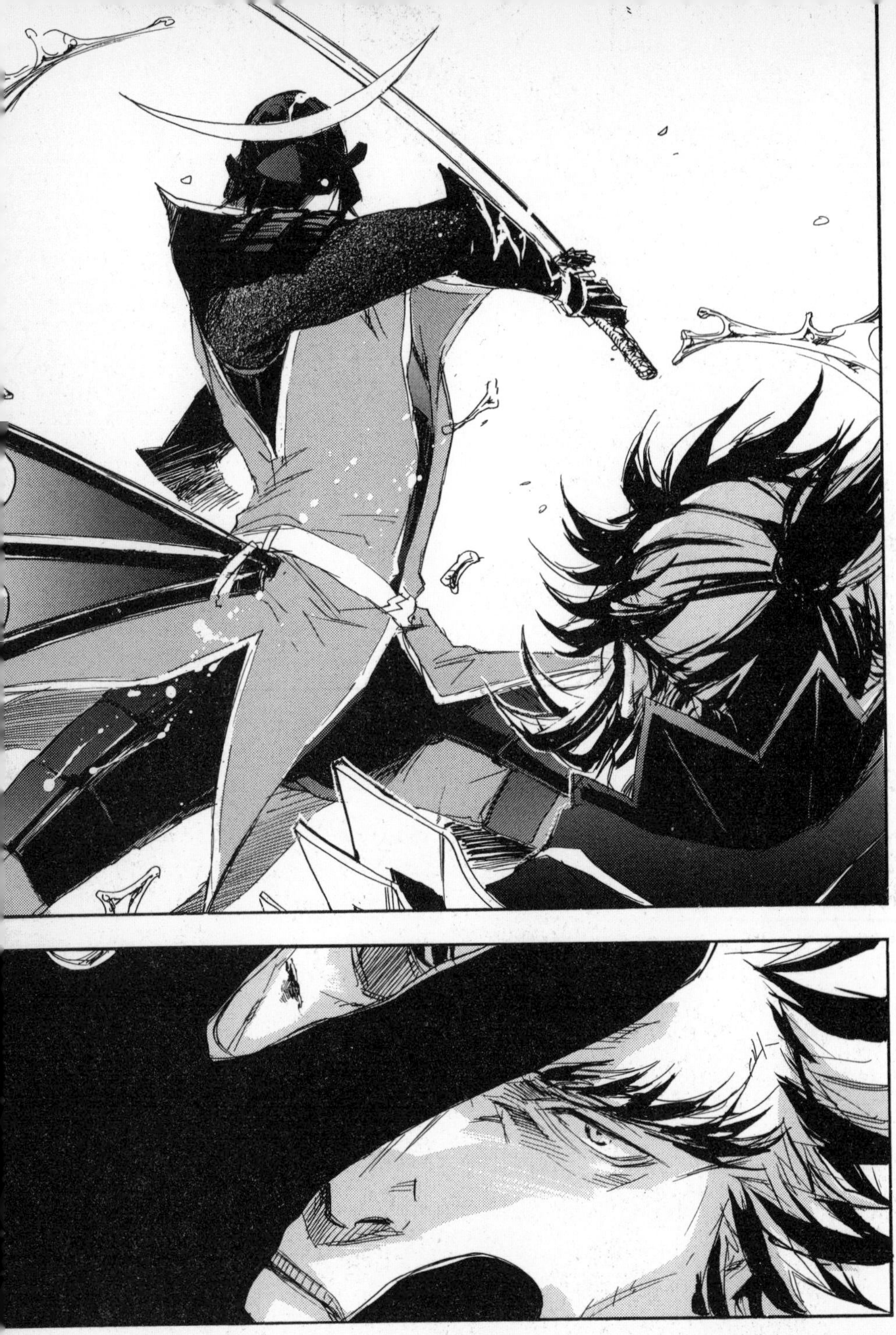

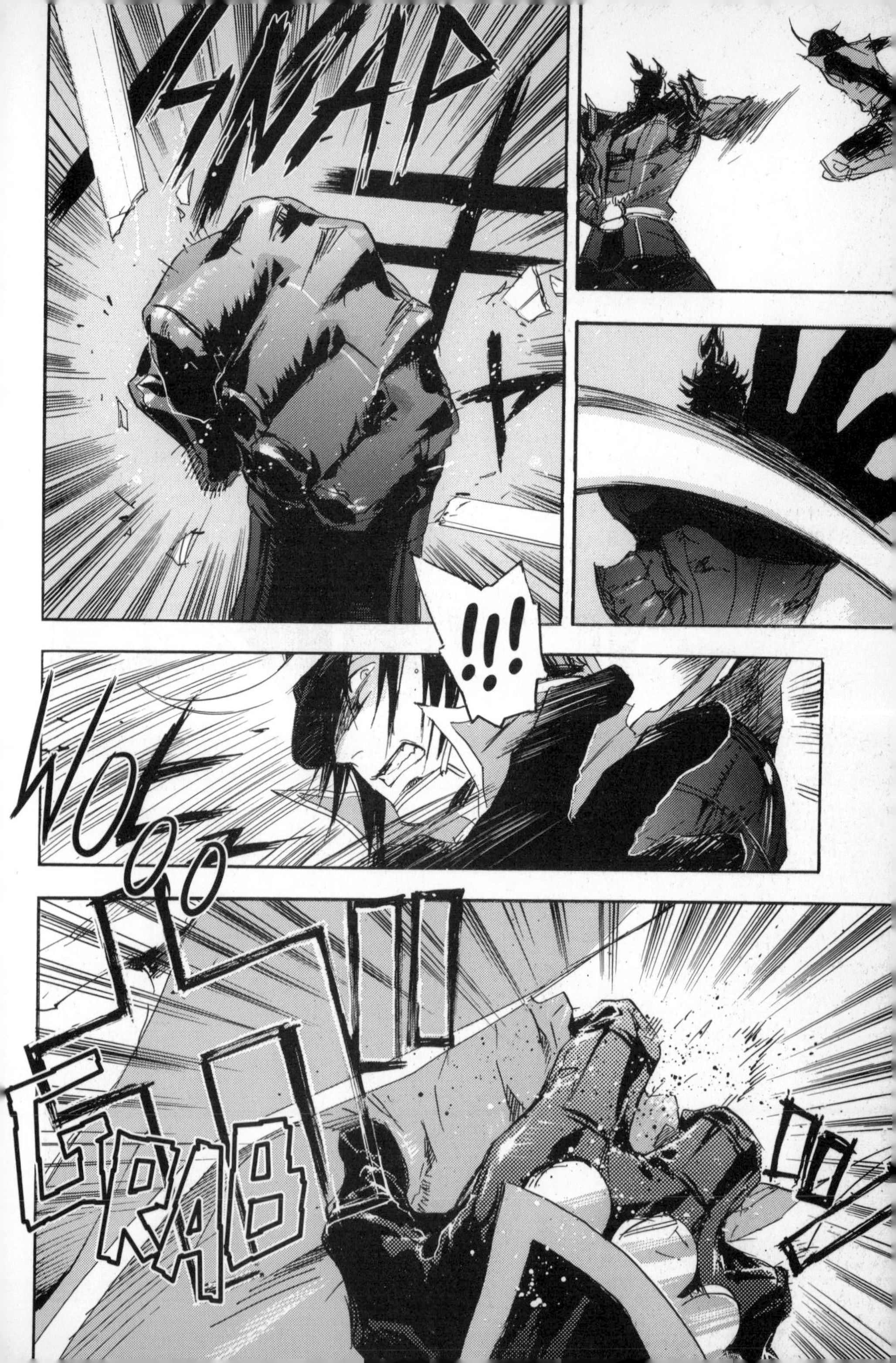
SNAP
!!!
WOOOO
DOO
GRAB

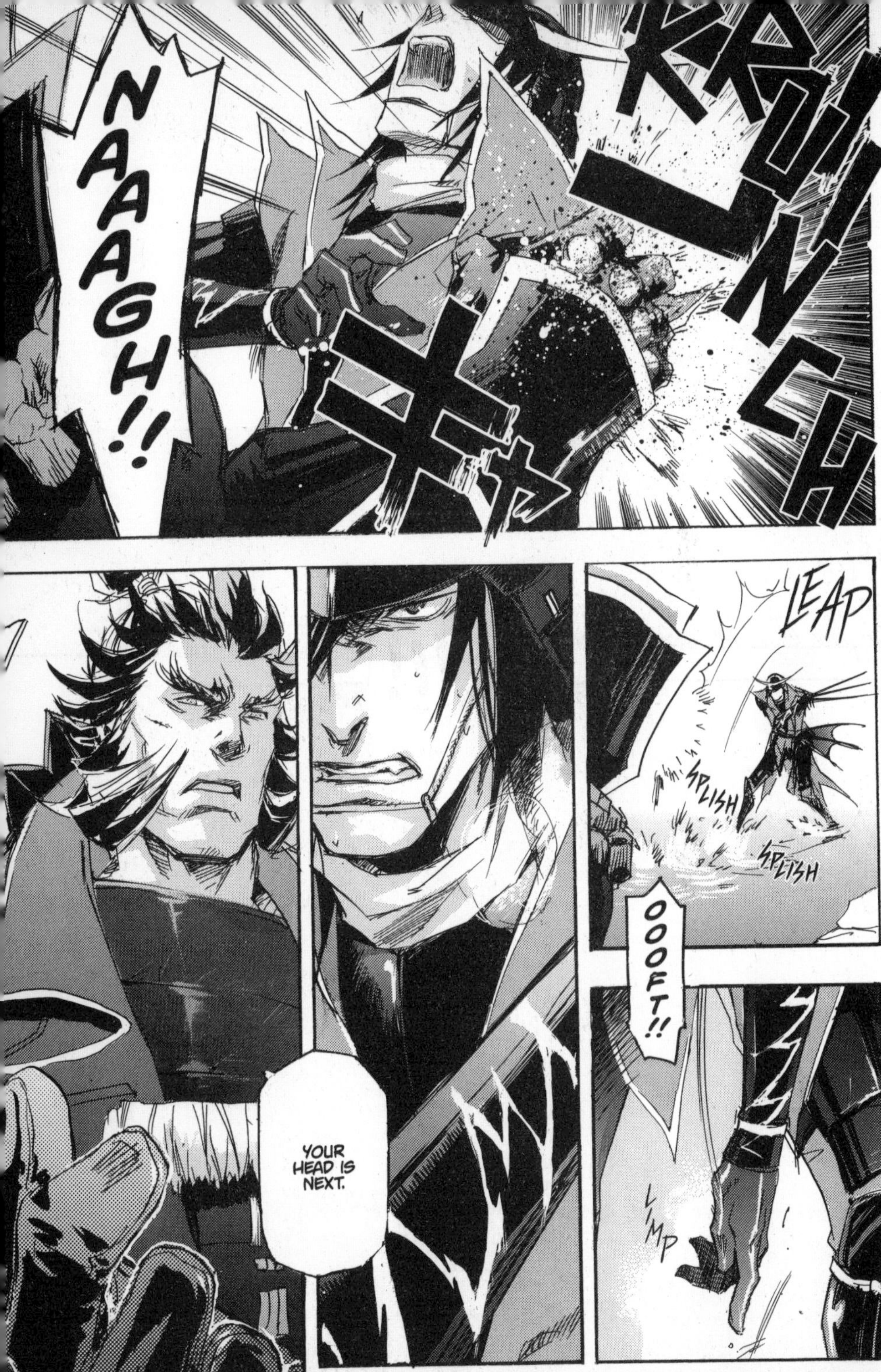
KRUNCH
ギャ
NAAAGH!!
LEAP
SPLISH
SPLISH
OOOFT!!
LIMP
YOUR HEAD IS NEXT.

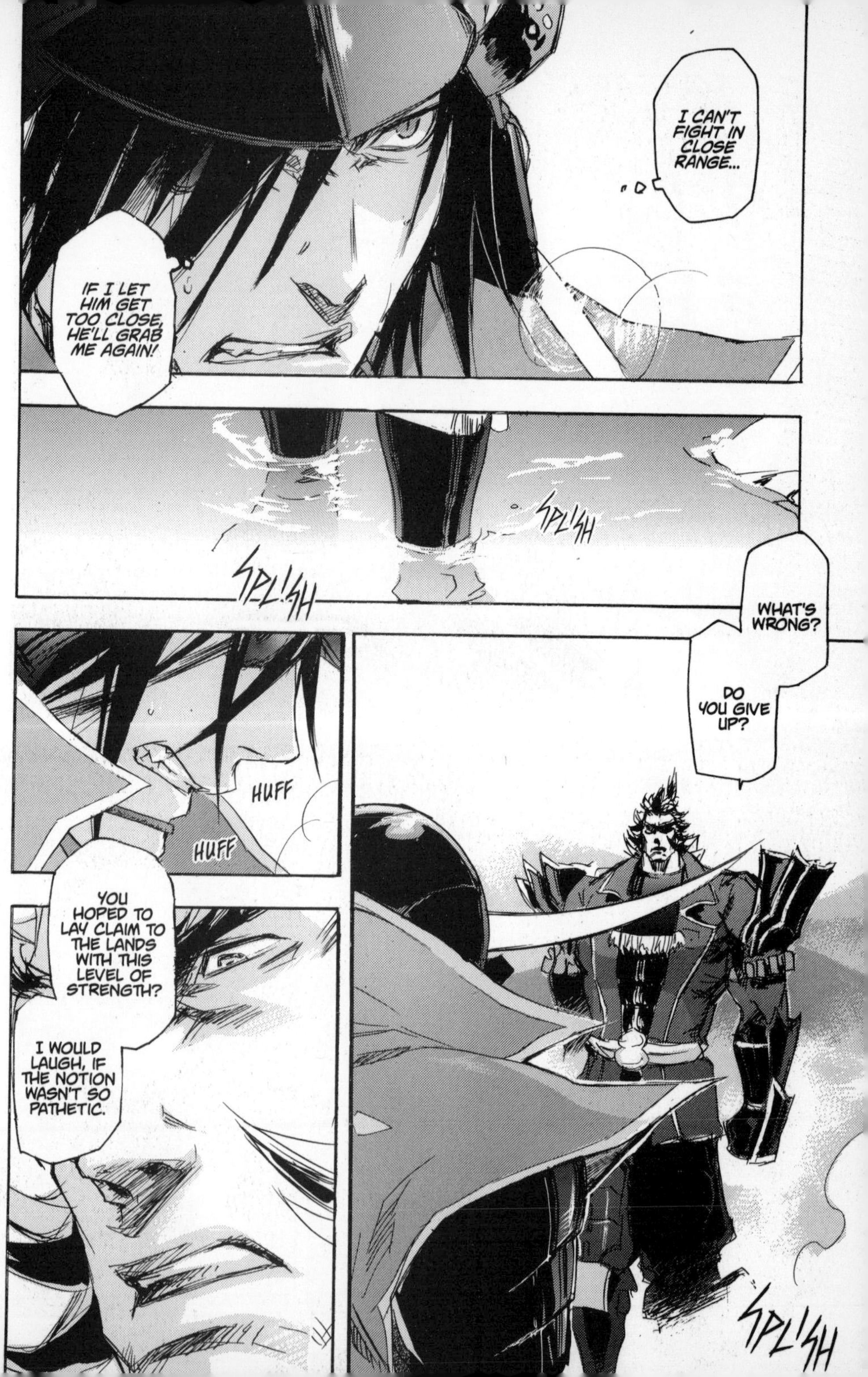
I CAN'T FIGHT IN CLOSE RANGE...
IF I LET HIM GET TOO CLOSE, HE'LL GRAB ME AGAIN!
SPLISH
SPLISH
WHAT'S WRONG?
DO YOU GIVE UP?
SPLISH
HUFF
HUFF
YOU HOPED TO LAY CLAIM TO THE LANDS WITH THIS LEVEL OF STRENGTH?
I WOULD LAUGH, IF THE NOTION WASN'T SO PATHETIC.

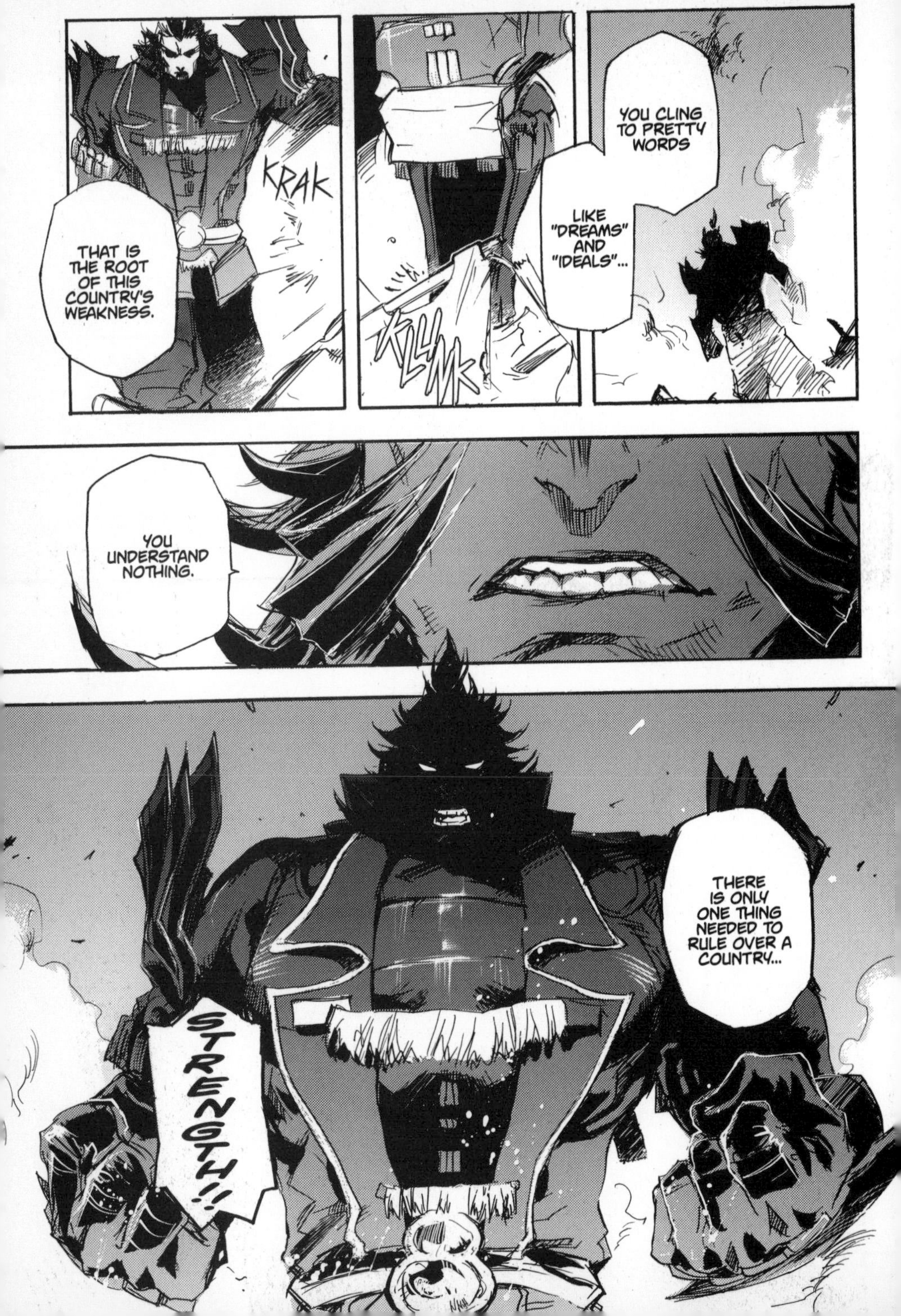
YOU CLING TO PRETTY WORDS
LIKE "DREAMS" AND "IDEALS"...
KLLUNK
KRAK
THAT IS THE ROOT OF THIS COUNTRY'S WEAKNESS.
YOU UNDERSTAND NOTHING.
THERE IS ONLY ONE THING NEEDED TO RULE OVER A COUNTRY...
STRENGTH!!

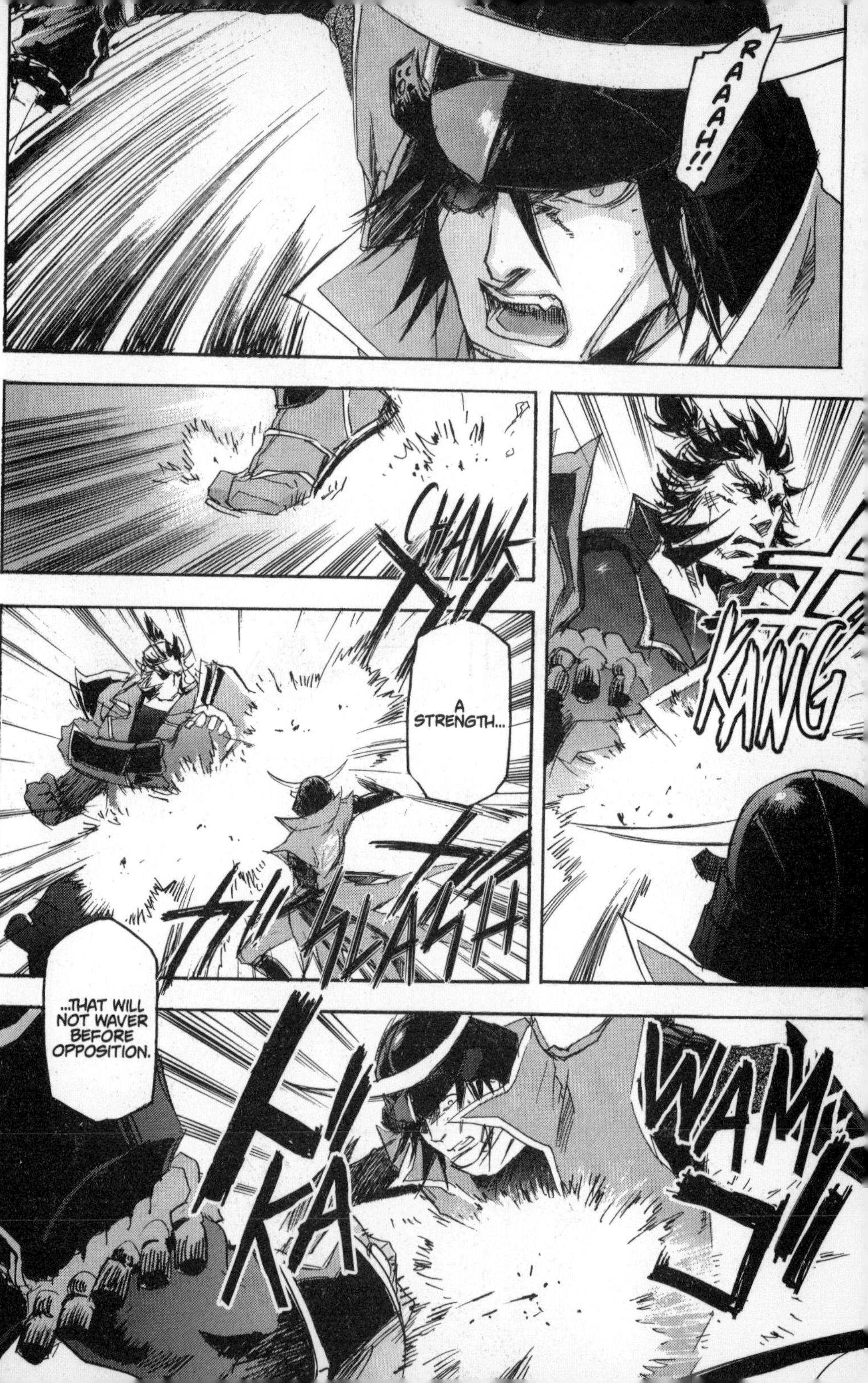
RAAAAH!!
KANG
CHANK
A STRENGTH...
SLASH
WAM
...THAT WILL NOT WAVER BEFORE OPPOSITION.

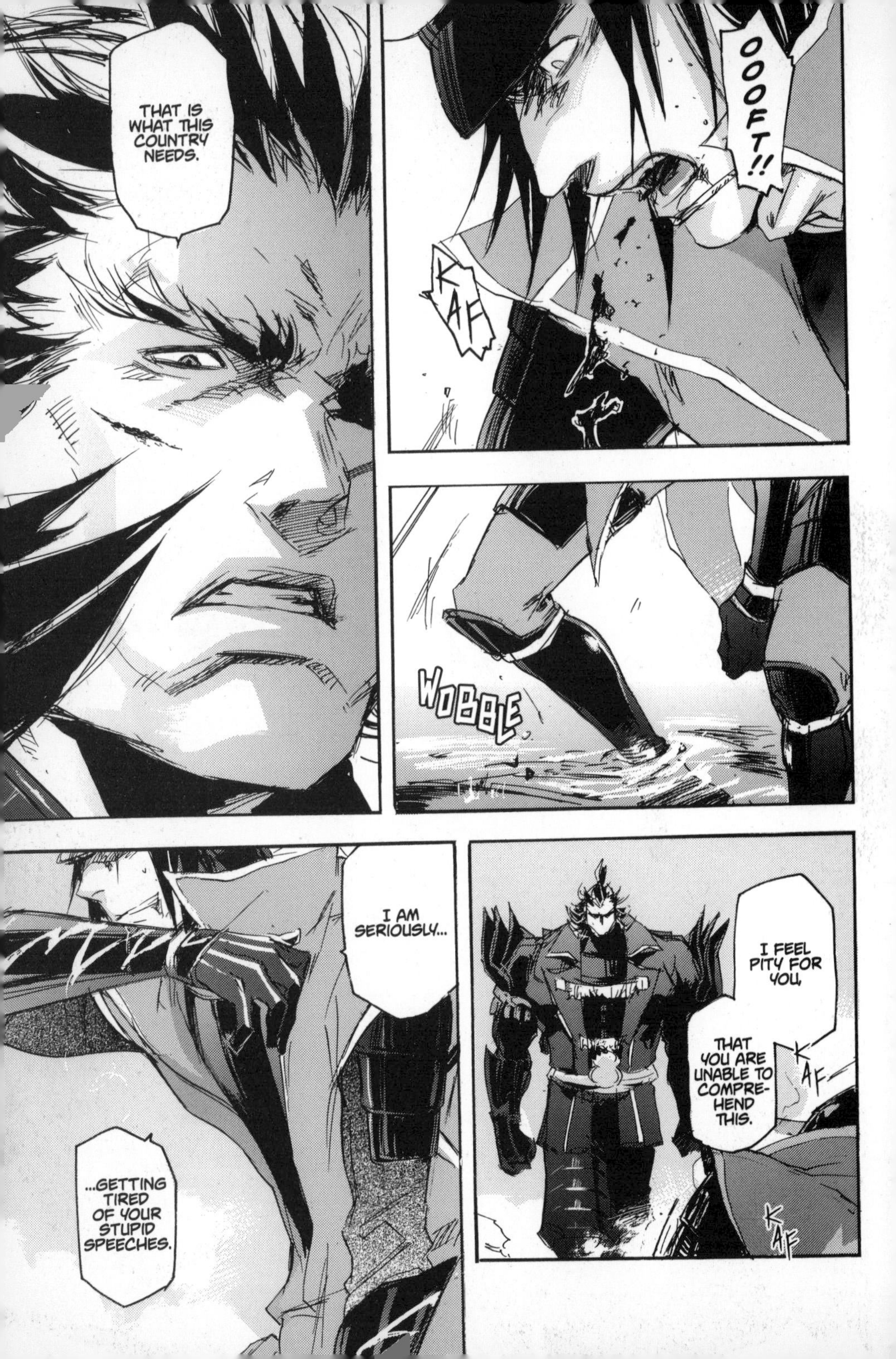
OOOFT!!
KAF
WOBBLE
THAT IS WHAT THIS COUNTRY NEEDS.
I FEEL PITY FOR YOU,
THAT YOU ARE UNABLE TO COMPRE-HEND THIS.
KAF
KAF
I AM SERIOUSLY...
...GETTING TIRED OF YOUR STUPID SPEECHES.

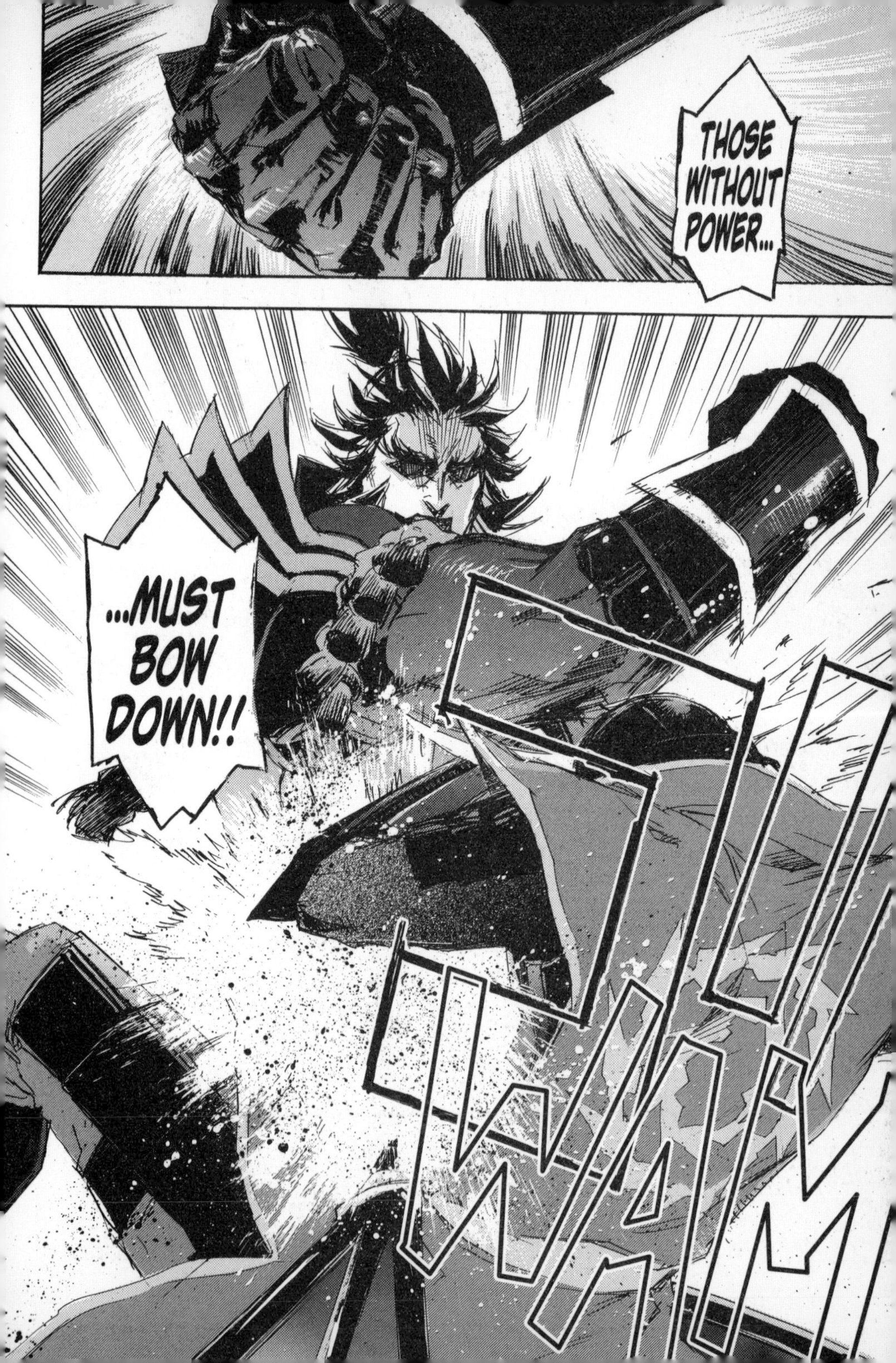
THOSE WITHOUT POWER...
...MUST BOW DOWN!!
WAM

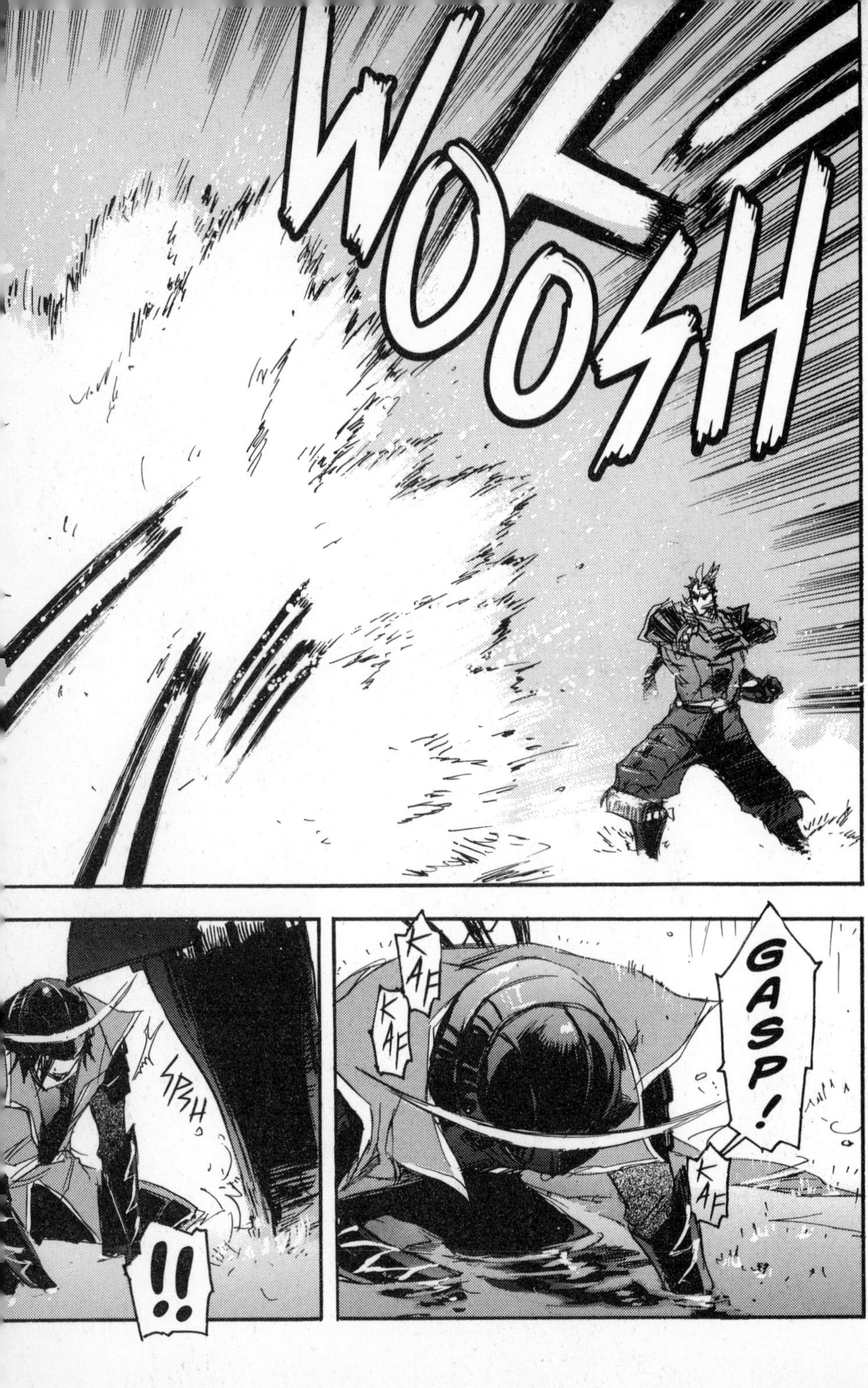
WOOSH
GASP!
KAF
KAF
KAF
SPSH
!!

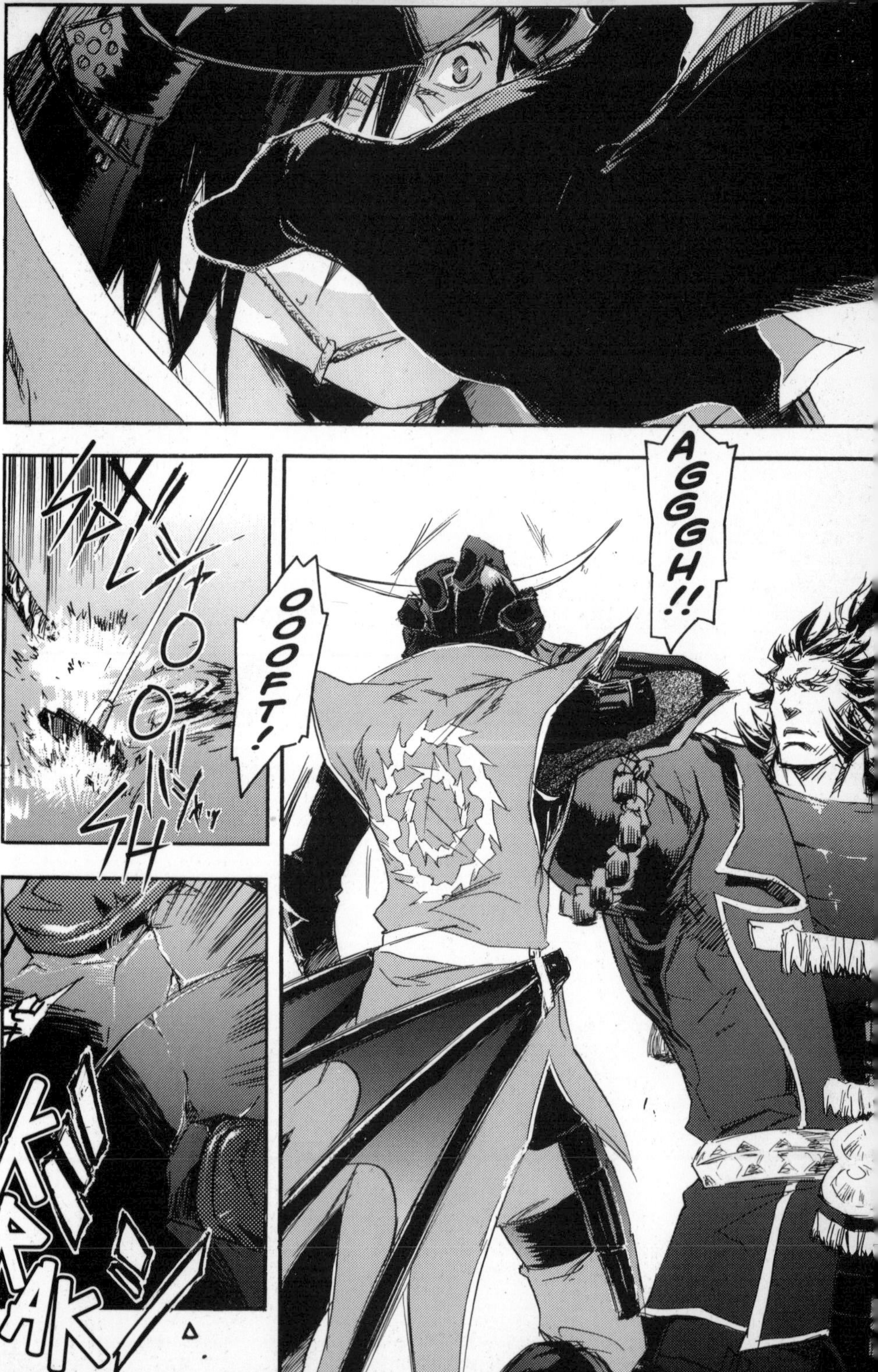
AGGGH!!
OOOFT!
SPLOOOSH
KRAK!!

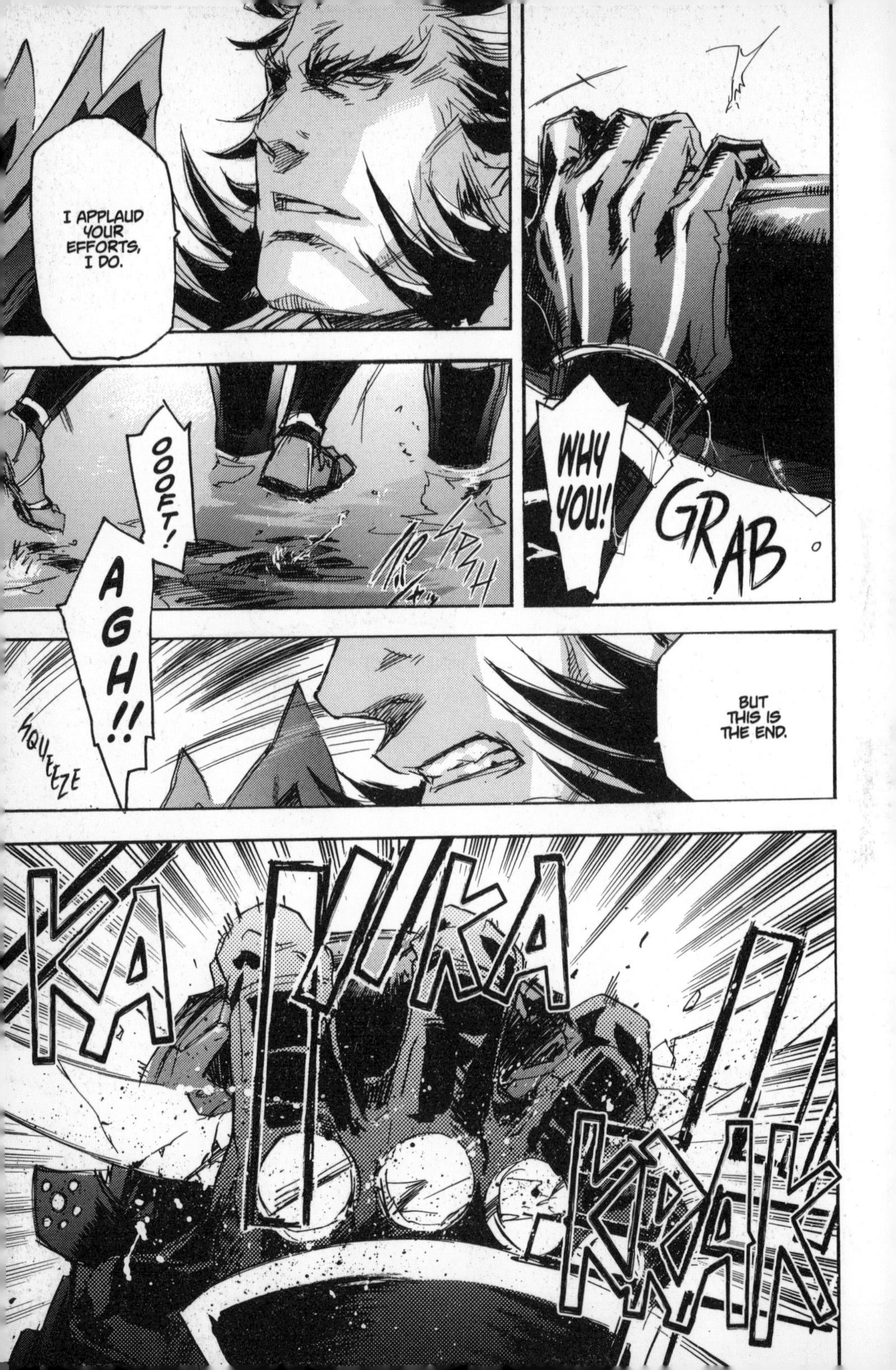
WHY YOU!
GRAB
I APPLAUD YOUR EFFORTS, I DO.
OOOFT!
SPSH
BUT THIS IS THE END.
AGH!!
SQUEEZE
KA
KRAK

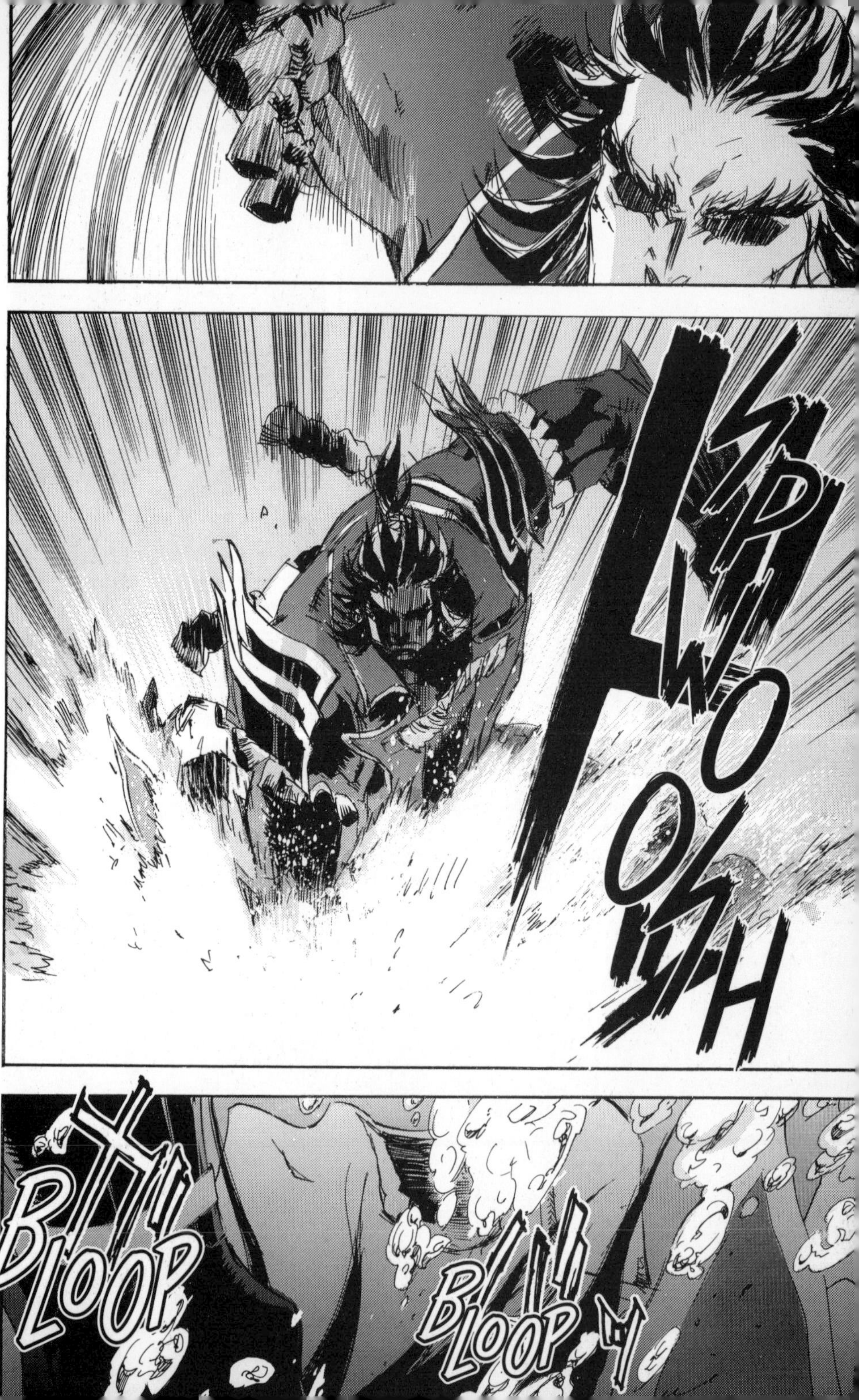
SPLWOOOSH
BLOOP
BLOOP

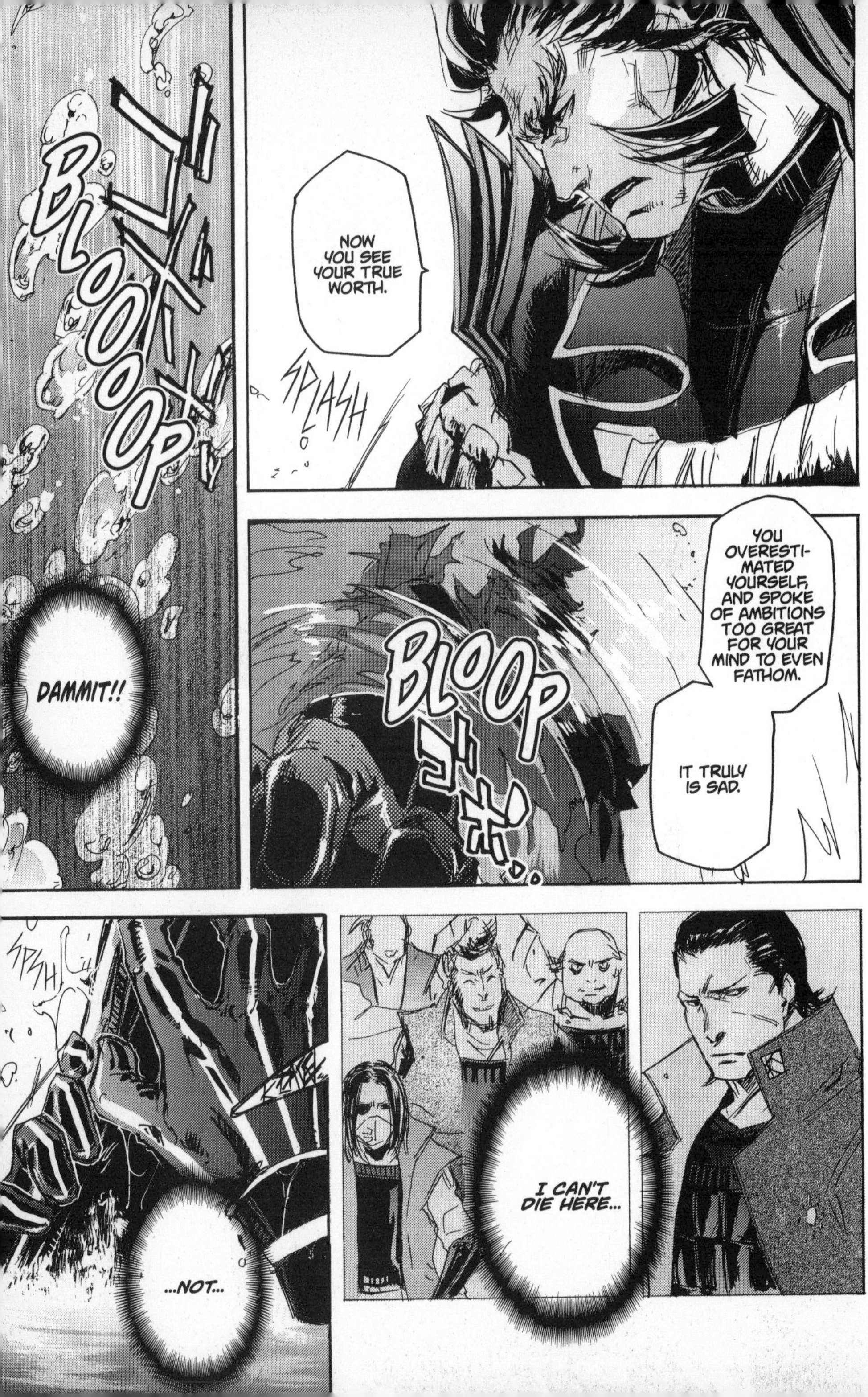

NOW YOU SEE YOUR TRUE WORTH.
SPLASH
YOU OVERESTIMATED YOURSELF, AND SPOKE OF AMBITIONS TOO GREAT FOR YOUR MIND TO EVEN FATHOM.
IT TRULY IS SAD.
BLOOP
BLOOOOOP
DAMMIT!!
I CAN'T DIE HERE...
SPLSH
...NOT...

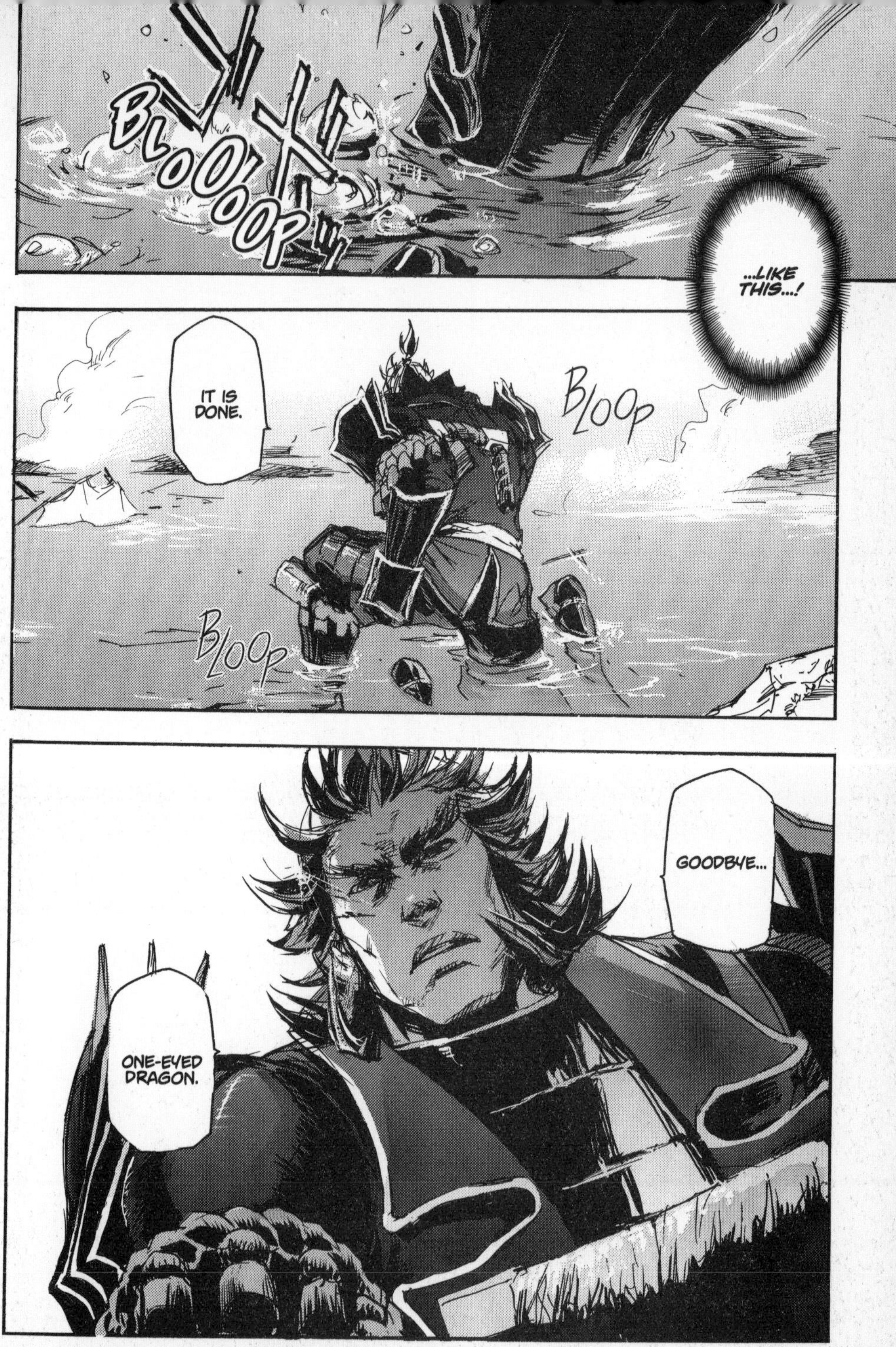
BLOOOOOP
...LIKE THIS...!
BLOOP
IT IS DONE.
BLOOP
GOODBYE...
ONE-EYED DRAGON.

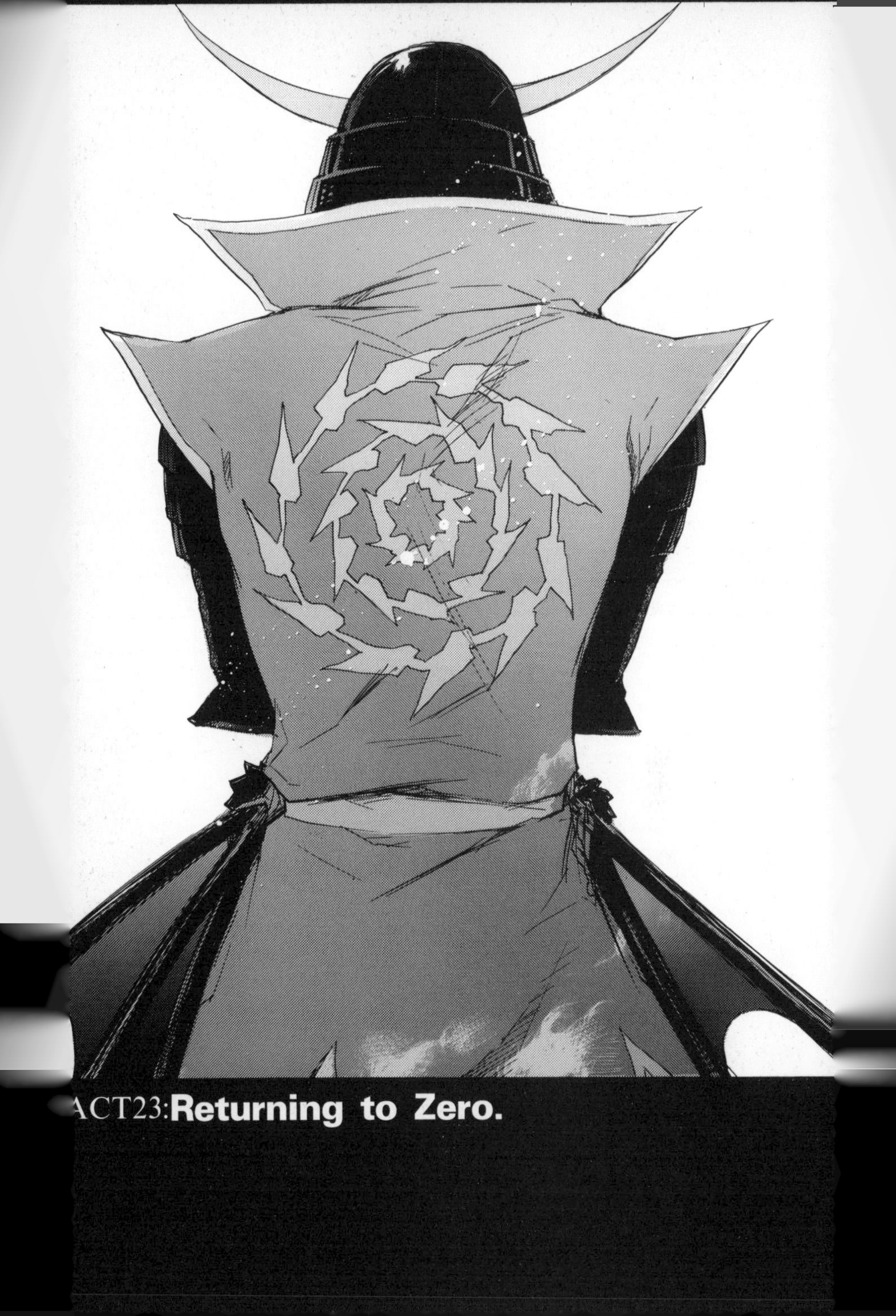

ACT23: Returning to Zero.

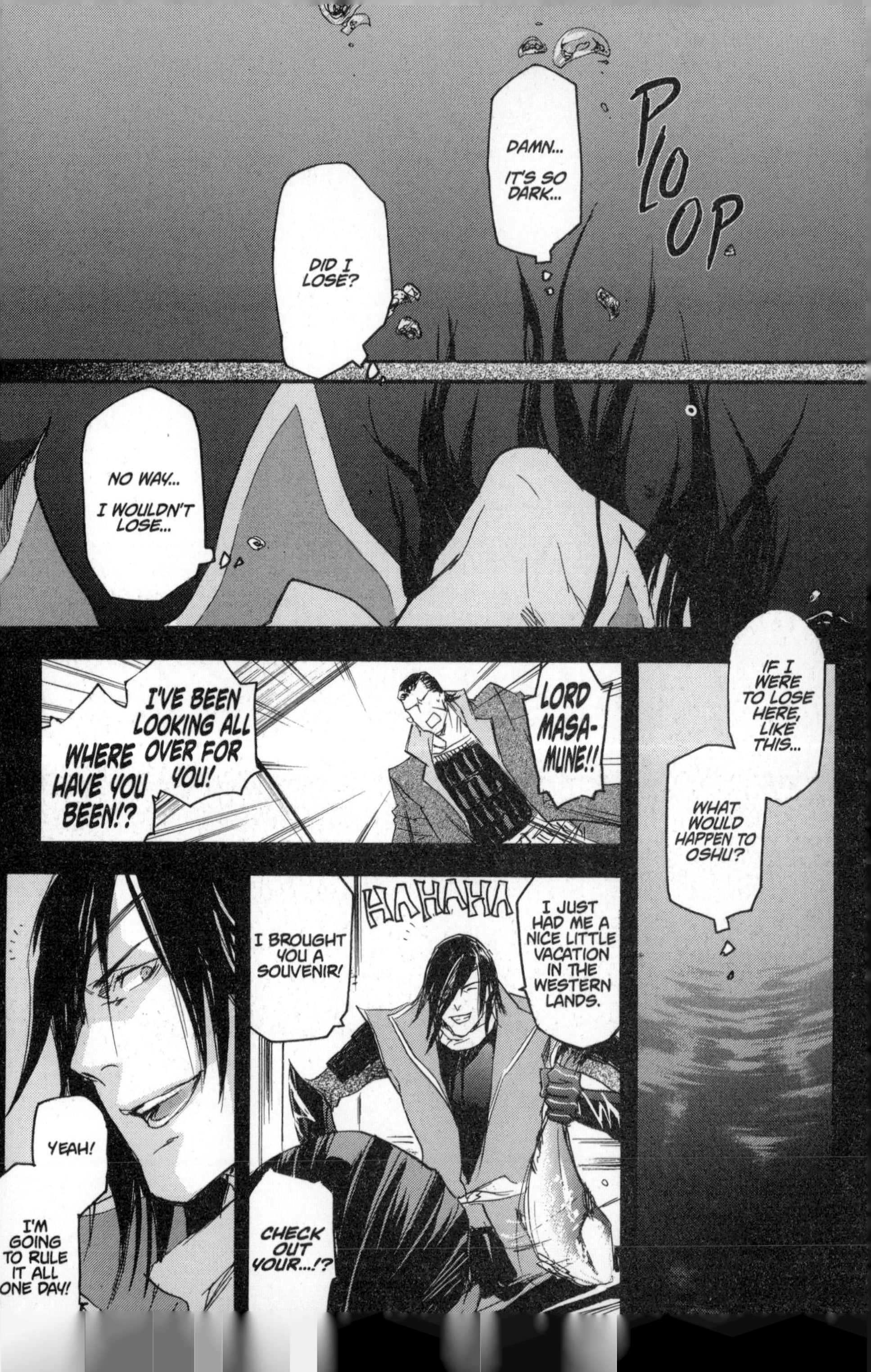
PLOOP
DAMN... IT'S SO DARK...
DID I LOSE?
NO WAY... I WOULDN'T LOSE...
IF I WERE TO LOSE HERE, LIKE THIS...
WHAT WOULD HAPPEN TO OSHU?
LORD MASAMUNE!!
I'VE BEEN LOOKING ALL OVER FOR YOU!
WHERE HAVE YOU BEEN!?
HAHAHA
I JUST HAD ME A NICE LITTLE VACATION IN THE WESTERN LANDS.
I BROUGHT YOU A SOUVENIR!
CHECK OUT YOUR...!?
YEAH!
I'M GOING TO RULE IT ALL ONE DAY!

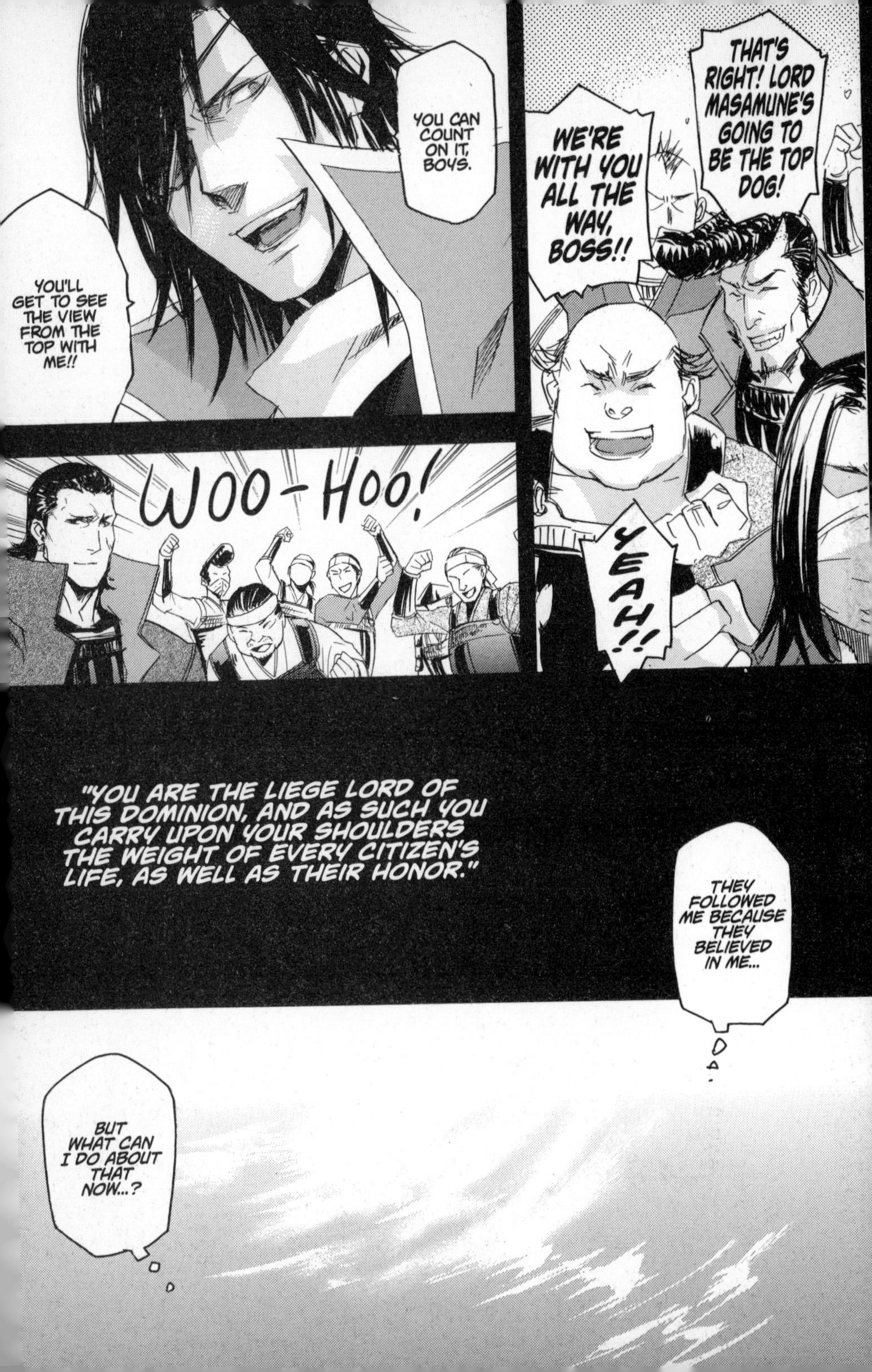
THAT'S RIGHT! LORD MASAMUNE'S GOING TO BE THE TOP DOG!
WE'RE WITH YOU ALL THE WAY, BOSS!!
YEAH!!
YOU CAN COUNT ON IT, BOYS.
YOU'LL GET TO SEE THE VIEW FROM THE TOP WITH ME!!
WOO-HOO!
"YOU ARE THE LIEGE LORD OF THIS DOMINION, AND AS SUCH YOU CARRY UPON YOUR SHOULDERS THE WEIGHT OF EVERY CITIZEN'S LIFE, AS WELL AS THEIR HONOR."
THEY FOLLOWED ME BECAUSE THEY BELIEVED IN ME...
BUT WHAT CAN I DO ABOUT THAT NOW...?

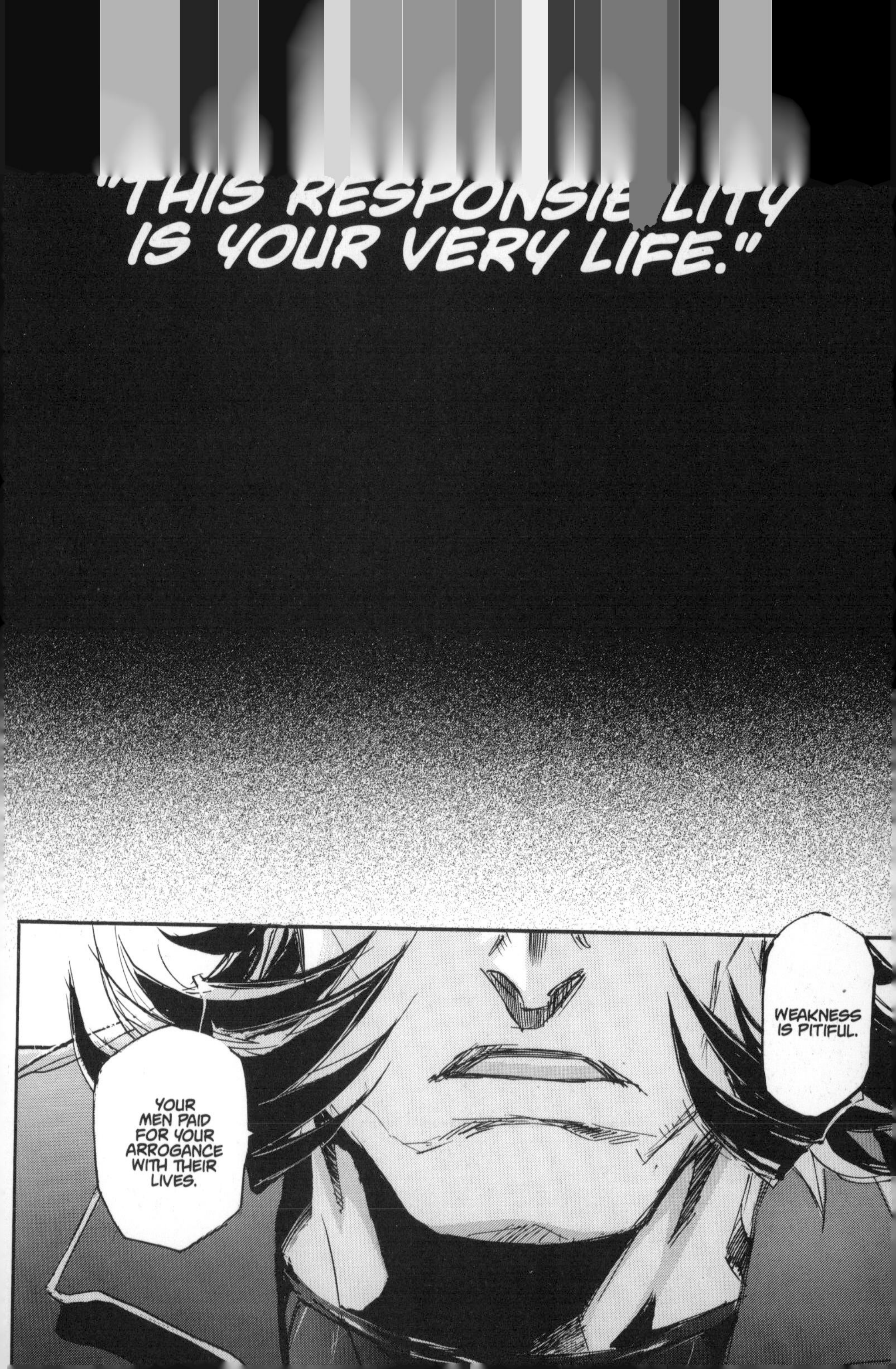
"THIS RESPONSIBILITY IS YOUR VERY LIFE."
WEAKNESS IS PITIFUL.
YOUR MEN PAID FOR YOUR ARROGANCE WITH THEIR LIVES.

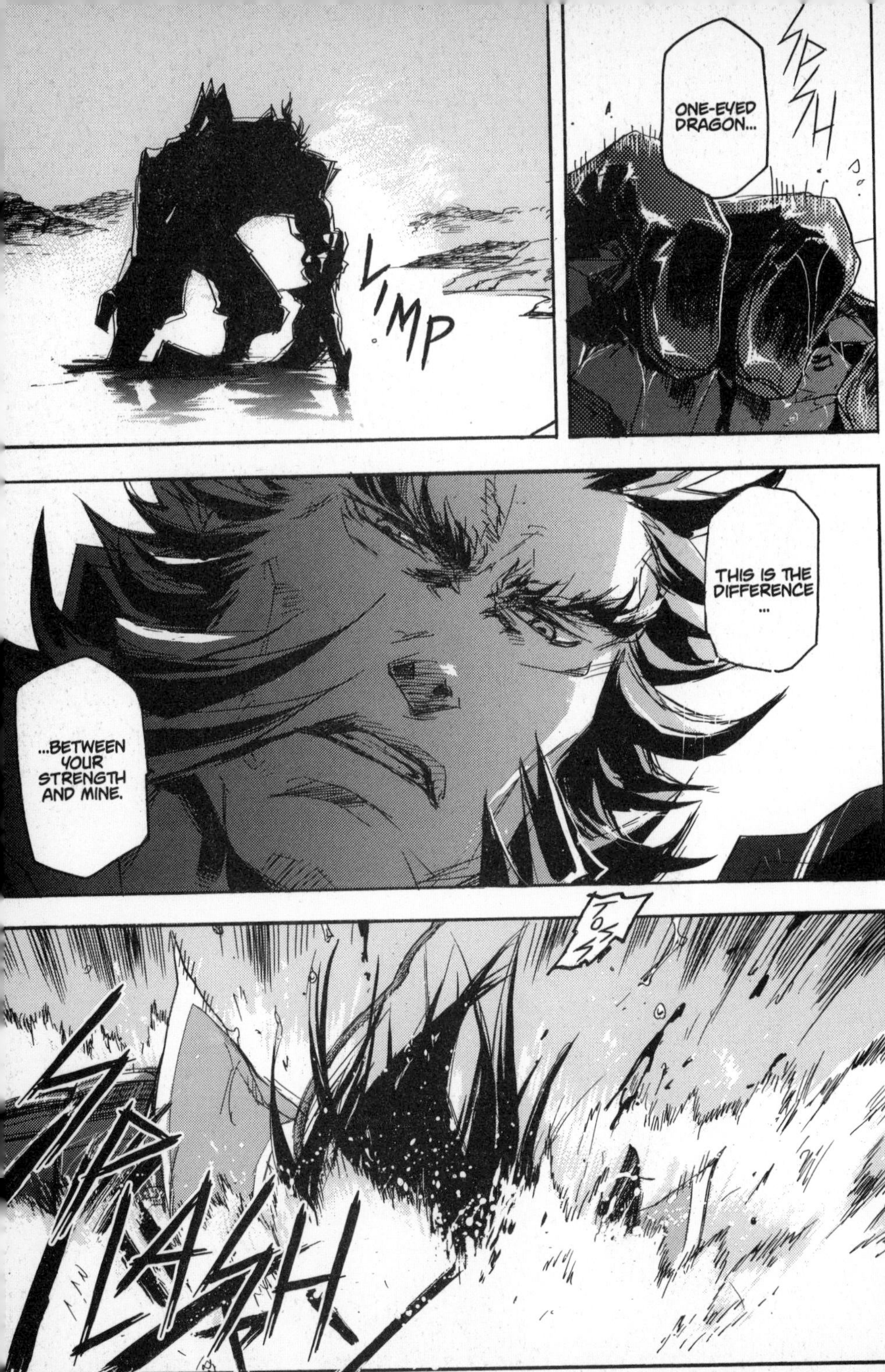
ONE-EYED DRAGON...
SPSH!
LIMP
THIS IS THE DIFFERENCE...
...BETWEEN YOUR STRENGTH AND MINE.
TOSS
SPLASH

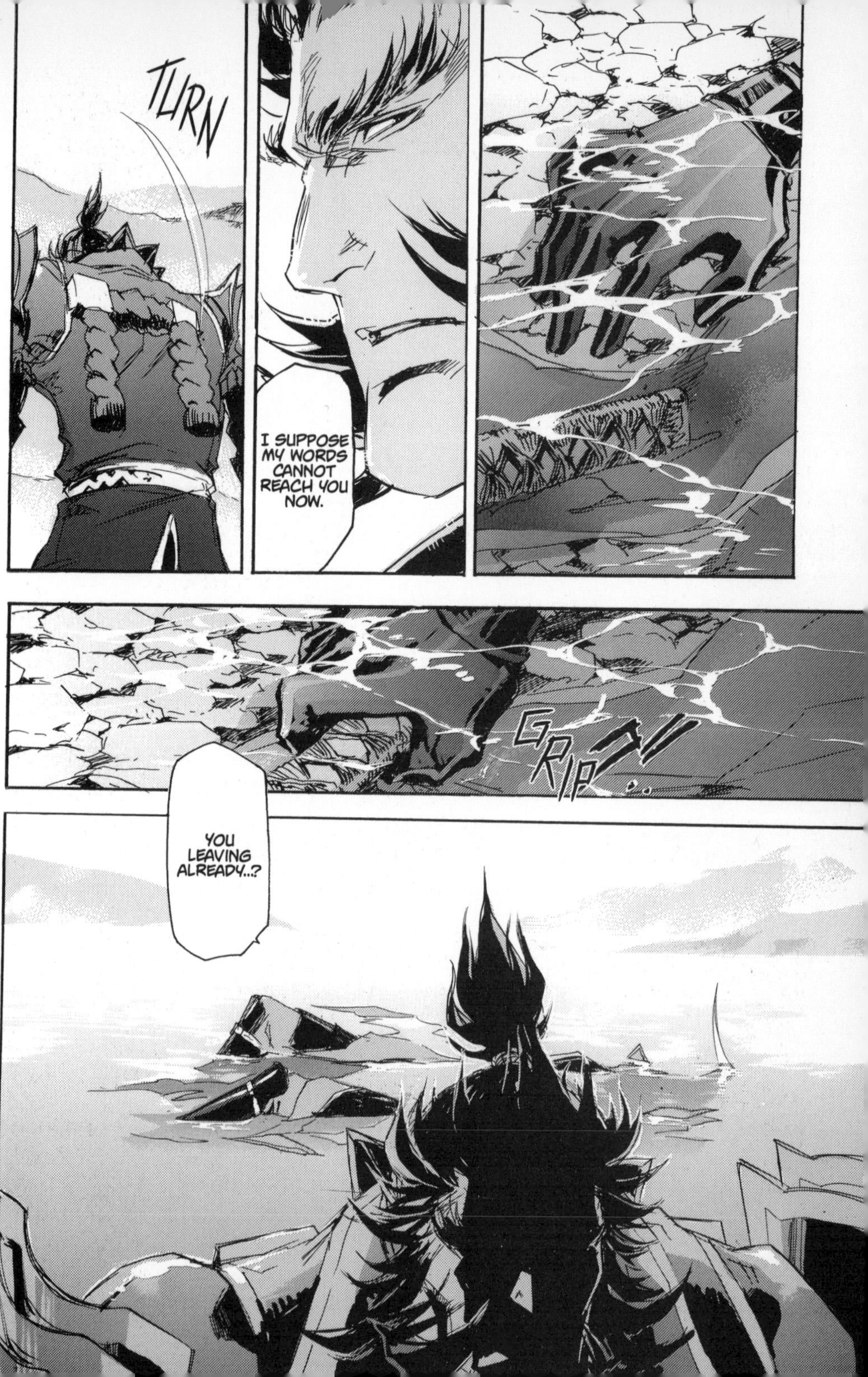
I SUPPOSE MY WORDS CANNOT REACH YOU NOW.
TURN
GRIP
YOU LEAVING ALREADY..?

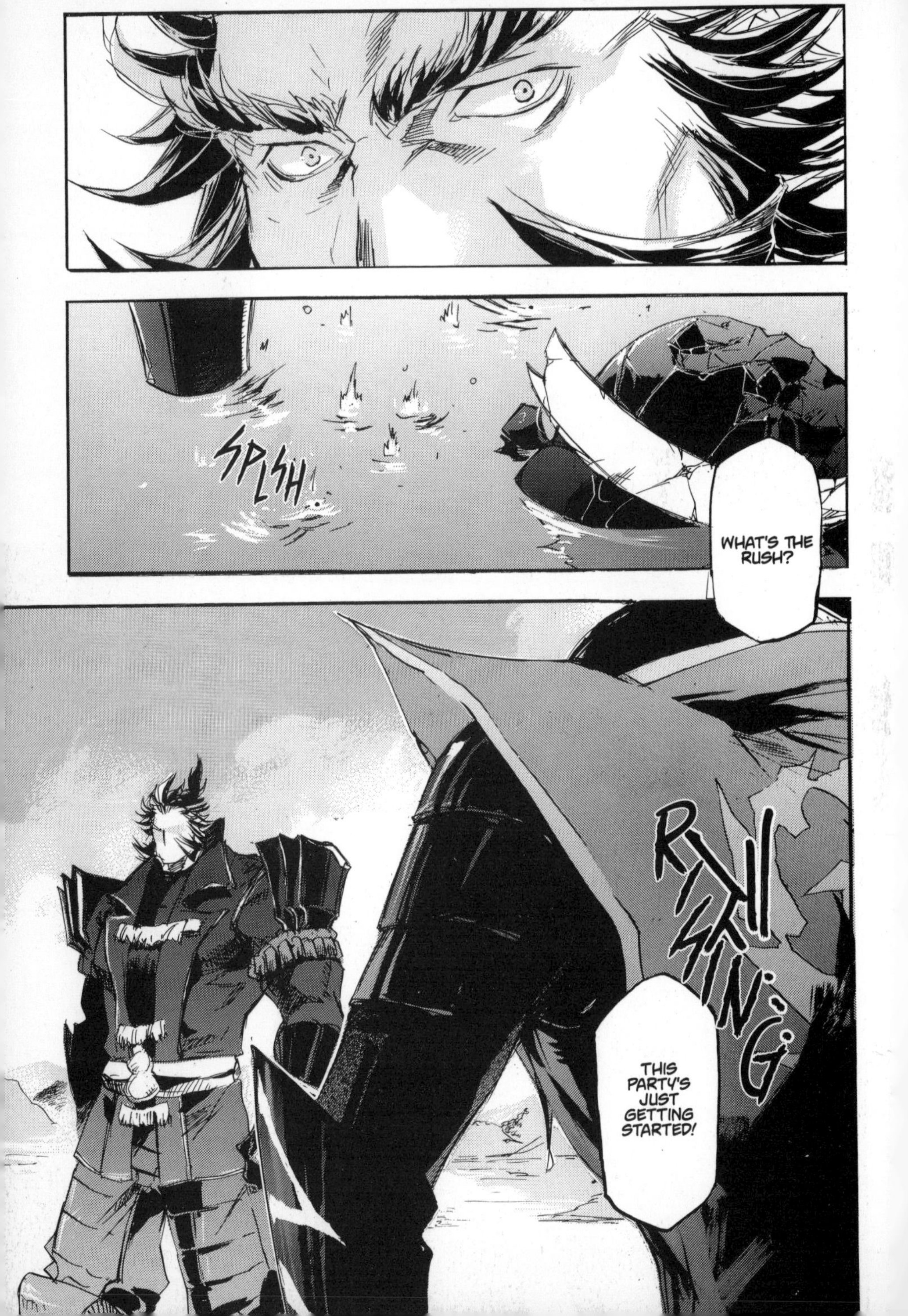
SPLSH
WHAT'S THE RUSH?
THIS PARTY'S JUST GETTING STARTED!

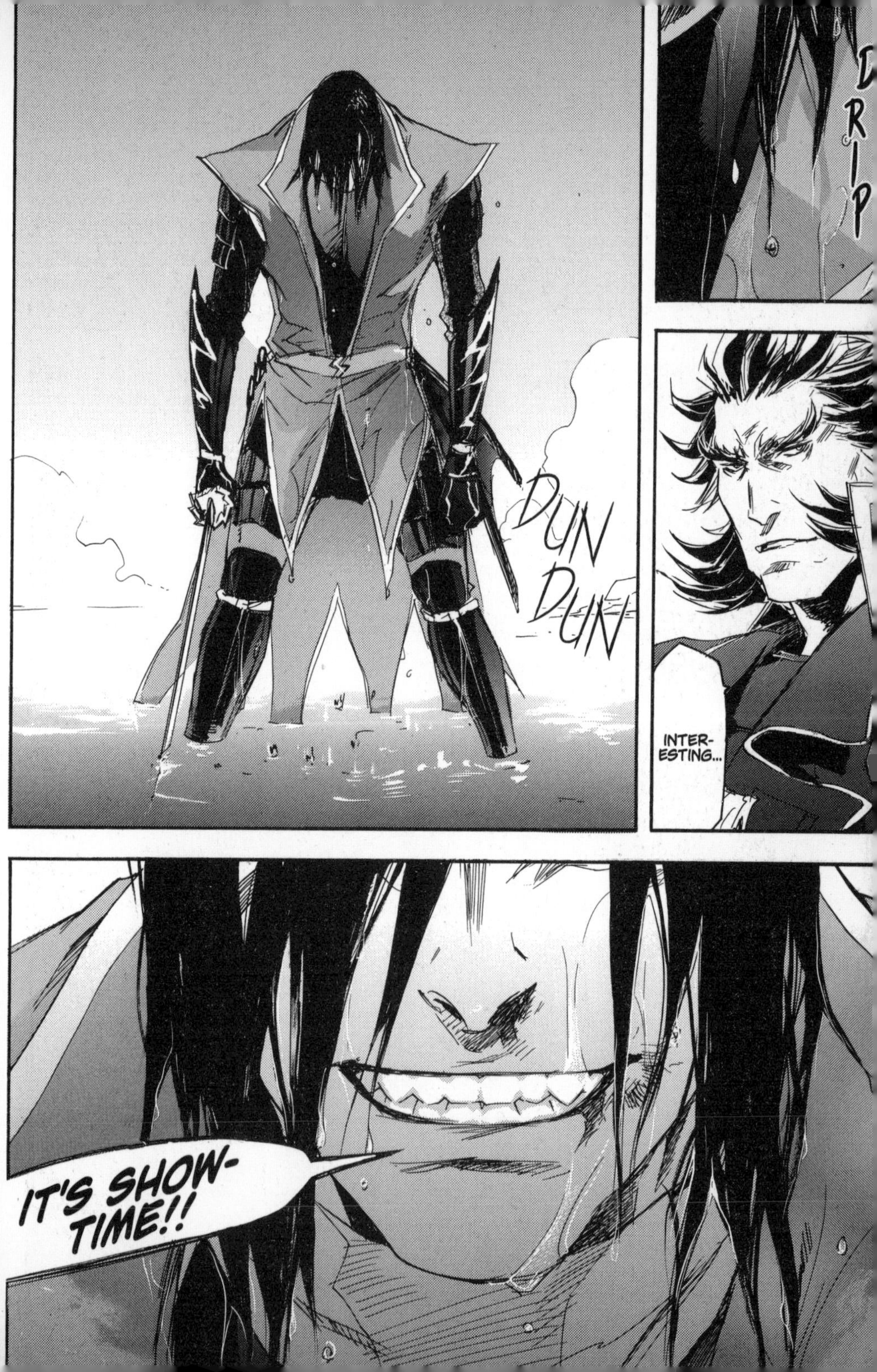
DRIP
INTER-ESTING...
DUN DUN
IT'S SHOW-TIME!!

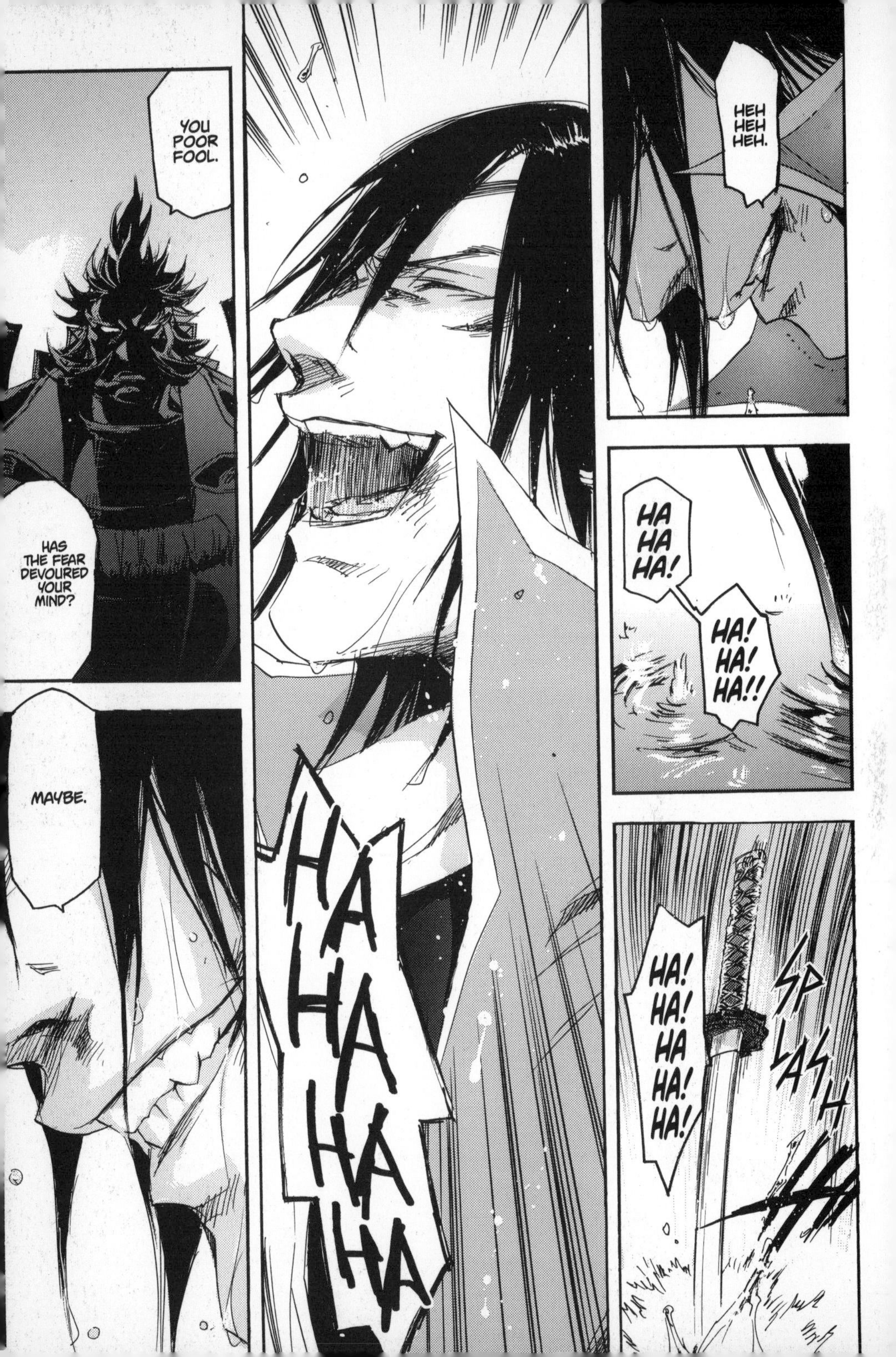
HEH HEH HEH.
HA HA HA!
HA! HA! HA!!
HA! HA! HA HA! HA!
SPLASH
HAHAHAHAHA
YOU POOR FOOL.
HAS THE FEAR DEVOURED YOUR MIND?
MAYBE.

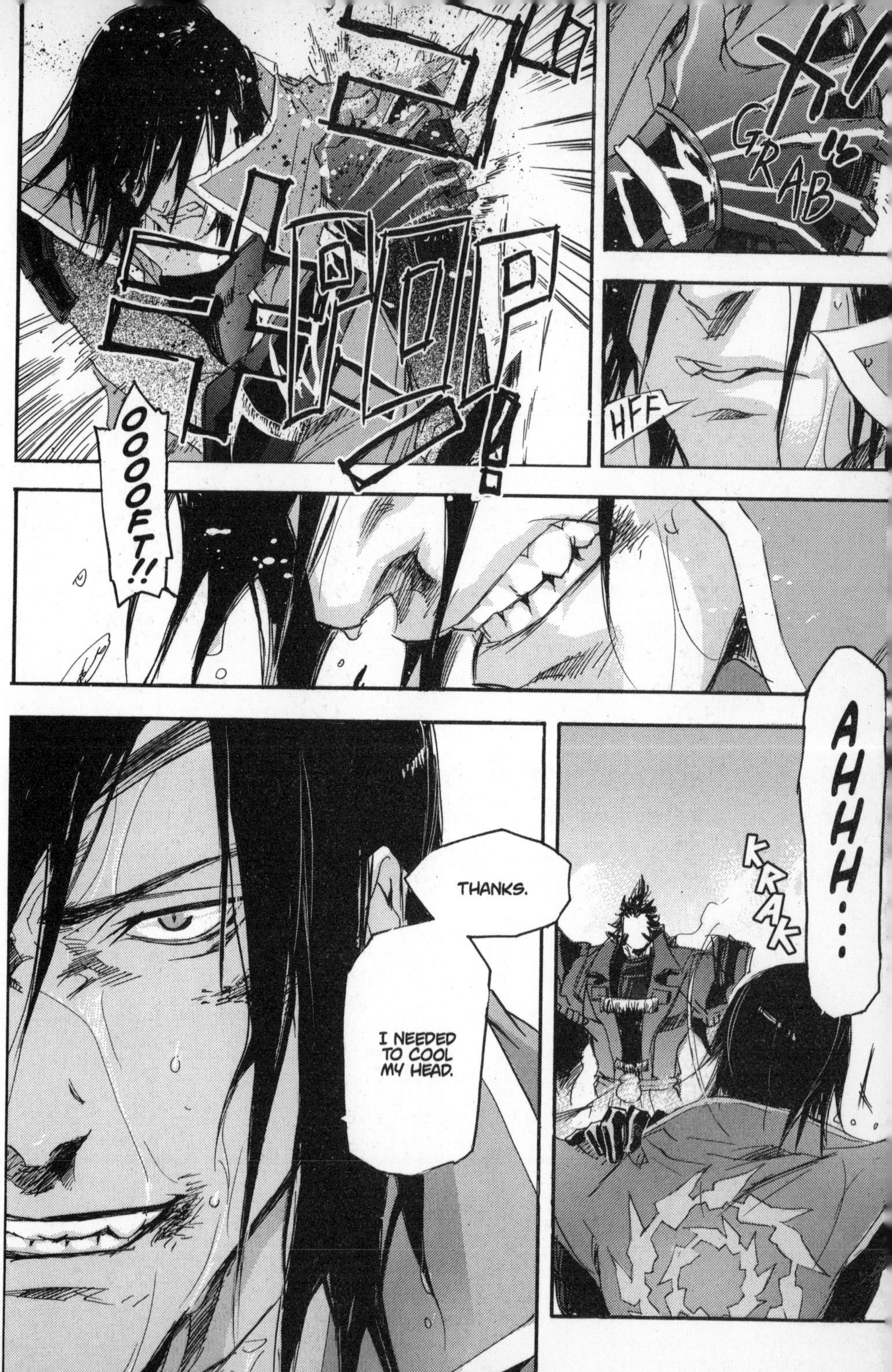
GRAB
HFF
POP!
OOOOOFT!!
AHHH...
KRAK
THANKS.
I NEEDED TO COOL MY HEAD.

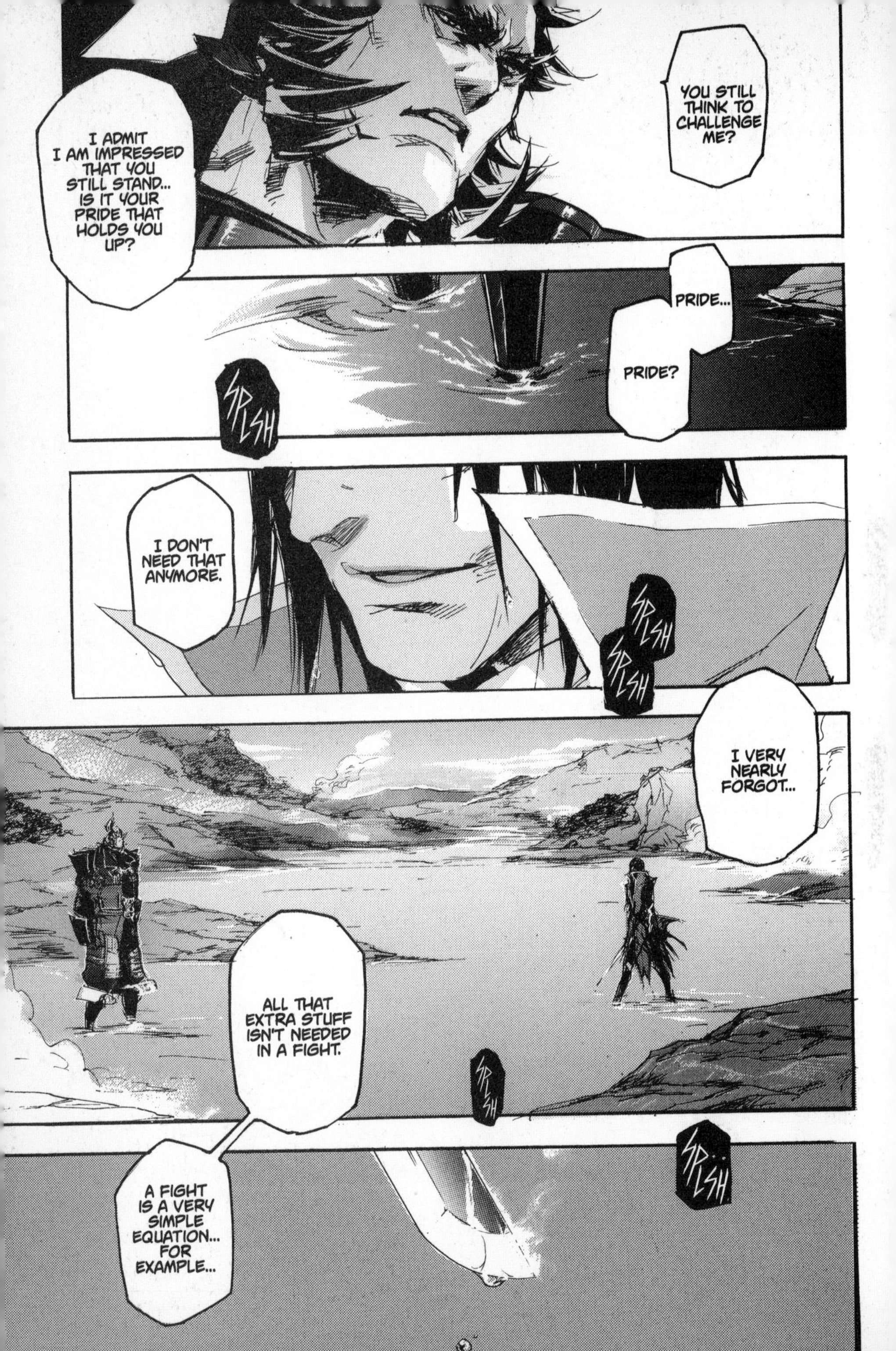
YOU STILL THINK TO CHALLENGE ME?
I ADMIT I AM IMPRESSED THAT YOU STILL STAND... IS IT YOUR PRIDE THAT HOLDS YOU UP?
PRIDE...
PRIDE?
SPLSH
I DON'T NEED THAT ANYMORE.
SPLSH
SPLSH
I VERY NEARLY FORGOT...
ALL THAT EXTRA STUFF ISN'T NEEDED IN A FIGHT.
SPLSH
SPLSH
A FIGHT IS A VERY SIMPLE EQUATION... FOR EXAMPLE...

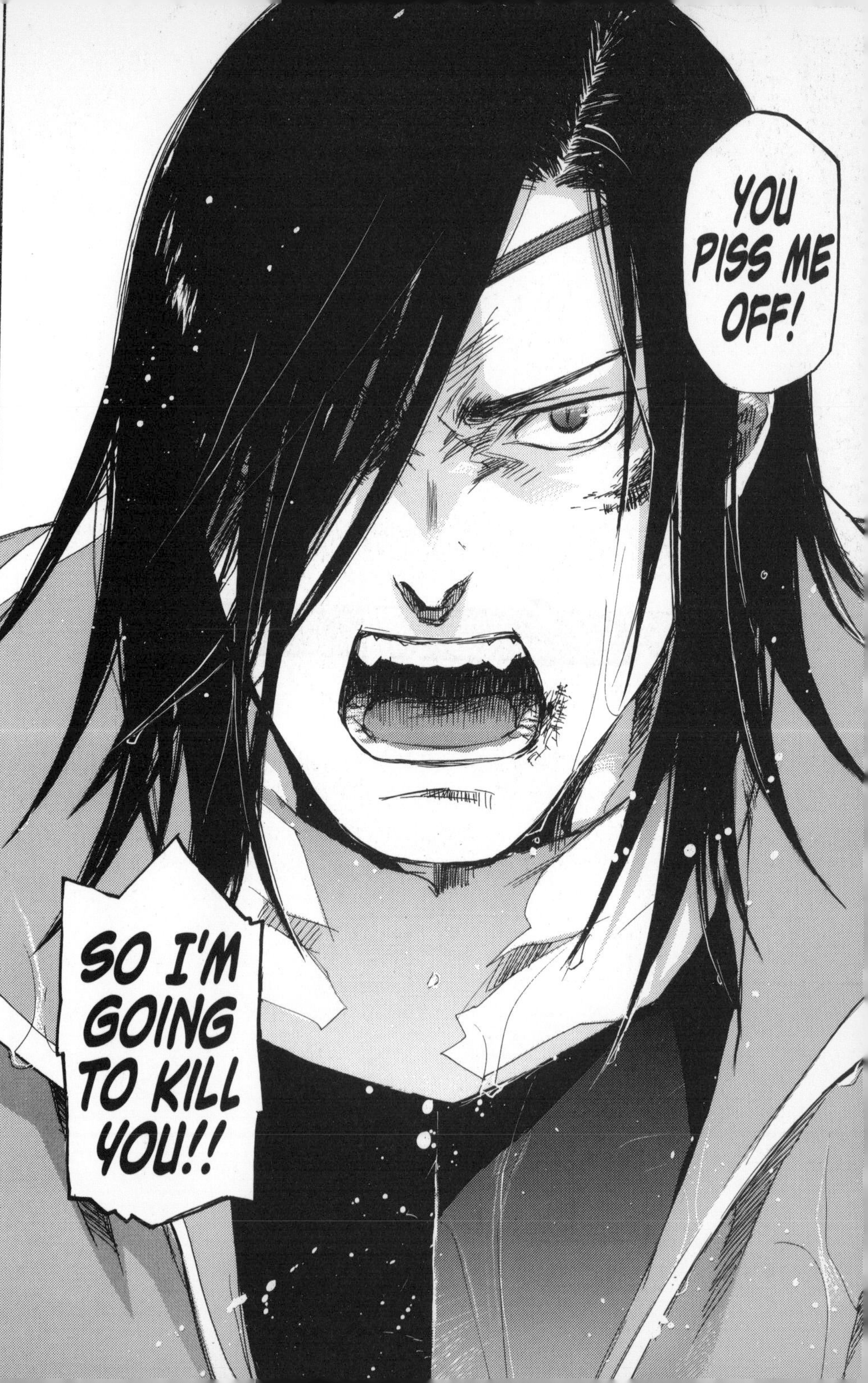
YOU PISS ME OFF!
SO I'M GOING TO KILL YOU!!

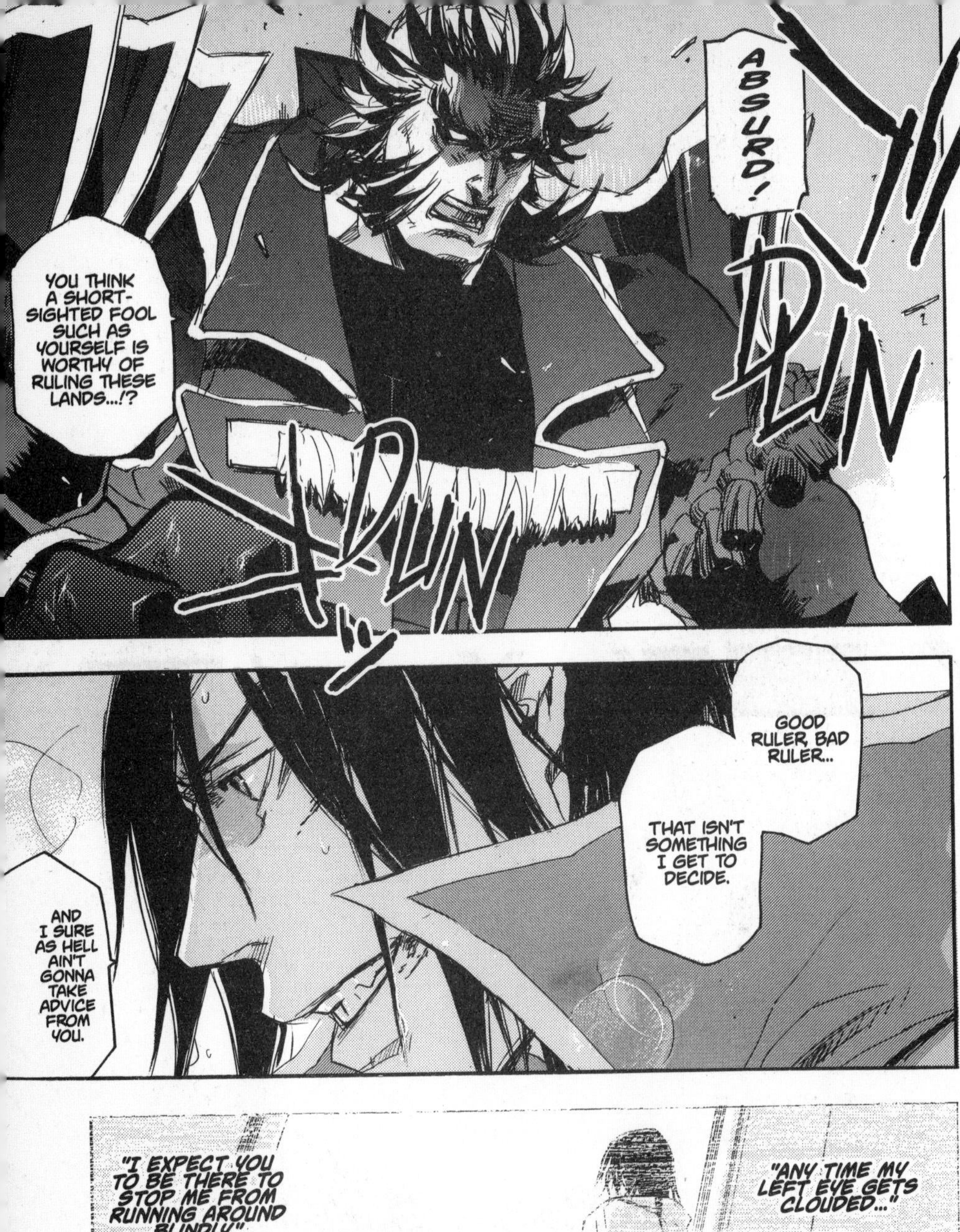
ABSURD!
DUN
DUN
YOU THINK A SHORT-SIGHTED FOOL SUCH AS YOURSELF IS WORTHY OF RULING THESE LANDS...!?
GOOD RULER, BAD RULER...
THAT ISN'T SOMETHING I GET TO DECIDE.
AND I SURE AS HELL AIN'T GONNA TAKE ADVICE FROM YOU.
"ANY TIME MY LEFT EYE GETS CLOUDED..."
"I EXPECT YOU TO BE THERE TO STOP ME FROM RUNNING AROUND BLINDLY."

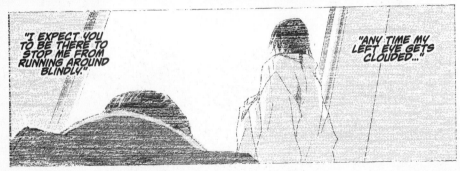

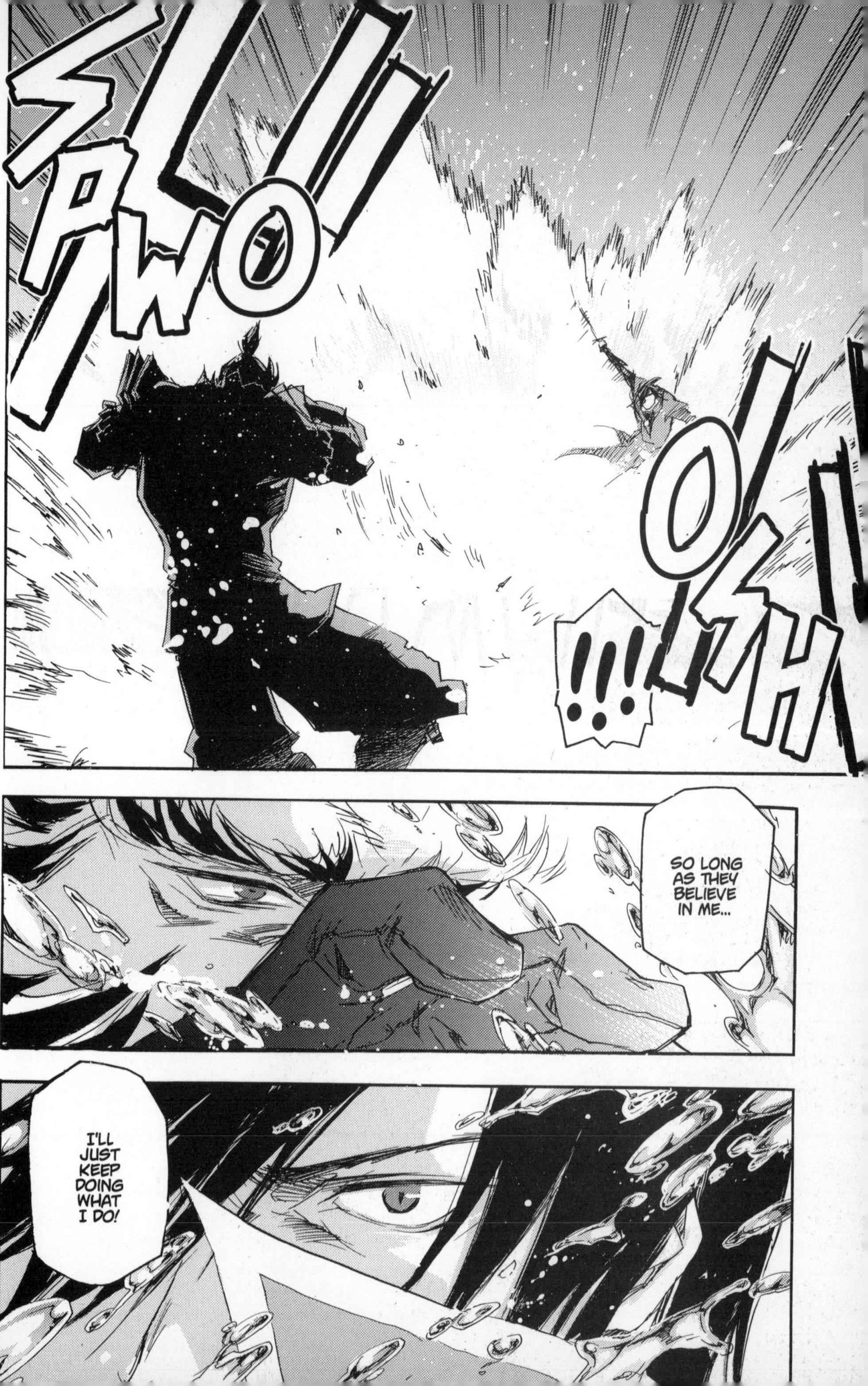
!!!
SO LONG AS THEY BELIEVE IN ME...
I'LL JUST KEEP DOING WHAT I DO!

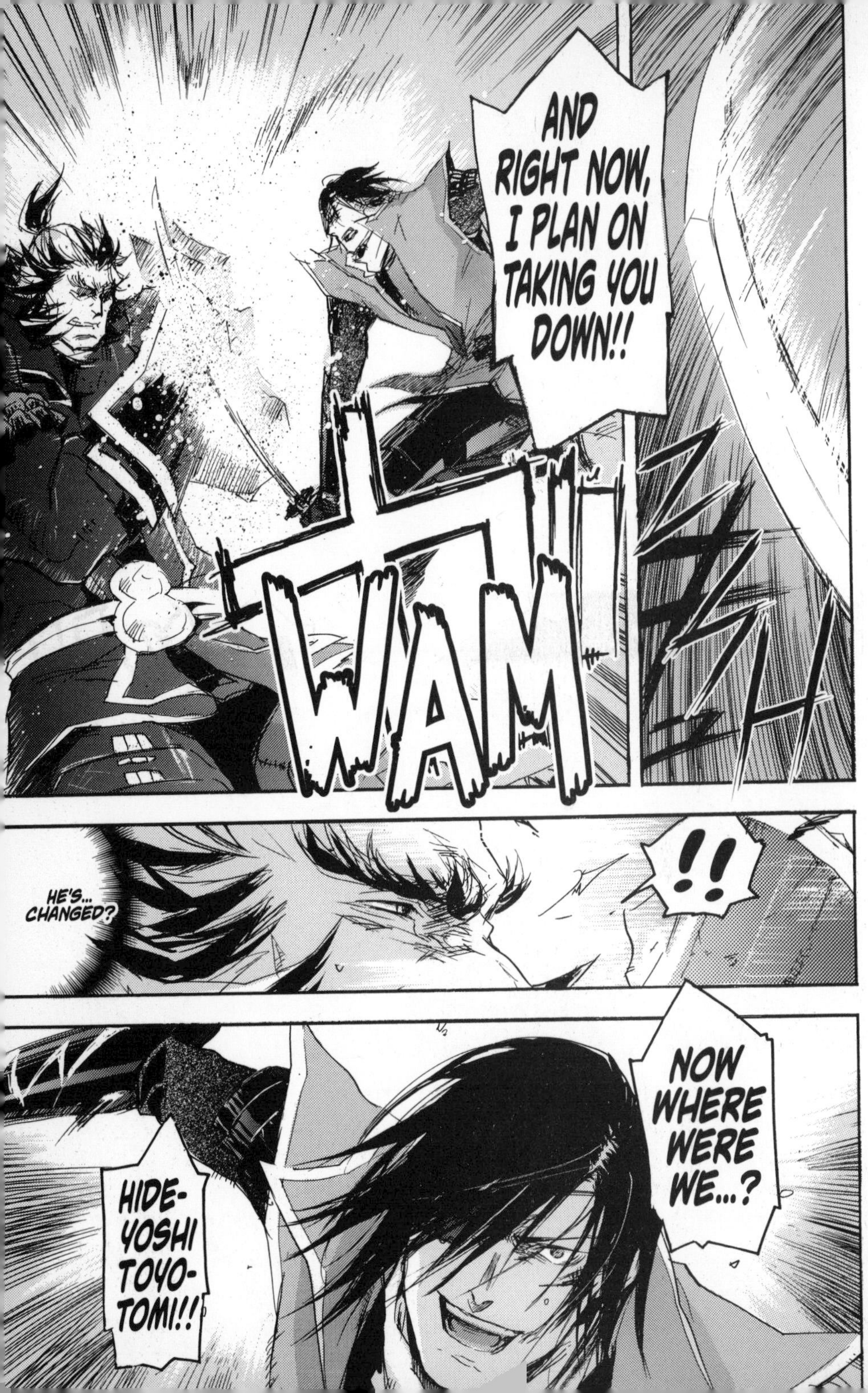
AND RIGHT NOW, I PLAN ON TAKING YOU DOWN!!
ZASH
WAM
!!
HE'S... CHANGED?
NOW WHERE WERE WE...?
HIDE-YOSHI TOYO-TOMI!!

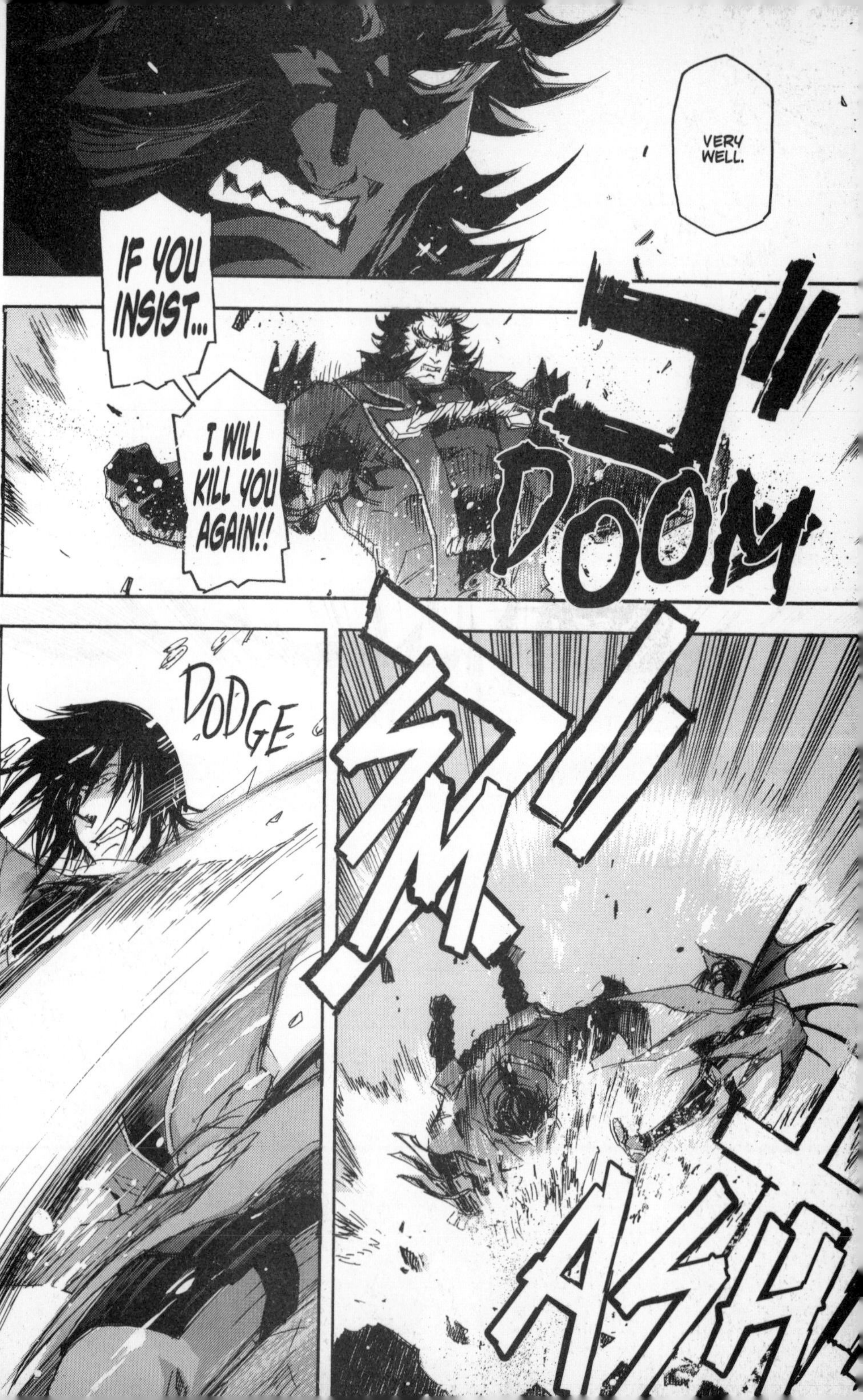
VERY WELL.
IF YOU INSIST...
I WILL KILL YOU AGAIN!!
DOOM
SM
ASH
DODGE

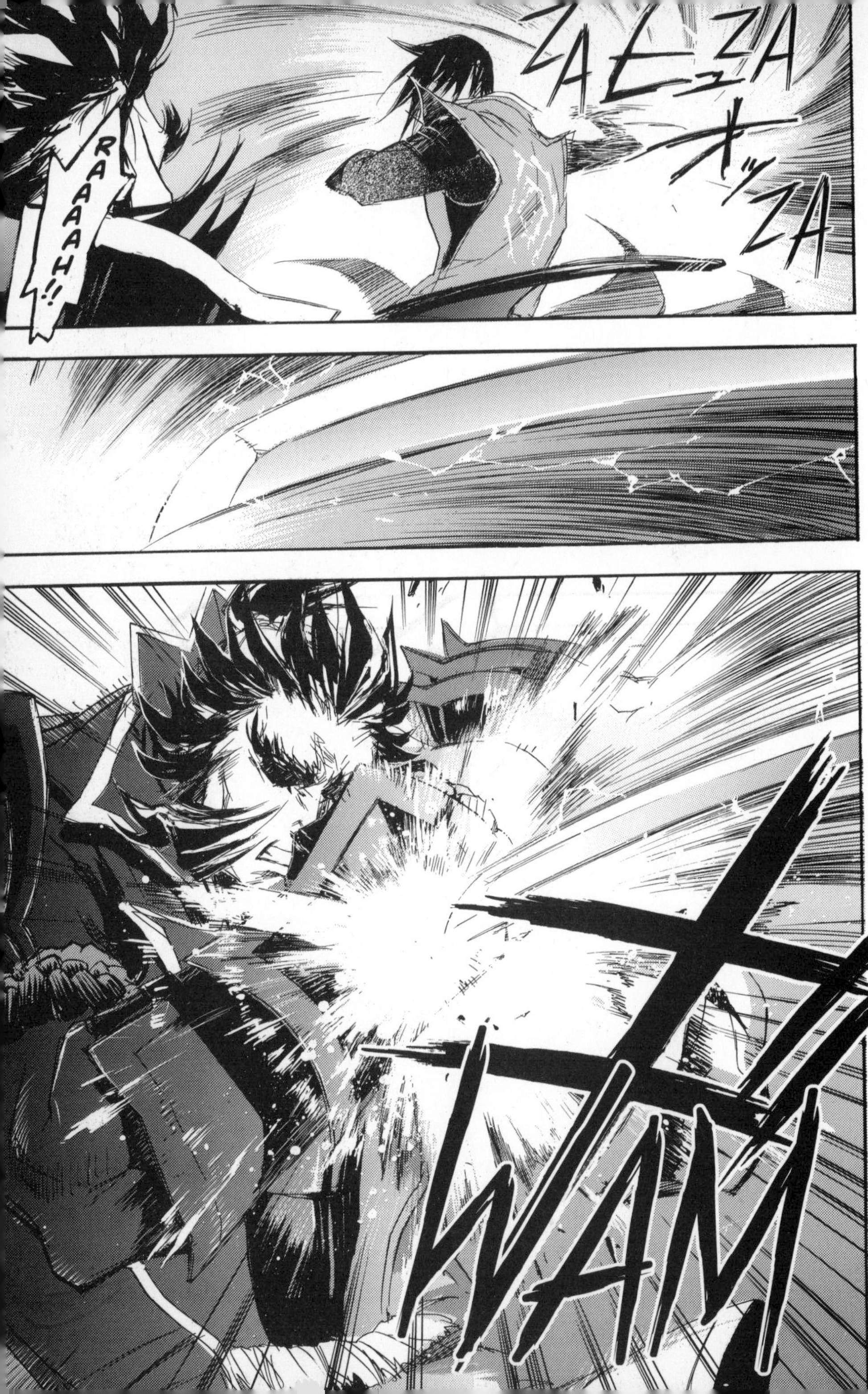
ZA ZA ZA ZA
RAAAAAH!!
WAM

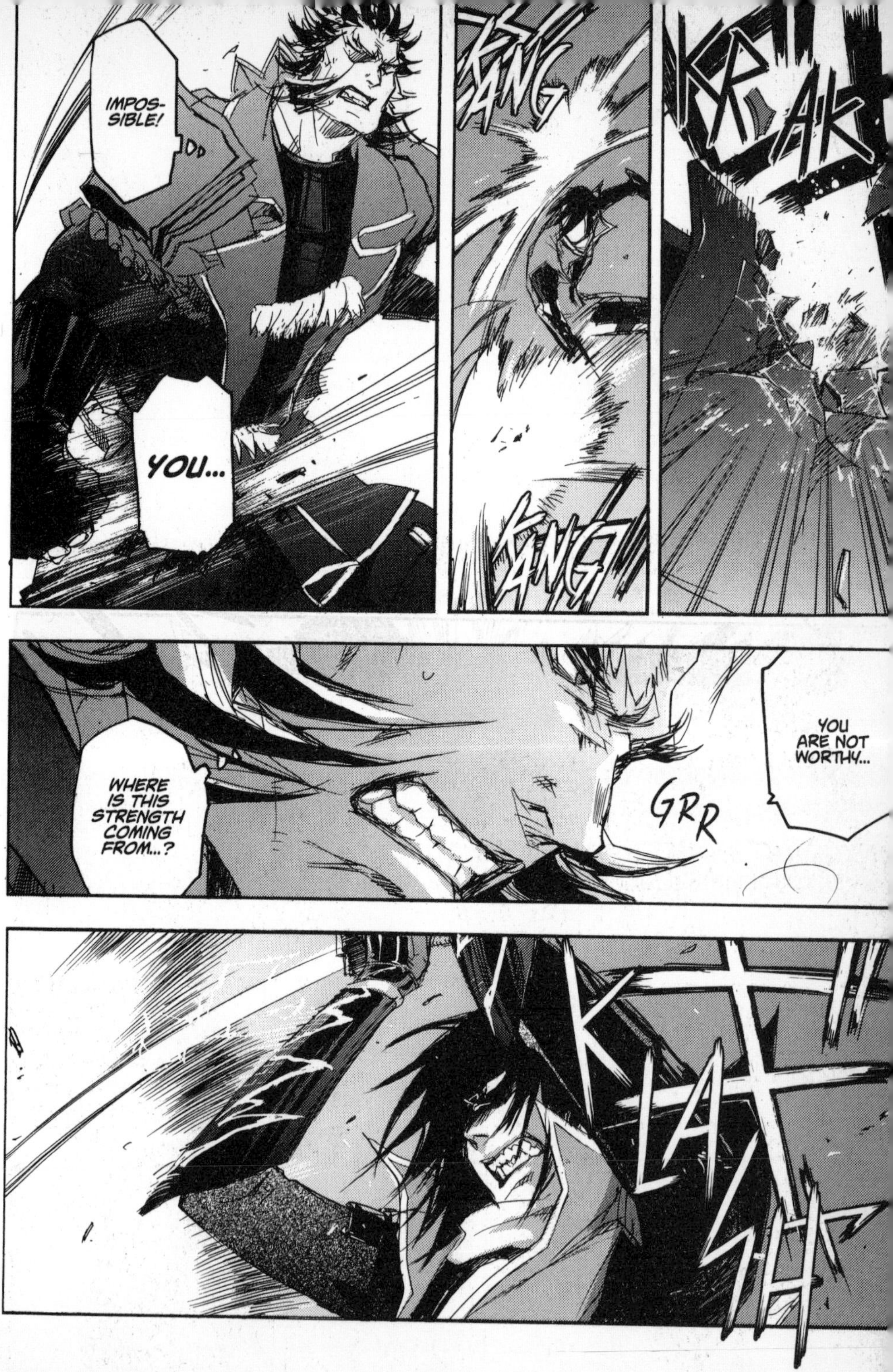
KRAK
KANG
KANG
IMPOS-SIBLE!
YOU...
YOU ARE NOT WORTHY...
GRR
WHERE IS THIS STRENGTH COMING FROM...?
KLASH

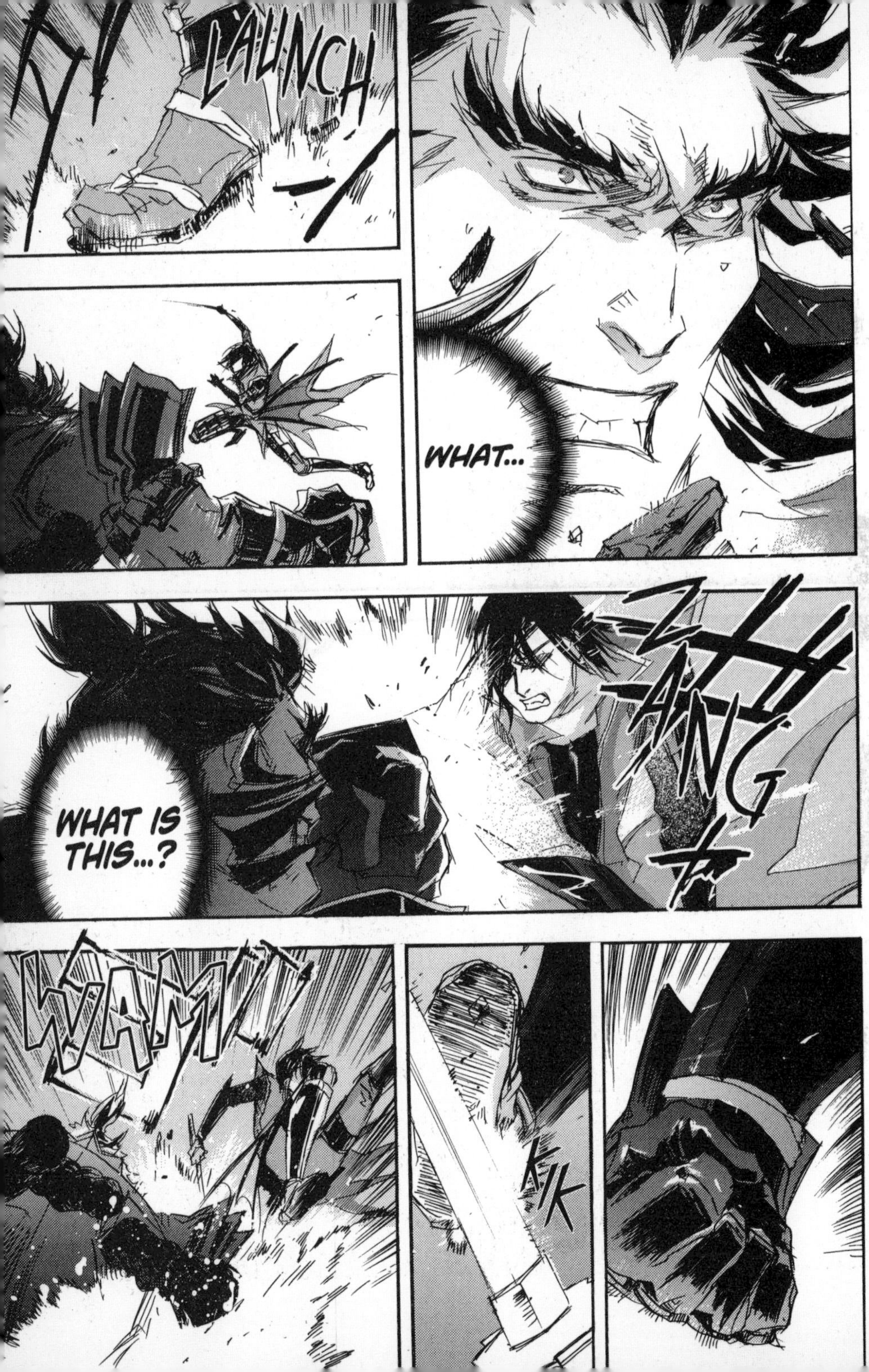
WHAT...
LAUNCH
ZHHANG
WHAT IS THIS...?
KIK
WAM!!

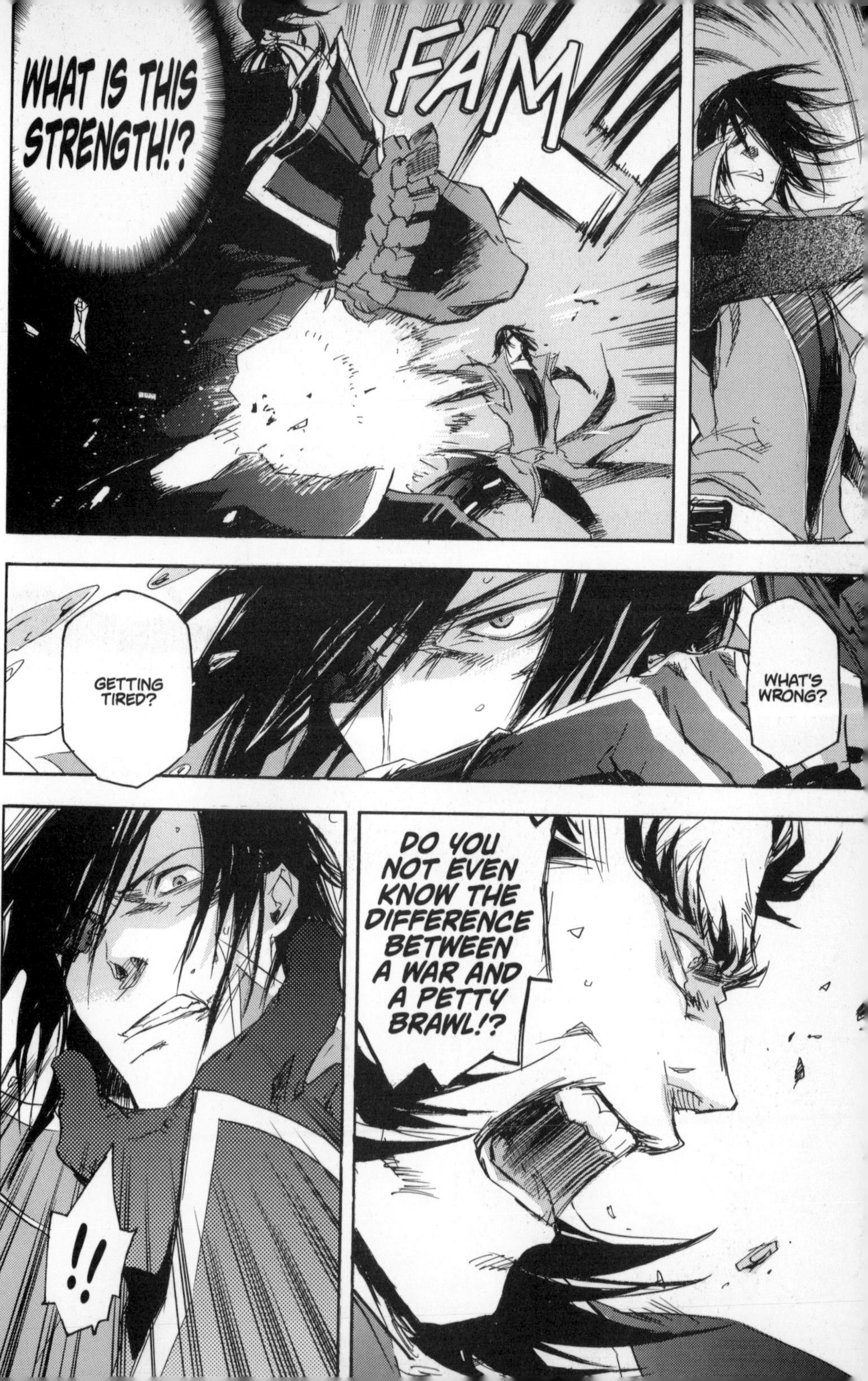
FAM
WHAT IS THIS STRENGTH!?
WHAT'S WRONG?
GETTING TIRED?
DO YOU NOT EVEN KNOW THE DIFFERENCE BETWEEN A WAR AND A PETTY BRAWL!?
!!

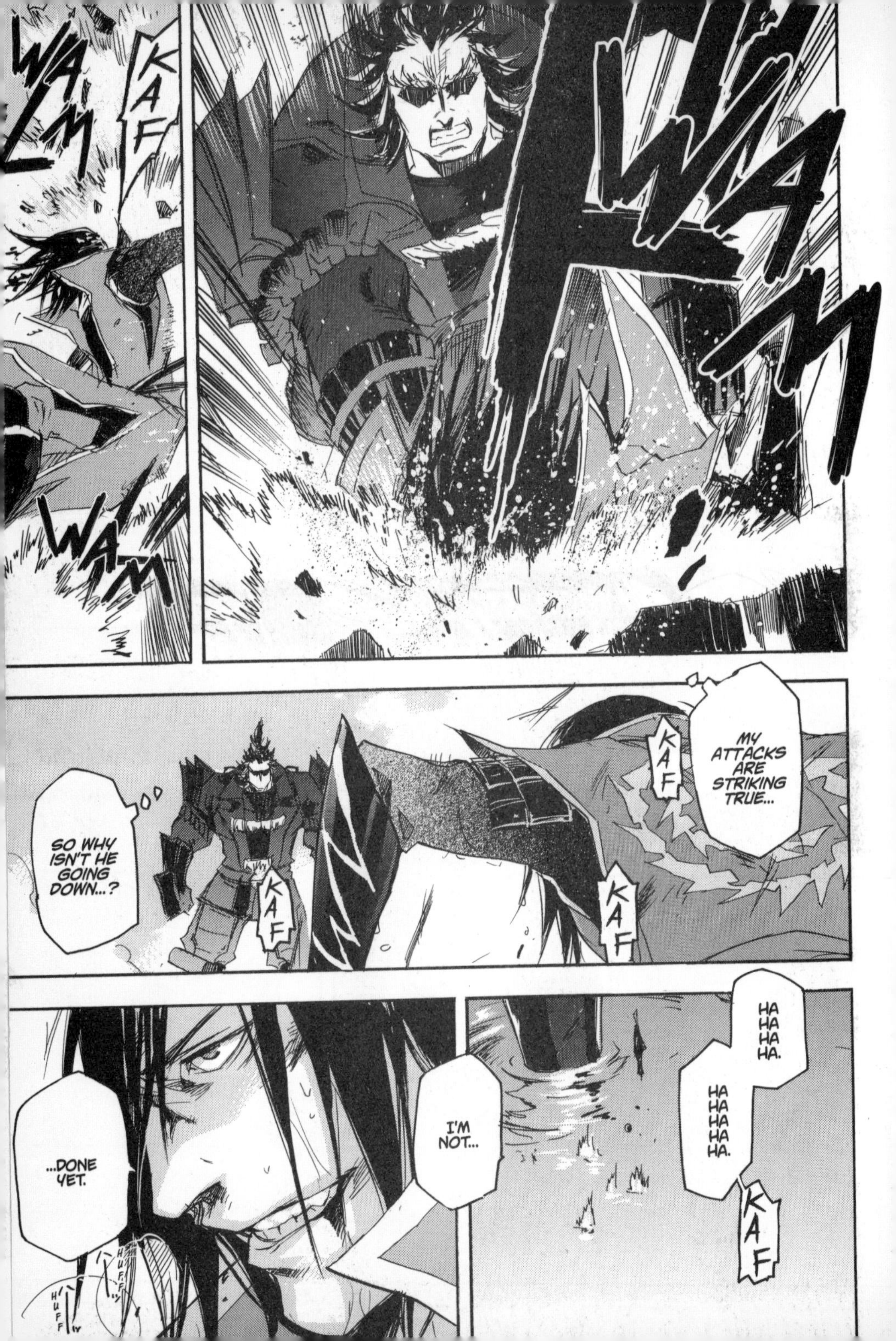
WAM
WAM
KAF
WAM
WAM
MY ATTACKS ARE STRIKING TRUE...
KAF
KAF
KAF
SO WHY ISN'T HE GOING DOWN...?
HA HA HA HA.
HA HA HA HA HA.
KAF
I'M NOT...
...DONE YET.
HUFF
HUFF

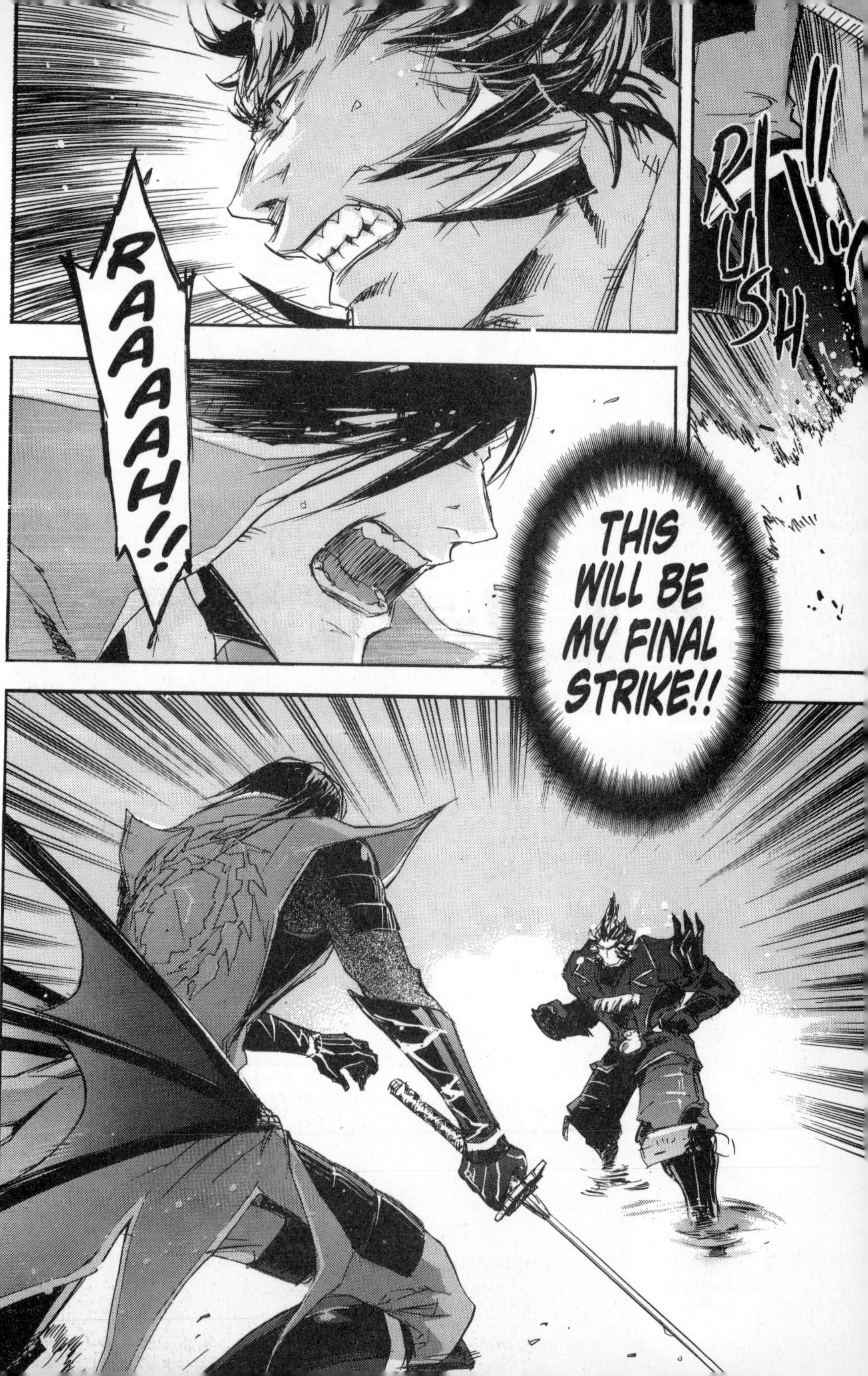
RUSH
RAAAAH!!
THIS WILL BE MY FINAL STRIKE!!

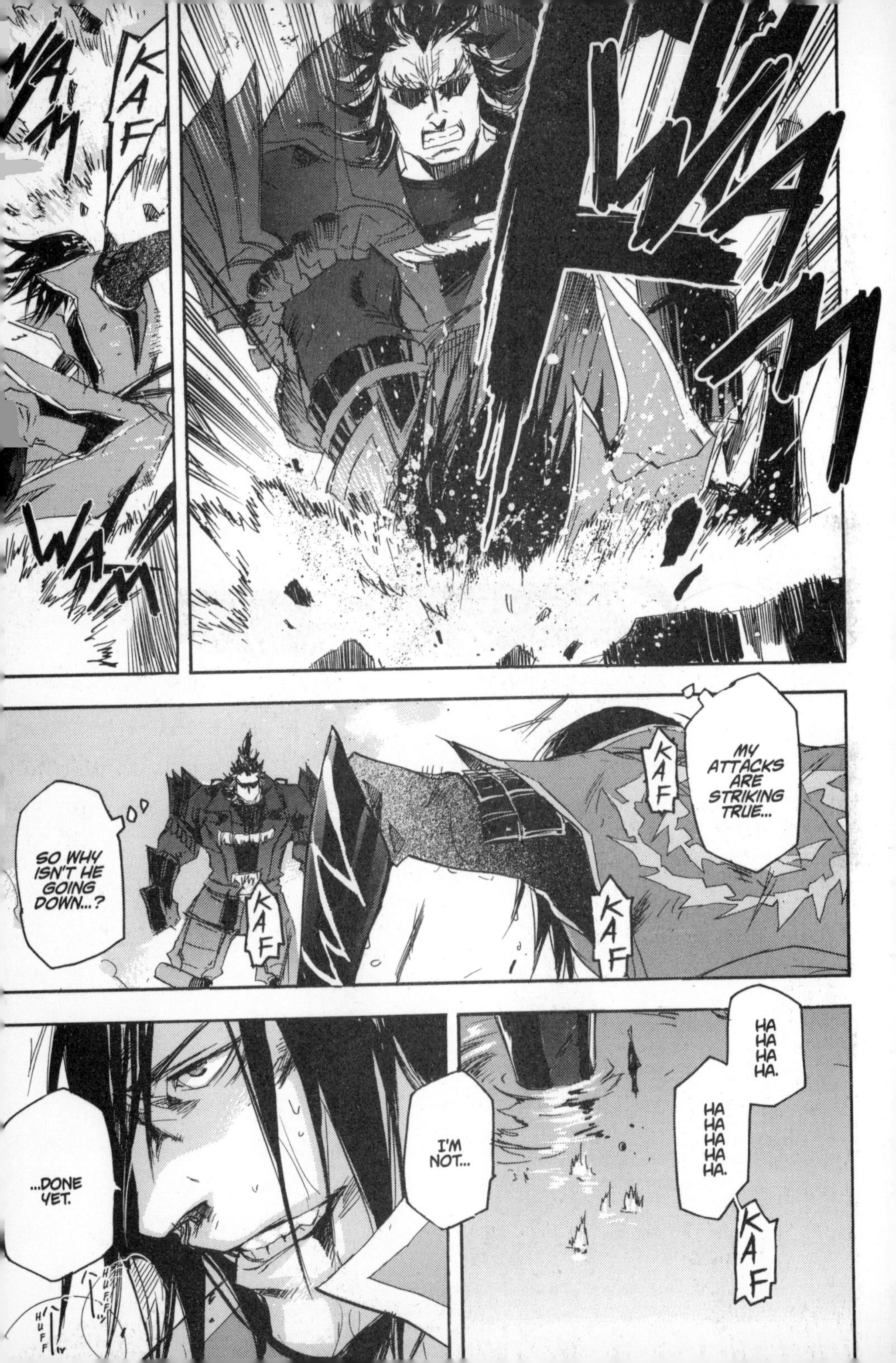
WAM
WAM
KAF
WAM
WAM
MY ATTACKS ARE STRIKING TRUE...
KAF
KAF
SO WHY ISN'T HE GOING DOWN...?
KAF
HA HA HA HA.
HA HA HA HA HA.
KAF
I'M NOT...
...DONE YET.
HUFF
HUFF
HUFF

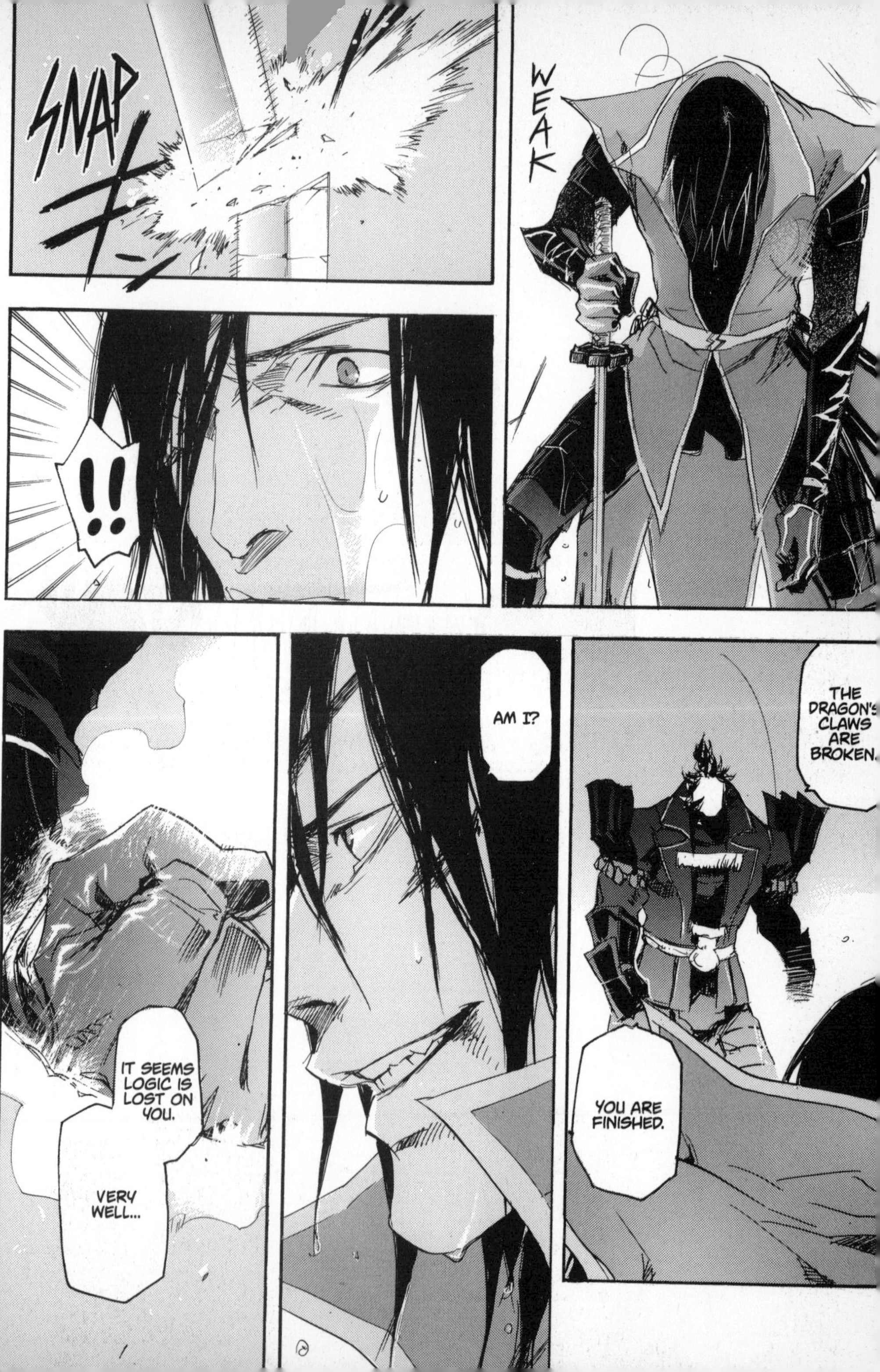
WEAK
SNAP
!!
THE DRAGON'S CLAWS ARE BROKEN.
YOU ARE FINISHED.
AM I?
IT SEEMS LOGIC IS LOST ON YOU.
VERY WELL...

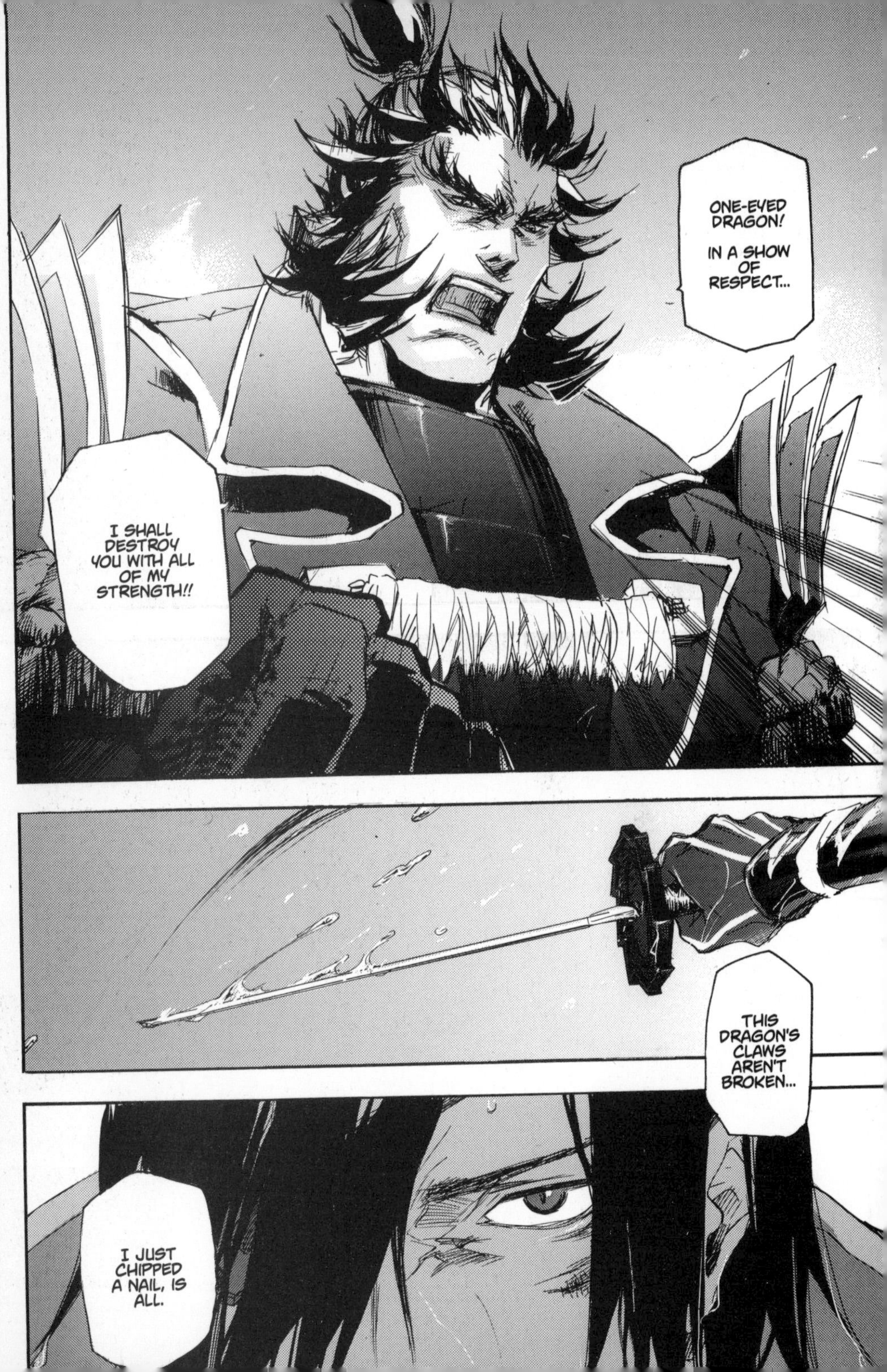
ONE-EYED DRAGON!
IN A SHOW OF RESPECT...
I SHALL DESTROY YOU WITH ALL OF MY STRENGTH!!
THIS DRAGON'S CLAWS AREN'T BROKEN...
I JUST CHIPPED A NAIL, IS ALL.

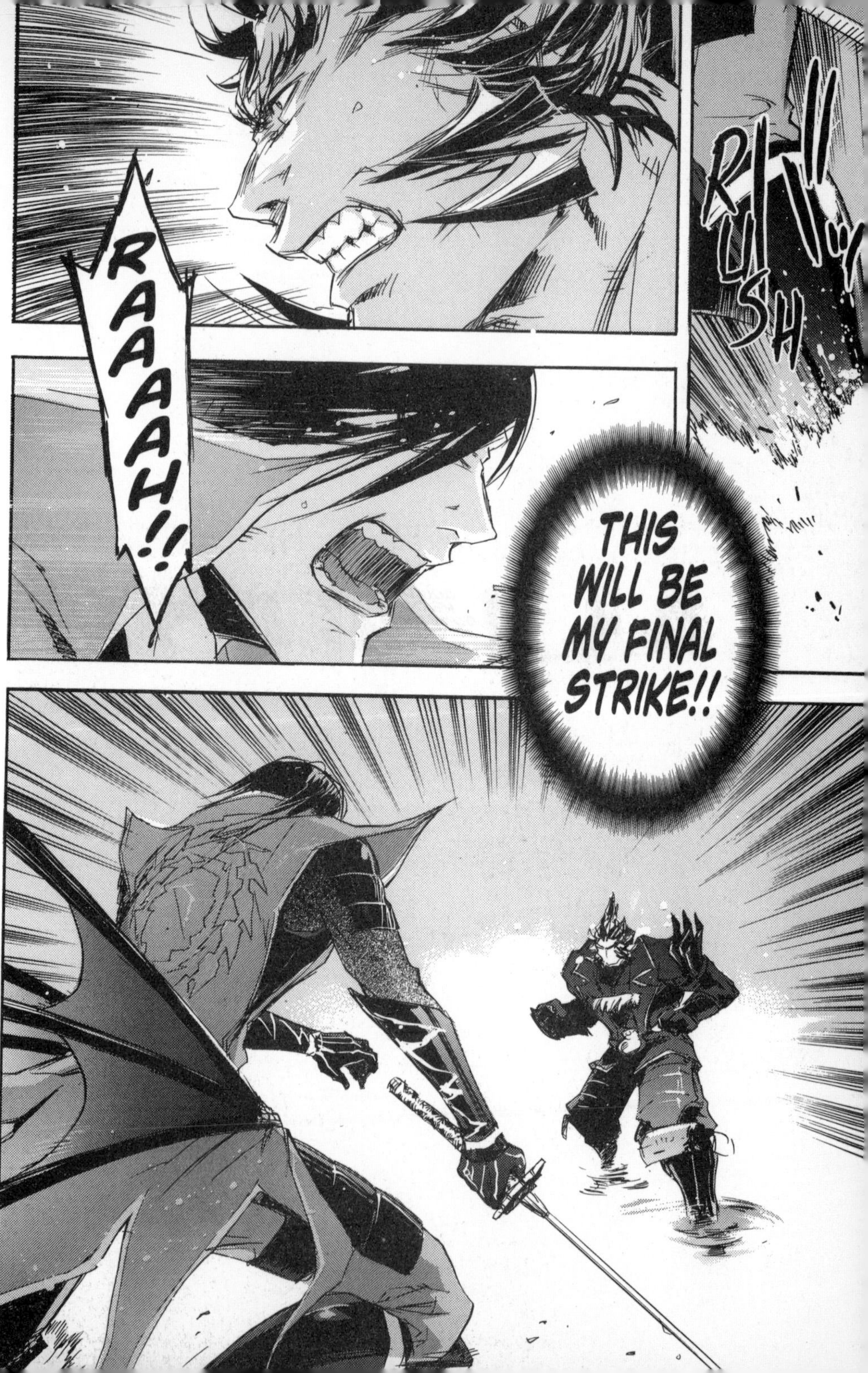
RUSH
RAAAAAH!!
THIS WILL BE MY FINAL STRIKE!!

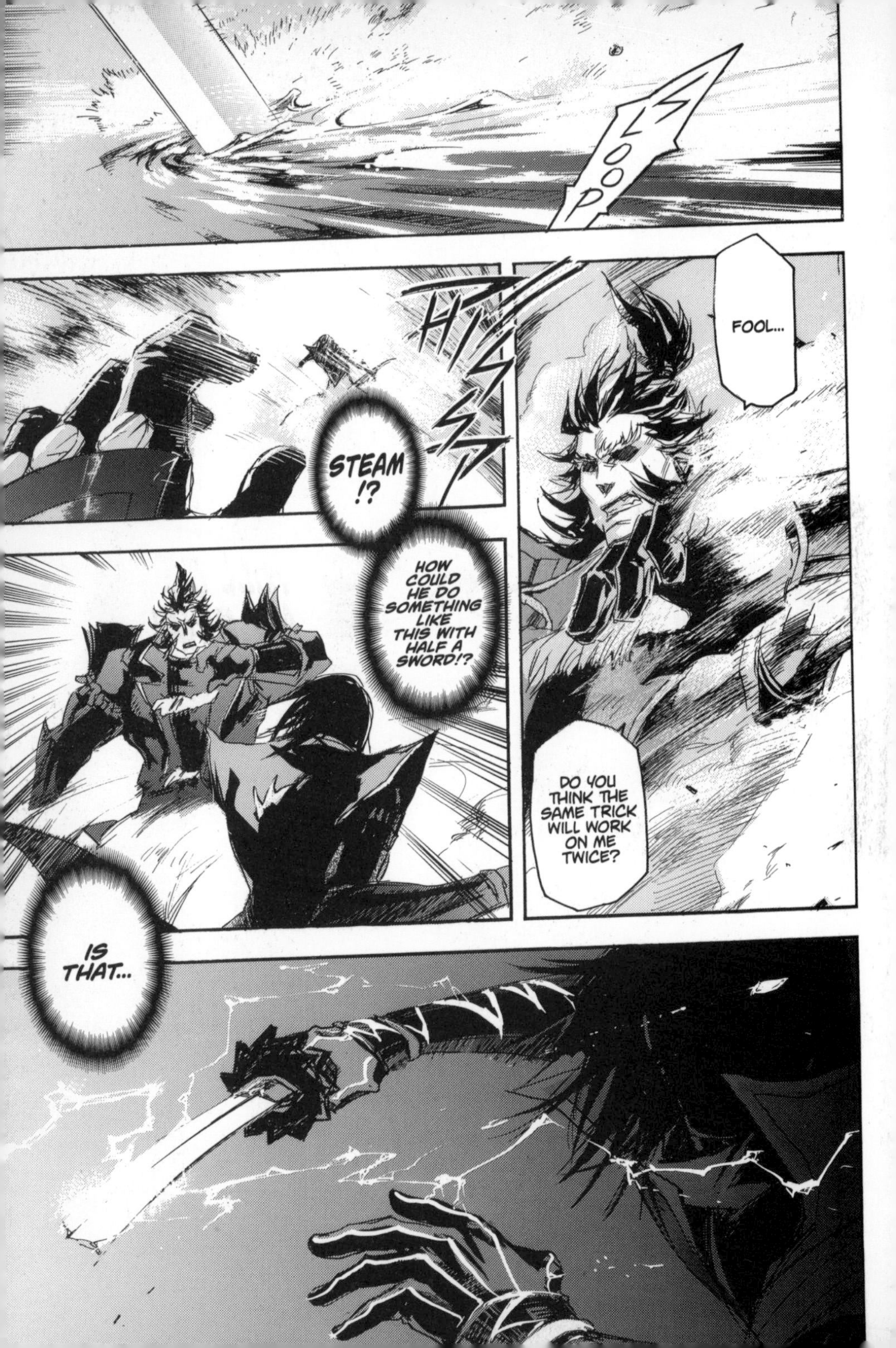
SLOOP
FOOL...
DO YOU THINK THE SAME TRICK WILL WORK ON ME TWICE?
HISSS
STEAM!?
HOW COULD HE DO SOMETHING LIKE THIS WITH HALF A SWORD!?
IS THAT...

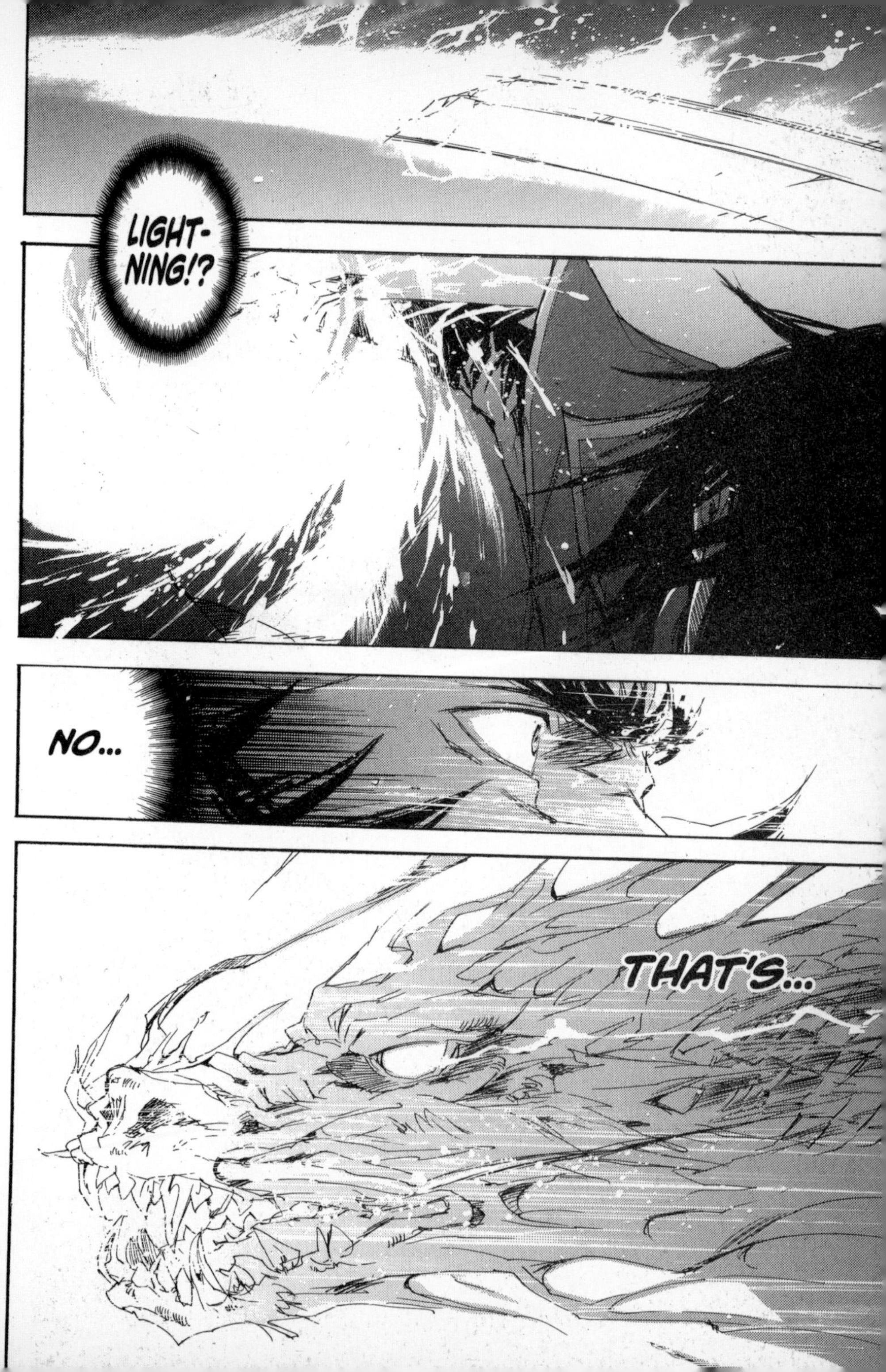
LIGHT-
NING!?
NO...
THAT'S...

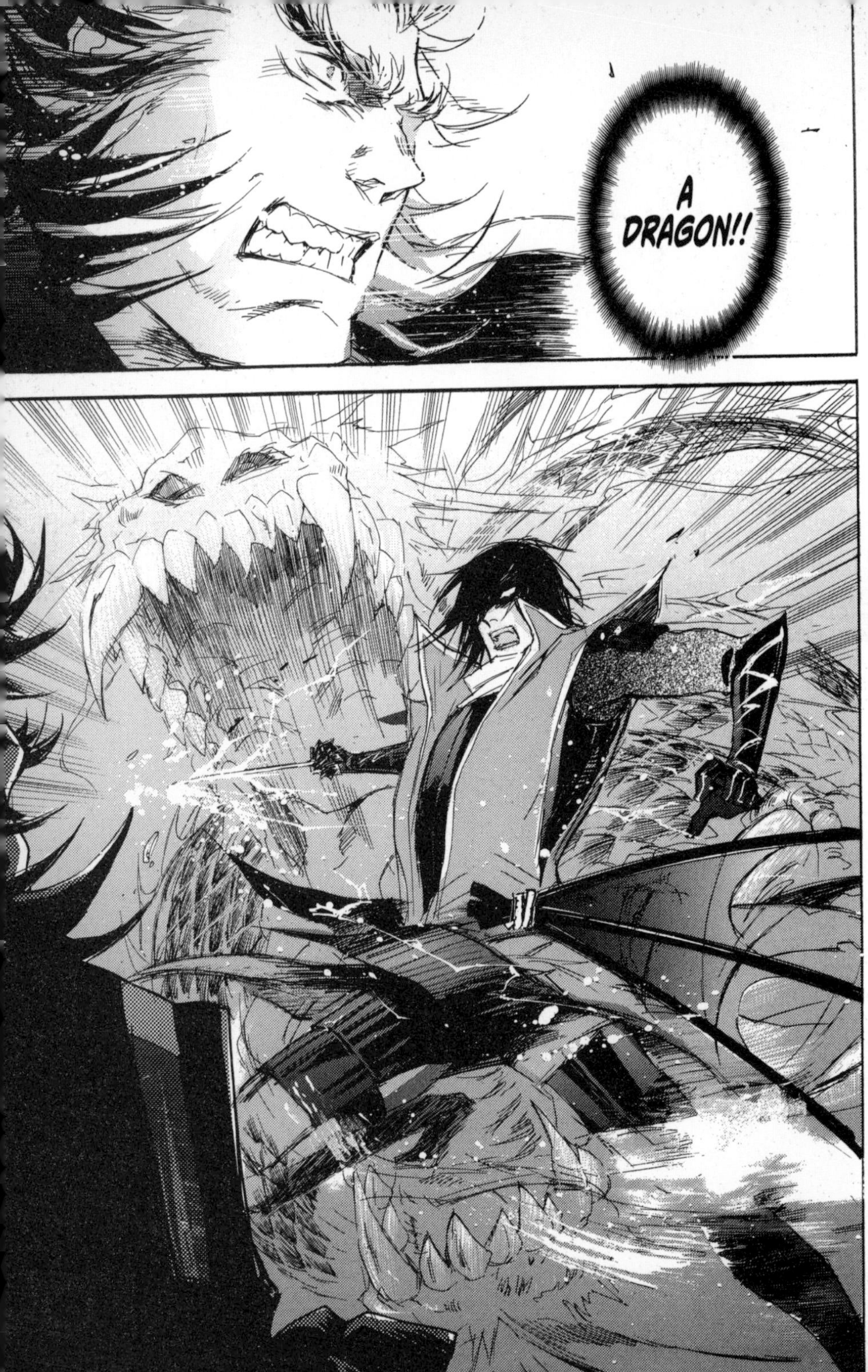
A DRAGON!!

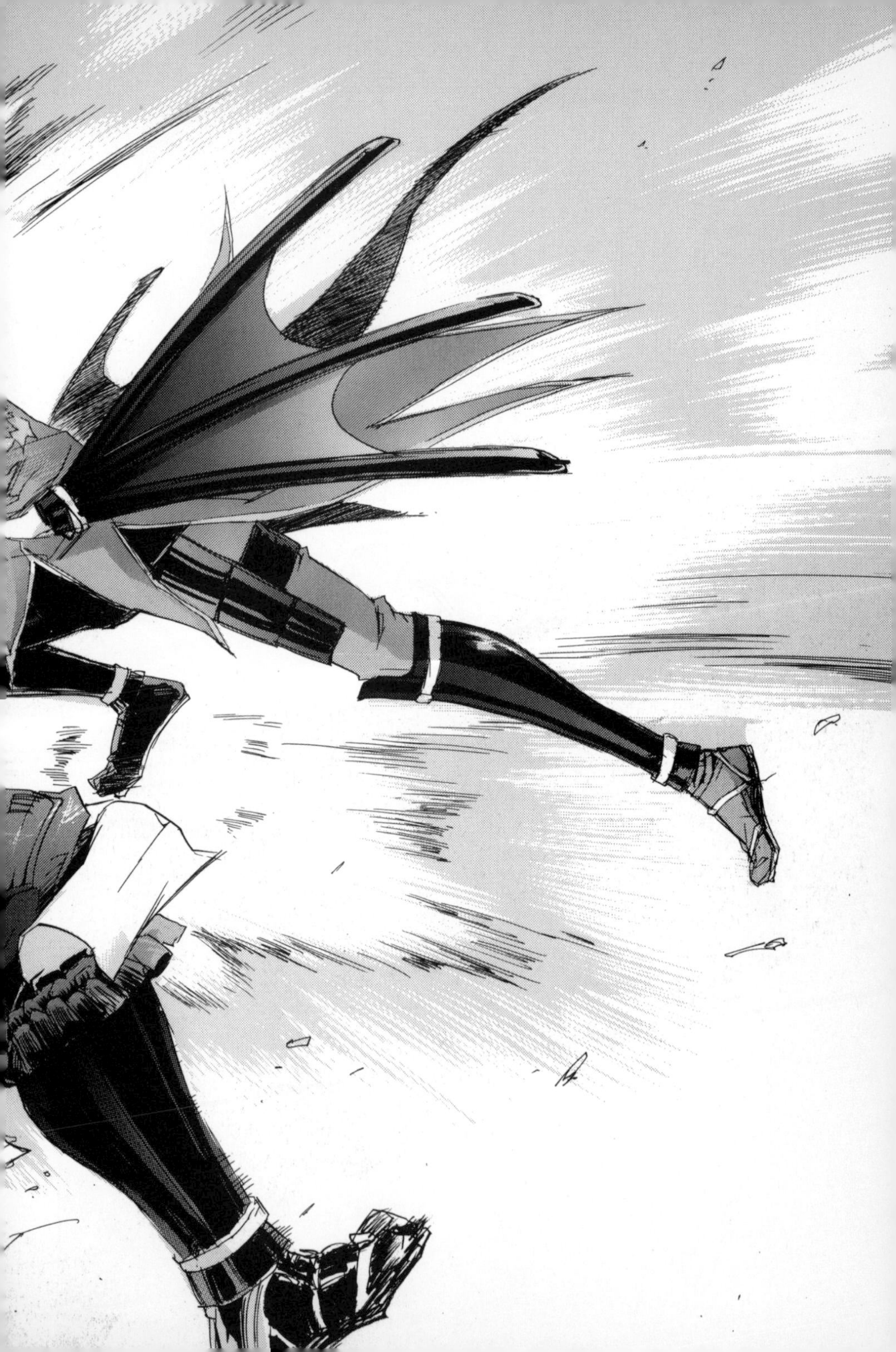

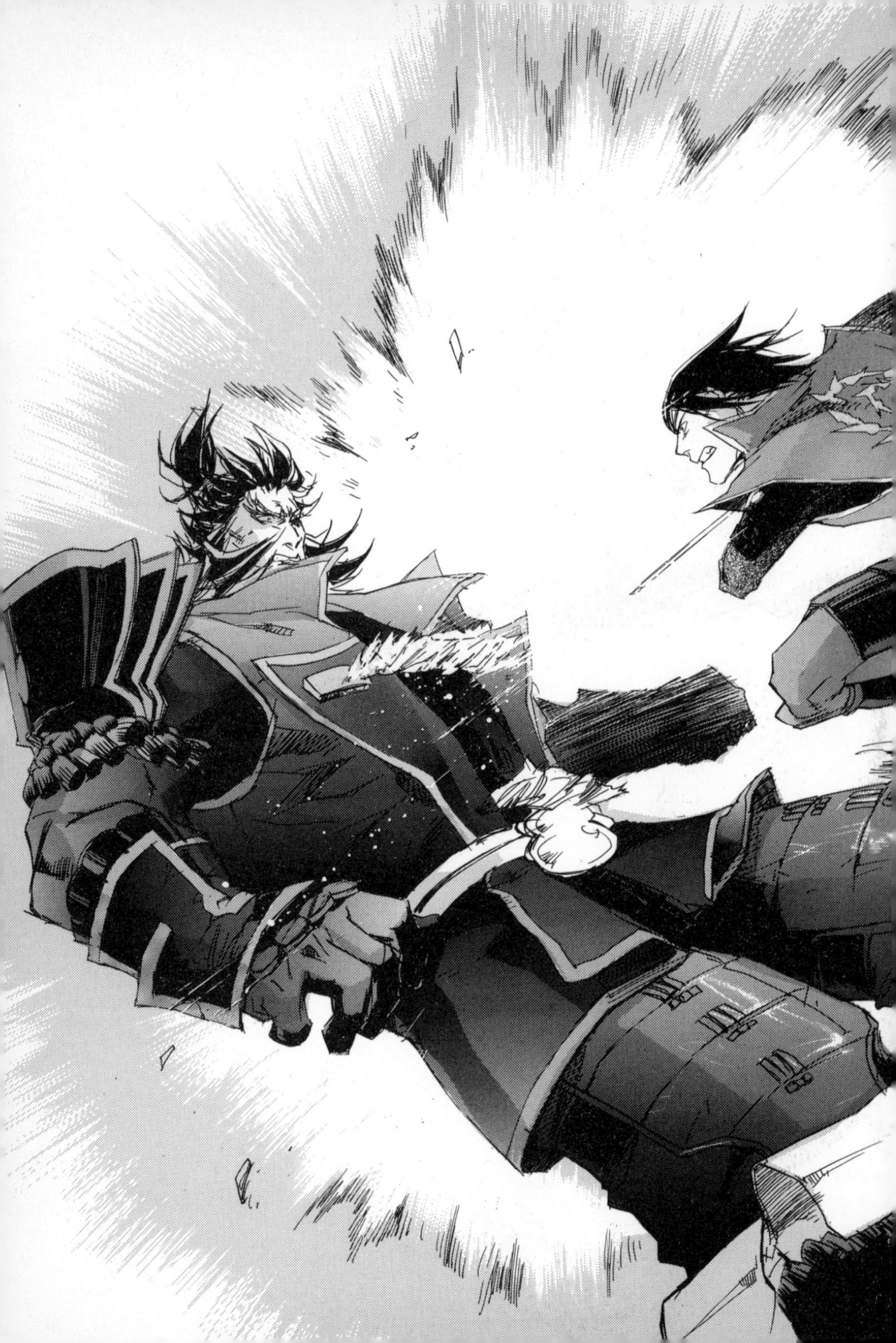

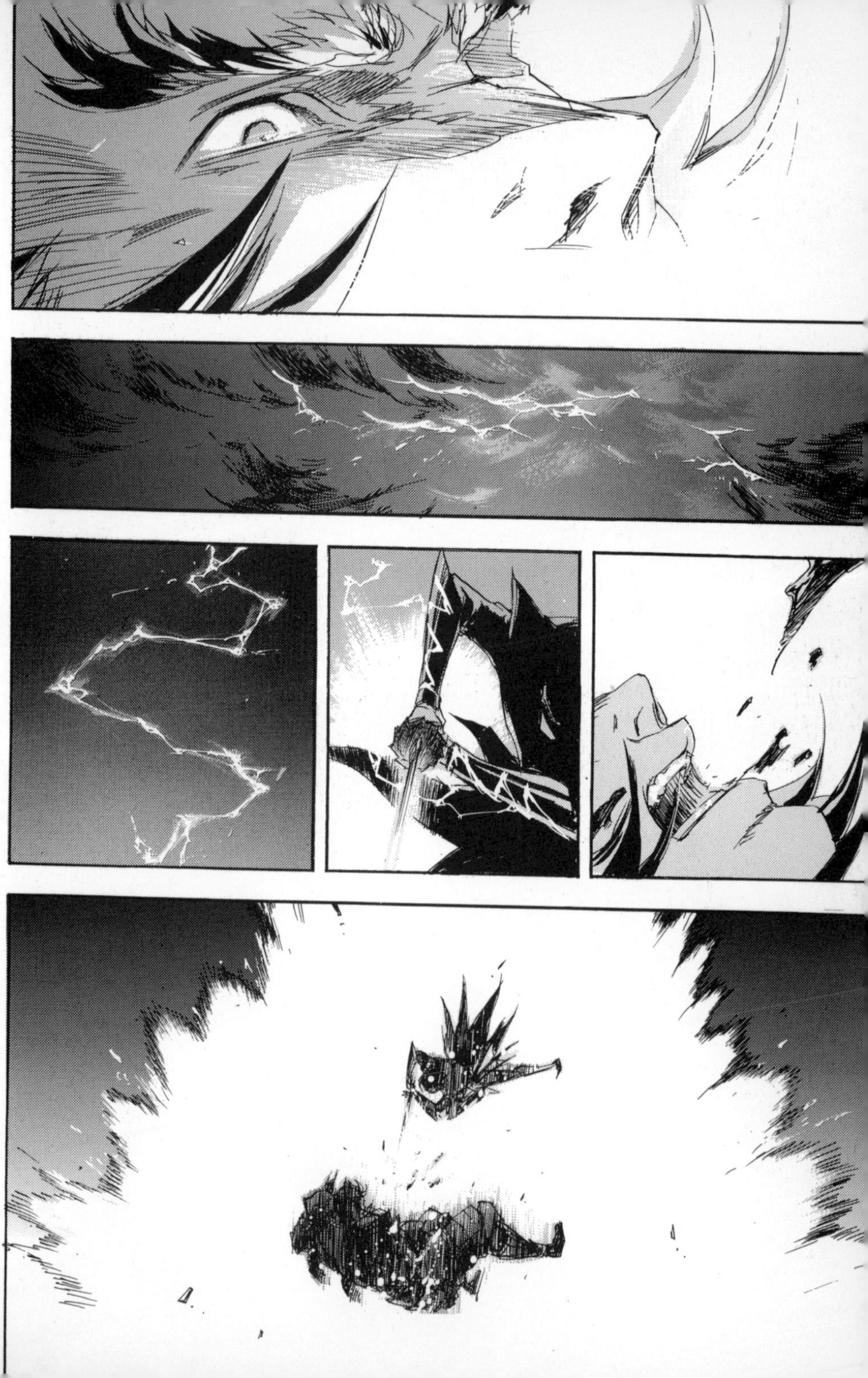

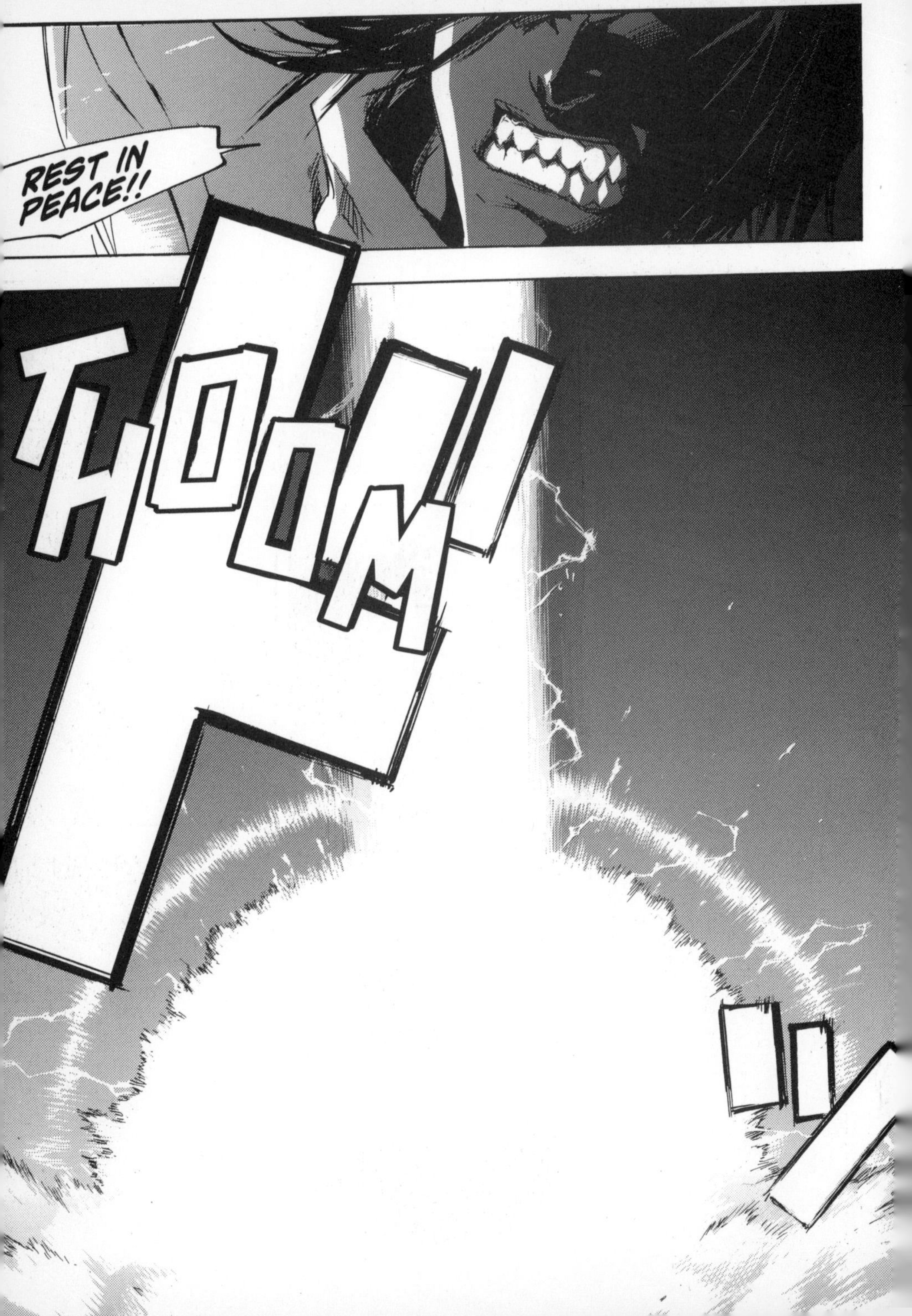
REST IN PEACE!!
THOOM!

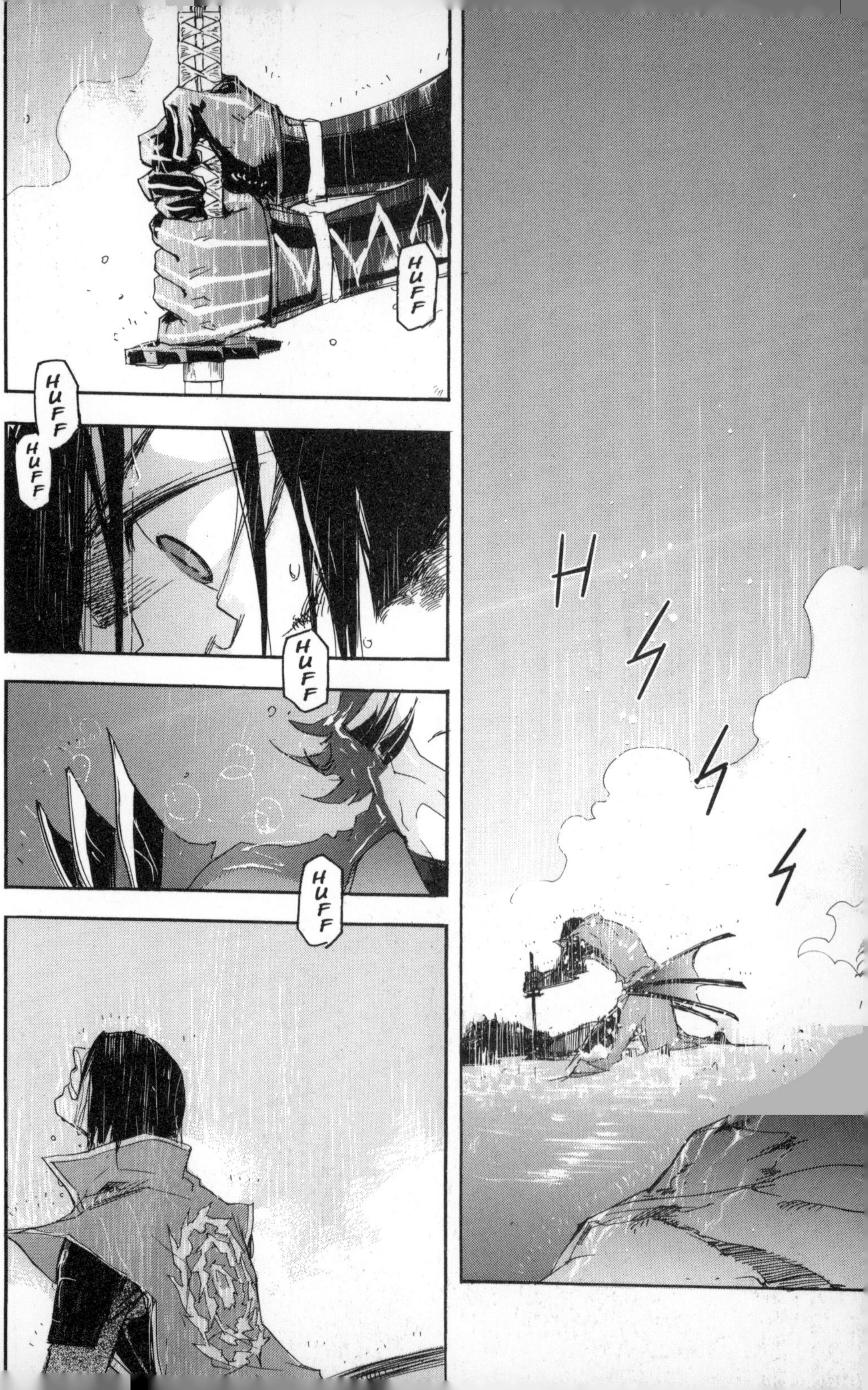
HSSSS
HUFF
HUFF
HUFF
HUFF
HUFF

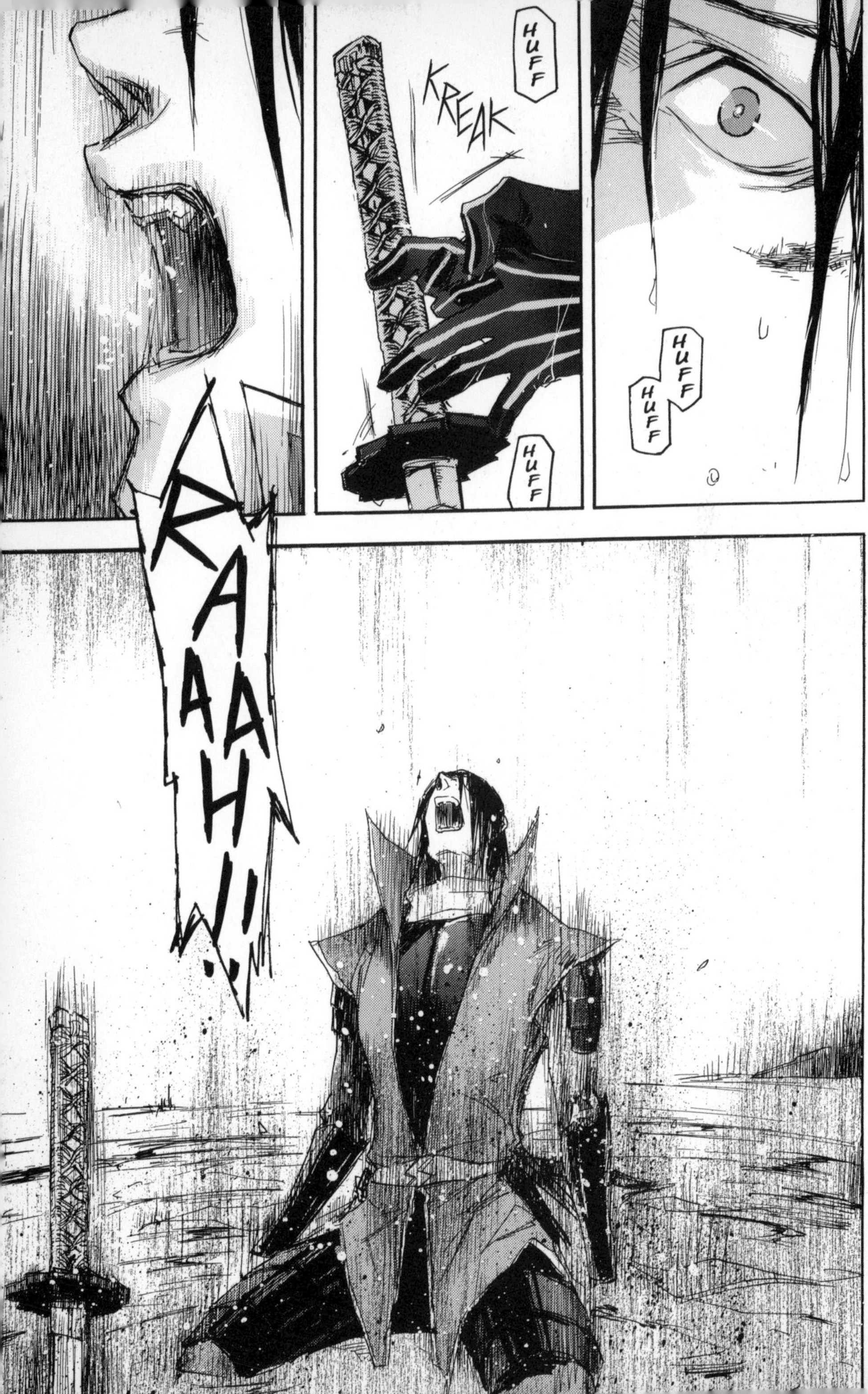
HUFF
HUFF
HUFF
KREAK
HUFF
KRAAAH!!

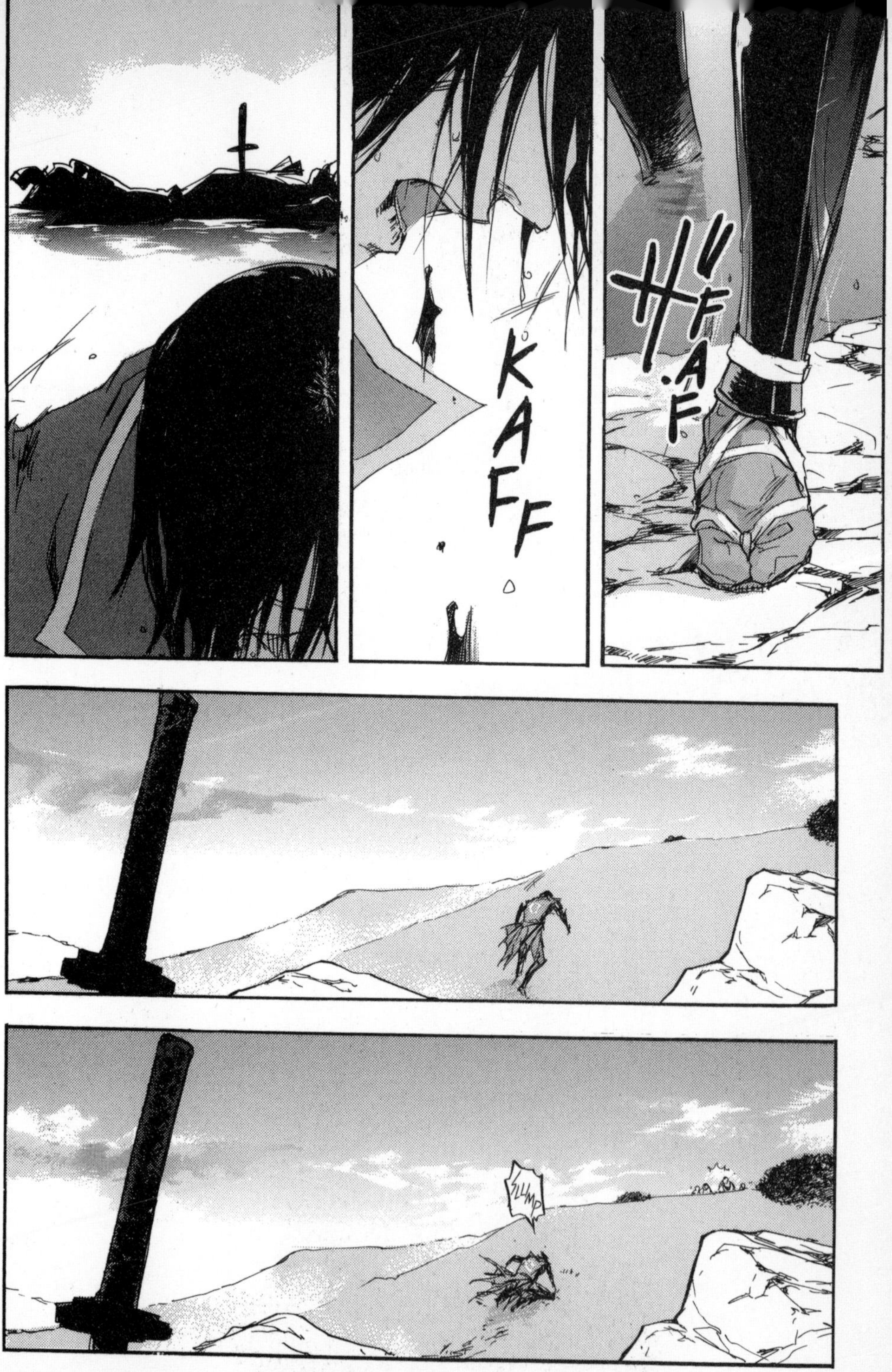
HUFAF
KAFF
SLUMP

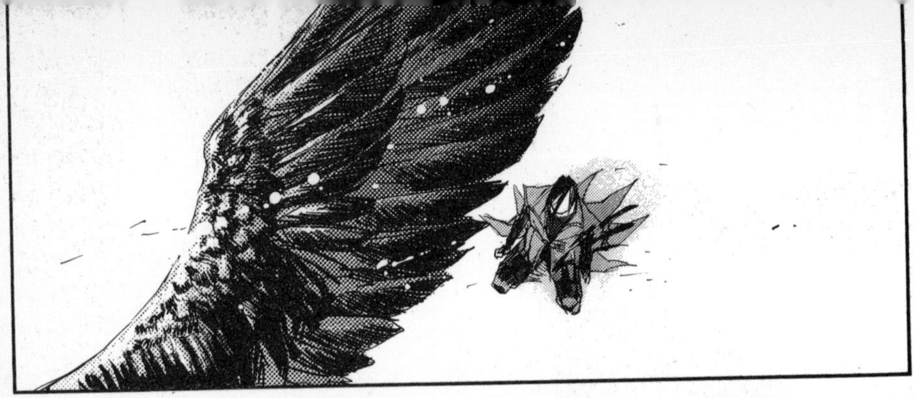
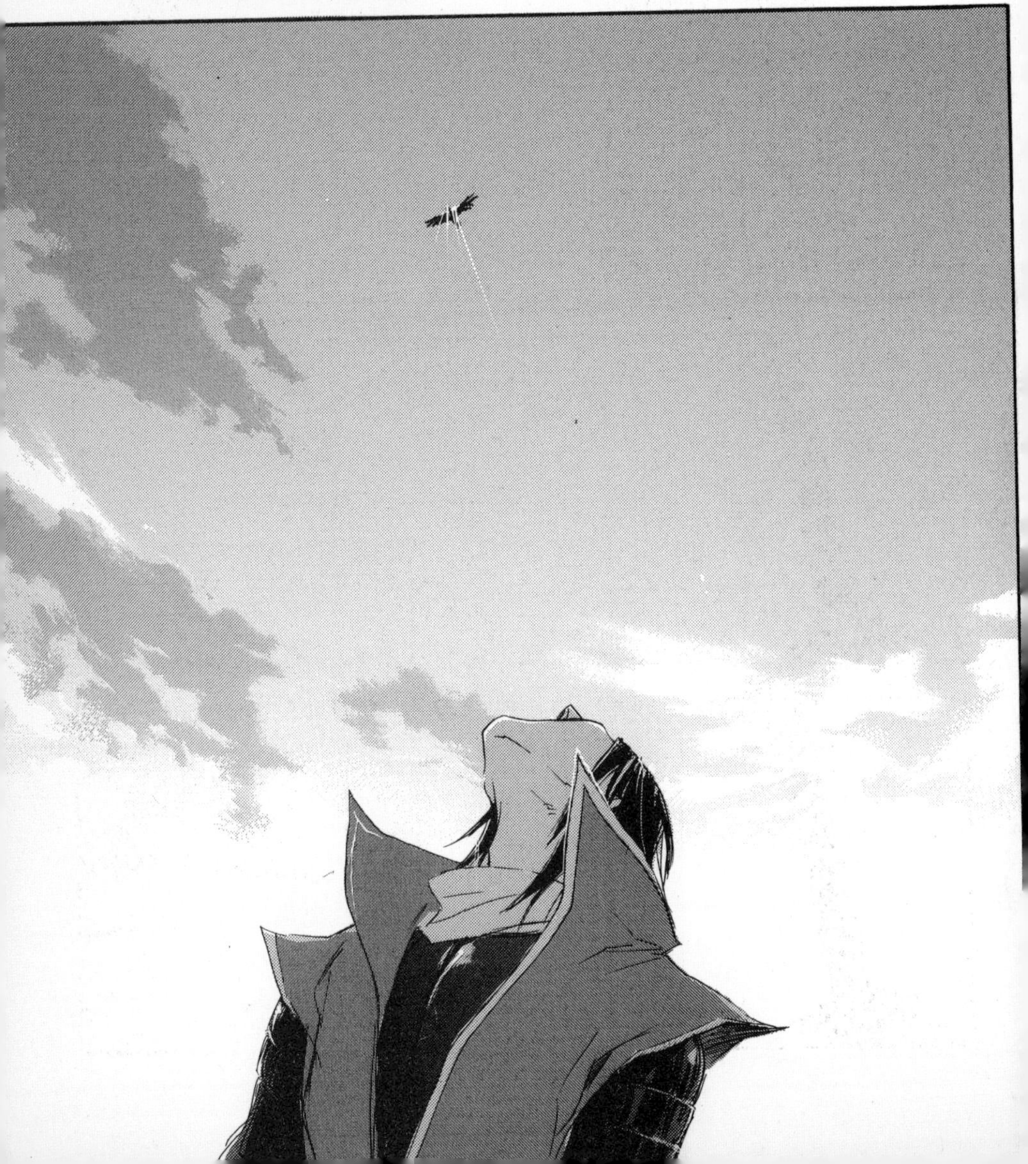

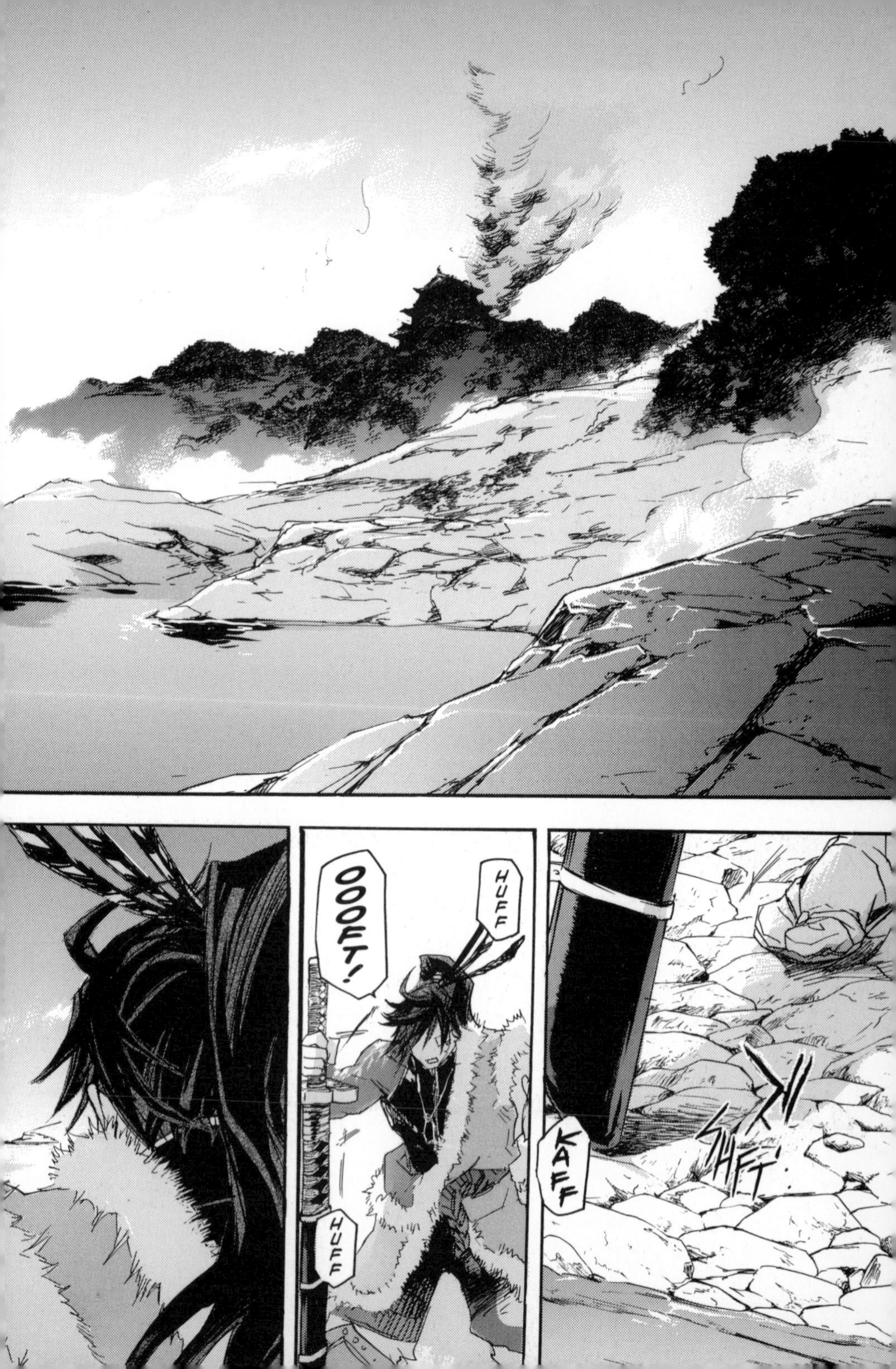
KK SHFT!
KAFF
HUFF
OOOFT!
HUFF

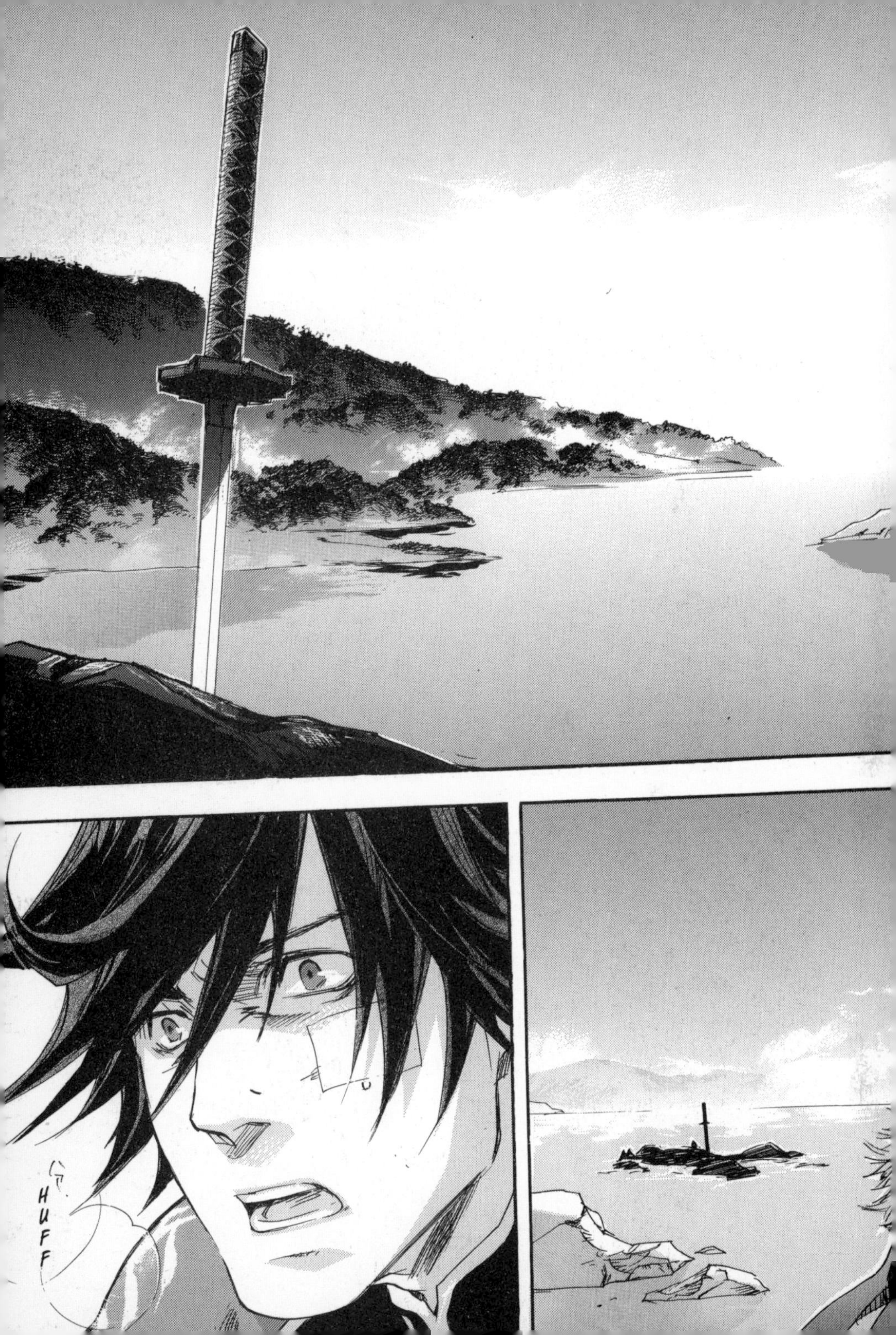
HUFF

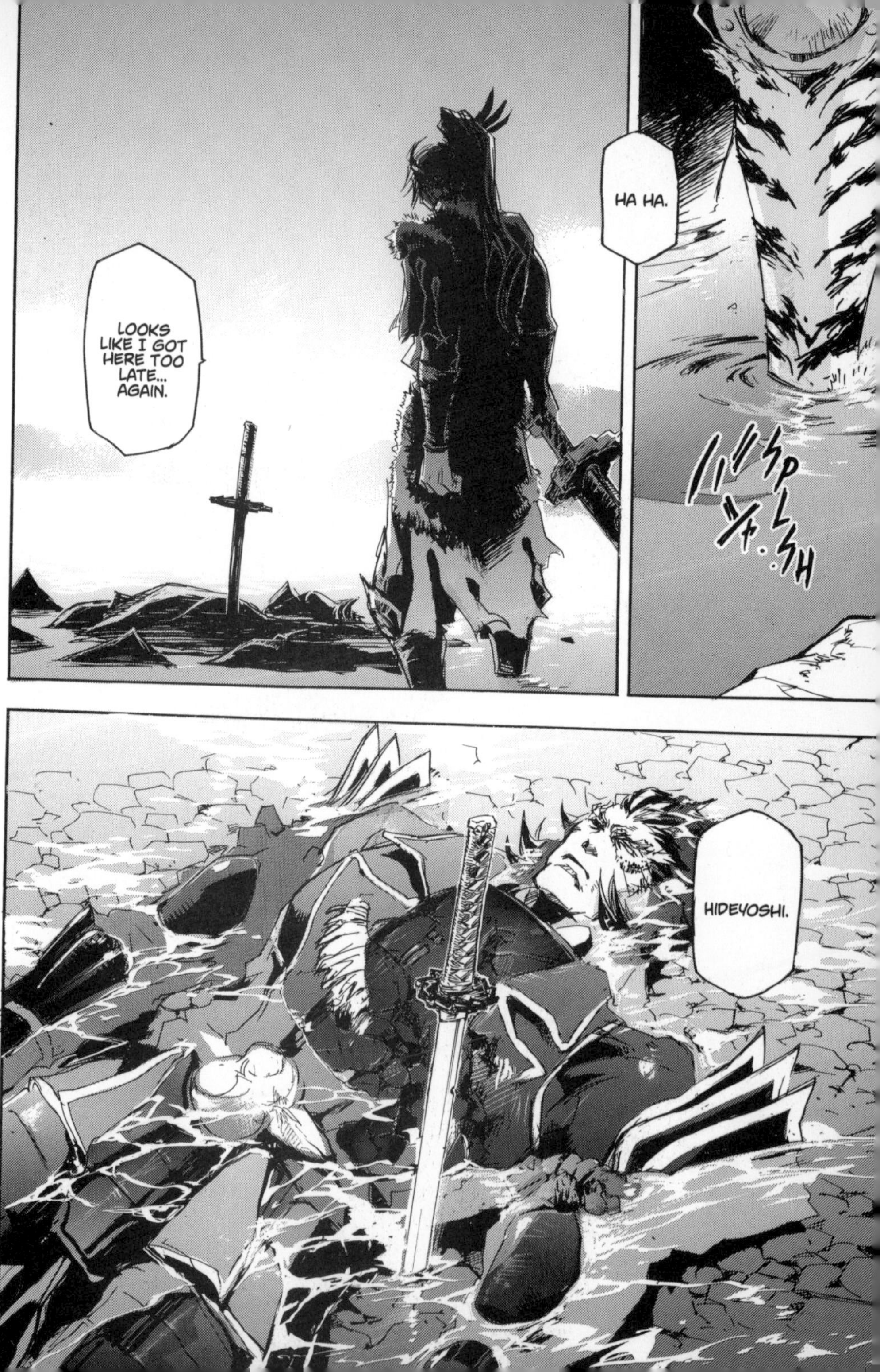
HA HA.
SPLSH
LOOKS LIKE I GOT HERE TOO LATE... AGAIN.
HIDEYOSHI.

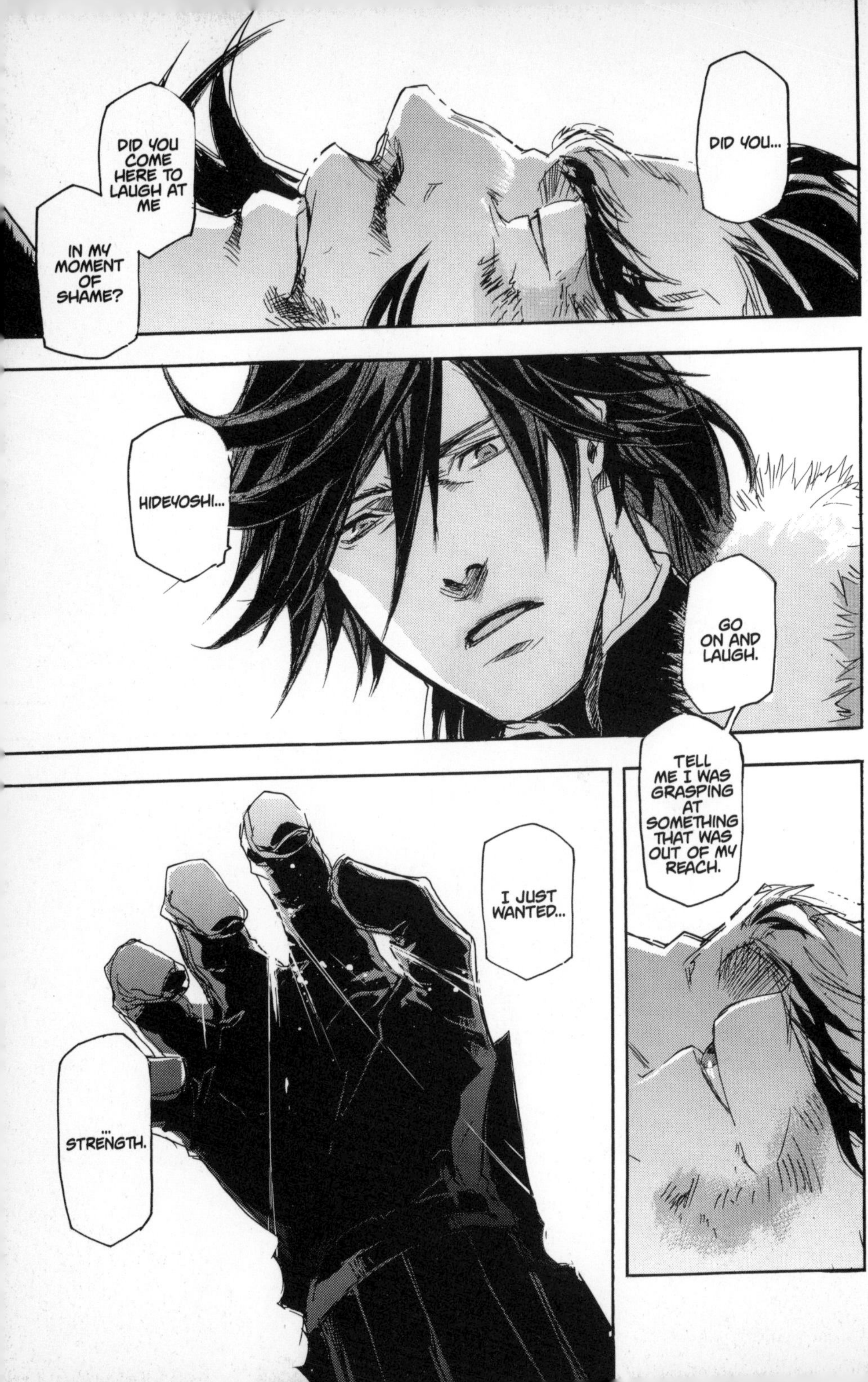
DID YOU...
DID YOU COME HERE TO LAUGH AT ME
IN MY MOMENT OF SHAME?
HIDEYOSHI...
GO ON AND LAUGH.
TELL ME I WAS GRASPING AT SOMETHING THAT WAS OUT OF MY REACH.
I JUST WANTED...
...STRENGTH.

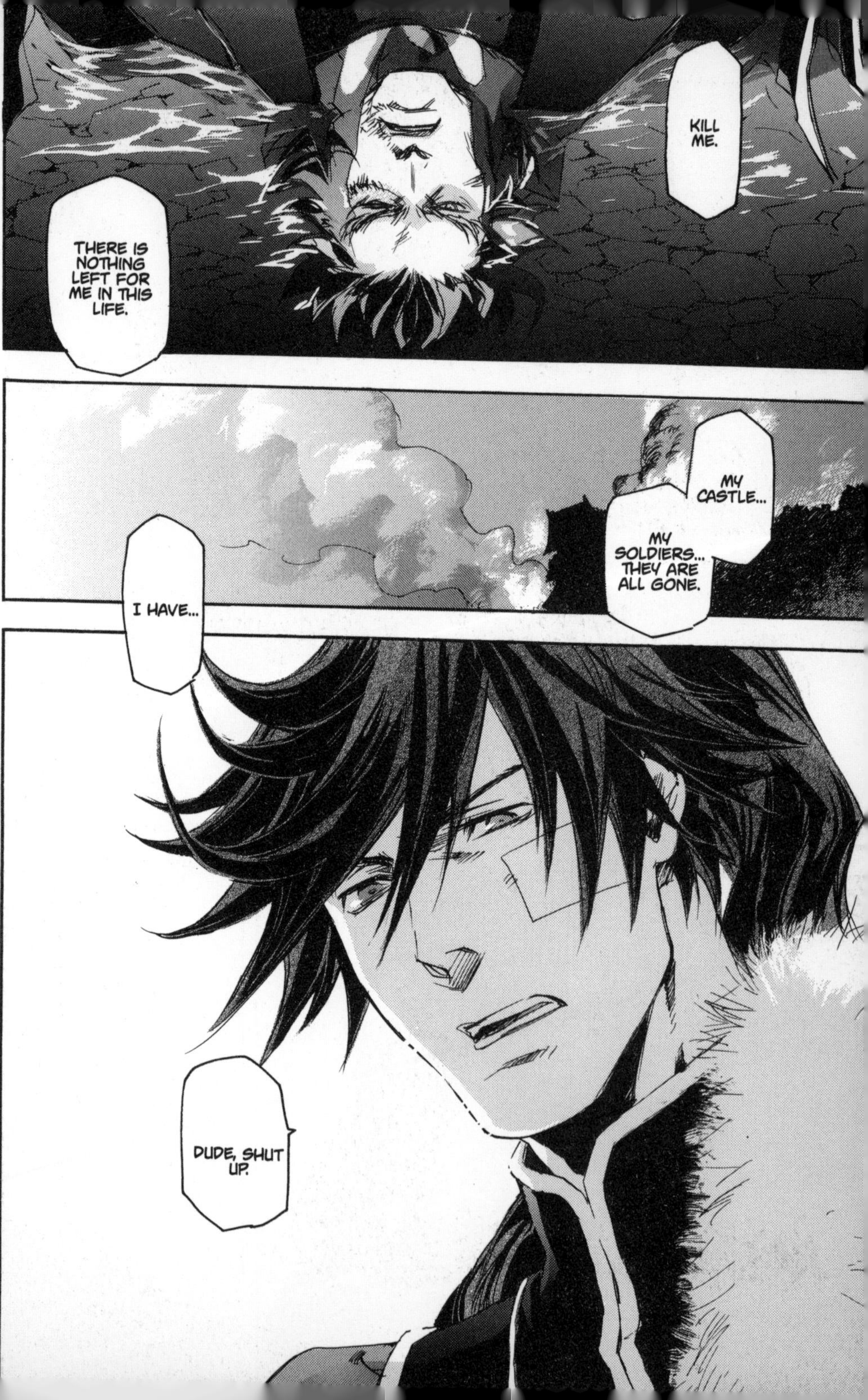
KILL ME.
THERE IS NOTHING LEFT FOR ME IN THIS LIFE.
MY CASTLE...
MY SOLDIERS... THEY ARE ALL GONE.
I HAVE...
DUDE, SHUT UP.

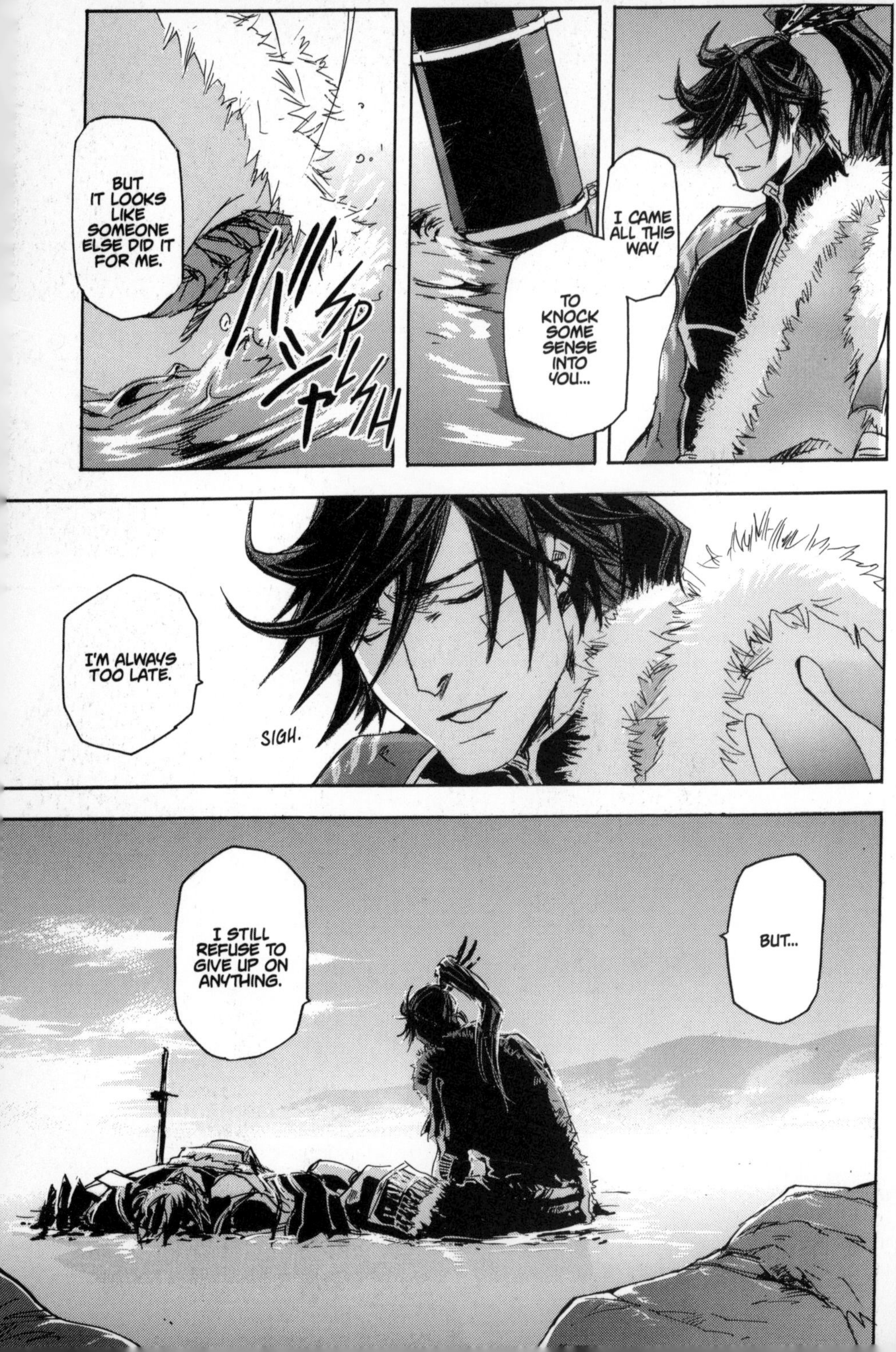
I CAME ALL THIS WAY
TO KNOCK SOME SENSE INTO YOU...
SPLSH
バシャ
BUT IT LOOKS LIKE SOMEONE ELSE DID IT FOR ME.
I'M ALWAYS TOO LATE.
SIGH.
BUT...
I STILL REFUSE TO GIVE UP ON ANYTHING.

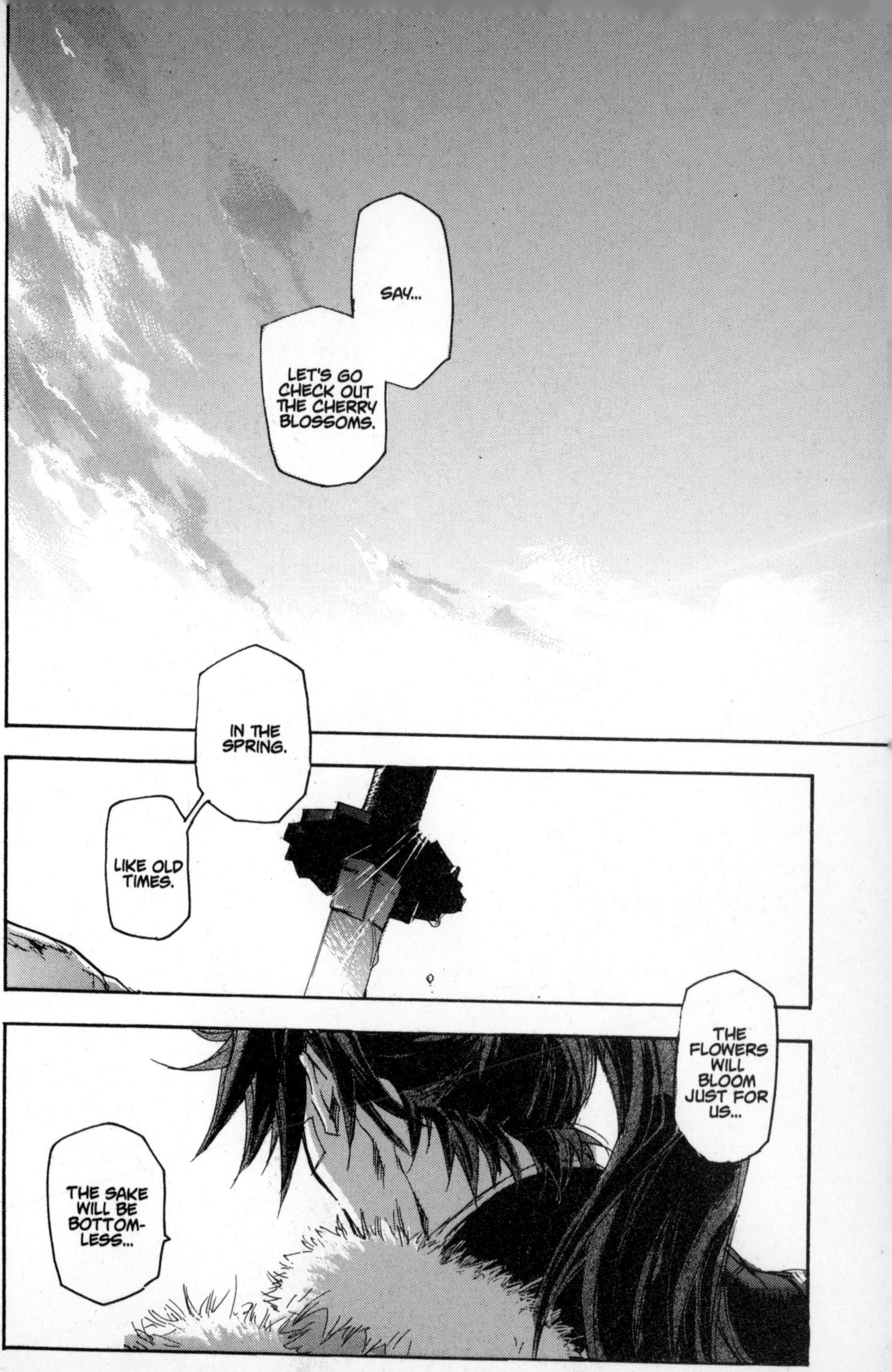
SAY...
LET'S GO CHECK OUT THE CHERRY BLOSSOMS.
IN THE SPRING.
LIKE OLD TIMES.
THE FLOWERS WILL BLOOM JUST FOR US...
THE SAKE WILL BE BOTTOM-LESS...

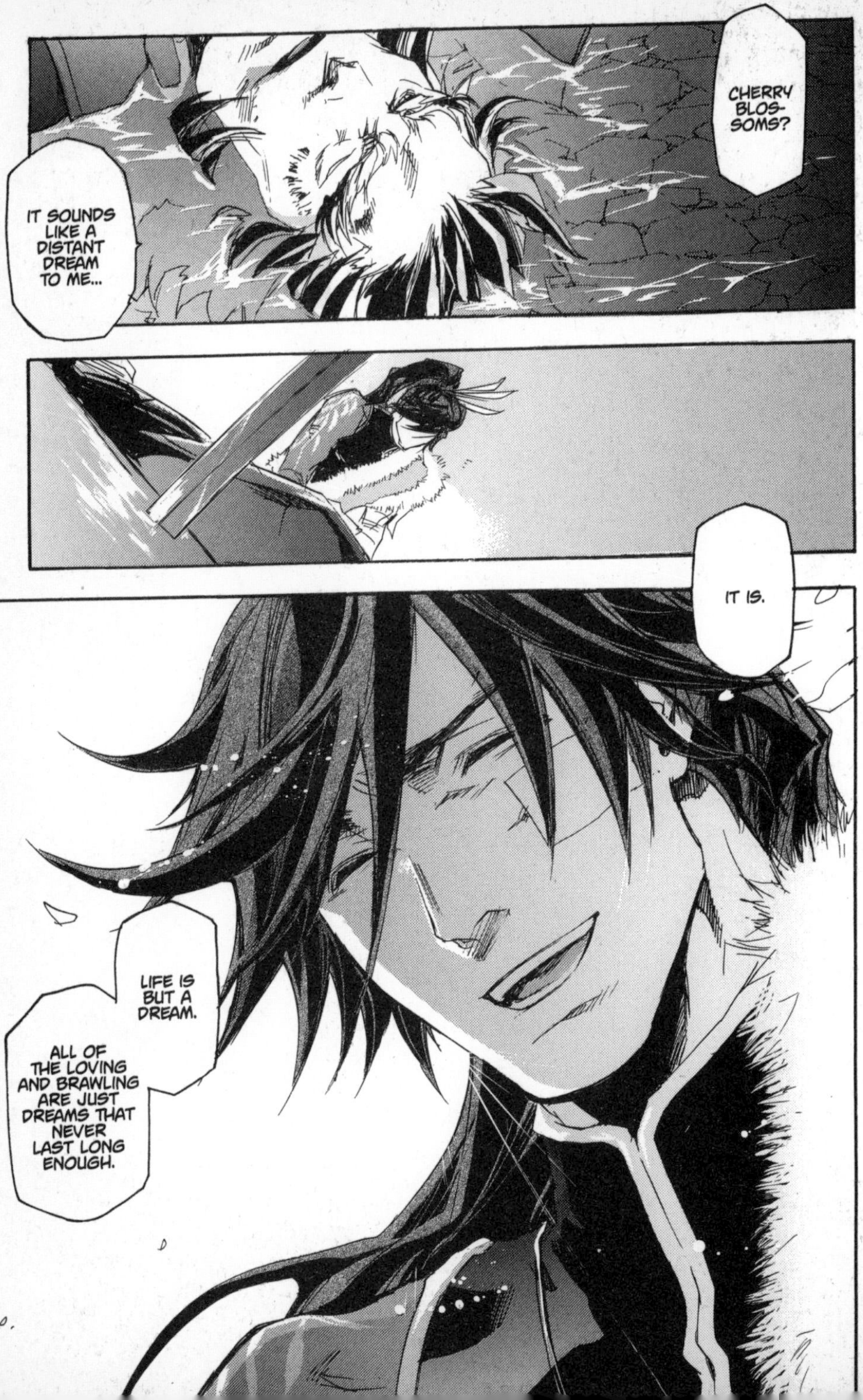
CHERRY BLOS-SOMS?
IT SOUNDS LIKE A DISTANT DREAM TO ME...
IT IS.
LIFE IS BUT A DREAM.
ALL OF THE LOVING AND BRAWLING ARE JUST DREAMS THAT NEVER LAST LONG ENOUGH.

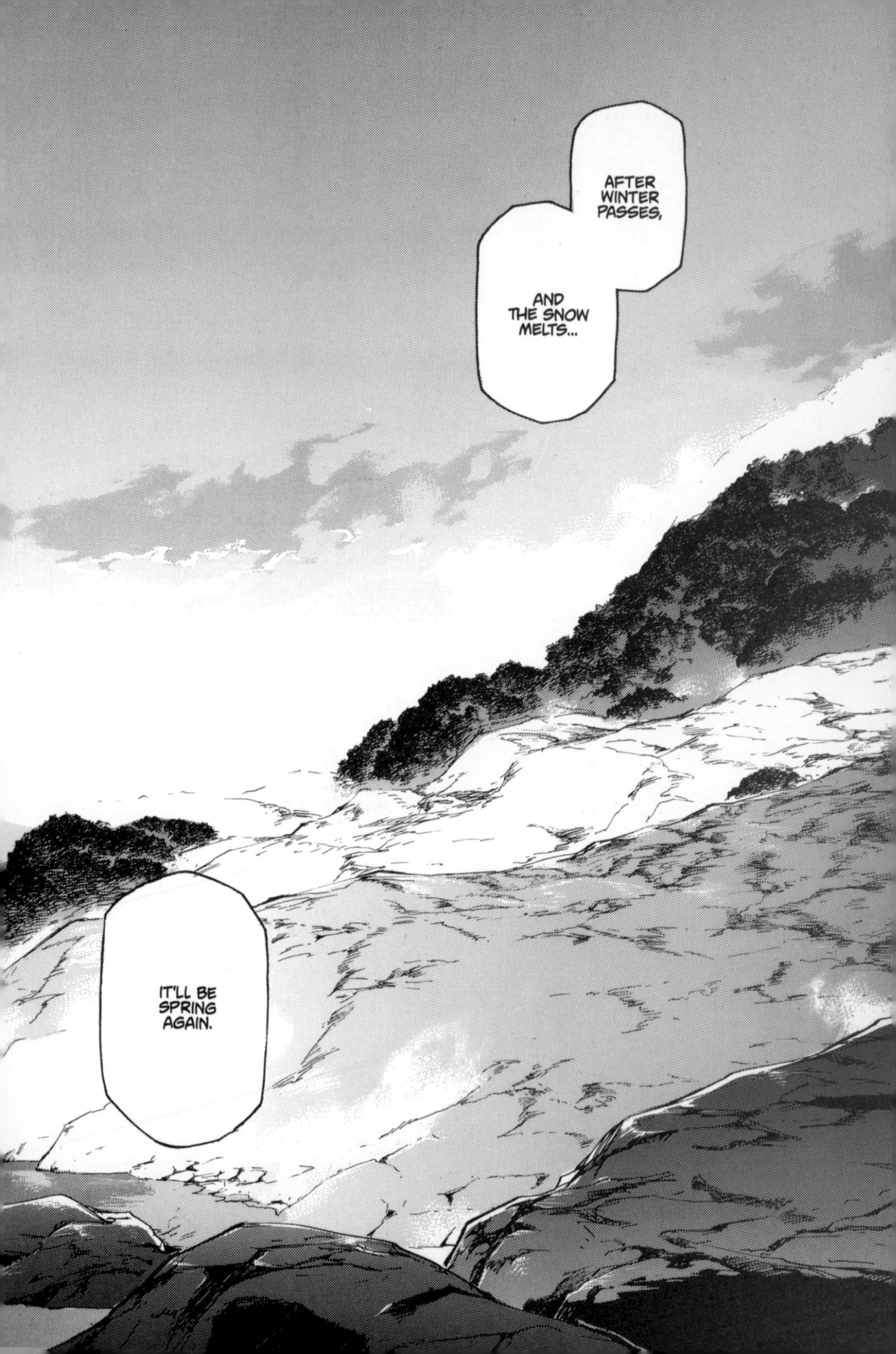
AFTER WINTER PASSES,
AND THE SNOW MELTS...
IT'LL BE SPRING AGAIN.

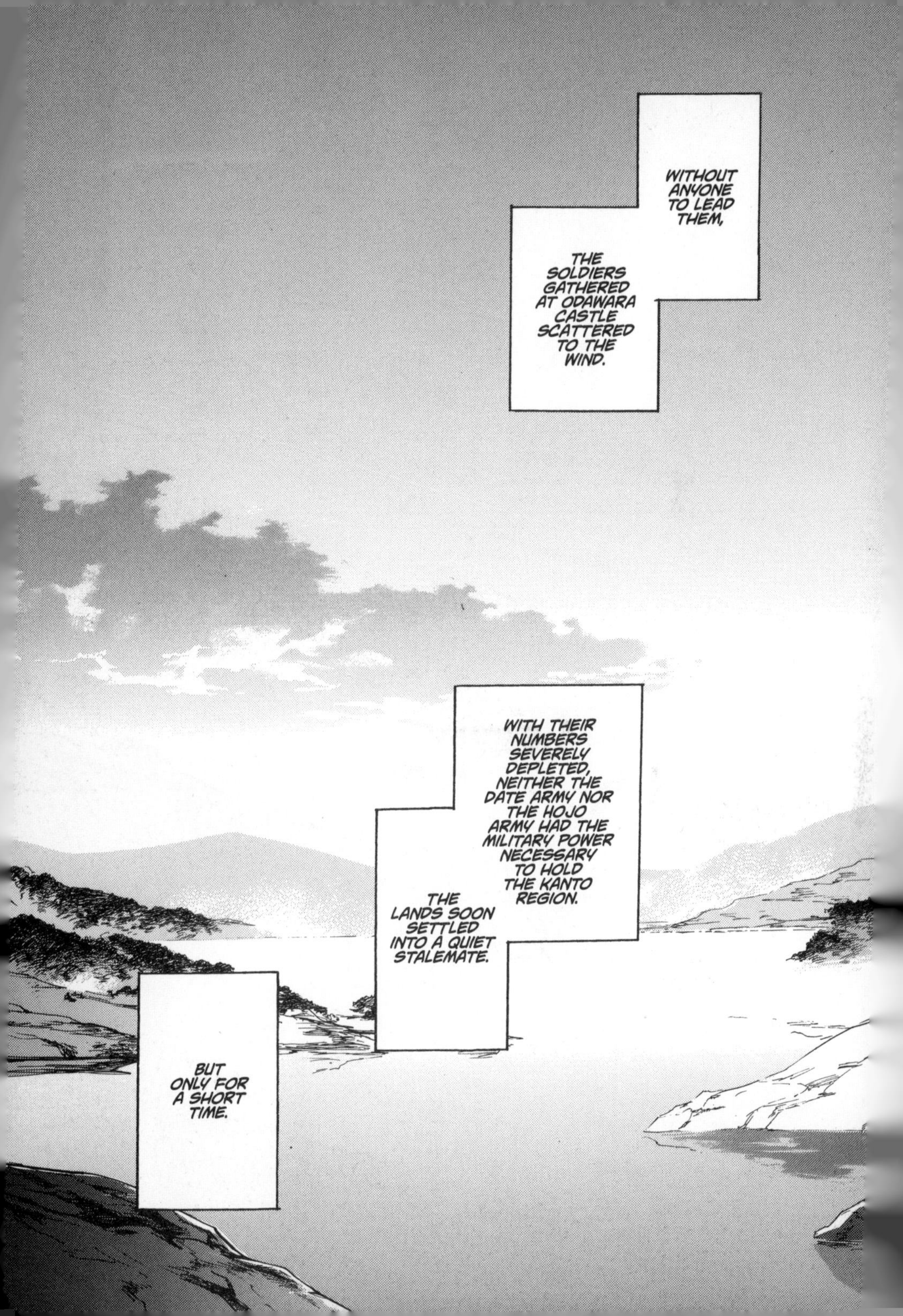
WITHOUT ANYONE TO LEAD THEM,
THE SOLDIERS GATHERED AT ODAWARA CASTLE SCATTERED TO THE WIND.
WITH THEIR NUMBERS SEVERELY DEPLETED, NEITHER THE DATE ARMY NOR THE HOJO ARMY HAD THE MILITARY POWER NECESSARY TO HOLD THE KANTO REGION.
THE LANDS SOON SETTLED INTO A QUIET STALEMATE.
BUT ONLY FOR A SHORT TIME.

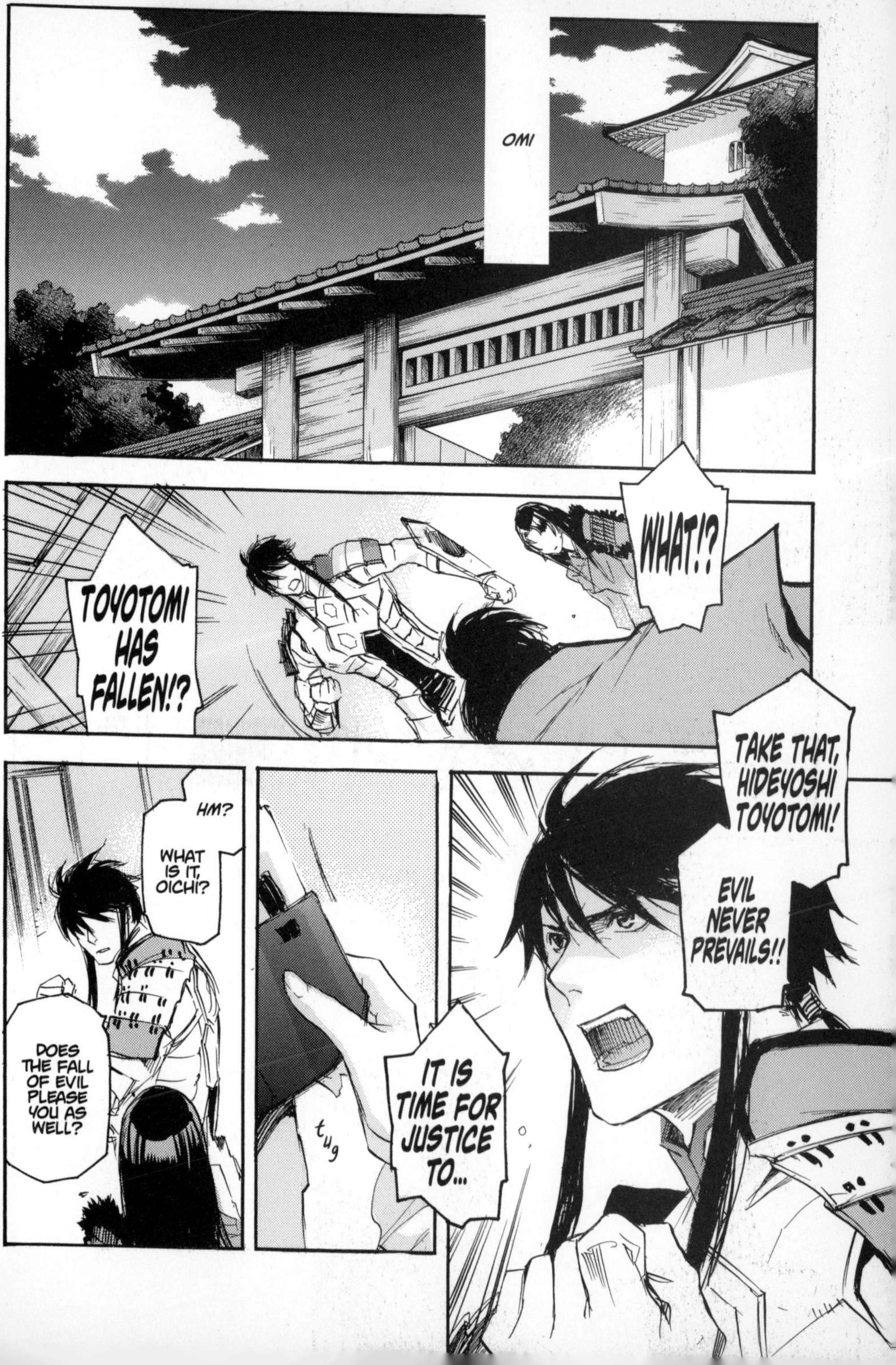
OMI
WHAT!?
TOYOTOMI HAS FALLEN!?
TAKE THAT, HIDEYOSHI TOYOTOMI!
EVIL NEVER PREVAILS!!
IT IS TIME FOR JUSTICE TO...
tug
HM?
WHAT IS IT, OICHI?
DOES THE FALL OF EVIL PLEASE YOU AS WELL?

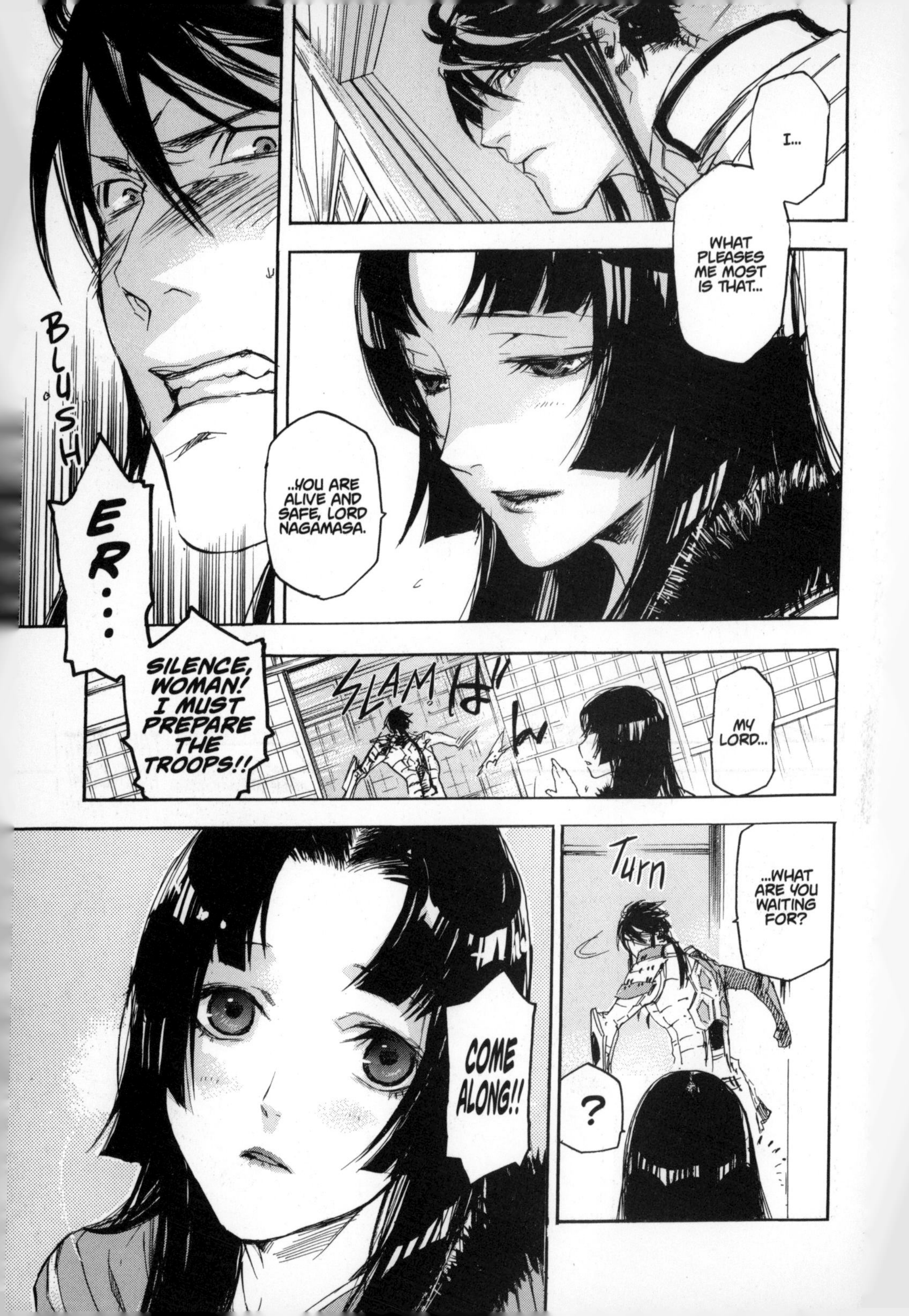

I...
WHAT PLEASES ME MOST IS THAT...
..YOU ARE ALIVE AND SAFE, LORD NAGAMASA.
BLUSH
ER...
MY LORD...
SLAM
SILENCE, WOMAN! I MUST PREPARE THE TROOPS!!
Turn
...WHAT ARE YOU WAITING FOR?
?
COME ALONG!!

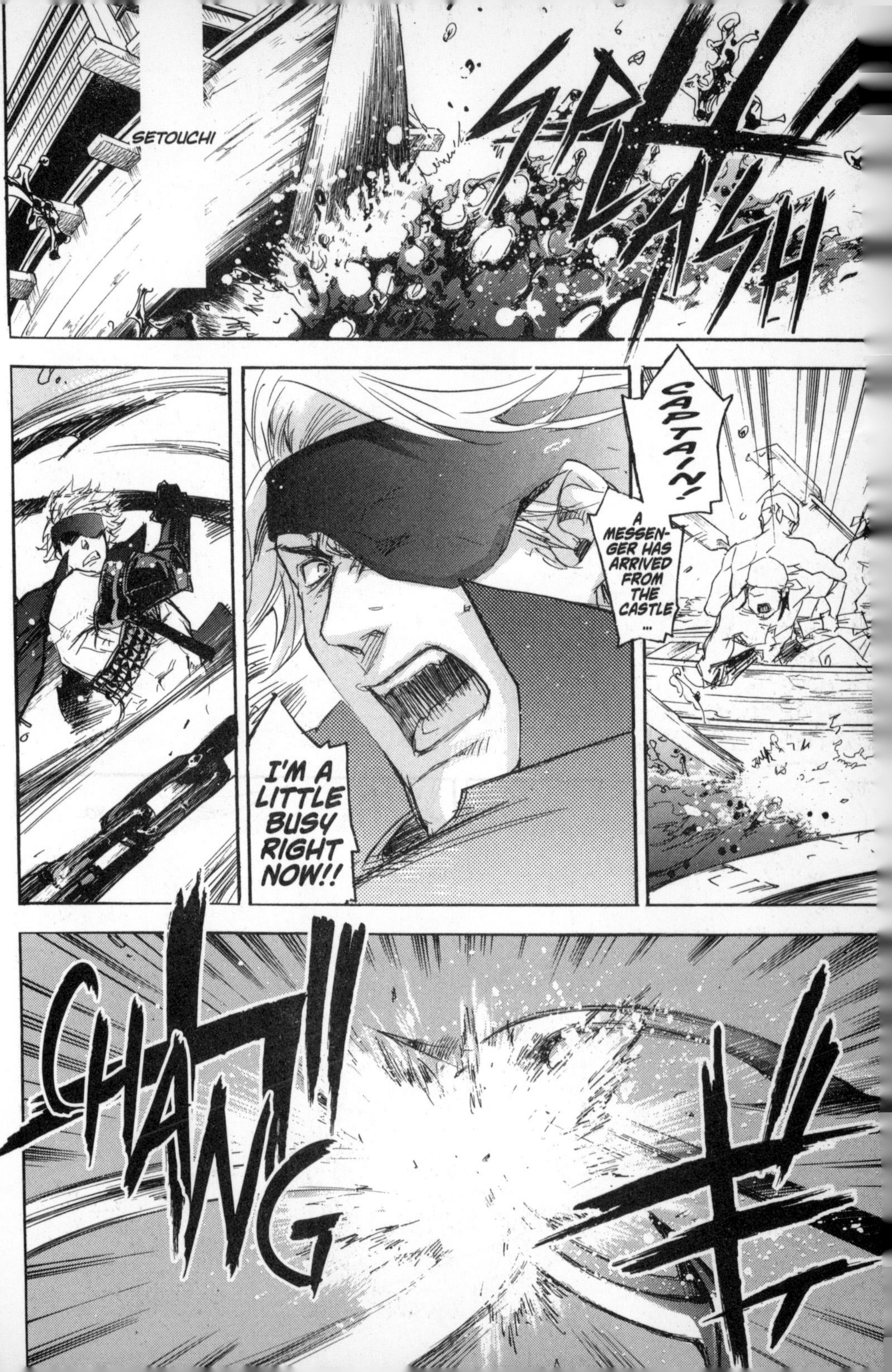
SETOUCHI
SPLASH
CAPTAIN!
A MESSENGER HAS ARRIVED FROM THE CASTLE...
I'M A LITTLE BUSY RIGHT NOW!!
CHAWNG!!

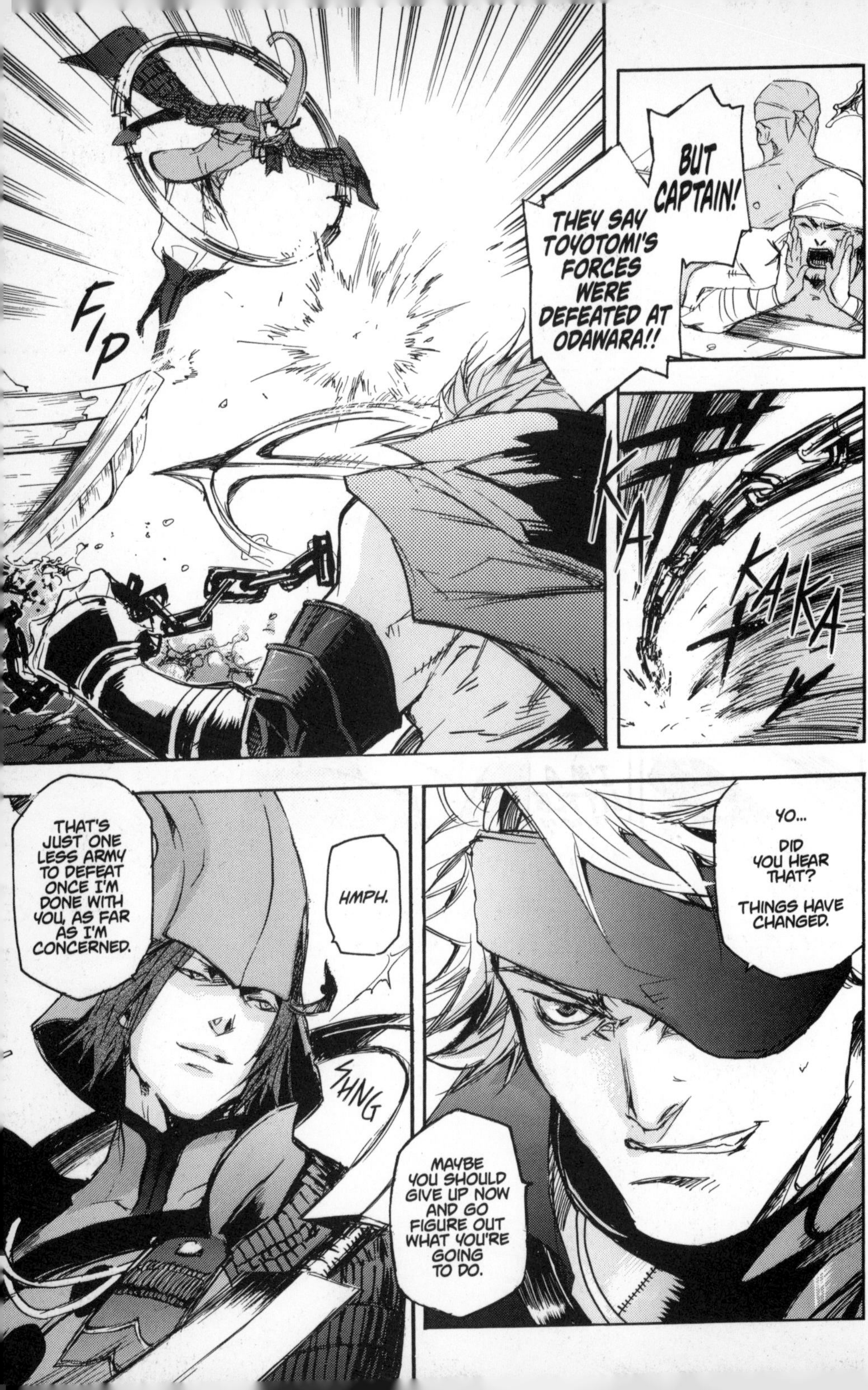

BUT CAPTAIN!
THEY SAY TOYOTOMI'S FORCES WERE DEFEATED AT ODAWARA!!
KA
KAKAKA
FIP
YO...
DID YOU HEAR THAT?
THINGS HAVE CHANGED.
MAYBE YOU SHOULD GIVE UP NOW AND GO FIGURE OUT WHAT YOU'RE GOING TO DO.
HMPH.
THAT'S JUST ONE LESS ARMY TO DEFEAT ONCE I'M DONE WITH YOU, AS FAR AS I'M CONCERNED.
SHING

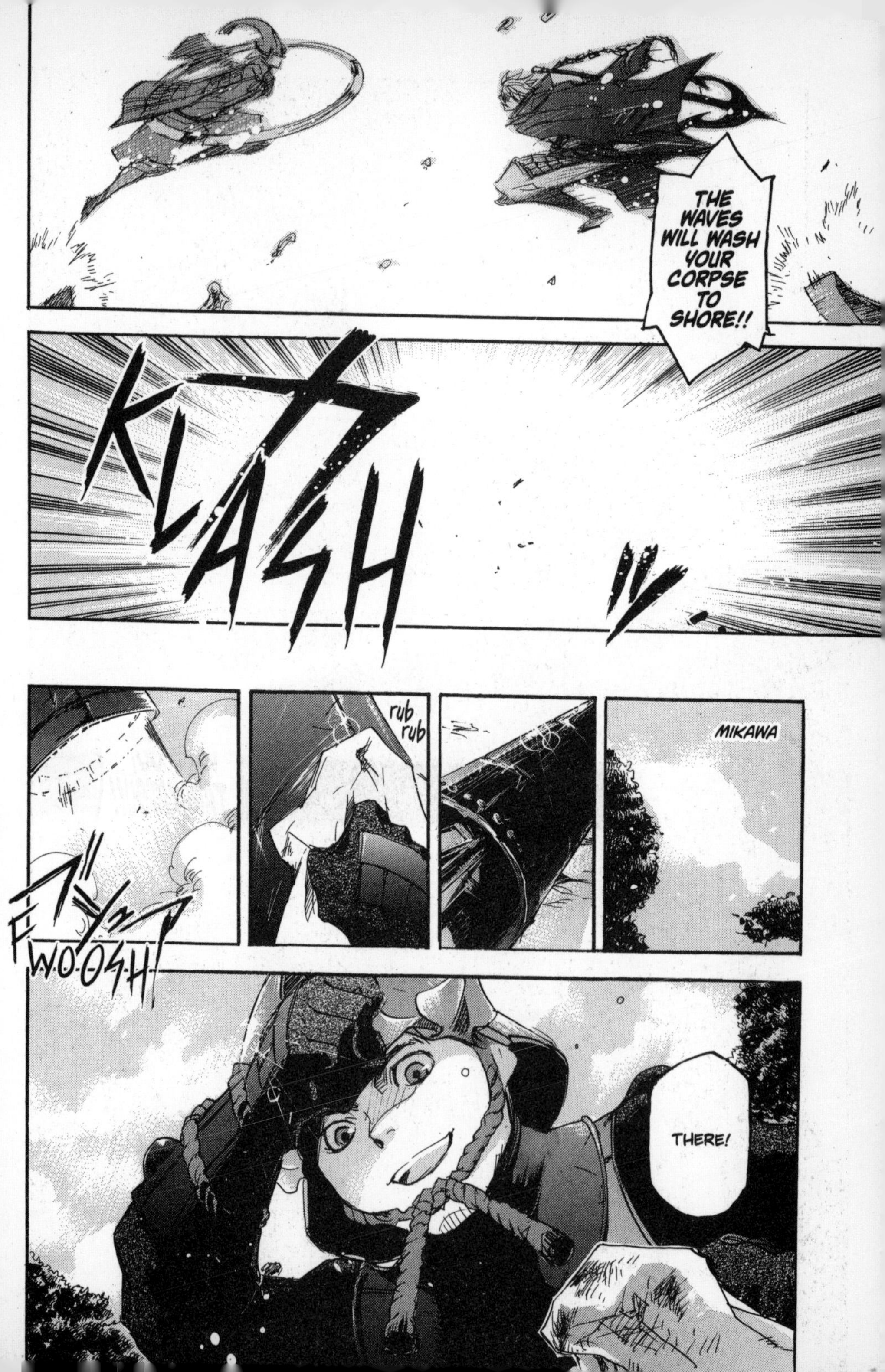
THE WAVES WILL WASH YOUR CORPSE TO SHORE!!
KLASH
MIKAWA
rub rub
FWOOSH
THERE!

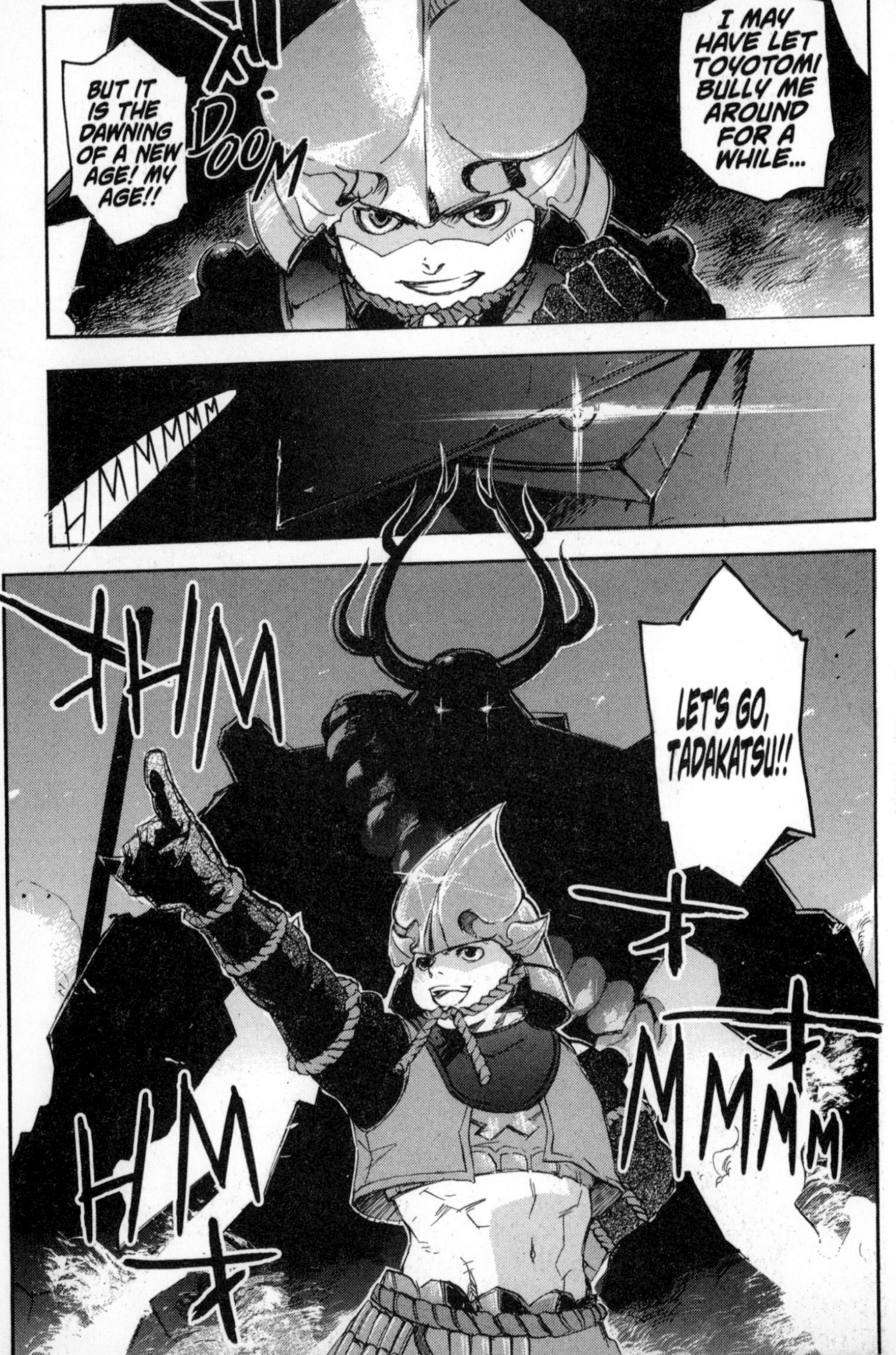
I MAY HAVE LET TOYOTOMI BULLY ME AROUND FOR A WHILE...
BUT IT IS THE DAWNING OF A NEW AGE! MY AGE!!
DOOM
LET'S GO, TADAKATSU!!

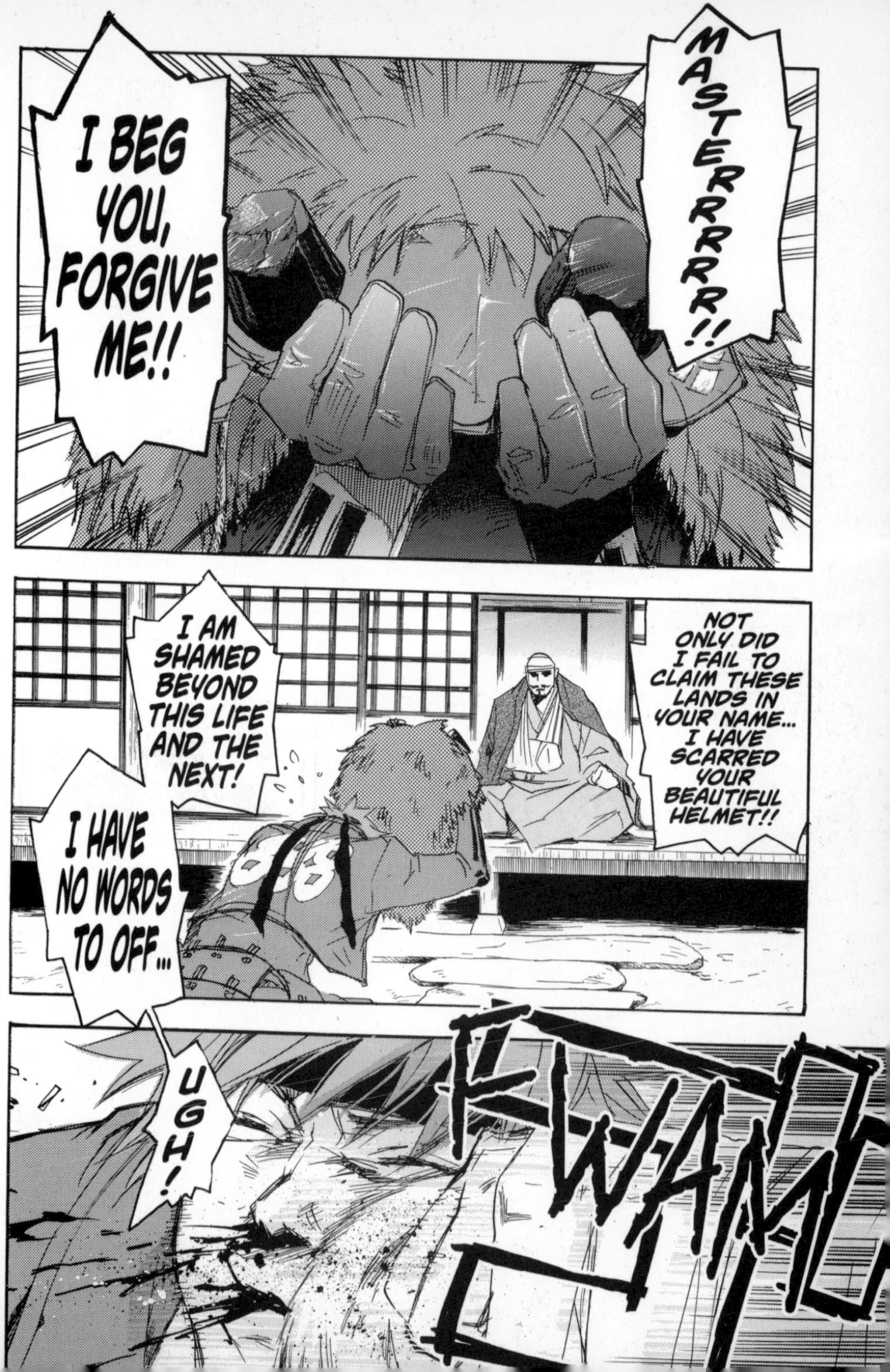
MASTERRRRR!!
I BEG YOU, FORGIVE ME!!
NOT ONLY DID I FAIL TO CLAIM THESE LANDS IN YOUR NAME... I HAVE SCARRED YOUR BEAUTIFUL HELMET!!
I AM SHAMED BEYOND THIS LIFE AND THE NEXT!
I HAVE NO WORDS TO OFF...
FWAM
UGH!

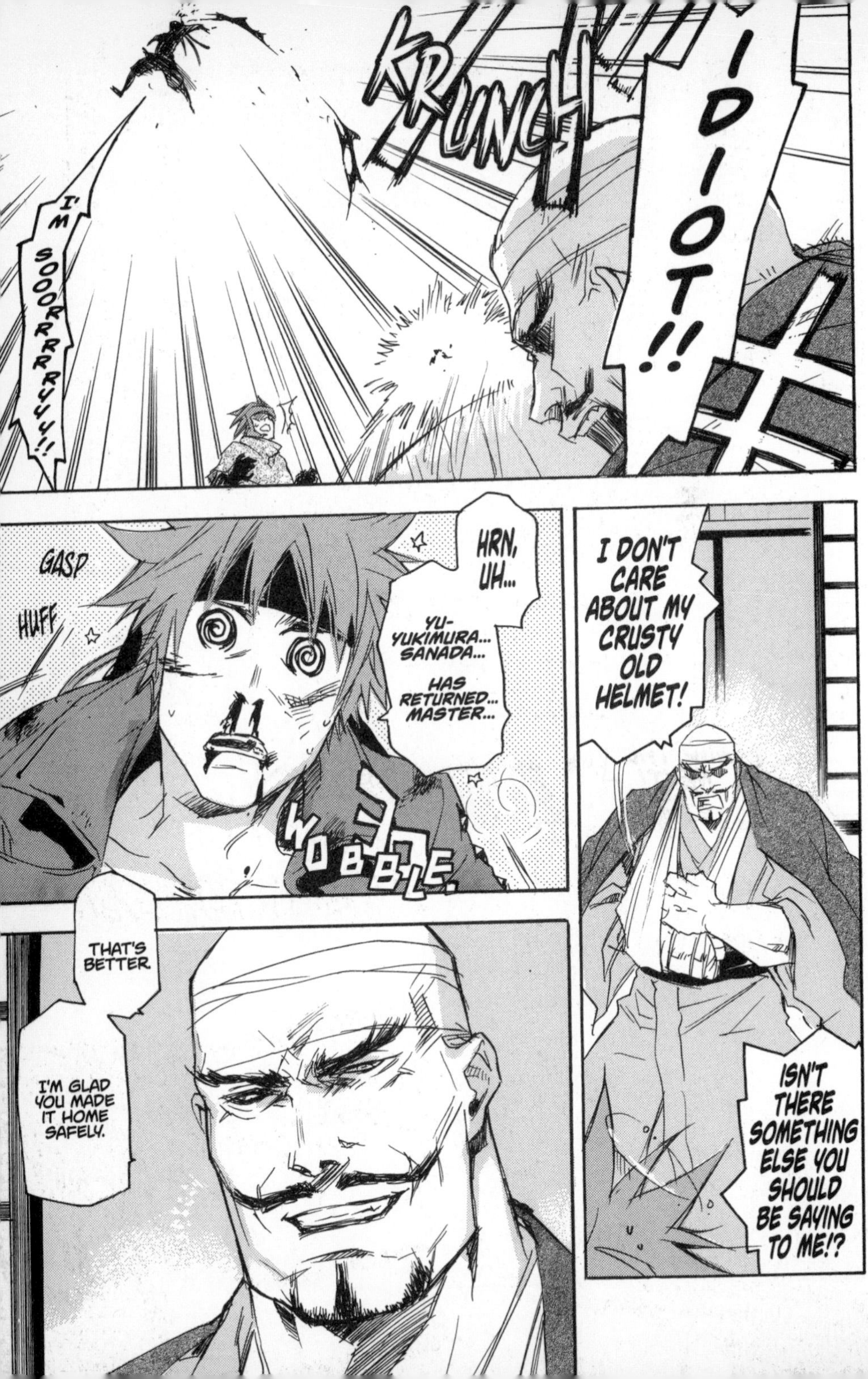
IDIOT!!
KRUNCH
I'M SOOORRRRYYYY!!
I DON'T CARE ABOUT MY CRUSTY OLD HELMET!
ISN'T THERE SOMETHING ELSE YOU SHOULD BE SAYING TO ME!?
HRN, UH...
YU-YUKIMURA... SANADA...
HAS RETURNED... MASTER...
GASP
HUFF
WOBBLE.
THAT'S BETTER.
I'M GLAD YOU MADE IT HOME SAFELY.

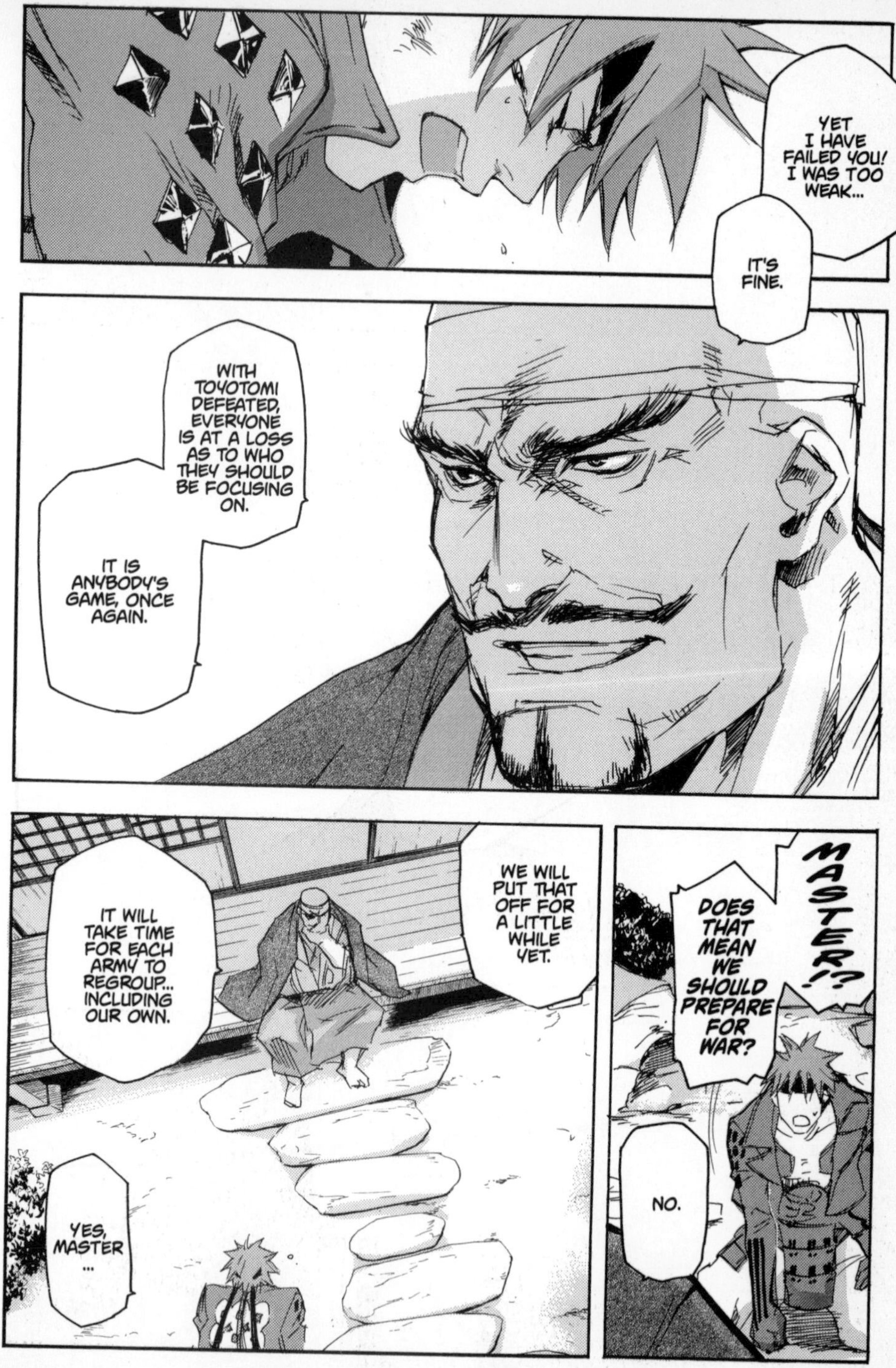
YET I HAVE FAILED YOU! I WAS TOO WEAK...
IT'S FINE.
WITH TOYOTOMI DEFEATED, EVERYONE IS AT A LOSS AS TO WHO THEY SHOULD BE FOCUSING ON.
IT IS ANYBODY'S GAME, ONCE AGAIN.
MASTER!?
DOES THAT MEAN WE SHOULD PREPARE FOR WAR?
NO.
WE WILL PUT THAT OFF FOR A LITTLE WHILE YET.
IT WILL TAKE TIME FOR EACH ARMY TO REGROUP... INCLUDING OUR OWN.
YES, MASTER ...

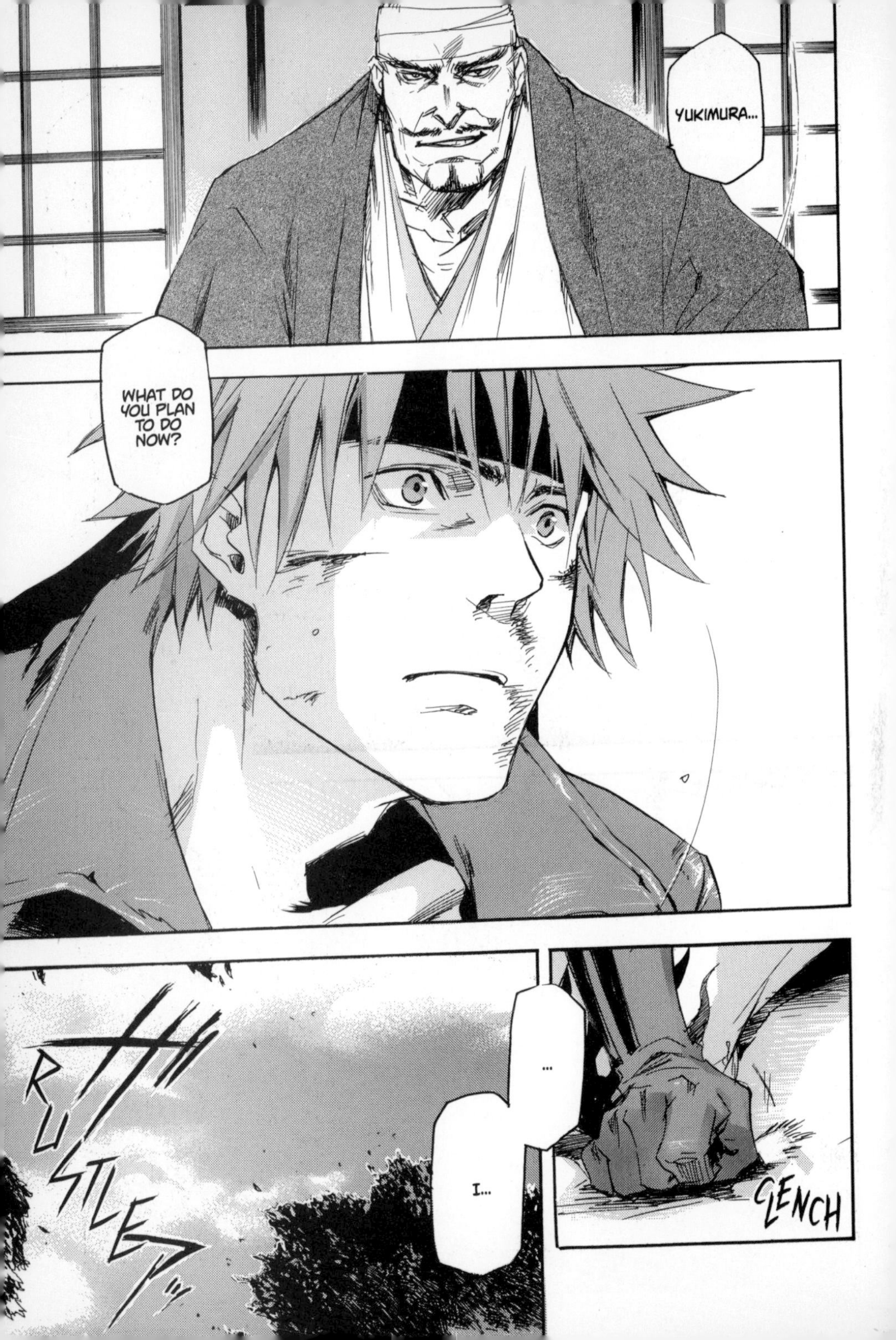
YUKIMURA...
WHAT DO YOU PLAN TO DO NOW?
CLENCH
...
I...
RUSTLE

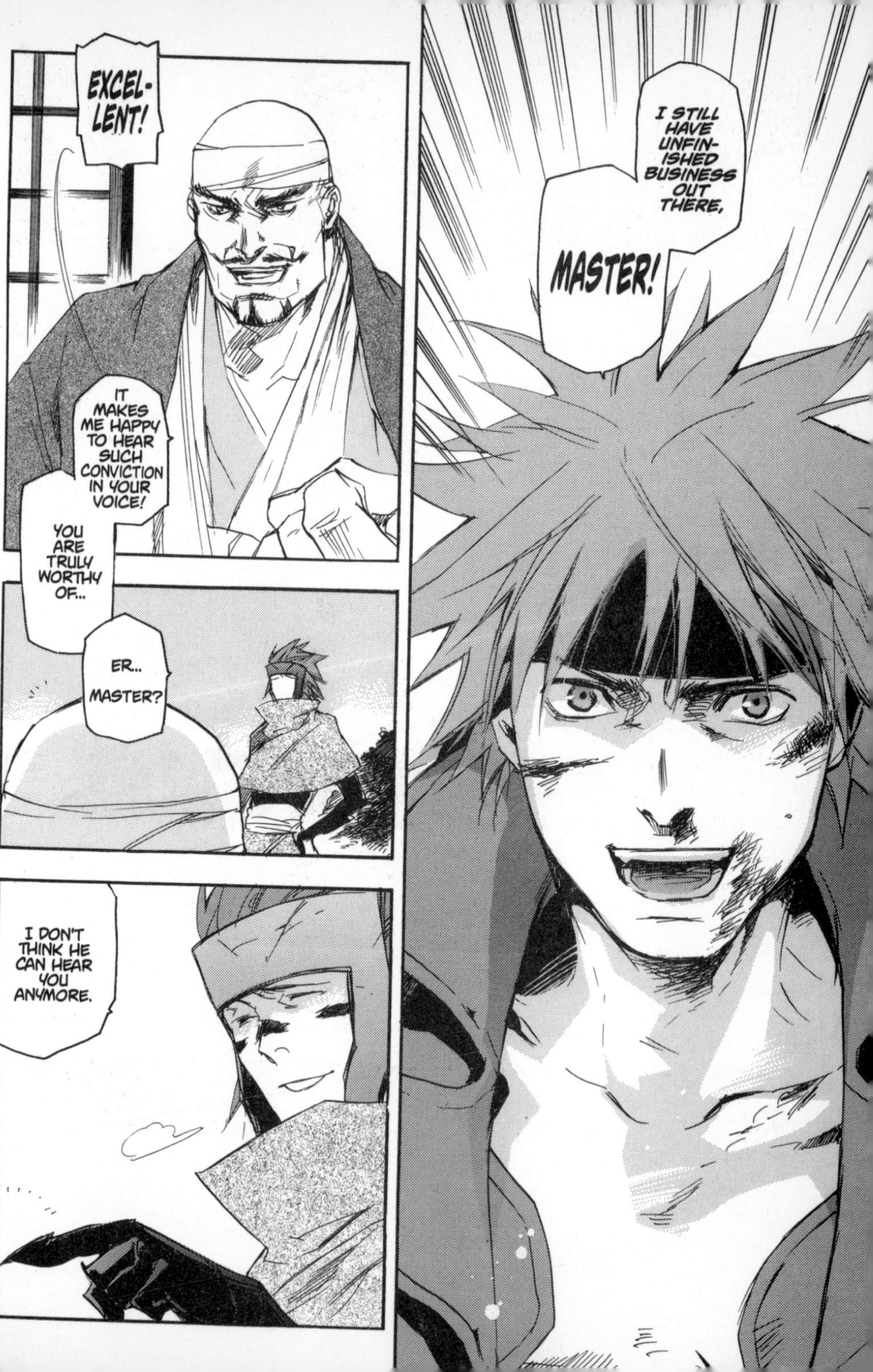
I STILL HAVE UNFINISHED BUSINESS OUT THERE,
MASTER!
EXCEL-LENT!
IT MAKES ME HAPPY TO HEAR SUCH CONVICTION IN YOUR VOICE!
YOU ARE TRULY WORTHY OF...
ER... MASTER?
I DON'T THINK HE CAN HEAR YOU ANYMORE.

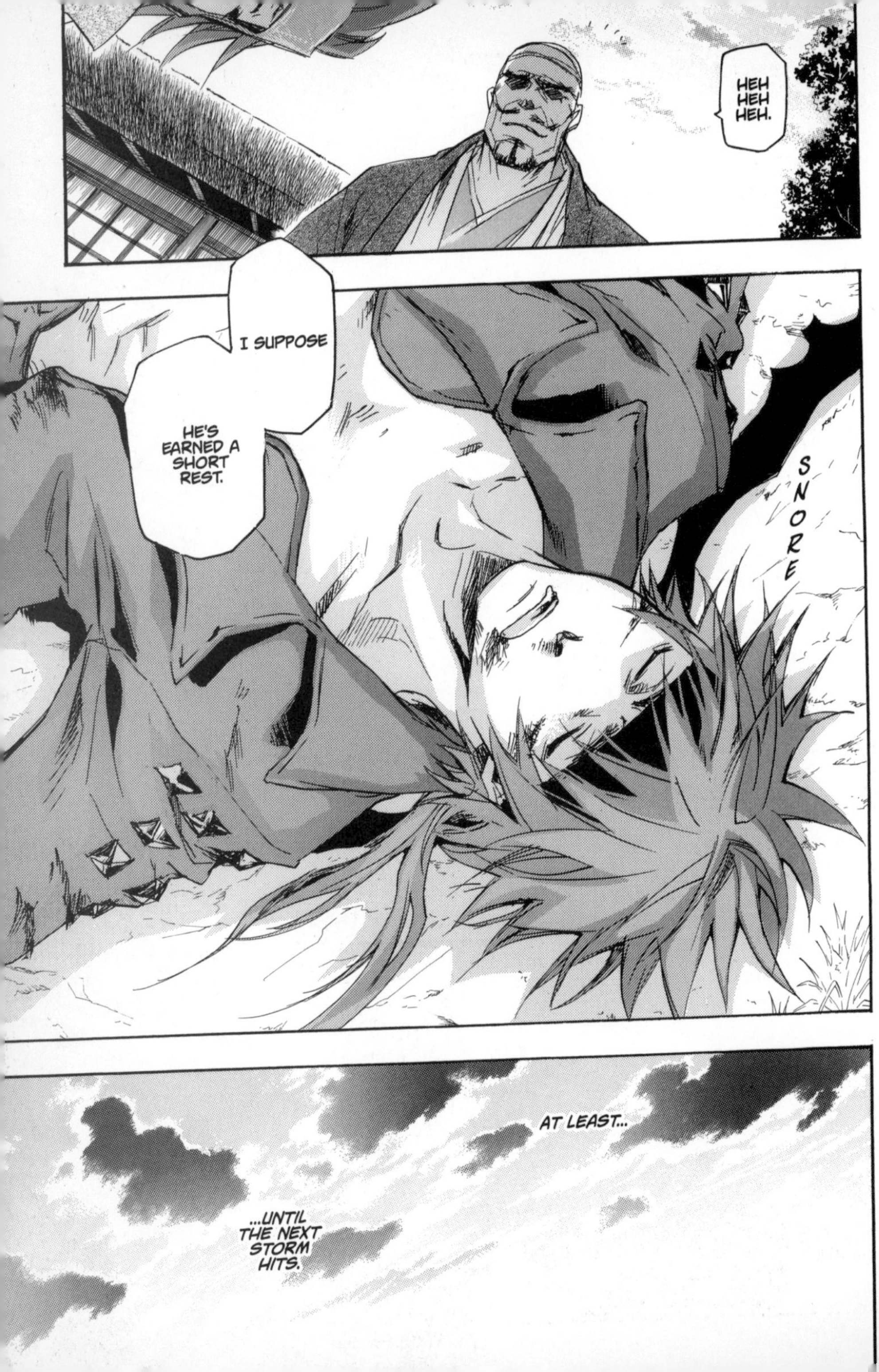
HEH HEH HEH.
I SUPPOSE
HE'S EARNED A SHORT REST.
SNORE
AT LEAST...
...UNTIL THE NEXT STORM HITS.

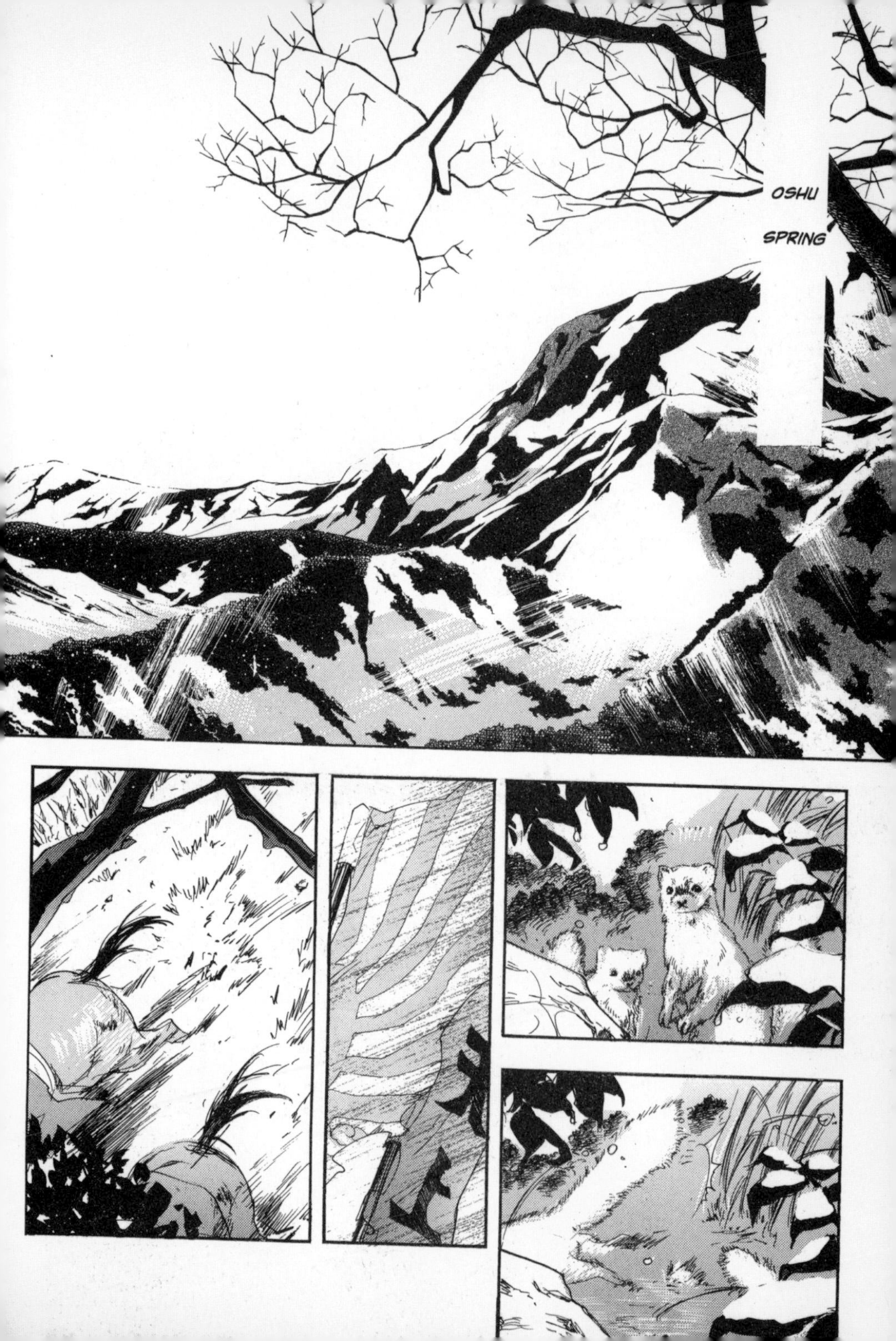
OSHU
SPRING

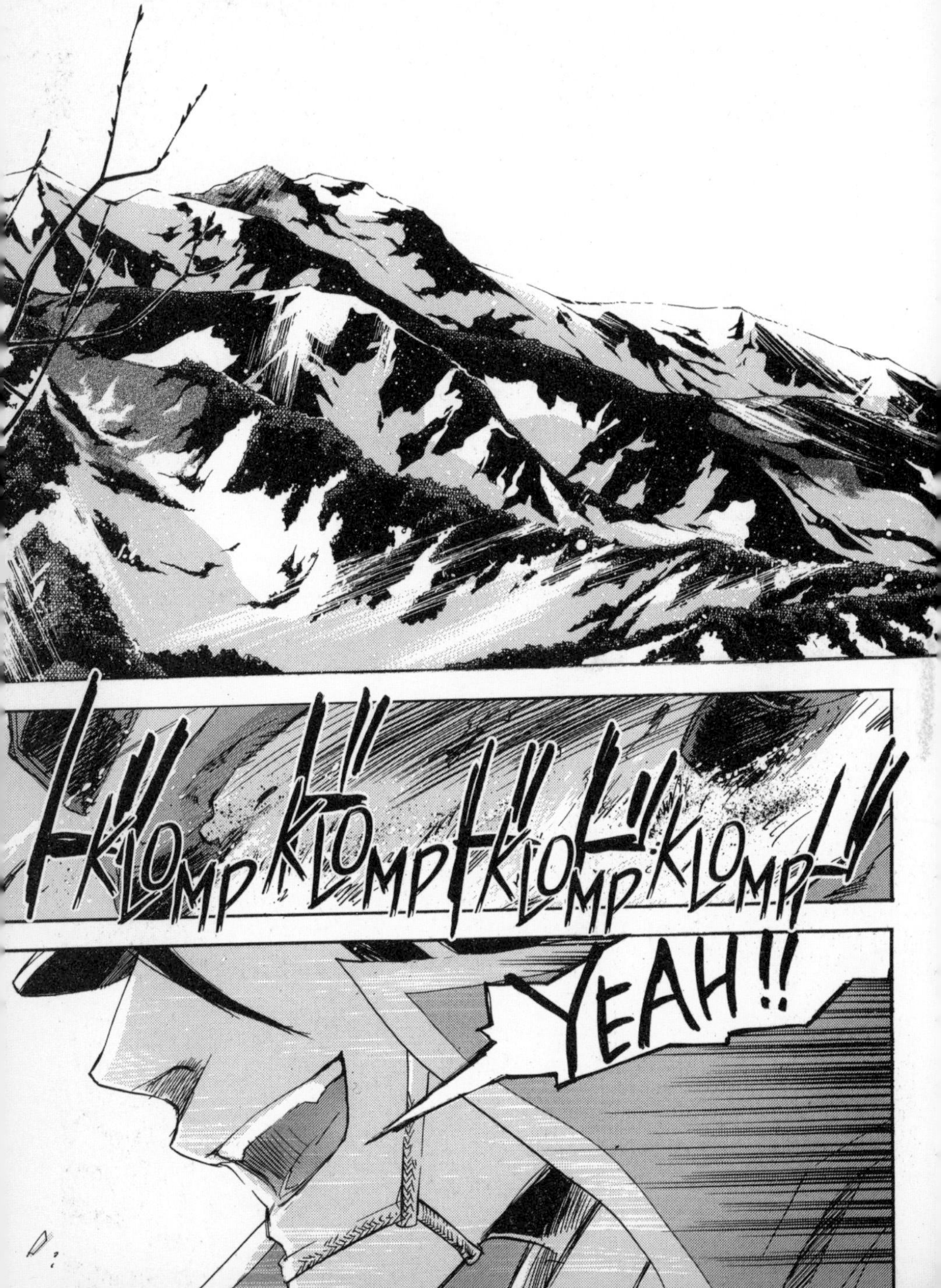
KLOMP KLOMP KLOMP KLOMP
YEAH!!

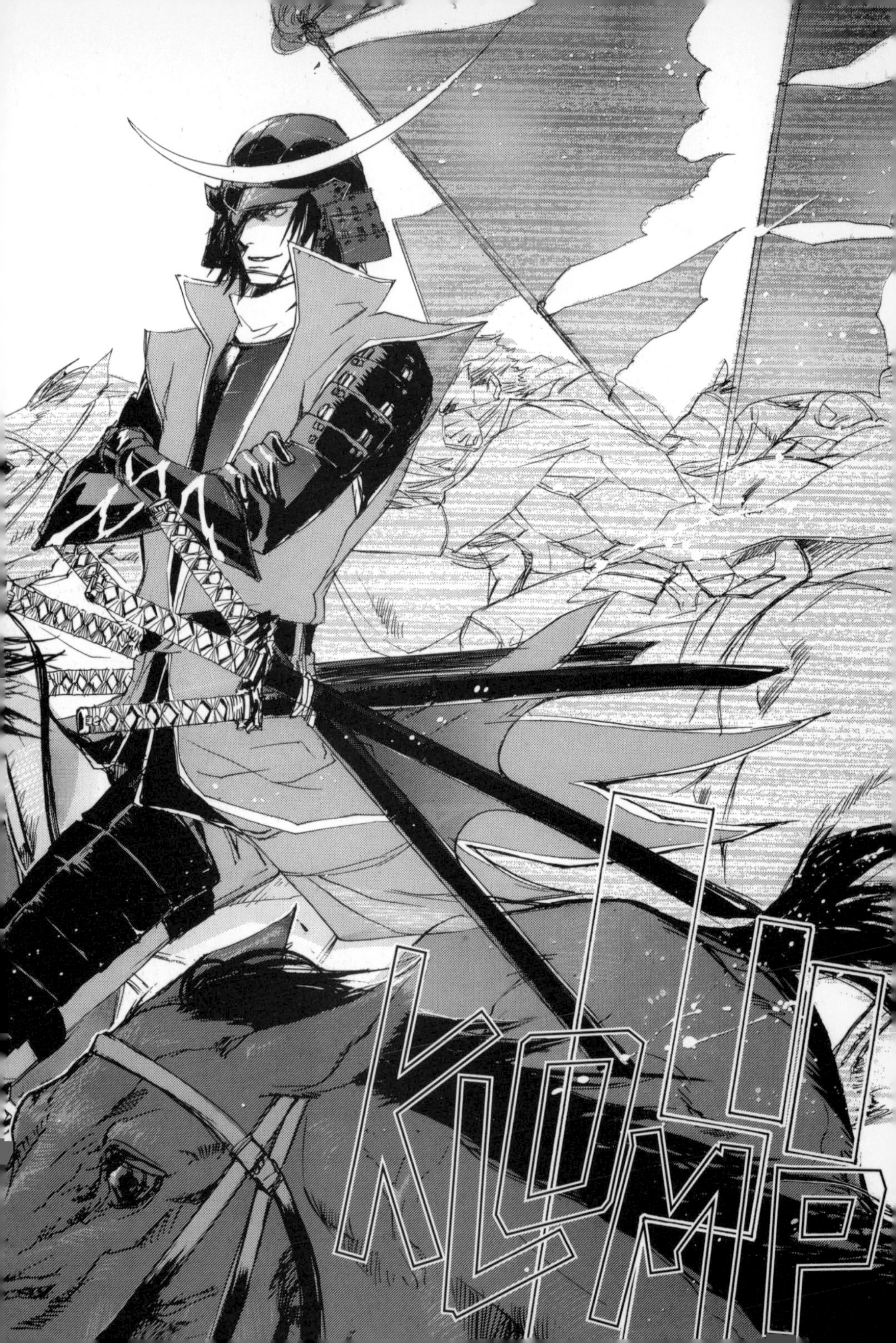
KLOMP
KLOMP

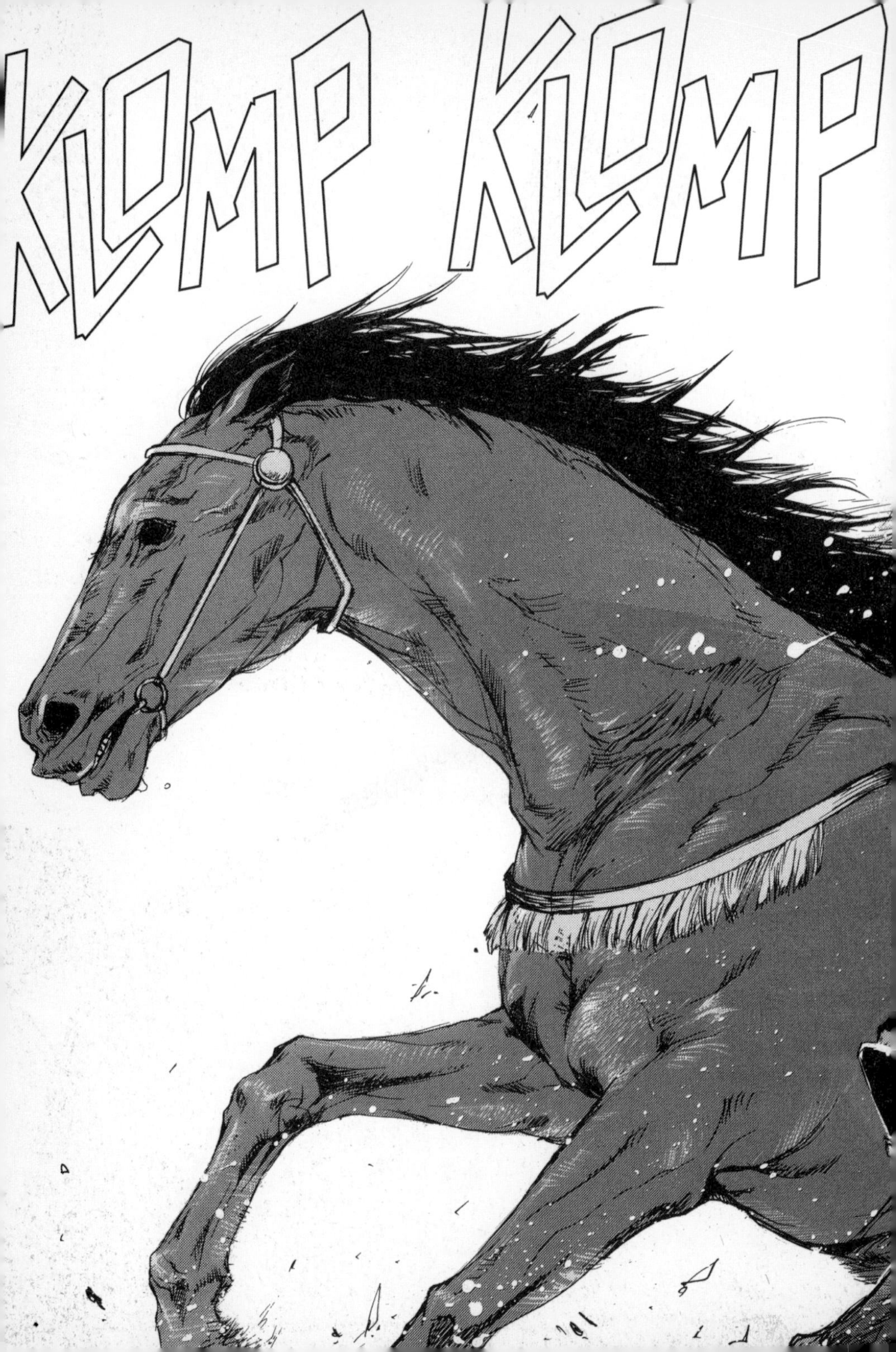
KLOMP KLOMP

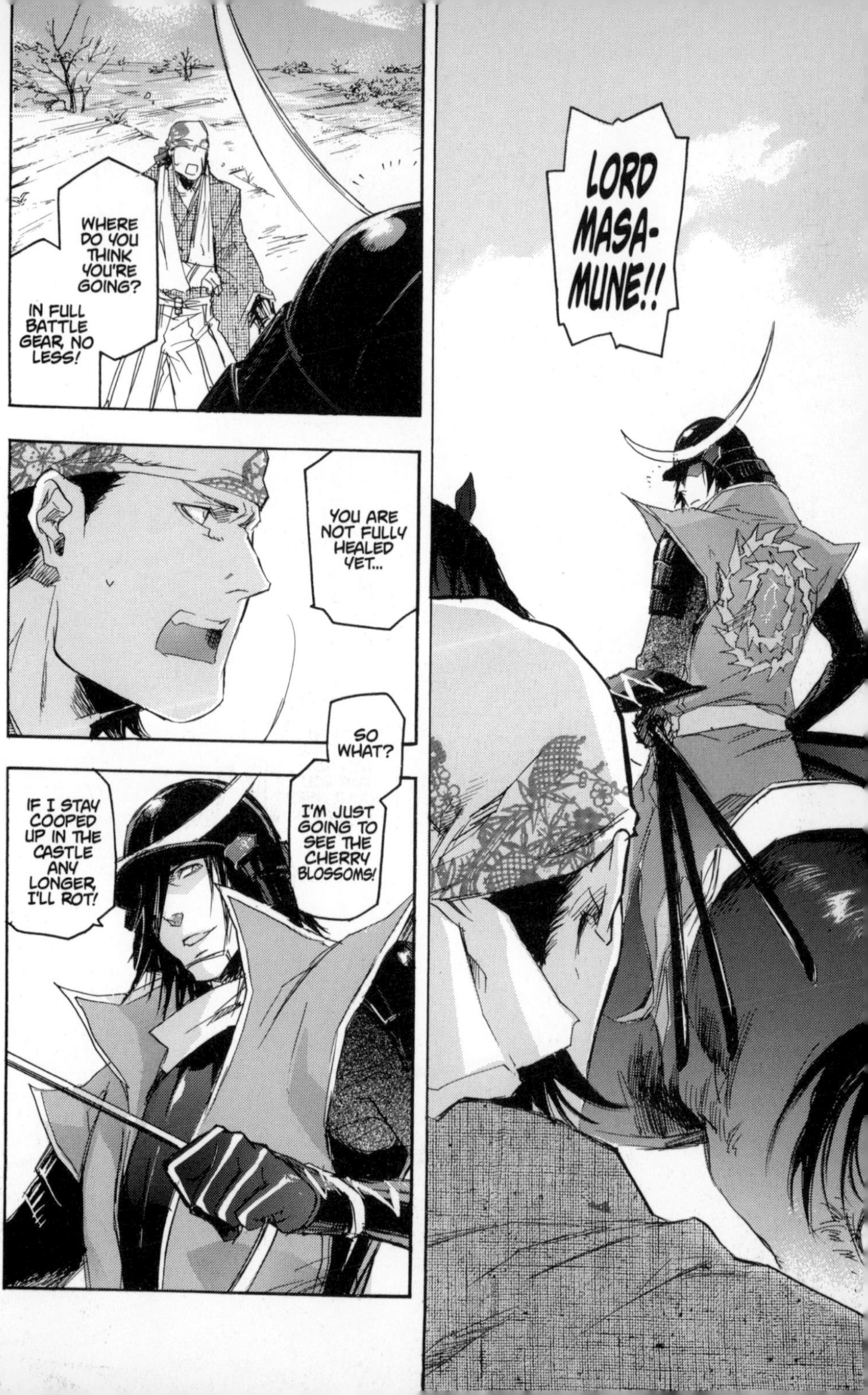
LORD MASA-MUNE!!
WHERE DO YOU THINK YOU'RE GOING?
IN FULL BATTLE GEAR, NO LESS!
YOU ARE NOT FULLY HEALED YET...
SO WHAT?
I'M JUST GOING TO SEE THE CHERRY BLOSSOMS!
IF I STAY COOPED UP IN THE CASTLE ANY LONGER, I'LL ROT!

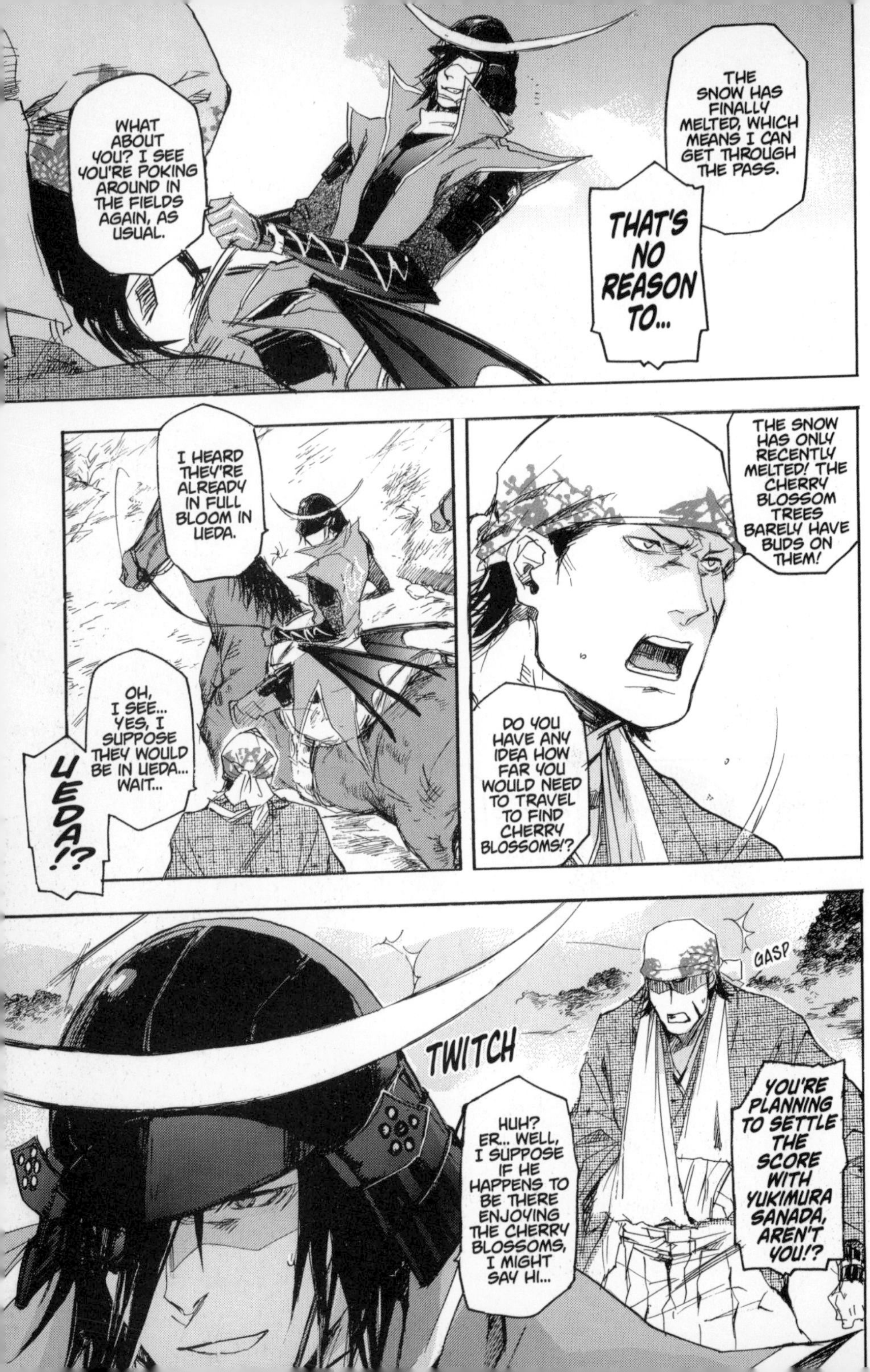
THE SNOW HAS FINALLY MELTED, WHICH MEANS I CAN GET THROUGH THE PASS.
THAT'S NO REASON TO...
WHAT ABOUT YOU? I SEE YOU'RE POKING AROUND IN THE FIELDS AGAIN, AS USUAL.
THE SNOW HAS ONLY RECENTLY MELTED! THE CHERRY BLOSSOM TREES BARELY HAVE BUDS ON THEM!
DO YOU HAVE ANY IDEA HOW FAR YOU WOULD NEED TO TRAVEL TO FIND CHERRY BLOSSOMS!?
I HEARD THEY'RE ALREADY IN FULL BLOOM IN UEDA.
OH, I SEE... YES, I SUPPOSE THEY WOULD BE IN UEDA... WAIT...
UEDA!?
GASP
YOU'RE PLANNING TO SETTLE THE SCORE WITH YUKIMURA SANADA, AREN'T YOU!?
TWITCH
HUH? ER... WELL, I SUPPOSE IF HE HAPPENS TO BE THERE ENJOYING THE CHERRY BLOSSOMS, I MIGHT SAY HI...

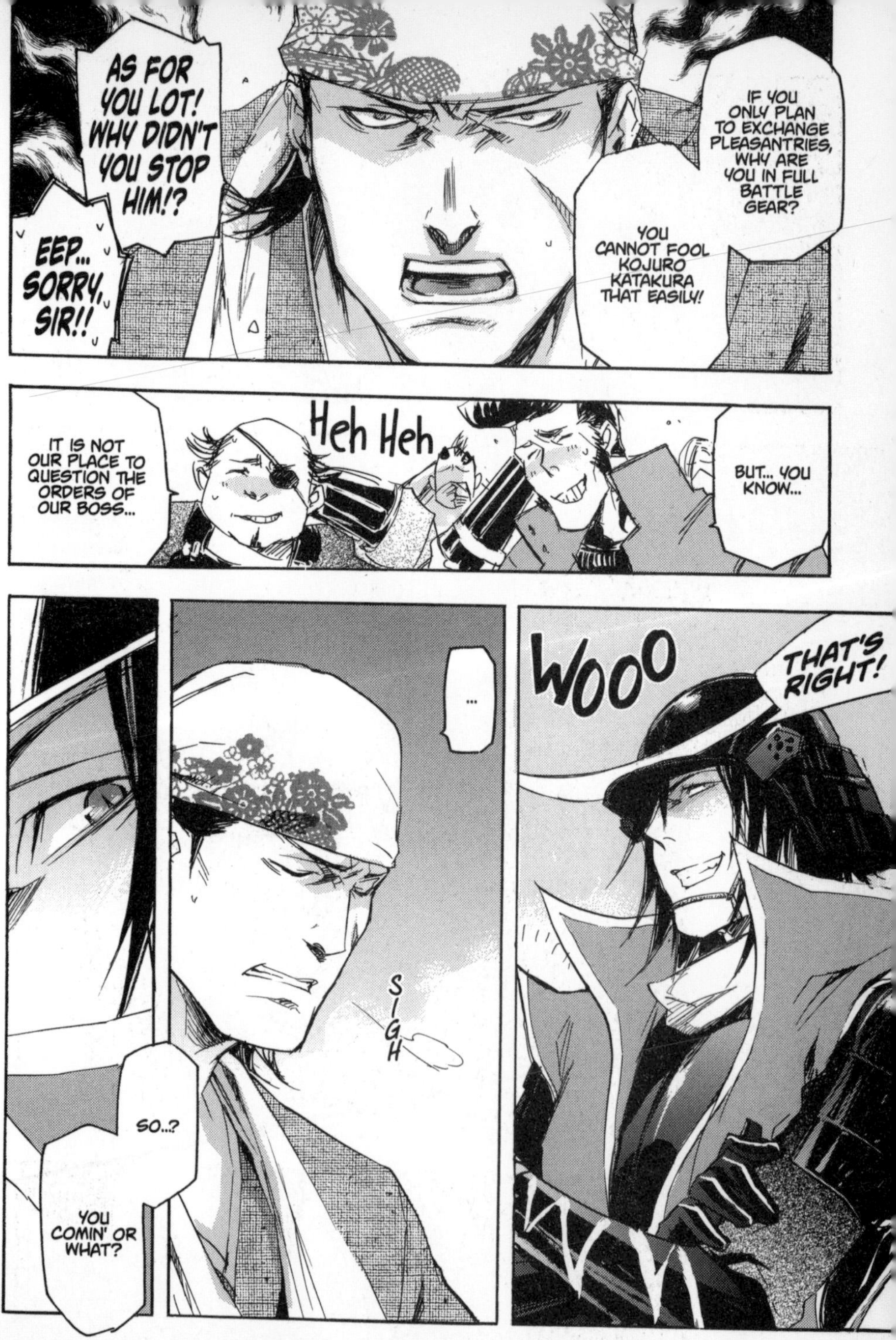
IF YOU ONLY PLAN TO EXCHANGE PLEASANTRIES, WHY ARE YOU IN FULL BATTLE GEAR?
YOU CANNOT FOOL KOJURO KATAKURA THAT EASILY!
AS FOR YOU LOT! WHY DIDN'T YOU STOP HIM!?
EEP... SORRY, SIR!!
BUT... YOU KNOW...
Heh Heh
IT IS NOT OUR PLACE TO QUESTION THE ORDERS OF OUR BOSS...
THAT'S RIGHT!
WOOO
...
SIGH
SO..?
YOU COMIN' OR WHAT?

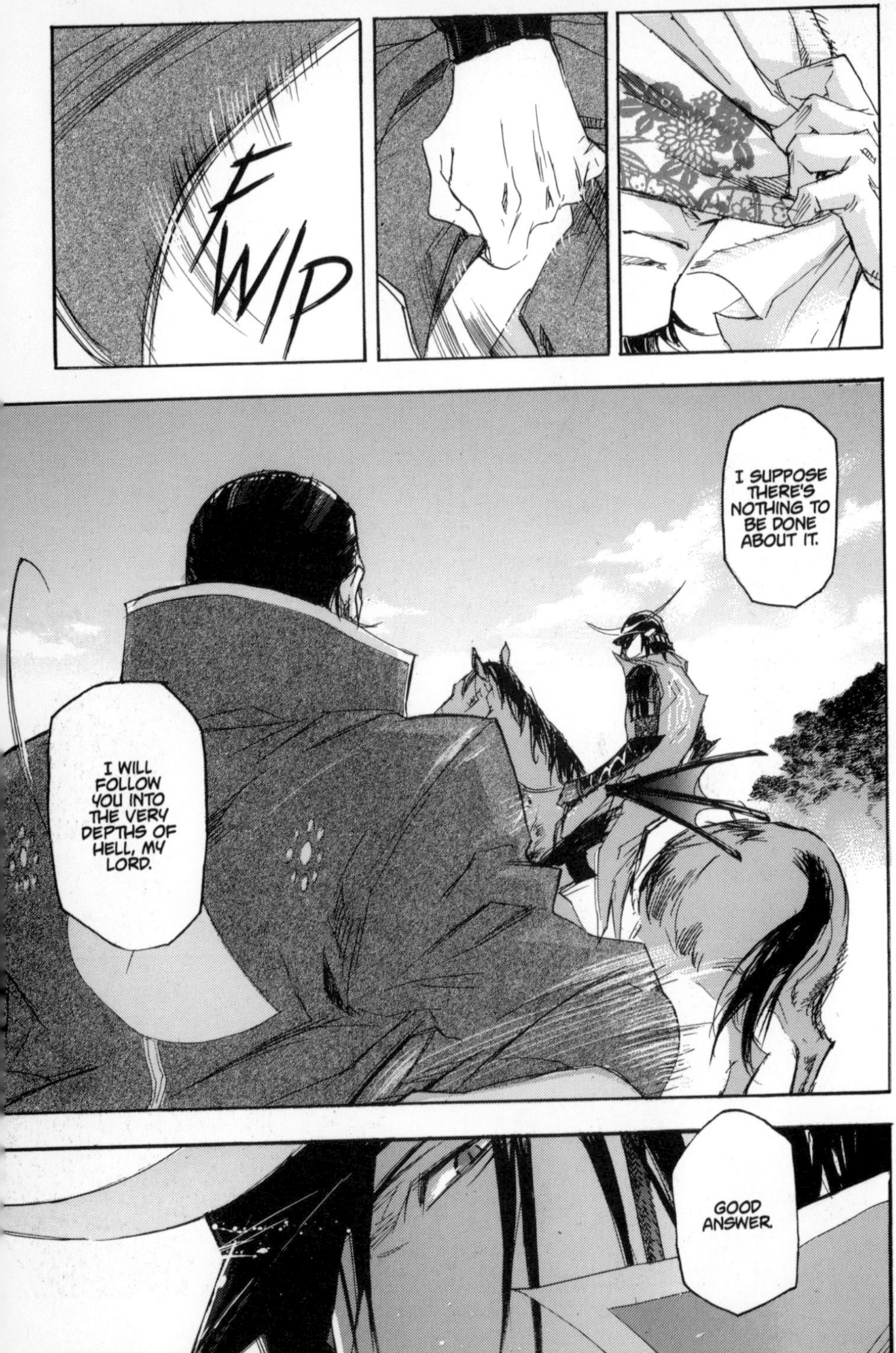
FWIP
I SUPPOSE THERE'S NOTHING TO BE DONE ABOUT IT.
I WILL FOLLOW YOU INTO THE VERY DEPTHS OF HELL, MY LORD.
GOOD ANSWER.

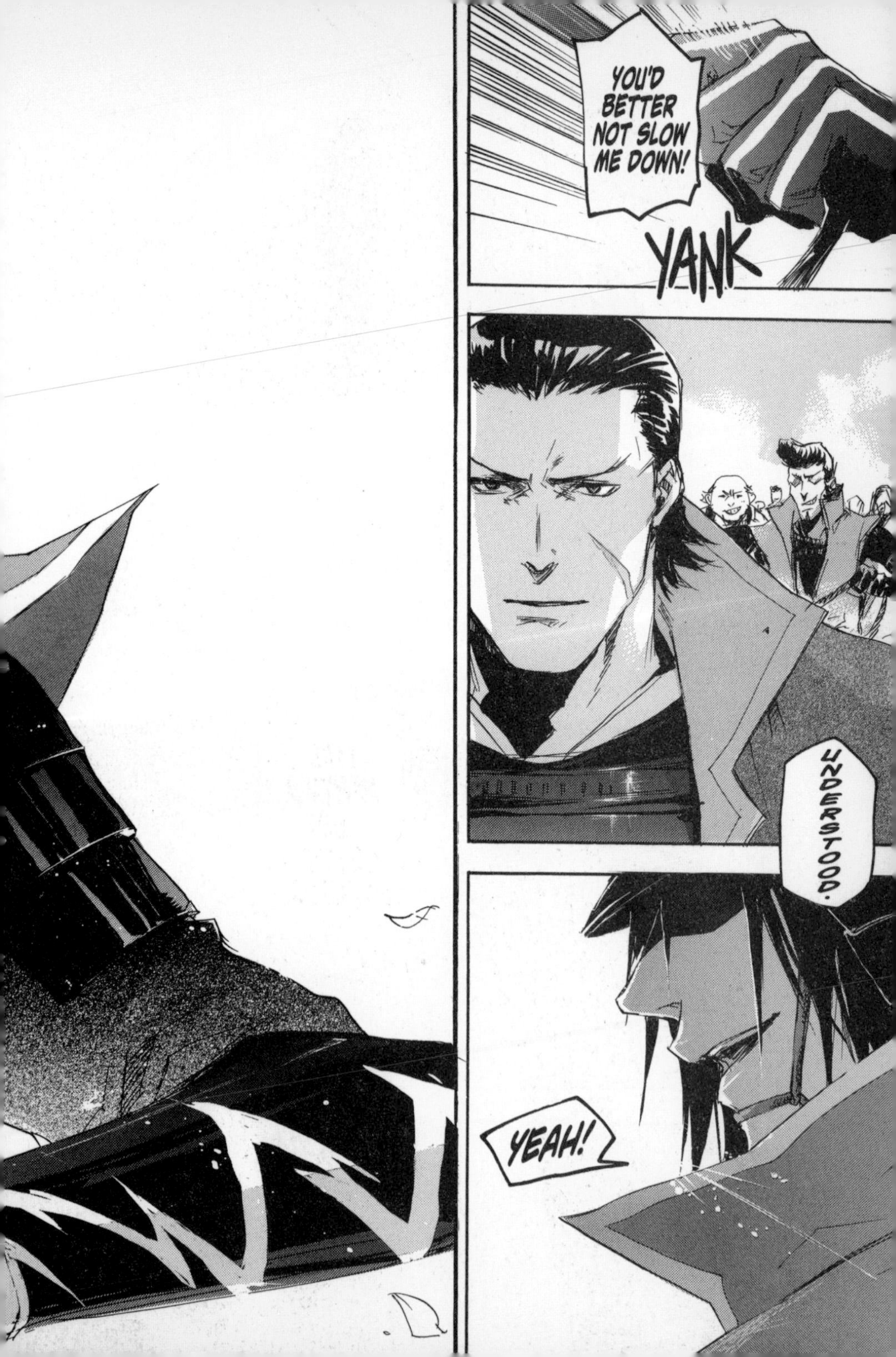
YOU'D BETTER NOT SLOW ME DOWN!
YANK
UNDERSTOOD.
YEAH!

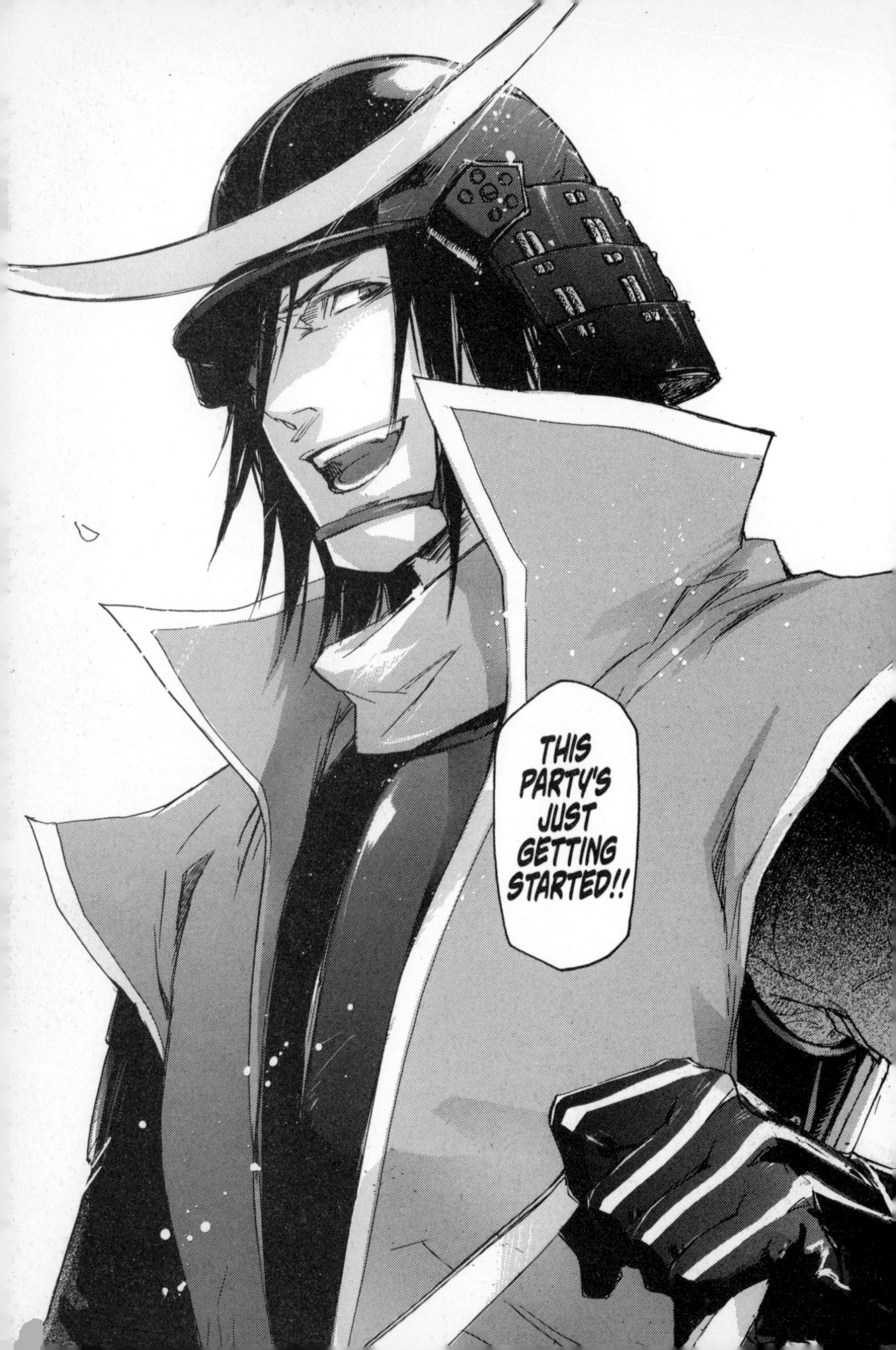
THIS PARTY'S JUST GETTING STARTED!!

Congratulations on the final volume! Haibara and everyone else who had a hand in this manga did a truly wonderful job! Haibara has a way of drawing characters that makes them so appealing and exciting. With the focus on Masamune, Yukimura, and Keiji as they faced the overwhelming challenges brought on by Hideyoshi Toyotomi and Hanbei Takenaka, Haibara also managed to give the other characters plenty of depth. As one of the creators of the game, I am very pleased with the content offered by this manga. Personally, Keiji is my favorite character... oh, and Matsu too! The climax was very thrilling, and I hope the game series will be able to carry on that sense of excitement. I hope you, the reader of this manga, and all of your friends will be enticed to check out our future endeavors with the "Sengoku Basara" game series. In conclusion, I'd like to take this opportunity to thank Yak Haibara! Thank you very much!

"Sengoku Basara" Series Director
Shin Yamamoto

The final volume! These past two years have been full of trial and error, but I had a lot of fun drawing this manga! I obviously still have a lot to learn, so I owe a debt of gratitude to the people over at Capcom who watched over me warmly as I floundered about, my editor for their limitless patience, and of course the readers who made it all worthwhile! Thank you all so very much!

Yak Haibara

SPECIAL THANKS
Chiyo Agata
Cha-
Kano Suigetsu
Tatsune Seno
My Editor
Everyone at Capcom

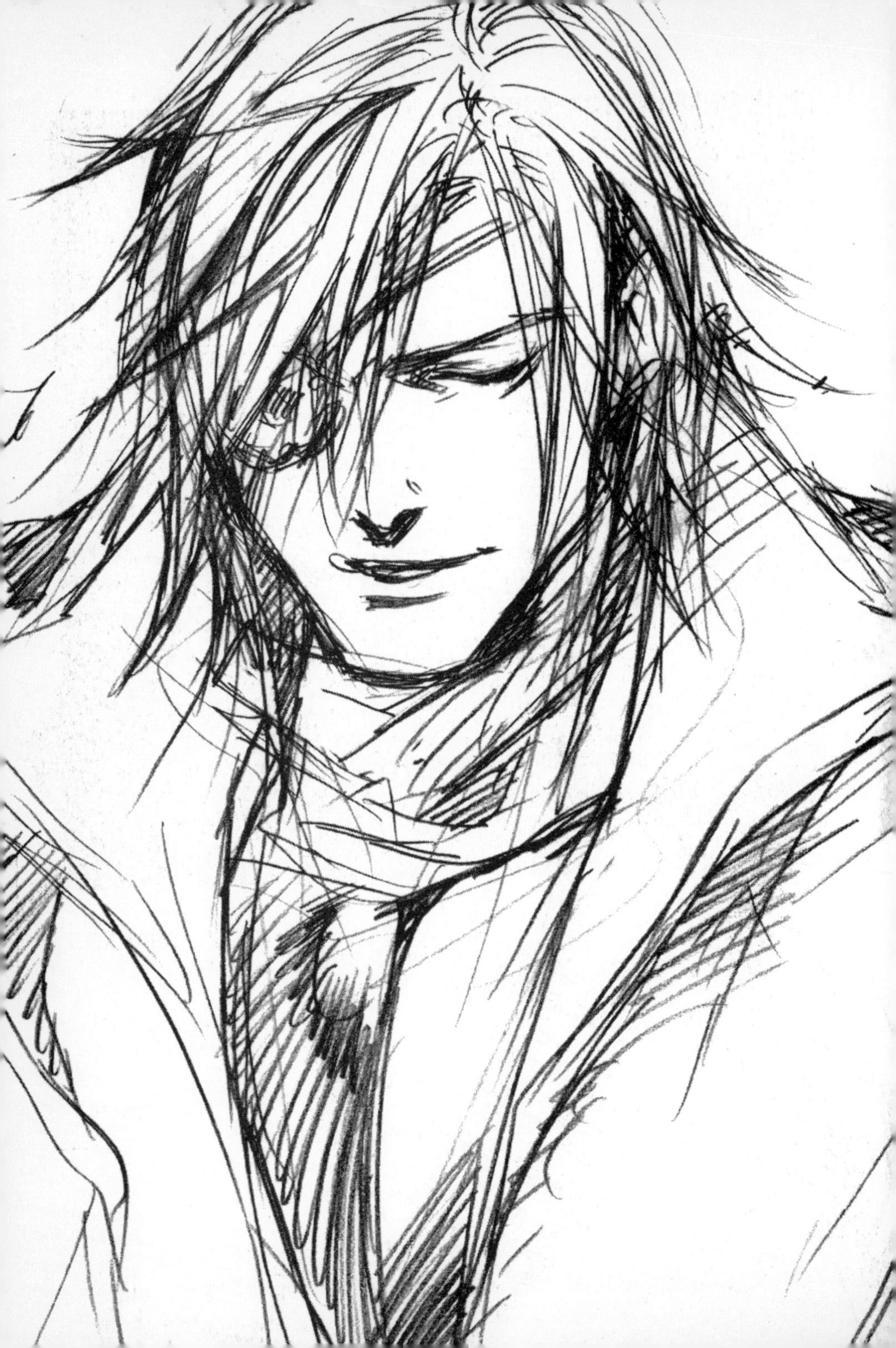

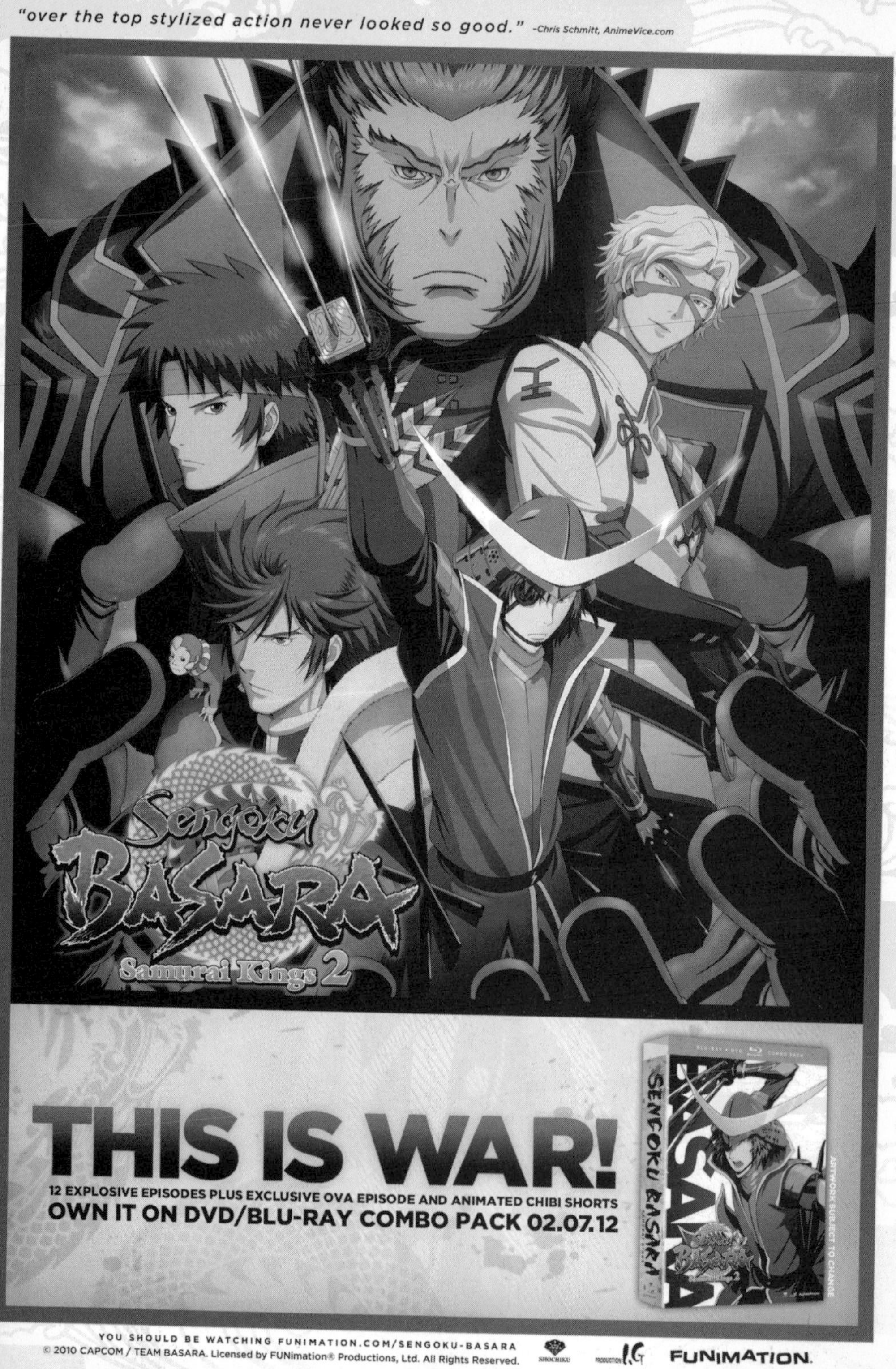
"over the top stylized action never looked so good." -Chris Schmitt, AnimeVice.com
Sengoku BASARA
Samurai Kings 2
THIS IS WAR!
12 EXPLOSIVE EPISODES PLUS EXCLUSIVE OVA EPISODE AND ANIMATED CHIBI SHORTS
OWN IT ON DVD/BLU-RAY COMBO PACK 02.07.12
SENGOKU BASARA
ARTWORK SUBJECT TO CHANGE
YOU SHOULD BE WATCHING FUNIMATION.COM/SENGOKU-BASARA
© 2010 CAPCOM / TEAM BASARA. Licensed by FUNimation® Productions, Ltd. All Rights Reserved.
SHOCHIKU
I.G
FUNIMATION

Samurai Heroes
OFFICIAL COMPLETE WORKS

Sengoku Basara Samurai Heroes: Official Complete Works collects the unique artwork behind the latest game in this landmark Capcom series. Included in this collection are character designs, rough sketches, promotional art, and an exclusive interview with the creators behind Sengoku Basara.

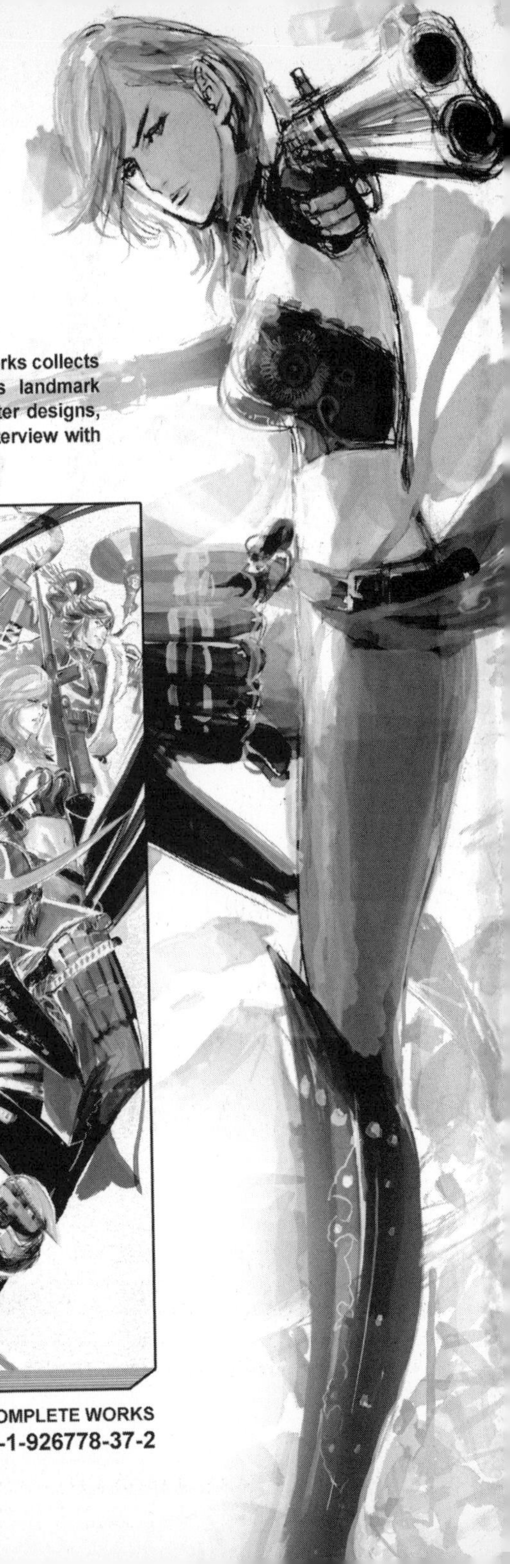

SENGOKU BASARA: SAMURAI HEROES - OFFICIAL COMPLETE WORKS
ISBN: 978-1-926778-37-2

ONIMUSHA
NIGHT OF GENESIS

Two Onimusha warriors embark on epic adventure! One sets off to overthrow the evil warlord Toyotomi Hideyoshi. The other seeks revenge on a traitor to her clan. These Onimusha warriors' paths are destined to intersect. Will they join forces to save the world from destruction at the hands of the monstrous Genma, or will the Omen Star finally descend and bring unending chaos to the world?

Vol.1 ISBN: 978-0973865257

Vol.2 ISBN: 978-0973865264